The Ebony Success Library

The Ebony Success Library

Volume I
1,000 Successful Blacks

By the Editors of Ebony

The Southwestern Company,
Nashville, Tenn.
By arrangement with
Johnson Publishing Company Inc., 1973

Library of Congress Cataloguing in Publication Data

Main entry under title:
1,000 successful blacks.

    (The Ebony success library, v. I)
     I. Negroes—Biographies.   I. Ebony.   II. Series.
E185.96.093   1973   920'.073   73-5828
ISBN 0-87485-060-6

R.R.D. 1-73

Publisher
John H. Johnson

Editor
Charles L. Sanders

Designer
Cecil L. Ferguson

Production Coordinator
Brenda M. Biram

Production Assistants
Editorial: Brenda J. Butler
Photographs: Basil O. Phillips

Introduction

Men of business, diplomacy, government; discoverers of a method of operating on the human heart, of synthesizing life-saving drugs; inventors of a clock, shoe-lasting equipment, the traffic light, the gas mask; planners of cities, builders of great houses, levees, roads; women of education; singers, artists, engineers, soldiers, poets. . . .

From the very beginning of their sojourn in what became the United States of America, black men and women have achieved success in almost every field of endeavor. The names are familiar: Benjamin Banneker, Jan Matzeliger, Garrett Morgan, Charles Drew, Percy Julian, George Washington Carver, Mary McLeod Bethune, Madame C. J. Walker, Benjamin O. Davis Sr., Richard Wright, W.E.B. DuBois, Ralph J. Bunche, Robert S. Abbott, Langston Hughes. . . .

Success for such black heroes was measured not merely in terms of the accumulation of wealth but in terms of achievement of goals—achievement despite all the restrictions that slavery and racism imposed. And it is in this light that we present the hundreds of stories in *The Ebony Success Library.*

We are aware that, for many black men and women of today, the word "success" has little relevance to what must be the commitments and pursuits of a people still largely denied enjoyment of the "American dream." Thus the stories in these three volumes are offered neither as testamentary evidence nor as praise for what black people have been permitted to accomplish as rewards of citizenship. They are stories—as are the stories of Banneker, Carver, DuBois, Bunche and the others—of goals set, of struggle toward those goals, of goals achieved. They are challenges to myths and lies, and they are inspirational examples for the young black American who feels that he has reason to defer dreams, to lose faith, to give up hope of achievement.

Herein the reader will find more than 1,100 stories of black men and women who have achieved success—in business and industry, in the sciences and arts, in sports, entertainment, government. . . .

Volume I contains one thousand stories told in biographical sketches, while in Volume II there are seventy-two illustrated articles about such persons as Mrs. Fannie Lou Hamer, the bold black liberationist in Mississippi; businessmen George E. Johnson, John H. Sengstacke and Henry G. Parks; heavyweight champion George Foreman, and Michael Jackson of the Jackson Five. In Volume III, scores of persons in various careers are featured, and hundreds of sources are listed for the student who is seeking scholarship aid.

Almost all the persons selected for inclusion in these volumes had their beginnings in circumstances not very different from those of black youths of today; in some instances those circumstances were many times worse. It must be remembered that American racism is as old as the republic itself and that black poverty is not new. Thus each person whose story is told in *The Ebony Success Library* represents yet another example of what a great people of courage and determination can achieve despite the most formidable odds. And each represents, we believe, what millions of young black Americans must become if they are to demand, and win, what is rightfully theirs.

These volumes were made possible through the cooperation of hundreds of individuals, organizations and business firms. We extend to each a very special thanks.

The Editors of Ebony

Contents

1,000 Successful Blacks

1,000 Successful Blacks

A

Hank Aaron

Kareem Abdul-Jabbar

Rev. Ralph D. Abernathy

Aaron, Henry (Hank), professional athlete, is a baseball player with the Atlanta Braves. Born Feb. 5, 1934 in Mobile, Ala., he began playing baseball professionally with the Indianapolis Clowns of the Negro American League immediately after graduating from high school in 1952. His contract was purchased during the same year by the Boston Braves. He was assigned first to the Eau Claire, Wis. team as a shortstop, then to the Jacksonville Fla. team as a second baseman. In 1954, he became a regular outfielder for the Boston Braves—which later became the Milwaukee Braves, then the Altanta Braves. He became the first player in history to score both 500 home runs and 3,000 hits (in May, 1970)—and began the 1973 season with 673 home runs, needing only 42 more to break the all-time record set by Babe Ruth. In 1972, he signed a three-year contract for $600,000, which made him the highest-paid player in baseball history. Divorced, he is the father of four children: Gaile, Henry Jr., Larry and Dorinda. Address: Atlanta Braves, Atlanta Stadium, Atlanta, GA 30312

Abdul-Jabbar, Kareem, basketball player, signed his first professional contract, for five years and $1.4 million, with the Milwaukee Bucks, a last-place expansion team in the 1968–69 season. In his first season with the team, Milwaukee became a top contender and then in 1970–71 won the National Basketball Association title. In the 1971–72 season, Mr. Abdul-Jabbar was the highest scorer in the NBA. Born Ferdinand Lewis Alcindor in New York City on April 16, 1947, he weighed 13 pounds and measured 22 and ½ inches at birth. Now standing 7 feet, 2 inches, he is one of the most agile men in the game. He graduated from UCLA where he led the basketball team to three national championships and only one game lost in three years. He became an orthodox Muslim in adopting his present name. Mr. Abdul-Jabbar is an earnest student of Afro-American history and deeply concerned about the destiny of black people. He is married to the former Janice Brown (Habiba) Address: 700 W. Wisconsin Ave., Milwaukee, WI 53233

Abernathy, The Reverend Ralph David, clergyman and administrator, is president of the Southern Christian Leadership Conference and has been pastor of the West Hunter Baptist Church in Atlanta, Ga. since 1961. He was born March 11, 1926 in Linden, Ala. He rose to national prominence when he and Dr. Martin Luther King Jr. (whom he succeeded as president of SCLC after Dr. King's death on April 4, 1968) led the famous Montgomery (Ala.) bus boycott in 1955 and 1956. He is a graduate of Alabama State College (B.A., 1950) and has done graduate study at Atlanta University. He has honorary degrees from Allen University (LL.D., 1960); Long Island University (LL.D., 1969) and Morehouse College (D.D., 1971). Rev. Abernathy has traveled and lectured extensively. He has addressed the Conference on Positive Action for the Peace and the Security of Africa in Ghana, and has toured Europe and South America. He and his wife, Juanita, have four children: Jaundalynn, Donzaleigh, Ralph David III, and Kwame Luthuli. Address: Southern Christian Leadership Conference, 334 Auburn Ave., N.E., Atlanta, GA 30303

Albert W. Adams Jr.

Edward B. Adams

John D. Adams

Luthermae E. Adams

Adams, Albert W. Jr., administrator, is personnel assistant-equal opportunity administrator at the Seven-Up Co. world headquarters in St. Louis, Mo. He is responsible for implementing policies and programs relating to Equal Employment Opportunity guidelines, for employment interviewing and for selection for salary and hourly positions. He is also involved in training, labor relations and personnel research. Born Nov. 22, 1948 in Detroit, Mich., he turned down an appointment to the U.S. Naval Academy in favor of a scholarship to Harris Teacher's College in St. Louis. He graduated in 1970 with a B.A. degree in elementary education. He has also completed one-fourth of the requirements for an M.B.A. degree. In 1972 he was corporate chairman for the United Negro College Fund and was cited for raising more than $50,000. He collects stamps and coins. He and his wife, Linda, have no children. Address: 121 S. Meramec, St. Louis, MO 63105

Adams, Edward B., administrator, is operations manager for IBM Corp., Information Records Division in Colorado, manufacturer of flexible magnetic media. He is responsible for the manufacture and engineering of computer tape, flexible magnetic disks, magnetic selectric typewriter cards and computer tape accessories. Previously, he was buying manager and industrial engineering manager for IBM. Born Jan. 31, 1939 in New York, N.Y., he is a graduate of New York University (B.I.E., industrial engineering, 1959) and did graduate study in industrial engineering at the Brooklyn Polytechnic Institute. He is a director of Productions, Inc., a member of the NAACP and Rotary International. He and his wife, Mary, have three children: Jennifer, Teddy and Michele. Address: P. O. Box 1900, Boulder, CO 80302

Adams, John D., supervisor, is a public relations supervisor and field services representative for American Oil Co. in Chicago, III. He assists the manager of public relations by writing press releases, coordinating press relations with news media and supervising community public relations activities. He was born March 16, 1943 in Oakland, Calif. He has a B.S. degree from Arkansas A.M. & N. Coll. (1964) and an M.B.A. degree from Calif. State Coll. (1965). He is a member of the Chicago Advertising Society and the Public Relations Society of America. Mr. Adams is active in the YMCA and in Boys Clubs of America. He is single. Address: Standard Oil Co. (Ind.), 200 E. Randolph St., Chicago, IL 60606

Adams, Luthermae E., organization head, is supreme basileus of Gamma Phi Delta. Previously, she was national financial grammateus and regional director of the international business and professional service organization. She also is resident agent (in Berkeley, Calif.) of Lewis Business College of Detroit, Mich. Born Jan. 12, 1916 in Orange, Tex., she studied business education at Hughes Business College in Texas and at Merritt College in Oakland, Calif. She has an honorary L.H.D. degree from Miller's University of the Bible Educational Association. She is a member of Elks of the World, Knights and Daughters of Tabor, the Berkeley Youth Advisory Board and the Household of Ruth. A widow, she has a daughter, Mrs. Effie R. Burgess, and three sons: John D. Reed, Arthur D. Reed and Calvin Watkins. Address: 2927-A Harper St., Berkeley, CA 94703

J. E. "Cannonball" Adderley

O. Rudolph Aggrey

William Aiken

Adderley, Julian Edwin, entertainer, is an alto saxophonist known to jazz fans as "Cannonball." A former Fort Lauderdale, Fla. high school music teacher and band director for eight years, he starred in nightclubs, at jazz concerts and on recordings. Born Sept. 15, 1928 in Tampa, Fla., he gained much of his musical training in high school. He attended the U.S. Naval School of Music in Washington, D.C. and has college credits from Florida A & M University. He conducted an army band in 1953 and, appearing with a small group, made his New York debut in 1955 at the Café Bohemia. He started to make recordings and, after becoming well-known, organized his own combo and toured until 1957. He then joined a group headed by trumpeter Miles Davis. Recognized as a competent professional by jazz fans, he started the Cannonball Adderley Quintet in 1959 and has played in Europe and at the Newport and Randall's Island jazz festivals. He was featured on an ABC-TV special and has won several awards. He is married to the former Olga James. Address: c/o John Levy Enterprises, 119 W. 57th St., New York, NY 10019

Aggrey, O. Rudolph, diplomat, is director of the office of West African Affairs at the Department of State in Washington, D.C. He has supervisory responsibility for United States relations with 13 West African nations. Mr. Aggrey was born July 24, 1926 in Salisbury, N.C. and received degrees from Hampton Institute (B.A., sociology) and Syracuse University (M.A., journalism). After newspaper and public relations work in Cleveland and New York, he joined the Foreign Service and served as information officer in Nigeria from 1951 to 1953. From there, he went on to become senior member of the American Embassy staff in the Congo and program manager for the United States Information Agency's motion picture and television service. In 1955, he earned the Meritorious Service Award for loyalty and devotion to duty with the USIA at Lagos, Nigeria. In 1964, Mr. Aggrey became the first black American Foreign Service officer to be named a fellow in the Center for International Affairs at Harvard University. He assumed his present position in 1970. He is a member of Sigma Delta Chi, a professional journalism society, the Federal City Club of Washington, D.C., and the Foreign Service Association. He and his wife, Francoise, have one child, Roxanne Rose. Address: U.S. Department of State, Washington, DC 20024

Aiken, William, certified public accountant, is president of the National Association of Black Accountants, Inc. and a partner of Aiken, Wilson & Brown, a black certified public accountant firm in New York, N.Y. He was born March 11, 1934 in New York City, and has degrees from City College (B.B.A., 1963), and Baruch College (M.B.A., 1970). As of 1973, he was serving on the board of directors of the Ethical-Fieldston Fund and the Business Advisory Board of the Borough of Manhattan Community College. He has been a state insurance examiner (N.Y.), then a senior accountant with Arthur Young and Co. He started his own firm in 1972. Since he became president of the NABA in 1971, that organization has increased its membership to 600 members and formed professional and student chapters across the country. He is the author of *The Black Experience in Large Public Accounting Firms*. He is married to the former Dorothy Harris. They have three children: Adrienne, William and Candice. Address: P.O. Box 726, FDR Post Office Station, New York, NY 10022

Alvin Ailey

Ailey, Alvin, choreographer and dancer, is founder and director of the Alvin Ailey American Dance Theater in New York, N.Y. This leading modern dance troupe has won world-wide acclaim, especially for its use of jazz music and popular dance idioms. Mr. Ailey was born Jan. 5, 1931 in Rogers, Tex. He studied dance in Los Angeles, Calif. and New York City. He performed on Broadway in *Jamaica* and other shows before organizing his dance troupe in 1958. Among outstanding works he has choreographed are *Revelations, Cry* and *The River*. He also was choreographer for the opera *Antony and Cleopatra* that opened at the Metropolitan Opera House (New York, N.Y.) in 1966 and for *Mass*, a dance-oratorio that opened at the J.F.K Center for the Performing Arts (Washington, D.C.) in 1971. Mr. Ailey's American Dance Theater has been a resident company of the Brooklyn Academy of Music and of City Center of New York. Address: 229 E. 59th St., New York, NY 10022

Robert L. Albert

Albert, Robert L., educational consultant, is president of Robert L. Albert & Associates, a higher education consulting firm in Sudbury, Mass., and is vice president of William Karp Consulting Co., Inc. in Chicago, Ill. Born Sept. 12, 1928 in New York City he attended the University of Washington and has an honorary L.H.,D from the same school. The Karp firm assists colleges and universities in developing programs to eliminate discrimination against minorities and women. It also develops employment recruitment programs involving the physically and mentally handicapped and the disadvantaged. Mr. Albert is also director of Equal Opportunity Intergroup Relations at Tufts University and is a special assistant to the school's president. He was a personnel analyst for the Washington State Department of Personnel (1958–66). He is a member of the Society of Personnel Administrators, and the State of Massachusetts-Technical and Vocational Advisory Council. He and his wife, Mildred, have five children: Michelle, Marsha, Lola, Keith and Kyle. Address: 79 Firecut Lane, Sudbury, MA 01776

Clifford L. Alexander Jr.

Alexander, Clifford L. Jr., attorney, is a member of the Washington, D.C. law firm of Arnold & Porter. He is a graduate of Harvard University (A.B., 1955) and Yale University Law School (LL.B., 1958). He was elected in 1969 to a six-year term on the Harvard Board of Overseers. Born Sept. 21, 1933 in New York, N.Y., he served as assistant district attorney for N. Y. County and was program and executive director of Harlem Youth Opportunities. He was foreign affairs officer of the National Security Council under President John F. Kennedy, and while under President Lyndon B. Johnson he was deputy special assistant (1964-65) and associate special counsel (1965-66). He was chairman of the Equal Opportunity Commission (1967-69). He is a member of the board of directors of several organizations and has received numerous honors and awards. He and his wife, Adele, have a daughter, Elizabeth, and a son, Mark. Address: 1800 G St., NW, Washington, DC 20506

Louis G. Alexander

Margaret Walker Alexander

Judge Raymond P. Alexander

Alexander, Louis G., executive, is a vice president of Amalgamated Trust & Savings Bank in Chicago, Ill. He was appointed to the position in 1967. Born Feb. 14, 1910 in Houston, Tex., he is a graduate of the Armour Institute of Chicago (B.S., electrical engineering, 1941) and had headed a number of electrical services firms before entering the banking field. He is vice president of the midwest region of the National Business League and is a member of the National Committee for Small Business Tax Reform. He is also treasurer of the midwest region of the Executive Reserves and is on the board of the Absalom Jones Theological Institute and the Interdenominational Theological Center. He is on the Chicago consultative panel of the National Academy of Sciences, and is a member of the American Veterans Committee. A widower, he has a son, Louis G. III. Address: Amalgamated Trust & Savings Bank, 100 S. State St., Chicago, IL 60603

Alexander, Margaret W., college administrator, is director of black studies at Jackson State College in Mississippi, and the author of *Jubilee,* a Civil War novel. Born July 7, 1915 in Birmingham, Ala., she is a graduate of Gilbert Academy, Northwestern University (A.B., English) and the University of Iowa (M.A., English; Ph.D., English). She has taught English since 1949 at Livingstone College, West Virginia State College and Northwestern University. Other books she has written include *For My People,* a volume of verse, and *Prophets for a New Day*, a book of poems. She has had many of her poems published in magazines and has edited several anthologies. She is in the process of completing, *Goose Island*, a collection of short stories, *Mother Boyer*, a novel, and *Epitaph For My Father*. She has won many prizes, including the Yale Award for Younger Poets and the Rosenwald Fellowship. She and her husband, Firnist, have four children: Marion Elizabeth, Firnist James Jr., Sigismund Walker and Margaret Elvira. Address: Jackson State College, Jackson, MS 39213

Alexander, Raymond Pace, jurist, is a senior judge of the Court of Common Pleas in Philadelphia, Pa. He was appointed a senior judge in 1970 after having served for eleven years as a judge of the Court of Common Pleas. Born Oct. 13, 1898 in Philadelphia, Judge Alexander graduated from the University of Pennsylvania (B.A., 1920) and Harvard University Law School (LL.B., 1923). He was elected to the Philadelphia City Council under the New Home Rule Charter in the mayoralty campaign in 1952 and served as chairman of its department of recreation from 1952 to 1956. He was chairman of Committee on Public Property and Public Works from 1956 to 1959. Of the thousands of cases Judge Alexander has presided over, many have become landmark decisions, the most important of which is the now famous Community Legal Services, Inc., case which laid the foundation for the establishment of government-supported legal services for the poor throughout the United States. Judge Alexander is a member of the Philadelphia Bar, the Pennsylvania Bar, and the American and National Bar associations. He has appeared as an active trial and appellate in all of the trial and appellate courts, state and federal, in the Philadelphia area and elsewhere in the North, South and East. He has travelled throughout Europe, Central and South America, the West Indies, the Republic of Haiti, the British Isles and Russia. Judge Alexander's wife, Sadie T. M., is an attorney. They have two daughters, Mrs. Mary Elizabeth Brown and Mrs. Rae Pace Minter. Address: One East Penn Square Bldg., Room 1004, Philadelphia, PA 19107

Alexander, Sadie Tanner Mossell, attorney, has practiced law in Philadelphia, Pa., since 1927. Born Jan. 2, 1898 in Philadelphia, she is the fifth generation of the Tanner family recorded in the United States Census as Free Negroes. She is an honors graduate of the University of Pennsylvania (B.S., education, 1918; M.A., economics, 1919; Ph.D., economics, 1921; LL.B., 1927). She was the first black woman in the United States to receive a Ph.D. and the first to earn a law degree from the University of Pennsylvania. She was admitted to the Philadelphia Bar in 1927, the first woman to practice in the Commonwealth of Pennyslvania, and was the second woman lawyer to hold the position of assistant city solicitor (1928–30 and 1934–38). Mrs. Alexander was appointed by President John F. Kennedy to the Lawyers Committee on Civil Rights. In 1972, she was elected president of the Philadelphia Bar Foundation, the first woman so honored. She is a member of the National Advisory Council of the American Civil Liberties Union, a member of the board of directors of the Greater Philadelphia Branch of American Civil Liberties Union, a founding member of the Advisory Committee to American Committee on Africa and a member of the National Committee for Support of Public Schools. She has travelled throughout Europe, the Far East, the West Indies, Hawaii, and the Philippines lecturing on the status of the American Negro. Mrs. Alexander's husband, Raymond Pace Alexander, is a judge. They have two daughters, Mrs. Mary Elizabeth Brown and Mrs. Rae Pace Minter. Address: 11 North Juniper St., Suite 830, Philadelphia PA 19107

Alexander, Theodore M. Jr., administrator, is deputy regional administrator of the U.S. Department of Housing and Urban Development's Atlanta regional office. Born June 22, 1932 in Atlanta, Ga., he is a graduate of Morehouse College (B.A., 1953) and New York University (M.B.A., business administration, 1956). Before assuming his present position, Mr. Alexander was director of HUD's office of unsubsidized insured housing programs. He also served as vice president of Alexander & Associates, a real estate company owned by his father. He is a member of a number of civic organizations, including the National Conference of Christians and Jews. He and his wife, Janis, have three children: Theodore III, Kimberly and Todd. Address: Department of Housing and Urban Development, Room 645, Peachtree Bldg., Atlanta, GA 30323

Alexander, William H., legislator and attorney, is a member of the Georgia House of Representatives in Atlanta, Ga. He was born Dec. 10, 1930 in Macon, Ga. Mr. Alexander studied at Fort Valley State College (B.S.); the University of Michigan (J.D.) and Georgetown University (LL.M.). He practices law in the state and federal courts and is a member of the Georgia and Michigan bars. Mr. Alexander was first elected to the House of Representatives in the 1965 special elections. He was reelected in 1966, 1968, 1970 and 1972. Mr. Alexander is a member of the board of directors of the Atlanta Crime Commission, the Lawyers Committee for Civil Rights Under Law; and is a former president of the American Civil Liberties Union of Georgia. He and his wife, Gayle, have one child, Jill. Address: 3725 Dover Blvd., SW, Atlanta, GA 30331

Sadie T. M. Alexander   T. M. Alexander Jr.   William H. Alexander

Marcus Alexis   Muhammad Ali   Aris T. Allen, M.D.

Alexis, Marcus, educator, is professor of economics and urban affairs at Northwestern University in Evanston, Ill. He has held teaching and research positions at six other colleges and universities. One of no more than 10 black economics professors teaching at major white institutions, Dr. Alexis first wanted to be a lawyer but changed his field when he received economics fellowships at two universities. Born Feb. 26, 1932 in Brooklyn, N.Y., he earned degrees from Brooklyn College (B.A.), Michigan State University (M.A.) and University of Minnesota (Ph.D.). His doctoral dissertation was a pioneering work on the study of black consumers. He did postdoctoral studies at Harvard University and Massachusetts Institute of Technology. He has written 29 articles in his field, published in major journals, and two books. He has delivered 22 papers before national and international meetings of such bodies as the Institute of Management Sciences and the American Marketing Association and is a member of numerous professional committees. Dr. Alexis and his wife, Geraldine, have three children: Marcus, Hilary and Sean. Address: Northwestern University, Evanston, IL 60201

Ali, Muhammad, boxer, was heavyweight champion of the world from 1964 to 1971. He turned professional after winning the Olympics light heavyweight championship in 1960 and won the heavyweight title from Sonny Liston on Feb. 25, 1964. He refused military induction on April 28, 1967, was stripped of his title by the World Boxing Association and was convicted in Houston, Tex. on June 20, 1967 of illegally refusing the draft. He returned to the ring in October, 1970 and lost the championship to Joe Frazier on March 8, 1971. On June 28, 1971 the U.S. Supreme Court overturned his conviction. Born Cassius Marcellus Clay on Jan. 18, 1942 in Louisville, Ky., he is a graduate of Louisville's Central High School. He and his wife, Belinda, have four children: Maryum, Reeshemah, Jamillah and Ibn. Address: Cherry Hill, NJ 08034

Allen, Aris T., M.D., physician and legislator, is in the private practice of medicine in Annapolis, Md. and has been a member (Republican, Annapolis) of the Maryland Legislature since 1966; he has been minority whip since 1968. Born Dec. 27, 1910 in San Antonio, Tex., he is a graduate of Howard University (M.D., 1944) and has studied at the University of Buffalo, the Joslin Clinic at Harvard University, the University of New Mexico Hospital, Cook County (Ill.) Hospital and New York University. He was a flight surgeon in the U.S. Air Force (1953–55). He is a member of several boards of directors, including Colonial Bank and Trust Co. of Annapolis (also a member of the executive committee), Citizens Housing and Planning Association, Parole Health Center, Chamber of Commerce and NAACP. He is a former member of the Anne Arundel County Board of Education. He is a member of numerous professional and civic groups. He is a member of the Anne Arundel General Hospital staff and is a Fellow of the American Board of Family Practice. He is the medical examiner for a number of insurance companies and organizations. He and his wife, Faye E. Watson Allen, M.D., with whom he practices medicine, have two sons, Aris Jr. and Lonnie. Address: 62 Cathedral St., Annapolis, MD 21401

Elbert E. Allen, D.D.S.

Allen, Elbert E., D.D.S., fraternity head and dentist, is supreme commander of the Supreme Camp of the American Woodmen with headquarters in Denver, Colo. Born Sept. 19, 1921 in Shreveport, La., he has degrees from Wiley College (B.S., 1942) and Meharry Medical College (D.D.S., 1947). Dr. Allen was elected in 1970 to head some 40,000 members of the fraternal benefit association. The fraternity has chapters in 23 states and the District of Columbia. A practicing dentist since 1945, Dr. Allen has held memberships in the National, Louisiana State and American Dental associations. He was the first black to hold public office in Shreveport after being elected to the Caddo Parish School Board in 1970. Some outstanding achievements by Dr. Allen include being named Honorary Citizen of New Orleans, La. (1959); receiving the Liberty Bell Award (Shreveport Bar Association, 1970), and becoming the first black to receive a Society of Dental Surgeons fellowship. He and his wife, Carolyn, live in Shreveport. Address: 1004 Sprague St., Shreveport, LA 71101

George L. Allen

Allen, George Louis, city official, is a member of the Dallas, Tex., city council and is president of Tecog Service Industries, a building maintenance firm. Since his appointment to the Council in 1968 (he was elected in 1969 and was reelected in 1971), he has initiated many major legislative programs, including a civil rights ordinance to provide public accommodations for all citizens in every type of business establishment, and the introduction of an open housing ordinance aimed at removing discrimination in the rental, sale and financing of housing. He was also a moving force in increasing employment of blacks in Dallas city government. Born Nov. 26, 1910 in New Orleans, La., he is a graduate of Xavier University (A.B., 1931) and the Institute of Insurance Marketing at Southern Methodist University. He is a certified public accountant and is a board member of Texas Southern University, Dallas County United Fund, Dallas Negro Chamber of Commerce and the North Texas Planning Council for Hospitals and Related Health Facilities. He is vice president and board member of both the Community Council of Greater Dallas and the Catholic Charities. He is the recipient of numerous citations and awards, including a 20-Year Service Award from Dallas Big Brothers, Inc., and the Distinguished Councilman's Award from the City of Dallas. He and his wife, Norma have four children: Don, George II, Norma, Arthur. Address: 2527 Ross Ave., Dallas, TX 75201

George M. Allen

Allen, George M., state executive, is a special assistant for minority affairs to the governor of Massachusetts. Born Nov. 14, 1933 in Boston, Mass., he attended various schools during his twenty-year U.S. Army career in the United States, Europe and Asia. He is president of the Roxbury Medical-Technical Institute Foundation and of the One Hundred Acres, Inc., a multi-racial resort complex he is erecting. He and his wife, Eva, have two children, James and Leslie. Address: The Commonwealth of Massachusetts, Executive Department, State House, Room 180, Boston, MA 02133

Milton Allen   William J. Allen   Rev. Willie B. Allen

Allen, Milton B., public official, is state's attorney for Baltimore Md. Elected in 1970 to a four-year term, he is responsible for the prosecution of all crimes that occur in the City of Baltimore. His staff includes 90 assistant state's attorneys. Born Dec. 10, 1917 in Baltimore, he is a graduate of Coppin State Teachers College (B.A., 1938; honorary LL.D., 1971) and the University of Maryland (LL.B., 1941; J.D., 1971). Prior to his election, he was a defense attorney in Baltimore for 25 years. He is a member of the National Bar Association, the American Bar Association, the American Civil Liberties Union, the National Bar Foundation and the Governor's Commission on Law Enforcement. He and his wife, Martha, have three sons: David, Peter and Milton Jr. Address: 204 Court House, Baltimore, MD 21202 **See article on Milton B. Allen in Volume II.**

Allen, William J., airline supervisor, is operating chief of passenger service for United Airlines at Cleveland-Hopkins International Airport in Cleveland, Ohio. His work involves administrative duties and the direction of about 200 supervisors, agents and other employees who serve the needs of passengers—sometimes as many as 1,000 a day who have been diverted to Cleveland because of weather problems in other cities. Mr. Allen has been with United since 1965 and has been a ticket agent, senior ticket agent trainer, and supervisor. He was promoted to his present position in 1971. Born August 21, 1939 in Cleveland, he attended Central State College (pre-medicine, 1958) and Fenn College in Cleveland for three years, and had on-the-job training in business and leadership. He is a member of the United Airlines Management Club and of Cleveland's Men, a social club. Divorced, he has a son, Deryck. Address: Cleveland Hopkins International Airport, Cleveland, OH 44135

Allen, The Reverend Willie B., clergyman, is pastor of Upper Room Baptist Church in Washington, D.C. He organized the church as a storefront congregation in 1957. Within six months, there were 200 members and a church building was purchased for $75,000. Eleven years later, the membership had increased to 1,900 and a new church building was built at a cost of $500,000. Previously, the Rev. Allen was pastor of Bethlehem Baptist Church in Washington. Born July 12, 1921 in Richmond, Va., he attended Virginia Union University. He is a member of the Progressive National Baptist Convention, the D.C. Baptist Convention and the Southern Baptist Convention. He is second vice president of the Baptist Ministers Conference of Washington and Vicinity. He and his wife, Anita, have four sons: George, Willie Jr., Stephen and Vincent. Address: 3760 Minnesota Ave., NE, Washington, DC 20019

R. Marchand Alphran

Charles Henry Alston

Larry C. Amos

Alphran, R. Marchand, promotion development manager, is in charge of development and implementation of consumer and trade promotions for Post Cereals at General Foods Corp. in White Plains, N.Y. He joined General Foods in 1967 and had served in the same position with its Jell-O Div. before appointment to his present position in 1970. Born in Chicago, Ill., he has an A.B. degree in psychology from Morehouse Coll. and a certificate of award from the Institute of Advertising Studies of Northwestern Univ. He was once an advertising representative at Johnson Publishing Co. in Chicago. He is a mem. of the Merchandising Executive Club of N.Y. He and his wife, Helen, have two children, Derek and Gina. Address: 250 North St., White Plains NY 10625

Alston, Charles Henry, artist, is a painter, sculptor, muralist, teacher and illustrator who has illustrated for a number of book publishers and such magazines as *Fortune, The New Yorker, Mademoiselle* and *Colliers.* As a member of the New York Art Commission, he helps approve all art work for city buildings, parks and other city properties as well as architectural designs for public works. Born Nov. 28, 1907 in Charlotte, N.C., Mr. Alston earned degrees from Columbia University (B.A., 1929; M.A., 1931) and is an associate professor at the City College of New York and an instructor at the Art Students League. He has won numerous prizes and awards, including the Dow Fellowship at Columbia in 1930 and the Rosenwald Fellowship in Painting (1938, 1939 and 1940), and has served on national and international advisory boards. Some of his works are in the permanent collections at the Metropolitan Museum, the Whitney Museum (Butler Institute of American Arts), University of Nebraska, Atlanta and Howard Universities. Mr. Alston also has murals in the Harlem Hospital, Museum of Natural History and the New York City College—all in New York City. He is married to Dr. Myra Logan Alston. Address: 1270 Fifth Ave., New York, NY 10029

Amos, Larry C., attorney, is a corporate lawyer with Brown & Williamson Tobacco Corp. in Louisville, Ky. He is responsible for advising the corporation and its subsidiaries on legal matters pertaining to labor relations, personnel, equal opportunity, insurance, traffic and contracts. Born July 28, 1935 in Atlanta, Ga., he attended Morehouse College, Lafayette College (B.S., 1957), Indiana University (M.B.A., 1958) and Indiana University School of Law (J.D., 1963). He is a member of the National Bar Association, American Bar Association and the Indiana and Kentucky Bars. While black corporate attorneys are very rare in proportion to the total number of black attorneys in the country, Mr. Amos sees increasing future opportunities in the corporate legal sector for well-prepared blacks. He and his wife, Nancy, have three children: Kevin, Delaina and Miles. Address: 1600 W. Hill St., Louisville, KY 40201

George A. Anderson

M. J. Anderson Sr.

Sarah A. Anderson

William H. Andrews

Anderson, George A., administrator, is a vice president of Draper & Kramer, Inc., a real estate management company, and is manager of Lake Meadows Apartments in Chicago, Ill. He is responsible for overall management of 10 high-rise buildings containing 2,007 apartments, a shopping center with 27 stores and a small office building. Previously, he was a Draper & Kramer branch office manager, and was manager of Prairie Shores Apartments (1,700 apartments). Born Nov. 25, 1923 in Chicago, he attended Howard University and took real estate courses at Roosevelt University and Central YMCA College in Chicago. He is a member of the Chicago Real Estate Board, National Real Estate Board, the Institute of Real Estate Management and the Apartment Building Owners and Managers Association and the South Side Planning Board, and supports La Rabida Children's Hospital, and the Jane Dent Home for the Aged. He and his wife, Gwendolyn, have a son, George Jr. Address: 500 E. 33rd St., Chicago IL 60616

Anderson, Marcellus J. Sr., businessman, is president of the Pan Texas Mortgage Investment Co. in Austin, Tex., and is president of the 300,000-member Federation of Masons of the World. He was born June 21, 1900 in Anderson, S. C., and is a graduate of Ohio State University (A.B.). He has taught at Livingstone College, Samuel Huston College, and Huston-Tillotson College. He is a director of Citizens National Bank of Austin, chairman of the board of directors of the Texas Association of Real Estate Brokers, and a director of United Mortgage Bankers of America, Inc. He and his wife, Ada, have two children, Sandra Joy and Marcellus Jr. Address: 3724 Airport Boulevard, Austin, TX 78722

Anderson, Sarah A., legislator (retired), served 18 years in the Pennsylvania House of Representatives until her retirement in 1972. Born in Jacksonville, Fla., she attended the Philadelphia High School for Girls and the Philadelphia Normal School and taught in the Philadelphia public schools. Representing the 193rd District in the state legislature, she served as chairman of the Health and Welfare Committee and was the moving force behind the establishment of the state's Commission on the Status of Women in 1964. She sponsored the Pennsylvania Equal Rights Amendment extending equal treatment under the law to women in all states and consistently fought for those who have been denied full voice in the government. Mrs. Anderson, widow of the late Dr. Adolphus W. Anderson Sr., has six children. Address: 226 N. 52nd St., Philadelphia, PA 19139

Andrews, William H., administrator, is director of Cleveland Metropolitan General Hospital in Cleveland, Ohio. He was born Oct. 16, 1919 in Wellston, Mo. Mr. Andrews is a graduate of Lincoln University (B.S., 1941). He studied accounting and personnel management at Loyola University in Chicago, Ill. (1948); and hospital adminstration at Washington University in St. Louis, Mo. (M.H.A., 1954). Prior to accepting his present position, Mr. Andrews was assistant director, 1964–65; deputy director, 1965–69 and has served in administrative positions at Homer G. Phillips Hospital 1941–54; DePaul Hospital, 1953–54; Peoples Hospital, 1954–55; George W. Hubbard Hospital of Meharry Medical College, 1955–59 and Forest City Hospital, 1959–64. He is a member of the American College of Hospital Administrators; a member of the American Hospital Association and a member of the Personnel Advisory Committee of Cleveland Welfare Foundation. He and his wife, Mildred, have two children, William and Brenda. Address: 3395 South Scranton Rd., Cleveland, OH 44109

Maya Angelou

Herbert Arlene

Martina Arroyo

Angelou, Maya, author, playwright and entertainer, is author of the 1970 best-selling autobiography, *I Know Why the Caged Bird Sings*. In the book, she says: " . . . a born loser—had to be: from a broken family, raped at eight, unwed mother at 16. . . ." Yet, from the date of her birth, April 4, 1928 in St. Louis, Mo., far from being a failure, Miss Angelou today is an author, poet, conductor, actress, singer, songwriter, playwright and film director. She was the first black woman to have an original screenplay produced, *Georgia, Georgia*, in 1971. She was also San Francisco's first black woman conductor in 1945. A woman of many careers and activities, she has written a volume of poetry, *Just Give Me A Cool Drink of Water Before I Die*, composed music and had some of her songs recorded by B.B. King. A turning point in her life came during a five-year stay in Africa, during which time she became associate editor of *The Arab Observer* in Cairo, Egypt, and later taught dance in Ghana. Of this African stint in the 1960s, she says: "Being black, female, non-Muslim, non-Arab, six feet tall and American made for some interesting experiences." A divorcee, Miss Angelou has one son, Guy Johnson. Address: Gerard Purcell Associations, 133 Fifth Ave., New York, NY 10003

Arlene, Herbert, legislator, is a Democratic member of the Pennsylvania Senate. Elected in 1966, he became the first black state senator in Pennsylvania. He represents the Third District (Philadelphia). He was a state representative (1958–66). Born Sept. 15, 1917 in Harrison, Ga., he is a graduate of the Philadelphia Business School and has an honorary LL.D. degree from Miller State College. He has been leader of Philadelphia's 47th Ward and executive secretary of the Democratic City Committee. He is chairman of the Senate Labor and Industry Committee, and vice chairman of the Military Affairs and Aeronautics Committee. Mr. Arlene a member of the boards of directors of the Wharton Neighborhood Community Center and the Greater Philadelphia Development Corp., and is a delegate on the Model Cities Neighborhood Council No. 15 and an officer of the Union A.M.E. Church. He is a 32nd degree Mason. He and his wife, Emma, have two children, Herbert Jr. and Clara. Address: 1710 W. Columbia Ave., Philadelphia, PA 19121

Arroyo, Martina, opera singer, is a leading American soprano who has performed in Israel and South America as well as in the United States and Europe. She was born in New York City. As a child, she showed remarkable talent as a singer, and attended Hunter High School in New York, a special school for gifted children. Later, at Hunter College (B.A., 1954), she was given special permission in her freshman year to sing with the school Opera Workshop. In 1959, she was one of four national winners in the Metropolitan Opera's Audition of the Air and won a guest contract. In 1963, she debuted with the New York Philharmonic, singing the lead role in the world premiere of Samuel Barber's *Andromache's Farewell*. She has appeared at the New York Metropolitan Opera every season since 1965. She was the first soprano in 20 years to sing two consecutive opening nights for the Met when she sang the role of Elvira in *Ernani* in 1971. She is married to Italian violinist Emilio Poggioni. They have no children. Address: c/o Maurice Feldman, 745 5th Ave., New York, NY 10022

Ashe, Arthur R., Jr., professional athlete-businessman, is a member of the touring professional group, World Championship Tennis, which conducts tournaments among its personnel. He is also president of Players Enterprises, Inc., in Washington, D.C. Born in Richmond, Va., in 1944, he was discovered and tutored by black tennis player Ronald Charity, who took him to Dr. Robert W. Johnson, a black physician and developer of young black tennis players in Lynchburg, Va. Mr. Ashe's application was refused by three major regional white tournaments when he was 15. But in 1961, at 18, he won the United States Lawn Tennis Association National Interscholastic Championship at Charlottesville, Va., without losing a set. A graduate of UCLA, he won two United States Intercollegiate championships while at the university. His many tournament victories include the United States Men's Hard Court, the United States Amateur, the Australian Open and the United States Men's Clay Court. He was a member of the team that won the Davis Cup in 1969. Mr. Ashe has been an executive of Philip Morris Co. and Hobson Paper Co. and is one of the owners of First Service, a Richmond insurance company. He served in the U.S. Army as an officer. Address: 888 17 St., N.W., Washington, DC 20006

Atkins, Hannah Diggs, legislator, is a state representative in the Oklahoma House of Representatives. She was the first black woman in the state's history to chair a committee (Mental Health and Retardation). Mrs. Atkins was born Nov. 1, 1923 in Winston-Salem, N.C. She received degrees from Saint Augustine's College (B.S.) and the Graduate School of Library Science at the University of Chicago (B.L.S.). She has also studied at Oklahoma City University Law School and the University of Oklahoma. From 1963 to the time of her election, Mrs. Atkins was employed at the Oklahoma State Library where she was chief of the general reference division and acting law librarian. She is a member of the Governor's Commission on the Status of Women, the State Advisory Committee to the State Board of Education, the executive board of the Oklahoma County Mental Health Association and the Executive Board of the Oklahoma City Symphony Society. Mrs. Atkins and her husband, Charles, have three children: Edmund, Charles and Valerie. Address: 501 State Capitol, Oklahoma City, OK 73105

Atkins, Thomas I., administrator and state official, is secretary of communities and development for the state of Massachusetts. Though blacks make up less than 3 percent of Massachusetts population, he is the chief administrative officer of the state for economic development and the only black member of the governor's cabinet. He was born March 2, 1939 in Elkhart, Ind. Mr. Atkins is a Phi Beta Kappa graduate of Indiana University (B.A., 1961); Harvard University (M.A., 1963; J.D., 1969), and was awarded an honorary doctorate degree from Northeastern University. He is the first black elected to the Boston City Council, 1969. He is a member of the NAACP, a member of the Urban League and a member of the Harvard Board of Overseers. Mr. Atkins is married to Sharon Annette. They have three children: Todd, Thomas Jr., and Trena. Address: 100 Cambridge St., Room 1303, Boston, MA 02202.

Arthur Ashe Jr.

Hannah D. Atkins

Thomas I. Atkins

14

J. Edward Atkinson

Pearline Atkinson

Richard H. Austin

Atkinson, J. Edward, public relations executive, is a senior public relations supervisor for the Carnation Co. in Los Angeles, Calif., and acts as a liaison officer between Carnation and the minority communities. He was promoted to his present position in 1970 after five years as a sales representative and public relations supervisor. Born Jan. 21, 1914 in Denver, Colo., he received a B.A. degree from Loyola University in Los Angeles and for many years he owned and operated two restaurants in the city. He is the author of *Black Dimensions in Contemporary American Art,* a record of the genius of 50 American black artists, which was published in 1971 and recognized by *Esquire* magazine and the Business Committee for the Arts for its outstanding contribution in promoting the arts. Mr. Atkinson is a member of the Area Advisory Board to the Mayor of the City of Los Angeles and the President's Advisory Board of Loyola University. He and his wife, Antoinette, have two children, Edward and Joy. Address: Carnation Co., 5054 Wilshire Blvd., Los Angeles, CA 90019

Atkinson, Pearline, administrator, is administrative assistant and executive secretary to the executive director of the United Negro College Fund in New York, N.Y. She assists the executive director, supervises the clerical staff, takes minutes at all board meetings, and ensures efficient operation of the UNCF office. She has the authority to make decisions in the absence of the executive director. Born April 15, 1938 in New York City, she has studied at Queens College, the City College of New York and Hunter College. Before joining UNCF in 1964, she was executive secretary at the U.S. Army Procurement District, and was a legal secretary for the U.S. Army Intelligence Corp. (1956–60). Divorced, she has a daugher, Kim. Address: United Negro College Fund, 55 E. 52nd St., New York, NY 10022

Austin, Richard H., state government official, is secretary of state for the state of Michigan. He is second in line of succession to the governor. As secretary of state, Mr. Austin heads a department of 2,400 employees and over 250 branch offices who serve Michigan residents through the issuance of automobile licenses and drivers' licenses, handling license appeals and overseeing elections. He is also keeper of the Great Seal and official records and archives of state government. Mr. Austin was born May 5, 1913 in Stouts Mountain, Ala. He studied business administration at Detroit Institute of Technology (B.S., 1937) and holds an honorary Doctor of Laws degree from Detroit College of Business (1971). In 1941, he became Michigan's first black certified public accountant and worked in his own firm until 1967. Mr. Austin received national attention as a candidate for mayor of Detroit in 1969. He led the field in the primary and received 49 percent of the vote in the non-partisan general election. He was elected secretary of state in 1970, thus becoming the first black secretary of state in the country. He is a member of the American Institute of Certified Public Accountants, president of the Michigan Area Bay Boy Scouts of America, chairman of the Randolph W. Wallace Kidney Foundation and a member of the boards of directors of ten organizations. He is also active in the NAACP and the Urban League. He and his wife, Ida, have a daughter, Hazel. Address: Treasury Bldg., Lansing, MI 48238

B

James S. Avery

John A. Axam

Warren H. Bacon

Avery, James S., public relation executive, is public affairs manager of the Exxon Co., U.S.A. in Pelham, N.Y. He is responsible for the planning, programming, and project development of the petroleum company's governmental, political, community and public relations programs within an eight-state region covering New York, New Jersey and the six New England states. Born March 24, 1923 in Cranford, N.J., he has degrees from Columbia College (A.B., history, 1948) and Columbia University (M.A., history and education, 1949). Active in numerous educational and civic affairs, Mr. Avery is grand basileus of the 40,000-member Omega Psi Phi fraternity, chairman of Union County N.J. Coordinating Agency for Higher Education, member of Past Presidents Advisory Council of the National Association of Market Developers and of Frontiers International. He and his wife, Marge, have two children, Sheryl and James Jr. Address: Exxon Co., U.S.A., Hutchinson River Parkway, Pelham, NY 10803

Axam, John A., librarian, is head of the stations department at the Free Library of Philadelphia, Pa. He is responsible for library service to institutions (hospitals, prisons, schools, etc.), to undereducated adults and young adults and to communities that are more than one-half mile from a branch or the central library. He established and directs The Reader Development Program. He was born Feb. 12, 1930 in Cincinnati, Ohio, and has degrees from Cheyney State College (B.S., 1953), and Drexel University (M.S., library science, 1958). He is a member of the Pa. Library Assn., and the American Library Assn., and is on the board of directors of the Crime Prevention Assn. and on the Youth Services Review Comm. He and his wife, Dolores, have no children. Address: 236 N. 23rd St., Philadelphia, PA 19103

Bacon, Warren H., administrator, is assistant director manpower administration for Inland Steel Co. of Chicago. Born Jan. 12, 1923 in Chicago, he is a graduate of Roosevelt University (B.A., 1948) and the University of Chicago (M.B.A., 1951). Before assuming his present position, Mr. Bacon was a vice president of administration for Supreme Life Insurance Co. in Chicago. He is a member of the American Iron and Steel Institute, a director of Hyde Park Federal Savings & Loan Association of Chicago, and president of Urban Ventures, Inc., an economic development corporation to aid minority entrepreneurs. In 1963 he was appointed a member of the Chicago Board of Education and is currently serving his second five-year term. His civic interests include membership in the Economic Club of Chicago. He is also a trustee of the Russell Sage Foundation and a director of Home Investment Fund and other organizations. He and his wife, Mary Lou, have three children: Warren, Roger and Randall. Address: 30 West Monroe St., Chicago. IL 60603

D'Army Bailey

Pearl Bailey

David N. Baker Jr.

James Baldwin

Bailey, D'Army, city official, is a member of the City Council of Berkeley, Calif. Born Nov. 29, 1941 in Memphis, Tenn., he is a graduate of Clark University in Worcester, Mass. (B.A., 1964) and the Yale University School of Law (LL.B., 1967). He practices law in Berkeley; he was national director of the Law Students' Civil Rights Research Council. He is single. Address: City Hall, 3284 Adeline St., Berkeley, CA 94709

Bailey, Pearl (Mae), entertainer, who has been singing professionally since 1933 and acting professionally since 1946, is one of America's best known entertainers. She has released numerous albums, appeared in Broadway shows, hosted her own television series and appeared in clubs and theaters in the U.S. and in Europe. Born March 29, 1918 in Newport News, Va., she attended public schools in Philadelphia, Pa. She began singing with various popular bands when she was 15. At 28, she made her stage debut in *St. Louis Woman.* Her acting career has included roles in the Broadway musical *House of Flowers* and the motion pictures *Variety Girl* and *Carmen Jones.* She has recorded with Columbia, Coral and Decca record companies. In 1967, she won a special Tony award for her performance in the Broadway musical, *Hello Dolly.* Her autobiography, *Raw Pearl,* was published in 1969. Her husband, drummer Louis Bellson Jr., frequently performs with her. They have two children, Tony and Dee Dee. Address: c/o William Morris Agency, 1740 Broadway, New York, NY 10019

Baker, David Nathaniel Jr., musician-composer-educator, is chairman of the jazz department at Indiana University, his alma mater (B.M.E.; M.M.E.). Born Dec. 21, 1931, in Indianapolis, Ind., he started his music education in the seventh grade learning to play tuba. In 1959, he received a Dizzy Gillespie Scholarship to attend the School of Jazz in Lenox, Mass., where Ornette Coleman and other names-to-be were his classmates, and where he joined the George Russell Sextet. Next, Mr. Baker studied trombone with the master, J.J. Johnson. He toured Europe with Quincy Jones in 1961 and has performed with many other important jazz ensembles, including those of Stan Kenton, Lionel Hampton and Wes Montgomery. Mr. Baker has composed 100 jazz and classical works, has been guest conductor with the Indianapolis Symphony, the Indianapolis Civic Orchestra and the Indiana University Symphony and has performed as a soloist with the Boston Symphony and the Evansville (Ind.) Philharmonic. He is the author of four books on musical improvisation and has received a long list of awards and citations. Mr. Baker and his wife, Eugenia, have one daughter, April Elaine. Address: Indiana University School of Music, Bloomington, IN 47401

Baldwin, James, author, is a novelist, essayist and lecturer. His novels include *Go Tell It on the Mountain* (1953), *Notes of a Native Son* (1955), *Giovanni's Room* (1956), *Another Country* (1963) and *Tell Me How Long The Train's Been Gone* (1968). His other works include two collections of essays, *Nobody Knows my Name* (1961) and *The Fire Next Time* (1964), and *Rap on Racism* (1971), his lengthy conversation with anthropologist Dr. Margaret Mead. His plays are *Blues for Mister Charlie* (1964) and *The Amen Corner* (1968). His collection of short stories, *Going to Meet The Man,* was published in 1965. His most recent work is *One Day When I Was Lost* (1973). He was born Aug. 2, 1924 in New York, N. Y. and became a Pentecostal Church preacher in Harlem as a teenager. In 1943, he moved to New York's Greenwich Village to work at various jobs and to write. Five years later, disillusioned by racism in the U. S., he went to Paris, France, and lived for a number of years. He returned to the U. S. and became an outspoken critic of racism and discrimination, then returned to Europe to divide his time between southern France and Istanbul, Turkey. He has received numerous literary awards. Address: c/o Dial Press, 750 3rd Ave., New York, NY 10003

Ernest (Ernie) Banks

Fred L. Banks Jr.

Kathleen F. Banks

Banks, Ernest (Ernie), baseball coach, is the first base coach and former player with the Chicago Cubs. Mr. Banks began playing professionally with the Negro American League in 1950 and in 1953 went with the Kansas City Monarchs. In 1954, Mr. Banks had his first full year with the Cubs turning in a .275 batting average. The following year the shortstop broke two major league records—44 home runs (more than any major league shortstop had ever hit in a season), five of which were grand slams, another major league record. He broke his own home run record in 1958. He was named Most Valuable Player in the National League in 1958 and 1959, played in 13 All-Star games and in 1971 was named to the Texas Sports Hall of Fame. Mr. Banks was born in Dallas, Tex., on Jan. 31, 1931. An executive with Seaway National Bank, Mr. Banks is on the board of managers of the Chicago Metropolitan YMCA and is member of the board of the Chicago Transit Authority. He is the author of a book, *Mr. Cub.* He and his wife, Eloyce, have three children: a daughter, Jan, and twin sons, Jerry and Joey. Address: 1060 W. Addison St., Chicago, IL 60613

Banks, Fred L. Jr., attorney, is a partner in Anderson, Banks, Nichols and Leventhal, a law firm in Jackson, Miss. The firm conducts a general law practice but specializes in civil rights cases as the Mississippi arm of the NAACP Legal Defense and Educational Fund, Inc. Taking over an office formerly funded by the Legal Defense and Educational Fund, Mr. Banks and his partners have established a self-supporting firm "able and willing to undertake major civil rights cases no other private firm in Mississipi will handle." Born Sept. 1, 1942 in Jackson, he attended Howard University (B.A., business administration, 1965) and Howard University School of Law (J.D., 1968). While in college, he worked part-time at U.S. government agencies and at Freedmen's Hospital. In 1966-67, as a Ford Foundation Fellow, he did research in civil rights cases at Howard Law School. He is president of the Jackson branch NAACP and is city attorney of Fayette, Miss. He and his wife, Taunya, have two children, Rachel and Jonathan. Address: 538 1/2 N. Farish St., Jackson, MS 39202

Banks, Kathleen F., writer, is a publicist with NBC-TV in Burbank, Calif. She handles publicity for "The Flip Wilson Show" and "The Dinah Shore Show." A journalist, she has worked as a newswriter and feature writer for several network news programs and for the *Los Angeles Times.* She teaches English at Los Angeles City College and at Los Angeles Southwest College. Born Nov. 21, 1941 in Chattanooga, Tenn., she is a graduate of Wayne State University (B.A.) and the University of California at Los Angeles (M.S.). She is a member of the Publicists Guild, the Writers Guild of America, Delta Sigma Theta and Sigma Theta Phi. Mrs. Banks and her husband, Shermont, have no children. Address: NBC Publicity, 3000 W. Alameda, Burbank, CA 91505

Baraka, Imamu Amiri (LeRoi Jones), writer and activist, is the director of Spirit House and spiritual leader of Temple Kawaida in Newark, N.J. Born Oct. 7, 1934 in Newark, he received his B.A. in English (1953) from Howard University and did graduate work at the New School for Social Research and Columbia University in New York City. Known as one of America's most distinguished poets and playwrights, he has also authored a book of essays, *Home,* and two critiques on black music. Among his early volumes of poetry are *Preface to a Twenty Volume Suicide Note* (1961) and *The Dead Lecturer* (1964). The more recent *Black Art* was published by his own company, Jihad Productions. His play, *The Dutchman,* won an Obie Award in 1964, and *The Slave* received second prize at the First Festival of Negro Arts held in Senegal in 1966. Both have been produced as films. In 1968, he established the Black Community Development organization in Newark to promote black nationalism, community control and Pan-Africanism. A powerful local political leader, he was an organizer of the National Black Political Convention held in Gary, Ind. in 1972 and is an official of the Congress of African People. He and his wife, Amini, live in Newark. He is the father of six children: Maisha, Asia, Obalaji Malik Ali, RasJua Al Aziz, Shani Isis Makeda and Amiri Seku Musa. Address: 33 Stirling St., Newark, NJ 07103

Barbee, Lloyd A., legislator, is a member of the Wisconsin State Legislature and a practicing attorney in Milwaukee, Wis. He was born Aug. 17, 1925 in Memphis, Tenn., and has degrees from LeMoyne College (B.A. social science, 1949) and the University of Wisconsin Law School (J.D., 1956). Representing a Milwaukee ghetto district (he was first elected in 1965), Mr. Barbee was the only black member of the 133-member Wisconsin legislature until reapportionment in 1972. Labeled a "radical" because of his innovative bills in the legislature, he was the first legislator to introduce bills calling for state reparations for blacks and American Indians, the abolition of all prisons, and permitting unmarried prisoners to have conjugal visits. He is also responsible for passage of a fair housing bill. Mr. Barbee is also the chairman of the Wisconsin State Black Political Caucus. In the legislature, he serves on the Joint Committee on Finance and the Board on Government Operations. Divorced, he is the father of three children: Finn, Daphne and Rustam. Address: 110 E. Wisconsin Ave., Milwaukee, WI 53202

Barkley, Rufus, fashion designer, is a designer at Teal Traina, a clothing manufacturer, in New York, N.Y. He designs three collections—ranging from sportswear to daytime and evening dresses—each season. He was born Jan. 11, 1949 in New York and graduated in 1970 from the city's Parsons School of Design. While a student, he worked part-time as a design assistant at Oscar de la Renta, International. After graduation, he continued as a full-time assistant. He has received several awards for his work, including the Don Simonelli Critics Award and the J.C. Penney Sportswear Award. He is single. Address: 550 Seventh Ave., New York, NY 10018

Imamu Amiri Baraka

Lloyd A. Barbee

Rufus Barkley

Barnes, Edward J., educator, is professor of psychology and associate dean at the College of Arts and Science of the University of Pittsburgh (Pa.). Born Oct. 12, 1933, in Oakland Calif, he served in the Armed Forces (1949-51) and then earned a B.A. degree (1954) from San Francisco State College. He received an M.A. degree from the University of California at Berkeley and a Ph.D. degree (1963) from Michigan State University. He constantly has been involved in educational research and has written numerous published articles. He is a member of the American Psychological Association and other groups. He and his wife, Norma, live in Pittsburgh. Address: 617 Cathedral of Learning, Pittsburgh, PA 15212

Barnes, Eugene M., legislator, is a member of the Illinois Legislature, representing Chicago's 29th District. He is a member of the Illinois Black Political Caucus. He has served on the board of directors of the National Society of State Representatives and the Midwest Association for Sickle Cell Anemia. He has been active in the fight against sickle cell anemia, and introduced one of the first legislative bills in support of sickle cell research. He was born July 24, 1931 in Chicago. He and his wife, Melody, have three children, Vikki, Eugina and Craig. Address: State Capitol, Springfield, IL 62706

Barrett, Brenetta Howell, state official, is director of human resources for the state of Illinois. Born June 28, 1932 in Chicago, Ill., she studied at the Chicago Loop College and DePaul University. She was appointed in 1973 by Illinois Gov. Daniel Walker. Previously, she was employed by the director for community and public relations at the Chicago Economic Development Corporation. Active in civic, political and community affairs, she served as national vice chairman for the 1972 First National Conference on Business Opportunities for Women. She was also a consultant to the State of Illinois House Contracts Compliance Committee, National VISTA program, various community action organizations, the business education office of Howard University, and the Citizens Relations Service of Chicago. She is a member of the board of the American Civil Liberties Union in Illinois and also served on the advisory board of the Illinois Citizens for Medical Control of Abortions and the National Organization of Women, Chicago chapter. Mrs. Barrett has received numerous honors, including awards and citations from the Chicago Business Opportunity Fair, Illinois Youth Commission, Merit Employment Committee, Chicago/CORE, and the Chicago branch of the NAACP. She has four children: Cynthia, Sharonne (Abiibi), Kevin and Viveca. Address: Illinois Department of Human Resources, Chicago, IL 60604

Barrie, Scott, fashion designer, is president of Barrie/Sport Ltd., a women's fashion manufacturer, and president of Barrie Plus, Ltd., manufacturer of women's accessories in New York, N.Y. Mr. Barrie's designs are offered for sale in such stores as Saks Fifth Avenue, Lord and Taylor, Henri Bendel, I. Magnin and Bloomingdale's. Born January 16, 1945 in Philadelphia, Pa., he attended the Philadelphia Museum College of Art and the Mayer School of Fashion in New York City. Mr. Barrie, who supervises a staff of 30, started his own business in 1969. He designed the costumes for the film *Blood.* Address: 530 Seventh Ave., New York, NY 10018

Edward J. Barnes

Eugene M. Barnes

Brenetta H. Barrett

Scott Barrie

Marion Barry

Mary Treadwell Barry

Richmond Barthé

Barry, Marion, public official, was elected as president of the Washington (D.C.) Board of Education in 1972. He is also director of operations for Pride, Inc., a federally supported work-training and job placement agency involving some eight-hundred black youths and men aged 14 to 27. He was one of the co-founders (with his wife, the former Mary Treadwell, and Carroll Harvey, an engineer) of Pride, Inc. in 1967. He was the first national chairman of SNCC and once headed its Washington office. Born March 6, 1936 in Itta Bena, Miss., he is a graduate of LeMoyne College (B.S., chemistry, 1958) and Fisk University (M.S., chemistry, 1960)—both on full academic scholarships. He has studied for a doctorate at the University of Kansas (1960–61) and the University of Tennessee (1961–64). He has been a member of the Third World Coalition Against the War, and is a member of Alpha Phi Alpha fraternity. He is chairman of the board of directors of Pride Economic Enterprises, a profit-making, diversified corporation (founded in 1968) which owns various businesses in the District of Columbia. Mr. Barry and his wife, who is executive director of Pride, Inc., live in Washington. Address: Board of Education, 415 12th St., NW, Washington, DC 20004

Barry, Mary Treadwell, administrator, is executive director of Youth Pride, Inc. and president of both Pride Economic Enterprises, Inc. and Pride Environmental Services, Inc.—all in Washington, D.C. Youth Pride was founded in 1967 as a program for the development and employment of inner-city black males. The other two Pride corporations provide employment and business ownership for disadvantaged blacks. Born April 8, 1941 in Lexington, Ky., she attended Fisk University and Ohio State University. She is a student at Antioch Law School in Columbia, Md. Before joining Pride, she was a buyer and merchandise coordinator for a department store chain. She was a board member and chairwoman of the National Capital Head Start and the National Committee on Household Employment. She is a member of the D.C. Chapter of the National Association of Market Developers, Inc., the District of Columbia Citizens for Better Public Education, Inc., the American Management Association, the Human Rights for Prisoners Association, and the International Institute of Women's Studies. In 1970, she founded INPUT (the Independent Political Union of Trust), a local-level political action group. She is married to Marion S. Barry Jr. Address: 1536 U St., NW, Washington, DC 20009

Barthé, Richmond, sculptor, is a preeminent artist whose works appear in collections around the world. He was the first black sculptor commissioned to do a public monument dedicated to a white person when he was asked by New York City to do a relief medallion portrait for the Fifth Avenue Memorial to *New York Evening Journal* editor-columnist Arthur Brisbane. He is one of the few black artists successful enough to make a full-time living from his art. He was born Jan. 28, 1901 in Bay St. Louis, Miss. He studied at the Art Institute of Chicago, and has honorary degrees from Xavier University (M.A., 1934) and St. Francis College (Doctor of Fine Arts, 1947). He began his artistic career as a painter, but changed to sculpture in 1928. He did the marble bust of Booker T. Washington for New York University's Hall of Fame and carved a large frieze entitled *The Green Pastures* on a Harlem housing project. For Haiti, he made monumental statues of liberators Toussaint L'Ouverture and Jacques Dessalines. Leading museums in Africa, Austria, Canada, England, France and Germany own his works, as do the Whitney Museum of American Art and the Metropolitan Museum of Art in New York and the Philadelphia Museum. He received Rosenwald and Guggenheim fellowships and was the recipient of the James J. Hoey award for Interracial Justice in 1945. Since the 1950s, he has resided in Jamaica in the British West Indies. Address: Cole Gale PO St. Ann Jamaica BWI

Nathaniel Bates

The Rt. Rev. H. I. Bearden

Romare Bearden

Bates, Nathaniel, city official, is the mayor of Richmond, Calif. Upon his election in 1972, he became the third black man to serve in that capacity. A city councilman since 1968, he was vice mayor during 1971. Mr. Bates is also the senior deputy probation officer of Alameda County, in Oakland, Calif., a position he has held since 1968. Born Sept. 9, 1931 in Cason, Tex., he attended San Francisco State College (B.A., psychology, 1963). He is president of the East Bay Division, League of California Cities, and vice chairman of the Human Resources Committee of that body. He is a member of the National League of Cities' Public Safety Committee, Black Probation and Parole Association, National Black Elected Officials Advisory Board, National Council on Alcoholism for Contra Costa County and the Regional Council on Criminal Justice. Mr. Bates and his wife, Shirley, have four children: Michael, Gail, Larry and Steven. Address: 24th & Barrett, Richmond, CA 94804

Bearden, The Right Reverend Harold I., clergyman, is bishop of the Third Episcopal District of the African Methodist Episcopal Church, comprising the states of Ohio and W. Va., and western Pa. Born March 8, 1910 in Atlanta, Ga., he has degrees from Morris Brown College (A.B.) and Turner Theological Seminary (B.D.), and honorary degrees from Kittrell, Daniel Payne, Campbell and Monrovia colleges, and Wilberforce University. Bishop Bearden was elected to his position in 1964. Under his administration, his district of the A.M.E. Church grosses $3 million annually. He and his wife, Lois, have six children: JoAnn, Harold, Gloria, Lloyd, Sharon and Richard. Address: African Methodist Episcopal Church, 1541 14th St., NW, Washington, DC 20005

Bearden, Romare H., artist, is one of America's most distinguished painters. His works have been exhibited in major museums, seen in some fifteen one-man exhibitions and in more than sixty group showings since he began painting seriously in the early 1930s. Intermittently, he was employed as a social worker with the New York City Department of Social Services. He has also written a number of songs. He was born Sept. 2, 1914 in Charlotte, N.C. After graduating from New York University (B.S., 1935), he studied at the Art Students League and had his first one-man show in 1940. In 1950, he went to Paris to study and paint. He began to create collages dealing with black themes in the 1960s. The Museum of Modern Art in New York gave him a major exhibition in 1971. He is art director of the Harlem Cultural Council and a founder of Cinque Gallery for young black artists. He is the author of a biography of the expatriate black artist Henry O. Tanner and co-author of *The Painter's Mind* (1969) and *Six Black Artists* (1972). Mr. Bearden is married to the former Nanette Rohan. Address 357 Canal St., New York, NY 10013

Belafonte, Harry, singer, actor and film director, heads his own motion picture production firm, HarBel. Born March 1, 1927 in New York, N.Y., he attended high school there and served with the U.S. Naval Reserve (1943–46). Again a civilian at age 19, he joined the American Negro Theatre, discovered his singing talent and was booked into nightclubs as a pop singer. Unhappy with the pop genre, he began to build a repertoire of folk ballads. He became an instant success at the Village Vanguard nightclub. A contract with RCA launched him as a recording star. He then starred in two films, *Bright Road* and *Carmen Jones*, followed by *Island in the Sun* in 1957. He starred in three of his own HarBel film productions: *The World, the Flesh and the Devil*, *Odds Against Tomorrow* and *The Angel Levine* and co-starred with Sidney Poitier in *Buck and the Preacher* in 1972. Also popular as a live performer, Mr. Belafonte starred in the Broadway production, *Three for Tonight*. His concerts have set many attendance records. Among his television successes, the 1959 special, ''Tonight with Belafonte'' won him an Emmy award for top musical performer. He and his wife, Julie. have two children, David and Gina. He has two daughters, Adrienne and Shari, by a previous marriage. Address: c/o The Mike Merrick Co., 9000 Sunset Blvd., Los Angeles, CA 90069

Bell, Al, business executive, is executive vice-president and board chairman of Stax Records, Inc. in Memphis, Tenn. Born March 15, 1940 in Little Rock, Ark., he is a graduate of Philander Smith College (B.S.; hon. L.H.D.). He was a disc jockey before joining Stax in 1966. He was named executive vice president in 1967. Mr. Bell is regarded as one of the most influential men in the recording industry. Through his management, the Stax Organization produces such international artists as Isaac Hayes, the Staple Singers, Rufus Thomas, the Dramatics, David Porter, The Bar-Kays, and Booker T. and the MGs. He and his wife, Lydia, have a son, Gregory. Address: 98 N. Avalon. St., Memphis TN 38104

Bell, Edward B., corporate executive, is coordinator of special projects in the merchandising department at Atlantic Richfield Co. in Philadelphia, Pa. He is responsible for the coordination of marketing programs and activities directed toward urban marketing areas. Born March 25, 1931 in Philadelphia, he is a graduate of the University of Pennsylvania (B.A., 1953). He is a former professional football player with the Philadelphia Eagles (defensive halfback, 1955–58), the Hamilton Tiger-Cats in Canada (defensive halfback-linebacker, 1959) and the New York Titans (linebacker, 1960). He was an instructor at the Guided Missile School at Fort Monmouth, N.J., and was a technician in the research laboratory of General Electric Missile & Space Agency. He is national treasurer and a board member of the National Association of Market Developers, and a board member of Urban Market Developers and the Philadelphia Sandlot Sports Federation. He is founder and vice president of Men Concerned, of Philadelphia, and is a member of the Crime Commission of Philadelphia. He and his wife, Barbara, have two children, Elmyra and Edward Jr. Address: 260 S. Broad St., Philadelphia, PA 19101

Harry Belafonte

Al Bell

Edward B. Bell

Edward F. Bell

Thomas M. Bell

George M. Bellinger

Lillian P. Benbow

Bell, Edward F., attorney, is a senior partner in Bell and Brown, a law firm in Detroit, Mich. He was born April 22, 1929 in Grand Rapids, Mich., and has degrees from the University of Michigan (B.A., 1951) and Detroit College of Law (J.D., 1954). He was a social worker with Children's Aid Society in Detroit (1956 to 1959) and was in private law practice (1959 to 1969). He served for three years as a Wayne County (Detroit) circuit judge. In 1972, he resigned to campaign for election as mayor of Detroit. He is a former president of the National Bar Association. He and his wife, Marilyn, have two children, Celeste and Whitney. Address: 1550 Guardian Building, Detroit, MI 48226

Bell, Thomas M., legislator and businessman, is a state representative in Ohio (10th District, Cleveland). He serves on the State Education Committee and the State Health and Welfare Committee. He is also supervisor and part-owner of Merchants and Industrial Security Agency, a private protection agency in Cleveland. Born Jan. 23, 1948 in Cleveland, he attended Cuyahoga Community College and Wilberforce University. Mr. Bell, who was first elected in 1972 at age 23, is a member of the executive committee of the 21st Congressional District Caucus and the Plus Club, and has participated in raising funds for numerous community agencies. He and his wife, Sharon, live in Cleveland. Address: Ohio House of Representatives, Columbus, OH 43215

Bellinger, George M., electrical engineer, is president of Bar-Pat Manufacturing Co., Inc. in Bridgeport, Conn. Born Aug. 18, 1932 in Brooklyn, N. Y., he attended New Haven College. After 20 years of experience in circuit board and electro-mechanical assemblies, etc., he opened his own electronics manufacturing firm in 1970. The company boasted profits of $120,000 for 1972 and expected to double that figure in 1973. Bar-Pat designs, engineers, manufactures, tests and installs various electro-mechanical assemblies. Its customers include GE, RCA, IBM and Western Electric. Mr. Bellinger is a member of Greater Bridgeport Business and Professional Association, and Bridgeport Mental Health Council. He and his wife, Barbara, have four children: George, Randy, Rudolph and Patricia. Address: 437 Howard Avenue, Bridgeport, CT 06605

Benbow, Lillian Pierce, administrator, is director housing programs of the Michigan Civil Rights Commission in Detroit, Mich. She is responsible for overall program development and implementation of the agency's housing program designed to broaden housing opportunities for minority groups. She is also national president of the 60,000-member Delta Sigma Theta sorority. Born in Vicksburg, Miss., she is a graduate of Le Moyne College (B.A., social science) and studied philosophy at the University of Michigan and law at the Detroit College of Law. She is a member of the board of directors of Detroit Home for Girls. She is a member of the Michigan League for Human Services, the National Association of Human Rights Workers, and a number of other professional and civic groups. She has received numerous citations and awards. Her husband, Edward D. Benbow, is drug coordinator for the Michigan State Board of Education. They have a foster son (a nephew), Thomas Edward McInnis. Address: 900 Cadillac Sq. Bldg., Detroit, MI 48226

Lerone Bennett Jr.

Rev. Marion D. Bennett

Edwin C. Berry

Bennett, Lerone Jr., journalist and historian, is senior editor of *Ebony* magazine in Chicago, Ill. Born Oct. 17, 1928 in Clarksdale, Miss., he is a graduate of Morehouse College (A.B., 1949; honorary Litt.D., 1965). After his graduation, he was a reporter for the *Atlanta Daily World* and was promoted to city editor in 1953. He joined Johnson Publishing Co. 1963 as an editor of *Jet* magazine. Later, he transferred to *Ebony* and was promoted to senior editor in 1958. He is the author of *Before the Mayflower: A History of Black America.* Since it was published in 1962, the book has sold more than 50,000 hardcover copies. By 1973, it was in its fourth revised edition. As of 1973, he had written six other books published by Johnson: *The Negro Mood* (1964); *What Manner of Man: A Biography of Martin Luther King Jr.* (1964); *Confrontation: Black and White* (1965); *Black Power U.S.A.: The Human Side of Reconstruction, 1867–1877* (1967); *Pioneers in Protest* (1968), and a collection of essay and speeches. *The Challenge of Blackness* (1972). He also was editor of the three-volume *Ebony Pictorial History of Black America* (1972). He has written numerous articles for *Ebony.* He is a lecturer, and has taught black history as an associate professor at Northwestern University (1968–69) and has been associated with the Institute of the Black World in Atlanta, Ga. His poetry has appeared in such volumes as *New Negro Poets: U.S.A.* edited by Langston Hughes. He and his wife, Gloria, have four children: Lerone III, Joy, and twins Constance and Courtney. Address: 820 S. Michigan Ave., Chicago, IL 60605 **See article on Lerone Bennett Jr. in Volume II.**

Bennett, The Reverend Marion D., clergyman and legislator, is pastor of Zion United Methodist Church in North Las Vegas, Nev. and is a member of the Nevada Legislature (Democrat, Las Vegas). Born May 31, 1936 in Greenville, S.C., he is a graduate of Morris Brown College (A.B.) and the Interdenominational Theological Center (M.Div.). He has also studied at the University of Nevada, Atlanta University and the Switzerland Ecumenical Institute. He was president of the Las Vegas Branch NAACP (1963–67), vice president (1967–69), treasurer (1969), and president (1971–73). He was chairman of the board of directors of Operation Independence (1969–71) and treasurer of the Economic Board of Clark County, Nevada (1969). He is a member of the board of directors of Black Methodists for Church Renewal and is active in numerous church and civic groups. In the legislature, he is chairman of the Health and Welfare Committee and a member of the Legislative Functions and Rules Committee. He and his wife, Gwendolyn, have two children, Marion Jr. and Karen. Address: 1911 Goldhill Ave., Las Vegas, NV 89106

Berry, Edwin C., corporate executive, is special assistant to the president of Johnson Products Co. and is director of the George E. Johnson Foundation. Born Nov. 11, 1910 in Oberlin, Ohio, he is a graduate of Oberlin College (B.A., 1934) and the University of Pittsburgh (M.A., 1943). He has been a teacher and guest lecturer at the University of Chicago, Northern Illinois University, Northwestern University, Roosevelt University, National College and Loyola University. He has been a human relations consultant to various industrial, religious and educational groups and has contributed articles to a number of professional publications. He was the first director of the Portland, Ore. branch of the Urban League (1945–55) and was executive director of the Chicago Urban League (1956–70). He is a member of the boards of directors of numerous organizations, including the Community Fund of Metropolitan Chicago. He and his wife, Betsy, live in Chicago. He has a son, Joseph. Address: 8522 S. Lafayette Ave., Chicago, IL 60619

Leonidas H. Berry, M.D.

Theodore M. Berry

Joseph G. Bertrand

Berry, Leonidas H., M.D., physician, is in the private practice of medicine in Chicago, Ill. and is senior attending physician at Cook County, Michael Reese and Provident hospitals in Chicago. He grew up in Norfolk, Va. and is a graduate of Wilberforce University (B.S., 1924), the University of Chicago (S.B., 1925), Rush Medical College (M.D., 1929) and the University of Illinois (M.S., pathology, 1933). He has an honorary degree from Wilberforce University (Sc.D., 1945). He is a member of the board of directors of the Service Federal Savings and Loan Co. in Chicago, Ill. He is a diplomate of the American Board of Internal Medicine, the Subspecialty Board of Gastroenterology and the National Board of Medical Examiners; a member of the American Medical Association, the American Gastroscopic Society; a Fellow of the New York Academy of Medicine; past president of the National Medical Association and past president of the Cook County Physicians Association. He has written numerous scientific articles for national and state medical journals and is a co-author of a book (scheduled to be published in 1973) on endoscopy; Dr. Berry is a pioneer in the field. He has received several awards, including the University of Chicago Alumni Achievement award, the Distinguished Service award of the National Medical Association and a Certificate of Merit for Scientific Exhibits from the Chicago Medical Society. He and his wife, Emma, have a daughter, Judith. Address: 2600 S. Michigan Ave., Chicago, IL 60616

Berry, Theodore M., city official, is a city councilman and in 1972 was elected as mayor of Cincinnati, Ohio. (Cincinnati has a city manager form of government; mayors are elected by their fellow-councilmen.) He was vice mayor of the city (1956–57). Born Nov. 8, 1905 in Maysville, Ky., he is a graduate of the University of Cincinnati (A.B., liberal arts, 1928; LL.B., 1931). He has served as a councilman for many years and is a member of two law firms—Goldman, Cole and Putnick, in Cincinnati, and Lawson, Lawson, Taylor and Phillips, in Washington, D.C. He has held numerous civic and governmental positions on the local, state and national levels and from 1965 to 1969 was director of community action programs with the U.S. Office of Economic Opportunity. He has been president of the Cincinnati Branch NAACP (1932–38 and 1943–46) and has served on the association's national board. He and his wife, Johnnie Mae, have four children: Faith, Darryl, Gail and Theodore. Address: City Hall, Room 150, 8th and Plum Sts., Cincinnati, OH 45202

Bertrand, Joseph G., city official, is city treasurer of Chicago, Ill. and is chairman and chief executive officer of Gateway National Bank of Chicago. He was president, chief executive and chairman of the board of Chicago's Highland Community Bank (1970–72) and was vice president of the city's Standard Bank and Trust Co. (1966–70). Elected as city treasurer on the Democratic ticket in April, 1971, he was the first black elected to a major city office in Chicago history. Born Oct. 27, 1931 in Biloxi, Miss., he is a graduate of the University of Notre Dame (A.B., economics, 1954), where he was the school's first black basketball All-American and attended Loyola University Law School in Chicago (1958–1960). He was named one of the Top Ten Young Men of 1965 by the Chicago Junior Association of Commerce and Industry. He is a member of a number of organizations, including the (Chicago) regional advisory council of the Small Business Administration, the (Illinois) Governor's Advisory Council for Economic Opportunity and the Highland Park Business Association. He and his wife, Joan, have six children: Joseph Jr., Joan, Jason, Justin, Jeffrey and Julian. Address: City Hall, Room 206, Chicago IL 60603

Andrew Billingsley

Billingsley, Andrew, educator, is vice president for academic affairs at Howard University in Washington, D.C. He is responsible for the coordination and administration of 15 academic units of undergraduate, graduate and professional instruction, including research and community service. Previously, he was assistant chancellor for academic affairs at the University of California (Berkeley). Born March 20, 1926 in Marion, Ala., he is a graduate of Grinnell College (B.A., political science, 1951), Boston University (M.S. social work, 1956), the University of Michigan (M.A., sociology, 1960), and Brandeis University (Ph.D., social welfare, 1964). He received the 1964 bi-annual National Association of Social Workers Award and the 1969 Michael Schwerner Memorial Award. He is author of *Black Families in White America*. He is a member of the board of directors of the Council on Social Work Education, the Publications Advisory Commission and the Child Welfare League of America. He and his wife, Amy, have two children, Angela and Bonita. Address: Howard University, Washington, DC 20001

Orzell Billingsley

Billingsley, Orzell Jr., jurist, is a municipal judge in Roosevelt City, Ala. and is a practicing attorney. Born Oct. 23, 1924 in Birmingham, Ala., he attended Talladega College (B.A., 1946) and Howard University (LL.B., 1950). He was one of the organizers and is general counsel of Alabama Cities and is a consultant for corporations, credit unions, cooperatives, etc. In 1967, he launched a movement to incorporate hundreds of largely black municipalities in the South, obtaining financial assistance from the federal government and from private foundations. Out of this movement evolved Roosevelt City, U.S.A., with Mr. Billingsley as its founder and municipal judge. As a civil rights attorney in 1968, he was responsible for the release of Johnny Coleman, imprisoned in 1961 by an all-white jury. Mr. Billingsley is the organizer of Afro Contractors Association of Alabama. He is a member of the Democratic executive committee of Jefferson County, on the board of directors of the Alabama State Conference of the NAACP, and the Jefferson County Committee for Economic Opportunity. Mr. Billingsley and his wife, Geselda, have a daughter, Shuane Elise. Address: 1630 4th Ave., Suite 510–12, Birmingham, AL 35203

Clyde Billington

Billington, Clyde, state legislator and realtor, is a member of the House of Representatives and president of Clyde Billington Realty, Inc., in Hartford, Conn. Mr. Billington directs his firm in the management of federally insured apartments and in home sales. He was elected in 1970 and 1972 to the legislature, where he represents the 7th Assembly District. Mr. Billington was born Aug. 29, 1934 in Hartford, Conn. He is a graduate of Lincoln University where he majored in chemistry and biology (B.S., 1958). He studied organic chemistry at the University of Connecticut and pharmacology at the University of Maryland. He has also studied at the University of Hartford and received his real estate license in 1965. Unable to get a job in the South, he joined Pratt and Whitney Aircraft Company as an assistant chemical engineer and became a controller in the Apollo Space Program. Mr. Billington is a member of the Greater Hartford Board of Realtors; a member of the American Chemical Society; and a member of the Certified Property Manager for FHA. He and his wife, Melora, have three children: Courtney, Christal and Mark, II. Address: 919 Albany Ave. Hartford, CT 06112

Myles E. Billups   Rev. Cecil Bishop   Joe Black

Billups, Myles E., administrator, is the only black member of the board of commissioners of the Virginia Port Authority, which has control of piers and docks in Virginia and supervises interstate and foreign commerce on piers and docks. Born Sept. 25, 1926, in Norfolk, Va., he worked his way up from dock worker to foreman and eventually to his present position, to which he was appointed in 1971 by the governor of Virginia. He is a former president of the Norfolk branch of the International Longshoremen Organization (AFL-CIO) and is the only union member on the port authority's board. He is a member of the advisory board of Eastern Virginia Medical College, the Virginia State AFL-CIO and the Health, Welfare & Planning Committee of Virginia. He and his wife, Dorothy, have seven children: Mrs. Alma C. Jackson, Mrs. Dorothy L. Brothers, Mrs. Myra J. Nixon, Myles Jr., Carolyn, Michael and Darlen. Address: Virginia Port Authority, 1222 Maritime Tower, Norfolk, VA 23320

Bishop, The Reverend Cecil, clergyman, is pastor of the Trinity A.M.E. Zion Church in Greensboro, N.C. Born May 12, 1930 in Pittsburgh, Pa., he is a graduate of Knoxville College (B.A., 1954), Howard University School of Religion (B.D., 1958) and Wesley Theological Seminary (S.T.M., 1960). Before assuming his present pastorate in 1960, he pastored the Clinton A.M.E. Zion Church in Rockville, Md. (1957–60). He was ordained a deacon in 1955 and an elder in 1957. He is director of the A.M.E. Zion Church's Division of Preaching Ministries (Department of Evangelism) and is a member of the Board of Home Missions. He is a member of the North Carolina State Advisory Committee of the U.S. Commission on Civil Rights, and is a member of national and state church organizations. He is chairman of the Greensboro Housing Authority and is active in several local civic groups. He and his wife, Wilhelma, live in Greensboro. Address: 631 E. Florida St., Greensboro, NC 27406

Black, Joe, corporate executive, is vice president of special markets of the Greyhound Corp. in Phoenix, Ariz. For this holding company of more than 90 subsidiaries with an annual gross of about $2.8 billion, Mr. Black is responsible for policies, practices and procedures that affect the black consumer market. He has been with Greyhound for 10 years and has been special markets representative; director of special markets, and vice president of special markets for Greyhound Lines, Inc., the corporation's transportation subsidiary. He has been in his present post for four years. Born Feb. 28, 1924 in Plainfield, N.J., Mr. Black has a degree from Morgan State College (B.S.) and pursued graduate studies at Rutgers University and Seton Hall University. Before joining Greyhound, he taught at the Management Training School of the 2nd Congressional District Business and Professional Women's Club of Chicago, Ill. Mr. Black is the father of Martha Jo and Joseph Frank. Address: Greyhound Tower, Phoenix, AZ 85077

Leona R. Black

Lucien E. Blackwell

Robert B. Blackwell

Black, Leona R., county official, is chief administrator of the Fraud-Complaint Division of the State's Attorney's Office of Cook County (Chicago), Ill. She is in charge of planning, programming and supervising all programs designed to eliminate consumer fraud. Born Jan. 5, 1924 in Galveston, Tex., she attended Prairie View A&M College, Cortez Peters Business College, Roosevelt University and the University of Chicago. In the 1972 election for state's attorney, she helped mobilize some 500,000 black voters on Chicago's South Side on behalf of the successful candidate, Bernard Carey. She was a delegate to the 1972 Democratic National Convention and is a member of the Illinois Democratic Women's Caucus and the Illinois Black Caucus. She is a widow. Address: 2600 S. California Ave., Chicago, IL 60008

Blackwell, Lucien E., legislator, is a member of the Pennsylvania House of Representatives from the 188th District (Philadelphia County). He was elected to the office in 1972. Born Aug. 1, 1931 in Whitset, Pa., he is a student of political science at St. Joseph's College. He has been a business agent for Local 1332 of the International Longshoremen's Association (AFL-CIO); a member of the Port Coordinating Council of Philadelphia and the District Council Port of Philadelphia; a committeeman of the 46th Ward (Philadelphia), which he served as chairman of the labor committee; an instructor with the Supreme Council of Cadets of America, and an organizer with the (Philadelphia) Neighborhood Youth Council. He is a member of Pyramid Temple No. 1 and Demolay Consistory No. 1 in Philadelphia. In 1949, as an amateur boxer, he won the novice diamond belt championship, and in 1953 the light middleweight title of the U.S. Army's 25th Infantry Division in Korea. He and his wife, Jannie, have four children. Address: Pennsylvania House of Representatives, Harrisburg, PA 17120

Blackwell, Robert B., public official, is mayor of Highland Park, Mich. (pop. 35,000). First elected in 1968, he was reelected in 1970 to a four-year term. He was born Nov. 4, 1921 in Meridian, Miss. and attended Talladega College, Howard University (B.A., 1949) and Detroit College of Law. Prior to his election as mayor, he was a city councilman and a member of the City Planning Commission, Police Commission and Fire Commission. He was elected in 1970 as chairman of the National Black Caucus of Local Elected Officials. He is a member of the executive board of the National League of Cities, member of advisory committees of the U.S. Department of Housing and Urban Development, and consultant to the President's Advisory Council on Management Improvements. He and his wife, Florrie, have four children: Brenda, June, Arthur and Bobbi. Address: 30 Gerald Ave., Highland Park, MI 48203

Eubie Blake

Ulysses B. Blakeley

Clarence W. Blount

Blake, James Hubert ("Eubie"), musician, is America's oldest living black composer. At 90, he has been in show business for 76 years. Born Feb. 7, 1883 in Baltimore Md., "Eubie" started playing the piano at six and professionally at 17. He was taught piano by Margaret Marshall, musical composition by Llewelyn Wilson and at the age of 66 completed a course in "the Schillinger System of Composition" at New York University. In 1915, he and Noble Sissle formed a partnership as lyricist and composer and later became the well-known vaudeville team of Sissle and Blake. In 1921, Mr. Blake and Mr. Sissle, together with another vaudeville team, produced the pioneer of black revues of Broadway, *Shuffle Along*. One song, "I'm Just Wild About Harry," is still popular. In the early 1930's Mr. Blake collaborated with Andy Razaf and wrote the musical score for *Blackbirds*. Out of this association came the still popular hit, *Memories of You*. In the early '40s Mr. Blake became musical conductor for the USO Hospital Unit, touring the nation for five years. He retired in 1946. In May, 1965, Sissle and Blake were honored by the American Society of Composers, Authors and Publishers. In August, 1965, the team were honored guests at the 36th Annual Chicagoland Music Festival. In 1969, Mr. Blake recorded a two record album entitled *The 86 Years of Eubie Blake*, and in 1972 he performed a solo concert at Alice Tully Hall in New York City. Mr. Blake and his wife live in New York. Address: 284-A Stuyvesant Ave., Brooklyn, NY 11221

Blakeley, The Reverend Ulysses Buckley Sr., religious executive, is executive secretary of Black Presbyterians United, the black caucus of the Presbyterian Church of America. Born Nov. 29, 1911 in Laurens, S.C., he attended Lincoln University (B.A., sociology and philosophy, 1926; B.S.T., 1939), the Harvard University Chaplain's School (1943), Temple University, the University of Pennsylvania and Parsons College (D.D., 1959) in Iowa. He was the first black pastor of First Presbyterian Church in Chicago, Ill. A trained community organizer, the Rev. Blakeley was among the founders of The Woodlawn Organization in Chicago, one of the pioneers of local social and political organization. He and his wife, Gwendolynne, have three children: Rebecca, Ulysses Jr. and Gwendolynne. Address: 9 S. Munn Ave., East Orange, NJ 07050

Blount, Clarence W., legislator and educator, is a Maryland state senator (Democrat, District 5, Baltimore) and is coordinator of the New Dunbar Development Team, a group of community persons and educators who are supervising the development of curriculum, the development of a management system, training staff, etc. for a new "open-space" school in Baltimore. Born April 20, 1921 in Beaufort County, N.C., Mr. Blount is a graduate of Morgan State College (A.B., political science) and Johns Hopkins University (M.A., liberal arts). He has taken four years of graduate courses in international law and international relations at Georgetown University, and has studied at Riverside (Calif.) College and the University of Florence (Italy). He is a former high school teacher and principal. He is chairman of the twelve-member Baltimore city senatorial delegation—a major achievement for a freshman senator (he was elected in 1970) and a "first" for a black legislator. He is a member of a number of education and civic groups, including the National Association of Secondary School Principals and the Academy of Political and Social Science. During World War II service in the U.S. Army, he was a defense trial lawyer, assisted in repatriating refugees and prisoners of war, and investigated claims against American acts of war. He and his wife, Gordine, have three sons: Michael, Edward and Mark. Address: 3307½ Liberty Heights Ave., Baltimore, MD 21215

Vida Blue

Wendell N. Bodden

James Boggs

Blue, Vida, professional athlete, is one of the leading pitchers with the Oakland Athletics of the American League. More than any other single player, he revitalized the national sport of baseball in 1971, his first full major league season. When he won both the Cy Young (he was the youngest player ever to do so) and Most Valuable Player awards, he significantly boosted the A's home attendance. Born July 28, 1949 in Mansfield, La., he took over most of his family responsibilities after his father died. Always a talented athlete, his first love was football and he set several records at DeSota High School. Although several college scouts wanted to sign him, he decided to attend Grambling College but left there before he graduated to sign with the then Kansas City Athletics. He played the 1971 season on a $13,500 contract and held out the following year for more money. He won only eight games that next season, but sparkled in relief appearances as the A's first beat the Detroit Tigers in the American League playoff games and then the Cincinnati Reds of the National League in the World Series. He is a bachelor. Address: Oakland Athletics, Oakland-Alameda County Coliseum, Oakland, CA 94621

Bodden, Wendell N., administrator, is in charge of the cooperative education and high school work/study programs for Grumman Aerospace Corp. His responsibilities include administration of program budgets, consultant to various colleges, planning, counseling, recruiting and developing cooperative education programs in the Long Island region of New York. Born March 8, 1930 in New York City, he attended C.W. Post College and the Armed Forces Institute and has participated in numerous management, insurance and human relations courses and seminars. Prior to his present position, Mr. Bodden served as assistant group leader and designer of structural systems for Grumman Aerospace Corp. He has been chairman of the educational committee of the NAACP in Long Island, vice president of the National Cooperative Education Association and has held various management and supervisory positions on and outside the job. Mr. Bodden notes that as of now there are about two or three blacks who direct programs in the business world throughout the country but the field is growing rapidly and will continue to grow. He is a member of the Wyandawch Development Cooperation, the Belmont Lake Civic Association and the Afro-American Republicans. He and his wife, Natalie, have three children: Mark, Wendell Jr. and Ingrid, Address: Grumman Aerospace Center, Dept. 327-Plant 39, Bethpage, NY 11714

Boggs, James, author, worked for 28 years in a Detroit, Mich. automobile plant before deciding to quit his job at age 48 to undertake "a theoretical analysis of the history of U. S. development and to project a vision of what we must do in this country to develop another way for man to live." Since publication in 1963 of his first book, *The American Revolution: Pages from a Negro Worker's Notebook*, he has continued to explore the concept of "black power" in relation to the cyber-cultural revolution. He also wrote *Racism and the Class Struggle,* and he and his wife, Grace, are at work (as of 1973) on a new book tentatively titled *The American Revolution and the Evolution of Humanity.* His books and articles have played a key role in the development of the ideology of the black revolution. Born May 28, 1919 in Marion Junction, Ala., he moved North after graduating from high school and became a laborer. He is self-educated. He and his first wife, Annie, had six children: James, Wayman, Donald, Jacqueline, Thomasine and Ernestine. Address: 3062 Field St., Detroit, MI 48214

Darwin W. Bolden

Dorothy Bolden

Julian Bond

Bolden, Darwin Willis, a corporate executive, is president of the New York-based Pan African Business Information Center, a non-profit center which serves as a "one-stop" business information agency for promotion of business development in Africa and the Caribbean, and of trade between Africa, the Caribbean and black America. He assumed the position in January, 1973 after resigning as national executive director of the Interracial Council for Business Opportunity, the well-known national business counseling organization that has assisted many black enterprise efforts. Mr. Bolden was born Aug. 8, 1932 in Niagara Falls, N.Y., and is a graduate of Syracuse University (BA, economics and political science, 1951) and Yale University Law School (LL.B., 1959). Under his leadership, ICBO grew from an agency serving fewer than 250 clients to one serving more than 2,100. Its offices increased from 4 to 14, and capital secured for clients grew from $350,000 to more than $20 million a year. Considered an authority on black economic development, Mr. Bolden was director of the Black Elected Officials Conference and was a member of President Nixon's Minority Enterprise Advisory Committee. He and his wife, Margaret, have two children, Faiz and Darwin. Address: Pan African Business Information Center, 575 Madison Ave., New York, NY 10016

Bolden, Dorothy (Mrs. Abram Thompson), administrator, is president of the National Domestic Workers Union and is director of the Homemaking Skills Training Program in Atlanta, Ga. She was a founder-organizer of the union. She recruits domestic workers for union membership and supervises a homemaking skills project that involves consumer rights, nutrition, child care, credit and budgeting, cooking and housecleaning and serving. Born in Fulton County, Ga., she attended high school and studied at the Chicago (Ill.) School of Dress Designers. "And I have 40 years of experience as a maid," she says. She is a member of the Atlanta Legal Aid Society, member of the board of directors of the Welfare Rights Organization and member of the League of Women Voters. She was a member of the Advisory Committee of the U.S. Commission on the Rights and Responsibilities of Women. She and her husband, Abram Thompson, have seven children: Frank, Avon, Dorothy, Altermiece, Anthony, Abram Jr. and Antonia. Address: 643 Delridge St., N.W., Atlanta, GA 30314

Bond, Julian, legislator, is a member of the Georgia House of Representatives and a nationally known civil rights and political personality. Born Jan. 14, 1940 in Nashville, Tenn., he is a graduate of Morehouse College (B.A., 1971), where he helped found the Committee for Human Rights (COHAR), a civil rights group whose sit-ins began the desegregation of lunch counters in Atlanta. In 1960, COHAR and other groups coalesced to form the Student Non-Violent Coordinating Committee (SNCC), which gained nationwide prominence for Mr. Bond and other members. Mr. Bond was elected to the Georgia legislature in November, 1965. During the national Democratic Convention in 1968, his name was placed in nomination for the office of vice president. A highly regarded poet, his work is included in *New Negro Poetry U.S.A.* He and his wife, Alice Louise, have four children: Phyllis, Janes, Horace and Michael. Address: Georgia Legislature, Atlanta, GA 30314

The Rt. Rev. I. H. Bonner

Arna W. Bontemps

James E. Booker

Bonner, The Right Reverend Isaiah Hamilton, clergyman, is presiding bishop of the Eighth Episcopal District of the African Methodist Episcopal Church. The District comprises Louisiana and Mississippi. Born July 27, 1890 in Camden, Ala., Bishop Bonner is a graduate of Knoxville College (A.B., B.D.) and has honorary degrees from the Morris Brown College (D.D.) and Allen University (LL.D.). After pastoring various churches, he was elected as a bishop in 1948 and was assigned to South Africa for four years. Before being assigned to the Eighth District he was sent to South Carolina where he helped raise more than $1 million for the church. He was the first Alabaman to be president (1961) of the Bishops' Council, the highest office of the A.M.E. Church. His wife, Mrs. Ida Belle Bonner, is Episcopal supervisor of the Women's Missionary Society of the Eighth District. Address: 1937 Peniston St., New Orleans, LA 70115

Bontemps, Arna Wendell, author and educator, has a career spanning more than three decades. He has written scores of novels, poems and biographies and has been a teacher at almost every educational level. He was born Oct. 13, 1902 in Alexandria, La. When he was a small child, his family moved to Los Angeles, Calif. He attended Union Pacific College (B.A., 1923), UCLA, Columbia University, New York University, and in 1943 received his M.A. from the University of Chicago. As a poet, he received the *Crisis* magazine prize in 1926, the Alexander Pushkin Prize, a Rosenwald Fellowship, and, in 1949–50, a Guggenheim Fellowship for creative writing. He has written or co-authored more than 22 books, among them: *God Sends Sunday* (1931) *Black Thunder* (1936); *Drums At Dusk* (1939); *Lonesome Boy* (with Langston Hughes), and *Famous Negro Athletes* (1964). He is one of the last survivors of the cultural black renaissance which flourished in Harlem in the 1920s. For many years, he was head librarian at Fisk University. In 1969, he accepted a distinguished visiting professorship at Yale University where he was a lecturer and curator in Afro-American studies. He later returned to Fisk as a writer-in-residence. He and his wife, Alberta, have six children: Joan Marie, Paul Bismark, Poppy Alberta, Camille Ruby, Constance Rebecca, Arna Alex. Address: 3506 Geneva Circle, Nashville, TN 37209

Booker, James E., public relations consultant, is president of James E. Booker Associates, Inc. in New York, N.Y. The firm specializes in civil rights, urban affairs, minority economic development, government relations and politics. For 18 years (1948 to 1966), Mr. Booker was a columnist and political editor of the *New York Amsterdam News.* He received more than 20 journalism awards. He was chief information consultant to the National Advisory Commission on Civil Disorders (which produced the 1968 Kerner Commission Report), and was consultant and director of information for the 1966 White House Conference on Civil Rights. He also has been a consultant to the New York State Commission on Human Rights. He is a lecturer at the New School for Social Research and is a commentator on community problems on "WWDT-Newsfronts," a weekly television show in New York City. Born July 16, 1926 in Riverhead, N.Y., he is a graduate of Howard University (A.B., 1947). He took special courses in journalism at New York University and the New School for Social Research, and graduated from the Armed Forces Information School and the U.S. Army Psychological Warfare School. He is a member of numerous organizations, including the National Press Club, the Newspaper Guild Club of New York, the American Newspaper Guild and the Capital Press Club. He and his wife, Jean, have a son, James Jr. Address: 527 Madison Avenue, Suite 301, New York, NY 10037

Booker, Simeon S., journalist, is Washington (D.C.) Bureau Chief of Johnson Publishing Company, Inc., and is a columnist for *Jet* magazine. Born Aug. 27, 1918 in Baltimore, Md., he is a graduate of Virginia Union University (B.A., English, 1942). He also studied radio, script writing and journalism at Cleveland College (1945–50). He was the second black man to win a Nieman Fellowship in journalism at Harvard University (1950) and was the first full-time black reporter for the *Washington Post* (1952–54). He is a member of the National Press Club, the Washington Speaker's Community and the Washington Press Club. He was a war correspondent in Vietnam and visited Africa with President Richard M. Nixon (1957), U.S. Attorney General Robert Kennedy (1962) and Vice President Hubert Humphrey (1968). He is a radio commentator for Westinghouse Broadcasting Co., and is the author of two books, *Black Man's America* and *Susie King Taylor, Black Nurse*. Divorced, he has three children: Simeon Jr., James and Theresa. Address: 1750 Pennsylvania Ave., NW, Washington, DC 20006

Booker, Sue, television producer, is host of the weekly news and public affairs television series, "Doin' It at the Storefront," on station KCET in Los Angeles, Calif. Born March 25, 1946 in Jersey City, N.J., she attended the University of Illinois (B.S., journalism) and Columbia University (M.S., journalism). She started in television as production assistant for "Children's Workshop" and later became co-producer of "The Black Frontier," a black history of the early West. Miss Booker won awards from The Associate Press (1971) for "Cleophus Adair," a documentary about the life of a black former drug addict in Watts and from The Atlantic International Film Festival, a Gold Medal Award for "Soledad," which she co-produced with Jesus Trevino. She is co-author of the book, *Cry at Birth*, an anthology of the writings of black youth (1972). Miss Booker is a member of the advisory board for the Office of Minority Affairs of the National Association of Educational Broadcasters and is acting vice chairman of the National Association of Black Media Producers. She is single. Address: KCET-TV, 4400 Sunset Dr., Los Angeles, CA 90027

Booker, Venerable F., banker, is president and chairman of the board of Freedom Bank of Finance in Portland, Ore. He was born in 1921 in Great Bend, Kan., and attended Portland State College and the Portland Conservatory of Music. He was a professional musician before he began developing a real estate business in 1960. In 1969, after weeks of discussions with business leaders, bankers, consultants and attorneys, he organized Freedom Bank of Finance with $600,000 in capital and $17,000 in deposits. Within a three-year period, the bank was "in the black"—with customers evenly divided between blacks and whites. Mr. Booker and his wife, Winfred, have three children, Venerable, Cheryl and Michael. Address: Freedom Bank of Finance, 2737 N.E. Union Ave., Portland, OR 97212

Simeon S. Booker

Sue Booker

V. F. Booker

Charles H. Boone

Rev. L. V. Booth

Rev. William H. Borders

Boone, Charles H., management specialist, is Market Manager-Southeast at Coca-Cola USA, in Atlanta, Ga. He is in charge of development of markets among blacks in the southeastern U.S. through his company's independent bottler system. He was formerly the company's sales and marketing representative in Columbia, S.C. He was born on March 13, 1932 in Summerville, S.C., and has a B.S. degree from Benedict College. He has also done special study in marketing at Harvard University. He is the former president of the National Association of Market Developers. He is active in youth programs, and served on the President's Task Force on Youth Motivation. He believes that opportunities in the field of business will open up quickly for those young blacks who prepare themselves at the college level. He and his wife, Margaret, have three children: Cheryl, Charlene and Crystal. Address: 164 Kevin Court, N.W., Atlanta, GA 30311

Booth, The Reverend L. Venchael, clergyman, is the pastor of the Zion Baptist Church in Cincinnati, Ohio and the president of the Progressive National Baptist Convention. He is also special secretary of the American Bible Society. Born Jan. 7, 1919 in Collins, Miss., he is a graduate of Alcorn A&M College (B.A., 1940), Howard University (B.D., 1943) and the University of Chicago (M.A., 1945). He has been pastor for 20 years. He is a contributor of book reviews to *The Journal of Religious Thought*, a scholarly publication at Howard University and is the author of *Who's Who In Baptist America* (1960). He is vice chairman of the Baptist World Alliance, the first black to serve as a member of the board of trustees at the University of Cincinnati and a member of the National Conference of Christian and Jews. He and his wife, Georgia, have five children: L. V. Jr., William, Anna, Georgia and Paul. Address: 630 Glenwood Ave., Cincinnati, OH 45229

Borders, The Reverend William Holmes, clergyman, has been pastor of the Wheat Street Baptist Church in Atlanta, Georgia, since 1937. Born Feb. 24, 1905 in Macon, Ga., he graduated from Morehouse College (B.A., 1929), Garrett Theological Seminary (B.D., 1932), Northwestern University (M.A., 1929) and holds honorary degrees from Gammon Theological Seminary, Morehouse College, Morris Brown, Shaw, Howard, Atlanta, and Wilberforce universities. In 1939, Rev. Borders was responsible for the hiring of black policemen and a black voter registration increase from 6,000 to 12,000. In 1945, he led the Atlanta black community in raising $11,000 to bury four Monroe, Ga., lynch victims and to offer a reward for the apprehension and conviction of their killers. He also led the movement in Atlanta which resulted in the hiring of black bus drivers in 1945. The Rev. Borders chaired the committee which initiated the desegregation of hotels, restaurants, and lunch counters in Atlanta. He is also responsible for the building of the Wheat Street Complex which includes a 522-unit, $5 million housing project, a Christian education building, a supermarket and a shopping center. His church has a credit union which is worth more than $300,000. The Rev. Borders has written seven books of sermons and poems and sold more than 100,000 copies. A widower, he has a son, William Holmes Borders Jr., and a daughter, Juel Pate Borders-Benson, are both physicians. Address: 24 Young St., N.E., Atlanta, GA 30301

35

Arnita Y. Boswell

Hildagardeis Boswell

Alvin J. Boutte

Boswell, Arnita Y., educator, is associate field work professor at the University of Chicago School of Social Service Administration in Chicago, Ill. She teaches graduate and Ph.D. students. She is also director of the school's Public Welfare Curriculum Development Program. Previously, she was a school social worker for the Great Cities Improvement Project (Chicago); special counselor for minority undergraduate students at the University of Chicago; human rights coordinator for OEO (Chicago), and director of social service for Project Headstart in Chicago. She was a visiting lecturer at George Williams College and Roosevelt University in Chicago, and supervised social work services for Project Headstart in black communities in the South, in Appalachia, Hawaii, Puerto Rico, the Virgin Islands and Guam, and on Indian reservations. Born in Detroit, Mich., she is a graduate of Kentucky State College (B.S., home economics) and Atlanta University (M.S.W., social work) and received an advanced certificate in social work from Columbia University School of Social Work. She is founder of the League of Black Women and is a member of numerous professional, civic and black-oriented groups. She has received a number of honors and awards. She and her husband, Paul Boswell, a physician, have a daughter, Bonnie Bell. Address: 969 E. 60th St., Chicago, IL 60637

Boswell, Hildagardeis, legislator, is a Maryland state representative, elected in 1970 to a four-year term. She is also a human relations specialist with the Maryland State Commission on Human Relations. She was born Jan. 12, 1934 in Daisytown, Pa. After studying at Barnard College of Columbia University, she graduated from Morgan State College (B.A., Pol. Science, 1961). Further study has been at N.Y. State School of Industrial and Labor Relations, Cornell University and University of Maryland Law School. She was a Scholar at Morgan State University's Institute for Political Education (1960-61). She "lost" her 1970 election to the Maryland House but, maintaining that she had been the victim of fraud, filed charges with the U. S. Dept. of Justice. She won her case and was seated. In the legislature, Mrs. Boswell has co-sponsored a controversial bill proposing three-year marriage contracts—with an option to renew. The bill emerged as the most requested piece of legislation in the history of Maryland's Department of Legislative Reference and brought Mrs. Boswell numerous invitations to speak on the subject. She is a divorcee. Address: State House, Annapolis, MD 21404

Boutte, Alvin J., banker, is the president of the Independence Bank of Chicago. He has been with the bank for eight years and was elected president in 1970 while he was vice chairman of the board. He was born Oct. 10, 1929 in Lake Charles, La. and received his education at Xavier University in New Orleans, (B.S., 1951). He is one of the founders of the Independence Bank, which was organized in 1964. There are 25 black presidents of banks, and he feels that the future opportunities are unlimited. During his service as president, the bank has grown from $13 million in total assets to its current size of $31 million in 1972. He is vice president of the Chicago Urban League, board member of the Better Business Bureau of Chicago, member of the Chicago Board of Education, and is finance chairman of the 1972 National Black Political Convention. He and his wife, Barbara, have four children: Janice C., Jeanette B. Gregory J. and Alvin J. Jr. Address: 7636 S. Cottage Grove, Chicago, IL 60619

Bowen, Ruth J., booking agent, is president and founder of Queen Booking Corp. in New York, N.Y. Born Sept. 13, 1930 in Danville, Va., she attended New York University and UCLA, majoring in business administration. A show business veteran and business confidante of the late Dinah Washington, Mrs. Bowen opened Queen Artists, a business advisory organization in 1965 on the advice of the singer. In 1969, Mrs. Bowen changed the nature (and the name) of her business to a theatrical booking agency. The only woman who heads her own booking agency, which annually tops the million dollar mark, she guides the careers of entertainers and books them into theaters, clubs and shows across the nation and around the world. Her acts include Aretha Franklin, Carolyn Franklin, Erma Franklin, Sammy Davis Jr., the Impressions, Stevie Wonder, Redd Foxx and Jerry Butler. Mrs. Bowen is a member, and past president, of the Rinkydinks Club (a social-charity group) and is a member of Operation PUSH. She is married to William ("Billy") Bowen. Address: Queen Booking Corp., 1650 Broadway, New York, NY 10019

Bowen, William F., legislator, is an Ohio state senator, representing the 9th District (Cincinnati). Appointed in February, 1970, he has since been elected to a four-year term. He serves on the Senate Committee for Environmental Affairs and the Committee on Commerce and Labor. He has assisted in the reform of the state's Rehabilitation and Correction Program, thus helping prison inmates secure employment after parole. He served in the Ohio House (1966-68) as representative of the 69th District and was Democratic Minority Whip of the 108th General Assembly. He has his own business, B. C. Services, which distributes black-manufactured products. Born Jan. 30, 1929 in Cincinnati, he studied business administration at Xavier University and accounting at the National Training Laboratory. He is chairman of the Hamilton County Black Caucus and chairman of the Governor's Task Force on Corrections, and is a member of numerous political, civic and fraternal organizations. He and his wife, Delores, a nursing supervisor for the Cincinnati Department of Public Health, have three sons: William, Kevin and Terrence. Address: State House, Columbus, OH 43215

Ruth J. Bowen

Boyd, Lucille Inman, organization head, is imperial commandress of the Imperial Court Daughters of Isis, an auxiliary group to the Shriners, in San Antonio, Tex. Born April 3, 1906 in San Antonio, Tex., she received degrees from Wiley College (B.A., 1928) and the University of California at Berkeley (M.Ed., 1940). Mrs. Boyd, who was a public school teacher for 41 years, held a variety of other positions in the Daughters of Isis before she was elected to head the organization in 1972. Her responsibilities include overall operation of the group, organization of new chapters and coordination of state and local lodges. She is a member of the Retired Teachers' Association, the Order of Eastern Star, Golden Circle and the Zeta Phi Beta sorority. She is married to Frank Boyd. Address: 220 Chestnut St., San Antonio, TX 78202

William F. Bowen

Lucille I. Boyd

Miller W. Boyd Jr.

William M. Boyd II

E. A. Boykins

Boyd, Miller W. Jr., psychologist, is co-director and a research psychologist at the Academy of Urban Service, Inc. in St. Louis, Mo. Born Sept. 16, 1934, he is a graduate of Fisk University (A.B., 1955), St. Louis University (M.S., research psychology, 1968; Ph.D., developmental psychology, 1970). He has also studied at the University of Tennessee (1955–56). Before assuming his present position in 1971, he was director of Experiment in Higher Education and assistant professor of psychology at Southern Illinois University (1969–71), special education instructor at Webster College (1968–69), psychology consultant of Project Follow Through and Head Start in St. Louis, Mo. (1968–69), and general psychology instructor at Parks Aeronautical College (1968). He has written numerous papers for various publications. He is a member of the National Association of Education for Young Children, National Council for Black Child Development, Council for Exceptional Children, American Psychological Association, Association of Black Psychologists, National Caucus on the Black Aged, Child Day Care Association of St. Louis, National Association of Non-White Rehabilitation Workers, and the Southwestern Psychological Association. Divorced, he has two children, Kevin and Kristin. Address: Academy of Urban Service, 2739 North Grand, St. Louis, MO 63106

Boyd, William M. II, educator, is executive director of the Educational Policy Center and is a member of the faculty of Queens College in New York City. He was born June 18, 1942 in Tuskegee, Ala. and has degrees from Williams College (B.A., 1963) and the University of California at Berkeley (M.A., political science, 1966; Ph.D., political science, 1972). His work at the center involves developing, implementing, and administering programs to increase opportunity for blacks in higher education. He was the first black on the board of trustees of Williams College (1969–72). He is a member of the board of directors of the Whitney M. Young Jr. Foundation, A Better Chance, and the Court Employment Project, and is steering committee chairman of the National Black Alliance for Graduate Level Education. He was a Peace Corps volunteer in Cameroun (1963-65). He and his wife, Arleen, have two children, William III and Danielle. Address: 400 Madison Ave., New York, NY 10017

Boykins, E.A., educator, is president of Mississippi State College in Itta Bena. Appointed in July, 1971, he was formerly the acting head of the science department (1958–61) and director of the division of Arts and Sciences (1970–71) at Alcorn A & M College. Born Oct. 5, 1931 in Vicksburg, Mississippi, he attended Xavier University (B.S., biology, 1953), Texas Southern University (M.S., 1958), the University of Connecticut (M.S., 1960) and Michigan State University (Ph.D., zoology, 1964). Dr. Boykins is a member of the American Council on Education, The American Institute of Biological Sciences, the Mississippi Conservation Educational Advisory Council and other professional organizations. He has published and presented papers on such subjects as "DDT in the Food Chains of Wild Birds" and "The Effects of DDT-Contaminated Earthworms in the Diet of Birds." The recipient of a number of honors and grants, Dr. Boykins has held consultant positions with the National Science Foundation Division of Undergraduate Education in Science and the Inter-Institutional Cooperative Program for College & Public Schools. Teachers of Disadvantaged Youth (University of Mississippi). He and his wife, Beverly, have four children: Darryl, Rhea, Connie and Karen. Address: Mississippi Valley State College, Itta Bena, MS 38941

Thomas Bradley

B. T. Bradshaw Sr.

Troy Brailey

Rev. Dorothy Sutton Branch

Bradley, Thomas, city councilman, is a member (since 1963) of the City Council of Los Angeles, Calif. In 1969, he was narrowly defeated (he received 47% of the vote) in the election for Mayor of Los Angeles. He was born Dec. 29, 1917 in Calvert, Tex., and attended the University of California at Los Angeles and Southwestern University Law School (LL.B., 1956). He was a member of the Los Angeles Police Department (1940-61) and was in the private practice of law (1961-63). He is on the board of directors of: Bank of Finance (in L.A.), California Center for Research and Education in Government, Greater Los Angeles Urban Coalition, Indian Culture and Education, and National League of Cities. He and his wife, Ethel, have two daughters, Lorraine and Phyllis. Address: Room 240, City Hall, Los Angeles, CA 90012

Bradshaw, Booker Talmadge Sr., insurance executive, is president-treasurer of the Virginia Mutual Benefit Life Insurance Co. in Richmond, Va. Born Feb. 26, 1904 in St. Louis, Mo., he has degrees from the University of Illinois (B.S.) and Virginia State College (LL.D.). Involved in the insurance industry since 1925, he was a founder of Virginia Mutual. He has been president of the company since 1933. He is a member of the board of directors of Consolidated Bank and Trust Co. and Jefferson Va. Townhouse Corp. He is a member and past president of the National Insurance Association. He and his wife, Emma, have a son, Booker Jr. Address: 112 E. Clay St., Richmond, VA 23219

Brailey, Troy, legislator, is a member of the Maryland House of Delegates. Born Aug. 26, 1916 in Lynchburg, S.C., he attended New York University. During 25 years as a representative of the Brotherhood of Sleeping Car Porters and six years as a legislator, he built a reputation as a "friend of the little people." In 1970, he was chosen as vice chairman of Baltimore's 43-member city delegation to the House, the first black ever named to one of the city's two leadership positions. He was honored as an Unsung Hero by the Maryland chapter of the American Labor Council in 1965, and in 1963, he served as chairman of the historic March on Washington. He is a former chairman of the Baltimore chapter of the American Labor Council. He and his wife, Chessie, have two children, Mrs. Alice Faye Toriente and Norman. Address: 2405 Baker St., Baltimore, MD 21216

Branch, The Reverend Dorothy Sutton, clergywoman, is pastor of the Commonwealth Community Church in Chicago, Ill. Born Feb. 4, 1922 in Chicago, she is a graduate of Judson Baptist College (B.S., sacred theology, 1938), Garrett Theological Seminary (M.A., religious education, 1941) and the University of Colorado (Ph.D., divinity, 1960). She also took graduate courses at the University of Chicago. She started preaching in 1934 at the age of 12, and in 1939 became pastor of the Junior Church of Cosmopolitan Community Church in Chicago. In 1942, she started the Youth Fellowship at Commonwealth Funeral Home, which later received a charter as the Commonwealth Community Church in 1946. She is on the board of the City Colleges of Chicago and is president of Douglas Park Development Corporation. She is also president of the Greater Lawndale Conservation Commission and the Lawndale Businessmen. She is a member of Alpha Gamma Psi. She and her husband, Lemmie C. Branch, a mortician, live in Chicago. Address: 140 W. 81st St., Chicago, IL 60620

Herman R. Branson

E. J. Brantley Sr.

Leo Branton Jr.

Branson, Herman Russell, educator and administrator, since 1970 has been president of Lincoln University in Pennsylvania. Previously, he was president of Central State University in Ohio (1968-70). A physicist, he was born Aug. 14, 1914 in Pocahontas, Va. He attended the University of Pittsburgh and is a graduate of Virginia State College (B.S., *summa cum laude,* 1936) and the University of Cincinnati (Ph.D., 1939). He has honorary Sc.D. degrees from Virginia State College (1967), the University of Cincinnati (1967) and Lincoln (Pa.) University (1969). He has taught mathematics, physics and chemistry at Dillard University (1939-41) and Howard University (1941-42). He was head of the physics department at Howard (1955-68). He was a National Science Foundation Faculty-Fellow at the University of Hamburg (Germany) and the French Atomic Energy Commission (1962-63). He has received several research grants and has been a consultant to the Atomic Energy Commission and other science-related agencies and projects. He was national president of the National Institute of Science (1956-57) and is a member of numerous professional societies and civic groups. He has written some 80 articles for scientific journals and education publications. Address: Lincoln University, Lincoln PA 19352

Brantley, Edward James Sr., educator, is president of Knoxville College in Tennessee. Born Dec. 12, 1923 in Lockland, Ohio, he has degrees from Howard University (B.S., psychology, 1948), Columbia University (M.A., student personnel administration, 1949) and the University of Colorado (D.Ed., guidance and counseling). He is a member of several organizations, including the American Personnel and Guidance Association and the Cooperative College Development Program. A divorcee, he has a son, Edward Jr. Address: Knoxville College, Knoxville, TN 37921

Branton, Leo Jr., attorney, has practiced law in Los Angeles, Calif. since 1949 and has established one of the most successful practices on the West Coast. He was born Feb. 17, 1922 in Pine Bluff, Ark. and is a graduate of Tennessee State University (B.S., 1942) and Northwestern University (J.D., 1949). While his participation in the successful defense of Angela Davis at her 1972 trial in California on charges of murder and conspiracy was his most recent involvement in a celebrated case, he has represented numerous Hollywood entertainers, a number of Communists, and many poor blacks, including some arrested during the 1965 rebellion in the Watts section of Los Angeles. He has also defended members of the Black Panther party as well as civil rights activists arrested in the South. He and his wife, Geri, have a son, Leo L. Address: 3450 Wilshire Blvd., Suite 1107, Los Angeles, CA 90010

40

Wiley A. Branton   Herbert J. Bridgewater Jr.   Andrew F. Brimmer

Branton, Wiley A., attorney, is a partner in Dolphin, Branton, Stafford & Webber, a law firm in Washington, D.C. and is affiliated with the Walker, Kaplan & Mays law firm in Little Rock, Ark. Born Dec. 13, 1923 in Pine Bluff, Ark., he has degrees from Arkansas A.M.&N. College (B.S., business administration, 1950) and the University of Arkansas School of Law (J.D., 1953). In 1957-58, he was chief counsel for the "Little Rock Nine," the black students who successfully desegregated Little Rock's Central High School. In 1962, he became director of the Voter Education Project in Atlanta, Ga. and helped register more than 600,000 black voters in 11 southern states during 1962-65. From 1965-67, he was special assistant to U.S. Attorneys General Nicholas Katzenbach and Ramsey Clark. His other work has included director, social program of the Alliance for Labor Action; director, Metropolitan Washington Community Action Agency, and executive secretary, President's Council on Equal Opportunity. He is a member of several bar associations, serves on many boards and commissions and has received numerous citations and awards for civil rights work. He and his wife, Lucille, have six children: Richard, Mrs. Toni C. Moore, Wylene, Wiley Jr., Beverly and Debra. Address: 666 Eleventh St., NW, Suite 500, Washington, DC 20001

Bridgewater, Herbert J. Jr., government employee and businessman, is a consumer protection specialist in the Federal Trade Commission regional office in Atlanta, Ga. He was born July 3, 1942 in Atlanta and has a B.S. degree from Clark College. He taught high school until 1967 when he became Relocation and Family Service Assistant with the Atlanta Housing Authority. As a consumer protection specialist, he seeks to curb unfair business practices that victimize consumers. He founded Bridgewater Enterprises, Inc., which includes public relations, counseling and telephone answering services. He writes a newspaper column, "Unsung Hero," which appears in the *Atlanta Daily World*. Address: Federal Trade Commission, Atlanta Regional Office, 730 Peachtree St., NE, Atlanta, GA 30308

Brimmer, Andrew F., economist, has been a member of the Board of Governors of the U.S. Federal Reserve System since 1966. Born Sept. 13, 1926 in Newellton, La. (his parents were sharecroppers), Dr. Brimmer earned degrees at the University of Washington (B.A., M.A.), Harvard University (Ph.D.) and Nebraska Wesleyan University (LL.D.). He also did postgraduate work as a Fullbright Fellow at the University of Bombay (India), and did further study at Marquette University. He was an economist at the Federal Reserve Bank of N.Y.; assistant professor at Michigan State University and University of Pennsylvania, and deputy assistant secretary, U.S. Department of Commerce. He is a member of the visiting committee (economics) of the Harvard Board of Overseers; the advisory committee of Atlanta University (Graduate School of Business), and the advisory council, Princeton University Department of Sociology. He has received numerous honors and awards and is a member of several professional organizations. His articles have appeared in a number of professional journals. Dr. Brimmer served with the U.S. Army from 1945-46. He and his wife, Doris, have one daughter, Esther. Address: Federal Reserve System, 20th and Constitution Ave., Washington, DC 20551

Sen. Edward W. Brooke

Deton J. Brooks Jr.

Gwendolyn Brooks

Brooke, Edward W., legislator, is U.S. senator from Massachusetts, elected in 1966 and reelected in 1972. He is a graduate of Howard University (B.S., 1941) and Boston University Law School (LL.B., 1948; LL.M., 1950). He has received 21 honorary degrees. A U.S. Army captain in World War II, he served with the Partisans in Italy and was awarded the Bronze Star and the Combat Infantryman's Badge. He was elected attorney general of Massachusetts in 1962 and reelected in 1964 with a majority of almost 800,000 votes. He is a member of the Senate Banking, Housing and Urban Affairs committee, the Committee on Appropriations, the Select Committee on Equal Educational Opportunity and the Special Committee on Aging. His honors include the Charles Evans Hughes award of the National Conference of Christians and Jews, the AMVETS Distinguished Service award and the Spingarn Medal of the NAACP. He is a fellow of the American Academy of Arts and Sciences and of the American Bar Association. He and his wife, Remigia, have two children, Remi and Edwina. Address: 421 Old Senate Office Bldg., Washington, DC 20510 **See article on Senator Edward W. Brooke in Volume II.**

Brooks, Deton J. Jr., administrator, has been commissioner of the Chicago (Ill.) Department of Human Resources since 1969. Previously, he was executive director of the Chicago Committee on Urban Opportunity (1964–69), research associate at the Loyola University School of Social Work (1961–64) and director of research and statistics at the Cook County Department of Public Aid (1958–64). From 1930 to 1958, he held positions ranging from public school teacher to personnel director to research associate. Born Jan. 14, 1909 in Chicago, Ill., he is a graduate of University of Chicago (B.S., mathematics, 1935) and Columbia University Teachers College (M.A., Ed.D., 1958). He has also studied international relations at the University of Chicago (1935–37). In 1970, he was elected president of the National Association for Community Development, a professional organization of community action program workers and directors. NACD sponsored the Mobilization for Domestic Unity, which brought 50,000 persons together in Washington in February, 1973 to protest President Nixon's elimination of many community action programs. He is a member of eleven professional organizations, including the American Academy of Political and Social Science and the American Public Welfare Association. He is a member of 27 civic groups and is chairman of Chicago's Third Ward Citizens Committee On Crime and Prevention. He has received numerous awards for community service. He and his wife, Mattie, have a daughter, Mrs. Mariam Sumlin. Address: 640 N. LaSalle St., Chicago, IL 60610

Brooks, Gwendolyn, poet, is a Pulitzer Prize winner and poet laureate of Illinois. She became the first black Pulitzer Prize winner when she received the award for poetry in 1950 for *Annie Allen,* her second volume of verse. Born June 17, 1917 in Topeka, Kan., she graduated from Wilson Junior College, Chicago, Ill. (1936). She has an honorary degree from Columbia College (L.H.D., 1964). She has been an instructor in poetry at Columbia College and Northeastern Illinois State College. She was named One of the 10 Women of the Year by *Mademoiselle* magazine (1945). She received the award for creative writing of the American Academy of Arts and Letters (1946). She was named a Guggenheim fellow for creative writing (1946) and received the Anisfield-Wolf award in 1969 when she was also named the Illinois poet laureate. She is a member of the Society of Midland Authors. Her works include *A Street in Bronzeville* (poetry, 1945), *Maude Martha* (novel, 1953), *Bronzeville Boys and Girls* (for children, 1956), *The Bean Eaters* (poetry, 1960), *Selected Poems* (1963), *In the Mecca* (1968), *Riot* (1969), *Family Pictures* (1970) and *Aloneness* (1971). She edits the magazine, *The Black Position.* She and her husband, Henry L. Blakely, have two children, Henry L. and Nora. Address: 7428 S. Evans Ave., Chicago, IL 60619 **See article on Gwendolyn Brooks in Volume II.**

Brooks, Brig. Gen. Harry W., Jr., military officer, is a brigadier general and Assistant Division Commander, 2nd Infantry Division of the U.S. Army. His work involves the planning, organizing and supervision of division activities. Promoted to brigadier general in Aug. 1972, General Brooks was director of Equal Opportunity Programs in Washington before assuming his present duties in January, 1973. He was born May 17, 1928 in Indianapolis, Ind. He attended four military schools and is a graduate of the University of Omaha (B.A., 1962; M.A., 1973). With twenty-five years of service in the army, he has won the Legion of Merit Award, the Bronze Star and the Army Commendation Medal. He recently completed a fact-finding mission on race relations on army installations in Europe, South Korea, Okinawa and Hawaii. General Brooks and his wife, Doris, have three children: Harry III, Wayne L. and Craig. Address: The Pentagon, Washington, DC 20310

Brown, Benjamin D., state legislator, is a member of the Georgia General Assembly to which he was first elected in 1965 at age 25. He is also a co-founder of Wright, Jackson, Brown, Williams & Stephens, Inc., an Atlanta public relations firm formed in 1968. He was elected first vice president of the Georgia delegation to the 1972 Democratic National Convention, the first black chosen as an officer of the regular delegation. Mr. Brown is active in the local Young Men's Christian Association, is vice chairman of the Atlanta Area Community Council, and serves as a member of both the Rules Commission and the Charter Commission of the Democratic National Committee. Born Nov. 14, 1939 in Montezuma, Ga., Mr. Brown earned degrees from Clark College (A.B.) and Howard University (J.D.) and was a Whitney Young Memorial Community Fellow at Massachusetts Institute of Technology. He and his wife, Lydia, have two children, Benjamin and Barry. Address: 100 Peachtree St., Atlanta, GA 30303

Brown, Dorothy Lavinia, M.D., physician, is a clinical professor of surgery at Meharry Medical College in Nashville, Tenn. She is also the director of Student Health Service at Meharry and Fisk Universities, and chief of surgery at Riverside Hospital. Born Jan. 1, 1919 in Philadelphia, Pa., Dr. Brown graduated from Bennett College (B.A., 1941), Meharry Medical College (M.D., 1948), and has an honorary doctorate from Russell Sage College in Troy, N.Y. She spent the first 12½ years of her life in an orphanage in Troy, N. Y., and rose to become the first black woman general surgeon in the South. Once a Tennessee state representative, Dr. Brown authored and sponsored the state's only attempt to update an abortion statute. It was defeated and so were her attempts to get back into the Tennessee assembly. She is a Fellow of American College of Surgeons, a member of the Nashville Academy of Medicine and the Governor's Commission on Status of Women. Dr. Brown is unmarried and was the first single woman in Tennessee permitted to adopt a child, Lola. Address: Meharry Medical College, Nashville, TN 37209

Brig. Gen. Harry W. Brooks Jr.

Benjamin D. Brown

Dorothy L. Brown, M.D.

George L. Brown

James Brown

Juanita Brown

Brown, George L., legislator, in 1956 became the first black man to be elected as a member of the Colorado State Senate. He was reelected in 1960, 1964, 1968 and 1972. He was appointed to the Colorado House of Representatives in 1955. He has been the chief sponsor of numerous bills, including those which strengthened Fair Employment Practices laws, repealed the State's miscegenation law, and improved public accommodations and housing statutes. Born July l, 1926 in Lawrence, Kan., he is a graduate of the University of Kansas (B.S., journalism, 1950) and has taken graduate courses at the University of Colorado. He was a reporter, rewrite man, aviation editor and night city editor of *The Denver Post* (1960–65); assistant executive director of the Denver Housing Authority (1965–69), and in 1969 was appointed as the first executive director of the Metro Denver Urban Coalition. In 1962, he conducted seminars and communications workshops in Europe and 14 African nations for the U.S. State Department. He has received a number of journalism awards. He is a member of the Governor's Advisory Committee, and of the board of directors of the Grandparents Program, the Metro Fair Housing Center, the C.F. Kettering Foundation, Denver Council of Boy Scouts and Labor's Community Agency. He is also a member of the National Urban Coalition Law and Government Task Force, the National Council for the Aged and the Governor's Coordinating Committee on Implementation of Mental Health and Mental Retardation Planning. He is instructor of a graduate course in black politics at the University of Colorado Denver Center, and is an instructor of urban affairs at the University of Denver. He and his wife, Rosemary, have four daughters, Gail, Cindy, Kim and Laura Nicole. Address: State Capitol, Denver, CO 80203

Brown, James, entertainer, is chairman of the board of James Brown Productions, James Brown Enterprises and Man's World, headquartered in Augusta, Ga. His organizations embrace two record companies, two real estate interests and three radio stations—WRDW in Augusta, Ga.; WEBB in Baltimore, Md., and WJBE in Knoxville, Tenn. Born May 3, 1933 in Augusta, he began performing at 12, picking up nickels and dimes as a singer and dancer for World War II soldiers stationed at Fort Gordon. For years, he entertained wherever he could get a "gig." In 1956, he recorded his first hit song and started on his way to becoming "Mr. Dynamite" in the rhythm and blues field and then "Soul Brother No. 1" in the soul music world. His 1968 gross income was $4.5 million. By 1971, his single records had sold over 39 million copies. In 1969 he was presented the Humanitarian Award by the Music and Performing Arts Lodge of B'nai B'rith in New York City and has been honored by heads of state. He and his wife, Deidre, have a daughter, Deanna. He is also the father of Terry, Daryl, Teddy, Venisha and Yamma. Address: 1122 Greene St., Augusta, GA 30902 **See article on James Brown in Volume II.**

Brown, Juanita, organization executive, is president of the National Association of Colored Women's Clubs, Inc., headquartered in Washington, D. C. She was born March 14, 1902 in Garden Grove, Iowa and is a graduate of Simpson College (B.A., music). She has taken courses in community and recreation work, and did graduate study at Chicago Musical College. She was NACWC recording secretary for nine years before being elected president in 1971. She is a former music teacher at Wilberforce University and Arkansas A.M.&N. College. She is a member of the Order of the Eastern Star and Delta Sigma Theta sorority. A widow, she has two children, Mrs. Anna Broomes and Robert Brown Jr. Address: 5808 16th St., NW, Washington DC 20011

Leroy J. H. Brown

Judge Lloyd O. Brown

Otha N. Brown Jr.

Brown, Leroy J. H., educator and architect, is a professor of architecture at Howard University and has his own firm of architects, engineers and planners in Washington, D. C. He was born Dec. 14, 1912 in Charleston, S. C. and is a graduate of South Carolina State College (B.S., mechanic arts), Howard University (B.S., architecture) and Catholic University (M.S., architecture). He was one of 11 black architects and engineers contracted to survey 5,900 buildings for possible rehabilitation in Washington, and was one of seven black architects retained to make a preliminary study of the future campus of Federal City College in Washington. He is a member of the Construction Specification Institute the National Technical Association and the American Institute of Architects. He and his wife, Angella, have no children. **Address:** 3310 Georgia Ave., NW, Washington, DC 20010

Brown, Lloyd Odom Sr., jurist, is a judge of the Cuyahoga County Court of Common Pleas in Cleveland, Ohio. He was appointed in Jan. 1973 after failing to win election to the Ohio Supreme Court on which he had served one year as an associate justice (appointed to fill an unexpired term). Both appointments were by Ohio's Governor John J. Gilligan. Previously, Judge Brown had been an elected judge of the Cleveland Municipal Court (1968-71). Born Dec. 12, 1928 in Little Rock, Ark., he is a graduate of Ohio State University (B.A., LL.B., JD.., 1955). He was assistant attorney general of Ohio (1958-59) and Cuyahoga County assistant prosecutor (1959-67). He began his law practice in Cleveland in 1955. He was a radioman in the U.S. Coast Guard (1946-49). He is a member of a number of professional and civic groups, including the Judicial Council of the National Bar Association and the Citizens League. He is an area chairman of Boy Scouts of America, manager of a Little League team, member of the advisory board of Cuyahoga County Child Welfare, and member of Commission on Public School Personnel Policies in Ohio. He and his wife Phyllis, have three children: Lloyd Jr., Raymond and Leslie. **Address:** Cuyahoga County Court House, 1 Lakeside Ave., Cleveland, OH 44113

Brown, Otha N. Jr., legislator, was first elected to the Connecticut House of Representatives in 1966. Born July 19, 1931 in Dequeen, Ark., he graduated *cum laude* from Central State University (B.S., history), received his M.A. degree from the University of Connecticut and a six-year professional diploma in educational administration from the University of Bridgeport (Conn.). Mr. Brown has pursued postgraduate and doctoral studies at New York University, Boston University, Springfield College (Mass.) and Queens College (N.Y.). For several years, prior to his political career, he was a Connecticut school counselor. He has worked in the legislature on behalf of improved educational opportunities for disadvantaged youth and more teacher benefits. **Address:** 208 Flax Hill Road, Apt. #6, South Norwalk, CT 06854

Robert J. Brown   Roscoe C. Brown Jr.   Tony Brown

Brown, Robert J., public relations executive, is a former special assistant to President Richard M. Nixon, and now heads his own public relations and marketing firm, B&C Associates, in High Point, N.C. Appointed presidential assistant in 1969, he served on the 14-man Council on Youth Opportunity which included nine cabinet members and was headed by Vice President Spiro T. Agnew. As the only black on the council, it fell largely to Mr. Brown to carry the message of opportunity to black youths. He was formerly a partner in Harlem Freedom Associates (commercial land development) of New York, N.Y., an agent of the Bureau of Narcotics, United States Treasury Department, and a law enforcement officer in the police department of High Point. Born Feb. 26, 1935 in High Point, N.C., Mr. Brown received his college education at Virginia Union University and North Carolina A&T University and holds six honorary degrees. He and his wife, Sallie, have no children. Address: B&C Associates, 1625 I St., NW, Suite 1010, Washington, DC 20006

Brown, Roscoe C. Jr., educator, is director of the Institute of Afro-American Affairs at New York University in New York, N.Y. Born March 9, 1922 in Washington, D.C., he has degrees from Springfield (Mass.) College (B.S.) and New York University (M.A., Ph.D.). He has written more than 50 articles on education and physical fitness for various publications. He is host of a weekly television series, "Black Arts," and a weekly radio series, "Soul of Reason," and is co-host of the Jersey City State College television program "Black Letters." He co-edited the book *Negro Almanac* (1967) and is co-author of *Classical Studies on Physical Activity* (1968) and *New Perspectives of Man in Action* (1969). He and his wife, Josephine, have four children: Doris, Diane, Dennis and Donald. Address: N.Y.U., Washington Pl., New York, NY 10003

Brown, Tony, educator and television producer, is the executive producer and host of National Educational Television's "Black Journal" and dean of the School of Communications at Howard University in Washington, D.C. Born Apr. 11, 1933 in Charleston, W. Va., he has degrees from Wayne State University in Detroit (B.A., sociology and psychology, 1959; M.S.W., psychiatric social work, 1961). A former city editor and drama critic for the *Detroit Courier*, he has served as a television and film producer at WTVS in Detroit and was a coordinator of the "March To Freedom With Dr. Martin Luther King Jr." on July 23, 1963. He also has published several magazines and newspapers and has owned a public relations and advertising firm. As executive producer of "Black Journal," the only national news and documentary television program on blacks, he received the 1972 Media Workshop Award and the 1972 Business Achievement Award from the Black Retail Action Group. The program itself received an Emmy award "for outstanding achievement in magazine-type programming" in 1970 and the 1970 Citation of Merit from the New York Urban League. Divorced, he has one son, Byron. Address: Black Journal, 10 Columbus Circle, New York, NY 10019

Willie L. Brown Jr.

James H. Browne

Robert S. Browne

Brown, Willie L. Jr., legislator, is an assemblyman of the 18th District of the California state legislature representing San Francisco, Calif. Born March 20, 1934 in Mineola, Tex., Mr. Brown studied political science at San Francisco State College (B.A., 1955), Hastings College of Law (J.D., 1958) and is an honorary fellow of Crown College. Elected to the California Assembly in 1964 after one unsuccessful race, he is one of the most influential members of the California state legislature. He is chairman of the state's powerful Assembly Ways and Means Committee which has a budget of $8 billion. Since 1959, Brown has practiced law, but decided to make politics foremost in his career. In 1964, he was admitted to practice before the United States Supreme Court. He led the fight in the 1968 Democratic National Convention to oust Georgia's Governor Lester Maddox. At the 1972 Democratic National Convention in Miami, Fla., he was chosen by South Dakota Senator George McGovern as a "co-chairperson" of the California delegation, a feat which gained him national prominence. His district—20 percent black—is said to be the most varied and cosmopolitan in the country, and, after current reapportionment, will include 249,500 people. He and his wife, Blanche, have three children: Susan, Michael and Robin. Address: State Capitol, Sacramento, CA 95814

Browne, James H., insurance executive, is president and chief executive officer of American Woodmen's Life Insurance Co. in Denver, Colo. He was born April 11, 1910 in Little Rock, Ark. He and his wife, Lucille, have two daughters: Mrs. Elaine Owens and Mrs. Rosalyn Welch. He was president of the National Insurance Association (1971-72) and now is chairman of the board. He also is chairman of the board of Douglas State Bank in Kansas City, Kan. He founded Crusader Life Insurance Co. and was president until it merged with American Woodmen's Life Insurance Co. in 1969. He is a member of the national board of governors of United Way of America; member, national advisory board of the Small Business Administration; member, President's Commission on Personnel Interchange; member, board of directors of Political Action Committee of Kansas City, Kansas City Area Chamber of Commerce, Wyandotte Hotel Corp. and Northeast Business Association. He is vice president, Kansas City Board of Public Utilities of Kansas City Kiwanis. His many awards include the B'nai B'rith Brotherhood Award (1962) and Kansas City's "Citizen of the Year" Award (1970). Address: 2100 Downing, Denver, CO 80205

Browne, Robert S., economist, is founder and executive director of the Black Economic Research Center in New York, N.Y., is a non-profit research and technical assistance organization founded in 1969 which researches aspects of the black economy, assists black economic development programs and publishes a quarterly journal. Born in 1924 in Chicago, Ill., he is a graduate of the University of Illinois (B.A., economics, 1944) and the University of Chicago (M.B.A., finance, 1947). He is completing his dissertation for a Ph.D. degree in economics from City University of N. Y. He has taught economics at Dillard University and Fairleigh Dickinson University. He was an economist with the U. S. foreign aid program in Cambodia (1955-57) and in Vietnam (1958–61). He resigned and made numerous speeches against U.S. policies in Southeast Asia. He was a planner of the 1967 Black Power Conference in Newark, N.J., and participated in the 1969 National Black Economic Development Conference in Detroit, Mich. He is a member of numerous organizations, including the National Sharecroppers Fund (vice-president) and the American Commission on Africa (member, board of trustees). He and his wife, Huoi, have four children: Hoa Mai, Alexi and Marshall. Address: 112 W. 120th St., New York, NY 10027

Joan M. Bryan

Bryan, Joan M., business woman, is system manager of special marketing affairs for Eastern Airlines in New York, N.Y. She develops programs for women's travel and assists with advertising and other means for mass communications in the minority market. She has been in her present position for nine months and prior to that was a sales representative with Eastern. Born Aug. 8, 1939 in Jamaica, N.Y., she attended Wilberforce University, is a graduate of Queens College (B.S.) and took Eastern Airlines' management training programs. Although she knows of no other black female who has the title of system manager in the airline industry, the job chances are excellent. She is a member and on the board of directors of the NAACP, the National Association of Media Women and Delta Sigma Theta Sorority. She enjoys gardening, reading, sewing and is interested in politics. She and her husband, Ernest, have two children, Aaron and Tamela. Address: 10 Rockefeller Plaza, New York, NY 10020

The Rt. Rev. Harrison J. Bryant

Bryant, The Right Reverend Harrison James, clergyman, is president of the Council of Bishops of the African Methodist Episcopal Church. Born Nov. 20, 1900 in Georgetown County, S.C., he left school in the sixth grade to work. He returned to the sixth grade at the age of 21, and worked his way through grammar school, high school and college as a house man and yard man. He is a graduate of Allen University (A.B.) and Payne Theological Seminary (B.D.), and has honorary degrees from Wilberforce University (LL.D. and D.D.). He is presiding bishop of the Fifth Episcopal District, which is comprised of fourteen states from Missouri, westward to Alaska. He has also served his church as pastor of various congregations. He was elevated to the episcopacy in 1964 and was bishop of the Republic of South Africa (1964-68). He is a 33rd degree Mason. He and his wife, Edith, have four children (two others are deceased): Mrs. Cynthia Pitts, Miss Hazel Bryant, The Reverend John Bryant and Mrs. Eleanor Graham. Address: 7419 Harrison St., Kansas City, MO 64131

James L. Buckner, D.D.S.

Buckner, James Lowell, D.D.S., dentist and business executive, is in the private practice of dentistry in Chicago, Ill. and is active in a number of business enterprises. He is a member of the board of advisors of Supreme Life Insurance Co. of America (1970–), member of the board of directors of Seaway National Bank of Chicago (1965–), secretary-treasurer of The Foodbasket, Inc. supermarkets (1969–) and was a founder of the State-51st Medical and Shopping Center (1962). He is vice president of the Chicago Urban League (1971–), treasurer of the Black Strategy Center 1971–), secretary-treasurer of the PUSH Foundation (1972–), member of the board of trustees of television station WTTW in Chicago, vice chairman of the Chicago Economic Development Corp. (1972–), chairman of the Chicago Financial Development Corp.'(1973–), a director of the CEDCO Capital Corp. (1972) and Ventures, Inc. (1970-) and a member of the President's Council on Minority Business Enterprise (1972–).He is also a director of Leadership Council for Metropolitan Open Communities, Southtown YMCA and the Leadership Council for Metropolitan Open Communities, and is a member of the board of advisors of Midwest Sickle Cell Anemia, Inc. He was president of the Lincoln Dental Society (1965–66) and secretary of the board of directors of the National Dental Association (1966–67). He is active in a number of other professional and civic groups, including Alpha Phi Alpha, Chicago Midwesterners, the Bonsomme Ski Club, U.S. Ski Association and the Sun Valley Ski Club. He has received numerous civic awards. Born July 29, 1934 in Vicksburg, Miss., he is a graduate of the University of Illinois (B.S.D., 1957; D.D.S., 1959). He is married to the former Gwendolyn Peaks. Address: 5050 S. State St., Chicago, IL 60609

Archie L. Buffkins

Sharnia Buford

William Buford

John A. Buggs

Buffkins, Archie L., educator, is chancellor of the University of Maryland (Eastern Shore Campus) in Princess Anne, Md. He was born March 30, 1934 in Memphis, Tenn. and has degrees from Jackson State College (B.A.) and Columbia University (M.A., Ph.D.). He has held academic and administrative positions at Rhode Island College, Texas Southern University, the University of Maine and at other schools. He is author of *An Intellectual Approach to Musical Understanding* (1965), and is currently writing a historical overview of Afro-American music. He and his wife, Carol Jane, have a daughter, LeRachel Harombe. Address: Chancellor's Residence, University of Maryland (Eastern Shore), Princess Anne, MD 21853

Buford, Sharnia, banker, is president of Douglass State Bank ($16 million in assets) in Kansas City, Kan. Born Feb. 3, 1939 in Bryans Mille, Tex., he has a B.A. degree from Texas College and has done graduate work at the University of Colorado. He has served in various capacities with the K.C. Urban Renewal Agency before joining Douglass State Bank in 1967 as vice-president. In 1968 he was promoted to senior vice-president and was elected president in 1972. Mr. Buford is a member of the American Banking Assn. and the National Bankers Association. He and his wife, Phyllis, have one child, Rhae Shawn. Address: 1314 5th St., Kansas City, KS 66101

Buford, William P., banker, is vice pres. and cashier of Vanguard National Bank in Hempstead, N.Y. He has full responsibility for operations, audit and cost control of the $11 million (in 1973) Interracial, but black-controlled, bank. Born Sept. 27, 1936, in New York, N.Y., he attended City College of N.Y. (A.A., math., 1959). He gained his banking experience during 17 years with First National City Bank of N.Y. and enrolled in advanced management and lending classes offered by the bank—at which he rose from clerk to assistant vice president. Mr. Buford and his wife, Minnie, have one daughter, Wylana. Address: 49 N. Franklin St., Hempstead, NY 11550

Buggs, John A., administrator, is staff director of the United States Commission on Civil Rights in Washington, D.C. The commission's responsibilities include reporting to the president and the Congress on the denial of equal protection of the laws to citizens because of their race, religion, sex or national origin. The commission also recommends to the president and Congress measures to combat discrimination. Prior to his present position, Mr. Buggs was deputy staff director of the commission, director of the Los Angeles County Commission on Human Relations for 13 years and deputy director of the Model Cities administration in the Department of Housing and Urban Development for two years. He won great community respect and national recognition for his leadership in easing tensions that followed the 1965 riots in the Watts section of Los Angeles. Born Nov. 20, 1915 in Brunswick, Ga., he is a graduate of Dillard University (A.B., history, 1939) and Fisk University (M.A., sociology, 1941). He is a member of numerous organizations, including the American Arbitration Association and the National Association of Human Rights Workers. He and his wife, Mary, have two children, Mrs. Zara Gale Taylor and Mrs. Diane Dorinda Dix. Address: 1121 Vermont Ave., NW, Washington, DC 20425

Ed Bullins

The Rt. Rev. Henry C. Bunton

The Rt. Rev. J. M. Burgess

Bullins, Ed, playwright, is associate director and resident playwright with the New Lafayette Theatre in New York, N.Y. He also is editor of *Black Theatre* magazine. Born July 2, 1935 in Philadelphia, Pa., he attended Los Angeles City College and San Francisco State University. He is the author of a number of plays, including *The Electronic Nigger*, *Clara's Ole Man*, *In the Wine Time*, *In New England Winter*, *A Son Come Home*, *Psychic Pretenders*, *Five Plays* and *The Theme is Blackness*. He also has published a number of books on drama, including *The Duplex* (1971), *The Hungered Ones* (1971). *Four Dynamic Plays* (1972), *Six Black Playwrights from the New Lafayette Theatre* and *New Plays from Black Theatre*, which he edited. Mr. Bullins is the recipient of the Vernon Rice Drama Award (1968) and an Obie award (1971) for distinguished playwriting. He has received Rockefeller grants (1968, 1970, 1973) and a Guggenheim Fellowship for Writing (1972). He has been a member of the faculties at Dartmouth and Fordham universities and has been visiting lecturer at Talladega College. Address: The New Lafayette Theatre, 2349 Seventh Ave., New York, NY 10030

Bunton, Henry Clay, clergyman, is bishop of the Seventh Episcopal District of the Christian Methodist Episcopal Church. His district includes Eastern Seaboard states from S.C. to the District of Columbia. Born Oct. 19, 1903 in Tuscaloosa, Ala., he has degrees from Florida A. & M. University (A.B.) and Denver University Iliff School of Theology (M.Th.). He also attended Garrett Theological Seminary of Northwestern University and Perkins School of Theology of Southern Methodist University, and has hon. degrees from Texas College (D.D.) and Miles College (C.H.D.). He pastored churches in Alabama, Florida, Arkansas, Texas, Colorado, and Tennessee, was presiding elder of the Kansas-Missouri Annual Conference, and was a U.S. Army chaplain before his election in 1962 as the 33rd C. M. E. bishop. He has increased church membership in his district by 100 percent and has assisted a number of young blacks to obtain scholarship aid. He is a trustee of Miles College and Paine College, and is a charter member of SCLC. He and his wife, Alfreda, have two daughters and two sons: Mattye, Marjorie, Henry and Joseph. Address: Christian Methodist Episcopal Church, 557 Randolph St., N.W., Washington, DC 20011

Burgess, Rt. Rev. John Melville, clergyman, is bishop of the Episcopal Diocese of Massachusetts. He is the only black diocesan bishop in the U.S. Born March 11, 1909 in Grand Rapids, Mich., he has degrees from the University of Michigan (A.B., 1930, M.A., 1931, sociology) and Episcopal Theological School in Cambridge, Mass. (B.D., 1934). His honorary degrees include D. Litt., LL.D., L.H.D. and D.D. He began his ministry in Grand Rapids in 1934. In 1946, he became a chaplain at Howard University and five years later a canon of the Washington Cathedral. He was archdeacon of Boston and superintendent of the Episcopal City Mission from 1956 until he became suffragan bishop in 1962. He was elected as bishop coadjutor of the Diocese of Massachusetts in 1969 and as bishop in 1970. He is a member of numerous church and civic organizations, including the National Council of Churches and the Massachusetts Civil Liberties Union. He and his wife, Esther, have two daughters, Julia and Mrs. Margaret Williams. Address: 1 Joy St., Boston, MA 02108

Judge Lillian W. Burke

Rep. Yvonne B. Burke

Arthur Louis Burnett

Burke, Lillian W., jurist, is a municipal court judge in Cleveland, Ohio. She was appointed to serve an unexpired term in January, 1969 and then won a full term in the November, 1969 election, thus becoming the first elected black female judge. She received an award from the American Woodsmen for this distinction in 1970. Born Aug. 2, 1917 in Thomaston, Ga., she is a graduate of Ohio State University (B.S., 1947) and Cleveland Marshall Law School (LL.B., 1951). She has served as assistant attorney general for the state of Ohio, president of the National Council of Negro Women and vice chairman of the Ohio Industrial Commission. She is a life member of the NAACP, as well as a member of the American Association of University Women, the Cuyahoga County and the Cleveland Bar Associations and Alpha Kappa Alpha sorority. She has received numerous awards, including the Award in Recognition of Outstanding Achievements in the Field of Law, presented by the National Sorority of Phi Delta Kappa. She and her husband, Ralph, have one son, Bruce. Address: Cleveland Municipal Court, City Hall, Cleveland, OH 44114

Burke, Yvonne Brathwaite, congresswoman, was elected Nov. 7, 1972 as a member of the U. S. House of Representatives from California (Democrat, 37th District, Los Angeles). She was the first black woman ever elected to Congress from California and the first woman in 20 years elected to the House from the State. Previously, she was a member of the California State Legislature (1966–72). Born Oct. 5, 1932 in Los Angeles, she is a graduate of UCLA (B.A., political science, 1953) and the University of Southern California School of Law (J.D., 1956). She began practicing law in Los Angeles in 1956. She was an attorney on the staff of the McCone Commission which investigated the Watts rebellions. She was a Fellow of the Institute of Politics at Harvard University. She and her husband, William A. Burke, live in Los Angeles. Address: House of Representatives, Washington, DC 20515 **See article Yvonne Brathwaite Burke in Volume II**

Burnett, Arthur Louis, attorney, is a magistrate of the U. S. District Court for the District of Columbia. Born April 15, 1935 in Spotsylvania County, Va., he attended Howard University (B.A., 1957) and the New York University School of Law (LL.B., 1958). Mr. Burnett was admitted to practice before the District Court in March, 1958 and before the U.S. Supreme Court in May 1964. He served as attorney-advisor and trial attorney in the criminal division of the U.S. Department of Justice (1958–65). He was assistant U.S. Attorney in Washington, D.C. (1965-69), then served as general counsel of the Metropolitan Police Department, a position he held until June 1969 when he was sworn in as United States magistrate. Mr. Burnett is vice chairman of the Criminal Law and Procedure Commission, the Bar Association of the District of Columbia, and was elected to membership on the executive council of the Young Lawyers Section. He has served as financial secretary of the Washington Bar Association and as chairman of the Program-Speakers, Membership and Law Day Committees. Mr. Burnett and his wife, Ann, have five children: Darnellena, Arthur, Darryl, Darlisa and Dionne. Address: United States Court House, 3rd St. and Constitution Ave., NW, Washington, DC 20001

Calvin W. Burnett

John M. Burnett

Willie Miles Burns

Lawrence C. Burr

Burnett, Calvin W., educator, is president of Coppin State College in Baltimore, Md. Born March 16, 1932 in Brinkley, Ark., he is a graduate of St. Louis University (B.S., political science and biology, 1959; Ph. D., social psychology, 1963). Prior to assuming his present position, he was employed in a number of administrative capacities with St. Louis University and Washington University, and has taught at Meramec Community College and Homer Phillips Hospital in St. Louis, at Catholic University of America in Washington, D.C. and at Southern Illinois University (Edwardsville). He is a member of the boards of directors of a number of organizations. He and his wife, Martha, have three children: Vera, Susan and David. Address: Coppin State College, 2500 W. North Ave., Baltimore, MD 21216

Burnett, John M., agency executive, is executive director of the Better Business Bureau of Harlem in New York, N.Y., where he was born in 1923. He develops and implements programs that assure that consumers obtain value on purchases. In 1972, the Bureau helped obtain a $75,000 fine (imposed by a federal court) of a Harlem furniture store accused of defrauding customers. Mr. Burnett attended City Coll. of the City Univ. of N. Y. He is a former police lieutenant. He and his wife, Thelma, have four children: Bruce, Carl, David and Gail. Address: Better Business Bureau of Harlem, 2090 Seventh Ave., New York, NY 10027

Burns, Willie Miles, publishing executive, is vice president and agency manager of the Johnson Publishing Co. in Chicago, Ill. She is in charge of billing distributors, publisher's statements to the Audit Bureau of Circulations and second class mailing arrangements with the U.S. Post Office for all Johnson Publishing Co. publications Mrs. Burns joined the firm in 1946. Born in Lake Village, Ark., she graduated with a B.S. degree from A. M. & N. College (now University of Arkansas at Pine Bluff). She is a member of the board of the Sears YMCA in Chicago and a member of the Cook County Hospitals Governing Commission, and the State Street Business and Professional Women's Club. Address: 820 S. Michigan Ave., Chicago, IL 60605

Burr, Lawrence C., state executive, is assistant general manager of the (New York) State Park and Recreation Commission for the City of New York (N.Y.). He attained his post through competitive state civil service examinations in 1968. His work includes planning recreational facilities and programs, and involving responsible community leadership in planning and developing a program for use of state parks by residents of the area. Born June 18, 1913 in Denton, Tex. he is a graduate of Langston Univ. (A.B., 1936) and George Williams Coll. in Chicago (M.S., 1945). He has studied at Columbia for a doctorate in educational administration. Prior to accepting his present position, he was a staff consultant with the Community Council of Greater New York. He has been a program officer at the African-American Inst. in New York City and was a member of the Intl. Comm. of YMCA's of N. America—based in Madras, India—spanning the period of Indian independence and the assassination of Mahatma Gandhi. He founded the YMCA Boys Town in Madras. Mr. Burr and his wife, Mildred, are parents of Mrs. LaRosa Burr Lumpkin and Marial and Marthal Burr. Address: 180 Madison Ave., New York, NY 10017

Burrell, Berkeley G., businessman, is president of the National Business League in Washington, D.C. He was elected in 1962 and is currently spearheading the NBL's restructuring program to develop the 72-year-old organization into a minority multi-trade association. He was born June 12, 1919 in Washington, D.C. He attended Howard University and received an honorary degree from Virginia College in Lynchburg, Va. He is vice chairman of the President's Advisory Council on Minority Business Enterprises. He is a member of the National Commission on Productivity, the National Business Council for Consumer Affairs and the National Minority Purchasing Council. He is a member of the board of directors of the Research Foundation of Doctor's Hospital, Council of Better Business Bureaus and the Industrial Bank, all in Washington, D.C. He is a partner in Graham Associates, builders of a proposed $20 million office building in Washington, D.C. He and his wife, A. Parthenia, have one son, Berkeley G. Jr. Address: 4324 Georgia Ave., NW, Washington, DC 20011

Burrell, Walter Price Jr., publicist and journalist, is a unit-publicist for 20th-Century-Fox studios in Hollywood, Calif. and is a magazine writer and columnist. Born Nov. 4, 1944 in Portsmouth, Va., he is a graduate of Compton College (A.A., music and English), Hampton Institute (B.A., English) and UCLA (M.A., creative writing). He is producer and moderator of his own syndicated radio show, "The Record." He has written two books, *Whatever Turns You On* and *The Black Entertainer Speaks Out*, and a collection of poems, *Poems of a Triple Scorpio*, and has acted in two of his own plays, *All For A Place* and *Free, Black and 21*. He and his wife, Enola, have two children, Tracey and Mario. Address: P.O. Box 900, Beverly Hills, CA 90213

Burris, Roland W., state official, is director of the Illinois Department of General Services. He is responsible for construction, telecommunications, space leasing, procurement, vehicles and the Illinois Information Services. Prior to his appointment by Governor Daniel Walker on January 8, 1973, he was a second vice president of the Continental Illinois National Bank and Trust Company, which he joined as a tax accountant in 1964. Born Aug. 8, 1937 in Centralia, Ill., he attended Southern Illinois University (B.A., political science, 1959); the University of Hamburg, Germany, (postgraduate course in international law); and Howard University School of Law (J.D., 1963). Before joining Continental, he worked as national bank examiner for the U.S. Treasury Department (1963–1964). He is a board member of the Southern Illinois University Foundation, a trustee of St. John Baptist Church in Chicago, a member of the Independent Voters of Illinois, the NAACP, the Cosmopolitan Chamber of Commerce, the National Business League and the Chicago South End Jaycees. His professional affiliations include the American, Illinois and Chicago bar associations, the American Institute of Banking and the Cook County (Ill.) Bar Association. He and his wife, Berlean, have two children, Rolanda Sue and Roland II. Address: 160 N. La Salle St., Chicago, IL 60601

Berkeley G. Burrell

Walter Price Burrell Jr.

Roland W. Burris

Margaret T. G. Burroughs

John H. Burton

John H. Bustamante

Philip Butcher

Burroughs, Margaret Taylor Goss, educator, artist, writer and museum administrator, a founder and is director of the DuSable Museum of African American History and Art in Chicago, Ill. Born Nov. 1, 1917 in St. Rose, La., she is a graduate of Chicago Teachers College and the Art Institute of Chicago (M.A., art education, 1948). She has done graduate work in art education at Columbia University (1959–60). She was one of the founders and assisted in the development of Chicago's South Side Community Art Center and was one of the organizers of the National Conference of Negro Artists (1959). She has won two national awards at the Annual Atlanta Exhibition of black artists. She has had articles published in professional art and education journals and is author of *Jasper the Drummin' Boy* and *What Shall I Tell My Children?,* and edited *Did You Feed My Cow?* and *Whip Me Whop Me Pudding.* She has travelled widely throughout Africa, Europe and Asia, and done extensive research in Ghana, Togo, Dahomey, Ivory Coast and Nigeria. She interned for one year (1968–69) at Chicago's Field Museum of Natural History (in museum management and technology), and has been a group leader for the American Forum for International Studies in Africa (1971–72). She and her husband, Charles, a writer, Russian linguist and curator of the DuSable Museum, have an adopted son, Paul Nexo Burroughs. Mrs. Burroughs has a daughter, Gayle Goss Toller. Address: 3806 S. Michigan Ave., Chicago, IL 60653

Burton, John H., union negotiator, is a representative of the International United Auto Workers Union (UAW) in Detroit, Mich. His work involves the negotiating of contracts, grievance procedures and community relations. Born July 18, 1910 in St. Louis, Mo., he attended college for two years and has had 16 years' on-the-job training. Mr. Burton was elected mayor of the city of Ypsilanti after having served on the city council for 18 years. He is a member of Board of Controls, the Medical Center of the University of Michigan; he is on the board of trustees of the Chelsea Medical Center and the executive board of directors of the Comprehensive Planning Council. Mr. Burton won the Man of the Year award of the Ford Motor Car Co. (Ypsilanti & Rawsonville plants), the Law Day award from the Washtenaw Bar Association, and Distinguished Service awards from the Michigan Association of Black Women's Clubs and the NAACP. He and his wife, Willie, make their home in Ypsilanti, Mich. Address: 9650 S. Telegraph Rd., Taylor, MI 48180

Bustamante, John H., attorney, is a partner in George, Pegg and Bustamante, a Cleveland, Ohio law firm specializing in corporate law, estates and trusts. Born Aug. 11, 1929 in Santiago, Cuba, he has degrees from Boston Univ. (A.B., J.D.), and Harvard Univ. (LL.M.). He represents the largest number of black-owned business firms in Cleveland and has several national corporations as clients. He is co-owner of a $28 million, 23-story building in downtown Cleveland and is forming a bank. He is a member of the American Bar Association, National Bar Association and numerous other professional and civic organizations, and has received numerous honors and awards. He is a former chairman of the board of trustees of Central State University and is credited with "saving" the school by leading it through a period of financial crisis and student rioting in the 1960s. He and his wife, Joy, have five children: Tuan, Sonali, Andre, Kamala and Joachim. Address: 33 Public Sq., Suite 1107, Cleveland, OH 44113

Butcher, Philip, educator, is dean of the graduate school and professor of English at Morgan State College in Baltimore, Md. He was born September 28, 1918 in Washington, D. C. and has degrees from Howard University (A.B., 1942; M.A., 1947) and Columbia University (Ph.D., 1956). He joined the English faculty at Morgan State College in 1947. He is a nationally recognized authority on the life of the writer, social critic and humanitarian, George Washington Cable, and is the author of more than 85 books, articles and reviews. His books are *George W. Cable: The Northampton Years* (1959), *George W. Cable* (1962) and *The William Stanley Braithwaite Reader* (1972). He and his wife, Ruth, have two daughters, Wendy and Mrs. Laurel B. Miles. Address: Morgan State College, Baltimore, MD 21239

Broadus N. Butler

Sawyer L. Bynam III

George S. Bynum

Butler, Broadus Nathaniel, educator, is president of Dillard University in New Orleans, La. He was born May 28, 1920 in Mobile, Ala. and majored in philosophy at Talladega College (B.A., 1941) and the University of Mich. (M.A., 1947; Ph.D., 1952). From 1953 to 1969, he was professor and/or official at St. Augustine's College (Raleigh, N.C.), Talladega College, Wayne State University and Texas Southern University. He became president of Dillard in 1969. He was an assistant to the U.S. Commissioner of education (1964-65) and was special assistant to the U.S. Associate Commissioner for Higher Education (1965-66). He was an author of Title III of the Higher Education Act of 1965 and established its basic guidelines, interpretation and operation for support of small colleges and economically disadvantaged students. He is a member of numerous professional and civic organizations and has received a number of honors and awards. He and his wife, Lillian, have two children, Bruce and Janet. Address: Office of the President, Dillard University, New Orleans, LA 70122

Bynam, Sawyer Lee III, building contractor, is contract developer and estimator for General and Sub-Contractors Association, a group of 75 non-white companies in Houston, Tex. Born Sept. 15, 1933 in Houston, he received a B.S. degree from Texas Southern University and a certificate in construction planning and estimating. He was with Jones and Bynam Building Contractors for 12 years before he assumed his current position. Mr. Bynam negotiates contracts between white-owned construction firms and minority contractors and promotes the full participation of minorities in the construction industry. He and his wife, Betty Ann, have a son, Keith Wayne. Address: General and Sub-Contractors Association, 2211 Wheeler St., Houston, TX 77004

Bynum, George S., labor official, is secretary-treasurer of Local 939, Chicago Barbers Union (Independent) in Chicago, Ill. The 1,000-member local became independent in 1946 when he led its members out of the parent International Journeyman Barbers, Hairdressers and Cosmetologists Union of America (AFL-CIO) over a pension dispute. Born Dec. 23, 1910 in Chicago, Mr. Bynum attended Chicago State Teachers College and took special labor courses at the University of Notre Dame (1956–58) and the University of Chicago (1957–60). He completed a labor management course at Cornell University (1958–59). Prior to establishing the independent union, he was vice president of the international union, the first black so elected. He was founder and editor of the *Illinois Union Barber*, a statewide union publication, and in 1962 was appointed secretary of the Illinois State Board of Barber Examiners. He has represented the U.S. Labor Department at an international meeting of labor leaders in Japan. He is a board member of Service Federal Savings & Loan Association in Chicago. He and his wife, June, live in Chicago. Address: Chicago Barbers Independent Union, 300 S. Ashland Ave., Chicago, IL 60607

Donald Byrd

James W. Byrd

Manford Byrd Jr.

James E. Caldwell

Byrd, Donald, musician and educator, is chairman of the Department of Jazz Studies at Howard University in Washington, D.C. He is a popular jazz trumpeter and is one of the leading authorities on black music. Born Dec. 9, 1932 in Detroit, Mich., he has degrees from Manhattan School of Music (B.A., M.A.), and studied composition in Paris with famed musicologist Nadia Boulanger. He has appeared with Thelonious Monk, Sarah Vaughan, Miles Davis, Dizzy Gillespie and others, and wrote the score for the 1970 movie *Montgomery to Memphis*, the story of Dr. Martin Luther King Jr.'s civil rights crusade. Mr. Byrd has four children: Michael, Toussaint, Jen-Ai and Donna. Address: Howard University, Washington, DC 20001

Byrd, James W., police official, is chief of police in Cheyenne, Wyo. Born Oct. 22, 1925 in Newark, N.J., he served in the U.S. Army during World War II and in the Korean conflict. He joined the Cheyenne Police Department as a rookie patrolman in June, 1949 and worked his way up through the ranks to his present position. In 1957, he became a detective and was promoted to juvenile officer a year later. In 1961, he passed the promotional examination for the rank of lieutenant and attained that rank in the fall of that year. He became a captain in 1963 and was appointed police chief in January, 1966. He is a former Grand Knight of the Third Degree of the Knights of Columbus, and was selected as 1968 Lawman of the Year by Kiwanis International for the entire Rocky Mountain District which includes Wyoming, Colorado, Nebraska and South Dakota. He is a member of the International Association of Chiefs of Police, the National Police Officers Association and other civic and professional organizations. He and his wife, Elizabeth, have three chldren: Robert, James and Linda. Address: Cheyenne Police Department, 1915 Pioneer Ave., Cheyenne, WY 82001

Byrd, Manford Jr., administrator, is deputy superintendent of the Chicago Public School System. He administers operations and programs of the system under direction of the general superintendent and is the system's chief operating officer. With 560,000 students, 44,000 employees, and an annual budget in excess of $800 million, the Chicago school system is the second largest in the United States. Mr. Byrd taught school in Quincy, Ill. (1949-54). In Chicago, he has been a teacher, master teacher, assistant principal and principal. In 1967, he was appointed as assistant to the general superintendent. He was promoted to his present position in 1968. Born May 29, 1928 in Brewton, Ala., he is a graduate of Central College in Iowa (B.A., 1949; honorary L.H.D., 1969) and Atlanta University (M.A., 1954). He has taken graduate courses in supervision and public school administration at DePaul University and the University of Chicago. He is a member of the board of directors of Chicago State University and the Joint Negro Appeal, and is a trustee of Central College. He and his wife, Cheribelle, have three children: Carl, Bradley and Donald. Address: 228 N. LaSalle St., Chicago, IL 60601

Caldwell, James E., attorney, is tax counsel for Standard Oil Company of Indiana, which has headquarters in Chicago, Ill. Born May 22, 1930 in Louisville, Ky., he is a graduate of the University of Pittsburgh (A.B., economics, 1952) and Howard University School of Law (LL.D., 1958). He was editor-in-chief of the Howard Law Review. He has attended Northwestern University and in 1973 was a candidate for a master's degree in business administration at the University of Chicago. Before assuming his present position in 1970, he was a senior trial attorney for the Internal Revenue Service (1959–70). He is a member of the West Chesterfield Association, the NAACP, Urban League, and legal advisor of the Christian Action Ministry of Chicago. He is also a member of the Illinois Bar Association, Cook County Bar Association, Chicago Bar Association, the Chicago Tax Club and the Reserve Officers Association. He is a lieutenant colonel in the U.S. Army Reserve and is a commanding officer of the 96th Judge Advocate General Detachment in Chicago. He and his wife, Dolores, have three children: Janelle, James and Randall. Address: Standard Oil Company (Indiana), 910 South Michigan Ave., Chicago IL 60605

Caldwell, Lewis A.H., legislator, was elected to the House of Representatives of the Illinois General Assembly in 1967 and has been reelected twice. He has sponsored 33 bills in the House, chiefly directed toward social and economic justice without regard to race, creed or color. Born in Chicago, Oct. 12, 1905, Mr. Caldwell graduated from Northwestern University (B.S., 1933; M.S., 1940). His book, *The Policy King*, was published in 1946. Rep. Caldwell served as a professional social worker for 16 years, has headed his own public relations firm and has been a newspaper editor and columnist since 1941. He is vice president for public affairs of the Cosmopolitan Chamber of Commerce in Chicago. Mr. Caldwell and his wife, Ruth, have two children, Mrs. Barbara Caldwell and Mrs. Phyllis Lumley. Address: 840 E. 87th St., Chicago, IL 60637

Callender, LeRoy, structural engineer, is proprietor of his own firm in New York, N.Y. Born Feb. 29, 1932 in New York City, he is a graduate of City College of the City University of New York (B.C.E., 1958). He attended Brooklyn Technical High School, noted for its academic excellence, and graduated in 1950 first in his class in architectural design. Attending City College at night, he worked as a draftsman for a major structural engineering firm. He was also drafted into the U.S. Army in 1952, assigned to a special drafting school and then sent to Korea where he designed small office buildings and other facilities. Honorably discharged, he completed college, joined another engineering firm and worked on the first nuclear power plant built in the East—the Consolidated Edison plant at Indian Point, N.Y. Founded in 1969, his own firm has provided consultation on the $3.2 million dormitory and student union buildings for Mary Holmes College in West Point, Miss.; the $6.3 million Whitney M. Young Complex in Yonkers, N.Y.; the $30-million Lindsay-Bushwick Houses in Brooklyn, N.Y., and the $14 million Douglas Circle project in Manhattan. Divorced, he has a son, Eric. Address: 401 E. 37th St., New York, NY 10016 **See article on LeRoy Callender in Volume II.**

Lewis A. H. Caldwell

Calloway, DeVerne Lee, legislator, is state representative of the 81st District in St. Louis, Mo. She first sought office in 1962 and has been reelected for six consecutive terms. Mrs. Calloway was born June 17, 1916 in Memphis, Tenn. and is a graduate of LeMoyne-Owen College (A.B., 1938). She did graduate studies in English at Atlanta University and at Northwestern University. In the legislature, she has been in the forefront of battles to win fair employment, equal pay for women, open housing, and has tried to increase community involvement in the operation of the St. Louis school board. Mrs. Calloway is very active as a member of many city and state committees. Both she and her husband, Ernest Calloway, have been commended by the St. Louis community for their efforts to educate the average citizens in the effectiveness and need for political participation on all levels—local, state and federal. The first black woman to be elected in Missouri, she concentrates on issues affecting the poor and the black. Address: 4309 Enright, St. Louis, MO 63108

LeRoy Callender

DeVerne L. Calloway

Godfrey Cambridge

Dick Campbell

Rev. A. J. Carey Jr.

Cambridge, Godfrey, entertainer, is a comedian and film actor. Born Feb. 26, 1933 in New York City, he graduated from Hofstra College and attended City College of New York. His first professional appearance was in the off-Broadway production, *Take a Giant Step* (1956). He has also appeared in numerous Broadway hits, including *Nature's Way, Detective Story, Lost in the Stars, The Blacks, Purlie Victorious, A Funny Thing Happened on the Way to the Forum* and *How to be a Jewish Mother.* Mr. Cambridge has played leading roles in such films as *The Last Angry Man, Gone are the Days!, The Troublemaker, The President's Analyst, The Busy Body* and *The Biggest Bundle of Them All* and *Watermelon Man.* He was co-star of *Cotton Comes to Harlem* (1970) and *Come Back Charleston Blue* (1972). He has made a number of guest appearances on television, including the Jack Paar, Johnny Carson, Merv Griffin and Ed Sullivan shows. He is a recipient of the Obie award (1961) and is the author of *Put Downs and Put-Outs* (1967). Address: c/o United Artists, 729 7th Ave., New York, NY 10019

Campbell, Dick, administrator and former entertainer, is executive director of the Sickle Cell Disease Foundation of Greater New York. The non-profit, educational foundation has helped focus national attention on the disease which mostly affects black persons. Mr. Campbell was born more than 65 years ago in Beaumont, Tex. He has degrees from Paul Quinn College (B.A., sociology) and Columbia University (M.A.), Beginning as a singer in the speakeasies in Los Angeles and later in Harlem, Mr. Campbell performed on Broadway in *Hot Chocolates* and in seven editions of *Blackbirds.* Mr. Campbell and his first wife, the late Muriel Rahn, organized the first Harlem Theatre Workshop and established the Rose McClendon Players. Established in 1937, the players produced about 30 plays during the next five years. During World War II, Mr. Campbell organized more than 65 all-black USO-Camp shows, sending thousands of black performers all over the world. In 1956, the State Department asked him to research and organize a cultural exchange program between the United States and Africa. He spent seven years touring Africa and setting up the program. He was manager of the African Pavilion at the New York World's Fair in 1964, and later worked with Operation Crossroads Africa until 1967, when he became director of public affairs for the Human Resources Administration in New York City. Mr. Campbell is married to the former Beryl Wilson of Trindad. Address: 144 W. 125th St., New York, NY 10027

Carey, The Reverend Archibald J. Jr., clergyman and jurist, has been a judge of the Circuit Court of Cook County (Ill.) since 1966, and has been a minister in the African Methodist Episcopal Church since 1929. Born Feb. 29, 1908 in Chicago, Ill., he attended the University of Chicago, the Lewis Institute (B.S., 1928), Northwestern University (B.D., 1932) and the Kent College of Law (LL.B., 1935). He is a member of Prescott, Taylor, Carey and Cooper, a Chicago law firm, and is pastor emeritus of Quinn Chapel A.M.E. Church in Chicago. He was pastor from 1949 to 1967. He was a member of the Chicago City Council (1947–55), U.S. delegate to the 8th General Assembly of the United Nations (1953), and a member of the President's Committee on Government Employment Policy (1955–61). He was chairman of the Committee after 1957. He has taught legal ethics at Chicago's John Marshall Law School and lectured at Roosevelt University. He is the recipient of numerous civic awards, and has honorary degrees from Wilberforce University (B.D., D.D., LL.D.) in Ohio and John Marshall Law School (LL.D.) in Chicago. Judge Carey and his wife, Hazel, have a daughter, Mrs. Carolyn Frazier. Address: 1605 Civic Center, Chicago, IL 60602

Charles V. Carr

Diahann Carroll

James Y. Carter

Carr, Charles V., city official and business executive, has been a member of the Cleveland (Ohio) City Council (Democrat, 17th Ward) since 1945 and is president of the city's Quincy Savings & Loan Co., the only black-owned savings and loan company in northern Ohio. He has been a chief sponsor or co-sponsor of all civil rights legislation passed by the City Council since the 1940s. He was a member of the all-black group which, in 1952, purchased the Quincy Savings & Loan Co. (established in 1919) in Cleveland. At the end of 1972 the firm had more than $9 million in assets. He was a founder of the Dunbar Life Insurance Company, which was later purchased by the Supreme Life Insurance Company of America. Mr. Carr has been in the private practice of law since 1929. Born Nov. 9, 1903 in Clarksville, Tex., he attended Fisk University and Cleveland State University (J.D.), and has an honorary LL.D. degree from Central State University. He is a member of the Greater Cleveland Growth Association, the Cleveland Citizens League, the John Harlan Law Club, the Cleveland Bar Association and the Elks. He is a Mason and a life member of the NAACP. He and his wife, Hortense, have two children, Leah and Cathleen, and he has two children by a previous marriage, Carol and Charles. Address: 7609 Euclid Ave., Cleveland, OH 44103

Carroll, Diahann, entertainer, is a singer and an actress who was the star of "Julia," the long-running television drama series. Born July 17, 1938 in New York, N.Y., she won a Metropolitan Opera scholarship when she was ten years old but took lessons only for a month because, at the time, she wanted to be world roller skating champion. After attending the High School of Music and Art, she enrolled in New York University. But when she appeared on a talent show, "Chance of a Lifetime," and won top honors and $1,000 for three consecutive weeks, her singing and acting career was launched. The first major Broadway production in which she appeared was *House of Flowers* in 1954. That same year, she played her first movie role as Myrt in *Carmen Jones* and made numerous television guest appearances. She starred in the New York musical *No Strings* created by Richard Rogers. She received *Cue* magazine's coveted Entertainer of the Year award for that performance and her successes in supper clubs and on the screen. Her other film achievements include *Porgy and Bess, Goodby Again* and *Paris Blues.* Miss Carroll is married to Fredde Glusman. She has a daughter, Suzanne Kay. Address: c/o Roy Gerber, 1100 Alta Loma Rd., Los Angeles, CA 90069

Carter, James Y., city official, is public vehicle license commissioner for the City of Chicago, a cabinet-ranked position in city government. He was the first black to head a city department in Chicago. Born April 20, 1915 in Raleigh, N.C., he attended Hampton Institute and is a graduate of Bates College (A.B., 1936) and Boston University (M.A. and LL.B. 1940). Admitted to the North Carolina Bar in 1940, he was the first non-white to pass the state's bar examinations in more than ten years. During World War II, he was a U.S. Army pilot with the 302nd Fighter Squadron and commanded the 618th Bomb Group of the 332nd Fighter Group. Prior to his military service, he taught law at North Carolina College for two years. Following World War II, he relocated in Chicago; he was admitted to the Illinois Bar in 1946. He was a hearing officer in the Illinois Revenue Department (1946–52) and was a representative from the 22nd District to the Illinois Legislature (1954–70). He and wife, Gloria, live in Chicago. He has one daughter, Christine. Address: City Hall, Chicago, IL 60601

Matthew G. Carter

Richard A. Carter

Brig. Gen. R.C. Cartwright

Carter, Matthew G., business executive, is manager of community affairs for the Hoffman LaRoche, Inc., a pharmaceutical firm in Nutley, N.J. A former mayor of Montclair, N.J., Mr. Carter was born Oct. 16, 1915 in Danville, Va. He attended Virginia Union University (A.B., B.D.). He has an honorary D.D. from Virginia Union and an honorary LL.D. from Bloomfield College. Mr. Carter was elected mayor in 1968 and served four years. Prior to that, he served on the Montclair Board of Commissioners during which time he held the posts of commissioner of public works and vice mayor. Mr. Carter has held various professional positions including that of a church minister. He and his wife, Nanette, have two daughters, Mrs. Bettye Freeman and Nanette. Address: Hoffman LaRoche, Inc., Nutley, NJ 07110

Carter, Richard A., legislator, is a member of the Illinois General Assembly from the 19th District (Chicago). Born in Chicago, Ill., he attended Morehouse College in Atlanta, Ga. He served in World War II with the famous 761st Tank Battalion, the first black tank battalion to fight in the war. He fought under the command of General George S. Patton and received five battle stars. He is manager of parking lots for the Chicago Department of Streets. He and his wife, Ruth, have a daughter, Irmgard Marie. Address: State Capitol, Springfield, IL 61106

Cartwright, Brig. Gen. Roscoe C., military official, is assistant division commander of U.S. Military Headquarters USAREUR and 7th Army, 3rd Infantry Division. Born May 27, 1919 in Kansas City, Mo., he has degrees from San Francisco State College (A.B.) and the University of Missouri (M.B.A.). He has been in service since 1941 and has received specialized military training from the Command and General Staff College and the Industrial College of the Armed Forces. His assignment in 1972 as assistant division commander made General Cartwright the second black man in military history to serve in that capacity. He is responsible for assisting in the training, administration and housing of 14,000 officers and men into combat ready forces. During his military tenure, he served tours in World War II, Korea and Vietnam. Included in his numerous military citations and decorations are World War II Victory, Meritorious Service, Armed Forces Honor, United Nations, Korean Service and Vietnam Campaign Medals. He and his wife, Gloria, have four children: Roscoe C. Jr., Stanley, Mrs. Phyllis Diehl and Cynthia. Address: Headquarters 3rd Infantry Division, Office of the Assistant Division Commander, APO 09036

Rev. W. Sterling Cary   Edmund C. Casey, M.D.   John L. Cashin Jr., D.D.S.

Cary, The Reverend W. Sterling, clergyman, is the first black president of the National Council of Churches. He was elected in December, 1972. The Reverend Cary says that U.S. churches preach but don't practice integration. The new NCC president has also been for more than four years the area minister of the Metropolitan New York United Church of Christ and is also the first black to serve in that elected capacity. As New York area minister, he is responsible for 100 local congregations. Upon his election to the presidency of the National Council of Churches, the Reverend Cary said one of his first moves would be to ease the tension between the so-called conservative and liberal interpretations of the faith. Other aims are to promote decent low-income housing for the poor, better opportunities for minorities and an overhaul of the welfare system. Born Aug. 10, 1927 in Plainfield, N.J., the Reverend Cary graduated from Morehouse College (B.A.) and Union Theological Seminary (B.D.). He and his wife, Marie, have four children: Yvonne, Sterling, Denise and Patricia. Address: 297 Park Ave., S, New York, NY 10010

Casey, Edmund C., M.D., physician, was elected in 1970 as chairman of the board of trustees of the National Medical Association. An internist in private practice in Cincinnati, Ohio he is an assistant professor of medicine at the University of Cincinnati and a member of the dean's committee on minority students. He is co-director of medicine at Bethesda Hospital and a member of the associate staff at Christ Hospital. Dr. Casey is on the board of trustees of the Hamilton County Tuberculosis and Respiratory Disease Association and chairman of its program development committee. He is also a trustee of the Heart Association of Southwestern Ohio, vice president of the Ohio Thoracic Society and a member of the Planned Parenthood Association's medical advisory committee. Born in 1923 in Marion, Ind., he earned his degrees at Earlham College and the University of Pennsylvania. He served four years in the U.S. Army during World War II and two years during the Korean conflict in the Medical Corps of the U.S. Air Force with the rank of captain. He and his wife, Lillian, have two daughters, Yvette and Yvonne. Address: 437 Melish Ave., Cincinnati, OH 45229

Cashin, John Logan Jr., D.D.S., dentist and political activist, is founder and chairman of the National Democratic party in Alabama. The NDPA, a predominantly black party, was formed in 1967 in opposition to the politics of Alabama Governor George Wallace. Dr. Cashin is also a practicing dentist in Huntsville, Ala. He was born April 16, 1928 in Huntsville and has degrees from Tennessee State University (B.S.) and Meharry Medical College (D.D.S.). His political organization has elected almost 100 blacks to public office in Alabama since its founding. Some of his significant achievements include the founding of the NDPA, winning the Greene County Special Election in 1969 in Alabama, and his courageous campaign against George Wallace for governor of Alabama in 1970. He and his wife, Joan, have three children: John, Carroll and Sheryll. Address: 507 Gallatin, Huntsville, AL 35801

61

Caviness, The Reverend E. Theophilus, clergyman, is pastor of the Greater Abyssinia Baptist Church in Cleveland, Ohio. Born May 23, 1928 in Marshall, Tex., he is a graduate of Bishop College (B.A.) and Eden Theological Seminary in Missouri (B.D.). Before assuming his present pastorate in 1961, the Reverend Caviness was pastor of St. Paul Baptist Church in East St. Louis, Ill. He is president of the Greater Abyssinia Baptist Church Federal Credit Union; historian and a member of the board of directors of the National Baptist Convention, U.S.A., Inc.; auditor of the Ohio Baptist General State Association; treasurer of the Northern Ohio Baptist District Association, and first vice president of the Baptist Ministers Conference of Cleveland. He is a member of the Zoning Board of Appeals of the City of Cleveland. He and his wife, Jimmie, have two children, Theophilus James and Theodosia Jacqueline. Address: Greater Abyssinia Baptist Church, 1161 E. 105th St., Cleveland, OH 44108

Chamberlain, Wilt (Wilton N.), professional basketball player, is the star center of the Los Angeles Lakers team. Born April 21, 1936 in Philadelphia, Pa., he attended Kansas University where he was twice selected All American. He left college after two years in 1958 to develop himself as a player with the Harlem Globetrotters. In 1959, he signed with the Philadelphia Warriors in the National Basketball Association. For seven successive seasons, he led the league in total points scored per season. In 1967, playing with the Philadelphia 76ers, he led his team to an NBA record 68 victories and the league championship. Traded to Los Angeles, he led the Lakers in 1972 to an NBA record 69 victories, 33 of them consecutive (an all-time pro sport record). He holds the all-time professional lead in points scored (more than 30,000) and the most points scored by an individual in one game (100 points). His annual salary exceeds $300,000, and he receives additional income from advertising endorsements and business interests such as the Big Wilt's Smalls Paradise nightclub in New York City. Address: Los Angeles Lakers, 3900 W. Manchester Blvd., Inglewood, CA 90306 **See article on Wilt Chamberlain in Volume II.**

Rev. E. T. Caviness

Chapin, Arthur A., governmental aide, is director of the Office of Equal Employment Opportunity, United States Department of Labor. He joined the department in 1961, was appointed by the secretary in 1963 as manpower specialist for minority group problems. Previously, he was for three years an executive staff member of the Democratic National Committee. Born in Philadelphia in 1915, Mr. Chapin is a product of the rank-and-file labor movement in New Jersey; he served, 1947–58, as assistant to the president of the New Jersey State CIO Council. He specialized in the study and drafting of state legislation dealing with civil rights, housing and unemployment compensation. He also acted as civil rights advisor to the mayor of Newark. Mr. Chapin is a member of the Urban League and the NAACP. He is a widower and has two daughters: Marjorie, Greta and two sons, Arthur and Rodney. Address: U.S. Department of Labor, 14th and Constitution Ave., Washington, DC 20212

W. N. (Wilt) Chamberlain

Arthur A. Chapin

Thomas William Chapman

Louis Charbonnet III

Ray Charles

Chapman, Thomas William, health specialist consultant, is a health care consultant in the management sciences division of Arthur D. Little, Inc., management and research consultants. His position involves overall consulting in health care matters requiring research analysis, developmental and implementation projects, organization evaluation and planning of health delivery systems. Born May 17, 1945 in New Haven, Conn., he attended Boston College School of Special Education, St. Anselm's College in Manchester, N.Y. (B.A., sociology, 1968). Mr. Chapman was administrative resident with the Children's Hospital Medical Center in Boston, Mass. He has an M.P.H. in hospital administration and the Yale University School of Epidemiology and Public Health (M.P.H., hospital administration, 1971). While at Yale, he evaluated a government-sponsored high school-college allied health careers program of the New Haven board of education. Mr. Chapman is a member of the American Hospital Association, the Massachusetts Hospital Association and Public Health Association. He and his wife, Erica Lynne, have one child, Justin Marc. Address: 25 Acorn Park, Cambridge, MA 02140

Charbonnet, Louis III, legislator and businessman, is a member of the Louisiana Legislature. Born March 12, 1939 in New Orleans, La., he took his place in the family business, Labat-Charbonnet Funeral Home, in 1957. He is a leader of the Black Legislative Caucus composed of five New Orleans representatives. In late 1972, he presented a proposal on behalf of the caucus to the New Orleans City Council calling for an end to the city police Felony Action Squad, rescinding a shoot-to-kill order, and creation of a police review board. To help seek a solution during a confrontation at predominantly black Southern University, he and two fellow lawmakers entered the administration building held by some 150 students and apparently de-fused a move by city police and Louisiana's governor to evacuate the building by force. The students left the building when the university vice president and dean resigned in response to their demand. Mr. Charbonnet is one of eight blacks in the 105-member legislature. He has a B.S. degree from Commonwealth College of Sciences. He and his wife, Simone Monette, have a daughter, Kim Marie. Address: 1607 St. Philip St., New Orleans, LA 70116

Charles, Ray, entertainer, is called a legend, a hero, a genius and a monument because of his talents as a singer, arranger, composer and bandleader. Mr. Charles has a bronze medallion which was presented to him by the French Republic. Born Ray Charles Robinson on Sept. 23, 1930 in Albany, Ga., he began playing the piano while still a small child. At seven, glaucoma blinded him. His mother told him, "You're blind, not stupid. You lost your sight, not your mind." When he was 10, young Ray lost his father, and his mother died when he was 15. At a school for the deaf and blind, he learned to read and write braille, to play some classical piano, to make mops and brooms—and that he was black. He left the school at 15 to tour with dance bands, and in two years got a job at a club in Seattle. At first he copied Nat "King" Cole's style, but he finally realized he must be himself as a musician. A road job with Lowell Fulsom led to New York and a personal booking at Harlem's Apollo Theatre. Back in Seattle, he formed the Swing-time Trio, had a television program and made some records. In 1954, he took his group, now numbering seven, to Atlantic Records and recorded *I Got A Woman*. Today, Ray Charles records for his own label, Tangerine, distributed by ABC Records. Mr. Charles and his wife, Della, have three sons: Ray Jr., David and Robert. Address: Queens Booking Corp., 1650 Broadway, New York, NY 10019

James E. Cheek

King V. Cheek

Madelyn Chennault

Cheek, James E., educator, is president of Howard University in Washington, D.C. Born Dec. 4, 1932 in Roanoke Rapids, N.C., he is a graduate of Shaw University (B.A., 1955), Colgate-Rochester Divinity School (B.D., 1958) and Drew University (Ph.D., 1962). He also has seven honorary degrees. Before assuming his present position in 1969, Dr. Cheek was a teaching assistant at Drew Theological School (1959–60), instructor in Western history at Union Junior College (1959–61), visiting instructor in Christian history at Upsala College (1960), assistant professor of New Testament and historical theology at Virginia Union University (1961–63) and president of Shaw University (1963–69). He is a member, director or trustee of more than 50 organizations, committees and commissions, including the National Council on Educating the Disadvantaged, the Educational Policy Center, Inc., the Joint Center for Political Studies, People United to Save Humanity (PUSH), Federal City Council, Drew University, the University of Miami, Common Cause Policy Council and Washington Home Rule, Inc. He and his wife, Celestine, have two children, James and Janet. Address: Howard University, Washington, DC 20001 **See article on James E. Cheek in Volume II.**

Cheek, King V., educator and administrator, is president of Morgan State College in Baltimore, Md. Born May 26, 1937 in Weldon, N. C., he is a graduate of Bates College (A.B., economics, 1959), the University of Chicago, (M.A., economics, 1960) and the University of Chicago Law School (J.D., 1964). He studied for a Ph.D. degree at the University of Chicago (1960-61) and has honorary LL.D. degrees from Bates College (1970), Delaware State College (1970) and the University of Maryland (1972). He was president of Shaw University (1969-71). At Shaw, he had been vice president of academic affairs (1967-69), dean of the college (1965-67) and assistant professor of economics (1964-65). He is a member of numerous professional and civic organizations and is a Grand Commander of the Order of the Star of Africa (conferred in 1971 by President William V.S. Tubman of Liberia). He is the author of several articles published in educational journals. He and his wife, Annette, have a son, King V. III. Address: Morgan State College, Coldspring Lane & Hillen Rd., Baltimore, MD 21212

Chennault, Madelyn, educator, is Calloway Professor of Educational Psychology and a professor of education at Fort Valley (Ga.) State College. She directs a "crisis clinic" for the college and the community, and teaches courses in psychology and mental retardation. She was born July 15, 1932 in Atlanta, Ga. and has degrees from Morris Brown College (B.S., 1957, elementary education and psychology); University of Michigan (M.A., 1961, educational psychology), Indiana University (Ed.S., 1965, mental retardation; Ed.D., 1966, mental retardation and psychology). Her doctoral internship in clinical psychology was done in 1971-72 at the University of Georgia. She continues to do research in her field and expected to become, by September 1973, one of about 10 black women in the U. S. to obtain a license to practice clinical psychology. She is a member of the Association of Black Psychologists, American Association of University Professors, and other professional organizations. She is a visiting lecturer at the University of Georgia. A number of her articles have been published in journals of education and psychology and she has been a consultant for several educational and psychological programs. Address: Box 1367, State College, Ft. Valley, GA 31030

Gwen S. Cherry

Judge Sammie Chess Jr.

Joseph A. Chester Sr.

Cherry, Gwen Sawyer, legislator, is a state representative in Florida (Democrat, 106th District, Miami). She was elected in 1970 and is vice chairman of the House Military and Veterans Affairs Committee and vice chairman of the Committee on Corrections. Born Aug. 27, 1923 in Miami, she is a graduate of Florida A&M University (B.S., science, 1946; J.D., 1965) and New York University (M.S., human relations, 1950). She has also studied on various fellowships at the University of California, Morgan State College and Fisk University. She has been in the private practice of law in Miami and has served as a legal assistance attorney for the U. S. Coast Guard. She has won a number of landmark cases in Florida courtrooms. She is a member of the American Association of University Women, the National Association of Women Lawyers, the Florida Women Lawyer's Association, The Democratic Women's Club of Dade County, the National Organization of Women, Sigma Gamma Rho, and numerous other professional and civic groups. She is co-author of *Portraits of Color* and has written articles for various professional journals. She has received a number of awards for her work. She and her husband, James L. Cherry, have two children, Mary and William. Address: 636 NW Second Ave., Miami, FL 33136

Chess, Sammie Jr., jurist, is judge of the Superior Court of the state of North Carolina. Born March 28, 1934 in Allendale, S.C., he has degrees from North Carolina Central University (A.B., LL.B.). He was appointed to his post by the governor in 1970 and is the first and only black in the South to serve in this capacity. He is admitted to practice before the U.S. and North Carolina Supreme Courts, the U.S. Courts for the Middle District of North Carolina and the Court of Appeals for the Fourth Circuit. Judge Chess is professionally affiliated with the American, North Carolina and High Point Bar Associations and the Southeastern and American Trial Lawyers Associations. He is a member of the board of high education for North Caolina, the Advisory Board of Salvation Army and formerly was commissioner of parks and recreation in High Point. He and his wife, Marlene, have two daughters, Marlene and Eva. Address: P.O. Box 107, High Point, NC 27461

Chester, Joseph A. Sr., legislator, is a member of the Maryland House of Delegates, representing the 2nd District (Baltimore). When elected in 1966, he was the first black to obtain public office in Maryland history. He was reelected in 1970. He is a member of the House Appropriations Committee. He was born March 4, 1914 in Wilson, N. C. and settled in Baltimore during the Depression. For 20 years, he was a driver-salesman for a transfer company. He began his political career in 1940 by knocking on doors in an effort to get people to register to vote. He became a ward executive and district leader, and in 1962 lost a race for City Council on an all-black ticket. Later, he founded and became president of the New Era Democratic Club. He is chairman of the Advisory Board of Hue Chemical Co., a maintenance supply firm owned by his son, William. He and his wife, Pearl, have seven children: Mrs. Fannie E.C. Alston, Mrs. Pearl B. McCants, Joseph Jr., Mrs. India Watkins, James A., William T. and Irvin E. Address: 2000 E. Hoffman St., Baltimore, MD 21213

Chester, William H., city official, was named to the Bay Area Rapid Transit District (BART) board of directors on Jan. 23, 1970 by the mayor of San Francisco. He served as its vice president in 1972 and is its 1973 president. The $1.4 billion Bay Area Rapid Transit System is the largest major transit development built in the last half a century and was dedicated Oct. 11, 1972. Mr. Chester is also a vice president of the International Longshoremen's & Warehousemen's Union. He joined the ILWU in 1938 and has been a member of Local 10 executive board since 1945, California regional director since 1951, and vice president-assistant to the president of the ILWU since 1968. Born in Shreveport, La., he attended public schools in Kansas City, Mo. and Western University in Quindero, Kan. Mr. Chester is a member of numerous civic and service organizations including the board of directors of the United Nations Association of San Francisco, the Northern Committee on Africa and the San Francisco Ballet. He is chairman of the mayor's Labor Advisory Committee, a member of the Commonwealth Club and the Bay Area Social Planning Council. He and his wife, Ethel, have two children, William H. Jr., and Kathy Ann. Address: 800 Madison St., Oakland, CA 94607

Chew, Charles Jr., legislator, is an Illinois state senator (29th District, Chicago). He is chairman of the Senate Transportation Committee and serves on five other committees and five Senate commissions. He is a member of the Governor's Advisory Board on Narcotics. He was elected to the Illinois Legislature in 1966. Born Oct. 9, 1922 in Greenville, Miss., he is a graduate of Tuskegee Institute. He is president of South Park Safe Deposit & Vault Corp. in Chicago and formerly was alderman of the city's 17th Ward. He is vice-president and treasurer of the National Center for Black Politics and is a life member of the NAACP. Senator Chew's leisure interests are "driving my Rolls-Royce and being with real people." He and his wife, Shirley, have a son, Lorenzo. Address: Civic Center, Chicago, IL 60602

Chisholm, Shirley A., congresswoman, is a U.S. representative from New York's 12th district. A Democrat, she was first elected in 1969. In 1972, she conducted a vigorous national campaign for the Democratic presidential nomination. Born Nov. 30, 1924 in Brooklyn, N.Y., she is a graduate of Brooklyn College (B.A. *cum laude*) and Columbia University (M.A.). She also has honorary degrees from Talladega College (LL.D.), Hampton Institute (LL.D.), North Carolina Central College (L.H.D.) and Wilmington College (L.H.D.). Prior to her election to Congress, she was a teacher and director of a nursey school, educational consultant to the Division of Day Care of the New York City Bureau of Child Welfare and a member of the New York State Assembly (1964–68). She has received numerous awards. She and her husband, Conrad, live in Brooklyn. Address: House Office Bldg., Washington, DC 20515 **See article on Shirley A. Chisholm in Volume II.**

William H. Chester

Charles Chew Jr.

Rep. Shirley A. Chisholm

Charles D. Churchwell

Rev. C. A. W. Clark

Kenneth B. Clark

Churchwell, Charles Darrett, administrator, is associate provost for academic services at Miami University in Oxford, Ohio. He is responsible for all academic support services, interdisciplinary studies and international programs. Born Nov. 7, 1926 in Dunnellon, Fla., he is a graduate of Morehouse College (B.S., mathematics, 1952), Atlanta University (M.S., library science, 1953) and the University of Illinois (Ph.D., library science, 1966). He has also studied at City College, Hunter College and New York University. Before assuming his present position in 1972, he was director of libraries at Miami University (1969–72), assistant director of libraries at the University of Houston (1967–69), assistant circulation librarian at the University of Illinois (1965–67), reference librarian in the circulation department of the New York Public library (1959–61) and library science instructor at Prairie View A & M College (1953–58). He was a Great Books discussion leader at New York Public Library (1960–61) and chairman of the Advisory Task Force on Academic Priorities at Miami University (1971–72). He is a life member of the American Library Association and the NAACP, and a member of the American Association of Higher Education. He is the author of *A History of Education for Librarianship, 1919–1939.* He and his wife, Yvonne, have two children, Linda and Cynthia. Address: 106 Roudebush Hall, Miami University, Oxford, OH 45056

Clark, The Rev. Caesar A.W., clergyman, is pastor of Good Street Baptist Church in Dallas, Tex. In 1970, the church completed construction of a new sanctuary and other facilities valued at $1 million. It also operates a day-care center for several hundred children and operates Good Haven Apartments, a 332-unit complex valued at more than $3 million. It makes annual contributions to Bishop College and a number of other institutions and projects. Dr. Clark was born Dec. 13, 1914 in Shreveport, La. and is a graduate of Bishop College (B.A.). He also has B. Th., LL.D. and D.D. degrees. He is a nationally known evangelist and is editor of the *National Baptist Voice,* the monthly newspaper of the National Baptist Convention U. S. A., Inc. He is a member of the board of directors of the Convention and is a member of numerous other church and civic groups. He is secretary of the board of directors of Bishop College. He has received a number of citations and awards. Divorced, he has a son, Caesar Jr. Address: 3110 Bonnie View Rd., Dallas, TX 75216

Clark, Kenneth Bancroft, psychologist, is director of the Metropolitan Applied Research Center (MARC) in New York, N.Y. The center was formed to conduct special research in community development and related social problems. Born July 24, 1914 in Panama, Canal Zone, he became a naturalized citizen in 1931. He is a graduate of Howard University (A.B., 1933; M.S., 1936) and Columbia University (Ph.D., psychology, 1940). With his wife, Dr. Mamie Phipps Clark, also a psychologist, he founded New York City's Northside Center for Child Development in 1946. During the 1960s, he organized Harlem Youth Opportunities Unlimited (HARYOU), a local self-help organization for young persons. Nationally prominent in psychological research, he contributed data cited by the United States Supreme Court in its landmark ruling in 1954, outlawing segregated schools. Dr. Clark is the author of *Dark Ghetto Dilemmas of Social Power,* a penetrating indictment of institutionalized racism. He has contributed to numerous professional journals, including the *Journal of Social Psychology,* the *Journal of Social and Abnormal Psychology* and the *Journal of Social Mental Hygiene.* The Clarks have two children, Kate and Hilton. Address: Metropolitan Applied Research Center, 60 E. 86th St., New York, NY 10028

Mildred Clark

Robert G. Clark

Walter H. Clark

Clark, Mildred, publishing executive, is vice president and controller of Johnson Publishing Co., Inc. in Chicago, Ill., publishers of *Ebony, Jet, Black Stars, Black World* and *Ebony Jr!.* magazines. She joined the company in 1944 as a secretary and has held the positions of subscription manager, bookkeeping assistant and bookkeeper. Born in Oskaloosa, Iowa, she has taken business courses and special courses at William Penn College. She also has had on-the-job training under a certified public accountant. Address: 820 S. Michigan Ave., Chicago, IL 60605

Clark, Robert G., legislator, is the first black man to serve in the Mississippi Legislature since Reconstruction. A member of the Mississippi Freedom Democratic Party, he was elected as a state representative (District 16, Holmes and Humphrys Counties) in 1967 and was reelected in 1971. Born Oct. 3, 1929 in Ebenezer, Miss., he has degrees from Jackson (Miss.) State College (B.S.) and Michigan State University (M.A.). A teacher-coach, he is athletic director and business manager at Saints Junior College in Lexington, Miss. During his years in the legislature, he has fought for improvements in public schools, and waged an unsuccessful one-man battle on the floor of the House in 1968 against raising tuition grants to private, segregated schools. He has served as president of the Holmes County Teachers Association and is founder and member of the board of Central Mississippi Incorporation of Community Action Programs. He is a member of the International Board of Basketball Officials and is a past president of the Central Mississippi Board of Athletic Officials. He and his wife, Essie, have a son, Robert Jr. Address: Box 184, Lexington, MS 39095

Clark, Walter H. executive, is senior vice president-finance of First Federal Savings and Loan Association in Chicago, Ill. The largest such firm in the Chicago area, its 1972 assets were $1.25 billion. Mr. Clark is administrator of all banking account relationships as well as the cash flow, the accounting systems, the budget and internal and external financial reports, and is manager of the security investment portfolio. Born June 5, 1928 in Athens, Ga., he has a B.A. degree from Southern Illinois University and an M.B.A. degree from De Paul University. He studied in the Harvard University advance management program in 1971. He is a member of the senior loan committee and assists in determining policy and planning. He also keeps management informed on economic trends and interests rates. He joined First Federal in 1955 and has held positions as treasurer and as vice president-treasurer. He was promoted in 1971. He is a member of a number of professional and civic groups, including the National Society of Controllers and Financial Officers. He and his wife Juanita, have two children, Hilton and Juanine. Address: 1 S. Dearborn St., Chicago, IL 60603

John Henrik Clarke

Joseph E. L. Clarke

Richard V. Clarke

Clarke, John Henrik, educator, is associate professor of African-American history at Hunter College of the City University of New York. He is the major professor and developer of courses in African and Afro-American history and culture in the Department of Black and Puerto Rican Studies. He is also Carter G. Woodson Distinguished Visiting Professor of African History at the Africana Studies and Research Center of Cornell University. Professor Clarke is the author or editor of nine books, including *Harlem, U.S.A.*, *The Lives of Great African Chiefs*, and *William Styron's Nat Turner: Ten Black Writers Respond*. Widely traveled in Africa, he was special consultant and coordinator of the CBS-TV series *Black Heritage*, for which he developed the original format. He was born Jan. 1, 1915 in Union Springs, Ala., finished high school in New York City, studied creative writing at Columbia University and soon began to be published in newspapers and magazines. On several occasions his stories have been listed in the annual anthology, *The Best American Short Stories*. He has an honorary LL.D. degree from the University of Denver. Professor Clarke and his wife, Eugenia, have two children, Nzingha Marie and Sonni Kojo. Address: 695 Park Ave., New York, NY 10021

Clarke, Joseph E. L., administrator, is director of sales for Supreme Beauty Products Company in Chicago, Ill. He is in charge of marketing and sales for Duke and Raveen, the second largest-selling black product line in the United States. Born Apr. 6, 1941 in New York City, he is a graduate of City College of New York (B.A., sociology, 1967). He has also studied at Bronx Community College (1959–60), Southern Illinois University (1960–63) and New York University (1967–68). Before assuming his present position in 1971, he was assistant sales director (1968–71), marketing research and merchandising representative for Johnson Publishing Company (1967–68) and eastern sales director of Supreme Beauty Products (1968–71). He was also office manager of the Livingstone Institute in New York City. He is a member of Alpha Phi Alpha Fraternity and the Cancer Society Steering Committee. He and his wife, Marion, have a daughter, Leslie. He has a daughter Bernadette by a previous marriage. Address: 645 North Michigan Ave., Chicago, IL 60605

Clarke, Richard V., business executive, is president of Richard Clarke Associates, Inc., minority executive recruiters, in New York, N.Y. with a branch office in Chicago, Ill. The firm has brought together numerous black job-seekers and industrial and corporate employers. It conducts Job Opportunity Centers in New York City, Chicago, Washington, D.C., Detroit, Mich., Atlanta, Ga. and Houston, Tex. Mr. Clarke established the firm in 1964 after operating Hallmark Employment Agency, which he founded in 1957. He publishes two magazines, *Opportunities for the College Graduate*, an annual, and *Contact*, a quarterly for employed black college graduates who wish to further their careers. He also operates Hallmark Holidays, a travel agency. Mr. Clarke was born in June, 1927 in New York City. He has a degree in business administration from City College of the City University of N.Y. (1955). He has been an employment consultant to many federal, state and private agencies, and is a member of numerous professional and civic groups. He is a member of the board of directors of Freedom National Bank in New York. He and his wife, Dr. Greta F. Clarke, a physician, have two children, Tracy and Richard Jr. Address: 1270 Avenue of the Americas, New York, NY 10020

Rep. William L. Clay

Xernona Clayton

Rev. Albert B. Cleage

Clay, William Lacy, congressman, is a Democratic member of the U.S. House of Representatives from the First District of Missouri (St. Louis). Born April 30, 1931 in St. Louis, he is a graduate of St. Louis University (B.S., history and political science, 1953). A former executive board member of the St. Louis Branch NAACP and a member of CORE, he organized hundreds of sit-ins and civil rights demonstrations and served 112 days in jail for contempt of court in one civl rights case. His credentials as a black activist for many years helped elect him to the St. Louis board of aldermen in 1959 and again in 1963. He was elected to Congress in 1968 and was reelected in 1972. He is a member of the House Committee on Education and Labor, the Ad Hoc Task Force on Poverty, and the House Democratic Steering Committee on Interest Rates. He is vice president of the Democratic Study Group and is a member of that organization's civil rights task force. He and his wife, Carol Ann, have three children: Vicki, William Jr. and Michelle. Address: U.S. House of Representatives, Washington, DC 20515

Clayton, Xernona, communications specialist, is producer and hostess of the "Xernona Clayton Show" on WAGA-TV in Atlanta, Ga., she was born Aug. 30, 1930 in Muskogee, Okla., and graduated from Tennessee State University (B.A., 1952). She taught in the public schools of Chicago and Los Angeles before joining the Southern Christian Leadership Conference with her late husband, Edward T. Clayton. After Mr. Clayton's death, she wrote the final chapter to his book, *Martin Luther King: The Peaceful Warrior.* An active civic worker, Mrs. Clayton is a consultant for the Atlanta Model Cities Program. She is a member of many professional organizations, including American Women in Radio and Television and the Atlanta Press Club. Address: 1551 Briarcliff Road, NE, Atlanta, GA 30302

Cleage, The Reverend Albert B. Jr., clergyman, is minister of the Shrine of the Black Madonna in Detroit, Mich. and national chairman of the Black Christian Nationalist Church, Inc., which seeks to "re-structure the theology and program of the black church in order that it may become relevant to the black liberation struggle." Born June 13, 1913 in Indianapolis, Ind., the Rev. Cleage is a graduate of Wayne State University (A.B.) and the Oberlin Graduate School of Theology (B.D.). He is the author of *The Black Messiah* and *Black Christian Nationalism* and has served on the national boards of the interreligious Foundation for Community Organization, National Committee of Black Churchmen, and the Commission for Racial Justice. He has adopted the name Jaramogi Adebe Ageyman ("liberator"). Some 2,000 persons, mainly young blacks, work with BCNC. The organization operates a large training center, a food co-op and a 50-acre farm, a counseling center and three religious and cultural centers. Divorced, the Rev. Cleage has two daughters, Mrs. Pearl Lomax and Mrs. Kristin Williams. Address: 13535 Livernois, Detroit, MI 48238

Kenneth W. Clement, M.D.

Fr. George H. Clements

Rev. James Cleveland

Clement, Kenneth W., M.D., surgeon, is assistant clinical professor of surgery at Case Western Reserve University School of Medicine in Cleveland, O. Born Feb. 24, 1920 in Pittsylvania County, Va., he is a graduate of Oberlin College (A.B., 1942) and Howard University (M.D., 1942). He was a U.S. Air Force flight surgeon (1951-53) and has been in the practice of general surgery in Cleveland since 1953. He is a diplomate of the American Board of Surgery. He was president of the National Medical Association (1963-64) and was the first black president of the Cleveland Baptist Association. From U. S. Presidents Kennedy and Johnson, he received appointments which involved formulation of Medicare legislation. Dr. Clement was director of the successful 1967 campaign of Carl B. Stokes for mayor of Cleveland, and was a 1970 candidate for election to the U. S. Senate. He has written some 36 papers and articles and has delivered more than 200 addresses on medical and social subjects. He has been a member of the board of directors of Mt. Pleasant Medical Center, Fair Housing Inc., Bardun Investment Corp., UAW Retired Workers Center and Great Lakes Mutual Life Insurance Co., and is a member of the board of trustees of Howard University and Kent State University. He is a member of the Board of Regents of the State of Ohio. He has received numerous awards and honorary degrees and is a member of 29 professional and civic organizations. Dr. Clement and his wife, Ruth, have a son, Michael, and twin daughters, Lia and Leslie. Address: 13645 Larchmere Blvd., Shaker Heights, OH 44120

Clements, Fr. George H., priest, is pastor of Holy Angels Church in Chicago, Ill. Born Jan. 26, 1932 in Chicago, he was the first black graduate of Quigley Seminary and is a graduate of St. Mary of the Lake Seminary in Mundelein, Ill. (B.A. and M.A., philosophy). He was ordained in 1957. Fr. Clements is highly active in community affairs and has organized several neighborhood associations and the Black Clergy Caucus. He serves on the boards of SCLC's Operation Breadbasket, the NAACP, the Urban League, the Better Boys Foundation and the Black Panther party. He is chaplain of the Afro-American Patrolmen's League, the Firemen's League and the Postal Workers' League, all in Chicago. Address: Holy Angels Church, 607 Oakwood Blvd., Chicago, IL 60653

Cleveland, The Reverend James, clergyman, recording artist and organization head, is pastor of the Cornerstone Institutional Baptist Church in Los Angeles, Cal., a well-known gospel recording artist on Savoy Records, and national president-founder of the Gospel Music Workshop of America, which meets annually and has a membership of some 10,000 church musicians. Born Dec. 5, 1931 in Chicago, Ill., he graduated from Marshall high school in Chicago and attended Roosevelt University. He began singing in various groups when he was a teenager. Later, he was piano accompanist for such groups as the Caravans and the Roberta Martin Singers. He has had his own group, The James Cleveland Singers, for many years. He ranks as one of the most successful gospel concert and recording artists in history. He has won several "gold records" and numerous awards. Address: 3701 Northland Drive, Los Angeles, CA 90008

James E. Clyburn

Jewel Plummer Cobb

LaVarne R. Cobb

Clyburn, James E., gubernatorial aide, is a special assistant (for human resource development) to Gov. John C. West of South Carolina. He is the first black appointed to the governor's staff since Reconstruction. Born July 21, 1940 in Sumter, S. C. He is a graduate of South Carolina State College (B.A., 1962) and attends the University of S. C. Law School. He has been executive director of the South Carolina Commission for Farm Workers, Inc. (1968-71), director of a Neighborhood Youth Corps (1966-68), counselor at the South Carolina Employee Security Commission (1965-66) and a high school history teacher (1962-65). He narrowly lost a 1970 election for the South Carolina House of Representatives. Shortly thereafter, he received his appointment from Governor West. He is a member of a number of political and civic organizations (in 1971, he was elected as the first black president of the South Carolina Young Democrats) and has received 11 citations and awards. He and his wife, Emily, have two children, Mignon and Jennifer. Address: Office of the Governor, Columbia, SC 29201

Cobb, Jewel Plummer, educator, is dean of Connecticut College in New London, Conn., where she is also professor of zoology. Born Jan. 17, 1924 in Chicago, Ill., she is a graduate of Talladega College (A.B., biology, 1944) and New York University (M.S., biology, 1947; Ph.D., cell biology, 1950). She holds honorary degrees from Lowell Technical Institute (D.Sc.) and Wheaton College (LL.D.) in Wheaton, Ill. Between 1945 and 1950, she was a biology instructor at New York University and from 1952 to 1954 an instructor of anatomy at the University of Illinois Medical School. In 1955, she returned to New York University as an instructor of research surgery and between 1956 and 1960 was assistant professor at Hunter College in New York City. She was professor of biology at Sarah Lawrence College, Bronxville, N.Y., from 1960 to 1969 and became dean of Connecticut College in 1969. She is a board member of the advisory committee of the National Institute for Dental Research and a member of the Institute for Educational Management and the National Center for Resource Recovery. Dr. Cobb is divorced and has a son, Roy Jonathan. Address: Connecticut College, New London, CT 06320

Cobb, LaVarne R., contractor, is president of Satisfactory Construction Co. in Detroit, Mich. The firm, which has 237 employees, is Michigan's third largest home improvement company. A businessman for 20 years, Mr. Cobb began his training in a two and a half year course in construction and estimating at the University of Michigan. Born April 26, 1935 in Alachua, Fla., he attended Gibbs Junior College and Florida A&M University, and is studying marketing in evening classes at the University of Detroit. He has taken three real estate courses at other schools and completed a four-year college course in business management at LaSalle Extension University in Chicago, Ill. This extensive education is his answer to "the black man's inability to obtain training from white companies in how to operate a large firm with 100 or more construction projects underway at one time." He wrote a home improvement sales and estimating book for the Metropolitan Contractors Association of Detroit and has taught classes in the subject for the Detroit Board of Education and for the Mayor's Committee for Human Resources. Mr. Cobb is divorced. Address: 7318 W. Warren Ave., Detroit, MI 48210

Cobb, W. Montague, M.D., medical educator and editor, is distinguished professor of anatomy at Howard University Medical School in Washington, D.C., and is editor of the *Journal of the National Medical Association.* Born in Washington, D.C .on Oct 12, 1904, he has served as president of the NMA, president of the American Association of Physical Anthropologists and the Anthropological Society of Washington, and vice president and chairman of the section for anthropology of the American Association for the Advancement of Science. He also served six terms as president of the Medico-Chirurgical Society of the District of Columbia. He is the author of more than 500 monographs, abstracts, editorials, scientific and popular articles, biographical sketches and other works. He graduated from Amherst College (A.B., 1925), Howard University (M.D., 1929) and Western Reserve University (Ph.D., 1932). He has also received honorary degrees from Amherst (D.Sc.) and Morgan State College (LL.D.) and some 40 citations for public service. As a distinguished educator, he believes that "the quality of teachers is much more important than anything else in importing a good education." He and his wife, Hilda, have two daughters, Mrs. Carolyn E. Wilkinson and Mrs. Hilda Gray. Address: Howard University Medical School, 520 W . St., NW, Washington, DC 20009

Cobbs, Clarence H., clergyman, is pastor of the First Church of Deliverance in Chicago, Ill. He founded the church in 1929 and a year later organized its still famous choir. The choir has made two European tours, and the church has broadcast its Sunday service each week since 1934. In addition to its sanctuary, it has built the Maggie Drummond Community Center (1956) and the 199-bed First Church of Deliverance Convalescent Home (1970). The staff of the $2.5 million home includes three doctors, a dentist, 30 nurses and 25 aides. Rev. Cobbs was born Feb. 29, 1908 in Memphis, Tenn. and has an honorary degree from Virginia Theological Seminary (D.D., 1971). He is international president of Metropolitan Spiritualist Churches of Christ, Inc., which has affiliated churches throughout the U. S. and in Africa. He is a member of a number of religious and civic groups. He is single. Address: 4315 S. Wabash, Chicago, IL 60653

Cobbs, Price M., psychiatrist, is a medical doctor with specialization in psychiatry. He has been practicing now for the past 11 years and is working in the area of group treatment for the effects of racism. Born Nov. 2, 1928 in Los Angeles, Calif., he has a B.A. from the University of California at Berkeley and an M.D. from Meharry Medical College. He is co-author of two popular books, *Black Rage* and *The Jesus Bag.* Dr. Cobbs is also a member of the National Medical Association, the American Psychiatric Association, the Institute of Medicine, and the National Academy of Science. He feels that there are more blacks in medical school now and more who are choosing psychiatry as a profession so that a black psychiatrist is not so rare today as he was five or 10 years ago. Dr. Cobbs and his wife, Evadne, have two children: Price Priester and Marion Renata. Address: 3528 Sacramento St., San Francisco, CA 94118

W. Montague Cobb, M.D.   Rev. Clarence H. Cobbs   Price M. Cobbs, M.D.

J. Otis Cochran

Elizabeth Cofield

James E. Cofield Jr.

Cochran, J. Otis, attorney, is national coordinator of the Dixwell Legal Rights Assn. in New Haven, Conn. He conducts paralegal training programs funded by the U.S. Office of Economic Opportunity and serves as consultant and instructor in training conferences across the United States. Born Aug. 10, 1944 in Atlanta, Ga., he received a B.A. degree from Morehouse College and a J.D. degree from Yale University. He was a participant in the southern civil rights movement of the early 1960s. He has been program coordinator of the Atlanta Council on Human Relations and a legal analyst for the U.S. Equal Employment Opportunity Commission. He has lectured and taught at Yale University and at Union College. He has been awarded a number of academic prizes and fellowships. Mr. Cochran is single. Address: 184 Dixwell Ave., New Haven, CT 06511

Cofield, Elizabeth, county official and educator, is the first black and the first woman to serve on the Wake County (N.C.) Board of Commissioners. She also holds the position of director of student life at Shaw University in Raleigh, N.C. As county commissioner, a post to which she was elected in November, 1972, her duties are largely budgetary, as the commission allocates funds for schools, levies taxes, issues bonds and provides water and sewer services. Born Jan. 21, 1920 in Raleigh, N.C., she received degrees from Hampton Institute (B.S.) and Columbia University (M.A.) and a diploma in administration and supervision. In 1969, she was elected to the Raleigh School Board for a four-year term. She and her husband, James, have twin sons, James Edward and Juan Medford. Address: Shaw University, Raleigh, NC 27602

Cofield, James E. Jr., management consultant, has parlayed his expertise in corporate finance, economics, corporate strategy and new venture analysis into a position as a consultant in the Management Counseling Division of Arthur D. Little, Inc. in Cambridge, Mass. Born May 16, 1945 in Norfolk, Va., he is a graduate of the University of North Carolina (B.S.) and the Stanford University Graduate School of Business (M.B.A.). He attended Howard University Law School. He considers his two most significant achievements to be determination to achieve in the face of adversities and successfully filing a $1 million class action suit against the prestigious Wall Street securities firm, Goldman, Sachs & Co. alleging employment discrimination. Stanford University, where Mr. Cofield was interviewed by the company's recruiter, has barred the firm's representatives from its campus. The New York Human Rights Division found "probable cause" to believe Mr. Cofield's charges, and the U.S. Equal Employment Opportunity Commission issued a right-to-sue letter. He and his wife, Joyce, live in Boston. Address: Arthur D. Little, Inc., Acorn Park, Cambridge, MA 02140

Joseph H. Cole

Charles A. Coleman

William T. Coleman Jr.

Cole, Joseph H., city official, is director of the District of Columbia Department of Recreation. He is responsible for the planning, administration and operation of the city's 160 recreation centers, 37 public swimming pools, 17 day camps, 1 resident camp and special programs for the handicapped, mentally retarded, mentally ill and senior citizens. Mr. Cole has been with the department since 1938 as a playground director, area director, director of city-wide programs and assistant superintendent. He was appointed to his present position in June, 1966. Born Feb. 13, 1913 in Philadelphia, Pa., he attended Howard University (B.S., health, physicial education and recreation, 1935), and completed one year of study toward a master's degree at Howard University and New York University. He also studied human relations at Catholic University and coaching at Holy Cross College. Mr. Cole is a member of the National Recreation & Park Association, Brookland Civic Association, the executive board of the Police Boy's Club, the C&O Canal Commission, Howard University Alumni Association, the NAACP and Omega Psi Phi fraternity. He and his wife, Laura, have two daughters, Mrs. Sylvia Ann Mackey and Mrs. Kathleen Teresa Mitchell. Address: 3149 16th St. N.W., DC 20010

Coleman, Charles A., administrator, is chief legal officer and executive assistant of the Commercial Department for Illinois Secretary of State Michael J. Howlett. Born Feb. 23, 1921 in Chicago, Ill., he is a graduate of Roosevelt University (B.S., accounting, 1949) and Chicago Kent College of Law (J.D., 1967). Before assuming his present position in 1973, he was in the private practice of law, supervisor of auditors for the Illinois Department of Revenue, and a cost accountant and supervisor of cost analysis for Rock Island Arsenal and Ford Motor Company. He is a member of the Chicago Bar Association, Cook County Bar Association, and the Archdiocese of Chicago School Board. He was a delegate to the Sixth Illinois Constitutional Convention (1969–70). He is former vice president of the West Chesterfield Community Association, director of Parish Credit Union, and an executive board member of the 21st Ward Regular Democratic Organization. He and his wife, Gwendolyn, have two children, Deborah and Pamela. Address: Centennial Bldg., Springfield, IL 62756

Coleman, William T. Jr., attorney, is senior partner in Dilworth, Paxson, Kalish, Levy & Coleman, a law firm in Philadelphia, Pa. During his legal career, he has been law secretary to Judge Herbert F. Goodrich of the U.S. Court of Appeals (Third Circuit), and U.S. Supreme Court Justice Felix Frankfurter. Born July 7, 1920 in Philadelphia, he graduated from the University of Pennsylvania (A.B., 1941) and Harvard University Law School (LL.B., 1946), and has studied at Harvard Business School. He is a member of the board of directors of Pan American World Airways, Penn Mutual Life Insurance Co., First Penn. Corp., First Penn. Banking and Trust Co., American Stock Exchange, Western Saving Fund Society and Brookings Institution. He is a trustee of the Rand Corporation. Mr. Coleman has held 23 United States and community appointive posts, including delegate to the United Nations General Assembly and senior consultant and assistant counsel to the President's Commission on the Assassination of President Kennedy. He is consultant to the U.S. Arms Control and Disarmament Agency and president of the NAACP Legal Defense and Educational Fund. He is a director and member of numerous professional and civic organizations. He and his wife, Lovida, have three children: William T. III, Lovida Jr. and Hardin L. Address: 2600 Fidelity Bldg., Philadelphia, PA 19109

Cardiss R. Collins

Cyrus J. Colter

Maurice L. Colvin

Collins, Cardiss Robertson, accountant, is the widow of George W. Collins, congressman from Illinois' 7th Congressional District (Chicago). Shortly after Congressman Collins' death in an airplane crash on Dec. 8, 1972, Mrs. Collins was endorsed for her husband's seat by the 24th Ward Regular Democratic organization and by the Cook County Central Democratic Committee. Born in 1932 in St. Louis, Mo., she is a graduate of Northwestern University (B.A. business, 1967). She worked successively as secretary, accountant and revenue auditor with the Illinois Department of Revenue; she resigned in January, 1973 after announcing her candidacy for the congressional seat. She is credited with assisting her late husband in a number of legislative duties, including the researching of housing and public health problems. She has one son, Kevin. Address: 3604 W. Roosevelt Rd., Chicago, IL 60624

Colter, Cyrus J., public official, is senior member of the Illinois Commerce Commission, a post he has held since 1950. He is also a novelist and short story writer whose collection of stories, *The Beach Umbrella,* won the 1970 University of Iowa School of Letters award. His published novels are *The Rivers of Eros* (1972) and *The Hippodrome* (1973). Born Jan. 8, 1910 in Noblesville, Ind., he attended Ohio State University (1928–30) Youngstown College (1930–1931), and Kent College of Law in Chicago (J.D., 1940). He has served under five governors on the Illinois Commerce Commission, beginning with the late Adlai E. Stevenson, who appointed him. He has also served with the Administrative Conference of the United States for the Study of Executive Agencies of the Federal Government; the Illinois Resources Planning Committee and the Railroads Committee of the National Association of Regulatory Utility Commissioners. From 1963 to 1969, he was chairman of the Illinois Emergency Transport Board. He is a member of many civic and community organizations, including the Friends of the Chicago Schools Committee, an advisory group established by the Chicago Board of Education. He is a member of Kappa Alpha Psi. He and his wife, Imogene live in Chicago. Address: State of Illinois Bldg., 160 N. LaSalle St., Chicago, IL 60602

Colvin, Maurice Lionel, human relations specialist, is administrative assistant to the city manager of Corpus Christi, Tex. and is administrator of the city's Human Relations Committee. He directs and coordinates programs designed to solve problems of racial and ethnic discrimination. He has the highest city job ever held by a black in the Gulf Coast city. Born Jan. 17, 1932 in Prairie View, Tex., he has degrees from Tuskegee Institute (B.S., social studies, 1954) and Texas A&I University (M.A., education, 1966). He has taken graduate courses at Texas Southern University. He worked his way through college on a five-year scholarship plan. He was one of the original members (and chairman) of the Human Relations Commission. Previously he was an administrator and supply technician for the U. S. Army Reserve in Sinton, Tex. He is a member of the National Association of Social Workers and several other professional and civic groups. He and his wife, Mary Ellen, have five children: Maureen, Karen, Gwendolyn, Maurice Jr. and Jacqueline. Address: P. O. Box 9277C, Corpus Christi, TX 78408

James P. Comer, M.D.

James W. Compton

James H. Cone

Comer, James P., M.D., educator, is associate professor of psychiatry at Yale University Medical School. His professional assignments have included seven years with the U.S. Public Health Service; appointment as a fellow in public health and preventive medicine at the Howard University College of Medicine, and clinical assignments to the District of Columbia Health Department and the National Institute of Mental Health in the career development program of the U.S. Public Health Service. Under the latter assignment, he was appointed to child study work at the Yale Medical Center, where he applies the principles of psychiatry and the behavioral sciences to the problem of inner-city school education and, in five years, has achieved significant improvements. Dr. Comer was born Sept. 25, 1934 in East Chicago, Ind. and has degrees from Indiana University (A.B., 1956), Howard University (M.D., 1960) and the University of Michigan School of Public Health (M.P.H., 1964). He received training in psychiatry at Yale's Department of Psychiatry and its Child Study Center. He completed his military service, in 1968 with the rank of surgeon (lieutenant colonel). He has written some 25 published articles and chapters of books and is the author of *Beyond Black and White.* Dr. Comer and his wife, Shirley Ann, have two children, Brian and Dawn. Address: Yale Child Study Center, 333 Cedar St., New Haven, CT 06510

Compton, James W., administrator, was appointed executive director of the Chicago Urban League in 1972. He joined the league in 1965 and has served as department executive director, program director, head of community services, director of the West Side office and as on-the-job training representative and employment counselor. In 1969, he left Chicago for 18 months to head the Urban League of Binghamton, N.Y. He taught for four years in the Chicago Board of Education Literacy Program and has lectured at universities on poverty and its effect on family life. Born April 7, 1939 in Aurora, Ill., he attended Morehouse College (A.B., political science, 1961) and won the Merrill Scholar Award (1959–61) for graduate study and travel. He has a diploma in French literature from the University of Grenoble (France) and took graduate courses in urban studies at Loyola University. He is on the board of directors of a number of professional and civic organizations, and is a member of numerous commissions. He won an award as one of the Ten Outstanding Young Men (1972) from the Chicago Junior Association of Commerce and Industry. Mr. Compton is divorced and the father of two children: James and Janice. Address: 4500 S. Michigan Ave., Chicago, IL 60653

Cone, James H., theologian, is professor of theology at Union Theological Seminary and is a lecturer in systematic theology at Woodstock College. Both schools are in New York, N.Y. His 1969 book *Black Theology and Black Power* introduced the phrase "Black Theology" and started a new theological movement in academic and church circles. He also authored *A Black Theology of Liberation* (1970) and *The Spirituals and the Blues: An Interpretation* (1972), and has contributed articles to numerous journals, magazines and anthologies. He is a contributing editor of the magazine, *Christianity and Crisis.* Born Aug. 5, 1938, in Fordyce, Ark., he has degrees from Philander Smith College (B.A., 1958), Garrett Theological Seminary, (B.D., 1961) and Northwestern University (M.A., 1963; Ph.D., 1965). He has taught and lectured at leading colleges and universities. He is a member of the board of directors of the National Committee of Black Churchmen; member, Black Methodists for Church Renewal, American Academy of Religion, Congress of African Peoples, and several other organizations. He and his wife, Rose, have two children, Michael and Charles. Address: 3401 Broadway, New York, NY 10004

Connor, George C. Jr., legislator and teacher, is one of the first nine black representatives elected to the Lousiana State House of Representatives since Reconstruction. Mr. Connor also teaches science at St. Augustine High School in New Orleans. Born May 28, 1921 in Baldwin, La., Mr. Connor earned his bachelor's degree in industrial arts at Xavier University in New Orleans which he attended with a track scholarship and where he was coached by the famous Ralph Metcalfe, now a U.S. representative from Illinois. Mr. Connor's college education was interrupted by military service which included duties in North Africa, Italy and the Philippines during World War II. Since 1951, he has been teaching at St. Augustine. He calls it fruitful work for 80 percent of the school's graduates go on into higher education. He was called into politics by a young man who came to his classroom and who was a member of the Community Organization for Urban Politics (C.O.U.P.). Mr. Connor and his wife, Marjorie, have three children: Jan, George and Terri. Address: 2600 London Ave., New Orleans, LA 70119

Conyers, John, congressman, is a U.S. representative from Michigan's first Congressional District. He was born May 16, 1929 in Detroit, Mich. He received his B.A. and LL.B. degrees from Wayne State University and spent his political apprenticeship as legislative assistant for three years to Congressman John Dingell. In addition to his duties as senior partner in the firm of Conyers, Bell and Townsend, he served as referee for the Michigan Workmen's Compensation Department, general counsel for the Trade Union Leadership Council, and a President John F. Kennedy appointee to the National Lawyers Committee for Civil Rights Under Law. Elected to Congress in 1964, he was reelected to his fifth consecutive term in 1972. Rep. Conyers is the first black to serve on the House Judiciary Committee, was co-sponsor of the Johnson Administration's Medicare program, and is an organizer of the Congressional Black Caucus. He is unmarried. Address: 222 Cannon House Office Bldg., Washington DC 20515

Cooper, Algernon J. Jr., city official, was elected mayor of Prichard, Ala., a suburb of Mobile, in 1972. Born May 30, 1944 in Mobile, he is a graduate of the University of Notre Dame (B.A., 1966) and New York University School of Law (J.D., 1969). He did postgraduate work at Spring Hill College, Roosevelt University and the University of Southern California. Before his election, he was a law clerk for Wilbur Trammel, judge of City Court in Buffalo, N.Y. (1964–65); a foreign affairs scholar at the U.S. State Department (1965–66); law clerk for Charles Conley in Montgomery, Ala. (1966–67); investigator for the Criminal Courts, City of New York (1967), and was on Senator Robert F. Kennedy's staff where he became responsible for minority group youths in the senator's presidential primary campaign in 1968. Mr. Cooper returned to Mobile in 1970 as an NAACP Legal Defense Fund attorney and was a partner in Crawford and Cooper, a law firm. His wife, Medora, is an economist. Address: P.O. Box 10515, Prichard, AL 36610 **See article on Algernon J. Cooper Jr. in Volume II.**

George C. Connor Jr.   Rep. John Conyers   Algernon J. Cooper Jr.

Peggy Cooper   Glenda L. Copes   Paul B. Cornely

Cooper, Peggy, consultant and attorney, is the developer of Workshops for Careers in the Arts, a federally funded program based in Washington, D.C. Previously, she was a consultant for Ashley, Meyer, Smith, an architecture firm in Washington. Born April 7, 1947 in Mobile, Ala., she is a graduate of George Washington University (B.A., 1968) and George Washington University National Law Center (J.D., 1971). She was the recipient of the Woodrow Wilson International Scholar Fellowship in 1971. She has received several distinguished awards and is a member of the Washington (D.C.) Bar Association, Federal City College board of trustees, and the Board of Higher Education, and is a trustee of the American Film Institute. Address: 1875 Mintwood Pl., NW, Washington, DC 20009

Copes, Glenda, L., executive, was appointed in 1971 as manager-urban affairs at Aetna Life & Casualty Co. in Hartford, Conn. She maintains close liaison with the community, provides technical assistance to senior management involved with urban affairs, proposes new programs, coordinates and motivates participation of Aetna employees in community activities and coordinates an educational partnership between Aetna and Hartford's Weaver High School. Previously Miss Copes was a community planner with The Greater Hartford Process, Inc. (a nonprofit planning and development organization), a supervisor of central records at Community Renewal Team, and director of administration at the Connecticut Housing Investment Fund. Born Oct. 18, 1943, in Hartford, she earned degrees at Smith College (A.B.) and Hartford College for Women (A.A.) and studied accounting at the University of Hartford. She is president of the Hartford Alumnae Chapter of Delta Theta Sigma Sorority, and is a member of the board of directors of Hartford Public Library. Address: 151 Famington Ave., Hartford, CT 06105

Cornely, Paul B., educator, is a professor at Howard University College of Medicine. He also does consultant work for voluntary and governmental agencies and research in the delivery of health care. Dr. Cornely was born March 9, 1906 in Guadeloupe, F.W.I. He has three degrees from the University of Michigan (A.B., 1928; M.D., 1931; Ph.D., 1934). He was awarded the Sedgewick Memorial Medal of the American Public Health Association in 1972. This is one of the highest honors in public health and the medal has been awarded annually since 1929 to outstanding public health leaders for the "advancement of public health knowledge and practice." Dr. Cornely is also assistant to the executive medical office of the United Mine Workers of America Welfare and Retirement Fund. He says that at the present time there are many opportunities for blacks in the medical profession. In the last 39 years, he has motivated thousands of medical students to improve health and health care for the disadvantaged. Dr. Cornely and his wife, Mae, have one child, Paul Jr. Address: Dept. of Community Health Practice, 520 W. Street, NW, Washington DC 20001

Bill Cosby

Bessie Coston

William Cousins Jr.

Cosby, Bill (William), entertainer, is star of the weekly television series, "The New Bill Cosby Show." He broke color barriers in television, becoming the first black in a "non-traditional" roll in 1965 when he co-starred in the series, "I Spy." He won the Emmy award in 1966 and 1967 as television's best male actor and he has since won two other Emmy awards. In 1969, he signed with NBC as executive producer and star of his own series, "The Bill Cosby Show" and he recently made several guest appearances on "The Electric Co." for the Children's TV Workshop. Mr. Cosby first achieved fame with humorous recordings of his childhood in Philadelphia, Pa., including *I Started Out As A Child*, *Why Is There Air*? and *Revenge*, for which he won a Grammy award in 1967. He now has a total of six Grammy awards. Born July 12, 1937 in Germantown, Pa., Mr. Cosby began his career doing comedy routines in the fifth grade. While in the 10th grade, he dropped out of school, but completed his high school education during a four-year hitch in the Navy. He then enrolled at Temple University on a track and football scholarship, quitting after his sophomore year to perform in Philadelphia coffee houses. He has since completed requirements for the bachelor's degree and has done graduate study at the University of Massachusetts. He is president of his own production company, Jemmin, Inc. He and his wife, Camille, have three children: Erika, Erinn and Ennis. Address: c/o Mariette Mandell, Warner Bros., 4000 Warner Blvd., Burbank, CA 91505

Coston, Bessie, administrator, is executive director of the YWCA in Youngstown, Ohio. She accepted the position in 1970 after serving as assistant executive director and program director. She supervises a staff of 31 (plus 56 part-time instructors) in carrying out a wide range of social service programs with an annual budget of $257,000. Born Nov. 29, 1916 in Jackson, Ga., she has degrees from Wilberforce University (B.A., social administration) and Ohio State University (M.A., social administration) and has done graduate study in counseling and guidance at Westminster College (Pa.). She has received a number of awards for community service; she is a member of the Youngstown Welfare Advisory Board. She attended the White House Conference on Children and Youth in 1970 and the White House Conference on Aging in 1971, and has worked with the League of Women Voters and the Mental Health Association. She is national president of Iota Phi Lambda sorority and is a member of the National Association of Social Workers, the NAACP and the Urban League. She and her husband, Floyd, have one child, Lynn Ruth. Address: 25 W. Rayen Ave., Youngstown, OH 44503

Cousins, William Jr., legislator-attorney, is an alderman (8th Ward) in Chicago, Ill. Elected in 1967, he serves on numerous City Council committees, including finance, judiciary, license and utilities. He has also maintained a private law practice in Chicago since 1953. Born Oct. 6, 1927 in Swiftown, Miss., he is a graduate of the University of Illinois (B.A., political science, 1948) and Harvard Law School (LL.B., 1951). He was an infantry platoon leader in the Korean conflict and is a major and staff judge advocate with the 425th Transportation Command in the U.S. Army Reserve. He is a member of the board of directors of several organizations, including the Cook County (Chicago) Bar Association, Operation PUSH, the Committee for Illinois Government, and Chicago Area Planned Parenthood. He is a member of the executive council of the United Church of Christ. He and his wife, Hiroko, have four children: Cheryl, Noel, Yul and Gail. Address: 29 S. LaSalle St., Chicago, IL 60603

Cowan, James Rankin, M.D., state official, is state commissioner of health in New Jersey. He is in charge of a department in excess of 1,000 persons and administers an annual budget exceeding $40 million. Dr. Cowan was the first black in the nation appointed to a governor's cabinet as commissioner of health, moving from senior attending physician at East Orange General Hospital. He is a member of the Essex County Medical Society, Medical Society of New Jersey and the New Jersey chapter of the Medical Committee on Human Rights. Born Oct. 21, 1916 in Washington, D.C., Dr. Cowan is a graduate of Howard University (B.S., 1937), Fisk University (M.A., 1940) and Meharry Medical College (M.D., 1944). He served in the U.S. Army from 1950 to 1953 and rose to become chief of surgery at the 26th Station Hospital in Regensburg, Germany. He was discharged as a captain. Dr. Cowan serves on numerous state governmental and advisory bodies. He and his wife, Juanita, a registered nurse, have three children: James R. Jr., Jay C. and a daughter, Jill W. Address: P.O. Box 1540, Trenton, NJ 08607

Cox, Wendell, D.D.S., dentist and broadcasting executive, has practiced dentistry in Inkster, Mich. since 1946, and is vice president of radio stations KWK in St. Louis, Mo. and WCHB and WCHD in Detroit, Mich. Born Nov. 7, 1914 in Charleston, S.C., he is a graduate of Talladega College (A.B.) and Meharry Medical College (D.D.S., 1944), and has taken graduate courses at Fisk University and Boston University. He is a member of both the American and the National Dental associations and the Detroit Mayor's Committee on Human Relations. He and his wife, Iris, have two children, Wendell Haley and Iris Marie. Address: 32790 Henry Ruff Rd., Inkster, MI 48141

Cream, Arnold ("Jersey Joe Walcott"), sheriff, was elected in 1971 as the chief law officer of Camden County, N. J. The former world heavyweight boxing champion (who fought under the name "Jersey Joe" Walcott) operates and supervises the county jail, provides personnel for court security, handles sheriff's sales and serves legal papers. Born in Camden, "Jersey Joe" turned professional boxer at 15 (his mother signed a statement that he was 18 so that he could get a license). He fought with fair success but without good purses until 1941, then "retired" to a shipyard job. In 1944, he met Felix Bocchiocchio who was to manage him to the crown. Many thought he should have been awarded the title on Dec. 5, 1947, when he knocked Joe Louis down twice but lost the controversial 15-round decision. In a return match, Louis knocked him out. Decisioned twice by Ezzard Charles for the title vacated by Mr. Louis, "Jersey Joe," in his third try in July, 1951, knocked out Charles with a left hook in the 7th round to become, at 37, the oldest man to win the world heavyweight championship. The next year, he defended his title against Charles by winning a decision. In Sept., 1952, he lost his crown to Rocky Marciano in a 13-round knockout. A deeply religious family man, Sheriff Cream feels that his present position gives him a "chance to help people." He and his wife, Riletta, live in Pennsanken, N. J. He is the father of six children. Address: Court House, Camden, NJ 08101

James R. Cowan, M.D.

Wendell Cox, D.D.S.

Arnold Cream

Judge George W. Crockett Jr.

Wardell C. Croft

Fred M. Crosby

Crockett, George W. Jr., jurist, is judge of Recorder's Court in Detroit, Mich. He was first elected in 1966 and was reelected in 1972. Born in Jacksonville, Fla. he attended Morehouse College (A.B., 1931; honorary LL.D., 1972) and the University of Michigan Law School (J.D., 1934). An outstanding jurist and leader in the black struggle in the United States, Judge Crockett has served as senior attorney for the U.S. Department of Labor, general counsel for the United Auto Workers–CIO and had a private practice before being elected to his present post in 1966. Fighting racism long before it was fashionable and safe to do so, he represented a case which won black auto workers entry into their Atlanta union and has set precedents in several cases involving black rights for his fellow members on the bench and even the U.S. Supreme Court. Judge Crockett has written articles for several law journals. His wife, Ethelene J. Crockett, is a physician. They have three children: Mrs. Elizabeth A. Hicks, George III, an attorney, and Ethelene II, a physician-surgeon. Address: Frank Murphy Hall of Justice, 1441 St. Antoine St., Detroit MI 48226

Croft, Wardell C., administrator, is president and board Chairman of Wright Mutual Insurance Co., in Detroit, Mich. One of 10 children, Mr. Croft was born July 3, 1918, in Gadsden, Ala. Grossly inadequate facilities provided a sketchy early education, but Mr. Croft learned business as a boy, overseeing family and hired cotton choppers, keeping time and payroll records. He learned the hard, cold side of selling, peddling blackberries and vegetables from door to door. Later, going north to Chattanooga to get summer work, he recruited himself into business as a special writer, was soon promoted to debit worker with a $100 monthly commission. Circumstances brought him in 1950 to Wright Mutual Insurance Company, Detroit, where he found a company about to go under. After two years, he was given the management responsibility and has placed the firm in a strong financial position. He was made president and chairman of the board in 1962. He attended Stillman College, Alexander Institute and the University of Michigan Extension Division. Mr. Croft and his wife, Theora, have one son, Robert. Address: 2995 E. Grand Blvd., Detroit, MI 48202

Crosby, Fred M., businessman, is president and owner of Crosby Furniture Co., Inc. in Cleveland, Ohio. The firm was founded in 1963. By 1972, it was grossing more than $500,000 a year. The firm began in 1963 as a used furniture store. It became so successful that it expanded to eight small stores, then to its present facility—a building occupying one-third of a city block. Now offering only furniture of above-average quality, it is one of Ohio's most successful black-owned businesses. Mr. Crosby was born May 17, 1928 in Cleveland. In 1972, he became the first black elected to the board of directors of the Ohio Council of Retail Merchants Association in its 50-year existence. He is also a member of the board of directors of the Greater Cleveland Growth Association and is a director/trustee of eight other business or civic organizations. In 1971, the governor of Ohio appointed him to the Ohio Fair Plan Advisory Board, and in 1972, the U.S. Department of Commerce presented him with an Award of Excellence in business; he received a personal letter of congratulation from President Nixon. Mr. Crosby and his wife, Phendalyne, have three children: Fred Jr., James and Llionicia. Address: 12435 St. Clair Ave., Cleveland, OH 44108

Judge James D. Crosson

Harold W. Cruse

Vincent T. Cullers

Crosson, James D., jurist, is a judge of the Circuit Court of Cook County (Ill.) Born March 8, 1909 in Newberry, S.C., he attended the Jewish People's Institute, the Lewis Institute of Chicago, and the John Marshall Law School (LL.B., LL.M.). He also has certificates in traffic conferences courses from Fordham University Law School and Northwestern University Law School. Before becoming a judge in 1962, he was administrative assistant to the chief justice of the Chicago Municipal Court (1954–61) and an attorney in the law firm of Gassaway, Crosson, Turner and Parsons (1946–54). During World War II, he was chief defense counsel of the General Courts-Martial of the Delta Base Sector and was legal officer with the provost marshal for the Port of Marseilles, France. He is a member of the board of directors of the Cook County Bar Association and a member of the American and Federal Bar associations. He is also a member of the American Judicature Society, a member of the Board of Appeals of the Selective Service System of Northern Illinois and a member of the board of trustees of the John Marshall Law School and a law member of Panel III of the Board of Appeals for the Selective Service System of Northern Illinois. He is a Mason. He and his wife, Jane, have a son, David. Address: Chicago Civic Plaza, Rm. 2401, Chicago, IL 60605

Cruse, Harold W., educator, is a professor of history and director of University Center for Afro-American and African Studies at the University of Michigan in Ann Arbor. A self-taught writer, historian, journalist, administrator, social critic and lecturer, Mr. Cruse oversees a staff of 20 plus a large number of students as director of the center of Afro-American and African studies. His work centers around developing approaches to inclusion of the black experience in the university academic framework. His authorship of *Crisis of the Negro Intellectual* established him in the literary and academic world. He has lectured at the universities of London, Sussex and Kent, England and Wales and the universities of Belgrade and Zagreb in Yugoslavia. He is listed in *Who's Who In America*. A veteran of World War II, Professor Cruse was born in Petersburg, Va. Address: Haven Hall, University of Michigan, Ann Arbor, MI 84104

Cullers, Vincent T., advertising executive, formed Vince Cullers Advertising Inc. in 1956 in Chicago, Ill. It was the first black advertising agency in America. A native of Chicago, Mr. Cullers attended the Art Institute of Chicago and the American Academy of Art (also in Chicago) and took business courses at the University of Chicago. He was promotional art director of *Ebony* magazine and was a freelance artist before opening his own agency. Johnson Products Co., Inc., a cosmetics manufacturer, (Ultra Sheen) is one of the firm's accounts. Another is People United to Save Humanity (Operation PUSH). Other major clients include P. Lorillard Co., Bristol-Myers Co., Ill. Bell Telephone Co. and Sears, Roebuck & Co. Mr. Cullers and his wife, Marian, have two children, Vincent Jr. and Jeffery. He enjoys football, baseball and golf. Address: 520 N. Michigan Ave., Chicago, IL 60605

D

Philip B. Curls

David Daniel

Walter C. Daniel

Curls, Philip B., legislator, is a Missouri state representative in Jefferson City, Mo.
Born April 2, 1942 in Kansas City, Mo., he is a graduate of Rockhurst College (B.S.,
B.A., accounting, 1965). He has also studied at Ohio State University, the University of
Kansas and Chicago University. Before his election in 1972, he was chief finance
administrator for Operation Upgrade of the Model Cities program (1970–71), and first
assistant to the clerk of the Jackson County Circuit Court (1967-70). He is
secretary-treasurer of Curls, Curls and Associates, a brokerage and appraising firm in
Kansas City, and is Third Ward coordinator of Freedom, Inc. As a state representative,
he is a member of the House Welfare and Medicaid Committee, the Urban Affairs
Committee, the State Institutions and Property Committee, and the Bank and Financial
Institutions Committee. He is a member of the Appraiser's Institute. He and his wife,
Melba, have two sons, Phillip II and Michael. Address: Missouri State Legislature,
Jefferson City, MO

Daniel, David, administrator, is director of the Cook County (Ill.) Department of Public
Aid. Born Jan. 2, 1906 in Columbia, Tenn., he is a graduate of Fisk University (B.A.
chemistry, 1928) and the University of Chicago (M.A. social service administration,
1954), and took additional courses in social service administration at the University of
Chicago (1955–56). He has been associated with the Department of Public Aid since
1938. He is a member of Alpha Phi Alpha, the National Association of Social Workers,
the Academy of Certified Social Workers, the American Public Welfare Association, the
Illinois Welfare Association, the National Conference on Social Welfare and the
National Association of City Welfare Directors. He and his wife, Mary, live in Chicago.
Address: 318 W. Adams St., Chicago, IL 60606

Daniel, Walter C., university official, is vice chancellor of the 23,000-student campus of
the University of Missouri at Columbia. Born in Macon, Ga. May 12, 1922, he attended
Johnson C. Smith University (B.A.), South Dakota State University (M.A.), Bowling
Green State University (Ph.D.) and holds an honorary degree from Lincoln University
of Missouri (L.H.D.). The educator and administrator was formerly president of Lincoln
Carolina Central University, St. Augustine's College and Bowling Green State
University. Dr. Daniels is a member of the Governor's Advisory Committee on
Comprehensive Health Planning and several other community service organizations.
He has published numerous articles in educational and literary journals throughout
the country. He is married to the former Launa Harris. Address: Office of the
Vice Chancellor, University of Missouri-Columbia, Columbia MO 65201

Barry R. Daniels   H. B. Daniels   Jesse Daniels

Daniels, Barry R., manufacturer, is president of Ric Daniels, Inc., manufacturer of men's shirts sold under the Foxey World label. The firm is located in New York, N.Y. Mr. Daniels and his wife, Gail, began the firm in 1970 and now have salesmen covering major cities throughout the U. S. and in the Caribbean. By 1972 they had developed what was considered as "one of the hottest" shirt lines in the world. Mr. Daniels was born May 14, 1950 in Washington, D. C. Both he and his wife attended New York's Fashion Institute of Technology, majoring in management techniques, apparel design, art and design. Address: Foxey World, 147 W. 40 St., New York, NY 10018

Daniels, Hayzel Burton, jurist, is the only black judge in Arizona (1973). Appointed in 1965, he is one of ten city magistrates in Phoenix. Previously, he was a state representative (1950–52) and assistant attorney general (1954–60). Born Feb. 7, 1907 in Fort Clark, Tex., he is a graduate of the University of Arizona (A.B., political science and history, 1939; M.A., education, 1941; J.D., 1948). He taught school at Fort Huachucha, Ariz. prior to enlisting in the U.S. Air Force, where he saw duty in the China-Burma-India Theatre in Special Services (1943–45). He received the Outstanding Alumnus award of the University of Arizona in 1968. He is a member of the American Bar Association, the Arizona Bar, the American Trial Lawyers Association, the North American Judges Association, the Arizona Magistrates Association, the NAACP and Omega Psi Phi fraternity. He and his wife, Grace, have two sons, Kirk and Kenneth. Address: Phoenix City Courts, 14 N. 4th Ave., Phoenix, AZ 85003

Daniels, Jesse, corporate executive, is president and owner of Jesern Enterprises Inc., in Piscataway, N.J. The firm, located in a 25,000 square foot building, specializes in the custom compounding of plastic materials. Born June 21, 1917 in Fallon, Okla., he was discharged from the U.S. Army in 1946 and began his career in the chemical industry with Manufacturers Chemical Corp. of Berkeley Heights, N.J. During the next 25 years, he also worked for Koppers Co. of Port Reading, N.J. and for Howard Polymers in Berkeley Heights. In 1969, he was named manager of the Howard plant in Hicksville, N.Y., and two years later was promoted to manager of the firm's Berkeley Heights plant. With the backing of the Interracial Council for Business Opportunity of New Jersey, Mr. Daniels and his general manager, Ernest Hazell, began the Jesern operation in 1972. He and his wife, Mildred, have four children: Deborah, Jesse Jr., Cynthia and Michael. Address: 1766 South 2nd St., Piscataway, NJ 08854

Daniels, Willie L., broker, is president and a director of Daniels & Bell, Inc. in New York, N.Y. On June 24, 1971, the firm became the first black-controlled member firm in the 179-year history of the New York Stock Exchange. By 1973 it owned two seats on the Exchange and was doing business throughout the U.S. and in Europe and Africa. The firm specializes in institutional sales and research. Born Sept 8, 1937 in Valdosta, Ga., Mr. Daniels is a graduate of Florida A & M University (B.A., 1960) and has taken advanced securities industry courses at the New York Institute of Finance. He began his career in securities in 1960 as a trainee in the research department of Francis I. duPont & Co. (now duPont, Glore Forgan & Co.). He became a securities analyst in less than three years, then joined Standard & Poor's as a senior financial statistician in 1966. He later worked at such firms as Bache & Co., and Shearson, Hammill and Smith Barney & Co. After competing an in-depth research and feasibility study of black ownership of business, he and his associates opened their own firm. He is an allied member of the New York Stock Exchange, a member of the Lawyers Club and a director of the Young Adult Institute & Workshop. He is single. Address: 64 Wall Street, New York, NY 10005

Dargan, Charles A., fund-raiser, is Imperial Potentate of the Ancient Egyptian Arabic Order, Nobles of the Mystic Shrine and is coordinator of the fraternal division for Opportunities Industrialization Centers of America, an organization that provides job training for thousands of persons—mainly low-income blacks. Mr. Dargan's work at OIC involves solicitation of funds to help the organization carry on its programs. As Imperial Potentate, he has helped develop programs that provide annual donations to the NAACP Legal Defense Fund and to Howard University for sickle cell anemia research. He also works with Chapin Day Care Center, a national organization that aids unwed mothers and orphans. Born in Daytona Beach, Fla., he attended Edward Waters College in Jacksonville, Fla. He is a widower. Address: 3224 16th St., NW, Washington, DC 20010

Darnell, Emma Ione, city official, is intergovernmental programs coordinator and chairman of the Grant Review Board for the city of Atlanta, Ga. She is a top ranking city official, advising the mayor and members of the Board of Aldermen on intergovernmental matters affecting Atlanta's citizens. Born March 1, 1937 in Atlanta, she is a graduate of Fisk University (B.A.), Columbia University (M.A.) and the Howard University School of Law (J.D.). Prior to being appointed to her present position, Miss Darnell was an assistant professor of psychology and education on the faculties of Morris Brown College and Atlanta University. She also served as a legal investigator for the U.S. Equal Employment Opportunities Commission. She is a member of the Atlanta chapters of the NAACP and the YWCA. Address: Office of the Mayor, 68 Mitchell St., Atlanta, GA 30303

Willie L. Daniels

Charles A. Dargan

Emma Ione Darnell

Ronald R. Davenport

Lt. Gen. B. O. Davis Jr. (Ret.)

Charles A. Davis

Davenport, Ronald R., educator and administrator, is dean of the Duquesne University Law School in Pittsburgh, Pa. Born May 21, 1936 in Philadelphia, Pa., he has degrees from Pennsylvania State University (B.S., economics, 1958), the Temple University Law School (LL.B., 1962) and Yale University (LL.M., 1963) Mr. Davenport is the only black dean in the country of a predominantly white law school. Having taught at Duquesne for seven years before his appointment (he continues to teach a course in constitutional law), Mr. Davenport also became the first non-Catholic and the first person under 40 years old to preside over the law school, which is considered one of the 20 best in the United States. He started his legal career as a clerk in a black Philadelphia law firm and later prepared the brief in the first "freedom riders" case (*Ralph Abernathy* vs. *Alabama*) as a staff attorney for the NAACP Legal Defense and Educational Fund. He is president of the Urban League of Pittsburgh and serves on the boards of the Allegheny Housing Rehabilitation Corp. and Allegheny General Hospital. Mr. Davenport and his wife, Judith Marylyn, have three children: Ronald Jr., Judith Allison and Susan Ross. Address: Duquesne University Law School, 600 Forbes Ave., Pittsburgh, PA 15206

Davis, Lt. Gen. Benjamin O., Jr., retired military officer, is assistant secretary of the U.S. Department of Transportation. He is director of civil aviation security. This presidential appointment in July, 1971 followed General Davis' retirement from the Air Force in 1970 and his service as director of public safety for the City of Cleveland. General Davis was born December 18, 1912 in Washington, D. C. He graduated from the United States Military Academy (B.S., 1936) with a commission as a second lieutenant in the U. S. Army Infantry. In 1942, after receiving his pilot's wings, he transferred to the Army Air Corps. During World War II he served as a commander of the 99th Fighter Squadron and the 332nd Fighter Group stationed in Europe and Africa (1943–45). Following World War II, he held a variety of commands, including chief of staff, United States Forces, Korea, and chief of staff, United Nations Command, 1965–67, commander of the Thirteenth Air Force at Clark Air Force Base in the Philippines and deputy commander-in-chief of the U. S. Strike Command at MacDill Air Force Base in Tampa, Fla. He was promoted to lieutenant general in 1965. He was a member of the President's Commission on Campus Unrest, has received honorary degrees from Morgan State College (Dr. Sci.), Wilberforce University (Dr. Mil. Sci.), and Tuskegee Institute (LL.D.). He and his wife, Agatha, live in Washington, D. C. Address: U.S. Department of Transportation, Washington, D. C. 20590

Davis, Charles A., administrator, is executive director of the National Insurance Association and president of Charles A. Davis and Associates, Inc., a public relations and marketing firm. Born Sept. 29, 1922 in Mobile, Ala., he studied at Roosevelt University in Chicago and West Virginia State College. He is the author of numerous articles and served as city editor and director of public relations at the *Chicago Daily Defender* before forming his own company. Mr. Davis is president of the American Association of Minority Consultants and is a member of the board of directors of many organizations including the National Conference of Christians and Jews, Chicago Theological Seminary, Comprehensive Health and Hospitals Governing Commission of Cook County, the board of governors of Illinois State Colleges and Universities and the Chicago Community Renewal Society. Mr. Davis and his wife, Rosalie, have two children, Charles Jr., and Daphne Kaye. Address: Charles A. Davis and Associates Inc., 2400 S. Michigan Ave., Chicago, IL 60616

Corneal A. Davis

Edward D. Davis

Georgia M. Davis

Davis, Corneal A., legislator, is a state representative and assistant minority leader in the Illinois General Assembly (22nd District in Chicago). He is the chief liaison for the Democratic party between the governor, key leadership and party members. First elected to the Illinois General Assembly in 1942, Mr. Davis is the senior black state legislator in the United States. He also was the first black elected assistant minority leader in a state assembly in 1970. Born Aug. 28, 1900 in Vicksburg, Miss., Mr. Davis has a degree from Tougaloo College (B.A.) and attended the John Marshall School of Law and the Moody Bible Institute. He was responsible for the introduction and passage of legislation in the assembly requiring the teaching of black history in Illinois public schools, requiring equal pay for black educators and calling for equal opportunity and fair housing practices. He was the first black to chair a legislative committee when he was named to head the Public Aid, Health and Safety Committee. As of 1973, Mr. Davis, who also is assistant pastor of the Quinn Chapel A.M.E. Church, was president of the Second Ward Regular Democratic Organization, and a board member of the McKinley House. He and his wife, Elma, have a daughter, Yvonne. Address: 3437 S. Indiana Ave., Chicago, IL 60616

Davis, Edward D., businessman, is chairman of the board and president of the Central Life Insurance Co. of Florida in Tampa. He was born Feb. 1, 1904 in Thomasville, Ga., and attended Paine College (B.A., 1928) and Northwestern University (M.A., 1934). Before starting his own mercantile and real estate business and subsequently working his way to the presidency of Central Life in 1965, Mr. Davis was on the faculties of Bethune-Cookman College and Florida A&M University. A high school principal for 15 years, he served as the president of the Florida State Teachers Association and was instrumental in that organization's successful legal suit demanding equal pay for black teachers in Florida. He later directed a nine-year effort to integrate the University of Florida. As president of the Florida Voters League, he spearheaded the increase of registered black voters in that state from 40,000 to more than 300,000 in 1964. A respected businessman, he is chairman of the budget committee of the United Fund of Greater Tampa and serves on trustee boards of Miles College and Paine College. Mr. Davis and his wife, LaRone, have six children: Edward Jr., Marie, Thelma, Charles, Samuel and Cynthia. Address: 1400 N. Boulevard, Tampa, FL 33607

Davis, Georgia M., legislator, was the first black and the first woman elected to the Kentucky State Senate. A Democrat, she was elected to her first term in 1967 and was reelected in 1971. Born Oct. 29, 1923 in Springfield, Ky., she attended Louisville Municipal College and has certificates from the Central Business School and the U.S. Government IBM Supervisory School. She owns and operates a restaurant, a laundry and a dry cleaning establishment in Louisville. A long-time civil rights activist, she was one of the organizers (1964) of Allied Organizations for Civil Rights, which urged passage of statewide public accommodations and fair employment laws (which passed in the Kentucky General Assembly in 1966). She was an organizer (1965) of the Kentucky Christian Leadership Conference (an affiliate of SCLC), and participated in numerous voter registration and civil rights campaigns during the 1960s. She is chairwoman of the Senate Committee on Health and Welfare and is vice chairwoman of the Committee on Labor and Industry. She is chairwoman of the Subcommittee on Wages and Hours and is a member of the Subcommittee on Narcotics. Divorced, she has a son, William. Address: 1036 S. 28th St., Louisville, KY 40211

Davis, Joseph M., administrator, is executive director of the National Office of Black Catholics in Washington, D.C. In this capacity, Mr. Davis is responsible for representing concern of blacks to officials of the Catholic church in an effort to bring about a redirection of the church's commitment of resources. He was born Aug. 17, 1927 in Macon, Ga., and has earned degrees from the University of Dayton (B.S., education, 1959), and the Catholic University of America (M.A., speech and drama, 1961). Mr. Davis belongs to the society of Mary (Marianists), a religious order, and has served as principal of St. Patricks College in Asaba, Nigeria, assistant prinicpal and dean of Studies Chaminade High School in Dayton, Ohio, and principal of St. James Elementary School also in Dayton, Ohio. Address: 734 15th St., NW, Washington, DC 20017

Davis, Lawrence A., educator, is chancellor of the University of Arkansas at Pine Bluff. Born July 4, 1914 in McCrory, Ark., he has degrees from the University of Arkansas (A.B., 1937; Ed.D., 1960) and the University of Kansas (M.A., 1941). He holds honorary degrees from Lane College (LL.D.), Morehouse College (LL.D.), Arkansas Baptist College (L.H.D.) and Hendrix College (LL.D.). Dr. Davis began his career at the University of Arkansas in 1937 as an English instructor. He was appointed dean of the college in 1942 and was elected to his current position in 1943. An active community leader, he is chairman of the association of State College Presidents, and holds memberships in many organizations, including the Advisory Commission of the National Junior Chamber of Commerce, National Planning Association, National Conference of Christians and Jews and numerous state commissions. He has written several articles and travels extensively. Dr. Davis and his wife, Rachel, have six children: Lawrence Jr., Larnell, Ronald, Michael, Gail and Janice. A daughter, Sharon, is deceased. Address: University of Arkansas at Pine Bluff, Pine Bluff, AR 71601

Davis, Nathan T., musician, composer and educator, is an assistant professor of music at the University of Pittsburgh, jazz saxophonist, and vice president of the Seque Recording Co. in Pittsburgh, Pa. Born Feb. 15, 1937 in Kansas City, Kan., he has a B.A. degree in music education from the University of Kansas. He has studied at the Kansas City Conservatory of Music and done graduate study at the Sorbonne in Paris. He was a Ph.D. degree candidate in ethnomusicology at Wesleyan University in Connecticut. In 1965, Mr. Davis, who lived and worked in Europe from 1960 to 1969, toured Europe and Africa for the U.S. State Department as soloist and arranger for a variety show from the University of Kansas. In 1962, he worked as a soloist for Radio Free Berlin and later joined the Kenny Clark Quintet. In 1964, he formed a group with trumpeter Woody Shaw, Billy Brooks and Larry Young and recorded three albums, *Happy Girl, Hip Walk* and *Peace Treaty.* Mr. Davis also was an instructor of jazz studies at the Paris American Academy of Music. Mr. Davis joined the faculty of the University of Pittsburgh in 1969. He and his wife, Ursula, have two children, Joyce Nathalie and Pierre Marc. Address: University of Pittsburgh, Jazz Studies Dept. Pittsburgh, PA 15232

Joseph M. Davis   Lawrence A. Davis   Nathan T. Davis.

Ossie Davis

Sammy Davis Jr.

Maurice A. Dawkins

Davis, Ossie, actor, is also a playwright and motion picture director perhaps best known for his role in *Purlie Victorious.* Born Dec. 18, 1920 in Cogdell, Ga., he attended Howard University in Washington, D.C., where Alain Locke, the black philosopher, suggested that he pursue a career in the theater. Over the last 30 years, Mr. Davis has appeared in 13 plays, including *Anna Lucasta* (1947), *Green Pastures* (1951), *A Raisin in the Sun* (1959) and *Purlie Victorious* (of which he was the author, 1962), eight motion pictures, and in numerous television plays. He also has written material for all these media and has been published in *Freedomways* magazine and in two anthologies, *Harlem U.S.A.* and *Soon One Morning: New Writing by American Negroes.* He directed the recent motion picture, *Black Girl.* He and his wife, actress Ruby Dee, have three children: Nora, Guy and LaVerne. Address: P.O. Box 1318, New Rochelle, NY 10802

Davis, Sammy Jr., entertainer, has been—as singer, dancer and actor—one of the most versatile and popular performers of stage, screen and television since the late 1940s. He was born Dec. 11, 1926 in New York, N.Y. At two, he became a regular trouper with his father and uncle in the family act, the Will Mastin Trio. When Sammy Jr. rejoined the trio following his World War II army service, the act scored a surprise hit at Slapsie Maxie's in Los Angeles, followed by one record-breaking date after another across the country. In 1948, Will Mastin and Sammy Davis Sr. retired from show business, and Sammy Jr. stepped onstage as a single. In November, 1954, he barely escaped death in an auto collision which cost him his left eye. He had a triumphal comeback a year later at Ciro's in Hollywood. A series of film roles followed, starting in 1959 with *Anna Lucasta* in which he co-starred with Eartha Kitt. Then came the coveted role of Sportin' Life in *Porgy and Bess* (1959); *Oceans 11* (1960) in which he co-starred with Frank Sinatra, Dean Martin and Peter Lawford; and the lead in *A Man Called Adam* (1966). He starred on Broadway in the long-running *Golden Boy* in 1964. He became a major television star in "Sammy Davis and His Friends," appearances on "Hullabaloo" and guest stints on a number of major variety shows. He has received many major honors as a performer and humanitarian. He and his wife, Altovise, live in Beverly Hills. Mr. Davis has three children: Tracey, Mark, and Jeff, by a previous marriage. Address: 9000 Sunset Blvd., Los Angeles, CA 90069. **See article on Sammy Davis Jr. in Volume II**

Dawkins, Maurice Anderson, administrator, is executive vice chairman of Opportunities Industrialization Centers of America Inc. Born Jan. 29, 1921, in Chicago, Ill., he is a graduate of Columbia University (B.A.), Columbia Teacher's College (M.A.) and Union Theological Seminary. He was minister of education and associate minister (1948–54) of the Community Church of New York and was pastor (1954–64) of the Peoples' Independent Church of Los Angeles, the oldest community church in the U.S. In 1964, he joined the Office of Economic Opportunity as an associate director of Vista. In that post he was responsible for establishing projects and assigning Vista volunteers to act in local anti-poverty programs throughout the country. He has served as president of the Los Angeles NAACP, was West Coast coordinator of the historic March on Washington and is a member of the California Commission on Urban Policy. He and his wife, Doris, have two children: Maurice K. and Susan. Address: OIC, 18 W. Chelton St., Philadelphia, PA 19144

James E. Dean

Walter R. Dean Jr.

Judge Russell R. DeBow

Dean, James E., legislator, is a member of the Georgia House of Representatives (76th District in Atlanta). Born in 1945 in Georgia, he has received degrees from Clark College in Atlanta (B.A., sociology, 1966) and Atlanta University (M.S.W., 1968). Mr. Dean also serves as director of alumni affairs at Clark College and project director for the Atlanta Urban League's New Thrust Program. He is a board member of the Metropolitan Atlanta Mental Health Association and is vice chairman of the Georgia House of Representatives Committee on Highways. He also serves on the welfare and labor committees in the House. Mr. Dean and his wife, Vyvyan, have two children, Sonya Velika and Monica Alexis. Address: 17 E. Lake Dr., NE, Atlanta, GA 30317

Dean, Walter Raleigh Jr., legislator and educator, is a Democratic member of the Maryland House of Delegates (Fifth District, Baltimore) and is an assistant professor of urban affairs at the Community College of Baltimore. Born Dec. 12, 1934 in Baltimore, Md., he is a graduate of Morgan State College (B.A., English, 1962) and the University of Maryland (M.S.W., 1968). Before his election in 1970, he was a reporter for the *Afro-American* newspaper (1962–64), a street club worker (1964–66) and a social welfare planner (1968–69) in Baltimore. He is a member of the National Association of Black Social Workers, the Junior Association of Commerce, the Black United Front and the Morgan State College Alumni Association. He has been active in political and civic groups in Baltimore, and is a member of the reform-minded New Democratic Coalition. He is single. Address: 2901 Liberty Heights Ave., Baltimore, MD 21207

DeBow, Russell R., jurist, has been a judge of the Circuit Court of Cook County (Ill.) since 1971. Born Aug. 5, 1913 in Lovejoy, Ill., he is a graduate of Illinois State Normal University (B.S., education, 1935) and DePaul University (J.D., 1954) and also attended Georgetown University. Prior to assuming his present position, he was administrative assistant to Chicago's Mayor Richard J. Daley (1965–71). He also was deputy commissioner of the city's department of investigation, a field representative for the *Chicago Defender* newspaper, director of recreation for the Works Progress Administration, assistant state director and assistant regional director of the National Youth Administration, assistant to the director of the federal office of Price Stabilization and assistant to the late U.S. Congressman Barrett O'Hara of Chicago. He and his wife, Dolores, have a daughter, Ruth. Address: Civic Center, Chicago, IL 60601

Ruby Dee

C. C. Dejoie Jr.

Robert A. DeLeon

Dee, Ruby, actress, has appeared in numerous legitimate and television plays and over a dozen motion pictures, including the Broadway productions of *Anna Lucasta* (1946), *A Raisin in the Sun* (1959) and *Boesman and Lena* (1971). Born Oct. 27, 1924 in Cleveland, Ohio, she attended Hunter College in New York, N.Y. Aside from her numerous legitimate stage credits, she has appeared in many motion pictures, including *The Jackie Robinson Story* (1950), *St. Louis Blues* (1957), *A Raisin in the Sun* (1960) and *Buck and the Preacher* (1971). Miss Dee collaborated with Jules Dassin and Julian Mayfield in the screenplay for *Uptight* and has edited an anthology of poems for the young, *Glow Child and Other Poems.* She has recorded and conducted recital tours of black poetry readings. She and her husband, actor Ossie Davis, have three children: Nora, Guy and Laverne. Address: P. O. Box 1318, New Rochelle, NY 10802

Dejoie, C. C. Jr., publishing executive, is president and publisher of the *Louisiana Weekly*, the only black newspaper in New Orleans and one of two black publications in the state of Louisiana. Born Oct. 25, 1914 in New Orleans, Mr. Dejoie earned degree's at Talladega College (B.A., 1937) and the University of Michigan (M.A., 1938). Prior to assuming his present position in 1969, he was editor and business manager at the newspaper where he has worked since 1938. In June of 1954, Mr. Dejoie was elected president of the National Newspaper Publishers Association. He was reelected for a second term in 1955 and served as treasurer of the organization for a number of years. Mr. Dejoie is a board member of the Amalgamated Publishers, Inc. and the Liberty Bank and Trust Co. He also is one of the corporate owners of the New Orleans Saints football team. Mr. Dejoie and his wife, Julia, have one son, Michael Charles. Address: Louisiana Weekly Publishing Co. 640 S. Rampart St., New Orleans, LA 70122

DeLeon, Robert Andrew, journalist, is managing editor of *Jet*, the weekly news magazine published by Johnson Publishing Co. in Chicago, Ill. Born October 14, 1950 in Oakland, Calif., he attended Morehouse College and Columbia University. He began his journalism career as a student at Morehouse when, at the age of 15, he was named editor of the school's yearbook. He worked for *Newsday*, the Long Island, N.Y. newspaper, and the *Atlanta Constitution* before joining *Ebony* magazine as an assistant editor in 1971. Six months later, at the age of 20, he was named managing editor of *Jet*, becoming the youngest managing editor of a major magazine in the U.S. He has served as president of the National Pre-Alumni Council of the United Negro College Fund, and is a member of the executive committee of the United Board for College Development in Atlanta, Ga. He and his wife, Barbara, have a daughter, Monica. Address: 820 South Michigan Ave., Chicago, IL 60605

Rep. Ronald V. Dellums

Judge James Del Rio

James DePreist

Dellums, Ronald V., congressman, is the U.S. representative from California (Seventh District). He was born Nov. 24, 1935 in Oakland, Calif. He received degrees from Oakland City College (associate of arts, 1958), San Francisco State College (B.A., 1960) and the University of California at Berkeley (M.A., social work, 1962). He has served in various local and state social agencies, and lectured part-time at San Francisco State and the University of California School of Social Work. "Instead of obtaining a Ph.D. at Brandeis in social policy," as he had planned, Rep. Dellums was persuaded to enter politics and was elected to the Berkeley City Council in 1967. His coalition of minority groups and students as well as Americans for Democratic Action, the AFL-CIO Committee on Political Education and a number of prominent liberal Democrats backed his successful 1970 campaign for U.S. congressman. In the House, he sits on the prestigious Foreign Affairs Committee and the District of Columbia Committee, and, by 1972, had co-sponsored nearly 200 pieces of legislation. Racism in the military, increased minimum wage levels, national health care, and child-care centers are among his priorities for congressional action. He and his wife, Leola, have three children: Piper, Eric and Brandy. He has two children, Michael and Pamela, by a previous marriage. Address: 1414 Longworth House Office Bldg., Washington DC 20515

Del Rio, James, jurist, is a Recorder's Court judge in Detroit and former member of the Michigan state legislature. Born in Detroit Jan. 30, 1924, he attended the Detroit Institute of Technology (B.A.) and received a degree from the Detroit College of Law (J.D., 1971). He holds an honorary degree from Union Baptist Seminary (D.L.). In 1946, he began a career in real estate as a salesman with the Crutcher Realty firm in Detroit. Six years later, he received his real estate brokers license and founded the Associate Brokers Investment Co., one of the largest black real estate companies in the country. In 1953, he became the first licensed black mortgage banker and organized the first black mortgage company in the United States. He was an executive for the Beneficial Life Insurance Co. and the Supreme Life Insurance Co. of America. Judge Del Rio is a vice president of industrial relations of Keystone Printing, and president of the Michigan Council for Political Education in Urban Areas, a political business and consulting firm. The recipient of numerous awards and citations, he is the author of a black history booklet entitled *The Conspiracy*. Judge Del Rio retired from the state legislature after serving for eight years when he was elected judge in 1973. He has a son, Alan. Address: Frank Murphy Hall of Justice, 1441 St. Antoine St. Detroit, MI 48226

DePreist, James, orchestral conductor, is associate conductor of the National Symphony Orchestra in Washington, D.C. Born Nov. 21, 1936 in Philadelphia, Pa., he is a graduate of the University of Pennsylvania (B.S., 1958; M.A., 1961). He also studied at the Philadelphia Conservatory of Music (1959-61). Before appointment to his present position in 1972, he was music director of the Contemporary Music Guild in Philadelphia (1959–62); American specialist in music for the United States State Department (1962–63); conductor-in-residence, Bangkok, Thailand (1963–64); music director of station WCAU-TV in Philadelphia (1965–66); music director of the summer music program of Westchester County, N.Y. (1965 and 1966) and assistant conductor to Leonard Bernstein, New York Philharmonic Orchestra (1965–66). He was guest conductor of the Rotterdam Symphony (1969) and made subsequent concert appearances with the Stockholm Symphony, the Philadelphia Orchestra and the New York Philharmonic. He won the first prize gold medal in the Dimitri Mitropoulos International Music Competition for Conductors (1964). He composed the ballet scores *Vision of America* (1960), *Tendrils* (1961) and *A Sprig of Lilac* (1964); the theme music for the *Eye on New York* series on WCBS-TV (1965) and the concert, *Requiem* (1965). He and his wife, Louise, have two daughters, Tracy and Jennifer. Address: National Symphony, 2480 16th St., NW, Washington, DC 20009 **(See article James DePreist in Volume II)**

Ophelia DeVore

Earl B. Dickerson

Rep. Charles C. Diggs Jr.

DeVore, Ophelia, business executive, is chairman of the board of Ophelia DeVore Associates, Inc. in New York, N. Y. The firm includes a model agency, a self-development charm school, a cosmetic company and a consultant service in marketing and public relations. The latter advises industry on products and promotions aimed at black women. Born August 12, 1926 in South Carolina, Miss DeVore attended New York University (mathematics and languages) City College of New York (fashion, writing and advertising) and the Vogue School of Modeling. The Ophelia DeVore School of Charm has many "page one" personalities among its alumnae, including actresses Diahann Carroll, Gail Fisher, Ellen Holly and Ena Hartman, and television personalities Joan Murray and Melba Tolliver. Miss DeVore is a member of several business organizations, including American Women in Radio and Television, the National Association of Market Developers and the National Business League. A widow, she is the mother of three daughters and two sons: Mrs. Carol P. Gertjegerdes, Mrs. Marie O. Henry, Cheryl, James and Michael Carter. Address: 1697 Broadway, New York, NY 10019

Dickerson, Earl Burrus, insurance executive, is honorary board chairman and financial consultant to the chief executive officer of Supreme Life Insurance Co. of America, with headquarters in Chicago, Ill. Born June 22, 1891 in Canton, Miss., he is a graduate of the University of Illinois (A.B., 1914) and the University of Chicago Law School (J.D., 1920). He has an honorary H.H.D. degree from Wilberforce University (1961). Mr. Dickerson has been associated with Supreme Life since 1921. He was general counsel (1921–55), executive vice president (1954–55), general manager (1955–62), president and chief executive officer (1955–71) and chairman of the board of directors (1971–73). He was an assistant corporation counsel of the City of Chicago (1923–27), an Illinois assistant attorney general (1933–39) and a member of the Chicago City Council (1939–43). During World War I, he was an infantry lieutenant in the American Expeditionary Forces, and was a founder of the American Legion. As a lawyer, his numerous courtroom victories include *Hansbury vs. Lee, et al*, a celebrated "restrictive covenant" case which opened up 26 city blocks on Chicago's South Side. He was a member of the President's Commission on Fair Employment Practice (1941–43). He is a member of the Chicago, Cook County, Illinois, American and National bar associations, and is affiliated with numerous professional and civic groups, including the University of Illinois Alumni Association and the University of Chicago Law School Association. He is a past grand polemarch of Kappa Alpha Psi fraternity. He and his wife Kathryn have a daughter, Mrs. Diane Dickerson Cohen. Address: 3501 S. Dr. Martin Luther King Jr. Drive, Chicago, IL 60653

Diggs, Charles C. Jr., congressman, is a member of the United States House of Representatives from Detroit, Mich. He was born Dec. 2, 1922 in Detroit and is a graduate of Wayne State University (B.S.). He has honorary degrees from Central State College and Wilberforce University. Mr. Diggs was elected in 1954 as Michigan's first black member of Congress. Previously, he was a two-term member of the Michigan State Senate. He is president of the House of Diggs, Inc., a mortuary establishment in Detroit. He is chairman (1973) of the House District of Columbia Committee and the House Foreign Affairs Subcommittee on Africa. He is dean of the Michigan Democratic delegation, founder and former chairman of the Congressional Black Caucus, president of the National Black Political Assembly and a former vice-chairman of the Democratic National Committee. He is married to Janet Elaine Hall. Mr. Diggs has three children: Charles III, Denise and Alexis. Address: 2464 Rayburn Bldg., Washington, DC 20515

Dilday, William H. Jr., television executive, is general manager of television station WLBT in Jackson, Miss. WLBT is an NBC affiliate and the largest commercial television station in Mississippi, and Mr. Dilday is responsible for the overall management of all areas of the station. He believes that he is the only black in such a position in the United States. Mr. Dilday was born Sept. 14, 1937 in Boston, Mass. and studied business administration at Boston University (B.S., 1960). He was personnel director for WHDH-AM/FM-TV in Boston before assuming his present position at WLBT. Though his original ambition was to be a journalist, Mr. Dilday believes that the management career in communications that he chose to follow is one where there are greater opportunities than in "on-camera" or "on-air" positions. He and his wife, Maxine, have two daughters, Erika and Kenya. Address: WLBT Television, P.O. Box 1712, Jackson, MS 39205

Dillard, Brig. Gen. Oliver W., military officer, is deputy director of the U.S. Army's Civil Operations and Rural Development Support at headquarters of the Military Assistance Command in Vietnam. He has been in the military service for 27 years and was the fifth black to achieve the rank of brigadier general of the army. He was the first black to attend the National War College (1964). Born Sept. 28, 1926 in Margaret, Ala., he attended Tuskegee Institute and is a graduate of Omaha University (bachelor of general education, 1959) and George Washington University (M.S., international affairs, 1965). He was inducted into the Army in 1945, was commissioned as a second lieutenant in 1947, and was promoted to his present rank in 1972. He has served in Europe, Africa and the Far East. He has received numerous citations and medals of honor—including the Purple Heart, the Silver Star and the Bronze Star—during his military career. He and his wife, Helen, have four children: Oliver Jr., Stephen, Dennis, and Diane. Address: The Pentagon, Department of the Army, Washington, DC 20310

Ditto, Frank, community leader, is director of the East Side Voice of Independent Detroit, a social action and service organization in Detroit, Mich. A founder of ESVID, Mr. Ditto was proposed as director by 26 churches of the community and was chosen from among 18 applicants. ESVID conducts 11 programs, including Citizens' Action Against Drug Abuse, Malcolm X Liberation School (providing supplemental academic and cultural education), "Blacktalk" (a TV program discussing people, programs and issues affecting the black community), *The Ghetto Speaks* newspaper, and the "Frank Ditto Show" and "Voices of East Side Youth" (radio programs). The organization also conducts a housing development division and a social service referral agency. Of 1,200 people treated at the drug clinic, some 800 reportedly have been helped toward rehabilitation,and 650 others are doing well. The clinic has the lowest recidivism rate of any clinic in Detroit. Mr. Ditto has received many awards for his community work. Address: 10833 Mack Ave., Detroit, MI 48214

William H. Dilday Jr.

Brig. Gen. O. W. Dillard

Frank Ditto

Dean Dixon

Isaiah Dixon Jr.

Julian C. Dixon

Mattiwilda Dobbs

Dixon, Dean, orchestra conductor, is conductor of the Frankfurt Radio Symphony Orchestra in West Germany. He was born Jan. 10, 1915, in New York, N.Y., and has degrees from The Juilliard School of Music (B.S.), and Columbia University (M.A.). At the age of 17, he founded the Dean Dixon Symphony Orchestra and the Dean Dixon Choral Society in New York. In August of 1941, Mr. Dixon made his debut as conductor of the New York Philharmonic Symphony Orchestra, becoming the first black and probably the youngest musician ever to conduct the orchestra. In 1948, Mr. Dixon received the Alice M. Ditson Award for Outstanding Contributions to Modern American Music, and in 1949 he was invited to conduct the Radio Symphony Orchestra of the French National Radio in Paris. In 1964, he was named musical director of the Sydney Symphony Orchestra, in Sydney, Australia. He has conducted concerts for the King of Sweden, the King of Denmark, the Queen of England, the Queen of Belgium and the Duke of Edinburgh. In 1970, after a 21-year absence from his native country, Mr. Dixon returned to the United States to conduct the New York Philharmonic Orchestra. He has conducted other orchestras in countries including, Japan, Spain, Italy, Israel, Mexico, Norway, Poland, Austria and Czechoslovakia. He has two daughters, Diane and Nina. Address: Hessischer Rundfunk, Frankfurt am Main, West Germany.

Dixon, Isaiah Jr., legislator, is a member of the Maryland House of Delegates (Fourth District in Baltimore) where he has served since 1967. As a legislator, he has introduced a bill calling for repeal of the one-year residency requirement for social aid in Maryland and a bill making Jan. 15 a state holiday in honor of the birth of the late Dr. Martin Luther King Jr. He was born Dec. 23, 1922 in Baltimore, Md., and attended Howard University, the University of Maryland and Morgan State College. In addition to being a state legislator, Mr. Dixon is a real estate and insurance broker. He and his wife, Marian, have a son, Isaiah III. Address: Maryland General Assembly, 1607 W. North Ave., Annapolis, MD 21404

Dixon, Julian C., legislator, is a Democratic assemblyman from the 63rd District (Los Angeles) in the California General Assembly. Born in Washington, D.C., he is a graduate of Los Angeles State College (B.S.) and Southwestern Law School (J.D.). Before his election in 1972, he was administrative assistant to State Senator Mervyn M. Dymally. He is a former special consultant to the Joint Committee on the Revision of the Election Code and a former consultant to the Senate Subcommittee on Human Needs and Resources. He is a member of Men of Tomorrow, the Brotherhood Crusade and numerous other community organizations, and has served on the statewide Sickle Cell Anemia Advisory Committee and the Advisory Board of the Joint Center for Community Studies at UCLA. He is a member of the Assembly's Education and Retirement Committee and is vice chairman of the Assembly Committee on Employment and Public Employees. Address: State Capitol, Sacramento, CA 95814

Dobbs, Mattiwilda, opera singer, is internationally known for her performing talents. Born and reared in Atlanta, Ga. she graduated from Spelman College in 1946. She then began four years of opera study in New York City under Lotte Leonard while studying Spanish at Columbia University (M.A., 1948). In 1947, she was awarded a Marian Anderson Scholarship, the first of a series of awards she was to receive for her singing talents. In 1951, Miss Dobbs won first prize in a music competition in Geneva, Switzerland. In the years that followed, she sang in Europe, the Soviet Union, Australia, India, Israel and many other countries. She was the first black artist to sing at La Scala in Milan, Italy, when she made her debut there in 1952. In 1954, she made her first concert tour of the U.S. and later gave a command performance for Queen Elizabeth II of England. Miss Dobbs has made numerous recordings and presently divides her time between concerts and recitals in Europe and engagements with the Metropolitan Opera in New York City. She is married to Bengt Janzon, a Swedish newspaper and public relations executive. Address: Vastmannagatan 50, Stockholm, Sweden 113 25.

Woodrow B. Dolphin

Jeff R. Donaldson

Linnaeus C. Dorman

Dolphin, Woodrow B., business executive, is founder and owner of W.B. Dolphin and Associates, consulting engineers, in Chicago, Ill. The firm provides engineering services for industrial, commercial, institutional and governmental clients. In 1972, there were about eight black-owned such firms in the U.S. Born Nov. 1, 1912 in Boley, Okla., Mr. Dolphin is a graduate of Wayne State University (B.S.E.E., 1937) and took specialized engineering courses at the Illinois Institute of Technology (1942–44). He has an honorary H.H.D. degree from Malcolm X College in Chicago (1970). As president of the National Technical Association in 1970, Mr. Dolphin persuaded the American Institute of Architects Task Force to provide a grant of $1.7 million to six black colleges for upgrading their architecture schools for national accreditation. He is a member of the National Technical Association. He and his wife, Edwina, have three children: Michele, Woodrow E. and Karl. Address: W.B. Dolphin and Associates, 130 N. Wells St., Chicago, IL 60606

Donaldson, Jeff R., artist and educator, since 1970 has been an associate professor of art, chairman of the Art Department and director of the galleries of art at Howard University in Washington, D. C. There are about 250 art majors at the university. Previously, Mr. Donaldson was a part-time lecturer in art history while studying for a Ph.D. degree at Northwestern University (1968-69). He was assistant professor of art at Northeastern Illinois State College in Chicago (1965–69); assistant professor of art at Chicago City College (1964-66), chairman of the art department at John Marshall High School in Chicago (1959–65) and a classroom teacher of art at Marshall High (1958–59). Born Dec. 15, 1932 in Pine Bluff, Ark., he is a graduate of Arkansas State College (B.S., art, 1954) and the Institute of Design of Illinois Institute of Technology (M.S., art education, 1963). He expected his Ph.D in art history from Northwestern in June, 1973. He was a creator of Chicago's original "Wall of Respect" (1967), has received several academic and professional awards, and is a member of a number of boards and associations. He and his wife, Arnicia, expected a child in early 1973. Address: Howard University, Washington, DC 20001.

Dorman, Linnaeus C., research specialist, is a research chemist with the Dow Chemical Co. in Midland, Mich. His specialty is the synthesis of polypeptides (organic compounds) for medical use. Dr. Dorman has been with the firm 12 years. Born June 28, 1935 in Orangeburg, S.C., he attended Bradley Univ. (B.S.), was a Dow Research Fellow at Indiana Univ. and earned his Ph.D. in organic chemistry there. The Dow company recruited him from college. While his work is in a rather specialized field, and black scientists with Ph.D.'s have been rare, he feels that opportunities for blacks as career scientists in chemistry are good, but the future in general for scientists (except the most gifted) is uncertain. Dr. Dorman has achieved recognition within the company as an authority in his field and has presented technical papers at local, state, national and international meetings. He and his wife, Phae, have two children, Evelyn and John. Address: Chemical Biology Research, 438 Bldg., Dow Chemical Co., Midland, MI 48640

Edmund Stanley Dorsey

Lawrence P. Doss

Herbert P. Douglas Jr.

Calvin A. Douglass

Dorsey, Edmund Stanley, broadcasting executive, is news director of radio station WIND in Chicago, Ill. Born Aug. 18, 1930 in Washington, D.C., he has a master of proficiency in language degree from Seoul University in Korea and a master's degree in political science from Keio University in Tokyo, Japan. He speaks eight languages, including Chinese and Vietnamese. While serving with the U.S. Army in Tokyo in 1949, he became the first black managing editor of *Stars and Stripes*, the military publication. In 1960, he became the first black White House broadcast correspondent while with radio station WWDC, and in 1963, he became the first black television news reporter in Washington while working as news director with radio-television station WOOK. He joined WIND in 1964 and was sent to Saigon in 1966, where he became the first black bureau chief for the Westinghouse Broadcasting Network. He heads a minority training program at WIND and had trained and hired twelve black reporters by 1973. He is a member of the National, Overseas and Capitol Press clubs, and is a member of the board of directors of the YMCA in Chicago, where he also teaches broadcasting at Malcolm X College. He and his wife, Louvenia, have four children: Michi, Toni, Kari and Edmund Jr. Address: 625 N. Michigan Ave., Chicago, IL 60611

Doss, Lawrence P., administrator, is president of New Detroit, Inc. in Detroit, Mich. The organization was established in 1967 when a number of citizens were called together to search for causes of the black rebellion and seeks cures for problems of poverty, discrimination, etc. Mr. Doss was appointed as president in June 1971. He directs all staff operations. Born June 16, 1927 in Cleveland, Ohio, he attended Fenn College in Cleveland, Ohio State University and American University, majoring in accounting, public administration and general management. He was with the Internal Revenue Service (1949-70) before being appointed as Detroit public school decentralization coordinator, helping to direct authority to local regional school boards and local school councils. He is chairman of the Michigan Neighborhood Education Authority and chairman of the Economic Development Committee of.the Detroit NAACP. He is a board member of the Inner City Business Improvement Forum, and is a member of many organizations, including the Presbyterian National Committee for Self Development, the Michigan Higher Education Commission and the United Health Organization. He and his wife, Juanita, have three children: Paula, Lawrence and Lawry. Address: 1515 Detroit Bank & Trust Bldg., 211 W. Fort St., Detroit, MI 48226

Douglas, Herbert P. Jr., business executive, is national vice president for special markets for Schieffelin & Co., importers of wines and spirits. He is one of two black vice presidents in that industry. Mr. Douglas was born March 9, 1922 in Pittsburgh, Pa. He has degrees from the University of Pittsburgh (B.S., 1948; M.Ed., 1949). While at the University of Pittsburgh, he was a member of the National Collegiate All-America Track and Field Team (1946), an Olympic medalist (London, 1948) and Athlete of the Year (1949). In 1950, he joined the Pabst Brewing Co. as a special representative and district manager. He joined Schieffelin & Co. as a special representative and district manager. He joined Schieffelin & Co. in 1963 as a control state representative and became a vice president in 1969. He holds membership in the NAACP, the National Association of Market Developers, the International Olympians Executive Committee and the Sales Executives Club of New York. He and his wife, Rozell, have two children, Herbert III and Mrs. Barbara Ralston. Address: Schieffelin & Co., 30 Cooper Sq., New York, NY 10003

Douglass, Calvin A., legislator, is a member of the Maryland House of Delegates (Four District, Baltimore). Born Sept. 1, 1909 in Baltimore, Md. he has degrees from Shaw University (B.S.) and the University of Maryland Law School (LL.B.), where he was only the second black admitted. Before being elected to the Maryland House of Delegates in 1967, Mr. Douglass served as assistant city solicitor and magistrate of the Northwestern and Western Police Court in Baltimore. He and his wife, Dorothy, have two children, Calvin and Mrs. Mercedes Rankin. Address: 1821 Pennsylvania Ave., Baltimore, MD 21217

John W. Douglass

Lewis C. Dowdy

Judge Edward R. Dudley

Lamar Dukes

Douglass, John W., legislator, is a member of the Maryland House of Delegates (Second District, Baltimore). Born March 19, 1942 in Princess Anne, Md., he attended Lincoln University (B.A., 1964) and Johns Hopkins University (M.A., chemistry, 1966). He taught chemistry at Morgan State College for two years (1966–68). While teaching at Morgan State, he became a salesman for R.L. Johnson Realty Company, a position he still holds. Mr. Douglass also is president of Chase Manhattan Contractors, Inc. The recipient of awards from numerous organizations, including the American Chemical Society and the American Legion, he is a past president of the Businessmen's League of Baltimore. He is married. Address: 1535 E. North Ave., Baltimore, MD 21213

Dowdy, Lewis C., educator and administrator, is chancellor of North Carolina A&T State University. Previously, he was dean of instruction and dean of the School of Education at the university. Born Sept. 1, 1917 in Eastover, S.C., he is a graduate of Allen University (A.B.), Indiana State College (M.A.) and Indiana State University (Ed.D.). He has honorary degrees from Allen University (Litt.D.) and Indiana State University (LL.D.). He was elected president (to assume office in November 1973) of the National Association of State Universities and Land-Grant Colleges, an organization of 118 institutions, including UCLA, Ohio State University and the University of Illinois. He is a member of the American Council on Education, the Association of American Colleges, the National Education Association and the North Carolina Association of Universities and Colleges. He and his wife, Elizabeth, have three children: Lewis Jr., Lemuel and Elizabeth. Address: North Carolina A & T State University, Greensboro, NC 27411

Dudley, Edward R., jurist, is a justice of the Supreme Court of the State of New York. He was elected in 1964. Admitted to the bar in 1941, he was a judge of the Domestic Relations Court of New York City (1955-60). He was President of the Borough of Manhattan (1961-65) and chairman of the New York County Democratic Committee (1963-65). He was director of the NAACP Freedom Fund (1953-55). Born March 11, 1911 in South Boston, Va., he is a graduate of Johnson C. Smith University (B.S., 1932) and St. John's University Law School (1941). He has honorary degrees from Johnson C. Smith, Morgan State College and the University of Liberia. He was U.S. ambassador to Liberia (1948-53) and started the first Point 4 program in Africa. He was made a Grand Commander, Order of Star of Africa. He was designated as administrative judge of Criminal Court of New York City in 1967 and as administrative judge of the New York Supreme Court (First Department) in 1971. He is a life member of the NAACP and is a trustee of the Fund for the City of New York. He and his wife, Rae, have one son, Edward Jr. Address: 549 W. 123rd St., New York, NY 10027

Dukes, Lamar, engineer, is manager of advanced communications and avionics engineering at Douglas Aircraft Co., a division of McDonald Douglas Corp., in Long Beach, Calif. He designs highly advanced communications systems for various commercial and military aircraft. In 1973, he was working on a special anti-submarine aircraft for the Canadian government. Born Nov. 6, 1925 in Pensacola, Fla., he attended Florida A & M University (1943–45) and is a graduate of the University of Pittsburgh (B.S., electrical engineering, 1953). He has taken advanced studies at New York University and St. John's University in New York, N.Y. and West Coast University in Los Angeles, Calif. Prior to his involvement with the anti-submarine design, he assisted in the design of an airborne warning and control system and an air-to-surface missile under a Douglas contract with the U.S. Air Force. He has also contributed to the development of the landing and rendezvous radars for the Apollo space mission's lunar lander. He is a member of St. Philomena Church in Long Beach and a member of a rumor control advisory board in the city. He and his wife, Juanita, have a daughter, Darlene Maria. Address: Douglas Aircraft Co., 3855 Lakewood Blvd., Long Beach, CA 90846

James R. Dumpson

Judge Robert M. Duncan

Robert Todd Duncan

Dumpson, James R., university official, is dean and professor of the Graduate School of Social Service at Fordham University in New York City. Born April 5, 1909; he has degrees from the State Teachers College at Cheyney, Pa. (B.S.) and the New School for Social Research (A.B. and M.A.). He has received honorary degrees from Howard University (L.H.D.), Tuskegee Institute (LL.D.), Fordham University (LL.D.) and St. Peter's College (L.H.D.). Mr. Dumpson's career as teacher and social worker includes 25 years of service in the New York Department of Welfare culminating in his appointment as commissioner of welfare for the city of New York in 1959. He resigned that post in 1965 to join the faculty of Hunter College School of Social Work of the City University of New York as professor and associate dean. His appointment as dean of the Fordham University Graduate School of Social Service came in 1967. He has received presidential appointments to national commissions on welfare, drug abuse and child care. He holds membership in numerous professional organizations and has written many articles for scholarly journals and anthologies. Mr. Dumpson and his wife, Goldie, have a daughter, Jeri. Address: Graduate School of Social Service, Fordham University at Lincoln Center, New York, NY 10023

Duncan, Robert Morton, jurist, is a judge of the U.S. Court of Military Appeals, the court of last resort for the armed services in Washington, D.C. Appointed by President Richard M. Nixon in 1971, he is the first black judge of the court. Previously, he was an associate justice of the Ohio Supreme Court (1969-71), judge of the Franklin County (Ohio) Municipal Court (1966-69), and a member of the staff of Ohio Attorney General William B. Saxbe (1963-66). Born Aug. 24, 1927 in Urbana, Ohio, he is a graduate of Ohio State University (B.S., 1948) and Ohio State University College of Law (J.D., 1952). He attended the 1969 Appellate Judges' Seminar at New York University and the 1961 National College of State Trial Judges at the University of Nevada. He is a member of the President's Commission for Observance of the 25th Anniversary of the UN and the President's Commission on White House Fellows. He is a member of numerous professional and civic organizations and is a member of the board of trustees of Defiance College and Franklin University. He and his wife, Shirley, have three children: Linn, Vincent and Tracey. Address: 450 E. St., N.W., Washington, DC 20001

Duncan, Robert Todd, concert singer and actor, was the original Porgy in George Gershwin's *Porgy and Bess.* His memorable performance as Porgy led to roles in the Broadway musicals *Cabin in the Sky,* (1940), and *Lost in the Stars* (1950) and the movie *Syncopation* (1940). Mr. Duncan also appeared in *Pagliacci* and *Carmen* with the New York City Center opera company. In 1950, he won the Critics Award for best male performance in a Broadway musical. He was born Feb. 12, 1903 in Danville, Ky. After graduating in 1925 from Butler University in Indianapolis, Ind., he taught English and music at Louisville Municipal College for Negroes. In 1930, he received his master's degree from Columbia University. He then joined Howard University as a professor of voice and head of the department of public school music, a position he held until 1945. He is presently a voice instructor and coach in Washington, D.C. He and his wife, Gladys, have one son, Charles. Address: 4130 16th St., N.W., Washington, DC 20011

Katherine Dunham

Dunham, Katherine, dancer—choreographer—educator, is director of the Performing Arts Training Center and Dynamic Museum at Southern Ill. Univ. in East St. Louis, Ill. She is also technical adviser on intercultural affairs at the John F. Kennedy Center for the Performing Arts in Washington, D.C. Born June 22, 1912 in Chicago, Ill., Miss Dunham has degrees from the University of Chicago (Ph.B.) and MacMurray Coll. (honorary L.H.D.). A world-renowned artist, Miss Dunham pioneered in introducing African and Caribbean dances to American audiences. In 1972 she directed (at Wolf Trap Farm for the Performing Arts, located in Virginia) *Treemonisha,* a ragtime opera by Scott Joplin, and has staged dozens of plays, films, television specials and operas, including *Green Mansions* and *Aida.* Among the books she has written are *Touch of Innocence* (1959) and *Island Possessed* (1969). She and her husband, John Thomas Pratt, have a daughter, Marie-Christine. Address: Southern Ill. Univ., East St. Louis, IL 62201

Robert W. Dunham

Dunham, Robert, restaurateur, is president of the McDonald's (hamburgers) franchise on 125th Street in Harlem, New York, N.Y. Harlem's McDonald's is the third most successful of nearly 2,800 McDonald's outlets in the U.S. Born in 1932 in Kannapolis, N.C. to a sharecropper family, Mr. Dunham joined the U.S. Air Force in 1951. Assigned to the Food Service School, he became such a good cook that he was transferred from the enlisted men's mess to the officers' mess. After discharge, he worked as a machine operator and then as a salad man at New York's Waldorf-Astoria Hotel. Eventually, he joined the police force and learned managerial—and physical—skills which proved helpful when he opened his establishment. He retired from the force after 14 years because of illness. He tried a restaurant venture but was unable to get financing. He then obtained his present franchise. Youth gangs at first threatened to drive the restaurant out of business, but a tough policy by Mr. Dunham and his two partners stopped the harassment. He and his wife have a son, Bradley. Address: 215 W. 125th St., New York, NY 10027 **(See article on Robert Dunham in Volume II.)**

Albert J. Dunmore

Dunmore, Albert J., administrator, is manager of the Urban Affairs Department at the Chrysler Corp. in Detroit, Mich. Born June 4, 1915 in Georgetown, S.C., he earned a degree at Hampton Institute (B.S., 1937). Mr. Dunmore served as a reporter and editor for thirty years with the *Pittsburgh Courier* and *Michigan Chronicle* newspapers. He is chairman of the United Community Services Metropolitan Area Planning Committee, co-chairman of the Urban Alliance, member of the board of directors of the Detroit Press Club Foundation, vice president of the Detroit Urban League board of directors and chairman of the urban affairs committee of the National Association of Market Developers. Mr. Dunmore and his wife, Josephine, have five children: Ruth, Charlotte, Jonathan, Gregory and Stephen. Address: 1200 Oakland, Highland Park, MI 48221

Barbara J. Dyce

Dyce, Barbara Jeanne, educator, is an instructor of medicine and pharmacology at the University of California School of Medicine in Los Angeles, Calif. She is also the laboratory director of research in biochemistry, and is a research associate. Her biochemical research has aided in the search for ways to detect and treat cancer and cystic fibrosis. She was born Feb. 17, 1928 in Chicago, Ill., and attended Loyola University, Evansville College, the University of Illinois, the University of Chicago and the University of Illinois Medical School. She received her M.Sc. degree from the University of Southern California School of Medicine in 1971. She is a member of several professional organizations, including the American Association for the Advancement of Science, and has had numerous papers published in scientific journals. She is founder and past president of the Feminine Touch, Inc., a group organized to support positive organizations in the black community. Divorced, she has a son, Clarence. Address: University of Southern California School of Medicine, 2025 Zonal Ave., Los Angeles, CA 90033

E

Mervyn M. Dymally

Marian W. Edelman

John W. Edghill

Dymally, Mervyn M., legislator, is a member of the California State Senate, where he has served since 1967. He was elected in 1962, the first black member of the California State Assembly, where he served four years. Born May 12, 1926 in Cedros, Trinidad, he has degrees from California State College in Los Angeles (B.A.) and Sacramento State College (M.A.). He was awarded an honorary LL.D. degree by the University of West Los Angeles. An innovative legislator and scholar, Mr. Dymally is chairman of the Senate Majority Caucus and the Senate Committee on Elections and Reapportionment. A visiting fellow at the Metropolitan Applied Research Center (MARC) in New York City, he also lectures at two California colleges and holds membership in the American Academy of Political and Social Science, the American Association of University Professors and the American Political Science Association. He is editor of the *Black Politician*, a quarterly journal, and author of *The Black Politician: His Struggle for Power.* Mr. Dymally is founder and board chairman of Consensus Publishers, Inc., a trade and college textbook company. He also organized the Urban Affairs Institute in California and Arizona, which sponsors minority student internship programs in government and public affairs, and the National Conference of Black Elected Officials. Mr. Dymally and his wife, Alice, have two children, Mark and Lynn. Address: 2622 S. Western Ave., Los Angeles, CA 90018

Edelman, Marian Wright, attorney, is co-editor (with Ruby G. Martin) of the Washington Research Project of the Southern Center for Public Policy, headquartered in Washington, D. C. The project is involved in litigation (mainly in the area of equal employment opportunity), monitoring various federal programs (child care, school desegregation, etc.) and in liaison with community groups. Mrs. Wright is also director of the Harvard University Center for Law and Education, part of the Office of Economic Opportunity's legal services program. The center's work is directed toward reform in education through research and action on the legal implications of educational policies. Mrs. Wright came into national prominence during 1964–68 when she was director of the NAACP Legal Defense and Education Fund, Inc. in Jackson, Miss. Born June 6, 1939 in Bennettsville, S.C., she is a graduate of Spelman College (B.A., 1960) and Yale University Law School (LL.B., 1963). Her junior year at Spelman was spent at the University of Geneva (Switzerland). She was a John Hay Whitney Fellow at Yale. She has received numerous honors and awards for her work and is a member of a number of professional, civil rights and civic groups. In 1971, she was elected a trustee of Yale University, one of only two women trustees in the school's 270-year history. She and her husband, Peter B. Edelman, have two sons, Joshua and Jonah. Address: 61 Kirkland St., Cambridge, MA 02138

Edghill, John W., business executive, is field sales manager for the American Tobacco Co., a division of American Brands, Inc. in New York, N.Y. He supervises and directs sales and marketing functions of district managers and salesmen throughout the United States. Previously, he was a sales representative, sales supervisor and field sales supervisor for the company. Born Sept. 13, 1921 in New York City, he is a graduate of West Coast University (B.S., art, 1948). A safety instructor with the New York State Conservation Department, he is a member of the Masons, the Shriners, the Elks, and the Roundtable of Commerce. He and his wife, Jeanne, have two children, John IV and Jacqueline. Address: 245 Park Ave., New York, NY 10017

Christopher F. Edley

Helen G. Edmonds

Alfred L. Edwards

Edley, Christopher Fairfield, administrator, is executive director of the United Negro College Fund. Born Jan. 1, 1928 in Charleston, W. Va., he is a graduate of Howard University (A.B., political science, 1948) and Harvard Law School (LL.B., 1953). Before assuming his present position in 1973, he was program officer of the Ford Foundation (1963–73), regional counsel for the Federal Housing and Home Finance Agency (1961–63), chief of the administration of Justice Division of the U.S. Commission on Civil Rights in 1960, a partner in the law firm of Moore, Lightfoot and Edley (1956–60), assistant district attorney of Philadelphia (1954–56), law clerk (1953–54) and a staff sergeant in the U.S. Army (1950–51). He was a member of the Pennsylvania Fair Housing Advisory Committee (1958–60), board member of the Philadelphia Fellowship Commission (1958–63) and a commissioner of the Philadelphia Commission on Human Relations (1956–63). Mr. Edley is a member of the Westchester County Drug Abuse Committee, National Bar Association, American Bar Association, and secretary of the Philadelphia Barristers Club. He has received numerous honors, including the 1960 Certificate of Appreciation from the U.S. Commission on Civil Rights, the 1959 Howard University Alumni Award, and the 1966 Distinguished Service Award of the Philadelphia Commission on Human Relations. He and his wife, Zaida, have two children, Christopher Jr. and Judith. Address: United Negro College Fund, 55 E. 52nd St., New York, NY 10022

Edmonds, Helen G., educator, is Distinguished Professor of History at North Carolina Central University in Durham, N. C. and is national president of The Links, Inc., a women's organization with 126 chapters in 34 states and the District of Columbia. She joined the NCCU faculty in 1941 as professor of history and has been graduate professor of history, (1948-64) chairman of the Department of History and Social Science, (1963-64) and dean of the Graduate School of Arts and Sciences, (1964-71). Born Dec. 3, 1911 in Lawrenceville, Va., she is a graduate of Morgan State College (A.B., history, 1933), Ohio State University (M.A., history, 1938; Ph.D., history, 1946). She did post-doctoral research in Modern European History at the University of Heidelberg (West Germany) during 1954-55. She was one of three members of the Interim Committee in Charge of Administration of NCCU (1966-67). She is a member of the Peace Corps (ACTION) National Advisory Council, has served the U. S. Government as a leader-specialist of various international education programs, and was U. S. Alternate Delegate to the UN General Assembly (1970). She has written numerous articles and is author of the book *Black Faces In High Places* (1971). She has received a number of honors, awards, fellowships and grants, and is a member of several professional organizations, including the American Historical Association, the Association for the Study of Negro Life and History, National Education Association and Southern Historical Association. Address: North Carolina Central Univ., Durham, NC 27707

Edwards, Alfred L., federal official, is deputy assistant secretary of the United States Department of Agriculture. Born Aug. 9, 1920 in Key West, Fla., Dr. Edwards earned degrees in economics from Livingstone College (B.A., 1948), the University of Michigan (M.A., 1949) and the University of Iowa (Ph.D., 1958). He taught for five years at Southern University in Baton Rouge, La., and later at the University of Iowa and the University of Nigeria in Nsukka. Dr. Edwards is a member of the American Economic Association, the Nigerian Economic Society, the Tax Institute of America and other learned and professional organizations. He and his wife, Willie Mae, have two children, Beryl Laurette and Alfred L. Jr. Address: U.S. Department of Agriculture, 12th St. & Independence Ave., SW, Washington, DC 20250

A. Wilson Edwards ·   George H. Edwards

Edwards, A. Wilson, city official, is director of public safety for the city of Louisville, Ky. He has overall responsibility for the police and fire departments. Born Feb. 19, 1908 in Frankfort, Ky., he has a certificate in police administration from the University of Louisville, a certificate in police sciences from the International Police School and a certificate in foreign services from the United States Foreign Service Institute. From 1935 to 1966, he was a police officer, patrolman, detective, sergeant and lieutenant commander of the Parks Section, and assistant director of safety on the Louisville police force. He has also served as chief of security for the late President William V. S. Tubman of Liberia (1958-60), advisor to Col. Tran Minh Cong, chief of police, Da Nang City, South Vietnam (1966-68) and security officer for the 1957 inauguration of President Dwight D. Eisenhower and the 1965 inauguration of President Lyndon B. Johnson. He served as security officer for the first meeting of the Organization of African States (1958). In 1963, he organized and commanded the Special Services Bureau of the Louisville Police Department. Two years later, he went to Liberia to organize and head the National Bureau of Investigation. He and his wife, Rosella, live in Louisville. Address: Office of Director of Safety, City Hall, Suite 102, Louisville, KY 40202

Edwards, George H., legislator, is state representative in the Michigan House of Representatives. He was born February 13, 1911 in Brunswick, Ga. and attended Morehouse College (A.B.) and Atlanta University and New York University for graduate study. He has participated in special institute study at Michigan State University and the University of Indiana. He was first elected to the Michigan legislature in 1954 and has been reelected nine times. As a senior member of the Michigan House of Representatives, he is chairman of the Corporations and Finance Committee, a senior member of the Revision and Amendment to the Constitution Committee, and is assistant majority floor leader. He has served as chairman of the Democratic Caucus Personnel Committee, vice president of the Budget and Expenditures Committee of the House of Representatives, coordinator of personnel, and was a member of the first legislative council when it was created by statute in 1965. He and his wife, Esther, have four children: Harry, Robert, Verne, and Pamela. Address: State Capitol, Lansing, MI 48901

Nelson Jack Edwards

Edwards, Nelson Jack, labor union official, is an international vice president of United Auto Workers in Detroit, Mich. Born Aug. 3, 1917 in Lowndes County, Ala., he is a high school graduate who worked in the fields between classes. At 17, he married his childhood sweetheart, moved into Montgomery and worked for the Southern Oil Co.—12 hours a day for 15¢ an hour. Two years later he moved to Detroit to find a better job. He got a 60¢ an-hour job at the Dodge Main Foundry and on the advice of his brother, joined the UAW union. Moving from Chrysler Corp. to Ford Motor Co., he became active in his new local (900) and within a year was elected chairman of the overwhelmingly white labor group. In 1948, he was appointed to UAW's international staff as representative of Region 1A. He was elected in 1962 as the first black member of UAW's International Executive Board. He is director of the UAW Councils at Alcoa, Budd, Allen Industries, Briggs, Electric Storage Battery and Kelsey-Hayes corporations, involving 300,000 workers. In 1963, as the official representative of the UAW, he worked with Dr. Martin Luther King Jr. in Birmingham at the height of the civil rights drive. He and his wife, Laura, have two children, Nelson Jack Jr. and Lorraine. Address: 8000 E. Jefferson Ave., Detroit, MI 48214 **See article on Nelson Jack Edwards in Volume II.**

Lloyd C. Elam, M.D.

Elam, Lloyd Charles, M.D., educator, has been president of Meharry Medical College in Nashville, Tenn. since 1968. After teaching psychiatry at the University of Chicago, he went to Meharry where he established and chaired the department of psychiatry from 1961 through 1968. In 1966–68, he also was dean of the school of medicine and designed and initiated many of the curriculum revisions now in effect at the school. Since Dr. Elam became president, Meharry has expanded its faculty, facilities and student enrollment. Two unique programs were also started, designed to bring more students into the health professions. Born Oct. 27, 1928 in Little Rock, Ark., he has degrees from Roosevelt University (B.S.) and the University of Seattle (M.D.) and was a resident in psychiatry at the University of Chicago. Dr. Elam serves on eight medical and advisory bodies including the National Board of Medical Examiners, the Advisory Committee to the National Academy of Sciences and the National Association for Equal Opportunity in Higher Education. He and his wife, Clara, have two children, Gloria and Laurie. Address: 1005 18th Ave., Nashville, TN 37208

Lonne Elder III

Elder, Lonne III, film writer, producer, and playwright, is best known as the writer of two highly acclaimed films, *Sounder* and *Melinda*, and as writer and producer of ABC-TV's "Movie of The Week." He was born in Americus, Ga, and attended New Jersey College State University and served in the U.S. Army. After discharge, he joined the Harlem Writers Guild along with contemporaries Lorraine Hansberry, Julian Mayfield, Douglas Turner Ward and John Oliver Killens. He appeared in the Broadway production of Lorraine Hansberry's *A Raisin in The Sun* while continuing to write. He was awarded a John Hay Whitney writing fellowship, a scholarship to study film-making at the Yale University Drama School, and a scholarship in playwriting from the Yale Drama School. His play, *Ceremonies In Dark Old Men*, produced by the Negro Ensemble Company, won the Circle award, the Vernon Rice Drama Desk award, the Stella Holt Memorial Playwrights award and the Los Angeles Drama Critics award. He has written for the "N.Y.P.D." and "McCloud" television series, and has shot his own films at the Yale School of Drama Audio Visual Center. A member of the Black Academy of Arts and Letters, the Harlem Writers Guild and the Black Artists Alliance, Lonne Elder and his wife, Judyann, have two sons, David and Christian. Address: 20th Century-Fox Films, 10201 W. Pico, Los Angeles, CA 90024

Duke Ellington

Daisy Elliott

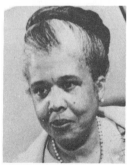

Effie O. Ellis, M.D.

Ellington, Edward Kennedy ("Duke"), bandleader-pianist-composer, is one of the world's greatest musicians. Born April 29, 1899 in Washington, D.C., he has honorary degrees in music from Wilberforce University (1949), Milton College (1964), College of Arts and Crafts (1966), Morgan State College (1967) and Yale University (1967). He made his first appearance as a jazz player in New York City in 1916. He has toured Europe, England, France, Japan, Latin America, the Far East and Australia. He has appeared in concert at Carnegie Hall (1943-50) and at the Metropolitan Opera House (1951). He and his band have performed a five-year engagement at the Cotton Club in Harlem (1927-32) and have appeared in such films as *Black and Tan* (1929), *Check and Double Check* (1930), *She Got Her Man* (1935), *Murder at the Vanities* (1935) and *The Hit Parade* (1937). His compositions and recordings include *Mood Indigo, Solitude, Caravan, Sophisticated Lady, Do Nothing Till You Hear From Me, Don't Get Around Much Any More, Black, Brown and Beige* and *Liberian Suite. He also* conceived and wrote *A Concert of Sacred Music,* which premiered at Grace Cathedral in San Francisco (1965), and the ballet score, *The River,* for the American Theatre Ballet (1970). He has received numerous awards, including the *Downbeat* musical poll (1967), critics poll (1968-70), International Jazz Critics Poll (1968-70), a Grammy (1967), the NAACP Spingarn Medal (1959) and the Medal of Freedom presented by President Richard M. Nixon (1969). He is a widower and has a son, Mercer. Address: 116 Central Park South, New York, NY 10019

Elliott, Daisy, legislator, is serving her fifth term in the Michigan legislature as state representative from Detroit. She was born Nov. 26, 1919 in Filbert, W. Va., received training at Detroit Institute of Commerce and studied at Wayne State University and the University of Detroit. She was elected a delegate to the Michigan state convention, and is author of the civil rights provision of the state constitution. Most of her legislation has been in the interest of education, senior citizens and juveniles. Mrs. Elliott Is a member of Zeta Phi Beta sorority and has received a number of awards, including the Distinguished Service Award from Black Legislators Clearing House, and the Woman of the Year award from the Michigan Federated Democratic Club. She and her husband, Charles Bowers Elliott, have two children, Doris and Robert. Address: Capitol Bldg., Rm. 219, Lansing, MI 48901

Ellis, Effie O'Neal, M.D., physician and administrator, is special assistant to the executive vice president for health services of the American Medical Association, which has headquarters in Chicago, Ill. She works with various medical societies and professional and community groups in an effort to improve the quality of health services. She is a liaison for the AMA with the National Medical Association and the Women's Medical Association. Born June 15, 1913 in Pulaski County, Ga., she is a graduate of Spelman College (A.B., biology and chemistry, 1933), Atlanta University (M.A., biology, 1935) and the University of Illinois (M.D., 1950). She served her residency in pediatrics at the University of Illinois Hospital and in pediatric cardiology at Johns Hopkins Hospital in Baltimore, Md. Before assuming her present duties in 1970, she was director of medical education at Provident Hospital in Baltimore, Md. (1954–56), regional director of maternal and child health for the state of Ohio (1960–1965), regional medical director for the U.S. Children's Bureau (1965–67) and regional commissioner for social rehabilitation for the U.S. Department of Health, Education and Welfare. She is a member of the American Public Health Association, the American Public Welfare Association, the American Association on Mental Deficiency, the American Association for Maternal and Child Health, Alpha Gamma Phi and Delta Sigma Theta. She has received numerous citations and awards for her work. She is married to James Solomon, a physician and they have a daughter, Mrs. Daniel Comegys. Address: 535 N. Dearborn St., Chicago, IL 60610

Ralph Ellison   Simon L. Estes

Ellison, Ralph, author and college professor, is a professor in the humanities at New York University, and an author and critic. He was born March 1, 1914 in Oklahoma City, Okla. and attended Tuskegee Institute. He has honorary degrees from Tuskegee Institute (Ph.D., humane letters, 1963), Rutgers University (Litt. D., 1966), University of Michigan (Litt. D., 1967), Grinnell College (L.H.D., 1967), Williams College (Litt. D., 1970), Adelphia University (L.H.D., 1971). Long Island University (Litt. D., 1971), College of William and Mary (L.H.D., 1972). He has been awarded a Rosenwald Fellowship (1945), a National Academy of Arts and Letters Fellowship in Rome (1955-57), and a visiting Fellow American Studies (Yale, 1966). He has taught at Bard College, the University of Chicago and Rutgers University and has lectured at numerous universities and colleges throughout the world. He is the author of the novel *Invisible Man* which won him the National Book Award, the National Newspaper Publishers Russwurm Award, and *Shadow and Act*, a collection of essays. In 1969, he was awarded the Medal of Freedom by President Lyndon B. Johnson, and an analysis of his works accredited him with the *Chevalier de l'Ordre des Artes et Lettres* awarded in France in 1970. His short stories and essays have been published in various literary journals and magazines since 1939. He is married to the former Fannie McConnell. Address: New York University, New York, NY, 10003

Estes, Simon Lamont, opera singer, is one of the two black male singers enjoying international success in opera. Born Feb. 2, 1938 in Centerville, Iowa, he attended the University of Iowa where he was a pre-medical student and later majored in theology and social psychology. He became a member of the University's Old Gold Singers and was awarded a scholarship to Juilliard School of Music. A grant from the Martha Bard Rockefeller Foundation made it possible for him to audition for the Deutsche Opera in Berlin. Subsequently, he became a member of the Lübeck and Hamburg opera companies. His successes include appearances at Moscow's First International Tchaikovsky Vocal Competition (winning the coveted Tchaikovsky medal), the San Francisco Opera, the American Opera Society in New York, and the San Sebastian Festival in Spain. His triumphant performances include singing all four of the Hoffman roles in Offenbach's *Tales of Hoffman, Macbeth's Banquo, The Magic Flute,* and *The Marriage of Figaro.* Mr. Estes is single and lives in New York. Address: 165 W. 57th St., New York, NY 10028

Samuel B. Ethridge

Mari Evans

Samuel L. Evans

Ethridge, Samuel B., administrative director and educator, is the director of the Teacher Rights Division of the National Education Association in Washington, D.C. Born Dec. 22, 1923 in Brewton, Ala., he has earned degrees from Howard University (B.A. 1948), and the University of Cincinnati (M.Ed., 1957). As of 1973, he was a cabinet member of the NEA and responsible for most of that organization's civil rights programs, including the DuShane Emergency Fund Division, the Center for Human Relations and the Professional Rights and Responsibilities Commission. He began his career as an English teacher at Central High School in Mobile, Ala., and he became principal at Prichard, Ala. and supervisor of secondary education in Mobile County. Since then, he was an assistant chief of intergroup relations with the National Foundation–March of Dimes headquarters in New York City. As a member of the NEA Professional Rights and Responsibilities Commission staff, he was project coordinator for a 17-state task force survey of displacement of black educators and helped to slow down the massive dismissal of black teachers under the guise of compliance with desegregation orders. He and his wife, Cordia, have four children: Samuel, Sherman, Camile and Steven. Address: National Education Association, 1201-16th St. NW, Washington, DC 20036

Evans, Mari, educator and poet, is the producer, director and writer for "The Black Experience," a weekly presentation on WTTV-TV in Indianapolis, Ind., a program which draws its participants from and speaks to the black community. Her poetry has been used on record albums, television specials, two Off-Broadway productions and in numerous textbooks and anthologies. Her book, *I Am A Black Woman* (1970), received the Indiana University Writers' Conference Award (1970) and the Black Academy of Arts & Letters 2nd Annual Poetry Award. Her children's books, *J.D., I Look at Me*, and *Rap Stories*, are scheduled for publication in 1973. A John Hay Whitney Fellow (1965–66), she received a Woodrow Wilson Foundation Grant (1968), and served as consultant in the (1969–70) Discovery Grant Program of the National Endowment of the Arts. Miss Evans has lectured and read at colleges across the country. A native of Toledo, Ohio, she attended the University of Toledo, and has been writer-in-residence and instructor in black literature at Indiana University, Purdue University, and visiting assistant professor at Northwestern University. Miss Evans is a member of the Literary Advisory Panel of the Indiana State Arts Commission. She is chairman of the Statewide Committee for Penal Reform, the Fall Creek Parkway YMCA board of directors and on the Region I board of the National Council of the YMCA. Address: 2003 Sheridan Rd., Rm. 1-336, Education Building, Evanston, IL 60201

Evans, Samuel London, administrator, is executive vice president of the Philadelphia 1976 Bicentennial. He was born Nov. 11, 1902 in Leon County, Fla., and educated himself through reading, a series of collateral courses in institutions of higher learning, a four-year course of integrated concepts of science, philosophy, and education, and a Columbia University World Study Tour (1948). He has been awarded an honorary doctorate in music. He is founder, president and chairman of the National Board of the American Foundation for Negro Affairs, the former chairman of the Philadelphia Anti-poverty Action Commission, and a member of the International Association of Impresarios and Festival Managers. Mr. Evans was responsible for the appearances of Marcel Marceau and Grace Bumbry, the Royal Philharmonic and many others before Philadelphia audiences. He is a member of the board of directors of the Philadelphia General Hospital, a member of the board and production manager of the Philadelphia Chamber Orchestra Society, founder of the Philadelphia Youth Movement (one of the first groups to picket discriminatory retail stores), the appointed coordinator of President Roosevelt's U. S. Division of Physical Fitness, and former secretary of the Pennsylvania State Athletic Commission. (He was responsible for the first black boxing referees in the ring.) He and his wife, Edna, have a daughter, Mrs. Retha Bright. Address: Allman Bldg., 17th and Walnut St., Philadelphia, PA 19103

Evans, W. Leonard Jr., publisher, is president and publisher of Tuesday Publications, Inc. in Chicago. His firm's two magazines, *Tuesday* and *Tuesday at Home* are each inserted once a month in 22 major newspapers in the United States and the Bahama Islands with a combined circulation of 2.3 million. Born Nov. 18, 1914 in Louisville, Ky., he attended Fisk University, the University of Illinois (B.S., business administration) and Kent College of Law in Chicago. Mr. Evans' honors include a Citation of Merit for Outstanding Contributions to Journalism from Lincoln University in 1968, a National Newspaper Week Award from the Poor Richard Club in 1970, a United States Navy Recruiting Service Award and selection as national honoree of Beta Gamma Sigma in 1971. He has lectured at the Wharton School of Finance and Commerce, University of Pennsylvania. In March, 1972, Mr. Evans was invited by Jerome H. Holland, United States Ambassador to Sweden, to visit that country to meet with media officials and publishers in Stockholm. His board memberships include the National Conference of Christians and Jews, the Advertising Council, Inc., Fisk University, the University of Chicago, and Mercy Hospital and Medical Center in Chicago. Mr. Evans and his wife, Maudelle, have two children, Leonard, and Midian. Address: 625 N. Michigan Ave., Chicago, IL 60611

Evers, James Charles, city official, is mayor of Fayette, Miss. He was born Sept. 11, 1922 in Decatur, Miss. and attended Alcorn A&M College (B.A., 1950). He has succeeded his brother, the late Medgar Evers, as director of the Mississippi branch of the NAACP. Before becoming director, he participated in the secret recruitment of local black NAACP memberships, served as the first field director, and launched intensive voter-registration campaigns. Because of pressure and harassment from white segregationists, it became necessary for him to move to Chicago, Ill. He returned to Jackson, Miss. after the assassination of his brother in 1963 to take over the NAACP position. His tireless efforts toward NAACP membership and black voter registration resulted in his 1969 mayoral victory in the town of Fayette. He has numerous business holdings—one of which is the Medgar Evers Shopping Center in Fayette. He and his wife, Nanie Laura, have five children: Patricia, Carolyn, Charlene, Sheila and Eunice. Address: P.O. Box 605, Fayette, MS 39069

Ewell, Raymond W., legislator, is a Democratic member of the Illinois General Assembly from the 29th District (Chicago). Born Dec. 29, 1928 in Chicago, he is a graduate of the University of Illinois (B.A., 1949; M.A., 1950) and the University of Chicago (LL.B., 1954). Elected in 1966, 1968, 1970 and 1972, he has been a practicing attorney in the city of Chicago and a teacher in the Chicago public schools. He is a member of the board of the Chicago Conference to Fulfill These Rights, and a member of the Federal Public Defender Program, the NAACP, the YMCA and the Cook County Bar Association. He and his wife, Joyce Marie, have three children: David, Marc and Raymond. Address: State Capitol, Springfield, IL 50701

W. Leonard Evans Jr.

James Charles Evers

Raymond W. Ewell

F

Rep. Walter Fauntroy

Robert H. Fentress

Cecil L. Ferguson

Fauntroy, Walter E., congressman, is the U. S. Congressional Delegate from the District of Columbia. He was born Feb. 6, 1933 in Washington, D. C., and is a graduate of Virginia Union University (A.B., history, 1955) and Yale University Divinity School (B.D., 1968). He has honorary degrees from Virginia Union University (D.D., 1968), Yale University (D.D., 1969) and Muskingum College (LL.D., 1971) Rep. Fauntroy was elected to Congress on March 23, 1971 and was reelected to a second term on November 7, 1972. He is also pastor of New Bethel Baptist Church in Washington, D. C. Mr. Fauntroy was director of the Washington Bureau of SCLC from 1960 to 1971. He was chairman of the Congressional Black Caucus Task Force for the 1972 Democratic National Convention and chairman of the Platform Committee of the National Black Political Convention held in 1972 in Gary, Ind. He is chairman of the board of directors of the Martin Luther King Jr. Center for Social Change, and is a member of the board of directors of SCLC. He is a member of the Yale University Council, and is a member of the board of trustees of Virginia Union University. He and his wife, Dorothy, have a son, Marvin Keith. Address: 1121 Vermont Avenue, NW., Washington, DC 20005

Fentress, Robert H., publishing executive, is vice president and circulation director of Johnson Publishing Co., Inc. in Chicago, Ill. His responsibility is to obtain maximum circulation for the five magazines which the company publishes, *Ebony, Jet, Black Stars, Black World* and *Ebony Jr!,* in the United States and abroad. He supervises 35 people including a field staff in distribution and promotion of the magazines. After doing newspaper circulation work, Mr. Fentress started with JPC as circulation representative (1950–53), was assistant circulation manager (1954–57), became circulation manager in 1958 and vice president in 1968. Mr. Fentress was born Oct. 24, 1921 in Brownsville, Tenn. and attended Tennessee State University. He and his wife, Alice, have a son, Robert, and a daughter, Barbara. Address: 820 S. Michigan Ave., Chicago, IL 60605

Ferguson, Cecil (Duke), graphic artist, is assistant art director of *Ebony* magazine, published by Johnson Publishing Co., Inc. in Chicago, Ill. He also was designer of *The Ebony Success Library* and other books, and participates in numerous design activities of Johnson Publishing and its various divisions and subsidiaries. On *Ebony,* he does many of the page layouts, and he does promotional illustrations and layouts for other Johnson publications. Born March 13, 1931 in Chicago, he attended the Art Institute of Chicago and the Institute of Design at the Illinois Institute of Technology, and is a graduate of the American Academy of Art in Chicago. He and his wife, Irene, have a son, Mark. Address: 820 S. Michigan Ave., Chicago, IL 60605

Herbert U. Fielding

Charles L. Fields

Hughlyn F. Fierce

Clarence C. Finley

Fielding, Herbert Ulysses, legislator, is a member of the South Carolina House of Representatives and vice president of Fielding Home for Funerals in Charleston. Born July 6, 1923 in Charleston, S.C., he received his B.S. degree in business administration from West Virginia State College in 1948 and in 1966 became the first black elected to the South Carolina House since Reconstruction. During his first term, he sponsored 28 bills, 23 of which passed, earning him the best record for effectiveness in the 124-member body. Most of the bills were designed to benefit blacks. In 1966, Mr. Fielding received the Charleston Business Men's Man of the Year award. He is founder of the Political Action Committee of Charleston. He was reelected to the legislature in 1972. Mr. Fielding and his wife, Thelma, have three sons: Julius, Herbert and Frederick. Address: 122 Logan St., Charleston, SC 29401

Fields, Charles L., business consultant, is founder and president of Fields, Freeman Associates (formerly Recruiting Management Consultants, Inc., a business consulting firm). Born Oct. 28, 1932 in Mt. Vernon, N.Y., he received a B.S. degree from Florida A&M University in 1957 and a master's degree from the Columbia University Business School in New York City in 1972. In June, 1970, Mr. Fields was awarded the outstanding alumnus award of Florida A&M. He has written several articles for various business magazines around the country and has been a guest speaker at numerous colleges and universities. In 1962, Mr. Fields was appointed by New York Mayor Robert Wagner as deputy commissioner and labor adjuster, and later served as director of the Mayor's Commission on Exploitation of Minority Workers and as a labor-management arbitrator. Mr. Fields created and totally financed the first black-owned consulting organization offering a wide range of services to corporations, government and educational institutions in the area of minority-group employment. Some of the clients of the company are Armour, Xerox, Eastman-Kodak, Standard Oil Co., the Urban League. Mr. Fields and his wife, the former Barbara Silva, have two children, Denise and Charles. Address: 51 E. 42nd St., New York, NY 10017

Fierce, Hughlyn F., bank executive, is vice president and commercial loan officer of the Chase Manhattan Bank in New York, N.Y. He joined the bank in 1962 and was promoted to his present position in 1971. Born in New York City, he is a graduate of Morgan State College (B.A., economics) and New York university (M.B.A., finance). He is a member of the Council for Business Opportunity and the Cerebral Palsy National Association. He and his wife, Jewel, have three children: Holly, Heather and Brooke. Address: Chase Manhattan Bank, 1411 Broadway, Nw York, NY 10004

Finley, Clarence C., corporation executive, is executive vice president of Burlington House Products Group, a subsidiary of Burlington Industries in New York, N.Y. His position is the most important ever held by a black man in a major American firm. Born in Chicago, Ill., he is a graduate of Northwestern University (B.S., accounting). He also attended John Marshall Law School. His first job with what became today's corporate entity was as a $12-a-week file clerk in 1942 at the Charm-Tred Co., a family-owned carpet business in Chicago. Eager to learn the business, he had become paymaster by the time he was drafted for military service in 1943. After discharge, he became Charm-Tred's controller by 1951. Following the company's acquisition by Burlington Industries in 1959, he became a vice president in 1961. As executive vice president, he is second-in-command of a division that had $235 million in carpet sales in 1972. Burlington House Products Group consists of six subsidiaries (with 6,500 employees) in the U.S., Canada, Japan and West Germany. Mr. Finley lives with his wife, Emma, and daughter, Beth, in Westchester County, N.Y. Address: 1345 Avenue of the Americas, New York, NY 10019 **See article on Clarence C. Finley in Volume II.**

Ernest A. Finney Jr.

Rev. Miles M. Fisher IV

Ella Fitzgerald

H. Naylor Fitzhugh

Finney, Ernest Adolphus Jr., legislator, is a partner in the law firm of Finney and Gray in Sumter, S.C., and is a member of the South Carolina Legislature (Democrat, Sumter). Born March 23, 1931 in Smithfield, Va., he is a graduate of Claflin College (A.B., 1952) and South Carolina State College (LL.B., 1954). He was chairman of the South Carolina Civil Rights Commission (1963) and was a member of the South Carolina Elections Committee (1968–72). He is chairman of the board of directors of Buena Vista Development Corp. He is a member of Alpha Phi Alpha, the Masons, the Shriners and the Sumter Black Political Caucus. He and his wife, Frances, have three children: Ernest III, Lynn and Jerry. Address: 110 S. Sumter, Sumter, SC 29150

Fisher, The Reverend Miles Mark IV, organization official, is executive secretary of the National Association for Equal Opportunity in Higher Education, in Washington, D.C. Born Sept. 25, 1932 in Huntington, W. Va., he was educated at Virginia Union University (A.B., religion, 1954; M.Div., 1959) and North Carolina Central University (M.A., 1968). He has done graduate work at the University of Chicago Divinity School. Before beginning his work at NAEOHE in 1969, he was special consultant for Publications and Dissemination of Information at the Institute for Services to Education, in Washington, D.C. Earlier, he was a public schoolteacher in Durham, N.C., and an assistant professor at Norfolk State College in Virginia. He is a member of the American Association for Higher Education, the American Academy of Political and Social Science, the American Academy of Religion, and the Technical Advisory Board of the Conference of Minority Public Administrators. Mr. Fisher is an ordained clergyman. He is single. Address: 2001 S St., N W, Suite 450, Washington, DC 20009

Fitzgerald, Ella, entertainer, is an internationally famous jazz singer. Born April 25, 1918 in Newport News, Va., she was orphaned at an early age and attended school at an orphan's home in Yonkers, N.Y. At 15 years of age, she entered an amateur contest at the Apollo Theatre in New York City. Chick Webb, the famous bandleader and drummer, was in the audience and promptly hired her as a singer for his band. Under his direction and guidance, she became a polished entertainer. With her recording, in 1938, of *A-Tisket a-Tasket*, a syncopated version of the well-known nursery song, she gained worldwide fame. She inherited the band in 1939 upon Chick Webb's death but three years later began appearing as a soloist. Her more popular recordings have included "Love You Madly," "Hard-Hearted Hannah," "He's My Guy" and many others, most of them featuring her specialty, "scatting," a vocal imitation of instrumental phrasing. Her four-year marriage to drummer Ray Brown was dissolved in 1953. She has a son, Ray Jr. Address: c/o Virginia Wicks, 236 E. 68th St., New York, NY 10021

Fitzhugh, H. Naylor, marketing specialist, is a marketing vice president and director of special market programs for the Pepsi-Cola Company in Purchase, N.Y. Mr. Fitzhugh attempts to relate the company's marketing efforts, as well as its community service programs, to the changing tastes and aspirations of its black consumers. Prior to joining Pepsi-Cola, Mr. Fitzhugh was a professor of marketing at Howard University, where he was faculty adviser to the school's business and marketing clubs. He has degrees from Harvard University (B.S., *cum laude*; M.B.A.), and Virginia State College (L.L.D.) and was the first executive director and a former national president of the National Association of Market Developers. He also has written a number of articles in the field of minority marketing and minority business. He and his wife, the former Thelma Hare, have three children: Dr. Naylor H. Fitzhugh Jr., Richard and Mrs. Judith F. Rice. Address: Pepsi-Cola Company, Purchase, NY 10577

William J. Fitzpatrick

Roberta Flack

Arthur Fletcher

Samuel L. Foggie

Fitzpatrick, William J., fraternal leader, since 1948 has been Most Powerful Sovereign Grand Commander of the National Supreme Council Ancient and Accepted Scottish Rite Masons. Previously, he was National Deputy and National Grand Secretary General. Born January 20, 1889 in Fitzpatrick, Ala., he is a graduate of Tuskegee Institute and has honorary degrees from Union Baptist Seminary in Birmingham, Ala. (D.D.) and Miller University in Philadelphia, Pa. (LL.D.) Among his numerous accomplishments on behalf of Masons has been his founding of the National Masonic Charity Relief Department (which donates funds to survivors of deceased Masons) and the National Educational Department (which awards scholarships to deserving students). He is a member of Federation of Masons of the World. He and his wife, Dr. Julia C. Fitzpatrick, who is National Grand Matron of the Order of Eastern Star (Scottish Rite affiliation) have two children: Lorraine and Dollie. Address: 5040 Joy Road, Detroit, MI 48204

Flack, Roberta, entertainer, is a nationally famous singer and recording star. Born Feb. 10, 1940 in Asheville, N.C., she attended Howard University, majoring in piano and private voice instruction (B.A.). Upon graduating, she worked as a piano teacher, an accompanist for an operatic school and as a folk singer at several small clubs in Washington. It was there that she was discovered by jazzman Les McCann who recommended her highly to Atlantic Records. Miss Flack signed a contract and has risen to the top of the pop music world. Her latest single, for example, "The First Time Ever I Saw Your Face," recently rode the top of the national pop charts for more than a month. She was named top female vocalist for 1971 by *Downbeat* magazine. She has been honored by Washington, D.C., where she grew up, with Roberta Flack Human Kindness Day. Miss Flack is a member of the Delta Sigma Theta sorority. She is divorced. Address: 600 New Hampshire Ave., NW, Washington, DC 22307

Fletcher, Arthur Allen, administrator, is chairman of President Richard M. Nixon's Domestic Council Cabinet Committee, which recommends ways to eliminate economic discrimination against minorities. He was executive director of the National Urban League from 1972 to 1973 and previously was U.S. alternate delegate to the United Nations General Assembly. He was assistant secretary for wage and labor standards, U.S. Department of Labor (1969–71). Born Dec. 22, 1924 in Phoenix, Ariz., he is a graduate of Washburn University (B.A., 1950) and took postgraduate courses at Kansas State University and San Francisco State College. He was a candidate for election as lieutenant governor of the State of Washington (1968) and was a special assistant to the governor of Washington (1969). He has received numerous awards and is a member of a number of professional and civic groups. He and his wife, Bernyce, live in Columbia, Md. He has six children: Phyllis, Sylvia, Arthur J., Paul, Phillip and Joan. Address: 5101 W. Running Brook Rd., Columbia, MD 21044

Foggie, Samuel L., banking executive, is president of the United Community National Bank in Washington, D.C. Born April 16, 1927 in Washington, D.C., he has degrees from Howard University (B.A.) and Rutgers University (M.B.A.). Mr. Foggie, who has been with the bank eight years, has headed the $20 million business since 1970. Before becoming president, he served as vice president and cashier and as executive vice president. He is on the board of regents of Rutgers' Stonier School of Banking and is a member of the executive committee of the Interracial Council of Business Opportunity. Mr. Foggie and his wife, Dorothy, have two children, Samuel Jr. and Carla. Address: United Community National Bank, 3940 Minnesota Ave., N.E., Washington, DC 20019

Bowles C. Ford

Rev. Jerry W. Ford

Johnny Ford

Ford, Bowles, C., insurance executive, is executive vice president and secretary of the Guaranty Life Insurance Co. in Savannah, Ga. In 1970, he was elected as the first black member of the Savannah City Council. Born Oct. 3, 1911 in Columbia, Ohio, he attended Ohio State University. He began work at Guaranty Life in 1936 as a field representative and was promoted from secretary-treasurer to his present position in 1962. He is a member of the National Insurance Association. He and his wife, Edwina, have a son, Bowles Jr. and a daughter, Mrs. Ruth Dale Ford Grant. Address: 460 W. Broad St., Savannah, GA 31406

Ford, The Reverend Jerry W., clergyman, is pastor of Bethel A.M.E. Church in Los Angeles, Calif. Born Oct. 30, 1921 in Pine Bluff, Ark., he is a graduate of Westminister College in Salt Lake City, Utah (B.A., B.D.) and has taken graduate courses at the University of Utah. Wilberforce University awarded him an honorary D.D. degree. He was ordained a church deacon in 1942 and was ordained an elder in 1944. He is a member of the General Board of the A.M.E. Church and serves on eight commissions of the board. He has been a delegate to every General Conference of the A.M.E. Church since 1952, and is a candidate for election to the bishopric in 1976. He was one of the founders of the Western Christian Leadership Conference, an affiliate of SCLC. He is a member of Omega Psi Phi fraternity. He and his wife, Marion, have two children, Jerry Jr. and Sherri. Address: Bethel A.M.E. Church, 7916 S. Western Ave., Los Angeles, CA 90047

Ford, Johnny, public official, is mayor of the city of Tuskegee, Ala. Born August 23, 1942 in Tuskegee, Mr. Ford attended Knoxville College (A.B., 1964), and in 1967 went to work for the Greater New York City Council of the Boy Scouts of America, where he was the youngest multi-man district executive in the nation. In 1968, he was a key advance strategist in the political campaign of the late Sen. Robert F. Kennedy. He returned to Tuskegee to accept a position in the Model Cities program. His experience in politics made him feel that he could best help shape the future of Tuskegee by taking an active role. He decided to run for mayor and on Oct. 2, 1972 assumed office. Mr. Ford is also seeking to bring new industry to the city and provide as much business for local blacks as possible. He was voted Outstanding Young Man of America by the Outstanding Young Men of America Foundation. He and his wife, Frances, have a son, Johnny Jr. Address: 214 Main St., Tuskegee, AL 36083

William R. Ford

George Foreman

LaDoris J. Foster

Ford, William Richard, federal executive, is director of the U. S. Agency for International Development's Mission to Nigeria. The AID pogram is aimed at stimulation of various nations' economic and social development through loans for U. S. commodities and grants for technical assistance programs in the fields of agriculture, education and manpower as well as population, health and public safety. U. S. commitment to such programs in Nigeria totals more than $30 million a year. Mr. Ford was born Dec. 29, 1933 in Highland Park, Mich., and has degrees from Michigan State University (A.B., 1957; M.A., 1959). He has studied at MSU for a Ph.D. degree. He formerly headed the Michigan Office of Economic Opportunity and was State Executive Director of the Michigan Catholic Conference. In 1969, he was appointed by Michigan Governor William Milliken as director of the Michigan Employment Security Commission. He has received numerous awards for achievement and excellence, including the Young Man of the Year award of the Detroit Junior Chamber of Commerce, and was selected for the National Kappa Psi Fraternity achievement award in 1969. He and his wife, A. Annette, have three children, Eric, Natalie and Todd. Address: U.S. AID-Lagos, c/o Dept. of State, Washington, DC

Foreman, George, boxer, won the world's heavyweight championship from Joe Frazier on Jan. 22, 1973. Born Jan. 22, 1948 in Marshall, Tex., he dropped out of the seventh grade at age 13. In 1965, he joined the Job Corps and was trained as a carpenter, bricklayer and electronics assembler at the Grants Pass, Ore., conservation camp. Persuaded to join the camp's recreational boxing program, he displayed impressive punching power and eventually won the Corps' Diamond Belt Tournament. Entering the Golden Gloves competition in 1967, he lost a split decision in the finals but won a berth on the U.S. Olympics squad. In the 1968 Olympiad at Mexico City, he won the heavyweight Gold Medal by a second-round knockout over Russia's Ionas Chepulis. He turned professional in July, 1969 after winning 19 out of 22 amateur bouts in two years. After winning 21 professional "tune-up" fights under the tutelage of manager Dick Sadler, he took three rounds in 1970 to knock out George Chuvalo, whom Joe Frazier in 1968 had knocked out in four rounds and Muhammad Ali in 1967 had decisioned in 15. He had completed a string of 37 straight professional wins—34 by knockout—when he entered the ring a 3½-to-1 underdog against Frazier in Kingston, Jamaica. At 1:35 of the second round, he scored a technical knockout after flooring the champion three times in each round. George Foreman and his wife, Adrienne, have a daughter, Michi. Address: 23900 Madeiros Ave., Hayward, CA 94541 **See article on George Foreman in Volume II.**

Foster, LaDoris J., business executive, is personnel director of Johnson Publishing Company, Inc., in Chicago, Ill. She interviews prospective employees, coordinates staff programs, maintains company personnel records, enforces personnel policies and acts as liaison between management and personnel. Born Oct. 31, 1933 in St. Louis, Mo., she joined Johnson Publishing Co. in 1957. Before assuming her present position in 1972, she was a receptionist, secretary and administrative assistant in the company's personnel department. She is a board member of the South Side Community Art Center in Chicago, a member of the advisory board of Amtrak and a member of the Women's Division of the Chicago Economic Development Corp. She is single. Address: 820 S. Michigan Ave., Chicago, IL 60605

Luther H. Foster

Walter Fountaine

Redd Foxx

Foster, Luther H., educator, is president of Tuskegee Institute in Tuskegee, Ala. Born March 21, 1913 in Lawrenceville, Va., he received a B.S. degree at Virginia State College, where his father was president, an M.B.A. degree from the Harvard School of Business Administration and a Ph.D. in educational administration from the University of Chicago. In 1953, Dr. Foster was recruited by Tuskegee to become the top executive of the school. During his tenure as president, he has broadened service programs for the disadvantaged, strengthened the school's financial base and added substantially to the institution's physical plant. Dr. Foster is a trustee of the United Negro College Fund and in 1970 was chairman of the Association of American Colleges. He and his wife, Vera, have two children, Adrienne and Hilton. Address: President's Office, Tuskegee Institute, Tuskegee, AL 36088

Fountaine, Walter, businessman, is a hair stylist, wig designer and fashion coordinator. He owns two beauty salons—Coif Camp, in New York, N.Y., and Splinters, in London, England. He was born in Cleveland, Ohio, and has studied at Ohio State University, Cleveland Institute of Art, Cleveland Institute of Music, Mexico City College, Grace Beauty School of N.Y., and the Art Students League of N.Y. He was one of the first black men to obtain national film credit as a hair stylist. His film assignments have included *The Slaves*, *Cotton Comes to Harlem*, *Shaft's Big Score* and *Super Fly*. His celebrity clients include singers Carmen McRae, Roberta Flack and Dionne Warwicke, actor Ron O'Neal, actresses Diana Sands and Cicely Tyson, Mrs. Betty Shabazz (the widow of Malcolm X) and millionairess Gloria Vanderbilt-Cooper. He was invited to Liberia in 1972 as the official hairdresser/makeup artist for the inaugural of President William R. Tolbert Jr. Mr. Fountaine and his wife, Lolli, have a daughter, Tasha. Address: Coif Camp, 203 W. 23rd St., New York, NY 10011

Foxx, Redd, comedian, is a television star in the highly rated series, "Sanford and Son." Born John Elroy Sanford, Dec. 9, 1922 in St. Louis, Mo., he attended DuSable High School in Chicago, Ill. Quitting after a year, he hopped a freight train with two friends to seek success with their washtub band in Chicago. They performed on street corners and in subways for up to $50 a night. When World War II broke up the group, Mr. Foxx worked as a busboy and a 7th Ave. garment cart pusher, and slept on rooftops when he was broke. In the early 1940s, he began to perform in clubs in New York and Baltimore, Md. He teamed up with Slappy White for four years on the black vaudeville circuit. In 1951, the pair joined Dinah Washington's show in California for a month before splitting up. Redd Foxx combined Los Angeles nightclub work with sign-painting to earn a living until 1955 when he recorded *Laff of the Party*, the first of 35 party records he made for Dootsie Williams, owner of Dooto Records. He then made 14 more party LPs for Frank Sinatra's Loma/Reprise Records. His 49 party albums have sold more than 10 million copies in 15 years. In 1964, he was "discovered" by television producers. After a hit on the "Today" show, he has been a guest on the Johnny Carson, Merv Griffin, Steve Allen, Mike Douglas, Virginia Graham and Flip Wilson shows, as well as the specials, "A Time for Laughter" and NBC-TV's 1968 "Soul." By 1968, he had become a top club attraction in Las Vegas. "Sanford and Son" premiered on Jan. 14, 1972 and soon was rated among television's top 10 shows. Mr. Foxx and his wife, Betty Jean, have a daughter, Debraca. Address: National Broadcasting Co., 3000 W. Alameda Ave., Burbank, CA 91505 **See article on Redd Foxx in Volume II.**

Erwin A. France

Aretha Franklin

John Hope Franklin

France, Erwin A., mayoral aide, is administrative assistant to Richard M. Daley, mayor of Chicago, Ill. and director of the Model Cities-Chicago Committee on Urban Opportunity Program. Previously, he was director of the Chicago Youth Opportunity Centers, the nation's largest; deputy director of the Illinois State Employment Service-metropolitan Chicago area, and assistant executive director of the Chicago Commission on Youth Welfare. Born Oct. 26, 1938 in St. Louis, Mo., he is a graduate of George Williams College (B.S., urban studies) and Loyola University (M.A.). A member of the board of trustees of Roosevelt University and George Williams College he has been an instructor in sociology (Loyola University), a lecturer in political science and sociology (George Williams College) and an instructor in public administration (Roosevelt University). A consultant to national organizations and municipal governments throughout the country, he is a member of numerous professional and community organizations. He and his wife, Loretta, have two sons, Mark and Eric. Address: 640 N. LaSalle St., Chicago, IL 60610

Franklin, Aretha, entertainer, is a world-renowned vocalist and recording artist. The "queen of soul" to her fans, she reigns over the pop music field. Born March 25, 1942 in Memphis, Tenn., she recorded her first single for Chess Records in 1954. In 1961, she signed a contract with Columbia Records and produced such albums as *The Electrifying Aretha Franklin, Laughing on the Outside, Runnin' Out of Fools,* and *Unforgettable.* In 1963, she appeared at the Newport Jazz Festival and at the Lower Ohio Jazz Festival. In 1966, she signed with Atlantic Records and in 1967, she recorded her first two million-seller albums, *I Never Loved a Man* and *Aretha Arrives.* Her other albums include *Lady Soul, Aretha Now, Aretha in Paris, The Tender, The Moving, The Swinging, Live at Fillmore West, Young, Gifted and Black* and *Amazing Grace.* Her single, "Respect," has won both the Grammy and the Golden Mike Awards. She opened the 1968 National Democratic Convention with her "soul" version of "The Star Spangled Banner." She was named Top Female Vocalist in 1967 and the Number One Female Singer in 1968. She has also received a special citation from SCLC for her support of various civil rights activities. She has four sons: Clarence, Edward, Teddy and Kecalf. Address: Queen Booking Corp., 1650 Broadway, New York, NY 10019

Franklin, John Hope, historian, is John Matthews Manly Distinguished Professor of History at the University of Chicago and is former chairman of the department of history. He is a fellow of the university's Center for Policy Study. Born Jan. 2, 1915 in Rentiesville, Okla., he has a B.A. from Fisk University and M.A. and Ph.D. degrees from Harvard University. Dr. Franklin received grants for post-doctoral research from the Social Science Research Council and the John Simon Guggenheim Memorial Foundation. Before joining the University of Chicago faculty in 1964, he taught at Fisk University, St. Augustine College, Howard University, and several other colleges in the United States. He is the author of a number of books, including *Land of the Free,* which he wrote jointly with John Caughey and Ernest May. *The Negro in the Twentieth Century,* which he co-edited, was published in 1967. He is also general editor of the University of Chicago Press Series of *Negro American Biographies and Autobiographies.* For 20 years, he has served on the editorial board of the *Journal of Negro History.* He and his wife, Aurelia, have a son, John Whittington. Address: University of Chicago, Department of History, 1126 E. 59th St., Chicago, IL 60637

Leonard G. Frazier

Frazier, Leonard G., legislator, is a member of the Connecticut House of Representatives, representing the 10th legislative district (Hartford). He also is the owner of a successful electronics firm in the city. Mr. Frazier was born in Allendale, S.C. He attended Temple University, majoring in electrical engineering, and has studied at the Electronics Material School in California and the AIEA Electronic School in Honolulu, Hawaii. Mr. Frazier is a member of the American Legion, the Masons and the Lions Club of Hartford and is on the executive board of the local NAACP. He and his wife, Marion, have two daughters, Patricia and Judith. Address: 630 Blue Hills Ave., Hartford, CT 06120

Marion "Boo" Frazier

Frazier, Marion ("Boo"), record company executive, is executive vice president of Perception/Today Records, Inc. in New York, N.Y. He coordinates promotion, sales and marketing for all the company's products and supervises recording of all jazz albums. Born April 23, 1936 in Cheraw, S.C., he worked as a bandboy for Dizzy Gillespie's band while a teenager. He later spent two years studying music at Winston-Salem (N.C.) State College and worked for Chess Records (as a shipping clerk), Vee Jay Records and Duke Peacock Records before moving to Mercury Records in Chicago, Ill., as promotions director in 1969. He and his partner, Terry Phillips, organized Perception/Today. Eleven of the company's releases have been included among the "Top 100" records in sales. Mr. Frazier is a member of the National Association for Radio and Television Announcers, the Fraternity of Record Executives and the National Association of Record Merchandisers. He and his wife, Brenda, have a daughter, Cheryl. Address: 165 W. 46th St., New York, NY 10036

Frankie M. Freeman

Freeman, Frankie M., attorney, is a member of the U.S. Commission on Civil Rights. Born in Danville, Va., she is a graduate of Howard University (LL.B., 1947). She has also studied at Hampton Institute (1933–36). Before assuming her present position in 1964, she was a practicing lawyer (1949–56), an instructor of business law at College Center of the Fingerlakes (1947–49), a statistician at the Office of Price Administration (1944–45) and a U.S. Treasury Department clerk (1942–44). She is associate general counsel of the St. Louis Housing and Land Clearance Authorities. She is a member of the American, National and Mound City bar associations, the Lawyers' Association of St. Louis, the National Association of Housing and Redevelopment Officials, the National Housing Conference, the League of Women Voters and she is a former president of Delta Sigma Theta sorority. She has received numerous honors, including the 1953 Outstanding Citizen award of the Mound City Press Club; Women of Achievement award from the National Council of Negro Women (1956 and 1965). She is also a board director of the National Council of Negro Women. She and her husband, Shelby, have a daughter, Shelbe Patricia. Address: 5391 Waterman Ave., St. Louis, MO 63112

Mary E. Frizzell

Frizzell, Mary E., fraternal leader, is president of the Women's Missionary Society of the A.M.E. Church with headquarters in Washington, D.C. Born in Mayfield, Ky., Miss Frizzell has a B.A. degree from Kentucky State College (A.B., 1947) and Howard University (M.A., 1970). She also has earned certification in religious journalism from the Christian Authors' Guide in Philadelphia, Pa. She has been involved in missionary work for the past twenty years. Miss Frizzell has served as director of the promotion and missionary education department of the society. Under her guidance, the department offered leadership courses in adult work, published inspirational literature and maintained a reference book service. She also established its correspondence school and edited its yearbook. Miss Frizzell has been cited for meritorious service by the Chapel of Four Faiths in Philadelphia, Pa. and received the Faithful Award from the Life Membership Committee of the Women's Missionary Society. Address: A.M.E. Church, 1541 14th St., NW, Washington, DC 20005

118

Wilson Frost

Henry E. Frye

Hoyt W. Fuller

I. Owen Funderburg

Frost, Wilson, city official, is a Democratic member of the City Council of Chicago, Ill. He represents the 34th Ward. He was elected to his second term of office in 1971. Mr. Frost had represented the 21st Ward. Born Dec. 27, 1925 in Cairo, Ill., he is a graduate of Fisk University (B.A., economics, 1950) and Kent College of Law (J.D., 1958). He was supervisor of the women's division of the Illinois Youth Commission (1952–60) and has been in the private practice of law since 1960. He is a member of a number of professional bodies, including the Legal Redress Commission of the NAACP, Kappa Alpha Psi fraternity and Phi Alpha Delta legal fraternity. He and his wife, Gloria, have a daughter, Mrs. Jacqueline Baldwin, and a son, Rhey Orme. Address: City Hall, City of Chicago, Chicago, IL 60601

Frye, Henry E., attorney, legislator and businessman, is senior partner in Frye, Johnson and Barbee, a law firm in Greensboro, N. C. He is also a member of the North Carolina House of Representatives. Elected in 1968, he was the state's first black legislator since Reconstruction. He was reelected in 1970 and 1972. He represents the 26th District (Guilford County). He was one of the principal organizers of Greensboro National Bank which opened in 1971. Born Aug. 1, 1932 in Ellerbe, N. C., he is a graduate of North Carolina A&T University (B.S., biology 1953) and the University of North Carolina Law School (J.D., 1959). He is a former assistant U. S. attorney for the Middle District of North Carolina and once taught law at North Carolina Central University. He and his wife, Shirley, have two sons: Henry Jr. and Harlan. Address: 804 Southeastern Building, Greensboro, NC 27401

Fuller, Hoyt W., journalist, is executive editor of *Black World* magazine, published by Johnson Publishing Co., Inc., in Chicago, Ill. Born Sept. 10, 1927 in Atlanta, Ga., he is a graduate of Wayne State University (B.A.). In 1965, he was awarded a John Hay Whitney Opportunity Fellowship and spent a year travelling and studying in Africa. His articles have been published in numerous books and magazines, and he is author of *Journey to Africa*, a book about his three-month stay in Guinea. He is vice chairman of the North American Committee of the second Black and African Festival of Arts and Culture, which will be held in Nigeria in 1974. He is a founder of the Organization of Black American Culture, a non-commercial writers' workshop in Chicago. Participants in OBAC have included Sam Greenlee, Don L. Lee, Carolyn Rodgers, Johari Amini, Cecil Brown, Barbara Mahone McBain and other contemporary writers. Address: 820 S. Michigan Ave., Chicago, IL 60605

Funderburg, Illon Owen, banker, is a member of the board of directors, chief executive officer and executive vice president of Gateway National Bank in St. Louis, Mo. He is responsible for major decisions involving personnel, makes management recommendations to the board of directors on such matters as investments and loans, and maintains the bank's financial soundness and its image in the community. He joined the bank in 1966 after 13 years as a member of the board of directors and cashier of Mechanics and Farmers Bank in Durham, N. C. (1953-66). He was also an instructor of banking and finance at North Carolina College in Durham (1955-60). Born Aug. 21, 1924 in Monticello, Ga., he is a graduate of Morehouse College (B.A. 1947) and Rutgers University Graduate School of Banking (1959). He also attended the graduate school of the University of Michigan (1947-48). He is a member of the board of directors of the National Urban League, the National Bankers Association, the Cooperative Assistance Fund and the National Urban Coalition, and is a member of numerous organizations, boards and committees. He and his wife, Rosemary, have two sons, Illon Jr. and Douglas. Address: 3412 N. Union Blvd., St. Louis, MO 63115

G

Lewis L. Gaiter Jr.　　　Kenny Gamble　　　Bertram E. Gardner

Gaiter, Lewis L. Jr., banker, is president of Skyline National Bank in Denver, Colo. He was principal organizer of the multi-racial institution which opened Dec. 29, 1971. He is responsible for all operations of the bank and for its growth and development. Born Sept. 27, 1933 in Fort Leavenworth, Kan., he attended the University of Denver (B.S., business administration, 1963; J.D., 1970). He gained banking experience as a loan operations officer at United Bank of Denver (1966-70) and as a national bank examiner for the U. S. Dept. of the Treasury (1963-66) before deciding to develop ''an establishment capable of providing a means for financial stability for all races, particularly those disadvantaged because of color.'' Mr. Gaiter serves on numerous community and national organizations, including the board of directors and executive committee of the American Cancer Society. He and his wife, Sandra, have three children, Lewis III, Byron and Kimberli. Address: 1645 Arapahoe St., Denver CO 80202

Gamble, Kenny, producer and songwriter, is co-owner of Gamble-Huff Productions, Inc. and Philadelphia International Records, Inc. in Philadelphia, Pa. Born Aug. 11, 1943 in Philadelphia, he spent much of his high school career studying to be a medical technician. He received his start in the music industry as a performer and singer with various local Philadelphia singing groups. In 1968 and 1969, his recording studios were named the best rhythm and blues producers of the year. In 1972, his studios produced five records in succession, each of which sold over a million copies. For this, his studios were awarded five Gold Records. He and his wife, Dione, live in Philadelphia. Address: 250 S. Board St., Philadelphia, PA 19102

Gardner, Bertram E., banker, is vice president of urban affairs at the Cleveland Trust Company. He joined the bank in January of 1970 after serving as executive director of the Community Relations Board on former Cleveland Mayor Carl B. Stokes' cabinet. Mr. Gardner has been educational secretary of the Indianapolis Young Men's Christian Association, program secretary of the Cedar Branch in Cleveland, is on the board of directors of the Urban League, Goodwill Industries, and on the board of trustees for the Kiwanis Foundation, University Hospitals, Dyke College and the Minority Enterprise Development Company. He serves as a guest lecturer at Case Western Reserve University and Cuyahoga Community College in the fields of sociology, police administration, and urban communications. Born in 1915, he has a B.A. (sociology) and M.S. (psychology) from Butler University, he has been voted Man of the Year by the Omega Psi Phi national fraternity. Address: Euclid Ave. and E. Ninth St., Cleveland, OH 44101

Phyllis T. Garland

Erroll Garner

Arthur G. Gaston Sr.

Garland, Phyllis T., ("Phyl") journalist, is a contributing editor of *Ebony* magazine, published by Johnson Publishing Co., Inc. in Chicago, Ill. She is also an associate professor and acting chairman of the department of black studies at the State University of New York (College at New Paltz). Born Oct. 27, 1935 in McKeesport, Pa., she is a graduate of Northwestern University (B.S., journalism). She is the author of *The Sound of Soul: The Story of Black Music*, a book used in many high schools and colleges as a supplementary text in music courses. She has two books in progress. In 1962, while a writer-editor for the *Pittsburgh Courier* newspaper, she received the Golden Quill award as "outstanding feature writer." Theta Sigma Phi (women in communications) selected her for its 1971 Headliner award as one of the outstanding women in the country in the field of communications. Miss Garland is an authority on black music and musicians. Address: State University College, Black Studies Department, New Paltz, NY 12561

Garner, Erroll, pianist-composer, is an internationally noted jazz performer and innovator. Born June 15, 1923 in Pittsburgh, Pa., he began to play the piano at age three and appeared regularly, when he was seven, over radio station KDKA with a group called the "Candy Kids." At 11, he substituted for pianists on riverboats and in his early teens, he played jobs in local taverns, nightclubs and restaurants. Occasionally, he would play with a band, "faking" the arrangements, and started to acquire his unique style. Mr. Garner moved to New York in the early 1940's and won attention in night spots. His recordings came to rank among the world's best sellers. On March 27, 1950 he did his first full-length concert in Cleveland's Music Hall and has since been playing concerts internationally. Called "The Picasso of the Piano" by music critics, Mr. Garner has received many honors, including the Grand Prix Du Disque from the French Academy of Arts. He has more than 200 compositions to his credit, including: "Misty," "Solitaire," "Dreamstreet," "That's My Kick," "Mood Island' and "Feeling is Believing". Address: 520 Fifth Ave., New York, NY 10036

Gaston, Arthur G. Sr., businessman, is board chairman and president of Booker T. Washington Insurance Co. and other enterprises headquartered in Birmingham, Ala. Born July 4, 1892 in Demopolis, Ala., he graduated from Tuggle Institute. He has received honorary degrees from six colleges and universities. After serving in the U.S. Army during World War I, he set out to make his fortune. Working for the Tennessee Coal, Iron and Steel Co. for $3.50 a day, he saved about two-thirds of his pay. He also sold peanuts and began lending money to fellow workers for 25¢ on the dollar. Soon, he and his father-in-law, A. L. Smith, started a burial society which rapidly grew into an insurance company and other businesses. He started a chain of funeral homes. When he found a shortage of clerks and typists for his operations, he started a business college. He founded the Citizens Federal Savings and Loan Association to serve blacks who could not otherwise get home financing. The Gaston enterprises also reach into the motel, cemetery, realty and investment, mortuary and other fields, with holdings totaling more than $24 million. Mr. Gaston has received 66 awards and citations including honors from Presidents Harry S. Truman, Lyndon B. Johnson and Richard M. Nixon. He is active in youth work and serves on the boards of 24 public service organizations. He and his wife, Minnie, have a son, Arthur G. Jr. Address: 1728 3rd Ave., N. Birmingham, AL 35203 **See article on Arthur G. Gaston Sr. in Volume II.**

Gault, Charlayne Hunter, journalist, is a reporter and Harlem Bureau chief for *The New York Times.* Born February 27, 1942 in Due West, S.C., she was the first black woman to be admitted to the University of Georgia (B.A., journalism, 1963). From 1963 to 1967, she was on the staff of *The New Yorker* magazine as contributor to the "Talk of the Town" column and fiction writer. In 1967, she accepted a Russell Sage Fellowship in graduate social science at Washington (D.C.) University, and during that year worked with WRL/NBC News, Washington, D.C. She joined *The New York Times* in 1968 and opened the Harlem Bureau of *The New York Times* "to provide stories about human beings rather than sociological stereotypes." She also teaches at Columbia University as adjunct professor of journalism. She is married to Ronald T. Gault and has two children, Susan Stovall and Ronald Charles. Address: The New York Times, 229 W. 43rd St., New York, NY 10036

Gay, Eustace Sr., publishing executive, is president and general manager of the *Philadelphia* (Pa.) *Tribune,* a black-owned newspaper. Born May 2, 1892 in Barbados, W.I., he moved to Philadelphia in 1914. He joined the *Tribune* staff in 1926 and was secretary to the editor, managing editor, editor, treasurer, member of the board of directors, vice president and secretary to the board before he succeeded the late E. Washington Rhodes as president. He has received several awards, including a citation of merit for outstanding performance in journalism in recognition of 39 years with the *Philadelphia Tribune* by Lincoln (Pa.) University in 1965; the Carter G. Woodson Award of Honor by the Philadelphia Chapter of the Association for the Study of Negro Life and History in 1968; the City of Philadelphia Citation in 1969, and the Boy Scouts of America Silver Beaver Award in 1964. He has an honorary degree from the Pillar of Fire College and Pentecostal Seminary in York, England (L.H.D., 1970). He has served as an officer and board member of several civic and religious organizations. He is assistant chairman of the board of directors of the Office of Industry & Commerce in Philadelphia, and is chairman of the Finance Committee of the Zion Baptist Church. He and his wife, Cleoria, have a son, Eustace Jr. Address: 1250 N. 12th St., Philadelphia, PA 19122

Gaynor, Florence R., administrator, is the executive director of the New Jersey Medical School Teaching Hospitals, College of Medicine and Dentistry, in Newark, N.J. She is the only black female to head a major teaching hospital. Born Oct. 29, 1920 in Jersey City, N.J., she has degrees from New York University (B.S., 1964; M.A., 1966) as well as certificates from the University of Oslo, Norway (1965) and the Harvard Graduate School of Business (1972). She is the former executive director of Sydenham Hospital in New York (1971), assistant administrator at Lincoln Hospital in Bronx, N.Y. (1967–69) and pediatric nursing coordinator at Albert Einstein College of Medicine at Lincoln Hospital (1966–67). She is a member of numerous organizations, including the National League for Nursing (co-chairman), the American Public Health Association, and the National Council of Negro Women. Address: c/o Martland Hospital, 65 Bergen St., Newark, NJ 07107

Charlayne Hunter Gault

Eustace Gay Sr.

Florence R. Gaynor

Zelma W. George

Edward A. Gibbs

Althea Gibson

George, Zelma Watson, manpower specialist, is executive director of the Cleveland Job Corps Center for Women. She is responsible for a residential training program to prepare young women aged 16 to 21 years for employment responsibilities. Mrs. George was born in December, 1903 in Hearne, Tex. She is a graduate of the University of Chicago (Ph.B., sociology, 1924), New York University (M.A., personnel administration, 1943), and received her Ph.D. in sociology and intercultural relations in 1954 from New York University. She has been dean of women and director of personnel administration at Tennessee State University and was founder and executive director of the Avalon Community Center in Los Angeles from 1937–42. She was awarded a research fellowship by the Rockefeller Foundation from 1942 to 1944. She also participated in the Accra Assembly in Ghana, West Africa in 1962 as an expert on the role of the United Nations in disarmament. She also has lectured for the American Association of Colleges. Mrs. George is a member of numerous professional organizations. In 1971, she was named by President Richard M. Nixon to the Corporation for Public Broadcasting. Dr. George is the widow of Clayborne George, attorney and longtime president of the Civil Service Commission. Address: Carnegia Ave. at 107th St., Cleveland, OH 44106

Gibbs, Edward A., city official, is assistant commissioner of the department of rent and housing maintenance of the Housing and Development Administration in New York, N.Y. Born Dec. 12, 1919 in New York City, he has a bachelor's degree from New York University School of Commerce and a juris doctor degree from New York Law School. In his city position, Mr. Gibbs directs all facets of neighborhood improvement programs. He estimates that there are less than 12 blacks in the country in positions similar to his. He believes that his supervision of the construction of the Lincoln Center for the Performing Arts complex, and the relocation to better housing of over 6,000 families to make way for the complex were his most significant achievements. Mr. Gibbs and his wife, Dicy, have a daughter, Beryl. Address: Housing and Development Administration, 2 Lafayette St., New York, NY 10007

Gibson, Althea, athlete, defeated poverty and illiteracy to break the color bar in lawn tennis in 1950. Born Aug. 25, 1927 in Silver, S.C., she grew up in Harlem, N.Y. and was educated at Florida A&M University (B.S., 1953). In 1942, Miss Gibson won her first tennis tournament which was sponsored by the predominantly black American Tennis Association. She won the American Tennis Association championship in 1947 and held the title for the next nine years. In 1949, Miss Gibson reached the quarter finals of the Eastern and National Indoor Championships. Under pressure, the United States Lawn was allowed to enter the national championships at Forest Hills, Long Island in 1950, becoming the first black to compete in major lawn tennis competition. Seven years later, she won the coveted Wimbledon and Forest Hills championships. She has taught health and physical education at Lincoln University (1953–55), worked as community relations representative for the Ward Baking Company (1959) and on the New York State Recreation Council (1964). Miss Gibson retired from professional tennis in 1958 and joined the Ladies Professional Golf Association. She is a member of Alpha Kappa Alpha sorority and the author of *I Always Wanted to Be Somebody* (1958). She married William Darben (1965). Address: 275 Prospect St., East Orange, NJ 07017

Robert Gibson

D. Parke Gibson

Harry H. C. Gibson

Gibson, Bob (Robert) professional baseball player, is a premier veteran pitcher for the St. Louis Cardinals. He was born Nov. 9, 1935 in Omaha, Neb. He spent four years at Creighton University in Omaha, majoring in sociology. In 1957, Mr. Gibson spent one year with the Harlem Globetrotters. He has been a major league pitcher for 14 years, during which time he set many records and won numerous awards. Among his accomplishments are eight All Star Games, one Most Valuable Player Award, two Cy Young awards, and seven Golden Glove awards. In 1968, he won the Cy Young Award and Most Valuable Player award in same year. When he is not pitching for the Cardinals, Mr. Gibson is usually taking an active part in the development of the black community in Omaha. He has helped develop the minority-owned radio station KOWH and the minority-owned County Bank of Nebraska, which boasts over 300 investors. Says Mr. Gibson, who earns more than $100,000 yearly with the St. Louis Cardinals: "I believe that our (blacks') only salvation is through economic development. Green (money) is the only thing that most people respect." He and his wife, Charline, have two children, Renee and Annette. Address: 3624 S. 94th St., Omaha, NB 68124

Gibson, D. Parke, marketing specialist, is president and senior consultant of D. Parke Gibson Associates, Inc., a national marketing and public relations consulting firm in New York, N.Y. Born in Seattle, Wash., Mr. Gibson acquired his marketing skills through a U.S. Air Force on-the-job training program, home-study courses and through various newspaper and magazine jobs. He publishes *The Gibson Report*, a monthly letter on marketing to nonwhite consumers, and *Race Relations and Industry,* a monthly letter on corporate practices and policies in race relations and communication. He is a frequent contributor to business publications and is the author of *The $30 Billion Negro*, a book dealing with purchasing power and the shaping of attitudes and opinions in the black community. He has also written a chapter, "Working and Communicating with Minority Groups," in *Lesley's Public Relations Handbook*. He is a member of the American Marketing Association, the National Association of Market Developers and the Public Relations Society of America. He is past president of the American Association of Minority Consultants, an organization of black-owned public relations firms, marketing consultants and advertising agencies throughout the United States. He is divorced. Address: 475 Fifth Ave., New York, NY 10017

Gibson, Harry H. C., insurance executive, is senior vice president and general counsel of the Supreme Life Insurance Co. of America, in Chicago, Ill. Born Oct. 8, 1913 in Atlanta, Ga., he is a graduate of the University of Illinois (A.B., 1933) and the University of Illinois College of Law (J.D., 1935). A practicing attorney since 1935, Mr. Gibson, prior to assuming his present position, served as associate general counsel of the United Mortgage Bankers of America; vice president and director of Fireside Mutual Life Insurance Co., in Columbus, Ohio; commissioner and (successively) secretary and vice chairman of the Chicago Land Clearance Commission; district chairman of the American Cancer Society, and a member of the Federations Reviewing Committee of the Community Fund of Chicago. He is a member of the American Bar Association, the Illinois State Bar Association, the Cook County (Ill.) Bar Association, the Bar Association of the Seventh Federal Circuit, the American Judicature Society, the Chicago Law Institute, the National Bar Association, the NAACP, the Chicago Urban League, the United Negro College Fund, Sigma Pi Phi and Kappa Alpha Psi fraternities, and the Druids Club. He and his wife, Mildred, have a son, Edward L., a physician. Address: Supreme Life Insurance Co. of America, 3501 S. King Dr., Chicago, IL 60653

Kenneth A. Gibson   J. B. ("Dizzy") Gillespie   Nikki Giovanni

Gibson, Kenneth A., municipal official, is the mayor of Newark, N.J., and the first black mayor of a major eastern city. He defeated incumbent Hugh Addonizio by 55,097 votes to 43,086 on June 16, 1970. He was born May 15, 1932 in Enterprise, Ala., and moved to Newark at the age of eight, where he was an honor student in the city's public schools. He is a graduate of the Newark College of Engineering (B.S., 1963) and has worked as engineer in charge of the Newark Housing Authority's urban renewal projects. As mayor, he successfully mediated a teacher's strike that kept about half of the city's 80,000 public school students out of classes for two months in 1971. He has two daughters, Cheryl and JoAnne, by his first marriage. He and present wife, Muriel, were married in 1960. Address: Mayor's Office, City Hall, Newark, NJ 07102

Gillespie, John Birks ("Dizzy"), entertainer, is a jazz trumpeter and a historically important figure in the development of modern jazz. Born Oct. 21, 1917 in Cheraw, S.C., he was given early instrumental training by his father, a bricklayer, who conducted a small band in the town. At 14, he had formed his own band and was noted for his proficiency as a trumpeter. He enrolled in the Laurinburg (S.C.) Institute, studying harmony and theory. He moved to Philadelphia, Pa. in 1935 and took a job with the Frank Fairfax band, imitating trumpeter Roy Eldridge after hearing him on radio. He subsequently played with a number of other groups led by Teddy Wilson, Cab Calloway, Benny Carter, Les Hite, Charlie Barnett, Earl Hines, Coleman Hawkins, Duke Ellington and Billy Eckstine. He earned his nickname for his "eccentric behavior." With bassist Oscar Pettiford, he founded his own band in New York. The band is credited as one of the innovators of the bebop style of jazz, considered the source of modern jazz. Mr. Gillespie has recorded dozens of record albums and has won rave reviews for his many concert appearances. He and his wife, Lorraine, live in suburban New York City. Address: c/o ABC, 445 Park Ave., New York, NY 10019

Giovanni, Nikki, poet, is a writer and lecturer. Born June 7, 1943 in Knoxville, Tenn., she has published numerous poems, books of poems and magazine articles as well as given many successful concerts and lectures. She is presently an editorial consultant for *Encore* magazine, and holds an honorary doctor of humanities degree from Wilberforce University in Ohio. She spent four years at Fisk University in Nashville, Tenn., where she received honors in history. She also put in a semester at the University of Pennsylvania Graduate School of Social Work and one year at the Columbia School of the Arts in New York. Miss Giovanni is also a member of the National Association of Negro Women. She is single and lives with her son: Thomas. Address: c/o Victoria Lucas Associates, 1414 Sixth Ave., New York, NY 10019

Francis E. Gipson   Robert G. Glover   Regina Goff

Gipson, Francis E., city official, is director of parks and recreation for the City of East Cleveland, Ohio. He plans programs, prepares the department budget and administers all city recreation activities, and supervises all Parks and Recreation personnel. He was vice city manager (January to March, 1973). Born April 25, 1923 in Huntington, W. Va., he is a graduate of Kentucky State College (B.S., business administration, 1950) and attended forums and workshops sponsored by the National Recreation and Parks Association. He is a former member of the East Cleveland Board of Education. He is a member of the Lake Erie Association, Amateur Athletic Union and several other professional organizations. He is a former assistant district manager for Equitable Life Assurance Society of the U.S. He and his wife, Clara, have five children: Francis Jr., Linda, Pamela, Teresa and Constance. Address: 14340 Euclid Ave., East Cleveland, OH 44112

Glover, Robert G., chemist, is owner of the Quality Printing Ink Co. in Houston, Tex. Born July 4, 1931 in Bradley, Ark., he received training at the Printing Ink Institution of LeHigh University in Philadelphia, Pa. After receiving a certificate from there, he worked in the institution's laboratory for eight years. He also received on-the-job training at St. Clair & Valentine Co., another printing ink manufacturer. He is the only black owner of a firm which manufactures printing inks of all types for distribution throughout the world. He is a member of the Litho Club, the Craftsman Club and the Parent-Teacher Association of Houston. He and his wife, Mary, have six children: Mary, Andrew, Alvin, Shirley, Dedra and Robert. Address: 1803 Cleburne, Houston, TX 77004

Goff, Regina, educator, is a professor in the College of Education at the University of Maryland. A former assistant commissioner of the U.S. Office of Education, she was the first black ever to attain such a position. Born Aug. 12, 1912 in St. Louis, Mo., she is a graduate of Northwestern University (B.S., education-English, 1934) and Columbia University (M.A., early childhood education, 1940; Ph.D., developmental phsychology, 1948). She served as consultant for the Ministry of Education in Iran from 1955 to 1957 and has contributed numerous articles to educational and psychological journals. She is a member of numerous organizations, including the American Psychological Association, the Association for Childhood Education, International and the New York Academy of Science. She and her husband, Josiah F. Henry, have no children. Address: College of Education, University of Maryland, College Park, MD 20742

Simeon Golar

Malvin R. Goode

Rev. K. O. P. Goodwin

Berry Gordy Jr.

Golar, Simeon, administrator, has been chairman of the New York City Housing Authority since January, 1970. Born Oct. 12, 1928 in Chester, S.C., he holds a B.B.A. degree from City College of New York (where he graduated *cum laude*), and an L.L.B. degree from New York University Law School. Mr. Golar is responsible for the construction and management of low and moderate income housing in New York City. The housing authority provides housing for some 550,000 people. Mr. Golar is the second black, in the 38-year history of the housing authority to hold the position of chairman. He is the regional officer of the National Association of Housing and Redevelopment Officials. Mr. Golar has two daughters, Charlotte and Katherine. Address: 250 Broadway, New York NY 10007

Goode, Malvin Russell, newsman, is television and radio news correspondent with the American Broadcasting Company in New York, N.Y. Born Feb. 13, 1908 in White Plains, Va., he has an A.B. degree from the University of Pittsburgh and a doctor of humanities degree from Shaw University. He has spent 14 years as a newspaperman with the *Pittsburgh Courier* and 13 years as a news broadcaster with various Pittsburgh radio stations. With ABC, he is a special United Nations network correspondent for WABC radio and television networks in New York. Mr. Goode holds more than 52 awards from colleges, civic organizations and fraternal groups. He and his wife, Mary, have six children: Malvin Jr., Robert, Richard, Roberta, Ronald and Rosalia. Address: American Broadcasting Co., 1330 Avenue of the Americas, New York NY 10020

Goodwin, The Reverend Kelly Oliver Perry, clergyman, is pastor of Mount Zion Baptist Church in Winston-Salem, N.C. Born Dec. 24, 1911 in Washington, D.C., The Reverend Goodwin is a graduate of Howard University (A.B.) and United Theological Seminary (M.Div.) of Dayton, Ohio. He also has an honorary degree from Shaw University (D.D.) and a counselling certificate from North Carolina Baptist Hospital School of Pastoral Care, Bowman Gray School of Medicine, Winston-Salem. The Reverend Goodwin served as college chaplain at Winston-Salem State University and as vice chairman and commissioner of Winston-Salem Housing Authority. He is a member of the American Academy of Political and Social Science, National Association of Housing and Redevelopment Officials and Omega Psi Phi fraternity. He and his wife, Emmalene H., live in Winston-Salem. Address: Ninth and File Sts., N.E, Winston-Salem, NC 27101

Gordy, Berry Jr., businessman, is board chairman and president of Motown Industries in Hollywood, Calif. Born in Detroit, Mich., he graduated from Northeastern High School in 1948. He had 15 fights as a Golden Gloves featherweight, then served with the U.S. Army in Korea. Discharged in 1953, he opened a short-lived record store and then worked in an auto factory. He and his sister, Mrs. Gwen Fuqua, wrote "Reet Petite" for singer Jackie Wilson and the song became the first Gordy hit. Later, Mr. Gordy decided to distribute and promote his records himself. He borrowed $800 and started the Tamla record label with Smokey Robinson and the Miracles as the first group. Their record, "Way Over There," sold 60,000 copies. A much bigger hit was "Shop Around," which sold more than a million copies. Mr. Gordy formed Motown Record Corp. and signed a stable of little-known singers who went on to become famous. Among them were the Temptations, the Four Tops, the Supremes and Martha Reeves and the Vandellas. In 1970, the company moved its headquarters to Hollywood. Motown Industries, which grossed an estimated $50 million in 1972, controls eight subsidiaries, including Motown Record Corp. as well as Motown-Weston-Furre Productions, formed to produce the movie, *Lady Sings the Blues*, starring Diana Ross. Motown Records is among the top three record companies in sales volume. Divorced, Mr. Gordy has three children: Berry IV, Terry and Hazel Joy. Address: 6464 W. Sunset Blvd., Los Angeles, CA 90028 **See article on Berry Gordy Jr. in Volume II**

Simon P. Gourdine

Russell Goward

Harry P. Graham

Gourdine, Simon P., sports executive, is vice president for administration of the National Basketball Association. He serves as a counsel and liaison between the commissioner's office and the teams in the leagues and as director of player relations. He was promoted to vice president in 1973 after two and a half years as assistant to the commissioner. His appointment followed the recommendation of an outside consulting firm that the NBA be restructured. Born July 30, 1940 in Jersey City, N.J., he attended Commerce High School in New York City's Lincoln Park area and has degrees from City College of New York (B.A., political science, 1962) and Fordham University Law School (J.D., 1965). He served two years in the Army, and did a tour of duty at Long Binh, South Vietnam, where he received the Army Commendation Medal. Before joining the NBA, he was an assistant U.S. attorney and later worked in the legal department of the Celanese Corporation. Mr. Gourdine and his wife, Patricia, have two children, David and Christopher. Address: Two Pennsylvania Plaza, New York, NY 10001

Goward, Russell, legislator, has been a Missouri state representative since 1966. Born in St. Louis, Mo., on Aug. 25, 1935, he attended Hubbard's Business College, Harris Teachers College and the University of Missouri at St. Louis. He sponsored legislation which sent Missouri's first black congressman to the House of Representatives. He is also responsible for the bill which increased membership on the Missouri State Board of Cosmetology from three to five and allowed a black woman to serve on the board. This was a first in Missouri state history. Mr. Goward is also pushing legislation to require the teaching of black history and culture in Missouri schools. He and his wife, Dolores, have one son, Russell II. Address: 4015 Fair St., St. Louis, MO 63115

Graham, Harry Pierson, educator and administrator, is president of Voorhees College in Denmark, S.C. He was born Feb. 8, 1929 in Gaffney, S.C., and is a graduate of South Carolina State College in business administration (B.S., 1950), Northwestern University (M.S., business education, 1958) and the University of Oklahoma (Ph.D., 1969). Dr. Graham has served as chairman of business administration, vice president and acting president of Voorhees. He is listed in the 1971 edition of *Personalities of the South* and the 1971 edition of *Outstanding Educators of America.* He is a member of several professional organizations, including the National Education Association, the American Association for Higher Education and the National Business Education Association. Dr. Graham is unmarried. Address: Office of the President, Voorhees College, Denmark, SC 29042

Shelton B. Granger

M. Earl Grant

Rear Adm. S. L. Gravely Jr.

Granger, Shelton B., civic official, is executive director of the health and welfare council in Philadelphia, Pa. Born Feb. 21, 1921 in Harrisburg, Pa., he earned degrees at Howard University (A.B., 1942) and Columbia University (M.S., 1947) and did additional study at Western Reserve University. He has served as director of the human resources development division of the Latin American bureau, Agency for International Development, as director of the youth development division of the children's bureau, Department of Health, Education and Welfare (HEW); as executive director of the Cleveland and the Minneapolis Urban Leagues, and as consultant and professor of political science at Macalester College in St. Paul, Minn. He is a member of the National Association of Social Workers, the American Association of University Professors and the American Political Science Association. Mr. Granger and his wife, Dorothy, have three children: Diane, Shelton and Richelle. Address: Seven Benjamin Franklin Parkway, Philadelphia, PA 19103

Grant, M. Earl, savings and loan official, is chairman of the board and president of the Family Savings and Loan Association in Los Angeles, Calif. The institution has more than $3 million in assets. Born May 23, 1891 in Parkersburg, W. Va., Mr. Grant completed a second grade education before he began working with the rest of his 14-member family as a sharecropper. At age 17, he moved to Pittsburgh, Pa., where he was a dishwasher. Later, he was a cook for various railroads, including the Rock Island Railroad Company, which he left at age 22 when he moved to Los Angeles. There, he purchased a truck for $160, started his own rubbish collection agency in 1923 and sold his rubbish to hog ranchers as feed. In 1928, he purchased his own hog ranch, a fifteen hundred dollar investment that yielded $300,000 when he sold it in 1952. When a white banker refused to loan Mr. Grant money to buy a house, he organized the Broadway Federal Savings and Loan Association, the largest black-owned savings and loan association in America today. In 1954, he founded the Watts Savings and Loan Association, which is now the Family Savings and Loan Association. He and his wife, Flora, have a son, Don. Address: 3683 Crenshaw Blvd., Los Angeles, CA 90016

Gravely, Rear Admiral Samuel L. Jr., military officer (U.S. Navy), is director of Naval Communications and commander of the Naval Communications Command, Office of the Chief of Naval Operations, in Washington, D.C. Born June 4, 1922 in Richmond, Va., he is a graduate of Virginia Union University (A.B., 1948). He enlisted in the U.S. Naval Reserve (1942) and completed midshipmen school at Columbia University (1944), becoming the first black man to be commissioned as an ensign in World War II. He was assigned to the submarine chaser PC 1264, on which he served successively as communications officer, electronics officer and personnel officer. Released from active duty in 1946, he completed college in 1948. In August, 1949, the Navy recalled him to active duty, and he saw both sea and shore duty during the Korean War. He transferred from the Navy Reserve to the regular Navy in 1955. In February, 1961, as temporary skipper of the destroyer UUS *Chandler*, he became the first black man ever to command a Navy ship. Rising to lieutenant commander, he was given his own ship, the radar picket destroyer, USS *Falgout*. Two other ship commands followed. He was promoted to captain in 1967, and to rear admiral and director of Naval Communications in 1971. He and his wife, Alma, have three children: Robert, David and Tracey. Address: Chief of Naval Operations, The Pentagon, Washington, DC 20530 **See article on Rear Admiral Samuel L. Gravely Jr. in Volume II**

Curtis M. Graves

Earl G. Graves

Rev. Arthur D. Gray

Graves, Curtis M., agency official, is a training officer at the Leadership Institute for Community Development in Washington, D.C., teaching state and local government procedures. He was born Aug. 26, 1938 in New Orleans, La., and attended Xavier University and Texas Southern University (B.B.A., 1962). He was awarded an honorary doctorate from Union Baptist Bible Seminary. Mr. Graves was manager of the Standard Savings Association of Houston (1962–66) until his election to the Texas House of Representatives, where he served from 1966–72. He has lectured at numerous colleges and universities and is national vice president of the L.Q.C. Lamar Society, on the board of directors of the Black Legislative Clearing House, a member of the Urban Affairs Institute of California, the Galena Park Alumni chapter of Kappa Alpha Psi fraternity and the Catholic Interracial Committee. He and his wife, Joanne, have three children: Gretchen, Christopher and Gizelle. Address: 2021 L St., NW, Washington DC 20036

Graves, Earl Gilbert, publishing executive, is founder and president of Earl G. Graves Publishing Co., Inc., in New York City. Born in Brooklyn, N.Y. in 1935, he is a graduate of Morgan State College (B.A.), and served on the late Senator Robert Kennedy's staff as an administrative assistant from 1966 until 1968 when he formed Earl Graves Associates. His company serves as consultant on programs related to urban affairs and economic development. It also publishes *Black Enterprise* magazine which provides information on minority economic development as well as practical guidelines for black businessmen. It received the Horace Sudduth Special Award for pioneering work in quality minority enterprise magazine journalism. Active in community affairs, Mr. Graves is a member of the Brooklyn NAACP's board of directors. He and his wife, Barbara, have three sons: Earl Jr., John Clifford and Michael Alan. Address: 295 Madison Ave., New York, NY 10017

Gray, The Reverend Arthur D., clergyman, is minister at the Congregational Church of Park Manor in Chicago, Ill. He also was minister of the church from 1944 to 1952 before he became president of Talladega College (1952–62). He was minister at Plymouth Congregational Church in Washington, D.C. (1934–44) and was assistant to the president of Talladega (1930–32). Born Jan. 17, 1907 in Sheffield, Ala., he is a graduate of Talladega (A.B., 1929) and Chicago Theological Seminary (M.V.D., 1934; honorary D.D., 1948). He is a trustee of Talladega, vice president and member of the board of directors of the Community Renewal Society, a member of United Church of Christ Ministers for Racial and Social Justice and a member of United Black Churchmen of the United Church of Christ. He is a former president of the Washington, D. C. Branch NAACP, former assistant national moderator and former chairman of the executive committee of the General Council of Congregational Christian Chruches, and former member of the board of directors of the United Negro College Fund. He and his wife, Edna, have a daughter, Clarice. Address: 7000 S. King Dr., Chicago, IL 60637

Gray, C. Vernon, educator, is chairman of the Department of Political Science at Morgan State College in Baltimore, Md. Born July 30, 1939 in Sunderland, Md., he has political science degrees from Morgan State College (B.A.), Atlanta University (M.A.) and the University of Massachusetts (Ph.D.). Before accepting his present position in 1972, he was director of research at the Joint Center for Political Studies in Washington, D.C. Previously, he was an instructor at Oakland University in Michigan and at Philander Smith College in Arkansas; a lecturer and teaching assistant at the University of Massachusetts, and a research assistant at the Bureau of Government Research. He is secretary of the National Conference of Black Political Scientists, and is a member of the American Political Science Association and the Southern Political Science Association. He has been author or co-author of a number of articles for scholarly journals. He and his wife, Sandra, have two children, Angela and Michael. Address: Department of Political Science, Morgan State College, Baltimore, MD 21233

Gray, Fred D., legislator and attorney, is senior member of Gray, Seay & Langford, a law firm with offices in Tuskegee and Montgomery, Ala. He is also a cooperation attorney with the NAACP Legal Defense Fund, Inc., and city attorney for the City of Tuskegee. Previously, he was general counsel for the Alabama State Teachers Association and served as special counsel for Alabama State University. Born Dec. 14, 1930 in Montgomery, Ala., he is a graduate of Alabama State University and Western Reserve University Law School (Ohio). He was elected in 1970 as a member of the Alabama House of Representatives. He has handled many cases involving the rights of blacks, including the historic *City of Montgomery* vs. *Rosa Parks* case that grew out of Mrs. Parks' refusal to relinquish her seat to a white man and which triggered the Montgomery bus boycott of 1955–56. He is a member of numerous professional and civic organizations and a recipient of the Alabama Civil Liberties Union Constitutional Award for his support of the United States constitution. He and his wife, Bernice, have four children: Deborah, Vanessa, Fred Jr. and Stanley. Address: P.O. Box 239, Tuskegee Institute, Tuskegee AL 36088

Grays, Mattelia Bennett, educator and administrator, operates the Will Rogers Research and Development Center for the Houston Independent School District. Her duties correspond to those of school principal. She has total responsibility for academic curriculum of enrollees, staff development and management functions. She was born July 26, 1931 in Houston, Tex. She is a graduate of Dillard University in New Orleans, La. (B.A., *cum laude,* education) and the University of Michigan (M.A. special education). She is a member of the International Association of Childhood Education and on the executive board of the National Pan Hellenic Council, Inc. She is the national president of Alpha Kappa Alpha Sorority, Inc. She and her husband, Horace, have a daughter: Karen. Address: 3101 Weslayan, Houston, TX 77027

C. Vernon Gray

Fred D. Gray

Mattelia B. Grays

William P. Grayson Sr.   Bill Greene

Grayson, William Preston Sr., publishing executive, is executive vice president of Johnson Publishing Co. and associate publisher of *Ebony, Jet* and *Black Stars* magazines. He was born Feb. 3, 1914 in Jones, La., and is a graduate of Los Angeles City College (A.A., 1936). He has also studied advertising and marketing at the City College of New York, at Columbia and Harvard Universities and at Poor Richards School in Philadelphia. He began his career in 1937 as an advertising salesman with the *Baltimore Afro-American* newspaper. He joined Johnson Publishing Co. in 1947 as an advertising salesman. He became advertising manager and was promoted to vice president in 1957, to executive vice president in 1968, and to associate publisher in 1972. He supervises Johnson Publishing Co.'s New York City office and its national advertising sales as well as its sales promotion and merchandising programs. For three years, he was a special guest lecturer at the School of Retailing of New York University. Separated, he has three children: William Jr., Gloria and Geraldine. Address: 1270 Sixth Ave., New York, NY 10020

Greene, Bill, legislator, is a member of the California General Assembly (Democrat, 53rd District). He is chairman of the Select Committee on Manpower Development vice chairman of the Welfare Committee, and is a member of the Subcommittee on Higher Education and the Education, Revenue and Taxation Committee. He was elected to the assembly in 1966. Born Nov. 15, 1931, in Kansas City, Mo., he attended Lincoln Junior College in Kansas City and the University of Michigan. He was the first black clerk to the California Assembly and has served as a consultant to the speaker and as a legislative assistant to Assemblyman (now Senator) Mervyn M. Dymally. He was a field representative with the Los Angeles County Democratic Central Committee, a regional director for the California Federation of Young Democrats, a business representative of Local 347 of the Los Angeles City Employees Union, and a delegate with the Los Angeles County Federation of Labor. He is a veteran of the U.S. Air Force, a former "freedom rider" and a former field representative with CORE. He and his wife, Yvonne, have two daughters, Alisa and Jan. Address: California General Assembly, Sacramento, CA 95814

Brig. Gen. Edward Greer

Brig. Gen. A. J. Gregg

Lucius P. Gregg Jr.

Greer, Brig. Gen. Edward, military officer, is deputy commanding general of the U.S. Army Training Center Engineer and Fort Leonard Wood (Fort Leonard Wood, Missouri). Born March 8, 1924 in Gary, W. Va., he is a graduate of West Virginia State College (B.S., biological sciences, 1948) and George Washington University (M.S., international affairs, 1967). He has served since 1947 in the military and has received special military training at Ground General School, Strategic Intelligence School, Command and General Staff College and National War College. Named to this post in 1972, he is one of two blacks to be assigned as deputy commanding general of the six Army training centers in the world. He assists in the command, direction and control of the 28,000 officers and men at that military site. He is affiliated with Kappa Alpha Psi fraternity, Association of the United States Army and the Reserve Officers Association. He was awarded the Silver Star, the Legion of Merit with Oak Leaf Cluster and the Bronze Star Medal with Oak Leaf Cluster. He and his wife, Jewell, have three children: Mrs. Gail D. Lyle, Michael and Kenneth, Address: Headquarters, U.S. Army Training Center Engineer and Fort Leonard Wood, Fort Leonard Wood, MO 65473

Gregg, Brig. Gen. Arthur J., general officer, is deputy director of supply and maintenance with the United States Army. Born May 11, 1928 in Florence, S.C. he has a B.S. degree from St. Benedict College in Atchison, Kan., where he graduated *summa cum laude*. He also attended graduate-level military schools, the Command and General Staff College at Fort Leavenworth, Kan. and the Army War College. In October of 1972, he was promoted to brigadier general. He feels that he can provide inspiration, guidance and assistance to young men, and also exercise considerable influence on Army policy and operations as a result of his new appointment. Gen. Gregg and his wife, Charlene, have two daughters, Sandra and Alicia. Address: U.S. Army, Washington, DC 20310

Gregg, Lucius P. Jr., administrator, is president of the First Chicago University Finance Corporation and vice president of the First National Bank of Chicago. Born Jan. 16, 1933 in Henderson, N.C., he is a graduate of the U.S. Naval Academy (B.S., electrical engineering, 1955) and the Massachusetts Institute of Technology (M.S., aeronautics and astronautics, 1961). He also attended the Catholic University of America (aerospace engineering, 1961–63). Before assuming his present position in 1972, Mr. Gregg was a U.S. Air Force pilot and aircraft commander (1955–59), a research scientist at the Massachusetts Institute of Technology (1960–61), an Air Force research administrator (1961–65), an associate dean of sciences at Northwestern University (1965–69), and program officer of the Alfred P. Sloan Foundation (1969–72). He has received numerous awards and citations from civic, fraternal and scientific organizations. He and his wife, Doris, have a son, Perry III. Address: One First National Plaza, Chicago, IL 60605

R. C. (Dick) Gregory

Sister M. de Porres Grey

Roosevelt Grier

Gregory, Dick (Richard Claxton), entertainer, is a nationally famous comedian and social satirist who has identified himself closely with civil rights activism. Born Oct. 12, 1932 in St. Louis, Mo., he attended Southern Illinois University in Carbondale before moving to Chicago to seek a career on the stage. In 1958, he gave five dollars to the master of ceremonies at a South Side nightclub to let him perform onstage, and his career as a stand-up comedian was launched. Success came quickly and he has been featured in the major nightclubs of the nation, on countless television shows and in concert halls, with a style of humor often described as "cerebral." Much of his material contains biting social commentary, a reflection of Mr. Gregory's intimate involvement with civil rights. He has worked closely with a number of civil rights groups, including SNCC and CORE. He also has been involved in the anti-war movement for many years. In 1966, he ran unsuccessfully for mayor of Chicago and in 1968 was a candidate for U.S. president on the Peace and Freedom Party ticket. Mr. Gregory has made a number of comedy recordings, including *Dick Gregory in Living Black and White, Dick Gregory East and West, Dick Gregory at Kent State* and others. His books include *Nigger, From the Back of the Bus, Write Me In, The Shadow That Scares Me.* He and his wife, Lillian, have nine children: Michele, Lynne, Paula, Pamela, Stephanie, Gregory, Miss, Christian and Ayanna. Address: 1415 E. 55th St., Chicago, IL 60615

Grey, Sister M. Martin de Porres, administrator, is executive director of the National Black Sisters' Conference, the only national organization of black nuns, with headquarters in Pittsburgh, Pa. Born in Sewickley, Pa., she has degrees from Mount Mercy College in Pittsburgh (M.A.), Antioch-Putnam Graduate School of Education in Washington, D.C. (M.A.) and the University of Pittsburgh (Ph.D.). Sister Grey's administrative responsibilities include the publication of the conference's quarterly. She is involved with an annual education conference, an educational program for developing community schools, an annual socio-religious retreat, a curriculum development for black schools, a prison reform program and a black political agenda. She is a member of the National Committee of Black Churchmen, the Pontifical Committee on Peace and Justice, Afro-American Educators Association and the World Council of Churches. Address: 3333 Fifth Ave., Pittsburgh, PA 15213

Grier, Roosevelt ("Rosey"), entertainer, is a television and film actor as well as a singer and nightclub entertainer. He was born in Cuthbert, Ga. and grew up in Roselle, N.J. He is probably best remembered for his professional football career with the New York Giants and the Los Angeles Rams, from 1955 until 1967. After a serious knee injury, he terminated his football career and turned to the world of entertainment. He has written, published and recorded more than twenty songs and has appeared on numerous television shows and in a number of movies. When he is not concentrating on his career in show business, he is actively involved in politics and is on the board of directors of Direction Sports and the Joseph Kennedy Foundation for Retarded Children. Address: Metro-Goldwyn-Mayer Inc., 10202 W. Washington Blvd., Culver City, CA 90230

Booker Griffin

Gilroye A. Griffin

Junius Griffin

Griffin, Booker, broadcast journalist, is news director and community relations director at radio station KGFJ in Los Angeles, Calif. He reviews news to be broadcast, designs and executes various community relations programs and coordinates public service announcements and the station's services to listeners. He is an extraordinarily popular news commentator and public speaker in the Los Angeles area, and is a feature columnist for the *Los Angeles Sentinel* newspaper. Born Oct. 1, 1938 in Gary, Ind., he has a B.A. degree in psychology from Baldwin-Wallace College in Ohio. He and his wife, Lynette, live in Los Angeles. Address: KGFJ, 5900 Wilshire Blvd., Los Angeles, CA 90036

Griffin, Gilroye A. Jr., corporate executive, is vice president of corporate administration and associate counsel at Kenyon & Eckhardt, an advertising agency in New York, N.Y. He was born in Columbia, S.C. on Aug. 22, 1938. He is a graduate of Dartmouth College (B.A., English, 1959) and Columbia University (J.D., 1962). In his position with Kenyon & Eckhardt, he directs the operations of the company's service departments for all of its domestic offices, serves as associate counsel in all of the company's corporate and advertising legal matters (both international and domestic), and acts as director of personnel for all domestic, Canadian and Mexican offices. In September, 1972, he was elected to the corporate board of directors of his firm. He and his wife, Judith, have a son, Gilroye III. Address: 200 Park Ave., New York, NY 10017

Griffin, Junius, public relations executive, is president of Junius Griffin Associates in Hollywood, Calif. Established by Mr. Griffin early in 1972, the firm provides public relations, corporate communications and advertising services. Mr. Griffin was an executive of Motown Records for five years and served for two years as director of public relations at SCLC and as public relations aide to Dr. Martin Luther King Jr. He is a former reporter for *Stars & Stripes*, the *Associated Press* and the *New York Times*, and was city editor of the *Atlanta Daily World*. Born Jan. 13, 1929 in Stonega, Va., Mr. Griffin attended Bluefield State Coll., Wayne State Univ., St. Sophia Univ. in Tokyo, Japan, the Navy School of Journalism at Great Lakes, Ill., and the Armed Forces Information School. He is pres. of the Beverly Hills-Hollywood Branch NAACP and has crusaded against "blaxploitation" by the motion picture industry. He is a mem. of the bd. of trustees and bd. of gov. of the Martin Luther King Center for Social Change and a mem. of the bd. of the U.S. Comm. on Civil Rights. He and his wife, Ragni, have two children, Zenzi and Pamela. Address: 1800 N. Highland Ave., Hollywood, CA 90028

H

Frank W. Hale Jr.

Rev. Phale D. Hale

Alex Haley

Hale, Frank W. Jr., administrator, is associate dean, Ohio State University Graduate School. He is in charge of admissions, fellowships and minority affairs. He is chairman of the school's fellowship committee. Born March 24, 1927 in Kansas City, Mo., he is a graduate of the University of Nebraska (A.B., 1950; and M.A., 1951) and Ohio State University (Ph.D., 1955). He did post-graduate study in English literature at the University of London (England). He was president of Oakwood College in Huntsville, Ala. (1966–71) after serving as public relations director (1952–53), head of the speech department (1955–59) and assistant to the president (1957–59). He was chairman of the department of English at Central State College (1959–66). He has been a director of numerous professional groups, and is a member of the American Association of Colleges and Universities, the American Association of School Administrators, and other organizations. He has written a number of articles for various publications and in 1971 was named one of the Outstanding Educators of America. He and his wife, Ruth, have three children: Ruth, Frank and Sherilyn. Address: 164 W. 19th Ave., Columbus, OH 43210

Hale, The Reverend Phale D., legislator, is a member of the Ohio House of Representatives and is pastor of Union Grove Baptist Church in Columbus, Ohio. Born July 16, 1915 in Starksville, Miss., he is a graduate of Morehouse College (A.B.), Gammon Theological Seminary (M.Div.) and the Cincinnati Baptist Theological Seminary (D.D.). The Reverend Hale believes that politics should be, an extension of his ministry to people. He says "there is no conflict between the two." He has served as pastor of Union Grove Baptist Church for 22 years, and is in his fourth term as a member to the Ohio House of Representatives. He is also the chairman of the Health & Welfare Committee. He and his wife, Cleo, have four children: Phale Jr., Janice Ellen, Marna A. and Hilton Ingram. Address: 266 N. Champion Ave., Columbus, OH 43203

Haley, Alex, author-lecturer, is the author of the best-selling book, *The Autobiography of Malcolm X* and numerous magazine articles. Born Aug. 11, 1921 in Ithaca, N.Y., he attended college two years before serving 20 years in the United States Coast Guard. He taught himself writing while in the USCG and spent a few years struggling as a professional writer after his retirement in 1959. He is currently writing a book, *Roots*, based on his seven-year tracing of his own maternal family lineage back to the Gambia (Africa) village from which his seventh-generation forefather (Kunta Kinte) came to the United States as a slave in 1767. Mr. Haley is founder and president of the Kinte Foundation in Washington, D.C., devoted to creating the nation's first black genealogical library. He is also a founding member of the Black Academy of Arts and Letters. He is divorced and has three children: Lydia, William and Cindy. Address: P. O. Box 2907, San Francisco, CA 94126

Hall, Kenneth, legislator, is an Illinois state senator from the 54th District (East St. Louis). Born May 20, 1915 in East St. Louis, he attended Park College in East St. Louis. He was appointed to the State Rent Control Board by Governor Adlai Stevenson in 1949. He was Commissioner of the St. Clair County Housing Authority for five years and served as chairman for three years. He was elected commissioner of the East St. Louis Park District in 1959. He is a former investigator in the St. Clair County Sheriff's Department and is a licensed insurance broker. Since 1954 he has been a member of the St. Clair County Welfare Service Committee. He is chairman of East St. Louis City Democratic Central Committee. He served two terms in the state House of Representatives before his election to the Senate in 1970. He is a member of the NAACP and the Knights of Columbus. He and his wife, Anne, have four sons: Kenneth Jr., Maurice, Mark and Thomas. Address: Illinois General Assembly, Springfield, IL 62706

Hamer, Fannie Lou, rights activist, is the founder of Freedom Farm Cooperative and a garment factory which provide food and jobs for residents of Ruleville, Miss. She is vice chairman of the Mississippi Freedom Democratic Party and a member of the Democratic National Committee for Mississippi. Born Oct. 6, 1917 in Ruleville, she was the youngest of 20 children in a poverty-stricken family. The lot of poor blacks in Mississippi was hers until well beyond childhood. In the early 1960s, her efforts at voter registration brought arrests, evictions, threatening phone calls, abusive letters and beatings. Though the delegation she led to the 1964 Democratic National Convention failed in its effort to be seated, she was one of 22 blacks in the 44-member group that unseated the regular (white) Mississippi delegation at the 1968 convention in Chicago, Ill. She has achieved housing, jobs, a new security and a new dignity for many in Mississippi. Address: 626 E. Lafayette St., Ruleville, MS 38771 **See article on Fannie Lou Hamer in Volume II**

Hamilton, Arthur N., jurist, is an associate judge of the Circuit Court of Cook County, Ill. He also serves as first vice president of the 6th Ward of the Cook County Democratic organization. Born Jan. 21, 1917 in New Orleans, La., he attended Wayne State University in Detroit, Mich. and Kent College of Law (LL.B., 1950) in Chicago. He was admitted to the Illinois and Federal Bar in 1950, and was in the general practice of law (1950–58). He was assistant corporation counsel for the City of Chicago (1953–55) and assistant Cook County state's attorney (1955–56). After returning to his law practice (1956–69), he became special assistant Illinois attorney general (1968-69) and first assistant general attorney of the Chicago Park District (1969–71). He became a circuit judge in 1971. He is president of the board of Parkway Community House in Chicago, a member of the board of the Church Federation of Chicago, and is active in a number of political and civic groups. He and his wife, Mary, have two children. Address: Cook County Circuit Court, Civic Center, Chicago, IL 60601

Kenneth Hall   Fannie Lou Hamer   Arthur N. Hamilton

Hamilton, Charles V., educator, is professor of government and Ford Foundation professor of urban politics in the department of political science at Columbia University in New York, N.Y., a position to which he was appointed in 1969. Born Oct. 29, 1929 in Muskogee, Okla. he has degrees from Roosevelt University (B.A., 1951), Loyola University School of Law (J.D., 1954) and the University of Chicago (M.A., 1957 and Ph.D., 1964). Two of Dr. Hamilton's four published books are *The Black Preacher in America* (1972) and *The Black Experience in American Politics* (1973). His many articles have appeared in leading publications including *The New York Times* magazine, *Harvard Educational Review, the Phi Delta Kappan* and *Black World.* He previously taught at Albany State College, Tuskegee Institute, Roosevelt University, Rutgers-Newark State University and Lincoln University. He is the recipient of many awards and is vice president of the American Political Science Association and a Russell Sage Foundation visiting scholar. Dr. Hamilton and his wife, Dona, have two children, Valli and Carol. Address: Columbia University, New York, NY 10027

Hamilton, Grace T., legislator, has been a member of the Georgia House of Representatives (112th District in Atlanta) since 1966. She is also vice chairman of the Atlanta Charter Commission. Born Feb. 10, 1907 in Atlanta, she has degrees from Atlanta University (B.A., 1927) and Ohio State University (M.A., 1929), and was a Rosenwald Fellow in Community Organization for Intergroup Cooperation (1947-48). She was executive director of the Atlanta Urban League from 1943 to 1961. In 1971, she became the first black to be named Atlanta's Woman of the Year in professions. She has volunteered her time to many community service organizations and has received many honors, including that of Georgia Speaker of the Year (1972) from Emory University. Mrs. Hamilton and her husband, Henry, have a daughter, Eleanor. Address: State Capitol, Capitol Square, S.W. Atlanta, GA 30334

Hamilton, Paul L., educator, is a former member of the Colorado General Assembly. He served from 1969 to 1973, representing the 9th District (Denver), but decided not to seek reelection. Currently, he is a teacher of black history at Manual High School in Denver. He was on special assignment at the school from 1968 to 1972 to develop an Afro-American history curriculum. Born April 1, 1941 in Peublo, Colo., he is a graduate of the University of Denver (B.A., sociology, 1964; M.A., secondary education, 1972). In 1964, he taught social studies at Lake Junior High School in Denver. Four years later, he was transferred to Manual High School. When he was elected to office in 1968, he had no previous political experience, but was a community worker. He was active with the Negro College Fund, the NAACP and CORE. He was on the board of trustees of the Motivation Against Poverty and on the advisory boards of Youth Services and Common Cause. He and his wife, Emma, have a son, John. Address: 2811 Vine St., Denver, CO 80205

Charles V. Hamilton

Grace T. Hamilton

Paul L. Hamilton

Leroy Hampton   Lionel Hampton   Allen C. Hancock

Hampton, Leroy, business executive, is manager of minority employee relations for Dow Chemical Company in Midland, Mich. He acts as liaison between management and minority employees and coordinates programs affecting minority employees. He was born April 20, 1927 in Ingalls, Ark. and has degrees from the University of Colorado (B.S., pharmacy, 1950) and Denver University (M.S., chemistry, 1960.). In 1951, he became a registered pharmacist in Colorado. He has been with Dow Chemical for 19 years and has held the positions of development chemist and recruiting manager. He was promoted to his present position in 1969. He is a member of the American Chemical Society. He enjoys reading and photography. He and his wife, Anne, have two children, Cedric and Candice. Address: 2020 Dow Center, Midland, MI 48640

Hampton, Lionel, jazz musician, is a bandleader who has specialized in including pandemonium among audiences since the late 1930s. His theme number, "Flying Home," caused so much stamping of feet that it often threatened to "bring the house down." Born April 30, 1914 in Birmingham, Ala. "Hamp" attended elementary and high school in Chicago and took two years of music theory at the University of Southern California. A job as a newsboy for the *Chicago Defender* brought him his first set of drums. While playing with Louis Armstrong, he discovered the "vibes" and, after "fooling around" for about 45-minutes, mastered and played them on the now famous recording of "Memories of You." He played vibraharp with the Benny Goodman Quartet for four years and directed the group's recording sessions. He made many recordings, some of which are now collectors' items. He started his own big band in 1940, with many jazz giants as members, and during the forties and fifties was at the top of the hit charts. In 1965, he cut his group to combo size and named it the Inner Circle. Mr. Hampton has made many world tours playing to adoring audiences. Israel inspired his major work, "King David," and the 18-minute, four-part symphonic jazz suite had its premiere under Dimitri Mitropoulos. He is a member of Alpha Phi Alpha, the Elks (grand bandmaster), the Friars and the Grand Street Boys Club of New York City. His wife, Gladys, for many years his business manager, died in 1971. Address: 3808 W. Adams Blvd., Los Angeles, CA 90018

Hancock, Allen C., educator, is president of Texas College in Tyler, Tex. He was formerly dean of Jarvis Christian College and director of graduate studies at Hampton Institute. He was born Feb. 27, 1908 in Cherokee County, Tex. and has degrees from Texas College (B.A., 1932) and the University of Colorado (M.Ed., 1947; D.Ed., 1951). He is a member of Phi Delta Kappa (Education Honor Society), Alpha Kappa Mu, the National Education Association and the National Vocational Guidance Association. He is an ordained minister in the Christian Methodist Episcopal Church. He and his wife, Jewell, have a daughter, Juanita. Address: 2404 N. Grand Ave., Tyler, TX 75701

Wayman E. Hancock Jr.   Freeman Hankins   Henry E. Hardin

Hancock, Wayman E., Jr., marketing representative, is senior marketing representative in Chicago, Ill. for Informatics, Inc. of Canoga Park, Calif. The firm is a major computer software company. Mr. Hancock's job involves the sale of the Mark IV File Management System—an automatic computer programming system—to industrial firms, universities and governmental agencies. He was honored in December, 1972 for attaining $1 million in sales of the system. Born Jan. 2, 1937 in Chicago, Ill., he is a graduate of Roosevelt University (B.S., mathematics, 1960). He taught high school mathematics for two years before becoming a computer programmer for International Harvester Company and an instructor in the International Business Machines Education Center in Chicago. He joined Informatics, Inc. in 1967 as an engineer. He has worked as a salesman for the Mark IV system since mid-1969 and was instrumental in the formation of the Computer Technical School for SCLC's Operation Breadbasket. Mr. Hancock is brother of jazz pianist Herbie Hancock. He and his wife, Janice, have three daughters: Kelly, Janice and Veronica. Address: 2222 Riverside Plaza, Chicago, IL 60606

Hankins, Freeman, legislator, is a Democratic member of the Pennsylvania Senate. Born Sept. 30, 1918 in Brunswick, Ga., he attended Temple University (1947–50) and is a graduate of Dolan's College of Embalming. He is a funeral director in Philadelphia and is active in civic and community affairs. Mr. Hankins was elected to the senate in 1966 after serving in the Pennsylvania House of Representatives (1961–66). He is married to the former Dorothy Days. Address: 4075 Haverford Ave., Philadelphia, PA 19104

Hardin, Henry E., educator and administrator, is president of Morris College in Sumter, S.C. The college is a private, Baptist-supported liberal arts institute. Born in 1912 in Fort Motte, S.C., Mr. Hardin earned degrees from Benedict College (B.A., 1944; B.D., 1945) New York University (M.A., 1947) and pursued additional graduate studies there, at Union Theological Seminary and City College of New York. Previously a professor and dean of instruction, he was elected by the trustees to head the college in 1970 after the death of its president, O. R. Reuben. As dean, he also directed the college financial aid program, recruited students in large numbers and expanded on-campus and extension programs. He is a member of numerous professional organizations. His special honors include membership on the staff of the Colgate-Rochester Seminar on Black Church Curriculum in 1969, and on the President's Commission on Equal Opportunity. He and his wife, Carrie, have two daughters, Mrs. Isadora Wallace and Mrs. Henrietta Butler. Address: Morris College, Sumter, SC 29150

Vincent Harding   Inge Hardison   Nathan Hare

Harding, Vincent, educator and administrator, is executive director of the Institute of the Black World in Atlanta, Ga. A writer and historian, he is completing a book-length study of black radicals from the first slave ships to the present. Born July 25, 1931 in New York, N.Y., he graduated *cum laude* from City College of New York (B.A., history, 1952); Columbia University (M.S., journalism, 1953) and the University of Chicago (M.A., 1956; Ph.D., history, 1965). His academic honors include the 1970 Harbison Award for gifted teaching, and research and writing grants from various foundations and scholarly organizations. Dr. Harding was a part-time lay pastor first for a Seventh Day Adventist Mission Church and later for the Woodlawn Mennonite Church, both in Chicago, Ill. During the civil rights movement, he was a negotiator and troubleshooter in the South with various movement organizations. Dr. Harding chaired the department of history and sociology at Spelman College (1965–69) and was chairman of the Advisory-Coordinating Committee for "Black Heritage" (1968–69), a series of 108 CBS television programs on Afro-American history. A former director of the Martin Luther King Jr. Library in Atlanta, Dr. Harding has written numerous books and essays, and more than 150 articles, fiction, reviews and poetry have appeared in major publications. He and his wife, Rosemarie, have two children, Rachel and Johnathan. Address: 87 Chestnut St., SW, Atlanta, GA 30314

Hardison, Inge, painter and sculptress, is one of America's most distinguished artists. In 1963, she began the first of an on-going series of historical portraits, "Negro Giants in History." Her inspiration came from her discovery that there was only one black in the Hall of Fame of Great Americans at New York University. Mrs. Hardison's six-inch busts of black leaders in cast stone include Dr. W. E. B. Du Bois, Dr. Martin Luther King Jr., Dr. Mary McLeod Bethune, Frederick Douglass, Harriet Tubman and a prototype black slave woman. A native of Portsmouth, Va., she studied under sculptor William Zorach at the Art Students League in New York. Before she discovered sculpture and her gift for the art, she worked as a photographer, actress, artist's model and teacher. Most of her work has been in the field of portraiture. Chidren are her favorite subjects. She is a founding member of the Black Academy of Arts and Letters. She has a daughter, Yolande. Address: 444 Central Park West, New York, NY 10025

Hare, Nathan, publishing executive, is founder and president of The Black World Foundation, publisher of *The Black Scholar* and author of *The Black Anglo-Saxon*. Born April 9, 1933 in Slick, Okla., he is a graduate of Langston University (B.A., 1954) and the University of Chicago (M.A., 1957; Ph.D., 1962). He has written articles in such periodicals as *Newsweek, Black World, Saturday Review, The Times of London, Ramparts* and *Social Education*. He has taught at Howard University, Virginia State College and San Francisco College, where he was the first coordinator to be hired for a black studies program in the United States. He is a member of the National Steering Committee of the African Liberation Day demonstration and an honorary member of the African People's Party. In addition to teaching, Dr. Hare has been a professional boxer under the name of Nat Harris. He is married to Julia Hare. Address: 2658 Bridgeway, Sausalito, CA 94965

Judge R. A. Harewood

William J. Hargrave Jr.

J. Archie Hargraves

John H. Harmon

Harewood, Richard Alexander, jurist, is a judge in the criminal division of the Circuit Court of Cook County (Ill.). Born June 25, 1900 in Barbados, W.I., he is a graduate of the University of Illinois (A.B., 1922) and the University of Chicago (J.D., 1926). He has been a resident of the United States since 1907 and became a naturalized citizen in 1918. He was assistant corporation counsel for the city of Chicago (1941–44), assistant state's attorney for Cook County (1944–47), a member of the Illinois House of Representatives (1937–38 and 1957–58), and a judge of the Cook County Superior Court (1962–70). He has been a trustee of the University of Illinois since 1959. He is a member of the Chicago, Cook County and American bar associations and the Law Institute. He and his wife, Patricia, live in Chicago. Address: Civic Center, Chicago, IL 60601

Hargrave, William J. Jr., legislator, is the only black member of the Iowa House of Representatives. He is a Democrat from Iowa City. Born July 11, 1930, in Clarksdale, Miss., he attended Lindbloom High School in Chicago and is studying at the University of Iowa. He is a licensed private investigator and was a Johnson County (Iowa City) deputy sheriff (1969–72). He is the owner-operator of Bill's Engraving and is a public relations analyst. He and his wife, Edith, have five children: Christine, Carlon, Clayton, Craig and Constance. Address: State House, Des Moines, IA 50319

Hargraves, J. Archie., educator, is president of Shaw University at Raleigh, N.C. Born Aug. 2, 1916 in Greensboro, N.C., he has degrees from North Carolina A & T State University (B.S., *magna cum laude*), Union Theological Seminary (B.D.), and Chicago Theological Seminary (D. Rel.). Dr. Hargraves was chairman of the Black Center for Strategy and Community Development, Inc. in Chicago 1969-71. A minister, he has served many church and community related agencies in areas of public relations, advertising, feature writing and lecturing. Among his many publications are *Stop Pussyfooting Through a Revolution*, *A New Kind of Cat*, *The Fire Right Here*, *The Meaning of Black Power*, and *Blackening Theological Education*. He is the founder of Halfway House in Brooklyn, N.Y.; the Bedford Area Project; the East Harlem Narcotics Program and has been a consultant for the National Commission on the Causes and Prevention of Violence. Dr. Hargraves has received the Saslow Medal in Social Sciences, and has honors from Kappa Phi Kappa National Debating Sciences, Gamma Tau Honor Society, and was awarded Doctor of Humane Letters from Lewis and Clark College. He and his wife, Inez, have a daughter, Jamet Delmanda. Address: 118 E. South St., Raleigh, NC 27602

Harmon, John H., economist, is founder and executive director of the Afro-American Cultural Foundation in White Plains, N.Y. The foundation is "an independent black voice formed to eliminate the distorted protrayal of black people, their history, culture, and economics. . . ." Born Sept. 15, 1906 in Houston, Tex., he has degrees from Howard University (B.S., commerce, 1926) and Columbia University (M.S., 1927). During World War II, he was a price economist in charge of price control programs for the New York Region. He is a former executive director of the National Business League and was owner (until 1971) of his own business, Harmon Information and Business Service, Inc. In 1931, he co-authored (with Dr. Carter G. Woodson) *The Negro As A Business Man*. Mr. Harmon is chairman of the Greater N.Y. Council for the Association for the Study of Negro Life and History, and is a member of the organization's executive council. He and his wife, Susie, have seven children: John III, William, Ronald, George, Robert, Gregory and Cornelia. Address: 394 Tarrytown Rd., White Plains, NY 10607

David B. Harper

Charles F. Harris

George S. Harris

Harper, David B., banker, is president of the First Independence National Bank in Detroit, Mich. The bank has $28 million in assets. Born Dec. 3, 1933 in Indianapolis, Ind., he studied accounting at Arizona State University (B.A., 1963) and business administration at Golden Gate College in San Francisco (M.A., 1968). He has an honorary degree from Eastern Michigan University (LL.D., 1970). He was the jury foreman (and the only black juror) in the widely-publicized 1968 trial of Black Panther Party leader Huey P. Newton in California. At age 14, he entered St. Augustine Seminary (Miss.) and studied five years for the priesthood. He left the seminary to study at Arizona State University but entered the U. S. Air Force after one year. He returned to ASU after completing military service and graduated in 1963. He was an operations and lending officer at Bank of America in San Francisco before moving to Detroit to organize (with 20 others) First Industrial Bank. A widower, he is the father of seven children: Daniel, Sharon, Ralph, Wanda, Lydia, Carol and David. Address: 234 State St., Detroit, MI 48226

Harris, Charles F., publishing executive, is executive director of Howard University Press in Washington, D.C. Born Jan. 3, 1934 in Portsmouth, Va., he is a graduate of Virginia State College (B.A., history, 1955) and did postgraduate work in statistics and economics at New York University. In 1956, he became one of the first blacks to work for a major publishing firm in an administrative or editorial capacity when he joined Doubleday and Co. in New York City as a research analyst. Promoted to editor in 1960, he originated Zenith Books, the first series to present minority histories for both the educational and general markets. He was vice president and general manager of Portal Press, a subsidiary of John Wiley and Sons in New York City, and, later, a senior editor at Random House (also in New York City), where he began *Amistad*, a paperback periodical designed to develop a multi-disciplinary approach to black studies. Since assuming his post at Howard in 1971, he has been responsible for developing the country's only black university publishing program. He and his wife, Sammie, have two sons, Francis and Charles Jr. Address: 2400 Sixth St. NW, Washington DC 20001

Harris, George S., insurance executive, is vice chairman of the board of directors of Chicago Metropolitan Mutual Assurance Company in Chicago, Ill. He has held the position since 1971, when he retired as president of the life insurance company. Born Aug. 8, 1898 in St. Louis, Mo., he entered the real estate field in 1923, specializing in land acquisition, financing, planning new construction and mortgage counseling. In 1940, he became president and general manager of the Parkway Amusement Corporation in Chicago. In 1949, he was named manager of the real estate department at Metropolitan. He later served the company as investment officer, assistant secretary, vice president, assistant secretary and member of the board of directors. He, was elected president in 1961. He was president of the National Association of Real Estate Brokers (1953–59). He is a member of the boards of directors of the Chicago Bank of Commerce, Metropolitan (Chicago) Fair Exposition Authority, Chicago Association of Commerce & Industry and many other business firms and civic groups. He and his wife, Dorothy, have a daughter, Mrs. Edwinna E. Cuyjet. Address: 4455 S. Dr. Martin Luther King Jr. Dr., Chicago, IL 60653

J. Robert Harris II

Harris, J. Robert II, marketing analyst, is Associate Director, International Marketing Research for PepsiCo, Inc., in Purchase, N.Y. He plans and supervises surveys, polls and studies in 130 countries in order to provide information necessary for marketing the company's food and beverage products around the world. Mr. Harris was born April 1, 1944 in Lake Charles, La., and has degrees from Queens Coll. (B.A., psychology, 1966) and City Univ. of N.Y. (M.A., sociology, 1969). A member of the American Marketing Assn., he was one of the organizers of that group's Minority Employment Program, which was instrumental in the hiring of many blacks and other minority members into the marketing research field. He is also a member of the European Society for Opinion and Market Research. He speaks Spanish and French. Mr. Harris and his wife, Nathaleen, have two children, Evan and April. Address: PepsiCo, Inc., Purchase, NY 10577.

Patricia Roberts Harris

Harris, Patricia Roberts, attorney, is a partner in Fried, Frank, Harris, Shriver & Kampelman, a law firm in Washington, D.C. Born May 31, 1924 in Mattoon, Ill., she is a graduate of Howard University (B.A., *summa cum laude*, 1945) and George Washington University Law School (J.D., 1960—John Bell Larner Prize). She took graduate courses in industrial relations at the University of Chicago (1945–47) and has studied at American University. She was a trial attorney with the U.S. Justice Department (1960–61). She was associate dean of students and lecturer in law (1961–63), professor of law (1963–69) and dean of the Howard University School of Law (1969). She was U.S. Ambassador to Luxembourg (1965–67). Mrs. Harris was chairperson of the Credentials Committee of the 1972 Democratic National Convention. She is a member of Phi Beta Kappa, Order of the Coif, Delta Sigma Theta and Kappa Beta Psi. She is a board member of several corporations, institutions, etc. She is married to William Beasley Harris, also an attorney. Address: 600 New Hampshire Ave., NW, Washington, DC 20037 **See article on Patricia Roberts Harris in Volume II.**

William S. Hart Sr.

Hart, William S. Sr., administrator, is mayor of East Orange, N.J. He was elected to a four-year term and assumed office Jan. 1, 1970. Born Nov. 19, 1925 in Irondale, Ohio, he attended Delaware State College (B.S., 1950) in Dover and Seton Hall University (M.A., 1958) in South Orange, N.J. Prior to assuming his present position, he had served in the East Orange city council between 1960 and 1962. He and his wife, Gloria, have five children: Mrs. Linda Norwood, Cheryl, June, William Jr. and Robert. Address: City Hall, 44 City Plaza, East Orange, NJ 07019

Rev. William J. Harvey III

Harvey, The Reverend William J. III, religious executive, is the corresponding secretary of the Foreign Mission Board of the National Baptist Convention. He supervises the employment of mission stations in seven African countries, Jamaica, the Bahamas and Nicaragua. Domestically, he supervises and coordinates fund-raising drives of state conventions, associations and conferences comprising the national membership of over six million persons attending 28,000 churches. He was born in Oklahoma City, Okla. and is a graduate of Fisk University (B.A.) and Chicago Theological Seminary (M.Div.) and holds honorary degrees from Payne Theological Seminary and Birmingham Baptist College. His interest in the ministry began at the age of nine. He was elected to his present position in 1961. He and his wife, Jean, have two children, William IV and Janice Faith. Address: 701 S. 19th St., Philadelphia, PA 19131

Mustafa Hashim

Richard G. Hatcher

James G. Haughton, M.D.

Hashim, Mustafa, political activist, is president of the African-American Repatriation Association in Philadelphia, Pa. The goal of the African-American Repatriation Association is to "obtain land in Africa so that all African slave descendants can voluntarily repatriate there and establish homes and businesses in what was originally their native land." This program is seen as "the most viable solution to the racial discrimination and injustice that oppresses blacks in America." The association has petitioned the U.S. government to "cooperate with willing African states in any and all programs that will facilitate the voluntary repatriation of African-Americans." Born March 18, 1935, Mr. Hashim attended the Islamic and African Institute of Pennsylvania (1958–62). He and his wife, Hamida, have three children: Ishmail, Munira and Rasheeda. Address: 5119 Chestnut St., Philadelphia, PA 19139

Hatcher, Richard Gordon, city official, is mayor of Gary, Ind. Born July 10, 1933 in Michigan City, Ind., he has degrees from Indiana University (B. S., 1956, economics and government) and Valparaiso University (J.D., 1959). Elected in 1967 and re-elected in 1971, he was one of the first black mayors of a major U. S. city. Previously, he served as legal advisor to the Gary chapter of the NAACP and has been a member of the NAACP Indiana state executive Board, chairman of National Commission of Inquiry, executive committee member of National Urban Coalition, member of the board of directors of U.S. Conference of Mayors, member of the board of directors of National League of Cities, chairman of National Black Elected Officials, and co-chairman of National Steering Committee of the National Black Political Convention. He is vice president of Muigwithania, a service organization he helped establish. He has received numerous awards and honorary degrees. Address: City Hall, 401 Broadway, Gary, IN 46402

Haughton, James G., M.D., hospital official, is executive director of the Health and Hospitals Governing Commission of Cook County, in Chicago, Ill. He is responsible for the administration and management of the world-famous Cook County Hospital, a 1,600-bed acute general hospital; Oak Forest Hospital, a 1,900-bed chronic disease hospital and extended care facility, and the Cook County Hospital School of Nursing. He also plans and implements health service programs for 1.25 million low-income citizens of Cook County. His salary of $67,150 a year makes him the highest paid state government official in Illinois. Dr. Haughton was born March 30, 1925 in Panama City, Panama. He is a graduate of Pacific Union College (B.A., 1947) and Loma Linda University (M.D., 1950), and studied general medicine at New York University Post-graduate Medical School (1959-60). He was a health official in New York City before coming to Chicago in 1970. Divorced, Dr. Haughton has two children, Paula and James Jr. Address: Cook County Hospital, 1900 W. Polk St., Chicago, IL 60612

Rep. Augustus F. Hawkins   Clarence L. Hayes   Isaac Hayes

Hawkins, Augustus F., congressman, has been a member of the U.S. House of Representatives of the 21st District of California since 1962. He was elected to his fifth term in 1972 with 94.5 percent of the vote, the highest percentage in the election. He was elected to the California State Assembly in 1934 and authored or co-authored more than 300 laws, including one establishing California's low-cost housing program and one which removed racial designations from all state documents. Born Aug. 31, 1907 in Shreveport, La., he graduated from the University of California (A.B., economics) and attended graduate classes at the University of Southern California Institute of Government. In Congress, he is chairman of the House Sub-committee on Equal Opportunity, and serves on the Education and Labor Committee and the Committee on House Administration. Representing a district with one of the highest unemployment rates in the country, he has taken an especially keen interest in various proposals to provide jobs. He sponsored the Economic Opportunity Act, the Vocational Educational Act and the Equal Employment Opportunity section of the 1964 Civil Rights Act. He is involved in many local community action programs, including the Southeast Los Angeles Improvement Action Council (IMPAC), of which he was a founder. He and his wife, Pegga, live in Los Angeles. Address: 2350 Rayburn House Office Bldg., Washington, DC 20515

Hayes, Clarence L., businessman, is owner of the most successful black-owned florist operation in Chicago, Ill. Operating from two shops, he serves hundreds of customers and supplies all the fresh flowers and live plants for the new Johnson Publishing Company Building in Chicago. His other corporate clients include the R. H. Donnelley Co., a large printing firm. Before starting his own business in 1933, Mr. Hayes was employed by another Chicago florist before starting his own business in 1933. He is a member of the board of directors of the Metropolitan Youth Organization and is a supporter of numerous civic organizations. He was born Jan. 7, 1907 in Selma, Ala. He is single. Address: 3949 S. Dr. Martin Luther King Jr. Drive, Chicago, IL 60653

Hayes, Isaac, entertainer and business executive, is known as "Black Moses" to his fans. He is one of the most popular singers in the world. He was born Aug. 20, 1942 in Covington, Tenn., and graduated from Manassas High School in North Memphis, Tenn. As a youth, he sang with various gospel and rhythm-and-blues groups, and played piano and saxophone in nightclubs. In 1962 he and a friend, David Porter, began writing songs for Stax Records in Memphis. Among their efforts were "Hold On, I'm Coming" and "Soul Man," written for Stax artists Sam and Dave. The songs became popular throughout the U.S. In 1968 Hayes began his rise to stardom with *Hot Buttered Soul*, a record album that has sold some four million copies. In August, 1969 he made his concert debut in Detroit, Mich. In 1971 he wrote the theme music for the film *Shaft*. He won numerous awards for the score, including a 1972 "Oscar" from the Academy of Motion Picture Arts and Sciences. Mr. Hayes is a vice president of Stax Records. He is divorced and has four children. Address: Stax Records, 98 N. Avalon, Memphis, TN 38104

146

Reginald C. Hayes

Rev. Robert E. Hayes, Sr.

Robert L. Hayes

Roland Hayes

Hayes, Reginald C., business executive, is director of public affairs at Johnson Publishing Co., Inc. in Chicago, Ill. He is in charge of all public relations and promotional activities for the company. Previously, he was a television producer-director and a public school teacher, and has been a columnist and business editor for the *Chicago Courier* newspaper. Born April 1, 1928 in Richmond, Va., he is a graduate of Virginia State College (B.S. business administration, 1952) and Chicago Teachers College (M.Ed, 1964). He is a major in the U.S. Army Reserve in Chicago. He is a member of the American Marketing Association, the Public Relations Society of America, the Chicago Press Club, the Military Government Association and the Reserve Officers Association of the United States. He and his wife, Frances, have three children: Jacquelyn, Jocelyn and Reginald Jr. Address: 820 S. Michigan Ave., Chicago, IL 60605

Hayes, The Reverend Robert E. Sr., educator, is president of Wiley College in Marshall Tex. Wiley is the oldest four-year black college west of the Mississippi River (it opened in 1873) and is supported by the United Methodist Church. Elected as president in 1971 (he was a trustee for 26 years), Dr. Hayes raised $525,000 (in gifts and grants) within 19 months to apply to a $1.2 million deficit. "Wiley College is now open because of this 'miracle,'" he says. Dr. Hayes was born on July 13, 1920 in Marshall, Texas and has degrees from Wiley (B.A., 1941; honorary D.D., 1969), Gammon Theological Seminary (B.D., 1946) and Boston University School of Theology (S.T.M., 1946). He is member of several professional organizations, including the Council of Black College Presidents. He has been a Methodist minister for many years, and he founded Chapel Methodist Church and Pleasantville United Methodist Church in Houston, Tex. He and his wife, Dorothy, have four children: Patricia, Kathleen, Laurie and Robert Jr. Address: Wiley College, Marshall, TX 75670

Hayes, Robert L., business executive, is president of Black American Travel Association, a San Francisco-based travel agency designed to accommodate the interests and concerns of the black traveler. Born in St. Louis, Mo., Mr. Hayes is a graduate of the University of Washington (B.S. political science 1960). After writing the *Black American Travel Guide* and providing a consultancy service for major airlines, Mr. Hayes, a former public relations specialist and general consultant, developed the B.A.T.A. concept and attracted a team of investors, headed by Randolph A. Hearst. Mr. Hayes, who incorporated B.A.T.A. in 1971, heads a staff of seven. The association, which is independent of travel agency status, designs tours, coordinates and provides a consultation service for conventions; offers tour and car rental discounts; and has a membership travel club and hotel rating agency. In 1972, the association received an award from the Association of Travel Executives in New York for Excellence in Research and Development of Tours Stimulating Black Travel. Mr. Hayes has a son, Mark. Address: 1347 Divisadero St., San Francisco, CA 94115

Hayes, Roland, concert artist, has been an internationally acclaimed *lieder* singer since the 1920s. Born June 3, 1897 in a plantation cabin in Curryville, Ga., he was 15 when he met Arthur Calhoun, a black pianist, who encouraged him to sing. He studied for four years at Fisk University (he sang with the Fisk Jubilee Singers), then went to Boston, Mass. to study with basso Arthur J. Hubbard and enrolled at Harvard University extension school. In 1916, he began a four-year U.S. concert tour, then went to Europe where he sang at a command performance in Buckingham Palace for King George V and Queen Mary of Great Britain, then went to Europe to study German *lieder.* While there he made numerous appearances and established a reputation as one of the world's great *lieder* singers. Mr. Hayes has appeared with every major orchestra in the world. A number of universities have awarded him honorary degrees, and he is a Fellow of the American Academy of Arts and Letters. He and his wife, Helen, live in Brookline, Mass. His daughter, Afrika Hayes Lambe, is also a concert singer. Address: 59 Allerton St., Brookline, MA 02146

Vertis C. Hayes

Eugene Haynes, Jr.

Arthur B. Heard

Hayes, Vertis C., artist, is a well-known painter and sculptor who works in Los Angeles, Calif. Born in Atlanta, Ga., May 20, 1911, he received his art training at the National Academy of Design, the Florence Kane School of Art and the Art Student's League in New York City where he was an active member of the Harlem Artists Guild and the American Artists Congress. Mr. Hayes taught for ten years at LeMoyne College in Memphis Tenn., and is the former executive director and founder of LeMoyne Federal Art Gallery. Among his sculptures are ''The Family,'' a caststone theme piece located at the Family Savings and Loan Association in Los Angeles, Calif., and ''Peace,'' a two-piece creation displayed at Harrison Ross Mortuary in Los Angeles. He was awarded an honorary bachelor of fine arts degree in 1971 by the Art Institute of Boston. He is a founding fellow of the Black Academy of Arts and Letters. Mr. Hayes and his wife, Florence, have two sons, Vertis Jr. and Gregory. Address: 5929 S. Figueroa St., Los Angeles, CA 90042

Haynes, Eugene Jr., educator and composer, is professor of music at Lincoln University (Mo.) and is internationally known as a concert pianist. He has been artist-in-residence at the university since 1960. He teaches advanced courses in piano, improvisation and music history. He also hosts a classical music program, ''The Wonderful World of Music,'' on radio station KSD in St. Louis, Mo. A native of East St. Louis, Ill., he earned his undergraduate and graduate degrees in composition and piano at the Juilliard School of Music in New York, where he was awarded the Maurice Loeb Prize for excellence in graduate studies. He made his New York City debut at Town Hall in 1958 and has since appeared there and at Town Hall. He has appeared in every major city of Europe and in Latin America, and has been featured on several television specials. His original compositions include *String Quartet*, *Song Cycle*, *Symphony* and *Fantasy for Piano and Orchestra*. He is single. Address: Lincoln University, Jefferson City, MO 65101

Heard, Arthur B., savings and loan official, is corporate secretary, managing officer, assistant legal counsel and member of the board of directors of Quincy Savings & Loan Co. in Cleveland, Ohio. The company, established in 1919, was purchased from its white owners by an all-black group in 1952. At the time of purchase, the assets were $351,000; in 1973, the assets were some $9 million. Mr. Heard was also appointed vice president of the Civil Service Commission of Cleveland by the city's former mayor, Carl B. Stokes. He was born Oct. 26, 1924 in Cleveland and is a graduate of Fenn College (B.A., accounting, 1959) and the Cleveland Marshall Law School (J.D., 1963). He passed the Ohio Bar in 1963. He is also a licensed real estate broker. Mr. Heard is a member of the executive board of Catholic Community Action Commission; trustee of Catholic Charities; member of the Knights of Columbus (Fourth Degree); trustee of Better Homes for Cleveland Foundation; trustee of the Hough Development Corporation, and treasurer of the Greater Cleveland Conference on Religion and Race. He served in the U.S. Marines (1943–46). He and his wife, Marion, have a son, Martin. Address: 7609 Euclid Ave., Cleveland, OH 44103

Dorothy I. Height

Elmer W. Henderson

Freddye S. Henderson

Height, Dorothy I., civil rights activist, is national president of the National Council of Negro Women, Inc. (NCNW) and director of the Center for Racial Justice of the Young Women's Christian Association. She has served as president of NCNW since 1957. Born March 24, 1913 in Richmond, Va., she has degrees from New York University (B.S., M.S.) and honorary degrees from Tuskegee Institute in Alabama (L.H.D.), Coppin State College (L.H.D.), Harvard University (LL.D) and Pace College (LL.D). In 1934, she was a caseworker with the New York City Welfare Department. In 1937, she began working with the YWCA, where she rose through the executive ranks to her present position. She became recognized as a social service expert and, as a result, served on numerous commissions and boards, including the New York State Social Welfare Board (1958–68), the U.S. Department of Defense Advisory Committee on Women (1952-55) and the American Red Cross board of governors (1964-70). A past president of the Delta Sigma Theta sorority (1947-58), she has written numerous articles and received 14 awards, including the Distinguished Service Award of the National Conference on Social Welfare (1971). She currently holds board membership with 15 organizations. Address: 815 Second Ave., New York, NY 10031

Henderson, Elmer W., government attorney, is general counsel of the Committee on Government Operations of the U.S. House of Representatives. Born June 18, 1913 in Baltimore, Md., he attended Morgan State College (A.B., 1937), the University of Chicago (A.M., 1939) and Georgetown University Law School (J.D., 1952). A member of the board of directors of the Supreme Life Insurance Co. of America, he was executive director of the Illinois Commission on the Condition of the Urban Colored Population created by the Illinois General Assembly in 1940. He served for nearly five years as the Chicago regional director of President Roosevelt's Fair Employment Practices Committee and became for seven years the executive director of the American Council on Human Rights in Washington, D.C. Mr. Henderson and his wife, Ethel, have three children: Lee, Stephanie and Jocelyn. Address: 1640 Upshur St., NW, Washington DC 20011

Henderson, Freddye Scarborough, business executive, is executive vice president of Henderson Travel Service, Inc. in Atlanta, Ga. The family-owned corporation grosses more than $1.5 million a year. Born Feb. 18, 1917 in Franklington, La., she is a graduate of Southern University (B.S.) and New York University (M.S.). She received her master's degree in fashion merchandising—the first black woman to do so. Her tour agency has won a number of "firsts." It was the first travel agency, black or white, to operate group tours to West Africa, beginning in 1957 when Ghana gained independence; the first black firm to receive the Africa Trophy (in 1972, for excellence in African tour production and operation), and the first to reach $1 million in volume 1970). Mrs. Henderson was the first black person appointed to the U.S. Travel Service. She and her husband, Jacob, have four children: Mrs. Carole H. Tyson, Jacob Jr., Gaynelle and Shirley. Address: 931 Hunter St., NW, Atlanta, GA 30314

Henderson, John M., administrator, is assistant sales coordinator for the Kaiser Cement and Gypsum Corporation in Oakland, Calif. Born July 25, 1942 in Bastrop, La. he attended California State College (B.A., 1967; M.A., 1972). Recruited by the Kaiser corporation in 1968, he had served as director of the Neighborhood Service Program, a large community civic service program for the city of Oakland from 1967 to 1968. Mr. Henderson is president of More Oakland Residential Housing, Inc., an organization set up to develop low and moderate income housing and create new economic opportunities for minority ownership. He and his wife, Joyce, are active in several community service groups including the West Oakland Action Committee and the West Oakland Planning Committee. Address: 300 Lakeside Dr., Oakland, CA 94612

Henderson, Lenneal Joseph Jr., educator, is director of ethnic studies and assistant professor of sociology and government at the University of San Francisco (Cal.). He directs a multi-ethnic faculty and staff and is in charge of curriculum and program development. He also teaches courses in sociology, ethnic studies and government. He was born Oct. 27, 1946 in New Orleans, La. and studied political science and public administration at the University of California in Berkeley (B.A., 1968; M.A., 1969). His Ph.D. degree in political science is expected from the University of California (Berkeley) late in 1973. He was dean of students and assistant professor of government at St. Mary's College (Cal.) and has also taught at Sonoma (Cal.) College, California State College (Hayward), College of Alameda (Cal.), University of California (Berkeley), John F. Kennedy University (Martinez, Cal.) and Xavier University in New Orleans. He has served as a consultant to the Joint Center for Political Studies in Washington, D.C. He is author of an anthology, *Black Political Life in the United States.* He is a member of many professional and civic groups. He and his wife, Beverly, a criminologist, have a son Anthony. Address: 2130 Fulton St., San Francisco, CA 94117

Henderson, Vivian Wilson, educator, is president of Clark College in Atlanta, Ga. He was born Feb. 10, 1923 in Bristol, Tenn. and has degrees from North Carolina College—now North Carolina Central University—(B.S., economics, 1947) and the University of Iowa (M.A., economics, 1949; Ph.D., economics, 1952). He is a member of eight boards of directors, including the Voter Education Project, the Potomac Institute and Citizens and Southern National Bank and is a member of the board of trustees of the Ford Foundation. He has served on numerous committees and commissions, including President Lyndon B. Johnson's Advisory Committee for the Study of Race and Ed. (1967-68) and Commission on Rural Poverty (1967-68). In 1970, he won the Medal for Distinguished Service (Teachers College of Columbia University. He is a member of the American Economic Association and the Southern Economic Association. He has written a number of articles and has contributed to several books. He and his wife, Anna, have four children: Wyonella, Dwight, David and Kimberly. Address: 240 Chestnut St., SW, Atlanta, GA 30314

John M. Henderson   Lenneal J. Henderson Jr.   Vivian W. Henderson

V. W. Henley

Isabel Morgan Herson

William H. Hicks

Judge A. L. Higginbotham Jr.

Henley, Vernard W., bank president, is president and trust officer of the Consolidated Bank and Trust Co. in Richmond, Va. Born Aug. 11, 1929 in Richmond, he is a graduate of Virginia State College (B.S.). He was hired in 1958 as one of the bank's cashiers. He later served as vice president and executive vice president before he was appointed to his present position in 1971. Previously, he was a note teller and assistant cashier and had directed the personal loan department of the Mechanics and Farmers Bank in Durham, N.C. He is on the advisory council of the Salvation Army Boys Club and is director of the Richmond Area Community Hospital. He also serves on the budget committee of United Givers Fund. He and his wife, Pheriby, have three children: Vernard, Wade and Adrienne. Address: P.O. Box 10046, Richmond, VA 23228

Herson, Isabel Morgan, educator, is a professor of education at Southern University in Baton Rouge, La. Mrs. Herson, who is a native of Baton Rouge, has degrees from Southern University (B.A.) and Columbia University (M.A., teacher education). She also studied administration at Colorado State College. She joined the staff of Southern University in 1944 as a supervising teacher and was appointed principal of the University Laboratory School, then chairman of the Department of Elementary Education. In 1966 she directed the university's effort to develop a degree program in early childhood education. Mrs. Herson is a member of Zeta Phi Beta sorority and has served as national grammaeus and as national first anti-basileus. A widow, she has a foster daughter, Robbye Lynne Thomas. Address: Southern University, Box 9823, Baton Rouge, LA 70807

Hicks, William H., legislator, is a member of the New Jersey General Assembly (elected in 1971) and is a new car salesman ($1 million worth each year) in Paterson, N. J. He was born Aug. 27, 1925 in Littleton, N. C. He considers as one of his most significant achievements his earning of a B. A. degree from William Paterson College which he attended for seven years of evening studies. He was the first black alderman in Paterson (he served three consecutive terms) and in 1970 was elected as president of the Board of Aldermen. He is a member of the board of directors of Damon House, an anti-drug agency, and is director of the Paterson Boys Club. His leisure interests include reading, music, politics and community involvement. He and his wife, Margaret, have three children, Chiquita, Patricia and Bill Jr. Address: 926 Market St. Paterson, NJ 07513

Higginbotham, A. Leon Jr., federal judge, is judge of the U.S. District Court for the Eastern District of Pennsylvania. He was sworn in on Jan. 6, 1964 and was the youngest person in 30 years to be appointed as a federal district judge. He was born Feb. 25, 1928 in Trenton, N.J., and is a graduate of Antioch College (B.A., 1949) and Yale University Law School (LL.B., 1952). He has honorary degrees from 13 colleges and universities. On Sept. 25, 1962, he was nominated by President John F. Kennedy for a seven-year term as a Commissioner of the Federal Trade Commission. He thus became the first black to be a commissioner of a federal regulatory agency and the youngest person to be named a commissioner of the FTC. He has received numerous awards, including the 1969 Russwurm Award of the National Newspaper Publishers Association. He is a trustee and/or director of more than 30 organizations. He and his wife, Jeanne, have three children: Stephen, Karen and Kenneth. Address: U.S. Court House, Philadelphia, PA 19107

Rev. M. J. Higginbothan

Higginbothan, The Reverend Maurice James, clergyman, is pastor of the Bethel A.M.E. Church in Detroit, Mich. Born June 14, 1914 in Chicago, he is a graduate of Lewis Institute of Chicago (B.A.) and Garrett Theological Seminary (B.D.). He has taken graduate courses at Chicago Theological Seminary and Roosevelt University. He has honorary degrees from Wilberforce University (D.D.) and Edward Waters College (L.H.D.). In 1973, the church was completing construction of a new $1.5 million sanctuary and a $3 million housing project which included a tower and townhouses. The Reverend Higginbothan assumed the Bethel pastorate in 1961 after pastoring churches in Chicago and Evanston. He is chairman of finance of the Michigan Annual A.M.E. Church Conference and chairman of the Fourth Episcopal District delegates to the General Conference of 1972. He is a trustee of Hutzell Hospital and is chairman of the Medical District Council, an urban renewal area citizens group which is participating in the development of a new medical center in Detroit. He and his wife, Marian, have a daughter, Mrs. Gloria Heddy, and a son, Thomas. Address: 5311 St. Antoine St., Detroit, MI 48202

Adelaide Cromwell Hill

Hill, Adelaide Cromwell, educator, is director of Afro-American studies and professor of sociology at Boston (Mass.) University. Born Nov. 27, 1919 in Washington, D.C., she is a graduate of Smith College (B.A.), the University of Pennsylvania (M.A.), and received a two-year certificate in social work from Bryn Mawr and Radcliffe colleges (Ph.D.). Dr. Hill, a member of Phi Beta Kappa, has received an honorary degree from Southeastern University. Her career as an educator has been duly recognized by Smith College (Alumnae Medal, 1971) and by her membership in numerous professional organizations including the International African Institute, American Sociological Society and the Black Academy of Arts and Letters. Mrs. Hill and her husband, Dr. Henry A. Hill, have a son, Anthony. Address: 138 Mountfort St., Brookline, MA 02146

Bobby L. Hill

Hill, Bobby L., legislator, is a member of the Georgia General Assembly representing the 94th District in Savannah, Ga. He serves on the education, judiciary and welfare committees. He is also an attorney with the law firm of Hill, Jones and Farrington. Mr. Hill was born in Athens, Ga. and is a graduate of Savannah State College (B.S., 1963); Howard University School of Law (J.D., 1966). He is a member of the National Assembly for Social Policy and Development; a member of the Savannah Area Chamber of Commerce; a member of the State Advisory Board and a former youth field director for Region V of the NAACP. Mr. Hill and his wife, Dolores, have one son: Ashley Conrad. Address: 208 E. 34th St., Savannah, GA 31401

Carl M. Hill

Hill, Carl M., educator, has been president of Kentucky State University in Frankfort since 1962. Under his administration, the college attained university status with an enrollment increase from less than 600 to almost 2,000. He was born in Norfolk, Va., and is a graduate of Hampton Institute (B.S., 1931) and Cornell University (M.S., 1935; Ph.D., 1941). He also studied at the University of Pennsylvania. He is the author of some 32 research papers which have been cited in three textbooks. Dr. Hill has taught at Hampton Institute (1931–34), North Carolina A&T College (1941–44) and Tennessee A&I State University (1944–62), where he was Dean of the Faculty, and Dean of the School of Arts and Sciences from 1958. He is a member of 12 national academic organizations, of 17 boards and commissions, and was in 1962 one of six recipients of the Manufacturing Chemists Association award of excellence in college chemistry teaching, and the American Association of School Administrators. Dr. Hill and his wife, Helen, have two children: Mrs. Doris H. McGhee and Ernest C. Rose. Address: Kentucky State University, Frankfort, KY 40601

Natalie Hinderas

Hinderas, Natalie, concert pianist, is one of the most distinguished international artists. During 1972 she played a series of concerts with the Philadelphia Orchestra and the Los Angeles Philharmonic Orchestra. She planned concerts with the Cleveland, Atlanta and New York symphony orchestras during 1973. Born in Oberlin, Ohio, Miss Hinderas attended Oberlin College, the Juilliard School of Music and the Philadelphia Conservatory. She made her first stage appearance at the age of three, gave a full-length piano recital in Cleveland, Ohio when she was eight, and played with the Cleveland Women's Symphony at the age of 12. She has made numerous tours of Europe and the United States. Among her recordings is *Natalie Hinderas Plays Music by Black Composers*. She is an associate professor of music at Temple University in Philadelphia, Pa. She is married to Lionel J. Monagas and has a daughter, Michelle. Address: c/o Joanne Rile, Artists' Representative, 424 W. Upsal St., Philadelphia, PA 19119

Carl R. Hines

Hines, Carl Richard, administrator, is executive director of the Housing Opportunity Center in Louisville, Ky. He was appointed in February, 1972. He is also a member of the Louisville Board of Education. Before joining the Center staff as its city director in 1970, he was district manager of Mammoth Life Insurance Co. His work involves helping the poor to find better housing, and aiding minority contractors. He was born March 23, 1931 in Louisville and attended the University of Illinois (1949-50), the University of Louisville in 1954 and 1960 and the University of Louisville School of Law (1960-62). He was in the Air Force from 1951 to 1953 and served as an aerial gunner in Korea. He is a member of the Mayor's Housing Task Force, the Education Committee of the Louisville and Jefferson County Human Rights Commission, and the National Advisory Committee of Housing Consultants. He has professional licenses as a real estate and insurance broker. He and his wife, Teresa, have four children: Carl Jr., Keith, Cheryl and Cory. Address: 1111 W. Broadway, Louisville, KY 40203

Charles Hobson

Hobson, Charles, broadcast journalist and educator, is director of mass communications at Clark College in Atlanta, Ga., where he is developing what he intends to be a major training center for blacks who are pursuing careers in mass communications media. He accepted the position in 1971 after several years as writer-producer of the weekly public affairs series, "Like It Is," on WABC-TV in New York, N.Y. The show won the television industry's 1969 "Emmy" award for excellence. Mr. Hobson has been a writer for various magazines and is a contributing editor of the newspaper supplement, *Tuesday.* He has served as a consultant to the Ford Foundation on journalism education, and taught at Vassar College and the New School for Social Research. Born June 23, 1936 in Brooklyn, N.Y., he attended Brooklyn College and studied film at the New School for Social Research. He began his broadcast career with New York radio station WBAI-FM, where he worked for three years as production director. In 1968, he moved to WNEW-TV, also in New York, and wrote what may well have been the nation's first black-produced community program, "Inside Bedford-Stuyvesant." He also served as a writer-producer for the National Educational Television series, "Black Journal." He and his wife, Cheryl, have no children. Address: Clark College, Atlanta, GA 30314

Holland, Jerome H., educator and diplomat, in 1972 became the first black man ever elected to the board of directors of the New York Stock Exchange. Born Jan. 9, 1916 in Auburn, N.Y., he is a graduate of Cornell University (M.A., sociology, 1938) and the University of Pennsylvania (Ph.D., 1950). At Cornell he was an All-American football end (1937–38). He was an instructor of sociology and physical education at Lincoln University (1939–42); director of personnel, Yard 4, Sun Shipbuilding and Dry Dock Co. (1942 46); director of the division of political and social sciences, director of education and football coach at Tennessee A. and I. State University (1947–51), and social research consultant to the Pew Memorial Foundation in Philadelphia, Pa. (1951–53). He was president of Delaware State College (1953–60) and of Hampton Institute (1960–70), and was ambassador to Sweden (1970–72). He is on the boards of directors of nine major corporations and is a member, director or trustee of 23 professional, charitable or public service organizations. He is the author of five sociological studies of black people. He and his wife, Laura, have four children: Lucy, Joseph, Jerome Jr. and Pamela. Address: 270 Park Ave., New York, NY 10017 **See article on Jerome H. Holland in Volume II.**

Hollingsworth, Cecil, publishing executive, is executive vice president of the Hollingsworth Group, Inc., the firm, based in New York, N.Y., which publishes *Essence* magazine. Mr. Hollingsworth is one of the principals in the firm and was a founder of the magazine. Born Jan. 17, 1942 in New York City, he attended Manhattan Community College, City College of New York and the New School for Social Research. He has taken courses in advertising, marketing, advanced mathematics, computer science and logic. He and his wife, Patricia, have a son, Jason. Address: Essence Magazine, 300 E. 42nd St., New York, NY 10032

Holloway, Herman M. Sr., legislator, is a state senator in the Delaware General Assembly (Democrat, Wilmington). He became the first black to serve in the state senate when he won election in 1964. Born Feb. 4, 1922, in Wilmington, Del. he attended Hampton Institute and has an honorary degree from Delaware State College (LL.D., 1969). Active in state politics at the district level for 20 years, he served one year in the Delaware House of Representatives in 1963 after being elected to serve out an unexpired term. He became the first black to serve on the Joint Finance Committee in the General Assembly and played an active role in the passage of Delaware's Public Accommodations Act. He also introduced legislation for correctional reforms and training programs for welfare recipients in the state. Mr. Holloway, who is a building inspector for the Wilmington Savings Fund Society, was the recipient of the 1972 Outstanding Citizen Award of the Alpha Phi Alpha fraternity, Delaware Chapter and the 1972 Distinguished Service Award of the Wilmington branch of the NAACP. He and his wife, Ethel, have three daughters and two sons. Address: 843 Market St., Wilmington, DE 19801

Jerome H. Holland

Cecil Hollingsworth

Herman M. Holloway Sr.

Ruth Love Holloway

Donald Lee Hollowell

Claude W. B. Holman

Holloway, Ruth Love, administrator, is educational director of the National Right to Read Program, whose headquarters are in Washington, D.C. She administers a national effort to eliminate illiteracy by 1980. Her staff works with local school districts, state departments of education, community groups, colleges, etc. Born April 22, 1932 in Lawton, Okla., she has degrees from San Jose State University (B.A.), San Francisco State University (M.A.) and United States International University (Ph.D.). She was appointed to her position in 1970, and is responsible for coordinating reading and literacy programs of the United States Department of Health, Education and Welfare. Previously, she was a consultant for various local, state and national educational programs. She was a project director for Operations Crossroads Africa (1962) and was a Fulbright exchange teacher in England (1960). She is a member of various professional organizations and has received a number of awards for her work. She is married to Dr. James A. Holloway. Address: DHEW/Office of Education, 400 Maryland Ave., SW, Washington, DC 20202

Hollowell, Donald Lee, federal executive, is regional director of the Equal Employment Opportunity Commission, in Atlanta, Ga. Born Dec. 19, 1917 in Wichita, Kan., he has degrees from Lane College (A.B.; hon. LL.D.) and Loyola University (J.D.) Appointed to this position in 1966, he is responsible for eliminating job discrimination in specific public and private sectors of the southeastern region (N.C., S.C., Ga., Fla., Ala., Miss., Tenn. and Ky.). Also a lawyer, Mr. Hollowell began private practice in Atlanta in 1952. During that time, he handled a number of school desegregation and public accommodation cases. He was legal representative for the late Dr. Martin L. King Jr., Dr. Ralph D. Abernathy and scores of other civil rights workers in the 1960s. He and his wife, Louise, live in Atlanta, Ga. Address: Citizens Trust Bank Building, 75 Piedmont Avenue, N. E., Atlanta, GA 30303

Holman, Claude Wiley Bell, city official and attorney, has been a member of the Chicago (Ill.) City Council since 1955 and has practiced law in Chicago since 1934. He became president *pro tempore* of the council in 1970 after serving as chairman of the Judiciary Committee (1963–70). He is vice chairman of the Finance Committee and chairman of the Health Committee. Born Jan. 31, 1904 in Topeka, Kan., he attended Crane Junior College in Chicago, Loyola University and John Marshall Law School (J.D., 1934). He was admitted to the Illinois Bar in 1934 and was secretary to U.S. Congressman A. W. Mitchell of Illinois (1935–37). (Congressman Mitchell was the first black Democratic congressman in U.S. history.) He was a secretary of Draft Board #3 in Chicago (1940–45) and was a master in chancery of the Superior Court of Cook County (1949–69). He has been Democratic committeeman of Chicago's Fourth Ward since 1953 and was a senatorial committeeman (1950–54). In 1956, he was the first Chicago alderman to have enacted a city civil rights ordinance. He worked from 1956 to 1963 to acquire the signatures of enough aldermen (26 of the 50 members of Council) to enact the Chicago Fair Housing Act of 1963, the first such ordinance in the Midwest. In 1973, he was considered to be the most powerful black public official in Chicago. He is a member of the American Bar Association, the National Bar Association, the Chicago Bar Association and the Cook County Bar Association. He is a member of Kappa Alpha Psi. Address: City Council, City of Chicago, Chicago, IL 60602

Holman, M. Carl, administrator, is president of the National Urban Coalition. Born June 27, 1919 in Minter City, Miss., he grew up in St. Louis, Mo. He graduated *magna cum laude* with a B.A. degree from Lincoln (Mo.) University, and received an M.A. degree from the University of Chicago and an M.F.A. degree from Yale University. He is a winner of the Blevin Davis Playwriting Prize and of the John Fiske Poetry Prize. A former professor of English and the humanities at Clark College in 1949-62, he also taught at Atlanta University and Hampton Institute. From 1960 to 1963, Mr. Holman was editor of the *Atlanta Inquirer*. He won a 1962 award for political affairs reporting from the American Academy of Political Science. Joining the United States Commission on Civil Rights in 1962, he was serving as deputy staff director when he left in 1968 to join the coalition as vice president for program development. Until his election as president, Mr. Holman also served as national co-chairman of the coalition with Andrew Heiskell, chairman of the Board of Time, Inc., and W. D. Eberle, president, American Standard, Inc. He succeeded to the post formerly held by A. Philip Randolph and the late Whitney M. Young Jr. Mr. Holman formed a broad series of initiatives uniting urban racial and ethnic minorities so they could work together on their common problems. He and his wife, Mariella Ama, have three children: Kerry, Karen and Kent. Address: 2100 M. St., NW Washington DC 20037

Holmes, David S. Jr., legislator, is a member of the Michigan House of Representatives. He has sponsored significant legislation on behalf of young blacks in the Detroit, Mich. district (72,000 residents) he serves. He is a former social worker and labor union official, and is chairman of the Michigan Democratic Black Caucus. Mr. Holmes was born August 11, 1914 in Covington, Ky. He is a graduate of Virginia State College (B.S.) and has attended the graduate school of the University of Michigan. He and his wife, Avis, have two children, Patricia and Andrew. Address: Capitol Building, Lansing, MI 48933

Holmes, The Reverend Zan Wesley Jr., clergyman, is district superintendent of the Dallas-Metropolitan District of the United Methodist Church with the responsibility of supervising and coordinating 26 churches in the Dallas, Tex., area. Rev. Holmes was also state representative for Dallas County in the Texas House of Representatives until December, 1972, when he chose not to seek reelection, though he is a continuing force in the civil rights struggle in Texas. Born Feb. 1, 1935 in San Angelo, Tex., he is a graduate of Huston-Tillotson College (B.A.) and Southern Methodist University (B.D., M.S.T.) and was awarded an honorary degree by Huston-Tillotson College (D.D., 1970). Rev. Holmes has served as assistant director of the Dallas War on Poverty and was the first black to become president of the Dallas Pastors' Association. He was also the first black to hold the position of district superintendent in the North Texas Conference, and the second black to be elected from Dallas County to the Texas House of Representatives. He is married to the former Dorothy Burse. Address: 3028 S. Oakland Ave., Dallas, TX 75215

M. Carl Holman

David S. Holmes Jr.

Rev. Zan Wesley Holmes Jr.

156

Frank Holoman

Clarence L. Holte

Morris Hood Jr.

Raymond W. Hood

Holoman, Frank, legislator, is an assemblyman from the 65th District in the California General Assembly. Born Jan. 10, 1934 in McCaskill, Ark., he attended Lincoln University (Mo.) and is a graduate of Washburn University (B.A., business administration). He has taken various graduate courses at UCLA, California State College and the University of Southern California. After serving in the U.S. Army (1955–57), he acquired sales, managerial and administrative experience as a manager for Thrifty Drug Store in Los Angeles, as a pharmaceutical representative for Warner Lambert Pharmaceuticals, and as an administrative assistant to Jess Unruh, former speaker of the California Assembly. He is chairman of the Assembly's Freshman Democratic Caucus, vice chairman of the Governmental Organization Committee and a member of several other committees, including Local Government and Urban Development. He is a former president of the Medgar Evers Democratic Club, was alternate delegate to the 1968 Democratic National Convention and is affiliated with several other political and civic organizations. He is a member of Alpha Phi Alpha. He is president of Frank Holoman and Associates Inc. in Los Angeles. He and his wife, Margaret, have three children: Lisa, Rochelle and Teresa. Address: State Capitol, Rm. 4141, Sacramento, CA 90044

Holte, Clarence LeRoy, publisher, is a pioneer advertising specialist in ethnic markets and is founder and president of the Nubian Press, Inc. in New York, N.Y. Born Feb. 19, 1909 in Norfolk, Va., he attended Lincoln University (Pa.), the American Institute of Banking and the New School of Social Research, both in New York City. He joined Batten, Barton, Durstine & Osborn, Inc., an advertising agency, in 1952, and continues to work for the company as an ethnic markets consultant. Prior to joining the advertising agency, he was a sales representative with Lever Brothers Co. The first product of Nubian Press, established in 1971, is *Nubian Baby Book*, intended to acquaint black children with their Afro-American heritage. An avid book collector, Mr. Holte has a $400,000 collection of 7,000 books—acquired from all over the world—on black literature and history. His is one of the largest and most valuable such private collections in the world. He and his wife, Audrey Mae, have a daughter, Mrs. Helen Ruth Manley. Address: 383 Madison Ave., New York, NY 10017

Hood, Morris Jr., legislator, is a member of the Michigan House of Representatives in Lansing, Mich. He is one of twelve blacks elected in 1973. Before his election, he spent much of his time as a precinct delegate and campaign manager. He was born June 5, 1934 in Detroit, Mich., and attended Wayne State University. Mr. Hood is a member of the Michigan Black Caucus and the Trade Union Leadership Council. He and his wife, Beverly, have two children, Denise and Morris III. Address: State Capitol, Room 320-J, Lansing, MI 48933

Hood, Raymond W., legislator, is majority whip in the Michigan House of Representatives, representing the 14th District (Detroit). He was elected in 1964 and is the youngest black legislator to be elected in the House. He was reelected in 1966, 1968, 1970 and 1972. Born Jan. 1, 1936 in Detroit, Mich., he attended Fullerton Junior College in Fullerton, Calif. A Democrat, he is chairman of the Public Health Committee, vice chairman of the Labor Committee and a member of the Elections Committee and the Conservation and Recreation Committees. He also serves on the Urban Affairs Committee. He and his wife, Beverly, have two children, Raymond Jr. and Roger. Address: House of Representatives, Lansing MI 48933

Rev. Benjamin L. Hooks

Robert Hooks

Rev. O. M. Hoover Jr.

Hooks, The Reverend Benjamin Lawson, federal official, is the first black commissioner of the Federal Communications Commission, the agency which grants all radio, television and cable television licenses. It also regulates interstate telephone and telegraph services in the United States, and regulates the communications satellite system, domestic and international. Born Jan. 31, 1925 in Memphis, Tenn., The Reverend Lawson attended LeMoyne College (1941–43) and is a graduate of DePaul University in Chicago, Ill. (J.D., 1948). Before his appointment by President Richard M. Nixon to the $38,000-a-year FCC post for a term of seven years (beginning July 1, 1972), he was assistant public defender in Memphis, the first black judge of Shelby County (Memphis) Criminal Court and a practicing attorney. A licensed minister, he is pastor of the Middle Baptist Church in Memphis and the Greater New Moriah Baptist Church in Detroit. He is a co-founder and vice president of the Mutual Federal Savings and Loan Association in Memphis. He has been active in the struggle for the liberation of black Americans; he has served on the board of directors of SCLC. He is a life member of the NAACP and a member of the Memphis-Shelby County Human Relations Council. He and his wife, Frances, have a daughter, Mrs. Patricia Louise (Gray). Address: 1860 South Parkway East, Memphis, TN 38114

Hooks, Robert, actor, is founder and executive director of the D. C. Black Repertory Company in Washington, D.C. The company "aims at giving the black community true black images and an honest portrayal of 'back to the roots' art." Mr. Hooks was born April 18, 1937 in Washington, D. C. and attended Temple University. He has appeared in a number of Broadway productions, including *A Taste of Honey*, *Where's Daddy*, *A Raisin in the Sun*, and *Hallelujah Baby*. For the latter, he was nominated for an Antoinette Perry ('Tony') Award as the best actor in a musical. In 1965, Mr. Hooks, playwright Douglas Turner Ward and producer Gerald S. Krone organized The Group Theatre Workshop and began producing black plays in New York, N. Y. This project led to a $434,000 Ford Foundation Grant and the founding of the Negro Ensemble Company in 1967. The N. E. C. resident company became one of the most respected theater groups in the U. S. Mr. Hooks has appeared in several television programs, including "N. Y. P. D.," and in numerous motion pircures. Divorced, he has three children, Kevin, Eric and Cecilia. Address: 4935 Georgia Avenue, NW, Washington, DC 20011

Hoover, The Reverend Odie Millard Jr., clergyman, is pastor of the Olivet Institutional Baptist Church in Cleveland, Ohio, and is one of the nation's leading evangelists and singers. He was born Sept. 21, 1921 in Nashville, Tenn. and is a graduate of Tennessee State University (B.S., 1946); American Baptist Theological Seminary (B.Th.), and Union Baptist Theological Seminary (M.Th.), and has studied at Boston University, the University of Chicago, Virginia Union University and Yale University. He also studied music at Fisk University under the direction of John Work Jr. He has an honorary degree from Wilberforce University (L.H.D., 1969). He accompanied Dr. Martin Luther King Jr., to Oslo, Norway in 1964 for the 1964 Nobel Peace Prize. Since coming to Olivet in 1952, he has built a modern sanctuary, a community center and a playground. He is a 33° Mason and a member of the board of the Martin Luther King Jr. Foundation, Operation PUSH, SCLC and the American Baptist Theological Seminary. He is the founder of the O.M. Hoover Rescue Mission for Boys and is an associate national grand chaplain of the IBPO Elks of the World. Divorced, he has three children: Carole, Patricia and Odie M. III. Address: 8714 Quincy Ave., Cleveland, OH 44106

Lena Horne

Odell Horton

Norman O. Houston

Horne, Lena, entertainer, has been a singer and actress since the 1930s. She was born June 30, 1917 in Brooklyn, N.Y. At 16, she secured a job as a chorus girl at the famous Cotton Club in Harlem to help her family during the Depression. She danced and sang at the club for two years, later appearing in a short-lived Broadway play, *Dance with Your Gods*, in 1934. Miss Horne sang in Noble Sissle's band for three years and appeared briefly in the 1939 *Blackbirds* revue. In 1941, she became a soloist at the Cafe Society in New York City. In 1942, she was signed to an MGM contract and was featured in the all-black *Cabin in the Sky*, *Stormy Weather* and *Broadway Rhythm*. She was a star of the Broadway musical, *Jamaica,* which ran successfully for two years. Miss Horne also became a frequent guest on television shows and co-starred in a memorable special with Harry Belafonte in 1970. Miss Horne is a widow. She has a daughter, Mrs. Gail Jones Lumet. Address: 45 E. 89th St., New York, NY 10028

Horton, Odell, administrator, is president of LeMoyne-Owen College in Memphis, Tenn. Born May 13, 1929, in Whiteville, Tenn., he is a graduate of Morehouse College (A.B., 1951) and Howard University Law School (J.D., 1956), and has an honorary L.H.D. degree from Mississippi Industrial College. He was appointed assistant U.S. Attorney for the Western District of Tennessee in 1962 by the late U.S. Attorney General Robert F. Kennedy. He was a judge of the Criminal Court of Shelby County (Memphis) from Jan. 1969 to Sept., 1970 and is credited with creating a progressive pre-trial release program for indigent persons charged with violations of criminal law. He is the recipient of numerous awards, including the Howard University Distinguished Alumni Award, and the 1970 Bill of Rights Award. He is a member of the American Council on Education, the Association of American Colleges and Universities, the Council on Higher Education and the American Bar Association. He and his wife, Evie, have two sons, Odell Jr. and Christopher. Address: 807 Walker Ave., Memphis, TN 38126

Houston, Norman O., insurance executive, is one of the founders, the former president and now the chairman of the board of Golden State Mutual Life Insurance Co. in Los Angeles, Calif. The company has assets of $45 million with more than $1 billion worth of insurance in force. Born October 16, 1893 in San Jose, Calif., Mr. Houston attended the University of California (Berkeley) and the University of Southern California. He began his career in insurance sales in 1920 with National Life Insurance Co. of U.S.A. Five years later, he co-founded (with William Nickerson Jr. and George A. Beavers Jr.) Golden State Guarantee Fund Insurance Co. The present name was adopted in 1931. Beginning as secretary-treasurer in 1925, Mr. Houston became president and controller in 1945, president in 1949, chairman and chief executive officer in 1967 and chairman of the board in 1967. He is a member of numerous professional and civic organizations and has received some 20 awards and honors. He and his wife, Edythe, have three children, Norman B., Ivan J. and Elizabeth. Address: 1999 West Adams Boulevard, Los Angeles, CA 90018

Robert B. Howard Jr.   T. R. M. Howard, M.D.   Rt. Rev. J. L. Howze

Howard, Robert B. Jr., city official, is fire commissioner of Buffalo, N.Y. He supervises all fire fighting forces. He was the first black firefighter in Buffalo (appointed in 1943) and was promoted to lieutenant in 1951 and to captain in 1960 before being appointed commissioner in 1966. Born March 29, 1916 in Barnesville, Ga., he attended college for two years. He is a member of the Buffalo Fire Department Officer Association, Local 282 of Uniformed Firefighters Association, the New York State Fire Safety Advisory Board, the International Association of Fire Chiefs, and numerous other professional and civic groups. He is a member of the board of regents of Canisius College and a member of the Knights of Columbus (4th Degree). He was elected as Man of the Year by the Greater Niagara Frontier Advertising Club (1969), the Jewish War Veterans Post (1968) and the Amvets Post (1972). He and his wife, Irene, have a daughter, Jean. Address: 2401 City Hall, Buffalo, NY 14202

Howard, Theodore Roosevelt Mason, M.D., physician, is founder and executive director of Friendship Medical Center, which opened in June 1972 in Chicago, Ill. Born March 4, 1908 in Murray, Ky., Dr. Howard is a graduate of Oakwood College Academy in Alabama (1927); Union College, Lincoln, Neb. (B.S., 1931); College of Medical Evangelists (M.D., 1936) and became a diplomate of the National Board of Examiners in 1937. He was medical director of Riverside Sanitarium and Hospital in Nashville, Tenn. (1937–39); surgeon-in-chief, Taborian Hospital in Mound Bayou, Miss. (1942–47). He is founder and chairman emeritus of the board of directors of the United Order of Friendship of America, and served as surgeon-in-chief and medical director of Friendship Clinic and Hospital in Mound Bayou (1947–56). He is a member of the board of directors of the Tri-State Bank of Memphis (Tenn.), and Universal Life Insurance Co. in Memphis. He is a past president of the National Medical Association (1956–57) and president emeritus of the Magnolia Mutual Life Insurance Co. of Mound Bayou. Dr. Howard is a world traveler and noted big game hunter. He and his wife, Helen, have a son, Barrette. Address: 850 W. 103d St., Chicago, IL 60643

Howze, The Right Reverend Joseph Lawson, clergyman, is auxiliary bishop of the Catholic diocese of Natchez-Jackson, Miss. Born Aug. 30, 1925 in Daphne, Ala., he attended Alabama State Junior College in Mobile and is a graduate of Alabama State University (B.S., education) in Montgomery. Before he became interested in Catholicism, he taught biology and chemistry in the public schools of Mobile. In 1950, he began his training for the priesthood at Epiphany Apostolic College in Newburgh, N.Y. In 1953, he entered the Preparatory Seminary in Buffalo, N.Y. and in 1959, he graduated from St. Bonaventure University in New York. When he was named an auxiliary bishop, he became one of the few black bishops in the history of the Catholic church in the United States and the second in contemporary history. He is active in civic and religious affairs of Mississippi. Address: P.O. Box 2248, Jackson, MS 39205

Donald Hubbard

Lincoln T. Hudson

Roy D. Hudson

Hubbard, Donald, shoe designer, is employed by Cantata Shoes, a division of Latinas, which has offices in Florence, Paris, and London. He designs the Projections line. Born April 26, 1943 in Gary, Ind., he attended the Traphagen School of Fashion in New York, N.Y. At age 17, he brought sketches of his shoe designs to a Chicago, Ill. salon and the owner advised him to seek a career in New York. Taking the advice, he moved to New York City, where he was employed by a shoe design studio. He mastered the techniques of high quality design and joined Cantata Shoes in 1966. He travels between Italy and Spain, supervising manufacturing aspects of the shoes he designs. He is a bachelor. Address: 43 Bramham Gardens, London S.W.6, England

Hudson, Lincoln Theodore, executive, is vice president and midwest advertising sales director for Johnson Publishing Co., Inc. in Chicago, Ill. He joined the company in 1953 and supervises a staff of nine salesmen and other personnel. Born March 12, 1916 in Okmulgee, Okla., he is a graduate of Loyola University (B.S., economics, 1951) in Chicago and has attended the University of Chicago Business School. During World War II, he served in Italy with the U.S. Army 332nd Fighter Group. In March, 1945, he parachuted from a disabled aircraft over Czechoslovakia during escort duty on a bombing mission to Germany. He was captured and imprisoned at Nuremburg, Germany until liberated by the allied forces a month later. He won the Purple Heart. He is a member of a number of organizations, including the Agate Club and the Air Force Association. He and his wife, Chestine, have three children: Lincoln Jr., Crystal and Chester. Address: 820 S. Michigan Ave., Chicago, IL 60605

Hudson, Roy Davage, educator, is president of Hampton (Va.) Institute. As chief administrator of the college, he is responsible for 800 employees and 2,700 students. Dr. Hudson, who was born June 30, 1930 in Chattanooga, Tenn., has degrees from Livingstone College, (B.S. *summa cum laude* 1955); the University of Michigan (M.S., zoology, 1957; Ph.D. pharmacology, 1966) and Brown University (honorary M.A.) Dr. Hudson, who was appointed to his present position Oct. 1970, had previously been the first black to hold a full faculty position in the Department of Pharmacology at the University of Michigan Medical School (1965–66). He also served as an associate dean of the Brown University Graduate School (1968–69). He is a member of the boards of directors of the Chesapeake and Potomac Telephone Company of Virginia, the Virginia Peninsula Industrial Committee and the National Association for Equal Opportunity in Higher Education. He and his wife, Constance, have two children: Hollye Lynne and David Kendall. Address: 612 Shore Rd., Hampton, VA 23368

Leon Huff

Huff, Leon, producer and songwriter, is co-owner of Gamble-Huff Productions, Inc. and Philadelphia International Records, Inc. in Philadelphia, Pa. Born in Camden, N.J., he began his career in the music industry as a studio musician, playing the piano for local singing groups. He now composes and produces songs for the nation's top recording artists and his recording studios are among the fastest growing and most popular in the country. In two successive years, 1968 and 1969, he and his associates were named the best rhythm and blues producers in the country by the National Association of Television and Recording Artists. In 1972, they were awarded five gold records within three months for such million-seller records as: "The Back Stabbers," (The O'Jays), "If You Don't Know Me By Now" (Harold Melvin and the Blue Notes), "Me and Mrs. Jones" (Billy Paul), "Power of Love" and "Drowning in a Sea of Love" (Joe Simon). He is a member of NATRA, Broadcast Music, Inc. and the National Association of Record Manufacturers. Mr. Huff and his wife, Juanita, have two children, Debbie and Detira. Address: 250 S. Broad St., Philadelphia, PA 19102

Richard Howard Hunt

Hunt, Richard Howard, sculptor, is the creator of avant-garde sculptures (chiefly metal), many of which are in the permanent collections of art museums in Chicago. Ill.; Cleveland, Ohio; Houston, Tex.; New York and Buffalo, N.Y.; Milwaukee, Wis., and in Israel. Born Sept. 12, 1935 in Chicago, Ill., he is a graduate of the Art Institute of Chicago (B.A., education, 1957) where he studied sculpture under Nelli Bar. He was also an undergraduate student at the University of Chicago (1953–55). His work was exhibited in the Artists of Chicago and Vicinity exhibition (1955–56) at the 62nd, 63rd and 64th American exhibitions of the Art Institute of Chicago, the Carnegie international exhibition in Pittsburgh, Pa. (1958) and the Museum of Modern Art in New York City (1959). He has had one-man exhibits in New York City and in Chicago. He participated in the exhibition, "Ten Negro Artists from the United States," at the 1966 First World Festival of Negro Arts, held in Dakar, Senegal. He taught at the School of the Art Institute of Chicago (1961) and at the department of architecture and art at the University of Illinois in Chicago (1962). He has been visiting professor or visiting artist at seven schools, including Yale University and Purdue University (1965), and Northwestern University (1968). He has received six major awards and fellowships. Divorced, he has one daughter, Cecilia. Address: 1503 N. Cleveland Ave., Chicago, IL 60610 **See article on Richard H. Hunt in Volume II.**

Clarence H. Hunter

Hunter, Clarence H., administrator, is the director of public relations and publications at Howard University in Washington, D. C. Appointed in July, 1971, he is responsible for the administration of the university's publicity and promotion activities. Born Nov. 1, 1925 in Raleigh, N.C., he is a graduate of New York University (B.S., journalism, 1959). Prior to joining the university, he was associate director of the Washington Journalism Center in Washington, D. C., and information officer with the U.S. Commission on Civil Rights. He was a staff reporter for the *Washington Evening Star,* the *Post-Tribune* in Gary, Ind., and an associate editor with *Ebony* magazine in Chicago. He is trustee of the Washington Journalism Center and of the National Cathedral Foundation of Washington, D. C. He and his wife, Mary, have four children: Karen, Beverly, Katherine and Andrew. Address: 2400 6th St., NW, Washington, DC 20001

James Hunter

Norman L. Hunter

Brig. Gen. B. L. Hunton

Hunter, James, business executive, is president and founder of BASE Enterprises, Inc. in Beverly Hills, Calif. The firm includes BASE Publications, BASE Ltd. and Black Associated Sports Enterprises, Inc. Mr. Hunter is also the executive producer of the BASE Sports Network, which televises Grambling College football games and the show, "Grambling College Football Highlights." Born May 27, 1936 in Bowling Green, Ky., he attended Butler University and the University of Paris (France). He was public relations director for Ohio Congressman Louis Stokes during his 1968 campaign, and as a publicist for Paramount Pictures in Hollywood, Calif. In 1972, Louisiana Governor Edwin G. Edwards appointed him as a "colonel and aide-de-camp" on his staff "for popularizing the State of Louisiana" through the Grambling football telecasts. Mr. Hunter and his wife, Blanche, have three children: Marti, Alan and Kelly. Address: 8692 Wilshire Blvd., Beverly Hills, CA 91001

Hunter, Norman L., graphic artist, is art director of *Jet* and *Black Stars* magazines, published by Johnson Publishing Co., Inc. in Chicago, Ill. He is also artist-designer for Supreme Beauty Products (a Johnson Publishing subsidiary) and for the JPC Book Division. He is designer of books by *Ebony* Senior Editor Lerone Bennett Jr., and designed the highly successful three-volume set of books, *Ebony Pictorial History of Black America* (1972). Also a photographer, his work appears often in *Jet, Ebony* and *Black Stars*. A photograph he took of the late President Lyndon B. Johnson and Chicago Mayor Richard J. Daley was accepted for the Johnson Library at the University of Texas. Born Aug. 28, 1932 in Eutaw, Ala., he joined Johnson Publishing in 1955 as an apprentice after three years of study at the Society of Arts and Crafts in Detroit, Mich. He also studied at the Art Institute of Chicago. His page layouts and cover designs for *Jet* won the National Newspaper Publishers Association's 1972 Merit Award for Best Typography and Makeup. Divorced, he has a son, K. Derek. Address: 820 S. Michigan Ave., Chicago, IL 60605

Hunton, Brig. Gen. (USAR) Benjamin L., educator and administrator, is assistant director of education and training for the Bureau of Mines, U.S. Department of Interior, Washington, D.C. He administers a nationwide health and safety training program for the mineral industries and oversees all education and training efforts assigned to the bureau under the Coal Mine Health and Safety Act of 1969. He was appointed to the post in 1970. He was promoted to brigadier general June 10, 1971, and assumed his duties as commander of the 97th Army Reserve Command in Fort George G. Meade, Md., in November, 1972. A career military man, he was commissioned during World War II, and is a graduate of the Army Command and General Staff College, Ft. Leavenworth, Kan. He is a graduate of Howard University (B.A., 1940; M.A., history 1942) and American University (Ph.D., public administration, 1954). From 1942-66, he was a teacher and administrator in the Washington, D. C. school system. He has written two studies which were published by the public schools of Washington, D. C.: "Study of Selected School Dropouts, 1963-1966" in 1967, and "Basic Track in Junior High School" in 1962. From 1966 to 1970, he served both the Department of Interior and HEW. His awards include the Meritorious Service Award, the World War II Victory Medal, the American Theatre Service Medal and the Armed Forces Reserve Medal with Hour-Glass. He is a member of the White House Committee on Civil Rights and Minority Affairs and the D. C. Commission on Academic Facilities. He and his wife, the former Jean Cooper, have a son, Benjamin. Address: U. S. Dept. of the Army - Headquarters, 97th ARCOM, Fort George G. Meade, MD 20755

Charles G. Hurst Jr.

Jean Blackwell Hutson

Edith J. Ingram

Hurst, Charles G. Jr., educator, is the former president of Malcolm X College in Chicago, Ill. Born June 14, 1928 in Atlanta, Ga. and raised in Springfield, Mass., he was a high school dropout at 15, returned to school at 23 and earned his B.S. (business administration, 1953), M.A. (communications science, 1959), and Ph.D. (audiology, 1961) from Wayne State University in Detroit, Mich. He was founder and director of the Communications Science Research Center at Howard University where he was a professor of audiology and associate dean in the College of Liberal Arts (1961–69). A consultant on education and human development to a number of federal government agencies and more than fifty city and state boards of education, Dr. Hurst is the author of *Passport to Freedom* and more than 100 professional articles. He has invented both an electronic language trainer and programmed talking toys for pre-school and elementary school classrooms. The father of eight children—Carolyn, Carolyn Remel, James, Frederick, Christopher, Robert, Chaverly, and Ronald Charles—he is married to his second wife, Beverly. Address: 6855 S. Euclid Ave., Chicago, IL 60649

Hutson, Jean Blackwell, librarian, has been a curator of the Schomburg Center for Research in Black Culture since 1949. A division of the New York (N.Y.) Public Library, the center houses the nation's largest and most comprehensive collection of books, records, etc., documenting the history, literature and art of peoples of African descent. Mrs. Hutson's duties include approving all materials purchased by the center or donated to it, and establishing all policies and procedures. Born Sept. 17, 1914 in Summerfield, Fla., she has degrees from Barnard College (B.A., 1935) and Columbia School of Library Service (M.A., 1936). She has taken numerous courses in black studies and has studied American Race Relations and African Contemporary Affairs at the New School of Social Research (1948-52). She also has studied African Antiquities at the Seifert Historical Library (1951-53). She has written numerous articles and has received several awards for her work, including the annual Heritage Award of the Association for the Study of Negro Life and History (1966). She was assistant librarian in charge of Africana at the University of Ghana during 1964-65. She is a member of the American Library Association, a Fellow of the African Studies Association, and a founding member of the Black Academy of Arts and Letters. A widow, she has a daughter, Jean. Address: 103 W. 135th St., New York, NY 10030

Ingram, Edith J., jurist, is judge of Hancock County Court of Ordinary in Sparta, Ga. She hears cases involving probate, guardianship, traffic, lunacy, and the administration of estates. She also performs marriages, is custodian of vital records, supervises county, state and federal elections, and issues writs of *habeas corpus*. Born Jan. 16, 1942 in Hancock County, Ga., she is a graduate of Fort Valley State College (B.S., 1963). She was an elementary school teacher (1963–68). She received an Outstanding Courage in the Southern Political Arena plaque from the Atlanta Branch NAACP (1969) and was selected as 1972 Woman of the Year by the *Mirror* newspaper of Augusta, Ga. She is a board member of the East Central Committee for Opportunity, and a member of numerous professional political and civic organizations, including the Hancock Concerned Citizens Club, the State Democratic Executive Committee and the Georgia Council on Human Relations. She is single. Address: P.O. Box 151, Sparta, GA 31087

Roy Innis

Ray Irby

K. Leroy Irvis

Innis, Roy, civil rights activist, is national director of the Congress of Racial Equality headquartered in New York City. The non-profit organization, with a network of chapters across the United States, is concerned with the social, political and economic institutions of the black community. Mr. Innis was born June 6, 1934 in St. Croix, Virgin Islands. Mr. Innis is a graduate of the City College of New York (B.S., chemistry, 1959). He became actively involved in the Harlem New York chapter of CORE in 1963 and was elected national director in 1968. Under his leadership, CORE drafted and presented to Congress in 1968 the Community Self-Determination bill calling for control of schools, businesses and social service agencies in the black community. In 1970, CORE's *amicus curiae* brief was accepted by the U.S. Supreme Court in connection with its deliberations involving the case, *Swann* vs. *the Charlotte-Mecklenburg Board of Education*. Mr. Innis is co-publisher of the *Manhattan Tribune*, a weekly newspaper serving New York City's Upper West Side and Harlem. He is on the boards of directors of the Pan-African Institute, the National Urban Coalitions, Who's Who in Black America, New Era Health, Education and Welfare, the New York Urban Coalition and the Harlem Commonwealth Council. He and his wife, Doris, have six children: Alexander, Cedric, Patricia, Corinne, Niger and Kimathi. Address: CORE, 200 W. 135th St., New York, NY 10030

Irby, Ray, business executive, is president and chief operating officer of Supreme Life Insurance Company of America, which is headquartered in Chicago, Ill. Born June 7, 1918 in Meridian, Miss., he began his career in insurance 31 years ago in Tuscaloosa, Ala. He was elected to his present position in 1973 after serving two years as vice president and agency director. Before joining Supreme, the largest black-owned firm in the North, Mr. Irby had climbed every rung on the ladder of insurance management success. He studied mathematics at DePaul University and in 1969 became a Chartered Life Underwriter (CLU), the highest credential in the insurance industry. (Fewer than 100 blacks are among the 20,000 CLUs.) He has numerous business and civic affiliations, including the Institute of Life Insurance, Life Agency Management Association, Cosmopolitan Chamber of Commerce, National Urban League, NAACP and Operation PUSH. He and his wife, Geraldine, have four children: Sherman, Mrs. Rosie Hedgeman, Mrs. Edna Purkington and Lisa. Address: 3501 S. King Dr., Chicago, IL 60616

Irvis, K. Leroy, legislator, is Democratic minority whip of the Pennsylvania House of Representatives. He assumed the position in 1973 after serving on two occasions as majority leader (1969–70 and 1971–72). Born Dec. 27, 1919 in Saugerties, N.Y., he finished high school at the age of 15. He is a graduate of New York State Teachers College (B.A. Education, 1938), New York University (M.A., 1939) and the University of Pittsburgh Law School (LLB and J.D., 1954). He served as assistant district attorney of Pittsburgh (1957–63). He was first elected to the House in 1958. As majority leader, he played a vital role in a number of significant legislative campaigns, including the passage of a controversial income tax in Pennsylvania. He is a member of the Order of the Coif, Phi Delta Phi law fraternity, and Phi Beta Kappa. He is a member of the NAACP Legal Redress Committee and the boards of Mercy Hospital, Point Park College, and the Pittsburgh Council for the Arts. He is honorary chairman of the Public Defender Association. He is a widower. Address: Pennsylvania House of Representatives, Harrisburg, PA 17120

J

Alphonse Jackson Jr.

Rev. Cameron W. Jackson

Emory O. Jackson

Jackson, Alphonse Jr., educator and legislator, is a member of the Louisiana State Legislature (representing the 2nd District) and is assistant executive secretary of the Louisiana Education Association in Baton Rouge, La. Born Nov. 27, 1927 in Shreveport, La., he is a graduate of Southern University (B.A., educational administration, 1950) and New York University (M.A., educational administration, 1958). Elected to the state legislature in 1971, he assumed the LEA position in 1966. As assistant executive secretary of the LEA, he is responsible for professional negotiations, legal programs, educational services and external relations with the state's education system. He has worked as a school principal and educational consultant and has directed a $2.5 million Head Start Program. He served on the advisory committee of the 1964 U. S. Civil Rights Commission and organized a black cultural program in northern Louisiana. He and his wife, Rubye, have two daughters, Lydia and Angela. Address: 1116 Pierre Ave., Shreveport, LA 71103

Jackson, The Reverend Cameron W., clergyman, is pastor of the First A.M.E. Zion Church in Columbus, Ohio. Born Sept. 8, 1939 in Chattanooga, Tenn., he is a graduate of Livingstone College (B.A.) and Hood Theological Seminary (M.Div.). He has also studied at Howard University and has a certificate in community studies from Temple University. He was ordained a deacon in 1959 and was ordained a church elder in 1962. He is executive vice president of the Ministers and Laymen's Association of Columbus, president of the Board of Black Campus Ministry at Ohio State University, secretary of the Budget and Finance Committee of the A.M.E. Zion Annual Conference, chairman of the Black Clergy Council of Columbus, chairman of the board of ECCO Development Corp., treasurer of the Central Citizens Organization, and a member of the Board of Christian Education. He is a member of Alpha Phi Alpha. He and his wife, Margaret, have four children: Stephen, Michael, David and Charles. Address: First A.M.E. Church, 873 Bryden Rd., Columbus, OH 43205

Jackson, Emory O., journalist, since 1943 has been managing editor of the *Birmingham World*, a black newspaper in Birmingham, Ala. He was born Sept. 8, 1908 in Buena Vista, Ga. and is a graduate of Morehouse College (A.B.). He has honorary LL.D. degrees from Morehouse, Daniel Payne College and Birmingham Baptist College. He is a member of the board of directors of Protective Industrial Insurance, the Birmingham Urban League and the National Newspaper Publishers Association; secretary of the Jefferson County Community for Economic Opportunity; vice-president of Metropolitan Business Association, and member of the Alabama Christian Movement for Human Rights, the Birmingham Press Club and Sigma Delta Chi. Address: Birmingham World, P.O. Box 10724, Birmingham, AL 35201

George E. Jackson

Jacquelyne J. Jackson

James S. Jackson

Jackson, George E., airline executive, is director of sales development at American Airlines Inc. in New York City. Born Jan. 29, 1931 in Tryon, N.C., he is a graduate of New York University (B.S., marketing, 1957). In his present position with American Airlines Inc., he is responsible for developing and coordinating corporate sales plans and programs to increase sales in selected markets. He joined the staff of American Airlines in July 1964 as a sales representative and later served as manager of public relations. Before joining American, he was associated with *Ebony* magazine and the *New York Amsterdam News*. He and his wife, Anne, have one daughter, Cheryl. Address: 633 3rd Ave., New York, NY 10017

Jackson, Jacquelyne Johnson, medical sociologist, is an associate professor of medical sociology at Duke University, Durham, N. C. Born Feb. 24, 1932 in Winston-Salem, N.C., she has degrees from the University of Wisconsin (B.S., M.S.) and Ohio State University (Ph.D.). With Duke University since 1968, she is engaged in sociological research on aged blacks and families headed by black women. Her book, *These Rights They Seek,* was published in 1962, and she has edited *Proceedings of the Research Conference on Minority Group Aged in the South*. The first and only black female employed at Duke, she has taught at Howard University, Jackson State College and Southern University. A recipient of the President's Citation of the American Association of Homes for the Aging (1972), she holds memberships in the Southern Sociological Society, the American Psychological Association and the North Carolina Sociological Association. She has chaired caucuses of the Black Sociologists and the Committee on Equality of Opportunity in Psychology. She is on the board of Carver Research Foundation and the National Council on Family Relations. She has a son, Murphy. Address: Box 3003, Duke University Medical Center, Durham, NC 27710

Jackson, James S., educator, is an assistant professor of psychology at the University of Michigan. He was born July 30, 1944 in Detroit, Mich. and is a graduate of Michigan State University (B.A., psychology, 1966), the University of Toledo (M.A., psychology, 1970) and Wayne State University (Ph.D., social psychology, 1972). He was a teaching fellow and research assistant at Wayne State (1968-71). He is national president of the Association of Black Psychologists and is a member of the American Psychological Association, Alpha Phi Alpha and Psi Chi national honor society in psychology. He was national president of the board of directors of the Black Students Psychological Association (1970-71) and has been active in various psychology groups since he was a college student. He has several research projects in progress. He is single. Address: 4134 Institute for Social Research, University of Michigan, Ann Arbor, MI 48106

Rev. Jesse L. Jackson

Johnny Jackson Jr.

Rev. Joseph H. Jackson

Jackson, The Reverend Jesse L., clergyman and administrator, is president of Operation PUSH (People United to Save Humanity) with headquarters in Chicago, Ill. The organization concluded covenants in 1972 with two corporations, General Foods and Schlitz Breweries, totaling more than $150 million, which cover employment of blacks, purchases of goods and services from blacks and deposits in black-owned banks. Operation PUSH has opened offices in New York City; Los Angeles, Calif.; Memphis, Tenn, and Columbus, Ohio and a number of other cities. Born Oct. 8, 1941 in Greenville, S.C., the Reverend Jackson is a graduate of North Carolina A&T University (B.A., sociology, 1964). He studied at Chicago Theological Seminary under a Rockefeller Foundation grant and was ordained a Baptist minister (1968). He also has honorary degrees from Lincoln University and Chicago Theological Seminary (D.D., 1969), Oberlin College and North Carolina A&T University (L.H.D., 1970) and Howard University (H.H.D., 1970). Before assuming his present position, he was associate minister of the Fellowship Missionary Baptist Church, director of field activities for the Coordinating Council of Community Organizations (1965–66), Chicago coordinator of the Southern Christian Leadership Conference's Operation Breadbasket (1966–67), director of special projects and economic development of SCLC (all in Chicago) and was appointed national director of Operation Breadbasket by Dr. Martin Luther King, Jr. (1967). He and his wife, Jacqueline, have four children: Santita, Jesse Jr., Jonathan and Yusef. Address: 930 E. 50th St., Chicago, IL 60615 **See article on Jesse L. Jackson in Volume II**

Jackson, Johnny Jr., legislator, is a member of the Louisiana Legislature. Elected in 1972, he is the youngest of eight blacks and one of the youngest members in the legislature. He was born Sept. 19, 1943 in New Orleans, La. and has a B.A. degree from Southern University (1965). A bill he introduced in the Legislature was the first one in the South, and second in the U.S., covering lead paint poisoning. He was also elected in 1972 as a delegate to the Constitutional Convention charged with rewriting the Louisiana State Constitution. He was one of the founders of the National Welfare Rights Organization and National Tenants Organization, and is a member of the Black Legislative Caucus. His leisure interests include bowling and working with neighborhood youths. He and his wife, Ora Jean, have one child, Juane. Address: 2643 Desire St., New Orleans LA 70117

Jackson, The Reverend Joseph H., clergyman, has been pastor of the Olivet Baptist Church in Chicago, Ill. since 1941 and president of the 6.5 million-member National Baptist Convention, U.S.A. since 1953. Born in Rudyard, Miss., he earned his degrees at Jackson College (B.A.), Creighton University (M.A.) and Colgate-Rochester Divinity School (B.D.). He did postgraduate work in theology at the University of Chicago. He has honorary D.D. degrees from Jackson College and Central State University and honorary LL.D. degrees from Bishop College and the College of Monrovia, Liberia. He is a member of Phi Beta Sigma fraternity. He gave his first sermon to a congregation of his fellow eight-year-olds. He has conducted preaching missions in more than 15 countries of Europe, Africa, Asia and South America, and has authored four books. He and his wife, Maude, have one daughter, Mrs. Kenny Jackson Williams. Address: 405 E. 31st St., Chicago, IL 60616

Rev. Lawrence R. Jackson   Maynard H. Jackson Jr.   Michael Jackson

Jackson, The Reverend Lawrence R., clergyman, is pastor of Lilydale Progressive Missionary Baptist Church in Chicago, Ill. Born June 18, 1910 in Mound City, Ill., he studied theology at Ideal Bible College in Chicago and is a graduate of Chicago Baptist Institute. Before assuming his present Pastorate, the Reverend Jackson was pastor of Mt. Olive M. B. Church in Chicago. He is a member of the National Baptist Convention, U.S.A., Inc., and director of the Adult Division of the Baptist General State Congress of Christian Education of Illinois. He and his wife, Eula Mae, have twelve children: Charles Edward, Dorothy Mae, Robert Lewis, Eula Mae, Wendell Allen, Myrna Evelyn, Maurice, William, Frederick George, Arzetta Felecia and twins, Loretta Renee and Uletta Denee. Address: Lilydale Progressive M. B. Church, 10706 S. Michigan Ave., Chicago, IL 60628

Jackson, Maynard Holbrook Jr., city official, is vice mayor of Atlanta, Ga. In that position, he serves as president of the board of aldermen and as the presiding officer of the city council. He was elected in 1970 after practicing law since 1965. Born March 23, 1938 in Dallas, Tex., he was graduated from Morehouse College (B.A., 1956) which he entered at age fourteen as a Ford Foundation Early Admissions Scholar. He also is a graduate of North Carolina Central University's School of Law *(cum laude,* 1964). Mr. Jackson is a member of numerous organizations, including the National Bar Association, the Atlanta Bar Association, the NAACP, the Atlanta Urban League and the National Black Caucus of Local Elected Officials. He and his wife, Bunnie, have three children: Elizabeth, Brooke and Maynard Holbrook Jackson III. Address: First Federal Bldg., Suite 917, 40 Marietta St., Atlanta, GA 30303

Jackson, Michael, entertainer, is the lead singer of the Jackson Five, a pop singing group. Born Aug. 29, 1958 in Gary, Ind., he and his brothers, Jackie, Marlon, Jermaine and Tito, were introduced to Motown recording star Diana Ross by Gary's Mayor Richard G. Hatcher. Miss Ross phoned Motown president Berry Gordy Jr., and the group went to Detroit and became the biggest hit in Motown history. The group was soon recording both single records and albums and appearing on "The Ed Sullivan Show," "Hollywood Palace," "The Andy Williams Show" and "Goin' Back to Indiana," their own popular special for ABC-TV. In 1970, the Jackson Five ranked top in single-record sales and in album sales for new artists. In the fall of 1971, the singing group was featured in animated cartoons on a television series. The Jackson Five started singing when they lived in Gary, where their father was a crane operator. Mr. Jackson used to relax by writing songs and singing to the guitar. Michael's good looks, great energy and showmanship sparks the act. The family, with nine children in all, now lives in Los Angeles, Calif. Address: Motown Record Corp, 6464 Sunset Blvd., Los Angeles, CA 90028 **See article on Michael Jackson in Volume II**

Judge Perry B. Jackson   Prince A. Jackson Jr.   Richard H. Jackson

Jackson, Perry B., jurist, who retired in 1972, is judge emeritus of the Cuyahoga Country Common Pleas Court in Cleveland, Ohio. Born Jan. 27, 1896 in Zanesville, Ohio, he has degrees from Adelbert College (A.B.), Western Reserve University (LL.B.; honorary LL.D.), Monrovia (Liberia) College (honorary LL.D.) and Cleveland State University (honorary LL.D.). He was elected in 1942 as the first black judge in Ohio. Previously, he was a state representative, city councilman, assistant police prosecutor and secretary to the state director of public utilities. He is a member of the American, National, Ohio State, Cleveland and Cuyahoga County bar associations, the American Judicature Society and the John Harlan Law Club. He is a member of Phi Beta Kappa. He has received numerous honors, including YMCA Man of the Year (1971), Silver Beaver Award and Silver Antelope Award of the Boy Scouts of America, Community Chest Distinguished Service Award and the Gold Gavel Award of the Ohio Common Pleas Judges Association. Judge Perry and his wife, Fern, live in Cleveland. Address: 1 Lakeside Ave., Cleveland. OH 44110

Jackson, Prince A. Jr., administrator, is president of Savannah State College in Savannah, Ga. He was the first black appointed by Governor Jimmy Carter to the Southern Regional Education Board. Born March 17, 1925 in Savannah, he is a graduate of Savannah State College (B.S., mathematics, 1949), New York University (M.S., mathematics, 1950) and Boston College (Ph.D., higher education, 1966). A member of numerous organizations, including the National Institute of Science, and the board of directors of the Boy Scouts of America and the YMCA, he is also the recipient of at least 10 civic awards. In 1970, he was named Alumnus of the Year by the Savannah State College Alumni Association. His highest honor, he considers, was being elected president of his alma mater after serving on the faculty for 15 years. He and his wife, Marilyn, have five children: Prince III, Rodney, Julia, Anthony and Phillip. Address: Savannah State College, Savannah, GA 31404

Jackson, Richard H., engineering executive, is vice president-engineering at Gits Brothers Manufacturing Co. in Chicago, Ill. He was born Oct. 17, 1933 in Detroit, Mich., and attended the University of Missouri, Lincoln University (Missouri) and the University of Wichita. He designed the alternate landing gear system and the thrust reverser fail-safe system for the Boeing 747 while an engineer at Boeing Corp., has designed numerous components for various other aircraft and space vehicles. He was the first black engineer at Beech Aircraft and was consultant to the National Aeronautics and Space Administration and the Department of Defense experiment team for Gemini space flights 5 through 12. He and his wife, Arlena, have three children: Deirdre, Gordon and Rhonda. Address: 1846 S. Kilbourn Ave., Chicago, IL 60623

Russell A. Jackson, Jr.   Samuel C. Jackson   Allix Bledsoe James

Jackson, Russell A. Jr., administrator, is superintendent of Roosevelt School District No. 66 (12,000 students) in Phoenix, Ariz. Born Feb. 26, 1934 in Philadelphia, Pa., he has degrees from Cheyney State College (B.S., elementary education, 1956) and Temple University (M.Ed., educational administration, 1962; Ed.D., educational administration, 1970). He has also attended the University of Vermont's National Science Institute in Mathematics for Elementary School Personnel. He was superintendent of public school in East Orange, N.J. (1968–72). He was in the U.S. Navy (1957–59) and in the Naval Reserve (1957–63). He was assistant superintendent of schools in Chester, Pa. (1966–68). Earlier, he was a teacher and elementary school principal in Philadelphia. He is an expert on early childhood learning (his doctoral thesis was on the subject), and has emphasized programs for the teaching of reading to very young children. He is president of the National Alliance of Black School Superintendents and is a member of a number of professional and civic groups. He and his wife, Elois, have two children, Cherryl and Charles. Address: 6000 S. 7th St., Phoenix, AZ 85040

Jackson, Samuel C., administrator, is general manager of the National Community Development Corporation in Washington, D.C. Born May 8, 1929 in Kansas City, Kan., he is a graduate of Washburn University (BA.., 1951; LL.B., 1954). Before assuming his present position in 1973, he was assistant secretary of the U.S. Department of Housing and Urban Development (1969–72), a position which made him one of the highest-ranking black men in the nation's capital, He was also one of five original presidential appointees to the U.S. Equal Employment Opportunity Commission (1965–68) and was head of a U.S. housing mission to Africa in 1971. He has been a member of the NAACP national board of directors and its national legal committee, and served as president of the Topeka (Kan.) NAACP. He also served as deputy general counsel of the Kansas Department of Welfare. He and his wife, Judith, have two children, Marcia and Brenda. Address: 1855 Upshur St., NW, Washington, DC 20011

James, Allix Bledsoe, educator, is president of Virginia Union University in Richmond, Va. Born December 17, 1922 in Marshall, Texas, he has degrees from Virginia Union University (A.B., 1944; B.D., 1946) and Union Theological Seminary (Th.M., 1949; Th.D., 1957). He has an honorary LL.D. degree from the University of Richmond (1971). He is chairman of the Richmond City Planning Commission and vice president of the National Association for Equal Opportunity in Higher Education. He is a member of the boards of directors of Virginia Electric and Power Co., Greater Richmond Chamber of Commerce, Richmond Area Community Council and Richmond Community Hospital. He has been at VUU for twenty-five years and was elected president in 1969. He is the recipient of the Distinguished Service Award of Links, Inc. (1972) and the Omega Psi Phi Citizen of Year Award (1972). He and his wife, Susie, have two children, Alvan and Portia. Address: Virginia Union University, 1500 N. Lombardy, Richmond, VA 23220

Maj. Gen. Daniel James Jr.

James, Maj. Gen. Daniel Jr. ("Chappie"), military officer (U.S. Air Force), is assistant secretary of defense. Born Feb. 11, 1920 in Pensacola, Fla., he is a graduate of Tuskegee Institute (B.P.E.). At Tuskegee, he also took flying lessons and became a licensed pilot and flight instructor of Army Air Corps cadets until January, 1943 when he entered the aviation cadet program himself. Commissioned in July, 1943, he entered fighter overseas combat training at Selfridge Field, Mich. He was assigned to Korea as a flight leader in July, 1950, where he became known as the "Black Panther," flying F-51s and F-80s. He flew 101 combat missions before his assignment to Otis Air Force Base in Massachusetts in July, 1951, as an all-weather jet pilot. After assignments as operations officer and commander of various squadrons, he attended the Air Command and Staff School, Maxwell AFB in Alabama in September, 1956. In July, 1957, he became an air staff officer in the Office of the Deputy Chief of Staff for Operations, Air Defense Division at Headquarters, U.S. Air Force, in Washington, D.C. After duties in England and Arizona, he became director of operations for the 8th Tactical Fighter Wing in Thailand. He led a total of 78 missions over North Vietnam. Among his 14 decorations are the Distinguished Flying Cross (with oak leaf cluster), the Air Medal (with seven oak leaf clusters) and the Presidential Unit Citation. He and his wife, Dorothy, have three children: Danice, Daniel III and Claude. Address: The Pentagon, Washington, DC 20301 **(See article on Daniel James Jr. in Volume II)**

Robert E. James

James, Robert E., banker, is president of Carver State Bank in Savannah, Ga. Born November 21, 1946 in Hattiesburg, Miss., he studied accounting at Morris Brown College (B.A., 1968) and at Harvard University Business School (M.A., 1970). Elected president of Carver at age 25, he formerly worked for Armco Steel Corporation of Middletown, Ohio and the Citizens and Southern National Bank of Atlanta, Ga. He is a director of the West Broad Street YMCA and a director of Savannah Area Chamber of Commerce. Mr. James and his wife, Shirley, have a son, Robert. Address: P.O. Box 1865, Savannah, GA 31402

Troy Lee James

James, Troy Lee, legislator, is representative from the 9th District (Cuyahoga County) in the Ohio Legislature. He attended Fenn College, Bethany College and Western Reserve College. He is a grocer. He is a board member of the Margie Homes for the Mentally Retarded, Eliza Bryant Home for Aged, Democratic Executive Committee and the board of Ohio State Legislators Society. He is president of the 11th Ward Democratic Club. He and his wife, Betty, have a daughter, Lora Smith. Address: 4616 Cedar Ave., Cleveland, OH 44103

Rev. William M. James

James, The Reverend William M., clergyman, is senior minister of Metropolitan Community United Methodist Church in New York, N.Y. Born June 4, 1916 in Meadville, Miss., he is a graduate of Mt. Beulah College (A.A.), Butler University (B.S. and Bachelor of Sacred Literature) and Drew University (B.D. and M.A., religion). He has taken graduate courses at the University of Chicago. Before assuming his present pastorate in 1952, he was pastor of Trinity United Methodist Church in Bronx, N.Y. He was ordained a deacon in 1938 and an elder in 1940. He has served as a member and officer of the National Board of Education of the Methodist Church and is the organizer and founder of the Ministerial Interfaith Association, which administers the Harlem College Assistance Program, the Harlem Interfaith Harlem Counseling Association and the Foundation of Harlem. He is a former president of the New York City Branch NAACP. He and his wife, Juanita, have a son, Edward. Address: United Methodist Church, 1975 Madison Ave., New York, NY 10017

Judith Jamison

Thomas D. Jarrett

Vernon D. Jarrett

Jamison, Judith, dancer, is the highly acclaimed lead dancer of the Alvin Ailey American Dance Theater. Born May 10, 1943 in Philadelphia, Pa., she studied dance with private teachers Marion Cuyjet, Nadia Chilkovsky and Joan Kerr (1949–61). She was also a student at Fisk University and at the Philadelphia Dance Academy. Before joining the Ailey Company in 1965, she was a member of the American Ballet Theater and the Harkness Ballet. She is a board member of the National Council of the Arts. She received *Dance* magazine's 1972 Annual Citation. She and her husband, Miguel, live in Manhattan. Address: Alvin Ailey American Dance Theater, 229 East 59th St., New York, NY 10022

Jarrett, Thomas Dunbar, educator and administrator, since 1968 has been president of Atlanta University in Atlanta, Ga. Born Aug. 30, 1913 in Union City, Tenn., he has degrees from Knoxville College (A.B., 1933), Fisk University (A.M., 1937) and the University of Chicago (Ph.D., 1947). Dr. Jarrett began his teaching career in 1933 at Central High School in Paris, Tenn. He was an assistant professor of English at Knoxville (Tenn.) College (1937-40) and at Louisville (Ky.) Municipal College (1941-43) before joining the Atlanta University faculty in 1947 as an assistant professor. Since then he has been associate professor (1950-55), professor (1955-67) and chairman (1957-67) of the English Department; acting dean of the School of Arts and Sciences (1957-60); dean of the Graduate School of Arts and Sciences (1960-67); chairman of the Interim Administrative Committee (1967-68) and acting president (1968). He was a Ford Foundation Fellow and lectured at the University of London, Oxford University and Cambridge University (1953-54). He was president of the National Association of College Deans and Registrars (1968-69) and serves on a number of boards and committees. He and his wife, Annabelle, have a daughter, Paula. Address: Atlanta University, Atlanta, GA 30314

Jarrett, Vernon D., journalist, is an editorial page columnist for the *Chicago* (III.) *Tribune* newspaper, and is a radio and television producer and moderator. His *Tribune* column appears three times a week; his weekly show, "Black On Black," featuring interviews with outstanding black people, is on the ABC-TV station in Chicago, and his radio show, "The Vernon Jarrett Report," a one-hour "talk show" is heard on Chicago's WGRT. Born June 19, 1921 in Saulsbury, Tenn., he is a graduate of Knoxville (Tenn.) College (B.A., sociology), and studied journalism at Northwestern University. He also studied television writing and producing at the University of Kansas City (Mo.), and urban sociology at the University of Chicago. He was nominated for the Pulitzer Prize in journalism in 1972 and 1973, and has won numerous awards for his reporting. He is a member of the board of governors of the Chicago Chapter of the National Academy of Television Arts and Sciences, and is a member of Sigma Delta Chi. He has been a visiting associate professor of history at Northwestern University and taught a television course in American history for the City Colleges of Chicago. He and his wife, Fernetta, have two sons, William and Thomas. Address: Chicago Tribune, 435 N. Michigan Ave., Chicago, IL 60611

Jeffries, LeRoy W., marketing consultant is president of Jeffries & Associates, Inc. in Los Angeles, Calif. His clients include a number of America's largest corporations. Before he began his own firm in 1971, he was, for 21 years, director of advertising and a vice president of Johnson Publishing Company, Inc. in Chicago, Ill. Earlier, he taught a graduate course at Columbia University and was director of industrial relations for the National Urban League in New York, N. Y. He was born Aug. 14, 1911 in Greensboro, N. C. but grew up in Washington, D. C. and New York City. He is a graduate of Wilberforce University (B.S., 1935) and Columbia University (M.A., 1944). An honorary L.H.D. degree was conferred on him in 1966 by Wilberforce University. On May 1, 1972, President William R. Tolbert Jr. of Liberia commissioned him as Counsel of the Republic of Liberia for Southern California. He is a founder and a past president of the National Association of Market Developers, and is a member of the Los Angeles Advertising Club, Los Angeles Area Chamber of Commerce, Urban League of Los Angeles, NAACP and SCLC. He and his wife, Vermont, live in Los Angeles. Address: 3540 Wilshire Blvd., Los Angeles, CA 90036

Jenkins, Howard Jr., government official, is the first black to serve as a member of the National Labor Relations Board, an independent federal agency which administers the nation's principal labor relations laws. Born June 16, 1915 in Denver, Colo., he has degrees from the University of Denver (A.B., L.L.B.). A former law professor and specialist in the fields of labor and administrative law, he was appointed to the NLRB in 1963 by President John F. Kennedy to serve a five-year term. He was re-appointed to a second term by President Lyndon Johnson in 1968. Except for a brief stint in the real estate business, his employment history has been primarily in the field of law. Licensed to practice in Colorado and the District of Columbia, he served as an attorney for federal agencies in the Rocky Mountain area (1942–46) and taught labor and administrative law at Howard University Law School (1946–56). He served in the U.S. Department of Labor (1956–63) and was director of the Office of Regulations (1959–62) and assistant commissioner of the Bureau of Labor-Management Reports (1962–63). He and his wife, Alice, have three children: Judith, Howard III and Lawrence. Address: 1333 Tuckerman St., NW, Washington, DC 20011

LeRoy W. Jeffries

Jewell, Jerry Donal, D.D.S., legislator and dentist, is a state senator (3rd District) in Arkansas. He was elected in 1972. Born Sept. 16, 1930 in Chatfield, Ark., he is a graduuate of Arkansas AM&N College and Meharry Medical College School of Dentistry. He is in the private practice of dentistry in North Little Rock, Ark. He is a member of the American Dental Association and the National Dental Association. He is president of All, Inc. and is president of Eagle Life Insurance Co. in Little Rock. A life member of the NAACP, he is a former president of the Little Rock branch. He is a member of Alpha Phi Alpha. He and his wife, Ometa, have five children: Eldin, Avelinda, Sharon, Jerrod and Kason. Address: 105 E. 2nd, North Little Rock AR 72114

Howard Jenkins Jr.

Jerry Donal Jewell, D.D.S.

Albert William Johnson

Rev. Arthur Lee Johnson

Constance V. B. Johnson

Johnson, Albert William, business executive, is president of Al Johnson Cadillac, Inc. in Chicago, Ill. Born Feb. 23, 1921 in St. Louis, Mo., he is a graduate of the University of Illinois (B.S., business administration, 1942) and the University of Chicago (M.A., hospital administration). In 1967 he became the first black man to be awarded an Oldsmobile dealership franchise by the General Motors Corporation, and in 1973 operated the nation's fourth largest Cadillac outlet. He was assistant administrator and business manager at Homer Phillips Hospital in St. Louis, Mo. (1947–67). While employed at the hospital, he was a part-time Oldsmobile salesman; in 1966 he decided to seek a new car agency of his own. He wrote a letter to the chairman of the board of General Motors, applying for consideration. The application won approval and he was awarded an Oldsmobile franchise in a predominantly black area on Chicago's South Side. Because of his success, within four years he was awarded a Cadillac dealership. In 1972, after only thirteen months of black ownership, his was the fourth largest Cadillac dealership in the United States. He is national treasurer of Operation PUSH and is a board member of the NAACP Legal Defense Fund. He is a member of various business and civic groups. He and his wife, Marian, have two children, Albert Jr. and Donald. Address: 1650 E. 71st St., Chicago IL 60649

Johnson, The Reverend Arthur Lee, clergyman, is pastor of St. Paul's Baptist Church in Philadelphia, Pa. Born July 21, 1928 in Orangeburg, S. C., he is a graduate of South Carolina State College (B. A.) and Eastern Baptist Theological Seminary of Philadelphia (B. D.). Before assuming his present position, he was assistant to the minister of the 1,000/member St. Paul's Baptist Church. He is a member of the Progressive National Baptist Convention, Philadelphia Baptist Association and American Baptist Convention, and is a director of Opportunities Industrialization Center, Zion Investments Association, Inc., and Downing Town Agricultural and Industrial School. He and his wife, Frances, have two children, April and Ava. Address: St. Paul's Baptist Church, 10th and Wallace St., Philadelphia, PA 19123

Johnson, Constance Van Brunt, magazine editor, is managing editor of *Ebony Jr!* mazagine, published by Johnson Publishing Co., Inc. in Chicago, Ill. The magazine, for black children six to twelve years old, began publication in 1973. Born July 29, 1949 in Los Angeles, Calif., Mrs. Johnson is a graduate of Sarah Lawrence College (B.A., psychology and mathematics, 1971) and Harvard University (master of arts in teaching, 1972). She was a John Hay Whitney Fellow and a Dwight D. Eisenhower Fellow at Harvard. A reading specialist, she did special research on literacy in the Republic of Guyana. She and her husband, Don, a law student, live in Chicago. Address: 820 S. Michigan Ave., Chicago, LI 60605

Judge E. C. Johnson

E. Marie Johnson

Eunice W. Johnson

Johnson, E. C., jurist, is a judge of the Circuit Court of Cook County (Ill.). Born June 1, 1920 in Chicago, Ill., he attended Loyola University and is a graduate of Roosevelt University (A.B.) and John Marshall Law School (J.D.). His interest in law developed while he was a secretary and law clerk at the Chicago law firm of Ellis, Westbrook and Holman. He began the private practice of law in 1952, continuing until he became a magistrate (now called judge) of the Cook County Circuit Court in 1965. He is a member of several church, civic and fraternal organizations, including the National Association of Claimants Counsels of America and the Chicago, Cook County and National bar associations. He is a member of the Judicial Council of the NBA. He and his wife, Olivia, have two children, Edward and Ella. Address: Civic Center, Chicago, IL 60602

Johnson, E. Marie, psychologist and businesswoman, is president and owner of E. Marie Johnson and Associates, a multi-service consulting agency concerned with research excellence in the social and psychological sciences. Born in Elizabeth City, N.C., Dr. Johnson has earned degrees in psychology from Virginia State College (B.A.), Roosevelt University (M.A.) and Northwestern University (Ph.D.). **She** is the only black female in the United States who has a successful consulting agency with a multi-racial staff, and has clients that include some of the top 500 companies in the country. She is a member of Alpha Kappa Mu national honor society, Pi Lamda Theta, Alpha Kappa Alpha sorority, Association of Black Psychologists, American Psychological Association, American Personnel and Guidance Association. Dr. Johnson is single. Address: 520 N. Michigan Ave. Suite 622, Chicago, IL 60611

Johnson, Eunice Walker, publishing executive, is secretary-treasurer of Johnson Publishing Co., Inc. in Chicago, Ill. and is director-producer of the Ebony Fashion Fair. Born in Selma, Ala., she is a graduate of Talladega College (B.A., sociology) and Loyola University (M.A., social services administration). She completed courses in Studies of the Great Books at the University of Chicago, took graduate courses in journalism at Northwestern University and studied at the Ray Vogue School of Interior Decorating. She has also taken courses in sewing, tailoring and fashion design. Since 1962, she has brought the Ebony Fashion Fair to thousands of persons in cities throughout the U.S. In 1964, two models she selected for haute couture designer Emilio Pucci became the first blacks to participate in a showing of fashions at the famed Pitti Palace in Florence, Italy. Active in many civic, community and professional organizations, Mrs. Johnson is a member of the Women's Board of the Art Institute of Chicago, member of the board of directors of Talladega College (which was founded by her maternal grandfather, Dr. William H. McAlpine), member of the board of directors of the Woman's Division of the United Negro College Fund, and member of the Midwest Ballet and the National Foundation for the Fashion Industry. She is a trustee of Harvard St. George School in Chicago, a director of the Adoptive Information Citizenry Committee, and a member of the Women's Board of the University of Chicago and the board of the Hyde Park-Kenwood Women's Auxiliary of the Illinois Children's Home and Aid Society. In 1972, President Richard M. Nixon named her as a special ambassador to accompany Mrs. Nixon to Liberia for the inauguration of the country's new president, William R. Tolbert Jr. She and her husband, John H. Johnson, president and editor of Johnson Publishing Co., Inc., have two children, John Harold and Linda. Address: 820 S. Michigan Ave., Chicago, IL 60605

George E. Johnson   Glenn T. Johnson   I. S. Leevy Johnson

Johnson, George E., businessman, is president of Johnson Products, Inc., in Chicago, Ill. Born June 16, 1927 in Richton, Miss., he graduated from Wendell Phillips High School in Chicago. After graduation, he worked as a production chemist for a black cosmetics firm, doubling in the evenings as a busboy. He developed a hair straightener for men and after 10 years left the cosmetics company to market it himself. His product won immediate and widespread acceptance, and in 1957 he incorporated Johnson Products to manufacture and market Ultra Wave Hair Culture. Within a year, he added three hair-straightening and conditioning women's products under the Ultra Sheen label. In 1970, the annual sales of Johnson Products were more than $12.6 million. In 1971, the company became the first black-owned corporation to be listed on a major stock exchange, the American Stock Exchange. He conducts major charitable and educational programs for blacks through the George E. Johnson Foundation. He is chairman of the board of Independence Bank of Chicago and a member of the boards of directors of Commonwealth Edison Co. and the U.S. Postal Service. He and his wife, Joan, have four children: Eric, John, George Jr. and Joan Marie. Address: 8522 S. Lafayette Ave., Chicago, IL 60620 **See article on George E. Johnson in Volume II**

Johnson, Glenn T., jurist, is a judge of the Circuit Court of Appeals in Chicago, Ill. He was appointed in April, 1972. Born July 19, 1917 in Washington, Ark., he is a graduate of Wilberforce University (B.S., 1941) and John Marshall Law School (LL.B., 1949; Ph.D., law 1950). Previously, he was in law practice (1950–57), assistant attorney general of the state of Illinois (1957–63), and assistant attorney for the Metropolitan Sanitary District of Chicago (1963–66) and judge of the Circuit Court (1966–72). He is a member of the American, Chicago, Cook County, National and Illinois bar associations; Reserve Officers Association, American Legion, Urban League, and the South Side Community Committee. He is a past president of the Cook County Bar Association, a board director of the Woodlawn Boys' Club, a trustee of the Woodlawn A.M.E. Church, and a member of the South Parkway Urban Progress Center Advisory Council. He has received numerous honors, including the 1970 John Marshall Law School Distinguished Alumni Service Award. He and his wife, Evelyn, have two children, Glenn Jr. and Evelyn. Address: Civic Center, Chicago, IL 60601

Johnson, I. S. Leevy, legislator, is a member of the South Carolina General Assembly. He is one of the first three black legislators in South Carolina since Reconstruction and is also a practicing attorney at law. Born May 16, 1942 in Richland County, S.C., he is a graduate of Benedict College in South Carolina (B.S., 1965), the University of South Carolina (J.D., 1968), and has an associate of mortuary science degree from the University of Minnesota. He is a licensed embalmer and funeral director. He is a former instructor at Benedict College. He and his wife, Doris, have one son, George. Address: 1107½ Washington St., Columbia, SC 29211

John H. Johnson

The Rt. Rev. J. A. Johnson Jr.

Johnson, John H., publishing executive, is president, publisher and editor of Johnson Publishing Company, Inc., which has headquarters in Chicago, Ill. and branch offices in New York, N.Y., Washington, D.C. and Los Angeles, Cal. The company publishes *Ebony, Jet, Black Stars, Black World* and *Ebony Jr!* magazines, and has various affiliates, including a book division, a book club, Ebony-Jetours (a travel service), Ebony Fashion Fair and Supreme Beauty Products. Mr. Johnson is also chairman of the board of directors of Supreme Life Insurance Company of America, and is a member of the boards of directors of The Marina City Bank of Chicago, Service Federal Savings and Loan Association of Chicago, Twentieth Century-Fox Film Corporation, and several civic and business organizations. In 1972 he opened the new $8 million Johnson Publishing Company building in downtown Chicago and announced the purchase of Chicago radio station WGRT. Born Jan. 18, 1918 in Arkansas City, Ark., he graduated with honors from DuSable High School in Chicago and attended the University of Chicago and Northwestern University. He has honorary degrees from a number of schools, including Syracuse University, Morehouse College, Shaw University, Central State College, Benedict College, North Carolina College, Eastern Michigan University and Upper Iowa College. Since 1951, when the U.S. Junior Chamber of Commerce named him one of the Ten Outstanding Young Men of the Year, he has won numerous other awards, including the NAACP's Spingarn Medal (1966), the National Newspaper Publishers Association's John Russwurm Award (1966), the Horatio Alger Award (1966) and the University of Chicago Alumni Association's Professional Achievement Award (1970). He was honored as a Fellow of Sigma Delta Chi professional journalistic society in 1970. In 1972, he became the first black publisher to be named "Publisher of the Year" by the Magazine Publishers Association, which awarded him its Henry Johnson Fisher Award for outstanding contributions to publishing. In 1957, he accompanied then Vice President Richard M. Nixon on goodwill trips to nine African countries, and in 1959 to Russia and Poland. President John F. Kennedy named him a special ambassador to the Ivory Coast independence ceremony (1961) and President Lyndon B. Johnson named him a special ambassador to the Kenya independence ceremony (1963). He is a member of several business and civic organizations, and is a 33rd degree Mason. He and his wife, Eunice, have two children, John Harold and Linda. Address: 820 S. Michigan Ave., Chicago, IL 60605 **See article on John H. Johnson in Volume II**

Johnson, The Right Reverend Joseph A. Jr., clergyman, is presiding bishop of the Fourth Episcopal District (Mississippi and Louisiana) of the Christian Methodist Episcopal Church. Born June 19, 1914 in Shreveport, La., he is a graduate of Texas College (B.A., 1938), Iliff School of Theology (M.Th., 1943; D.Th., 1945) and Vanderbilt University (B.D., 1955; Ph.D., 1958). He has honorary degrees from Morris Brown College (D.D., 1961) Mississippi Industrial College (D.D., 1963) and Miles College (LL.D., 1969). He was the first black to be admitted to Vanderbilt University, the first to graduate and the first to receive a Ph.D. from that institution. He is chairman of the board of trustees of Mississippi Industrial College and has served on the boards of Texas College, Phillips School of Theology and Vanderbilt University. He has pastored churches in Tennessee, Colorado and Louisiana. He is chairman of the Board of Missions of the Christian Methodist Episcopal Church and is author of *The Soul of the Black Preacher* (1971). He is currently working on a translation of the New Testament. He and his wife, Grace, have three children: Joseph III, Charles and Patricia. Address: 109 Holcomb Dr., Shreveport, LA 71103

Rev. Joy J. Johnson

LaMont Johnson

Ralph C. Johnson

Johnson, The Reverend Joy Joseph, clergyman and state legislator, was elected in 1970 to the North Carolina House of Representatives, the second black to take a seat in the state's General Assembly since Reconstruction. In 1971 the assembly passed two significant bills he introduced. His Equal Employment Opportunity bill, approved by the House 99 to 0 and by the Senate without debate, made N.C. the first southern state to enact such a law. The other bill restores citizenship to anyone who has forfeited it through a crime, after he has been pardoned or completed his sentence. In 1966, he became the first black elected to the Town Board of Fairmont where he lives and is pastor of First Baptist Church. Born Nov. 2, 1922 in Scotland County, N.C. to a share-cropper family, the Reverend Johnson worked his way through his first four years of college. He is a graduate of Shaw University (A.B., hon. LL.D.) and Friendship College (D.D.). He and his wife, Omega, have a daughter, Deborah. Address: P.O. Box 455, Raleigh, NC 27202

Johnson, LaMont, film producer and musician, is executive producer, president and chairman of Filmethics International, Inc., film distributors in Los Angeles, Calif. Born Oct. 1, 1941 in New York, N.Y., he quit his chemistry studies at Manhattan College to join the U.S. Air Force. After his basic training, he was assigned to the Air Force Security Service as a German and Rumanian linguist. He had studied languages at Syracuse University following basic training and was able to identify 27 Eastern European languages, including Polish, Serbo-Croatian, Latvian and Lithuanian. Following his discharge in 1962, he embarked upon a career as a jazz pianist. He played with jazz stars Eric Dolphy, Roland Rahsaan Kirk, Ornette Coleman and Archie Shepp, and was featured with the Jackie McLean Quartet for nearly three years. He has worked as conductor, road arranger and organist for the Friends of Distinction singing group, as organist for the Fifth Dimension and Hugh Masakela, and as arranger for R. B. Greaves. He has composed film scores for nine featurette films and for a television pilot, a musical play and a feature film. He owns an independent record company, Sun, Moon and Stars, and Filmethics, which is the first black distribution company for feature films in the nation. Mr. Johnson and his wife, Carolyn, have two children, Astrid-Brett and Neil Collin-Keith. He is a minister in the Church of Scientology. Address: Filmethics International, Inc., Suite 706, 1800 N. Highland, Los Angeles, CA 90028

Johnson, Ralph C., certified public accountant, is founder of the Ralph C. Johnson Co. in Kansas City, Mo. The firm, opened in 1971, employs all the three black certified public accountants in the area. Born Dec. 4, 1941 in Pittsburg, Tex., Mr. Johnson is a graduate of Oakwood College in Alabama (B.S., business administration, 1964) and Wichita State University (M.S., accounting, 1967). He was licensed as a certified public accountant in Kansas in 1966 and in Missouri in 1971. He was associate professor of business administration at Alabama A.&M. College (1967-68) and was assistant professor of accounting at Wichita State University (1968-70). He was a staff accountant (1964-71) at Elmer Fox & Co., certified public accountants, in Kansas City. He is a member of several professional groups, including the American Institute of Certified Public Accountants. He and his wife, Nadine, have one child, Stacie. Address: 4900 Swope Parkway, Suite 301, Kansas City, MO 64130

Robert E. Johnson   Benjamin E. Jones

Johnson, Robert E., journalist, is executive editor of *Jet* magazine, published by
Johnson Publishing Co., Inc. in Chicago, Ill. Born Aug. 13, 1922 in Montgomery, Ala.,
he is a graduate of Morehouse College (B.A., sociology, 1948) and Syracuse
University (M.A., journalism, 1952). Although he was founder-editor of his high school
newspaper, *The Westfield Trail Blazer*, while in the 10th grade, he aspired to be a
lawyer, but a white racist joke led him to a career in journalism. To stem a protest
against the U.S. Navy's newspaper, *The Masthead*, which published a racist joke that
offended blacks, Mr. Johnson, who was in the Navy, was transferred to editorial duties
and soon became the newspaper's first black managing editor. He began his
professional career with the *Atlanta Daily World* as a reporter. He became city
editor. He joined *Jet* in 1953. He is a member of Sigma Delta Chi journalism fraternity,
Alpha Kappa Delta national honorary sociology society and Alpha Phi Alpha fraternity.
He has travelled extensively in the United States, Europe and Israel on editorial
assignments. In May, 1972, he was among the journalists who accompanied President
Richard M. Nixon to Russia, Poland and Iran. He and his wife, Naomi, have three
children: Bobbye, Janet and Robert III. Address: 820 S. Michigan Ave.,
Chicago, IL 60605

Jones, Benjamin E., administrator, is executive vice president of Capital Formation,
Inc. in New York, N.Y. CF provides managerial and technical assistance to minority
entrepreneurs. Mr. Jones joined the company in October, 1971 as director of
marketing. In April, 1972, he became vice president of administration, and in February,
1973 was named to his present position. Previously, he was a program director for the
Interracial Council for Business Opportunity. Born Sept. 8, 1935 in New York City, Mr.
Jones earned a B.A. degree in economics at Brooklyn College and a certificate in
government at Fordham University. He is a candidate for an MBA degree (1973) at
Pace College Graduate School. He is a member of the Council of Concerned Black
Executives, the executive committee of SCLC's Black Expo, SCLC's Operation
Breadbasket, Operation PUSH-New York, and the National Association of Market
Developers. He is a director of MBA Management Consultants, Inc. of Columbia
University's Graduate School of Business, and is a director of the Alumni Association
of Brooklyn College. Address: 5 Beekman Street, New York, NY 10038

Clarence B. Jones

James Earl Jones

John P. Jones

Jones, Clarence B., publishing executive, is editor and publisher of the New York *Amsterdam News*, the nation's largest black weekly newspaper in New York, N.Y. He is also chairman of the board and chief executive officer of AmNews Corp., the newspaper's parent company, and is chairman of the board of Inner City Broadcasting Corp., which owns and operates New York City's radio station WLIB. Previously, he was an allied member of the New York Stock Exchange and was a director and vice president of CBWL-Hayden, Stone, Inc., a New York City investment and brokerage firm. For several years, he was a lawyer specializing in entertainment and copyright law, corporate finance and organization, state and federal civil rights litigation. He was once a partner in Lubell, Lubell and Jones, a New York City law firm, and was a special counsel to Dr. Martin Luther King Jr. and the Southern Christian Leadership Conference. He was a New York delegate to the 1968 Democratic National Convention and a delegate-at-large to the 1972 convention. He is a member of numerous boards, civic and civil rights groups. He was a member of the Observers Committee in the Attica prison massacre in 1971. He was born Jan. 8, 1931 in Philadelphia, Pa. and is a graduate of Columbia University and Boston University Law School. He and his wife, Charlotte, have four children: Christine, Clarence Jr., Dana and Alexia. Address: 2340 Eighth Ave., New York, NY 10027

Jones, James Earl, actor, received the Tony award as best actor of 1969 for his stage role of heavyweight champion Jack Johnson in *The Great White Hope,* a part he also portrayed in the film version. He had already achieved international fame as an actor in more than two dozen stage productions, including *Romeo and Juliet, Sunrise at Campobello, The Cool World, King Henry V, The Blacks, The Tempest, Macbeth, Othello, The Winter's Tale* and *Bloodknot*. He also appeared in the movie *Dr. Strangelove*, and has played TV roles in "The Defenders," "East Side/West Side" and other series. He received The *Village Voice* Off-Broadway award and the *Theatre World* award in 1962. He is actor/director of the New York Public Theatre and actor/host of the TV feature "Black Omnibus." Mr. Jones was born Jan. 17, 1931 in Tate County, Miss. He has a degree from the University of Michigan (B.A., 1953) and a diploma from the American Theatre Wing (1957). He has also received honorary degrees (Litt. D.) from Fairfield University and the University of Michigan. Address: care of Lucy Kroll Agency, 390 West End Ave., Apt. 9-B, New York, NY 10024

Jones, John P., educator and administator, is president of Jarvis Christian College in Hawkins, Tex. Born March 1, 1915 in Tyler, Tex., he has degrees from Texas College (A.B.) and the University of Chicago (A.M.). He was appointed president of the institution in 1972 after serving for ten years as head of the English department, chairman of the division of humanities and assistant to the president. Listed in the *Directory of American Scholars* and *Who's Who in the South and Southwest*, he is director of a language project with the Endowment for the Humanities. He and his wife, Nola, have two children, Rhoda and John. Address: Jarvis Christian College, Hawkins, TX 75765

Johnnie A. Jones

Judge Mark Elmer Jones Jr.

Nathaniel R. Jones

Jones, Johnnie A., legislator and attorney, is a member of the Louisiana state legislature representing the 67th District (Baton Rouge). Born Nov. 30, 1919 in Laurel Hill, La., he is a graduate of Southern University (B.S., psychology, 1949) and Southern University Law School (J.D., 1953). A practicing attorney, he is a member of the Louisiana State Bar Association and the National Baton Rouge Bar Association. He is on the board of directors of numerous organizations including the Ada Bullock-Blundon Association, the Baton Rouge Council of Human Relations, the Boy Scouts of America, and is president of the board of directors of Community Advancement Inc. He and his wife, Sebell, have four children: Johnnie A. Jr., Adair, Adal, and Ann Sarah. Address: 1261–65 Government St., Baton Rouge, LA 70802

Jones, Mark Elmer Jr., jurist, is a judge of the Circuit Court of Cook County, Ill. He is also a prize-winning abstract painter and has exhibited his work in the Chicago area. Born Oct. 15, 1920 in Indianapolis, Ind., he is a graduate of Roosevelt University (A.B., political science, 1948) and Loyola University in Chicago (J.D., 1950). He was assistant Cook County state's attorney (1951–56). After seven years of private law practice, with the firm of McCoy, Ming & Leighton in Chicago, he was named associate judge of the Chicago Municipal Court, a position he held until his present election on Jan. 1, 1964. He is treasurer and a member of the executive committee of the judicial council of the National Bar Association, the black counterpart of the American Bar Association, and is on the executive committee of the Chicago branch of the NAACP. He is also a member of Urban Gateways and the Institute for Cultural Development. He has been published in a number of law reviews. For four years during World War II, he was with the U.S. Navy. His paintings have won first prizes from the Chicago Bar Association (on three occasions) and the South Side (Chicago) Art Center. He and his wife, Jeanne, have four children: Marquita, Marcus, Marvin and Julie. Address: Cook County Circuit Court, Civic Center, Chicago, IL 60601

Jones, Nathaniel R., attorney and administrator, is general counsel of the NAACP. Born May 13, 1926 in Youngstown, Ohio, he is a graduate of Youngstown University (B.A., 1951 and LL.B., 1956). He also has honorary degrees from Youngstown University (LL.D., 1970) and Syracuse University (LL.D., 1972). Before assuming his present position in 1969, Mr. Jones was executive director of the Fair Employment Practices Committee of the City of Youngstown (1966–69) and was in private law practice. As assistant U.S. attorney for the Northern District of Ohio, he became one of Ohio's top trial lawyers, handling the prosecution of a variety of crimes. In 1967, he was appointed deputy general counsel of the President's Commission on Civil Disorders. He headed a three-man team which investigated grievances of black servicemen in West Germany. His recommendations for military justice reform caused his appointment in 1972 as co-chairman of the Civilian-Military Task Force on Military Justice. Following the Task Force report, Mr. Jones was offered the position of deputy assistant secretary of defense for equal opportunity. Believing his highest duty was to remain with the NAACP, he told the Defense Department, "I'm not available." He and his wife, Jean, have two children, Pamela and Stephanie. Address: 1790 Broadway, New York, NY 10019 **See article on Nathaniel R. Jones in Volume II**

Paul R. Jones

Quincy Jones

R. W. E. Jones

Jones, Paul R., federal executive, is southern regional director of ACTION, the citizens service corps established in 1971 to coordinate federal volunteer programs in the U.S. and overseas. From his office in Atlanta, Ga., he directs all ACTION domestic programs in eight southeastern states. ACTION's programs are the Peace Corps, Volunteers in Service to America (VISTA), Foster Grandparent Program, Service Corps of Retired Executives (SCORE), Active Corps of Executives (ACE), Retired Senior Volunteer Program (RSVP) and University Year for ACTION. Former deputy director of the Peace Corps in Thailand, he was executive director of the Committee for Reelection of the President in 1972 and has been director of the Office of Civil Rights of the National Highway Safety Bureau and executive director of the Charlotte (N.C.) Model Cities Program. Born in 1930 in Bessemer, Ala., he attended Alabama State College and Howard University (B.S. and M.S., government) and studied for a doctorate at the University of California School of Criminology in Berkeley, Calif. He and his wife, Bess, have a son, Paul R. Jr. Address: 730 Peachtree St., N.E., Atlanta, GA 30308

Jones, Quincy, musician, is one of the foremost composers of musical scores for motion pictures in the United States. By 1973, he had scored more than 40 major films. Born March 4, 1933 in Chicago, Ill., he attended Seattle University. He began playing the trumpet at 14, performing with a small group formed by singer Ray Charles. At 18, he won a scholarship and received formal lessons at the Berklee School of Music in Boston. Two years later, he joined Lionel Hampton's band and then Dizzy Gillespie's band, which he had helped organize. He spent a year and a half in Paris composing, arranging and conducting for Barclay Records. He studied in Paris under the well-known musicologist Nadia Boulanger. Back in the U.S., he was musical director for the short-lived Harold Arlen blues opera *Free and Easy.* However, his all-star jazz orchestra made a highly successful concert tour of Europe. His first break in film music came with his score for the 1961 Swedish movie, *The Boy and the Tree.* After he scored his first U.S. film, *The Pawnbroker,* in 1965, critics hailed the music, and movie score offers poured in. He is the recipient of the Grammy and a number of other awards. He and his wife, Ulla, have two children, Martina-Lisa and Quincy III. He has a daughter, Jolie, by a previous marriage. Address: 1416 N. La Brea, Hollywood, CA 90028 **See article on Quincy Jones in Volume II**

Jones, Ralph Waldo Emerson, educator, is president of Grambling College, La. Born Aug. 6, 1905 in Lake Charles, La., he is a graduate of Southern University in Baton Rouge (B.S., 1924), Columbia University (M.A., 1935), and Louisiana Technical University (Ph.D., 1969). Dr. Jones has been with Grambling for 46 years, during which time he has served as an instructor, dean of men, academic dean, band director, coach, and director of development. He was appointed president of the college in 1936. He is a member of the Prince Hall Masons, Elks, and the Phi Beta Sigma fraternity, the Southwest Regional Education Board and the Southern Education Development Laboratory. He is a widower and has two sons, Ralph Jr. and John. Address: Grambling College, Grambling, LA 71245

Judge Sidney A. Jones Jr.

Theodore A. Jones

Virginia L. Jones

Jones, Sidney A. Jr., jurist, has been an associate judge of the Circuit Court of Cook County (Ill.) since 1964. Born July 2, 1909 in Sandersville, Ga., he attended Atlanta University (B.A., 1928) and graduated with honors from Northwestern University (J.D. 1931). He was a member of the legal staff of the U.S. Department of Labor (1939–46), was a member of the Chicago City Council (1955–59), representing the 6th Ward. In 1960, he was appointed judge of the Municipal Court of Chicago. He is a trustee of Atlanta University and is a member of the board of directors (and past president) of the Cook County Bar Association. He is a member of numerous community organizations, including the Chicago Boys Club, of which he is vice president and a member of the board of directors. He is a member of Alpha Phi Alpha, the NAACP (life member) and Prince Hall Masons. He and his wife, Roma, have two daughters, Mrs. Roma Steward and Mrs. Laurel Boyd, and a son, Sidney III. Address: Civic Center, Chicago, IL 60601

Jones, Theodore A., broadcasting executive, is president and a member of the board of directors of radio station WGRT in Chicago, Ill. Born Nov. 14, 1912 in Pueblo, Colo., he is a graduate of the University of Illinois (B.S., accounting and business management, 1933) and has taken graduate courses in business management at Northwestern University. He is a certified public accountant. He is a former chairman of the board (now a member) and president of the Chicago Branch NAACP. He was director of the Illinois Department of Revenue (1967–69) and senior vice president and general manager of Supreme Life Insurance Company of America (1955–67). He is treasurer and a director of Service Federal Savings & Loan Assn. of Chicago (1951–   ), treasurer and a director of Burr Oak Cemetery Assn. of Chicago (1955–   ), and a partner in Jones, Anderson & Co., C.P.A.'s (1940–   ). He is a trustee emeritus of the University of Illinois, a trustee of Talladega College, and a director of Operation PUSH. He is a member of numerous business and civic groups. He and his wife, Beatrice, have two daughters, Janice and Lynn. Address: 221 N. LaSalle St., Chicago IL 60601

Jones, Virginia L., librarian, is director of the School of Library Science at Atlanta University. Born June 25, 1912 in Cincinnati, Ohio, she is a graduate of Hampton Institute (B.S., library science, 1933; B.S., education, 1936), the University of Illinois (M.S., library science, 1938) and the University of Chicago (Ph.D., 1945). Before assuming her present position in 1945, she was assistant librarian (1934–36) and librarian (1936–37) at Louisville Municipal College; circulation department assistant at Hampton Institute Library (1935–36); director of the department of library science at Prairie View A & M College (summers of 1936–39); catalog librarian (1939–41), instructor in the School of Library Service (1941–43) and dean (1943–45) at Atlanta University. She is a member of the President's Advisory Committeee on Library Training and Research, and a member and former president of the Association of American Library Schools and the American Library Association. She is a member of Delta Sigma Theta and Beta Phi Mu. In 1971, she was elected to the executive board of American Library Association. She and her husband, Edward, live in Atlanta. Address: School of Library Science, Atlanta University, Atlanta, GA 30314

Rep. Barbara Jordan   Rt. Rev. F. D. Jordan

Jordan, Barbara, congresswoman, is U.S. representative from the 18th District of Texas
(Houston). Born Feb. 21, 1936 in Houston, she is a graduate of Texas Southern
University (B.A. *magna cum laude,* political science and history, 1956) and Boston
University School of Law (LL.B., 1959; LL.D., 1969). Before her election to Congress,
she had practiced law since 1959 and was elected a Texas state senator in 1966. She
was the first black to serve in the Texas senate since 1883. Unanimously elected
president *pro tempore* of the Texas legislature on March 28, 1972, she became the
first black woman ever elected to preside over a legislative body in the United States.
As a state senator, she drew praise from former president Lyndon B. Johnson as being
"the epitome of the new politics in Texas." She was instrumental in defeating a highly
restrictive voter registration act, in giving Texas its first minimum wage law ($1.25 per
hour), in bringing the first raise in workman's compensation in 12 years, and in setting
up the state's department of community affairs. She is single. Address: House Office
Bldg., Washington, DC 20515 **See article on Barbara Jordan in Volume II**

Jordan, The Right Reverend Frederick Douglass, clergyman, is a bishop and chief
ecumenical officer of the African Methodist Episcopal Church. The Church's Office of
Urban Ministries and Ecumenical Relations was established at his request "to provide
an effective instrument of Mission and Cooperation at the highest level in the church
and to assist local congregations to deal more effectively with the pressing problems of
modern society." In his position, Bishop Jordan is chairman of the Commission on the
Consultation on Church Union, chairman of the Commission on Union of Black
Methodist Churches, member of the executive committee of the World Methodist
Council, vice president of the Methodist Historical Society, member of the executive
committee and governing board of the National Council of the Churches of Christ in
the U.S.A., and a member of the World Council of Churches. He has been extremely
active in establishing the A.M.E. Church in Africa. He was ordained an elder in 1924
and was elected a bishop in 1952. Born Aug. 8, 1901 in Atlanta, Ga., he studied at
North Carolina A. & T. College, Howard University, Northwestern University (A.B.),
Garrett Theological Seminary (B.D.), the University of Chicago Divinity School
and UCLA. He has a number of honorary degrees. He was first vice president of the
National Council of Churches of Christ in the U.S.A. (1969–72). He is a 32nd degree
Mason, a life member of the NAACP and a member of Alpha Phi Alpha and Sigma Pi
Phi fraternities. He is married to the former Artishia Wilkerson. Address: 5151 Franklin
Ave., Hollywood, CA 90027

Jack Jordan

Orchid I. Jordan

Vernon E. Jordan Jr.

Jordan, Jack, film producer, is a partner (with Quentin Kelly) in Kelly-Jordan Enterprises, Inc., in New York, N.Y. Born Aug. 21, 1929 in New York, he attended Columbia University and the New York School of Performing Arts. He was an artist's manager and producer in Sweden before forming his own production company with Mr. Kelly. The company has exclusive film rights for all of author James Baldwin's works and has produced the critically acclaimed *Georgia, Georgia*, starring Diana Sands. The films, *Caged Bird*, *Honey Baby*, *Honey Baby* and *The Inheritance*, all by Mr. Baldwin, are scheduled to be produced by the company. Divorced, Mr. Jordan has two children, Hilarie and John. Address: Kelly-Jordan Enterprises, 342 Madison Ave., New York, NY 10002

Jordan, Orchid I., legislator, is a state representative from Missouri (25th District, including Kansas City). She began her career as a politician in 1970 when she assumed the seat of her husband, the late Leon M. Jordan, who died that year. Since then, Mrs. Jordan has been reelected to the legislature twice on her own merit. Born Aug. 15, 1910 in Clay Center, Kan., she has a degree in education from Wilberforce University (Ohio). She and her husband spent many years in Monrovia, Liberia before they returned to Kansas City in 1955 to go into business for themselves. While in Monrovia, she helped her husband set up a fingerprint bureau for the government of Liberia. She was able to assist him because of training she had received with the Kansas City Police Department. She then became a travel agent and office manager for Pan American World Airways in Monrovia. Three years prior to the death of her husband, she helped him found Freedom, Inc., the first black political organization in Kansas City. Address: 2745 Garfield Ave., Kansas City, MO 64109

Jordan, Vernon E. Jr., administrator, is executive director of the National Urban League, which has headquarters in New York, N.Y. Born Aug. 15, 1935 in Atlanta, Ga., he is a graduate of DePauw University (B.A., political science, 1957) and Howard University (J.D., 1960). He also has honorary degrees from Brandeis University, Howard University, Michigan State University, Morris Brown College, Tougaloo College, Tuskegee Institute, Bloomfield College and Wilberforce University. Before assuming his present position in 1972, he was executive director of the United Negro College Fund (1970–71), director of the Voter Education Project of the Southern Regional Council (1964–70), attorney and consultant for the U.S. Office of Equal Opportunity and Georgia Field Director of the NAACP (1962–64). He is a member of the boards of director of the American Museum of Natural History, Bankers Trust Company, Celanese Corporation, Clark College, John Hay Whitney Foundation, National Multiple Sclerosis Society, National Urban Coalition, New World Foundation, Rockefeller Foundation, Twentieth Century Fund, and The Urban Institute. He was a presidential appointee to the Council of the White House Conference (1966), the National Advisory Commission on Selective Service (1966–67) and the American Revolution Bi-Centennial Commission (1972). He has received numerous honors, including fellowships at Harvard University's Institute of Politics, the John F. Kennedy School of Government and the Metropolitan Applied Research Center. In 1969, he was awarded DePauw University's Old Gold Goblet for "outstanding achievements." He and his wife, Shirley, have one child, Vickee. Address: National Urban League, Inc., 55 East 52nd St., New York, NY 10022

E. J. Josey

Percy L. Julian

Josey, E. J., librarian, is chief of the Bureau of Academic and Research Libraries for the Division of Library Development of the New York State Education Department in Albany, N.Y. Born Jan. 20, 1924 in Norfolk, Va., he has degrees from Howard University (A.B., 1949), Columbia University (M.A., history, 1950) and the State University of New York (M.S.L.S., 1953). In the department since 1966, Mr. Josey plans, coordinates and supervises the promotion and development of colleges, universities and specialized research library services. Author of the books *What Black Librarians Are Saying* and *The Black Librarian in America*, he was the first chairman of the Black Caucus of the American Library Association. He is a member of the American Library Association, the New York Library Association, American Association of University Professors, the Association for the Study of Negro Life and History, and the NAACP (life member). He organized the first NAACP college chapter in the South (1963). He has won a number of awards for his civil rights, youth and library work. He has written more than 100 articles for professional journals, magazines, etc. He has a daughter, Elaine. Address: 99 Washington Ave., Room 505, Albany, NY 12210

Julian, Percy L., research chemist, is president of Julian Associates and director of the Julian Research Institute in Franklin Park, Ill. Born April 11, 1899 in Montgomery, Ala., he is a graduate of DePauw University (A.B., 1920), Harvard University (A.M., 1923) and the University of Vienna (Ph.D., 1931). He has 15 honorary degrees and is a member of Phi Beta Kappa and Sigma Xi honor societies. After graduation from DePauw, he was an instructor in chemistry at Fisk University for two years. He then received an Austin Fellowship for graduate studies at Harvard. He was a chemistry professor at West Virginia State College. In 1928 he became an associate professor and head of the chemistry department at Howard University. In 1929, with a General Education Board fellowship, he studied under the world-famous Professor Ernst Spath in Vienna and returned to Howard in 1931 with his Ph.D. and a full professorship. In 1932, he became a research fellow at DePauw for four years. Despite his now brilliant reputation, he was unable to secure a faculty appointment there or at any other major (white) school. Disillusioned, he became a research director of the soya products and the vegetable oil and food divisions of the giant paint manufacturer, the Glidden Company of Chicago. In 1954, he founded Julian Laboratories, Inc. in Chicago, with subsidiaries in Mexico City and Guatemala. In 1961 he sold the firm for $2,338,000. He founded his present organizations in 1964. He is credited with 162 scientific publications and 105 patents. Among his many discoveries are the successful synthesis of physostigmine, used in treatment of glaucoma; synthesis of the female sex hormone progesterone, and synthesis of a compound from soybean sterols permitting low-cost, wide availability of cortisone. He is the recipient of numerous honors and awards. Dr. Julian and his wife, Anna, have two children, Percy L. Jr. and Faith. Address: 9352 Grand, Franklin Park, IL 60131 **See article on Dr. Percy L. Julian in Volume II**

K

Kay, Ulysses, educator and musician, is a distinguished music professor and composer of concert music. He was born Jan. 7, 1917 in Tucson, Ariz., and has degrees from the University of Arizona (B.A., 1938), and the Eastman School of Music at the University of Rochester (M.Mus., 1940). He has studied at Yale University and has been the recipient of honorary doctorate degrees from Lincoln (Ill.) College, Bucknell University, University of Arizona, and the University of Rochester (Alumni Award, 1972). Other honors include a Ditson Fellowship, a Rosenwald Fellowship, a Ford Foundation grant, an American Academy of Arts and Letters grant, a Fulbright scholarship, and the Prix de Rome from the American Academy at Rome. Mr. Kay's compositions for voice, chamber groups, and orchestra include *Concerto for Orchestra, Sinfonia in E, A Short Overture, Serenade for Orchestra,* and *The Boor* (an opera). Mr. Kay and wife, Barbara, have three children: Virginia, Melinda, and Hilary. Address: 143 Belmont St., Englewood, NJ 07631

Kean, Daniel Gardner, business executive, is equal employment opportunity administrator for Gulf Oil Corp. in Pittsburgh, Penn. The first college-educated black person employed by Gulf, he maintains programs related to equal employment opportunity, develops minority group recruiting programs and assists in the training and developing of minority group employees. Previously, he was special marketing representative and public relations representative for Gulf. He was born December 1, 1912 in Louisville, Kentucky. He is a member of the National Association of Market Developers, and a member of the American Tennis Association. Mr. Kean is a graduate of the University of Michigan (A.B., sociology; M.A., mathematics) and advanced graduate work. Mr. Kean is single. Address: Gulf Building, Pittsburgh, PA 15219

Keith, Damon J., jurist, is a United States District judge in Detroit, Mich. Born July 4, 1922 in Detroit, he has degrees from West Virginia State College (A.B., 1943), Howard University Law School (LL.B., 1949) and Wayne State University (LL.M.) and an honorary LL.D. from West Virginia State College. Public offices have included appointment to the Committee of Manpower Development and Vocational Training and Coordinating, and as chairman of the Subcommittee of Administration and Organization of the Citizens Advisory Committee on Equal Educational Opportunities for the Detroit Board of Education. He is a member of the Detroit Housing Commission, chairman of the Michigan Civil Rights Commission, a member of Wayne County Board of Supervisors, and a member of the legal staff of the Detroit Board of Education in conservation matters. He assumed office as United States District Court judge on Oct. 12, 1967. Two of his rulings have been upheld by the Supreme Court—the desegregation of the Pontiac, Mich., school system and denial of the right to the attorney general to tap wires in domestic cases without a court warrant. Judge Keith was selected as one of the 100 Most Influential Black Americans by *Ebony* magazine in April, 1971. He and his wife, Rachel, have three daughters: Cecile, Gilda and Debbie. Address: 231 W. Lafayette St., Detroit, MI 48226

Ulysses Kay

Daniel Gardner Kean

Judge Damon J. Keith

George D. S. Kelsey

James Horace Kemp

Maida Springer Kemp

Kelsey, George Dennis Sale, educator, is Henry Anson Butts Professor of Christian Ethics at Drew University in Madison, N. J. He was born July 24, 1910 in Columbus, Ga. and is a graduate of Morehouse College (A.B., 1934), Andover Newton Theological School (B.D., 1937) and Yale University (Ph.D. 1946); Harvard University, 1958-59. He has studied at the London (England) School of Economics and Political Science (1965-66). Morehouse College awarded him a D. D. degree in 1970. He was professor of religion and philosophy at Morehouse College (1938-45) and director of the School of Religion (1945-48); associate director of Field Department National Council of Churches (1948-52) and associate professor of Christian Ethics at Drew University (1952-57). He is the author of *Racism and the Christian Understanding of Man* (1965) and *Social Ethics Among Southern Baptists, 1917–1965* (1973). He and his wife, Leola, have a son, George. Another son, Everett, is deceased. Address: Drew University, Madison, NJ 07940

Kemp, James Horace, labor union official, has been president of Local 189, Building Service Employees Union (AFL-CIO) in Chicago, Ill. since 1946. Born Aug. 18, 1912 in Muskogee, Okla., he attended Crane Junior College, Lewis Institute and John Marshall Law School in Chicago. He has been business representative of the General Service Employees Union since 1940, a member of the executive committee of the Chicago Federation of Labor since 1959, and a member of the executive board of the Chicago Branch NAACP since 1940. He is a member of the board of directors of Service Federal Savings & Loan Association in Chicago, a trustee of Talladega College and a member of Omega Psi Phi fraternity. He was elected as a delegate to the 1969–70 Illinois Constitutional Convention. He and his wife, Maida, live in Chicago. He has a daughter, Mrs. Beverly Helm. Address: 300 S. Ashland Ave., Chicago, IL 60607

Kemp, Maida Springer, labor leader, is consultant for The African Labor History Center, on leave from the International Ladies Garment Workers Union, where she has been a general organizer and member of the International staff since 1959. Born May 12, 1910, in Panama City, Panama, she is a naturalized American citizen. Educated in Brooklyn (N.Y.) public schools, she has taken numerous special courses in labor and management at Wellesley College, Rand School of Social Sciences in New York, and under the auspices of the education department of the International Ladies Garment Workers Union. She joined Local 22 of the Dressmakers Union (AFL-CIO) in 1933 and was a member of its executive board (1938–42). During World War II, she was a captain in the Women's Health Brigade (1942–44). In 1945, she accompanied an AFL trade union delegation to England. In 1959 she became an international representative in the Department of International Affairs, AFL-CIO, assigned to Africa, and served in both East and West Africa until 1965. From 1965–68 she was a general organizer for the ILGWU, assigned to the Southeastern Region of the United States and from 1969–72, she was on loan from the ILGWU to the A. Philip Randolph Institute where she set up the Midwestern Regional Office, based in Chicago, handling voter registration and education, and developing a coalition between the labor movement and the community for social action. Since January, 1973, she has been delegated by ILGWU as consultant to the African Labor History Center to work primarily in black educational institutions. She is a vice president of the National Council of Negro Women, a member of the board of the DuSable History Museum and a life member of the NAACP. She is married to James H. Kemp, a labor leader, and has one son, Eric W. Springer: Address: 345 E. 46th Street, New York, NY 10017

Richard C. Kennard Jr.

William J. Kennedy III

Robert J. Keyes

Kennard, Richard C. Jr., executive, is co-chairman of the board, president and chief executive officer of Capital Formation, Inc. in New York, N.Y. CF provides managerial and technical assistance to minority entrepreneurs. Mr. Kennard joined Capital Formation in May, 1969 as director of special projects. In July, 1969, he was promoted to vice president; in January 1970 he became president. Previously, he was a special agent (and a million-dollar producer) for Prudential Life Insurance Company. In October 1970, Capital Formation and the National Bankers Association were selected to administer President Nixon's Minority Bank Deposit Program. Mr. Kennard and CF executives mobilized support for the program, and by the end of December, 1971, deposits in 36 minority banks increased by some $242.2 million. Mr. Kennard was born May 14, 1933 in New York City and attended Williams College and Columbia School of General Studies. He is co-founder and chairman of the board of National Youth Movement, chairman of the Commercial Division of Operation PUSH-New York, chairman of the National Minority Chamber of Commerce and a member of the boards of the Council of Concerned Black Executives, the Negro Ensemble Company, the Lorraine Hansberry Peoples Theatre and the Community Film Workshop Council. Address: 5 Beekman Street, New York, NY 10038

Kennedy, William J. III, insurance executive, is president of North Carolina Mutual Insurance Co., the world's largest black-owned business, in Durham, N.C. Born Oct. 24, 1922 in Durham, he is a graduate of Virginia State College (B.A., business administration, 1942), the University of Pennsylvania (M.B.A., insurance, 1946) and New York University (M.B.A., finance and investment, 1948). He took additional graduate courses at New York University (1946–48). Mr. Kennedy, the son of William J. Kennedy Jr., fourth president of North Carolina Mutual, joined the company in 1950. He became controller in 1959, vice president in 1970, and president and chief executive officer in 1972. He is a member of the board of directors. He is vice president of the North Carolina Society of Financial Analysts. He is a member of the boards of directors of RCA Corporation, the Mechanics and Farmers Bank of Durham, the Urban National Corporation of Boston and the Galaxy Fund, Inc. of New York. He is a member of the board of directors, chairman of the finance committee and a member of the executive committee of United Durham, Inc., a modular homes construction firm. He and his wife, Alice, have a son, William IV. Address: Mutual Plaza, Durham, NC 27701

Keyes, Robert J., administrator, is corporate director of urban affairs at Lockheed Aircraft Corporation in Burbank, Calif. He coordinates minority recruiting and training with special emphasis on salaried jobs, and works with civil rights organizations for equal employment opportunity at local, state and national levels. Previously, he was a professional football player for the San Francisco 49ers (1959–60), a high school teacher and coach, an insurance salesman, and an assistant to California state officials, including Governor Ronald Reagan. He was recruited for his present position in December, 1972. Born April 13, 1936 in Bakersfield, Calif., he is a graduate of Antelope Valley Junior College in California (A.A.) and of the University of San Diego (B.B.A., 1962), and is studying (1973) for a master's degree at United States International University. He is a member of the President's Advisory Council on Minority Business Enterprise. He and his wife, Marva, have four children: Angelique, David, Denise and Robert. Address: Lockeed Aircraft Corp., 2555 N. Hollywood Way, Burbank, CA 91502

Mae Street Kidd

Rev. Thomas Kilgore Jr.

Martin Kilson

Kidd, Mae Street, legislator and public relations consultant, has been a member of the Kentucky House of Representatives since 1968, representing the 41st District, Jefferson County-Louisville, Ky. Her best known legislation is Kentucky House Bill 27, a major proposal establishing a state agency to promote and finance low-income housing in the state. The measure, sponsored by Mrs. Kidd, was passed and signed into law in 1972. Born in Millersburg, Ky., she is a graduate of Lincoln Institute (Lincoln Ridge, Ky.), and has studied public relations at American University. Before entering politics, she worked with Mammoth Life and Accident Insurance Co. as a supervisor of policy issue, sales representative and public relations counselor (1935–64). She received national recognition as the company's outstanding producer in ordinary sales for three consecutive years. Since 1964, she has been a consultant for Supreme Life Insurance Co. of America, receiving a gold plaque in 1966 for qualifying as a member of the Half Million Dollar Club. She also serves as a consultant for William L. Higgins Property Management Co., Inc. Mrs. Kidd, who has a broad community service background, served as a board member of the local branch YMCA for 12 years, and has spearheaded fund-raising drives for the Girl Scouts, the NAACP Legal Fund and other causes. A member of a number of professional and civic organizations, she has received many awards and honors. Mrs. Kidd and her husband, J. Meredith Kidd III, have no children. Address: House of Representatives, Frankfort, KY 40601

Kilgore, The Reverend Thomas Jr., clergyman, is a senior pastor of the Second Baptist Church, Los Angeles, Calif. (the oldest black Baptist church in Los Angeles). Born Feb. 20, 1913 in Woodruff, S.C., he has earned degrees from Morehouse College (A.B., 1935) and Union Theological Seminary (B.D., 1957). Honorary degrees have been awarded to him from Shaw University (D.D., 1956), Morehouse College (D.D., 1963), University of Southern California and Virginia Union University (LL.D., 1972). In 1971, he was elected first black president of the American Baptist Convention. As president, he has initiated a multi-million-dollar movement, Fund of Renewal (FOR), which will serve black churches across the country. Dr. Kilgore and his wife, Jeanetta, have two children, Lynn Elda and Jini Medina. Address: 2412 Griffith Ave., Los Angeles, CA 90011

Kilson, Martin, educator, is a professor of government at Harvard University. Born Feb. 14, 1931 in Rutherford, N.J., he received his B.A. degree from Lincoln University (Pa.) and his M.A. and Ph.D. degrees from Harvard. He was the first black appointed as a full professor on the Harvard Faculty of Arts & Sciences. He published his monograph in 1966, *Political Change in A West African State* (Harvard University Press). He is a member of the NAACP, a Fellow of the American Academy of Arts and Sciences, and a Fellow of the Black Academy of Arts and Letters. He and his wife, Marion, have three children: Jennifer, Peter and Hannah. Address: Department of Government, Harvard University, Cambridge, MA 02138

191

King, André Richardson, commercial designer, is a senior graphics designer and programmer with Skidmore, Owings & Merrill, architects, engineers and planners, in Chicago, Ill. Born July 30, 1931 in Chicago, he attended the University of Chicago School of Architecture, the Art Institute of Chicago (B.F.A., education, 1959) and Chicago Technical College for Engineering and Architecture. He served in the U.S. Air Force (1952–55), where he attained the rank of staff sergeant. In 1956 he opened his own design studio, and in 1959 joined Skidmore, Owings & Merrill. He is a member of Chicago Forum, and the Consular Corps of Chicago; he is acting consul for Barbados. He and his wife, Jan, have two children, Jandra and André. Address: Skidmore, Owings & Merrill, 30 W. Monroe, Chicago, IL 60605

King, B. B. (Riley B.), singer-guitarist, is one of the best known contemporary blues singers. He perfected his craft in relative obscurity for almost twenty years—touring seamy bars and dance halls. Not until the late 1960s did he suddenly find himself in demand by young white audiences, eager to hear authentic blues. Born Sept. 16, 1925 on a Mississippi Delta cotton plantation near Indianola, Miss., he bought a guitar and formed a quartet of spiritual singers as a teenager. Later, he began singing and picking the blues on street corners in Indianola. In 1947, he hitchhiked to Memphis, Tenn., where he was able to secure a job at WDIA, Memphis' black radio station, singing commercials and subsequently becoming a disc jockey. In 1949, he started recording on RPM, a minor label, and after several releases, came up with a hit "Three O'Clock Blues." In 1950, after the record had been on top of rhythm and blues charts for four months, he gave up his disc jockey job to go on the road. In 1968, he made his first European tour and played his first extended New York nightclub engagement at the Village Gate. He has since made many network television appearances and performed in Carnegie Hall. Address: B.B. Productions, 1414 Avenue of the Americas, New York, NY 10014

King, Coretta Scott (Mrs. Martin Luther King Jr.), lecturer-author-concert singer, is president of the Martin Luther King Jr. Center for Social Change in Atlanta, Ga. She is the widow of the late civil rights leader. Born April 27, 1927 in Marion, Ala., she holds degrees from Antioch College (B.A.) and the New England Conservatory of Music (B.A., music) and has a number of honorary degrees from universities, including Boston University, Marymount-Manhattan College, and Keuka College (Litt.D.); Brandeis University and Northwestern University (L.L.D.); and Morgan State College and Northeastern University, (Litt.D.). She has received numerous awards and honors, including the Annual Brotherhood Award of the National Council of Negro Women, the first annual Louise Wise Award of the American Jewish Congress Women's Auxiliary, the Wateler Peace Prize, and other national and international peace awards. She is the author of *My Life with Martin Luther King Jr.* (1969). Mrs. King has four children: Yolanda Denise, Martin Luther III, Dexter Scott and Bernice Albertine. Address: 234 Sunset Ave., NW, Atlanta, GA 30314

Andre R. King   B. B. King   Coretta Scott King

Edward B. King Jr.

Helen H. King

John O. Taylor King Sr.

King, Edward B. Jr., business executive, is a senior associate and director of the Office of Minority Manpower at the Association of American Publishers which is a voluntary confederation of some 260 book publishers in New York, N.Y. Mr. King is responsible for developing nationwide recruitment and training programs to assist publishers in employing, training and promoting black and other minority professional personnel. Previously, he was assistant to the president of Hofstra University (1968-70). Born August 17, 1939 in Roanoke, Va., he attended Detroit State College, Kentucky State College, Virginia Union University, Wilberforce University, the University of Dayton and Hofstra University. He was among the students who founded SNCC (1960), which he later headed. His work as a black activist has been cited by several historians, and he has received a number of honors and awards. Address: One Park Avenue, Suite 1810, New York, NY 10016

King, Helen H., publisher, is president of Let's Save The Children, Inc., a children's textbook company in Chicago, Ill. Born Oct. 15, 1936 in Clarksdale, Miss., she is a graduate of the University of Michigan (B.A., English and education, 1957). Before founding Let's Save The Children in 1972, Mrs. King was a free-lance writer, a writer for *Jet* (1960–61) and *Ebony* magazines (1969–71). She was an elementary school teacher in Pontiac, Mich. and in Chicago. She is a member of the National Association of Media Women. She is also the author of two books for black children, *Willy* (1971), and *the Soul of Christmas* (1972). Divorced, she has two children, Chad and Fenote. Address: Let's Save the Children, Inc., 645 N. Michigan Ave., Chicago, IL 60611

King, John O. Taylor Sr., educator, is president of Huston-Tillotson College in Austin, Tex. He joined the faculty of the college in 1947 and was a professor of mathematics (1952–65) and dean of the college (1960–68). Born Sept. 25, 1921 in Memphis, Tenn., he has degrees from Fisk University (B.A., 1941), Huston-Tillotson College (B.S., 1947), De Paul University (M.S., 1950) and the University of Texas (Ph.D., 1957). He was awarded an honorary (LL.D.) degree by Southwestern University in 1970. A veteran of World War II, he served as an army captain in the Pacific and now holds the rank of colonel in the U.S. Army Reserve. He has been a delegate to each General and Jurisdictional Conference of The United Methodist Church since 1956 and is president of the General Council on Ministries. He has co-authored four mathematics textbooks and has contributed many articles to professional and religious journals. He is co-author, with his wife, of *Stories of Twenty-Three Famous Negro Americans*. He and his wife, Marcet, have four children: John Jr., Clinton, Marjon and Stuart. Address: 1820 E. 8th St., Austin, TX 78702

Lawrence C. King

Rev. M. L. King Sr.

George Kirby

King, Lawrence C., business executive, is regional sales manager for General Foods Corp. in New York, N.Y. He directs the activities of four district managers who, in turn, direct the work of 60 sales supervisors, account managers and sales representatives. The region for which Mr. King is responsible includes Texas, Kansas, Iowa, Oklahoma, South Dakota, Arkansas and Louisiana. Previously, he was associate market research manager, senior product manager, district sales manager and sales development manager with the company. Born in Washington, D.C., he is a graduate of Howard University (B.A., economics 1951). He is a member of the Urban League and Kappa Alpha Psi. He and his wife, Beulah, have two sons, Larry and Craig. Address: 250 North St., White Plains, NY 10605

King, The Reverend Martin Luther Sr., clergyman, is pastor of the 3,500-member Ebenezer Baptist Church, Atlanta, Ga. Father of the late civil rights leader, he has been pastor of the church since 1932. Born Dec. 19, 1899 in Stockbridge, Ga., Rev. King is a graduate of Morehouse College School of Religion (B.Th.). He has honorary doctoral degrees from Morris Brown College (D.D., 1945); Wilberforce University, (L.L.H.D., 1965); Morehouse College (D.D., 1969) and the University of Haiti. He was named Clergyman of the Year by the Georgia Region of the National Conference of Christians and Jews in 1972 and has received many other awards and honors. Past moderator of the Atlanta Missionary Baptist Association, he serves on the boards of SCLC, the Citizens Trust Co., and the Carrie-Steele-Pitts Children's Home. He is also a trustee of Atlanta University, Morehouse College and the Interdenominational Theological Center. He and his wife, Alberta, have one daughter, Christine. Two sons are deceased: Dr. Martin Luther King Jr. and Rev. Alfred D. Williams King. Address: Ebenezer Baptist Church, 407-413 Auburn Ave., NE, Atlanta, GA 30312

Kirby, George, entertainer, is a popular comedian and impressionist. Born in Chicago, Ill., he also began his career there at the Club Delisa. He has his own weekly television show. He has worked with Cab Calloway, Lena Horne, Sarah Vaughan, and Billy Eckstine. In 1956, he toured Australia with Nat ("King") Cole, after which he went out alone in a series of appearances in American supper clubs that resulted in his spectacular rise to prominence as a major comedian. He has appeared on the "Johnny Carson Tonight Show," "Tom Jones Show," "Jackie Gleason Show," "Pearl Bailey Show," and many other television specials. He has performed at major state fairs throughout the country, and costarred with Rosalind Russell in the film, *Oh Dad, Poor Dad.* His record album, *The Real George Kirby,* is on the Cadet label. He is a golf enthusiast, and is invited to play in leading pro-am-celebrity tournaments, such as the Andy Williams, Glenn Campbell, Danny Thomas, and Bill Harrah events. He and his wife, Rosemary, live in Chicago. Address: CMA Press Dept., 211 East Chicago Ave., Chicago, IL 60611

Elizabeth D. Koontz   Francis A. Kornegay

Koontz, Elizabeth Duncan, administrator, became director of the Women's Bureau of the U. S. Department of Labor in 1969. She resigned in late 1972 but agreed to remain in her post until a successor was appointed. Born June 3, 1919 in Salisbury, N. C., she is a graduate of Livingstone College (A.B., 1938; honorary L.H.D., 1967) and Atlanta University (M.A., 1941). She also has honorary degrees from Pacific University, Bryant College, Howard University, American University, Coppin State College, Eastern Michigan University, Northeastern University and other schools. She was a public school teacher in North Carolina from 1947 to 1968; was president of the North Carolina Association of Classroom Teachers (1958-62), president of the department of classroom teachers of the National Education Association (1965-66), vice president of the N.E.A. (1967-68) and national president of the N.E.A. (1968-69). She is a member of Zeta Phi Beta and a number of other professional and civic organizations. She and her husband, Harry Lee Koontz, maintain a home in Salisbury, N. C. Address: 418 S. Caldwell St., Salisbury, NC 28144

Kornegay, Francis A., social agency official, is executive director of the Detroit, Mich. Urban League. He joined the league in 1944 as vocational secretary, became the assistant executive director in 1956 and was appointed executive director in 1960. Born Sept. 14, 1913 in Mt. Olive, N.C., he has degrees from North Carolina Central University (B.S., biology and mathematics, 1935) and the University of Michigan (M.A., 1941; Ph.D., 1972). He also has honorary degrees from Wilberforce University (H.H.D., 1965), Grand Valley State College (L.H.D., 1970) and Eastern Michigan University (H.H.D.). Mr. Kornegay has worked in the U.S. Treasury Department in Washington, D.C. and was commandant of boys and head of science at the Downingtown Industrial School. He toured Europe in 1952 and in 1955, lecturing on the problems of youths, and participated in the International Conference on Social Welfare and Human Rights (1968) in Helsinki, Finland. He is a trustee of Virginia Union University and Florida Memorial College and a member of the Economic Club of Detroit. Mr. Kornegay and his wife, Geraldine, have two sons, Francis Jr. and John Dancy. Address: 208 Mack Ave., Detroit, MI 48201

195

L

Joyce A. Ladner

Jewel S. R. Lafontant

Anna R. Langford

Ladner, Joyce A., sociologist, is an associate professor of sociology at Howard University in Washington, D.C. Born Oct. 12, 1943 in Waynesboro, Miss., Dr. Ladner is a graduate of Tougaloo College (B.A., 1964) and Washington University in St. Louis, Mo. (M.A., 1966; Ph.D., 1968). Dr. Ladner did postdoctoral research at the University of Dar es Salaam in Tanzania. She is the author of *Tomorrow's Tomorrow* and editor of *The Death of White Sociology* due for publication in April, 1973. Her articles have appeared in many leading newspapers and periodicals. Dr. Ladner is a member of the board of directors of the Twenty-first Century Foundation, the Caucus of Black Sociologists, the American Sociological Association and is a contributing and advisory editor to *The Black Scholar*. She is single. Address: Howard University, Washington, DC 20001

Lafontant, Jewel S. R., federal official, is deputy solicitor general of the United States. She argues U.S. Government cases before the U.S. Supreme Court. She is the first female to hold the position and is one of the highest-ranking black persons in the nation's capital. Born in Chicago, Ill., she is a graduate of Oberlin College (B.A., political science, 1943) and the University of Chicago (LL.D., 1946). Before being appointed to her position in 1973 by President Nixon, she was U.S. Representative to the United Nations (1972–72), a member of the President's Council on Minority Business Enterprise (1970–72), vice chairman of the U.S. Advisory Commission on International Educational and Cultural Affairs (1969–72), and a partner in the law firm of Stradford, Lafontant, Fisher and Malkin in Chicago. She is a trustee of Lake Forest College, Alumni Board member of the University of Chicago, vice president of the board of trustees of Provident Hospital and Training School Association, and a director of the Harvard St. George School. She has been a director of Jewel Companies, Inc., Trans World Airlines, Inc., Foote, Cone and Belding Communications and the United Nations Association. She was assistant U.S. Attorney for the Northern District of Illinois—the first black woman appointed to the position (1955–58). She was an alternate delegate to the 1960 Republican National Convention where she seconded the nomination of Vice-President Nixon. She was vice president of Woman's National Republican Club of Chicago (1970–72). She has received numerous awards. She and her husband, H. Ernest Lafontant, an attorney, live in Chicago. She has a son, John Rogers Jr., by a previous marriage. Address: U.S. Department of Justice, Suite 5125, 10th and Constitution Aves., Washington, DC

Langford, Anna R., attorney and alderman, in 1971 became one of the first two women (and the first black woman) ever elected alderman in Chicago, Ill. Elected from the 16th Ward, she defeated the candidate of the regular Democratic organization. She has been practicing law for some 16 years and is considered by colleagues and judges one of Chicago's best criminal lawyers. Born Oct. 27, 1910 in Springfield, O., she attended Roosevelt College and John Marshall Law School (LL.B., J.D.). Long an activist, she has received many citations for her work on behalf of human rights. She was vice co-chairman of the Illinois-delegation to the 1972 Democratic National Convention. She is a member of People United to Save Humanity (PUSH), the National Bar Association and many other professional and civic organizations. Divorced, she has a son, Lawrence Jr. Address: 1249 W. 63rd St., Chicago, IL 60621

Janet F. Langhart

Annie L. Lawrence

Rev. George Lawrence

Langhart, Janet Floyd, television personality, is hostess of the interview talk show, "Controversial Issues," on WISH-TV in Indianapolis, Ind. and is the weather reporter on WBBM-TV in Chicago, Ill. She attained her positions by auditioning and by special requests from employers. She is a former Ebony Fashion Fair model. Born Dec. 22, 1941 in Indianapolis, Miss Langhart attended college for two years on an academic scholarship. She was chosen "Miss Sepia 1966," "Miss Chicagoland 1967," and "Miss International Auto Show 1968." Though opportunities for blacks in television are growing, she feels that the improvement is "only because of FCC rulings on employment of minorities" and that "the pace is not fast enough." She is a member of American Women in Radio & TV and Chicago Women in Broadcasting. She is divorced. Address: 630 McClurg Ct., Chicago, IL 60611

Lawrence, Annie L., state official, is assistant nursing education coordinator for the State of Illinois Department of Registration and Education. Born Feb. 13, 1926 in Madisonville, Va. she is a graduate of DePaul University, (B.S.N., M.S.N.) and is studying toward a Ph.D. at the University of Chicago. Her work involves approving all schools of nursing in Illinois for licensure; surveying the schools and providing guidance on problems; improving nursing education; establishing new schools of nursing; evaluating rules and regulations to implement the Illinois Nursing Act; administrating state board examinations and participating in research and studies in nursing. She is advisor to the president of the Illinois State Nurse's Association, and is a member of the Board of Directors of the Washington Park YMCA. She feels that her most significant achievement has been helping many underprivileged women become nurses. Her husband, George W. Lawrence, is an attorney. They have no children. Address: Illinois Dept. of Registration and Education, 160 N. LaSalle St., Chicago, IL, 60603

Lawrence, The Reverend George, clergyman, is pastor of the Antioch Baptist Church (3,500 members) of Brooklyn, N.Y. He was born Sept. 21, 1927 in Trenton, N.J. He is recognized as one of the nation's most articulate spokesmen for the cause of black freedom and human dignity. Before assuming his present pastorate in 1959, he was executive director of the Empire State Baptist Convention (1957–59), press secretary of the National Baptist Convention (1953–55) and community relations director of Tabernacle Baptist Church in Dayton, Ohio (1950–53). He has been a regional representative of SCLC, director of communications for the Progressive National Baptist Convention, chairman of the Social Action Commission of the Protestant Council, president of the board of directors of the House of Friendship Community Center and Mental Health Center of Harlem, and board member of the New York and Brooklyn branches of the NAACP. He was Man of the Year of the Hudson Civic Association and the All-Brooklyn Poll winner cited by the *New York Recorder*. He has received achievement awards from the Brooklyn Urban League and the New York chapter of Omega Psi Phi fraternity. Address: Antioch Baptist Church, 828 Greene Ave., Brooklyn, NY 10021

James R. Lawson

Judge Marjorie M. Lawson

Don L. Lee

Lawson, James Raymond, educator, is president of Fisk University in Nashville, Tenn. Prior to becoming president in 1967, he was head of the department of physics for several years and then vice president. When the former head of the university resigned, Dr. Lawson was appointed to take his place, by the unanimous vote of the board of trustees. Born Jan. 15, 1915 in Louisville, Ky., he studied physics at Fisk University (A.B., 1935); University of Michigan (M.S., 1936; Ph.D., 1939). He has received such honors as Sigma Xi and Phi Beta Kappa and has active professional memberships in the American Physical Society, Optical Society of America, Society of Applied Spectroscopy and American Association of Physics Teachers. He has done considerable research in the field of infrared spectroscopy, and has published a number of articles in this subject. He also serves on the board of directors of the National Association for Equal Opportunity in Higher Education, is a member of the Nashville Chamber of Commerce and on the board of Trustees of the Southern Association of Colleges and Schools. He and his wife, Lillian, have four children: Ronald, Daryl (Mrs. Russell Miller), James and Elizabeth. Address: Fisk University, Nashville, TN 37203

Lawson, Marjorie McKenzie, attorney, is a partner (with her husband, Belford V. Lawson Jr.) in Lawson & Lawson, a law firm in Washington, D.C. Born in 1912 in Pittsburgh, Pa., she is a graduate of the University of Michigan (B.A. and certificate in social work) and the Columbia University School of Law (J.D.). She has been appointed to various positions by Presidents Kennedy, Johnson and Nixon, including: member, the President's Commission on Equal Employment Opportunity (1962); associate judge, D.C. Juvenile Court (1962–65); U.S. Representative to the U.N. Commission for Social Development (1965–69); member, President's Task Force on Urban Renewal (1969), and member, the Commission on the Organization of the Government of the District of Columbia (1970). She is a director of the National Bank of Washington, the Federal City Council, the Mayor's Committee on Economic Development, the Washington Urban League and the Housing Opportunities Council of Metropolitan Washington. She is a founder and trustee of the Educational Foundation of the National Council of Negro Women, and a founder of the Model Inner-City Community Organization, Inc. She and her husband have a son, Belford III. Address: 1140 Connecticut Ave., NW, Washington, DC 20036

Lee, Don L., poet, is writer-in-residence at Howard University, where he also teaches black literature and political science. Born Feb. 23, 1942 in Little Rock, Ark., he is publisher and editor of Third World Press, executive director of the Institute for Positive Education, and editor of the *Black Books Bulletin*, a quarterly discussing books, education, psychology, technology and history. He also was on the executive council of the Congress of African People and was vice chairman (1972–73) of the African Liberation Day Support Committee. He sees the survival of black people as the most important thing in his life and is attempting to bring unity to blacks of the world through his writings, teaching, publications and his educational institution. His published works include *Think Black* (1967), *Black Pride* (1968), *Don't Cry, Scream* (1969), *We Walk the Way of the New World* (1970), *Directionscore: Selected and New Poems* (1971), *Dynamite Voices: Black Poets of the 1960s* (1971) and *From Plan to Planet: Life Studies, the Need for African Minds and Institutions.* Address: Third World Press, 7850 S. Ellis Ave., Chicago, IL 60619

Howard N. Lee

Lena K. Lee

Rev. Thomas F. Lee

Lee, Howard N., city official, is mayor of Chapel Hill, N.C. He was elected in 1969 by a 450-vote margin and was reelected in 1971 by a landslide. He is also director of the Office of Human Development at Duke University. His work involves providing educational opportunities and career development for non-academic employees. Born July 28, 1934 in Lithonia, Ga., he attended Clark College (1953-56), Fort Valley State College (B.A., sociology, 1959) and the University of North Carolina School of Social Work (M.A., 1966). After graduation he was employed at Duke University as Director of Youth Services (1966-68). During 1968 and 1969, he was director of Employee Relations at Duke as well as assistant professor of sociology at North Carolina Central University. He is a member on many boards, commissions and committees, including; the Southern Regional Council, National Association of Social Workers and the North Carolina Heart Association. He has received numerous awards and honors. He was awarded the Doctor of Laws Degree by Shaw University in 1971. He and his wife, Lillian, have three children: Angela, Ricky and Karin Alexis. Address: Duke University, P.O. Box 3712, Durham, NC 27706

Lee, Lena K., legislator, is a member of the Maryland House of Delegates from the 4th District (Baltimore). A Democrat, she was first elected in 1967. Born in Pennsylvania, she is a graduate of Morgan State College in Baltimore (B.S., 1939), New York University (M.A., 1947) and the University of Maryland School of Law (LL.B., 1952). She has also attended Cheyney State College in Maryland. She is a member of the (Baltimore) Mayor's Committee on Procedures for Handling Legal Proceedings Under Emergency Conditions, the Mayor's Committee on Housing Code Enforcement, the League of Women Voters, the American Judicature Society, the International Platform Association, the National Order of Women Legislators and the National Association of Parliamentarians. She is the founder and a past president of the Baltimore chapter of the Cheyney Alumni Association. She is listed in *Who's Who of American Women, Who's Who of Women in the East, Who's Who in American Politics, Who's Who in World Industry* and the *Dictionary of International Biography.* She is a member of numerous civic organizations, including the Lafayette Square Recreation Association and Camp Mohawk Mothers of the YMCA, which she founded. She is a widow. Address: Maryland House of Delegates, Annapolis, MD 21401

Lee, The Reverend Thomas F., clergyman, is pastor of Emmanuel Baptist Church in Chicago, Ill. Born Feb. 6, 1925 in Tuscaloosa, Ala., he attended Crane Junior College, Shield Business College and Chicago State College, and is a graduate of the theological seminary of the Chicago Baptist Institute. He is a member of the American Baptist Convention and the Progressive National Baptist Convention. He is a member of the board of directors of the Church Federation of Chicago and the Chicago Baptist Association, and is chaplain and a board member of the Fraternal Order of Police. He is a deputy sheriff of Cook County Department of Corrections. He is a Prince Hall Mason and is active in numerous Chicago area church and civic groups. He and his wife, Willie Nell, have four children: Clifford, Michael, Franchon and Eric. Address: 6820 S. Emerald Ave., Chicago, IL 60621

Walter J. Leonard   Aubrey C. Lewis   Byron Lewis

Leonard, Walter J., educator, is a special assistant to the president of Harvard University. Prior to his appointment in 1971, he was the assistant dean and assistant director of admissions and financial aid at the Harvard University Law School (1969–71). He handled many of Harvard's problems concerning the admission of women, helped to get more black students admitted to its law school and directed the symposium on "The Black Lawyer in America Today" at Harvard. Born Oct. 3, 1929 in Alma, Ga., he attended Savannah State College (1947–50), Morehouse College (1959–60), the Graduate School of Business Administration at Atlanta University (1961–62) and the School of Law, Howard University (J.D., 1968). Mr. Leonard is the recipient of many honors including the National Bar Asssociation President's Award for Distinguished Service (1972). He is a member of the Association of American Law Schools, Council on Legal Education Opportunity, the American Association of University Professors and the Howard University Law School Alumni Association. The author of numerous articles and papers, he has delivered speeches at major law schools and organizations. He and his wife, Betty, have two children, Anthony and Angela. Address: Massachusetts Hall, Harvard University, Cambridge, MA 02138

Lewis, Aubrey C., business executive, is assistant vice president of F. W. Woolworth Co. in New York City in charge of security and shrinkage control. He develops and oversees measures relating to loss of company's merchandise, cash and other assets. He has been with the company since 1967 and was formerly executive personnel representative. Before joining Woolworth, he was a special agent with the FBI. Born in Montclair, N.J. in 1937, he is a graduate of Notre Dame University (B.S.) and has taken courses at the FBI Academy, Cornell University and New York University (business). An all-round athlete, he has coached both football and track, and was a scout for the Chicago Bears. He is commissioner of the N.J. Sports and Exposition Authority and a member of numerous other civic organizations. He and his wife, Ann, have five children: Lauren, Aubrey Jr., Lisa, John and Gary. Address: 233 Broadway, New York NY 10007

Lewis, Byron, advertising executive, is president of UniWorld Group, Inc., an agency that specializes in marketing, advertising and public relations. The firm seeks to reach and motivate black consumers. Mr. Lewis has held this position for three years. Born Dec. 25, 1931 in Newark, N.J., he is a graduate of Long Island University, (B.A., journalism, 1953). He attended New York University Graduate School where he studied administration and public relations. He is a member of the National Marketing Association. He was vice president and advertising director (1964–69) for *Tuesday,* a newspaper supplement. Mr. Lewis feels that "if blacks retain their special identity, they can become more valuable as productive people, with specialized knowledge and skills in two marketing areas rather than one." Divorced, he has a son, Byron Jr. Address: 62 W. 45th St., New York, NY 10036

Edward Lewis

Edward S. Lewis

Elma I. Lewis

Lewis, Edward, publishing executive, is publisher and chief executive officer of *Essence* magazine in New York, N.Y. Born May 15, 1940 in New York City, he is a graduate of the University of New Mexico (B.A., political science, 1963; M.A. international relations, 1965). He has taken postgraduate courses in public administration at Georgetown University (1965–66) and New York University (1967–69). Before he and his partners founded *Essence* in 1970, he was administrative assistant to the city manager of Albuquerque, N.M. (1964) and taught international relations to Peace Corps volunteers at the University of New Mexico (1964–65). He was a financial analyst for the First National City Bank of New York (1967–69). He is a bachelor. Address: *Essence*, 300 E. 42nd St., New York, NY 10017

Lewis, Edward S., educator, is dean of cooperative education and community relations of the Borough of Manhattan Community College in New York. Born Aug. 17, 1901 in Platte City, Mo., Dr. Lewis is a graduate of the University of Chicago (Ph.B., 1925), University of Pennsylvania, (M.A., 1939) and New York University (Ph.D., 1961). He also holds an honorary (LL.D.) degree from the University of Cincinnati, (1970). He has been a teacher of social science at Florida A&M College in Tallahassee; executive secretary of the Kansas City, Mo., Urban League, and executive director of the Urban League of Greater New York. In addition to being elected the first black president of the National Cooperative Education Association in 1970, he is the author of many book reviews and special feature stories and has contributed articles to educational and scoiological journals. Dr. Lewis has travelled in West Africa, India, Japan, China and Western Europe. He and his wife, Mary, have two children, Carol Jean and Raphael. Address: 134 W. 51st St., New York, NY 10020

Lewis, Elma I., administrator, is founder and director of the National Center of Afro-American Artists in Dorchester, Mass. For 22 years she has directed the Elma Lewis School of Fine Arts which has become the teaching division of the National Center of Afro-American Artists founded in 1968. Born Sept. 15, 1929 in Boston, Mass., she is a graduate of Emerson College (B.L.I., 1943) and Boston University (M.Ed., 1944). She holds honorary degrees from Harvard University, Colby College, Boston College, Anna Maria College and Emerson College. As teacher, administrator, lecturer, choreographer and writer for the NCAAA, she has received numerous honors. Under her direction, the National Center of Afro-American Artists has taught 5,000 black children in classes, workshops and seminars. The school is the prototype for many similar organizations now operating around the country. She is single. Address: National Center of Afro-American Artists, 122 Elm Hill Ave., Dorchester, MA 02121

Elsie M. Lewis

Henry Lewis

James E. Lewis

Lewis, Elsie Makel, educator, is professor of American history at Hunter College in New York, N. Y. She is a specialist in 19th Century and Afro-American history. A college professor since 1956, she has taught at Sweet Briar College (Va.), Emory University and Earlham College (Ind.). In 1971, she visited universities in Kenya, Uganda, Tanzania, Ethiopia and Egypt. Born May 2, 1914 in Little Rock, Ark., she is a graduate of Fisk University (B.A., 1932), University of Southern California (M.A., 1933) and University of Chicago (Ph.D., 1946). American history was her major at each school. Dr. Lewis has written a number of articles, and has presented numerous scholarly papers. She was admitted to Phi Beta Kappa and is a member of several professional organizations, including the American Historical Association and the Association for the Study of Afro-American Life and History. She is married to Joseph F. Makel. Address: Hunter College, 695 Park Ave., New York, NY 10017

Lewis, Henry, orchestra conductor, has been director of the New Jersey Symphony Orchestra in Newark, N.J. since 1968, and is in demand as a guest conductor of numerous orchestras. In 1972, he became the first black to conduct the Metropolitan Opera Orchestra. Born in 1932 in Los Angeles, Calif., he became a member of the Los Angeles Philharmonic Orchestra while still a student on a music scholarship at the University of Southern California. At 18, he was the youngest double bass player in the orchestra's history. He later was appointed as associate conductor. He founded the Los Angeles Chamber Orchestra in 1958 and was musical director of the Los Angeles Opera Co. (1965–68). He conducted the ballet-cantata *Gershwiniana* at La Scala Opera House in Milan, Italy in 1965. He was a bassist with, and later conductor of, the Seventh Army Symphony Orchestra (U. S. Army) in Stuttgart, Germany (1955–57). He is a founder of the Black Academy of Arts and Letters. He and his wife, opera and concert singer Marilyn Horne, have a daughter, Angela. Address: New Jersey Symphony, 1020 Broad St., Newark, NJ 07102

Lewis, James E., artist and educator, is chairman of the art department and director of the art gallery at Morgan State College in Baltimore, Md. Born Aug. 4, 1923 in Phenix, Va., he is a graduate of Philadelphia College of Art (B.F.A.), Temple University in Philadelphia (M.F.A.) and has done advanced studies at Syracuse and Yale universities. He was appointed to the Maryland Fine Arts Commission in 1962. He sculptured a monument dedicated to the memory of the black American soldier, which was erected at Battle Monument Plaza in Baltimore, Md. on June 12, 1972. He and his wife, Jacquelin, have two children, James Jr. and Cathleen. Address: Morgan State College, Baltimore, MD 21239

John Lewis

John G. Lewis Jr.

C. Eric Lincoln

Lewis, John, administrator, is executive director of the Atlanta-based Voter Education Project (VEP), a civil rights group which encourages blacks and other minority-group members to become registered voters and use politics as a means to positive social, economic and political change. Born Feb. 21, 1940 in Troy, Ala., Mr. Lewis graduated from the American Baptist Theological Seminary (B.A., 1961) and Fisk University (B.A., 1963). Arrested 40 times, he was one of the original participants of the CORE-sponsored Freedom Rides in 1961 and was clubbed down at Rock Hill, S.C., and again at Montgomery, Ala. In Mississippi, he was thrown into Parchman State Penitentiary. In 1963, he was one of the major speakers at the March on Washington, as head of the Student Non-Violent Coordinating Committee. As a young man in his early twenties, he dealt directly with two presidents. In 1965, he was in Selma, Ala., where the most brutal of all civil rights confrontations took place. The bloodshed at Selma helped to bring about the 1965 Voting Rights Act which outlawed the literacy tests and other devices which hampered black voting. Since then, more than one million blacks have been registered in the South. Mr. Lewis and his wife, Lillian, pursue political affairs as a leisure interest. They have no children. Address: 52 Fairlie St., NW, Suite 361, Atlanta, GA 30303

Lewis, John Gideon Jr., organization head, is Grand Master and Sovereign Grand Commander of the Prince Hall Masons (Southern Jurisdiction). Living in Baton Rouge, La., he is the director of the fraternal and social programs of the Prince Hall Lodge in Louisiana and of the Southern Jurisdiction of the United Supreme Council, ancient and Scottish Rite of Freemasonry. Born Dec. 9, 1903 in Natchitoches, La., he is a graduate of Fisk University (A.B.) and has an honorary (L.H.D.) degree from Central State College. He was Delta Man of the Year in 1960 and won the National Urban League Equal Opportunity Award in 1961. He is a life member of both the NAACP and the Louisiana Education Association. He and his wife, Amelia, have a daughter, Veraldine. Address: 1335 N. Boulevard, Baton Rouge, LA 70802

Lincoln, C. Eric, educator, is a professor of sociology and religion at Union Theological Seminary and an adjunct professor of religion at Columbia University, both in New York City. Born June 23, 1924 in Athens, Ala., he received degrees from LeMoyne College (B.A., 1947), Fisk University (M.A., 1954), the University of Chicago (B.D., 1956), and Boston University (M.Ed. and Ph.D., both 1960). He has also received an honorary LL.D. degree from Carleton College (1968). He has taught or served as an administrator at more than 15 educational institutions; guest lectured or presented papers at nearly 150 schools and professional organizations, and contributed to numerous American and German books and periodicals. His published books include *The Black Muslims in America*, *A Profile of Martin Luther King* and *The Blackamericans*. A member and the first president of the Black Academy of Arts and Letters, he edits a black religion series, bearing his name, for Doubleday and Co. He and his wife, Lucy, have a daughter, Hilary Anne, and son, Less Charles II. Dr. Lincoln also has two children, Cecil Eric and Joyce Elaine, by a previous marriage. Address: Union Theological Seminary, Broadway and 120th Sts., New York, NY 10027

Richard Linyard

Arthur C. Littleton

James B. Lockhart

Charles H. Loeb

Linyard, Richard, banker, is executive vice president and a member of the board of directors of the Seaway National Bank of Chicago, Ill. Born Nov. 16, 1930 in Maywood, Ill., he attended Northwestern University, received standard and advance certificates of the American Institute of Banking, and received a diploma from the Graduate School of Banking at the University of Wisconsin. In 1950, he began working at Oak Park (Ill.) Trust and Savings Bank as a janitor. He became, successively, an elevator operator, savings bookkeeper, teller, general bookkeeper and assistant manager of the savings department. He was elected assistant cashier in January, 1964. In December, 1964, he joined the Seaway National Bank as cashier. Later, he became vice president and cashier. He is president of the Chicago chapter of the American Institute of Banking. He and his wife, Maggie, have a daughter, Linda, and two sons, Lance and Timothy. Address: 645 E. 87th St., Chicago, IL 60619

Littleton, Arthur C., research psychologist, is president of Urban Behavioral Research Associates, a social science research and consulting firm in St. Louis, Mo. The firm, which has various skilled black specialists working as a team, serves as a catalyst between minority communities and the major social institutions. It has been engaged in consultation, curriculum development, staff training for various programs, and data interpretation. Born Sept. 25, 1940 in St. Louis, Dr. Littleton is a graduate of the University of Missouri (B.A., education, 1962; M.Ed., counseling, 1963) and St. Louis University (Ph.D., educational psychology, 1969). Before starting his own firm in 1971, he was assistant professor of education (1969–71) and an instructor (1968–69) at the University of Missouri at St. Louis. Earlier, he worked as an educational consultant, researcher, youth counselor and public school teacher. He has spoken at a number of national conferences of professional organizations, and his published works include a book, *Black Viewpoints* (co-editor with M.W. Burger) and articles in various scholarly journals. He was chairman (1972) of the black caucus of the American Educational Research Association. He and his wife, Paula, have three sons: Stephen, David and Jeffrey. Address: 2739 N. Grand, Suite 312, St. Louis, MO 63106

Lockhart, James B., business executive, is vice president-general counsel and secretary of the Budget Rent-a-Car Corporation of America in Chicago, Ill. He was elected to the position in December, 1972. Born May 27, 1936 in New York, N.Y., he is a graduate of Boston University (B.A. and B.S., business administration, 1957; J.D., 1959). Prior to assuming his present position, he was a partner in the law firm, Rivers, Lockhart & Lawrence. He also has served as an attorney and advisor in the chief counsel's office of the Bureau of Public Debt, U.S. Treasury Department; and as assistant corporation counsel for the City of Chicago. He is a member of the Chicago, Cook and American Bar Associations. He has served on the board of Lawrence Hall-Randall House (Episcopal Charities of Chicago). He and his wife, Reba, have one son, Marc. Address: Budget Rent-a-Car, 35 E. Wacker Dr., Chicago, IL 60601

Loeb, Charles H., newspaper executive, is vice president-advertising of the *Cleveland Call and Post*, a black-owned weekly newspaper in Cleveland, Ohio. He also writes editorials and a column. He was born April 2, 1905 in Baton Rouge, La. and attended Howard University for several years. He worked on the New York *Amsterdam News*, the *Atlanta World* and the *Cleveland Eagle* before joining the staff of the *Call and Post* in 1933. He was a war correspondent during World War II. Involved in civil rights, political and civic activities in Cleveland for many years, he is a member of the NAACP, the Urban League, and the Cleveland Opera Association. He has numerous journalism awards, including the 1966 Citation of Merit for Outstanding Performance in Journalism conferred by Lincoln University in Missouri. He and his wife, Beulah, have two daughters, Mrs. Jennie Dericotte and Mrs. Stella Munson. Address: 1949 E. 105th St., Cleveland, OH 44108

Herman H. Long   Joe Louis

Long, Herman H., educator, is president of Talladega College in Talladega, Ala. He is also director of Community Self Surveys and is a race relations consultant. Born May 2, 1912 in Birmingham, Ala. Mr. Long has degrees from Talladega College. (A.B., *cum laude* 1935) the School of Religious Education, Hartford Seminary Foundation (M.A., 1936) and the University of Michigan (Ph.D., 1949). Dr. Long was appointed to his present position in 1964 after serving as the director of the race relations department and the Race Relations Institute of Fisk University since 1947. He is the author of several scholarly articles, including "Social Psychology and Innovations in Education," "The Role of Government in Race Relations," "Community Research and Intergroup Adjustments," and a book titled *The Higher Education of Negroes: A Look Forward*. Dr. Long is a member of numerous civic and professional organizations, including the American Psychological Association, and the National Association for Intergroup Relations. He served as president of the United Negro College Fund in 1970. Dr. Long and his wife, Henrietta, have a daughter, Ellen. Address: Talladega College, Talladega, AL 35160

Louis, Joe (Joseph Louis Barrow), former heavyweight champion, held the world heavyweight boxing championship longer (12 years) and defended it more often (25 times) than anyone else. At his peak, polls showed he was better known throughout the world than any American other than President Franklin D. Roosevelt. He was born May 13, 1914 in Lexington, Ala. In 1932, he became Detroit's light heavyweight Golden Gloves champion, reached the finals of the national boxing championship a year later, and in April, 1934 became America's amateur light heavyweight boxing champion. Turning professional, he was managed by three Detroit blacks who molded him into a champion. In his first professional fight, in 1934, Mr. Louis knocked out Jack Kracken in the first round. In 1935, he knocked out the former champion Primo Carnera in the sixth round at Yankee Stadium. In 1937, he met James J. Braddock for the world championship and knocked him out in the eighth round, making Joe Louis, at 23, the youngest heavyweight champion of all time. In 1938, he knocked out Max Schmeling in two minutes and four seconds of the first round. During World War II, he risked his title in two fights and donated his entire purse to charity—fighting Buddy Baer for Navy Relief and Abe Simon for Army Relief. He retired as undefeated champion in March, 1949. He and his wife, the former Martha Malone Jefferson, an attorney, have an adopted son, Jo Jo. Mr. Louis has two children by a previous marriage, a daughter, Jackie, and Joe Jr. Address: c/o Martha M. Jefferson, 9350 Wilshire Blvd., Beverly Hills, CA 90212

Love, Clarence C., legislator, is state representative for the 35th District (Kansas City) of Kansas. He was elected in 1972 to his fourth term. Born February 24, 1922 in Weir, Kan., he studied architectural engineering for one year before having to leave school to support his family. After serving in World War II, he opened a dry cleaning business and became active in church and civil rights work. He is a 33° Mason. In the Kansas legislature, he led a successful effort to increase, from six to seven, the number of members on local school boards—an effort that resulted in the immediate appointment of 12 blacks to school boards in the state. He and his wife, Travestine, have four daughters: Mrs. Marva Roberson, Mrs. Cheryl Thompson, Mrs. Travestine Moore and Lynn, and a son, Clarence Jr. Address: Kansas State House, Topeka, KS 66612

Lowery, Robert O., city official, was appointed fire commissioner of New York City, N.Y. on Jan. 1, 1966. Born April 20, 1916 in Buffalo, N.Y., he attended the College of the City of New York and studied at New York University's School of Public Administration and at the Michigan State University National Institute on Police and Community Relations. Joining the department in 1942 as a fireman, he rose to commissioner through promotions to lieutenant, fire marshal and deputy fire commissioner. He is the first black appointed administrator of a fire department of a major city. The 15,000-member department is the largest fire-fighting organization in the world, has the largest annual budget ($330 million) and is the busiest, recording 280,000 alarms in 1971. He has launched programs to educate people about fires and to encourage better relations between the department and the public. He is attempting to recruit more blacks—currently only 4 per cent (600 men) of the firemen under his command are black. Indicative of his leadership is a quotation in a *New York Times* survey on corruption among New York City civil servants: "The Fire Department is the most honest agency in the city. It is well known that you can't bribe a Fire Department inspector." A widower, Commissioner Lowery has two daughters, Mrs. Lesie Ann Strickland and Mrs. Gertrude Erwin. Address: 110 Church St., New York, NY 10007
See article on Robert O. Lowery in Volume II

Lucas, Florence V., attorney, is deputy commissioner of the New York State Division of Human Rights. As chief of staff for all intra-agency coordination, she is responsible for seeing that all division policies are implemented by 260 professional, technical, and clerical employees. She became deputy commissioner in 1972 after six years of work at the division. Mrs. Lucas was born October 10, 1915 in New York, N.Y. She has degrees from Hunter College (B.A.) and Brooklyn Law School (J.D.). She is a member of the Judicial Council of the United Methodist Church and is national first vice president of the National Association of Negro Business and Professional Women's Clubs, Inc. She is married to David Rex Edwards. Address: 270 Broadway, New York, NY 10007.

Clarence C. Love

Robert O. Lowery

Florence V. Lucas

Victoria Lucas

Leonard Everett Lyles

Charles A. Lyons Jr.

Lucas, Victoria, public relations executive, is president of Victoria Lucas Associates in New York, N. Y. She formed her agency in 1968 with blues singer B. B. King as her first client. Since then she has never had to solicit an account. Other clients include peotess Nikki Giovanni; singer Donny Hathaway, Gladys Knight and the Pips, Irene Reid, Labelle, Gene McDaniels and the Patterson Singers. Besides entertainers, she has also had such clients as Defense Atty. F. Lee Bailey and *Encore* magazine. Miss Lucas has been a public relations and promotions specialist for more than 20 years. In 1971, she was named "Media Woman of the Year" by the National Association of Media Women. She is a member of the Publicity Club of N.Y., National Association of Media Women and Women Executives in Public Relations. Born in Chicago, Ill., she studied liberal arts at Wilson Junior College in Chicago, and business administration at City College of New York. Address: 1414 Ave. of the Americas, New York, NY 10019

Lyles, Leonard Everett ("Lenny"), business executive, is personnel manager at the Louisville factory of Brown & Williamson Tobacco Corp. in Louisville, Ky. Previously, he was the company's college sales representative, assistant to the national sales manager, and training coordinator. Born Jan. 26, 1936 in Nashville, Tenn., he is a graduate of the University of Louisville (B.S.) and has attended various managerial seminars sponsored by Brown & Williamson. He set a number of records in track and football at the University of Louisville, and played professional football with the Baltimore Colts and the San Francisco 49ers. He retired from football in 1969. He has received numerous awards and was the first black appointed to the Jefferson County Police Merit Board. He is director and vice chairman of the Louisville Association of Concerned Businessmen. He and his wife, Faith, have three sons: Leonard Jr., Michael and Christopher. Address: 1600 W. Hill St., Louisville, KY 40201

Lyons, Charles A. Jr., educator and administrator, is chancellor of Fayetteville State University in Fayetteville, N.C. He was born April 5, 1926 in Conetoe, N.C. Dr. Lyons is a graduate of Shaw University (A.B., history, 1949), and Ohio State University (M.A., political science, 1954; Ph.D., political science, 1957). He spent a year in India as a Fulbright Scholar, an experience which he feels helped to clarify his career plans. He left that country resolved to devote himself to the teaching of black youth. He has taught at Ohio State University (1951–56), Grambling College (1956–59) and Elizabeth City State University (1959–62). Prior to assuming his present position, he was director of admissions at Howard University (1964–69). He is a member of the South Carolina State Citizens Advisory Committee Institute for Alcohol Studies, and is a member of the Policy Commission, Institute for higher Educational Opportunity, Southern Regional Education Board in Atlanta, Ga. He and his wife, Rosa, have three children: Yvonne, Brenda and Charles. Address: Fayetteville State University, Fayetteville, NC 28301

M

Jackie "Moms" Mabley

William A. McClain

Ernestine McClendon

Mabley, Jackie ("Moms"), entertainer, is one of America's best known comediennes. Born Loretta Mary Aiken in Brevard, N.C., she graduated from high school in Washington, D.C. She started portraying funny characters in church pageants in North Carolina, starred in school plays, and at 13 was the community's favorite young comedienne. Seeing a touring vaudeville troupe convinced her, at 14, that her future lay in entertainment. After completing high school, she shared a boarding house life with show business friends in Buffalo, N.Y. Her gift for mothering disconsolate friends won her the nickname "Moms." She met the comedy team of Buck and Bubbles who steered her to her first role in a touring show, *The Rich Aunt from Utah.* Perfecting her own comedy monologue, she played with Tim Moore, Dusty Fletcher and Pigmeat Markham. By 1923 she was appearing in New York City, often sharing the stage with Louis Armstrong, Duke Ellington, Count Basie and Cab Calloway. She began playing to packed houses across the country—college auditoriums, concert halls, Playboy clubs and big-city theaters such as Harlem's Apollo and Chicago's Regal. In 1960, her first record album of jokes sold over a million copies. Ten other highly successful albums had been released by 1973. Her popularity landed her a role in the film *Boarding House Blues.* She has been a guest on the Mike Douglas, Bill Cosby, Merv Griffin, Smothers Brothers and Flip Wilson television shows. She has three daughters and six grandchildren. Address: 445 Park Ave., New York, NY 10022 **See article on Jackie ("Moms") Mabley in Volume II.**

McClain, William A., attorney, is a corporate lawyer with Keating, Muething & Klekamp, a law firm in Cincinnati, Ohio. He joined the firm in 1972 after leaving office as city solicitor of Cincinnati, a position he had held since 1963. Previously, he was deputy city solicitor (1957-63) and assistant city solicitor (1942-57). He was acting city manager of Cincinnati from April 13, 1968 to June 24, 1968 and from Jan. 16, 1972 to June 1, 1972. Born Jan. 11, 1913 in Sanford, N. C., he is a graduate of Wittenberg College (A.B., 1934) and the University of Michigan Law School (J.D., 1937). He is a member of the Ohio State Bar Association, National Bar Association, American Bar Association, American Judicature Society and other professional organizations. He is a member of the board of directors of Central Clinic, Cincinnati General Hospital, Council of Christian Communions of Greater Cincinnati, Cincinnati Area Chapter of American National Red Cross, and Cincinnati Chapter of National Conference of Christians and Jews. He is a trustee of Allen Temple A.M.E. Church; South Ohio Conference, 3rd Episcopal District of the A.M.E. Church (he is also general counsel), and McCall Edison Foundation of Cincinnati. He is a 33° Mason. He has received numerous citations, awards, honorary degrees, etc., is a member of a number of civic organizations, and has authored several published articles. He and his wife, Roberta, have no children. Address: 18th Floor, Provident Tower, Cincinnati, OH 45202

McClendon, Ernestine, artists' manager, is owner of Ernestine McClendon Enterprises, with offices in New York and Los Angeles. A theatrical agent for 12 years, she represents nearly 100 clients, including actors in television, radio, theater and movies, directors, writers and variety acts. She was the first in her field to be franchised by all unions as a theatrical agent and is largely responsible for getting blacks into television commercials. Born August 17, 1921 in Norfolk, Va., she attended Virginia State College in Petersburg. A former actress, she has appeared both on television and in live theater. She has taught acting in the Harlem Workshop, which she organized. She won the Woman's Award (1969) and was named one of Two Thousand Women of Achievement (1970). She and her husband, George Wiltshire, have a daughter, Phyllis. Address: 56 W. 45th St., New York, NY 10036

Billy Q. McCray

Judge Wade H. McCree Jr.

Geraldine McCullough

McCray, Billy Q., legislator, is a senator in the Kansas House of Representatives. He is also the chief industrial photographer for the Boeing Airplane Co. in Wichita, Kan. He has been a state senator for six years and has been with the Boeing company for 21 years. Born Oct. 29, 1929 in Geary, Okla., he attended Langston University (1945–47), Colorado University (1948–49) and the Lowry School of Photography in Denver, Colo. where he graduated with top honors. He was elected to his position as senator on the Democratic ticket in 1966. There have been only three black senators in Kansas since statehood. He believes his most significant achievement was being elected to the Kansas State Senate from a district composed of 60 percent white and 40 percent black and other minorities. He is a member of the Prince Hall Masons. Most of his work has been in the area of religious leadership training and civil rights for black citizens. He and his wife, Wyvette, have four children: Frankieleen, Anthony, Melody and Kent. Address: 3800 South Oliver, Wichita, KS 67210

McCree, Wade H. Jr., jurist, is a U.S. Circuit Judge. Born in Des Moines, Iowa, July 3, 1920, he is a graduate of Fisk University (B.A., 1941), Harvard University Law School (LL.B.) and has received honorary degrees (LL.D.) from Tuskegee Institute, Wayne State University, Detroit College of Law, University of Detroit, Michigan State University, University of Michigan and Harvard University. He practiced law in Detroit, Mich. and served as workmen's compensation commissioner prior to becoming Circuit Judge in Michigan in 1954. In 1961, he was appointed to the U. S. District Court, and in 1966 he was appointed to the U. S. Court of Appeals for the Sixth Circuit where he currently serves. He has been an adjunct faculty member of Wayne State University Law School, a member of the law faculty of the Salzburg Seminar in American Studies, a member of the summer faculty of the Law School of the University of Indiana, a fellow of the American Bar Foundation, a former director of the American Judicature Society, a director of the Federal Judicial Center, member of the Institute of Judicial Administration and a member of the Advisory Board of the American Bar Association. He and his wife, Dores, have three children: Mrs. Kathleen Lewis, and twins, Karen and Wade. Address: 700 Federal Building, Detroit, MI 48207

McCullough, Geraldine, painter-sculptress, is chairman and professor of the art department at Rosary College in River Forest, Ill. Born Dec. 1, 1922, in Kingston, Ark., she holds degrees from the Art Institute of Chicago, (bachelor of art education, 1948, and master of art education, 1955). As a student at the Art Institute, she was awarded the John D. Steindecker Scholarship, the Memorial Scholarship and won a figure painting citation. After teaching at Wendell Phillips High School for 14 years, she accepted the art professorship at Rosary College. She won honors as a painter and exhibited in national galleries, winning a Purchase Award in 1959, and first prize in 1961 at the Annual Art Exhibit of Atlanta University. She made her debut as a sculptress at the Century of Negro Progress Exposition held in Chicago in 1963. Her sculpture entitled "Phoenix," which was awarded the George D. Widener Memorial Gold Medal for the "most meritorious work" in sculpture at the 159th annual exhibition of the Pennsylvania Academy of Fine Arts in 1964, was a welded steel and copper abstraction of 250 pounds of solid metals. This annual exhibit is one to which only established artists are "invited" to enter their works. Mrs. McCullough, however, entered the competition without invitation—and won. She was commissioned to do a sculpture of Dr. Martin Luther King Jr. by the West-Side Developing Company. The sculpture was unveiled Jan. 15, 1973, on the anniversary of Dr. King's birthday. She is a member of Illinois Art Educators, Alumni Association of the Art Institute of Chicago, American Association of University Professors and appeared in *Who's Who of American Women*, 1966–72 and *American Negro Heritage*, 1968. Mrs. McCullough and her husband, Lester, have one son, Lester Jr. Address: 7900 W. Division, River Forest, IL 60302

McGee, Henry W., postal official, is district manager of the Chicago (Ill.) Metropolitan Area Postal Service. Born Feb. 7, 1910 in Hillsboro, Tex., he is a graduate of Illinois Institute of Technology (A.B., 1949) and the University of Chicago (M.A., 1961). Before assuming his present position in 1972, he had been the first black man to be postmaster of Chicago's main post office with 28,000 employees, "the world's largest mail processing facility under one roof." He joined the post office in 1931 as a substitute clerk-carrier and "was in good shape" if he made $10 a week. His persistence in pursuing an education while working undoubtedly had much to do with his advancement to supervisor, personnel director, postmaster and district manager, starting at a time when opportunities for blacks in the post office were much circumscribed. When he was appointed postmaster by President Lyndon B. Johnson in 1966, he inherited massive problems: ever-increasing mail volume, difficulty in recruiting capable employees and racial discrimination in hiring and promotion. He greatly improved efficiency and increased the number of black supervisors from about 200 to more than 700, while making it clear that there would be no reverse discrimination. Formerly president of the Chicago NAACP chapter, he is president of the Joint Negro Appeal and a director of the Community Fund of Chicago. He and his wife, Attye Belle, have three adult children: Henry Jr., Penny and Sylvia. Address: 120 S. Riverside Plaza, Chicago, IL 60688 **See article on Henry W. McGee in Volume II**

McGee, James, sales manager, supervises 11 retail stores of the Firestone Tire and Rubber Co. as retail sales manager of the Chicago, Ill. District which extends to South Bend, Ind. His responsibilities include recruiting, training, promotions, advertising and sales promotion, and all phases of store operation. Previously, he was a retail salesman, office mgr., credit mgr., service mgr., asst. store mgr. and store mgr. Born Nov. 26, 1934 in New Orleans, La., he attended the Milwaukee School of Engineering (Assoc. degree in elect. engrg.) and completed Firestone's advance management training in problem solving. He feels that opportunities for Blacks are unlimited in retail store positions, store management and middle management. He and his wife, Darlene, have four children: James III, Damon, Melanie and Erikka. Address: 2710 W. 79th St., Chicago, IL 60652.

McGehee, Nan Elizabeth, educator and administrator, is associate chancellor of the University of Illinois (Chicago Circle Campus). Previously, she was associate dean of faculties (1970–72) and associate professor of psychology. She was director of the University Honors Program (1967–70), she has been a member of the University faculty since 1961. Born in Chicago, she is a graduate of the University of Chicago (A.B.) and Northwestern University (M.S. and Ph.D.). She is a member of Alpha Kappa Alpha, the American Psychological Association and other professional and civic organizations. Address: University of Illinois, Circle Campus, Box 4348, Chicago, IL 60680

Henry W. McGee

James McGee

Nan E. McGehee

Rosalie J. McGuire

Donald C. McKayle

Rev. Samuel B. McKinney

McGuire, Rosalie J., educator, is president of the National Association of Negro Business and Professional Women Clubs, Inc., and is the retired principal of Bentalou Elementary School in Baltimore, Md. Previously, she was national education chairman and national first vice president of NBPWC. Born Jan. 27, 1910 in Baltimore, she is a graduate of Morgan State College (B.A.) and New York University (M.A., administration and supervision) and has done post-graduate work at Johns Hopkins University and Columbia University. She has served as first vice president of the Maryland League of Women's Clubs, basileus of Phi Delta Kappa sorority and co-chairman of Baltimore's Provident Hospital Development Program. She is a member of the National Council of Women of the United States, the President's Committee on the Employment of the Handicapped and the Provident Hospital board of directors. She and her husband, John McGuire, live in Baltimore. She has two sons, Elwyn and Marsden Rawlings. Address: 3411 Lynchester Rd., Baltimore, MD 21215

McKayle, Donald Cohen, choreographer, is one of America's most distinguished choreographers. Born July 6, 1930 in New York, N.Y., he enrolled at City College of New York in 1946 but left after his sophomore year to take dance lessons and to perform. He made his debut as a dancer in the spring of 1948, appearing in the works of Sophie Maslow and Jean Erdman at the Mansfield Theatre. For several years during the 1950s, he appeared with several choreographers, including the famed Martha Graham, and danced in Broadway shows. Like many modern dancers, he started to choreograph almost as soon as he began performing. In 1963, he received the Capezio Dance Award for his "translation of American folk material into theatre dances of interracial cast." For his staging of the dances and the much acclaimed prize fight scene in the Sammy Davis Jr. show *Golden Boy* (1964), he was nominated for an Antoinette Perry (Tony) Award. He also has choreographed a number of television shows for such entertainers as Bill Cosby and Leslie Uggams. He did his first film choreography for the 20th Century-Fox version of James Earl Jones' *The Great White Hope*. His company was chosen to perform at the 1960 Festival of Two Worlds in Spoleto, Italy. Throughout his career, Mr. McKayle has worked to gain recognition for black artists and has explored themes of black cultural identity. In 1965, he married Leah Levin, who dances professionally as Lea Vivante. They have a son, Guy. Mr. McKayle has two daughters, Gabrielle and Liane, by a previous marriage. Address: William Morris Agency, 151 El Camino Dr., Beverly Hills, CA 90212

McKinney, The Reverend Samuel B., clergyman, is pastor of the Mt. Zion Baptist Church in Seattle, Wash. Born Dec. 28, 1926 in Flint, Mich., he attended the public schools of Cleveland, and has degrees from Morehouse College (A.B., political science, 1949) and Colgate-Rochester Divinity School (M.Div., 1952). He is a Martin Luther King Fellow in black church studies at Colgate-Rochester/Bexley Hall/Crozer Theological Seminaries, and studied in Nigeria and Ghana in 1972. In 1970, he received an honorary doctor of divinity degree from Linfield College in McMinnville, Ore. He is founder of the Liberty Bank of Seattle, the first black bank in the Pacific Northwest. Rev. McKinney is president of Black American Churchmen, chairman, of the Seattle Opportunities Industrialization Center and principal of Harrison Elementary Education Center. He and his wife, Louise, have two daughters, Lora-Ellen and Rhoda Eileen. Address: Mt. Zion Baptist Church, 19th Ave. at E. Madison St., Seattle, WA 98122

Floyd B. McKissick

Fr. A. J. McKnight

Dunbar S. McLaurin

McKissick, Floyd B., land developer, is the president of Floyd B. McKissick Enterprises, Inc. in Soul City, N.C., a national company formed to help organize and finance black businesses. He is also president of Warren Regional Planning Corporation, Inc., the technical planning arm of the company, whose major project is the development of Soul City, a new town in North Carolina, the cost of which is estimated at $90 million. Born March 9, 1922 in Asheville, N.C., he worked his way through Morehouse College. He attended the Law School of North Carolina College (J.D., 1951) and was admitted to the North Carolina Bar in 1952 and the United States Supreme Court in 1955. He is also licensed to practice before the Federal Communications Commission, the Federal District Court of Appeals, the United States Court of Appeals and the United States Customs Court. In 1963, Mr. McKissick was elected national chairman of the Congress of Racial Equality and in 1966 he became its national director. He raised more than $3 million for the organization and used his past experience as receiver and trustee in bankruptcy to revamp its affairs. In 1968, he resigned from CORE to spend full time helping to build the black economy. Mr. McKissick is a lecturer and public speaker and has written many articles and essays. He is chairman of both the National Conference of Black Lawyers, the National Committee for a Two-Party System, Inc. and a member of Alpha Phi Alpha fraternity. He and his wife, Evelyn, have four children: Joycelyn Myers, Andree Y. Kennard, S. Charmaine and Floyd B. Address: P.O. Box 188, Soul City, NC 27553

McKnight, Fr. Albert J., financier and priest, is president of the Southern Cooperative Development Fund with headquarters in Lafayette, La. Born Aug. 8, 1972 in Brooklyn, N.Y., he has degrees from Saint Mary's Seminary (B.A., B.T.) and received seminary training under the Holy Ghost Fathers in Pennsylvania and Connecticut. In 1970, Fr. McKnight was appointed president of the financial institution that meets the needs of over 125 low-income cooperatives in the South. In residence at St. Paul's Church in Lafayette since 1970, he has served on numerous Louisiana economic development task forces. Included are Southern Consumers' Cooperative, Goals for Louisiana Task Force, United States Office of Economic Opportunity Task Force and People's Enterprise, Inc. He also helped to organize over 10 credit unions in the state and in 1963 was appointed diocesan director of Credit Unions. Fr. McKnight has also been associated with Our Lady of Lourdes, Immaculate Heart of Mary and Saint Martin de Porres Churches in Louisiana. Address: P.O. Box 3005, Lafayette, LA 70501

McLaurin, Dunbar S., economist and attorney, has been a successful businessman since 1942. He started his career in the Philippines and, in two years, at the age of 27, had built a $2 million business consisting of an import-export company, a motion picture company and an automotive and heavy equipment company. Born 1915 in Oklahoma City, Okla., he attended Southwest College (A.B., business administration, 1931), the University of Illinois (A.M., economics, 1932; Ph.D., economics, 1936, and Brooklyn Law School, J.D., 1953). He was a founder of Harlem's Freedom National Bank (1964). He is president of Ghettonomics, Inc., a consultant firm formed in 1968. He also perfected the Ghetto Economic Development and Industrial Plan (GHEDIPLAN), designed to help black businesses and enterprises through the use of small business association loans and bank deposits. He is chairman of the board, director and organizer of the Universal National Bank, the second minority bank ever to be given a charter in New York City in the past fifty years, and the first in the Wall Street area. He is a member of the New York Bar and has lectured and written extensively in the fields of minority economic development and minority banking .He has been an economic consultant to the city of New York and to the federal government. He and his wife, Liz, live in Mount Vernon, N.Y. Address: Universal National Bank, 15 Park Row, New York, NY 10038

James A. McLendon

C. J. McLin Jr.

E. Duke McNeil

Cirilo A. McSween

McLendon, James A., legislator, is a member of the Illinois General Assembly from the 24th District (Chicago) and is serving a third term of office. Born in Washington, Ga., he is a graduate of Fisk University in Nashville, Tenn. (A.B., 1928) and Northwestern University (J.D., 1932). He is a former master in chancery of the Cook County Superior Court and has been an arbitrator for the Industrial Commission and a staff attorney for the Chicago Transit Authority. He and his wife, Elnora, live in Chicago. Address: Illinois General Assembly, Springfield, IL 62706

McLin, C. J. Jr., legislator, is a state representative in Ohio (Democratic, Dayton). He was first elected in 1966. Born May 31, 1921 in East St. Louis, Ill., he attended Virginia Union University and graduated from the Cincinnati College of Embalming. He is president of McLin Funeral Home, Inc. in Cincinnati. Active in Democratic politics in Ohio, he was the first black elected president of the Gem City Democratic Club, a county-wide Democratic organization. In 1967 he was chairman of the Mayor's Committee for the Study of Riots. In 1968 he became the first black appointed to the State of Ohio House Rules Committee. He is a special advisor on Minority Affairs to the Governor of Ohio, and is secretary of the State Democratic Executive Committee. He is a board member of Unity State Bank in Dayton, Ohio, and holds memberships with the Boy Scouts of America, Catholic Interracial Council of Miami Valley, Dayton Chamber of Commerce, and Goodwill Industries of Dayton, Inc. He is also a member of the Montgomery County Funeral Directors Association, National Funeral Directors and Morticians Association, Inc. and Ohio Funeral Directors Association, Inc. Address: 1130 Germantown St., Dayton, OH 45408

McNeil, Ernest Duke, attorney, is senior partner in the law firm of E. Duke McNeil and Associates and president of The Woodlawn Organization in Chicago, Ill. Born Oct. 9, 1936 in Memphis, Tenn., he received degrees from Fisk University (B.A., history, 1957), Tennessee State University (B.S., political science) and De Paul University (J.D., 1965). Recently, Mr. McNeil was one of the first persons Illinois Governor-elect Dan Walker invited to join his cabinet. He is also chairman of the Black Businessmen's Association (an organization of 200 black entrepreneurs), president of Hustlers Discount Records, and co-founder and treasurer of UHURU, a legal foundation, and the Organization of Black American Culture. In 1972, he was honored by Power, Inc. for Outstanding Contributions for Black Liberation. Mr. McNeil and his wife, Sandra, have two children, Stephen and Julia. Address: T.W.O., 1135 E. 63rd St., Chicago, IL 60637

McSween, Cirilo A., insurance counselor and analyst, is president of Cirilo A. McSween and Associates in Chicago, Ill., and is among the top insurance salesmen of New York Life Insurance Co. Born July 8, 1929 in Panama City, Panama, he is a graduate of the University of Illinois (B.A., economics, 1954) where he won three varsity athletic letters in track and field. In 1957, he became the first black in the United States to represent a major life insurance firm, and also the first black to sell $1 million worth of life insurance for any company within one calendar year. He surpassed this feat every consecutive year since then, his highest total sales in any one year being $3,500,000. In December, 1966, he was the top ranking New York Life agent among the firm's 8,000 agents in the United States, Canada and Puerto Rico. In 1952, he was a member of the Republic of Panama Olympic Team and became captain in 1953. He is a vice president and a member of the board of directors of Independence Bank of Chicago and is national treasurer of the Southern Christian Leadership Conference, a post in which he succeeded the Reverend Ralph David Abernathy, now president of the organization. Mr. McSween is a life member of the insurance industry's Million Dollar Round Table, and is a North Central regional vice president of the Top Club of New York Life Insurance Co. He and his wife, Gwendolyn, have two children, Esperanza and Veronica. Address: 471 E. 31st St., Chicago, IL 60616

213

Pearl I. J. Madison

Robert P. Madison

Geraldyn H. Major

Joseph F. Makel

Madison, Pearl I. Johnson, businesswoman, is president of Christian Benevolent Burial Association, Inc. and Christian Benevolent Funeral Home, Inc. in Mobile, Ala. Born in Mobile, she was one of the founders of the businesses—the burial association in 1926, the funeral home in 1929—which now gross some $700,000 a year. She employs 80 persons. She is a member of the Mobile Area Chamber of Commerce, the National Insurance Association and is a sponsor of the Mobile Sheriff's Department. She is a widow. Address: P. O. Box 511, Mobile, AL 36601

Madison, Robert P., architect, is president of Madison-Madison, International, an architectural firm in Cleveland, Ohio. His brother, Julian C. Madison, is a partner. The firm, founded in 1954, has designed many buildings, including the U.S. Embassy Office Building in Dakar, Senegal, and the Engineering and Nuclear Facility at Tuskegee Institute in Alabama. Born in Cleveland on July 28, 1923, Mr. Madison earned degrees at Western Reserve University (B. Architect, 1948) and Harvard University (M. Architect, 1952) and did research in Paris under a Fulbright Fellowship. He is a member of the American Institute of Architects and is on the board of directors of the Northern Ohio Bank and the Industrial Bank of Washington (D.C.). He and his wife, Leatrice, have two daughters, Jeanne and Juliette. Address: 1900 Euclid Ave., Cleveland, OH 44115

Major, Gerri (Geraldyn H.), journalist, is a senior staff editor at the New York bureau of Johnson Publishing Company, Inc. A 20-year employee, she writes a weekly society column for *Jet* magazine and is a senior staff editor of *Ebony.* Born July 29, 1894 in Chicago, Ill., she graduated from the University of Chicago (Ph.B.), and has a degree in education from Chicago Normal College. She did further study at Columbia University and New York University. Mrs. Major has been managing and women's editor of several New York newspapers and once directed her own specialized publicity bureau. She is a member of the National Council of Negro Women, Actors' Equity Guild, Alpha Kappa Alpha sorority, the Urban League, and a life member of NAACP. She has travelled, on assignment, to all the major cities of the United States, Europe, Africa, Asia, Mexico, South America and the West Indies. She has honors and citations from all over the world and was voted "Foremost Woman in Communication." Address: 2235 Fifth Ave., Apt. 10-C, New York, NY 10037

Makel, Joseph F., sales executive, is assistant to the vice president of sales at Fromm and Sichel, Inc. in San Francisco, Calif. The firm is sole worldwide distributor for the Christian Brothers wines and spirits. Mr. Makel travels throughout the U. S. developing sales markets, especially among blacks. Born July 6, 1908 in Frederick County, Maryland, he attended elementary and high schools there and studied at Lincoln University (Pa.). He was a salesman for General Electric Co. (1934-36) and was a salesman (later National Sales Representative) with Calvert Distillers (1941-57) before joining Fromm and Sichel in 1957. He is co-author of the sales program "Men of Distinction" and has trained a number of black salesmen for his industry. He is a member of Omega Psi Phi fraternity, the NAACP (life member) and the Urban League. His wife, Dr. Elsie Lewis, is professor of American History at Hunter College. He has one son, Christopher. Address: 1255 Post St., Suite 505, San Francisco, CA 94109

Huey Perry Malone

Kenneth M. Maloney

Lenton Malry

Albert E. Manley

Malone, Huey Perry, engineer, is research fuels engineer at Gulf Oil Corp. in Harmarville, Pa. He develops refining processes for conversion of crude petroleum oils, coal and shale oil into non-polluting products such as gasolines, fuel oils and other useful oils. He was previously a research chemist with the company and worked for two years in petroleum refining at Universal Oil Products Corp. in Des Plaines, Ill. Born Feb. 3, 1935 in Bude, Miss., he is a graduate of Roosevelt University (B.S., 1958) and the University of Illinois (Ph.D., 1970). He is a member of the board of directors of the Urban League of Pittsburgh and is a member of the American Chemical Society, the American Petroleum Institute and the NAACP. He and his wife, LaVergne, have a daughter, Kathryn. Address: P. O. Box 2038, Pittsburgh, PA 15230

Maloney, Kenneth M., scientist, is a research physical chemist at General Electric Co. (Lamp Business Division) in Cleveland, Ohio. Born Oct. 11, 1941 in New Orleans, La., he is a graduate of Southern University (B.S.) and the University of Washington in Seattle (Ph.D.). In September, 1972, three people received General Electric's Corning Award, two men for their team effort and one individual. Dr. Maloney was the individual whose research provided additional guidelines for optimum use of titanium, and he has given valuable guidance to engineers for further perfection of General Electric jet engines and gas turbines. His principal field has been reaction kinetics and the fundamentals of metal-oxygen combustion phenomena. The recipient of numerous other awards, he has had scientific papers published in the *Journal of Physical Chemistry*. He was recruited by General Electric over a period, while an undergraduate at Washington and while a senior research scientist at Battelle-Northwest Research Center. Dr. Maloney and his wife, Yolanda, have two children, Sean and Shana. Address: General Electric Co., Lamp Business Division, Nela Park, Cleveland, OH 44112

Malry, Lenton, legislator and educator, is a member of the New Mexico Legislature, representing Bernalillo County (Albuquerque). He is also director of Cross-Cultural Awareness for Albuquerque Public Schools. First elected to the legislature in 1968, he has been re-elected twice by his 99 per cent white district. His legislative achievements include passage of a drug abuse bill and an anti-bias bill. Born Sept. 30, 1931 in Shreveport, La., he earned degrees at Grambling College (B.S., 1952), Texas College (M. Ed., 1957) and the University of New Mexico (Ph.D., 1968). He joined the Albuquerque school system as a junior high school teacher and became principal of John Marshall School and later La Mesa School. He and his wife, Joy, also a teacher, have one son, Lenton Jr. Address: 1500 Walter St., SE, Albuquerque, NM 87102

Manley, Albert Edward, educator, is president of Spelman College in Atlanta, Georgia. Appointed in 1953, he is the first male president of the women's college. Born Jan. 3, 1908 in San Pedro Sula, Spanish Honduras, he came to the United States in 1919 and became a naturalized citizen in 1939. He has degrees from Johnson C. Smith University (B.S., 1930; honorary LL.D.), Columbia Teachers College (M.A., 1938) and Stanford University (Ed.D., 1946). He also studied at the University of Chicago (1942). He was a teacher at Stephens-Lee High School in Asheville, N.C. from 1931 to 1934 and principal from 1935 to 1946. He then became state superintendent of black high schools in North Carolina (1941-1945) and dean of the College of Arts and Sciences and professor of education at North Carolina College (1946-53). He is chairman of the Council of Presidents of the Atlanta University Center and chairman of the Council of Presidents of the University Center in Georgia. He is a member of the Georgia Commission on Interracial Cooperation and is a director of the United Negro College Fund. He has written a number of articles that have been published in educational journals. He is married to the former Audrey Elaine Forbes. Address: Spelman College, Atlanta, GA 30314

William A. Manney

David Manning

Hubert V. Manning

Judge Thurgood Marshall

Manney, William A., broadcast executive, is general manager of radio station WBEE in Chicago, Ill. He was born July 12, 1931 in Springfield, Ark., and is a graduate of Philander Smith College in Little Rock, Ark. (B.A.). He began his broadcasting career in 1964 as an account executive with radio station WAAF (now WGRT) in Chicago. He joined WBEE as sales manager in 1966 and was promoted to general manager in 1970. He enjoys being able to train and develop young people for the industry. Mr. Manney is on the board of directors of the Cosmopolitan Chamber of Commerce in Chicago, and is second vice president of the Jane Dent Home for the Aged. He is a member of the National Association of Market Developers and of Black Media Representatives. He and his wife, Alice, have a daughter, Pamela. Address: 75 E. Wacker Dr., Chicago IL 60601.

Manning, David, banker, is executive vice president of the North Milwaukee State Bank in Milwaukee, Wisconsin. Previously, he was personnel director. He was born March 19, 1945 in Tulsa, Okla., is a graduate of the University of Missouri (B.A., economics and banking, 1969) and has completed several banking courses at the American Institute of Banking. He is a member of Alpha Phi Alpha fraternity and the U.S. Air Force Reserve. He and his wife, Paula Diane, have a daughter, Pamela Denise. Address: 2741 W. Fond du Lac, Milwaukee, WI 53210

Manning, Hubert V., educator and administrator, is president of Claflin College in Orangeburg, S. C. He was born Aug. 2, 1918 in Cheraw, S. C. He is a graduate of Claflin College (B.A., social science, 1940), Gammon Theological Seminary (D.D., 1945) and Boston University (M.A., history, 1947). He has served as ministry representative of the Southeastern Jurisdiction of the United Methodist Church, and was one of 12 college presidents selected to make a comparative study of higher education in eastern and western Europe. He was elected as president of Claflin while serving as pastor of Wesley United Methodist Church in Charleston, S.C. The 1969 Distinguished Alumnus Award, was conferred on him by Boston University School of Theology. He is a member of the board of directors of Orangeburg County United Fund, chairman board of directors of Triangle Association of Colleges of South Carolina and Georgia, member Phi Beta Sigma, and member of the advisory council of the South Carolina Higher Education Facilities Commission. He and his wife, Ethel, have two children: June (Mrs. Richard Thomas) and Michelle. Address: Claflin College, Orangeburg, SC 29115

Marshall, Thurgood, jurist, is an associate justice of the U.S. Supreme Court. Born July 2, 1908 in Baltimore, Md., he is a graduate of Lincoln University (A.B. *cum laude*, 1930) and Howard University Law School (LL.B. *magna cum laude*, 1933). He also has 19 honorary degrees. Before his Supreme Court appointment by President Lyndon B. Johnson in 1967, he was in private practice in Baltimore (1933–38). He was a part-time assistant to Charles H. Houston, NAACP special counsel (1936–38). He was NAACP special counsel (1938–62). He was judge of the U.S. District Court for the Second Judicial Circuit (New York), appointed by President John F. Kennedy (1962–65). He was solicitor general of the U.S. (1965–67). As NAACP counsel, Justice Marshall prepared the 1938 Supreme Court brief, granting a black student, Lloyd Gaines the right to enter the University of Missouri Law School. He won such key Supreme Court cases as *Smith* vs. *Allwright* (1944) ending segregated primaries; *Morgan* vs. *Virginia* (1946) invalidating state laws segregating interstate passengers; and *Sweatt* vs. *Painter* (1950) which resulted in admission of black law students to the University of Texas. His greatest victory was the 1954 school desegregation decision. His first wife, Vivian, died in 1955. In 1956, he married Cecilia Suyat. They have two sons, Thurgood Jr. and John. Address: U.S. Supreme Court, Washington, DC 20543 **See article on Thurgood Marshall in Volume II**

Martin, Louis Emanuel, newspaper executive, is vice president and editorial director of Sengstacke Newspapers in Chicago, Ill. The firm publishes the *Chicago Daily Defender*. Mr. Martin was a reporter (1936) and editor-in-chief (1947–59) of the *Defender*, and editor and publisher of the *Michigan Chronicle* (1936–47) in Detroit, Mich. He assumed his present position in 1969 after serving as deputy chairman of the Democratic National Committee (1961–69). He was editorial advisor to Amalgamated Press, Ltd. in Nigeria (1959-60). Born Nov. 18, 1912 in Shelbyville, Tenn., he attended the University of Michigan (B.A., 1934) and has honorary degrees from Harvard University (LL.D., 1970) and Wilberforce University (LL.D., 1951). He is a member of the board of directors of Chicago City Bank and Trust Co., and Service Federal Savings and Loan Association, and is vice president of the Michigan Chronicle Publishing Co. He is chairman of the board of directors of the Joint Center for Political Studies in Washington, D.C. and is a member of the board of trustees of the De Paul University. He is a member of the Federal City Club and the National Press Club in Washington, D.C., the Overseas Press Club in New York and the Chicago Press Club. He and his wife, Gertrude, have five daughters: Trudy, Anita, Toni, Linda and Lisa. Address: 2400 S. Michigan Ave., Chicago, IL 60616

Martin, Peggy Smith, legislator, is a Democratic Illinois state representative from the 26th District (Chicago). She was elected in 1972. Born May 22, 1931, in Corinth, Miss., she attended the University of Chicago (1952–54) and Kennedy-King College (1966–70). She is state chairman of the Illinois Council on Hunger, Health and Nutrition and is a member of the Public Welfare Coalition. She is a volunteer worker for Operation PUSH. She has two children: Genedric and Sandra. Address: Illinois General Assembly, Springfield, IL 62706

Marvin, Murray, insurance executive, has been vice president (for corporate planning and communications) of North Carolina Mutual Life·Insurance Company in Durham, N.C. since 1970. Born June 15, 1913 in Green County, Ohio, he is a graduate of West Virginia State College (B.S., education, 1936) and the University of Chicago (M.B.A., 1960). He began his career in 1946 as public relations director of Parkway Management Company in Chicago. In 1947, he and his wife founded Marvin & Marvin, a public and industrial relations consulting firm. He was executive director of the National Insurance Association for eleven years before joining North Carolina Mutual in 1961 as planning director. He was staff coordinator and owner's representative during construction of the company's new $5 million home office building (1961–65). He is a member of the American Management Association, the American Institute of Management, the Life Advertisers Association, the Public Relations Society of America and Kappa Alpha Psi. He and his wife, Dolores, live in Durham. Address: Mutual Plaza, Durham, NC 27701

Louis E. Martin

Peggy Smith Martin

Murray Marvin

Hans J. Massaquoi

Helen M. Mayes

Curtis Mayfield

Benjamin E. Mays

Massaquoi, Hans J., journalist, is managing editor of *Ebony* magazine, published by Johnson Publishing Co., Inc. in Chicago, Ill. Previously, he was assistant managing editor of *Ebony* and an associate editor of *Jet*. Born Jan. 19, 1926 in Hamburg, Germany, he immigrated to the United States in 1950 and became a naturalized citizen in 1960. Overcoming the language barrier to master English, he attended Elgin (Ill.) Community College, the University of Illinois (B.S., journalism, 1957) and Northwestern University. He was a parachutist in the U.S. Army (82nd Airborne Division from 1951–53. He has travelled widely in Europe and Africa for *Ebony*. In 1971, he received the Immigrant Achievement Award from the Immigrant Protective League of Chicago. He is a member of the board of directors of Travelers Aid of Metropolitan Chicago. Divorced, he has two sons, Steve and Hans Jr. Address: 820 S. Michigan Ave., Chicago, IL 60605

Mayes, Helen M., college official, is director of admissions and records at Albany (Ga.) State College. Born May 28, 1918 in Waycross, Ga., she is a graduate of Savannah State College (B.S., business administration, 1938) and New York University, where she completed a special program for admission officers and registrars (M.A., 1961). She has been secretary of the National Association of College Deans, Registrars and Admissions Officers since 1963, and in 1971 was elected to a one-year term as the first black president of the Georgia Association of Collegiate Registrars and Admissions Officers. She is a member of the Georgia Teachers and Education Association, the National Education Association and Alpha Kappa Alpha. A widow, Mrs. Mayes has a son, Nathaniel. Address: Albany State College, Albany, GA 31705

Mayfield, Curtis, entertainer, is a singer, composer and recording artist, who owns Curtom, a record company and publishing firm in Chicago, Ill. He formed the firm in 1970 after 12 years as lead singer of The Impressions. He wrote and sang the theme music for the 1972 film, *Super Fly*. Born June 3, 1942 in Chicago, he began singing as a teenager with The Alphatones and with gospel groups and choirs. Later, he joined The Roasters, a group which changed its name to The Impressions. Its members included the singing star Jerry Butler. The group's first best-selling record was *For Your Precious Love* (1958). In 1961, the group was reorganized and recorded another best-seller, "Gypsy Woman," written by Mr. Mayfield. His other compositions include "Keep on Pushing," "This Is My Country," "Amen" and "People Get Ready." Address: 5915 N. Lincoln Ave., Chicago, IL 60659

Mays, Benjamin Elijah, educator and administrator, is president of the Atlanta (Ga.) Board of Education and president emeritus of Morehouse College. Born Aug. 1, 1895 in Epworth, S.C., he is a graduate of Bates College (B.A., 1920) and the University of Chicago (M.A., 1925; Ph.D., 1935). He also has honorary doctorate degrees from a number of schools, including Morehouse College, Harvard University, Boston University, Virginia Union University and the University of Liberia. He became the first black elected president of the Atlanta Board of Education after retiring as president of Morehouse (1940–67). He joined the Morehouse faculty in 1922 as a mathematics teacher. He was dean of the School of Religion at Howard University (1934–40), and is former president of the United Negro College Fund. He is the author of several books, including *Born To Rebel* (his autobiography) and *The Negro Church* (written in 1933 in collaboration with the Reverend J. W. Nicholson). He has written numerous articles for magazines and professional journals and has contributed a weekly column to the *Pittsburgh Courier*. He has served on dozens of commissions, committees, boards, etc., and has been the recipient of scores of citations and honors. He is a member of Phi Beta Kappa. Delta Sigma Rho, Delta Theta Chi and Omega Psi Phi. He is a widower. Address: 3316 Pamlico Dr., SW, Atlanta, GA 30311

Mays, Willie Howard Jr., professional athlete, as of 1972 was the only baseball player in the history of the game to reach both 600 home runs and 3,000 hits during a career. His amazing feats as a centerfielder, his batting and his base running combine to make him one of the most exciting all-around players in the history of baseball. He was born May 6, 1931 in Westfield, Ala. By the time he was 14, he was playing for a semi-pro steel mill baseball team. In 1968, his father, William Howard Mays, arranged a tryout for him with the Birmingham Black Barons of the Negro National League. Willie was hired at $300 a season. In 1950, he was signed by the New York Giants (now San Francisco) system. He played for the Trenton (N..J) team (1950-51) and for the Minneapolis Millers (1951). He was called up by the Giants in 1951 and began setting numerous records. By 1966, he was earning $125,000 a year, the highest salary ever paid a baseball player. He left the Giants in 1972 and joined the New York Mets. He and his wife, Mae Louise, still live in San Francisco, Calif. He has a son, Michael. Address: New York Mets, 126th St. and Roosevelt Ave., Flushing, NY 11368

Meek, Russell C., columnist, civil rights activist, and radio and television personality, is president of Search for Truth, Inc. in Chicago, Ill. He is also secretary of Concerned Citizens for Police Reform, a prison consultant and broadcasts programs on WVON radio station in Chicago. He is the director of The Dravidian School of Black Karate and has black belts in goju and jiu jitsu. Search for Truth conducts a center for children and young adults, publishes a newspaper and conducts radio programs in prisons, allowing inmates to talk to the community. The organization is not funded. Born in Springfield, Ill., Sept. 9, 1933, Russell Meek is a broadcasting pioneer, producer of his own radio show, and is the host and producer of the documentary "The Way It Is" television show which has been shown in 123 major cities as part of a series called "Crisis in the Cities" whch won an Emmy Award in 1968. He is the author of *Poems for Peace, Justice and Freedom* (1969) and *The Message* (1967) Mr. Meek is the father of four children. Address: P. O. Box 24066, Chicago, IL 60624

Melton, Mitchell W., legislator, is a member of the Pennsylvania House of Representatives from Philadelphia. Elected to a five-year term in 1968, he has been reelected twice. Born April 6, 1943 in Philadelphia, he graduated from the Pennsylvania Institute of Criminology and received a certificate for the action course in practical politics. He has served on the House committees on education, labor relations and transportation safety. He has fought for the creation of state-run rehabilitation centers for drug users and wages a relentless battle against crime. He is a member of the Philadelphia Chamber of Commerce, the board of directors of the Mental Health/Mental Retardation Association, Inc., and the Temple University board for Community Mental Health. He and his wife, Evelyn, have two children, Tyrone and Donna. Address: 1843 N. Taney St., Philadelphia, PA 19121

Willie H. Mays Jr.   Russell C. Meek   Mitchell W. Melton

Louise Meriwether

Rep. Ralph H. Metcalfe

Henry M. Micheaux Jr.

Arthur J. Miller

Meriwether, Louise, author, is a free-lance writer living in New York, N.Y. Born in Haverstraw, N.Y., she was reared in Harlem in circumstances similar to those depicted in her successful 1970 novel *Daddy Was a Number Runner.* She has degrees from New York University (B.A.) and UCLA (M.A.). She has written numerous short stories and three children's books: *The Freedom Ship of Robert Smalls* (1971), *The Heart Man: The Story of Daniel Hale Williams* (1972) and *Don't Take the Bus on Monday: The Rosa Parks Story* (1972). While pursuing her writing career, Miss Meriwether was a legal secretary and worked at Universal Studios in Hollywood, Calif. as the first black story analyst. She is an organizer and member of Black Concern, a group seeking to influence American blacks against any accommodation with the Republic of South Africa. Miss Meriwether is single. Address: Prentice-Hall (Publishers), Englewood Cliffs, NJ 07632

Metcalfe, Ralph H., congressman, was elected in 1970 as a member of the U.S. House of Representatives from Illinois (1st District, Chicago). Previously, he was a member of the Chicago City Council (1955–71). Born May 29, 1910 in Atlanta, Ga., he is a graduate of Marquette University (B.Ph., 1936) and the University of Southern California (M.A., physical education, 1939). A former world famous athlete, he was a member of the U.S. track teams in the 1932 and 1936 Olympics. He was track coach and political science instructor at Xavier University in New Orleans, La. (1936–42); director of the department of civil rights, Chicago Commission on Human Relations (1945–49), and commissioner, Illinois Athletic Commission (1949–52). He is founder of the Ralph H. Metcalfe Foundation in Chicago, and is active in numerous athletic, youth and civic groups. He is a director of the Illinois Federal Savings & Loan Association and the North Bank of Chicago. He and his wife, Madalynne, have a son, Ralph Jr. Address: Room 1110, Longworth House Office Building, Washington, DC 20515

Micheaux, Henry McKinley Jr., legislator, is a member of the North Carolina General Assembly, representing the 16th District (Durham County). Born Sept. 4, 1930 in Durham, N.C., he is a graduate of North Carolina Central University (B.S., 1952; J.D., 1964). He was chief assistant solicitor for the 14th Solicitorial District (Durham) before his election to the legislature. He has served as assistant prosecutor for the Durham County District Court. He is affiliated with many organizations, including Durham Human Relations Housing Committee, Durham Chamber of Commerce, Durham Merchants Association, Omega Psi Phi, North Carolina State Bar Association, American Bar Association, American Judicature Society and the National Bar Association. He and his wife, Joyce, have a daughter, Jocelyn. Address: 1722 Alfred St. Durham, NC 27707

Miller, Arthur J., banker, is a second vice president at Chase Manhattan Bank in New York, N. Y. He manages a computer programming and systems analysis department with 50 employees. Previously, he was a programmer analyst and operations supervisor. Born Oct. 7, 1934 in New York City, he attended college, took various computer and systems courses and completed courses offered by the American Institute of Banking. A humorous aspect of his position, he says, is "the shocked look on the faces of job applicants entering my office and seeing a black man." His standard comment: "I'm for real. Have a seat!" He feels that the computer field is highly receptive to blacks, but sees no great increase of opportunities at his management level. A widower, he lives in East Orange, N.J. Address: One Chase Manhattan Plaza, New York, NY 10005

Frederick E. Miller

Isaac H. Miller Jr.

John J. Miller

Miller, Frederick E., administrator, is executive director and senior vice president of Opportunities Industrialization Centers of America, Inc., a national movement—based in Philadelphia, Pa.,—which provides manpower training and is engaged in minority economic development. By 1973, it was active in 104 American cities and, since its founding in 1964, has trained thousands of previously hard-to-employ persons. Mr. Miller is chief administrative officer and oversees all OIC activities. He is also president of the business and economic development division. He was recruited from Temple University (where he was on the faculty) by OIC's founder and chairman, the Reverend Leon H. Sullivan. He held several other positions in the organization before becoming executive director in 1964. Born Jan. 28, 1931 in Paulsboro, N.J., he is a graduate of Rutgers University (B.A., economics and business administration) and Temple University (Ed.M., secondary and special education). He is a doctoral candidate (educational psychology and administration) at Temple, and has done additional graduate study there in management and finance. He has won several awards for his work and has been a manpower and education consultant to the U.S. Government. He is a member of the OIC board of directors and the executive committee, and is active in other professional and civic groups. He and his wife, Jean, have four children: Fred Jr., Darryl, Kathleen and Felicia. Address: OIC, 18 W. Chelten Ave., Philadelphia, PA 19144

Miller, Isaac H. Jr., administrator, is president of Bennett College in Greensboro, N.C. He was born Sept. 26, 1920 in Jacksonville, Fla. He is a graduate of Livingstone College (B.S., chemistry, 1938) and the University of Wisconsin (M.S. and Ph.D., biochemistry, 1948 and 1951). He was a professor of biochemistry at Meharry Medical College in Nashville in 1962. He held the Lederle Medical Faculty Award at Meharry for three consecutive years. Dr. Miller is a member of the American Chemical Society, the Botanical Society of America, the American Association for the Advancement of Science and the Association of Southeastern Biologists. He is a former visiting scientist at the Oak Ridge Institute of Nuclear Studies and a panelist for the National Science Foundation Program on Research Participation for High School Teachers. He and his wife, Effie, have five children: Isaac III, Kevin, Eric, Keith and Kay. Address: Bennett College, Greensboro, NC 27420

Miller, John J., legislator, is an assemblyman from the 17th District (Berkeley) in the California Legislature. Born July 28, 1932 in Savannah, Ga., he is a graduate of Talladega College (A.B., 1954) and the Howard University School of Law (LL.B., 1957). He was a Walter Perry Johnson Graduate Research Fellow in Law at the University of California at Berkeley (1957–59) where he later became a candidate for the LL.M. degree. He is a partner in Miller and George, a law firm in Berkeley. He has served as a member and president of the Berkeley Board of Education, and as a member of the Berkeley NAACP board, the Berkeley Board of Library Trustees, and the Berkeley Housing Advisory and Appeals Board. He is a member of the American Academy of Political and Social Sciences, the American Bar Association, the California Bar Association, the National Lawyers Guild and the National Bar Association. He served as Assembly Democratic Leader from April, 1970 to January, 1971, and has served as vice chairman of the Criminal Justice Committee and as a member of the Ways and Means Committee, the Natural Resources & Conservation Committee and the Welfare Committee. He and his wife, Joyce, have two children, Duncan and Heather. Address: State Capitol, Sacramento, CA 95814

Billy G. Mills

Luna I. Mishoe

B. Doyle Mitchell

Mills, Billy G., city councilman and lawyer, is president *pro tempore* of the Los Angeles (Calif.) City Council. He was elected to the council in 1963 and was elected president *pro tempore* in 1969. He was born Nov. 19, 1929 in Waco, Tex. He attended UCLA (B.A., 1951; LL.B., 1954; J.D., 1968). Mr. Mills is a member of numerous legal and law enforcement groups and is on the board of directors and advisory boards of several organizations. He has received numerous awards for his work in Los Angeles communities. He and his wife, Rubye, have five children: Karol, Karen, Billy, John and James. Address: Room 237, City Hall, 200 North Spring St., Los Angeles, CA 90012

Mishoe, Luna I., educator and administrator, is president of Delaware State College and ranks among America's most distinguished mathematicians and physicists. Born Jan. 5, 1917, In Bucksport, S.C., he is a graduate of Allen University (B.S., 1938), University of Michigan (M.S., 1942), and New York University (Ph.D., 1953). In 1942, he entered the United States Army and in four years rose from private to first lieutenant. He has been professor of mathematics and physics at Delaware State College and chairman of the natural sciences department at Morgan State College. His doctoral dissertation in mathematics brought him a 1955 invitation to do advanced theoretical research at Oxford University, England, and an appointment as consultant to the Army's Ballistics Research Laboratory, Aberdeen, Md. He made an important mathematical discovery on which he co-authored a paper, with B. Friedman, which was published in the July 1963 *Quarterly of Applied Mathematics*. Dr. Mishoe has presented papers before the American and Canadian mathematical societies. When he became president of Delaware State College in 1960, he found 346 students, a faculty of 40, low teachers' salaries, a deficient curriculum and physical plant, inadequate state budget and no private or corporate support. Today, in all these areas, Delaware State College is in the mainstream of American higher education. In 1972, Dr. Mishoe became the first black appointed to the advisory board of the United States Coast Guard Academy and the first black on the advisory board of the Farmers' Bank of Delaware. He is a member of the American Mathematical Society and the Mathematical Association of America. Dr. Mishoe and his wife, Hattie, have four children: Bernellyn, Luna II, Wilma and Rita. Address: Delaware State College, Dover, DE 19901

Mitchell, Benson Doyle, bank executive, is president and chairman of the board of directors of the Industrial Bank of Washington, D.C. He was elected in 1954 after 20 years of service in various capacities. Born August 22, 1913 in Washington, D.C., he is a graduate of Howard University (B.S., mathematics, 1933) and attended Wharton School of Finance at the University of Pennsylvania (1933–34). He is a retired U.S. Army colonel and since 1950 has been assigned to the D.C. Selective Service Reserve Unit. He was president of the National Bankers Association (1959–66). He is secretary and board member, Northwest Securities Investors, Inc., treasurer National Business League, board member, Dolphin & Evans Settlements, Inc., and member of the executive committee of the National Bankers Association. He is a member of several other professional, civic and social groups. He received the 1971 Howard University Alumni Award for Outstanding Service in Banking and Community Service. He and his wife, Cynthia, have two children, Patricia and Benson Jr. Address: 4812 Georgia Ave., N.W., Washington, DC 20011

Clarence M. Mitchell Jr.

Clyde D. Mitchell

L. Pearl Mitchell

Mitchell, Clarence M. Jr., attorney, is director of the Washington (D.C.) Bureau of the NAACP. He has headed the bureau since 1950. He is also legislative chairman of the Leadership Conference on Civil Rights. In 1969 he was awarded the NAACP's Spingarn Medal for his efforts in obtaining passage of landmark civil rights acts—from the 1957 Civil Rights Act to the 1968 Civil Rights Act. He was a leader of the successful efforts to force the withdrawal of the nominations of Judges Clement Haynesworth and G. Harrold Carswell to the U.S. Supreme Court. Mr. Mitchell earned degrees at Lincoln University (A.B.) and the University of Maryland Law School (LL.B., J.D.). He did graduate work at Atlanta University and at the University of Minnesota. Born March 8, 1911 in Baltimore, Md., he has been a newspaper reporter, executive director of the Urban League of St. Paul, Minn., and an employee of several federal agencies. He and his wife, Juanita, an attorney, have four sons: Clarence, Keiffer, Michael and George. Address: 422 First St., S.E., Washington, DC 20003

Mitchell, Clyde D., training supervisor, is director of the Manpower Training Programs in Newark, N.J. and international president of Frontiers International, a black service organization. He is responsible for the supervision, coordination and budgets of On-Job-Training and the Neighborhood Youth Corps. Born Aug. 24, 1914 in Greenville, S.C., he attended Rutgers University, New York University, Syracuse University and Cornell University. He was director of the Essex County Youth and Economic Rehabilitation Commission in New Jersey. He served as an executive secretary to the mayor of Newark. He and his wife, Juanita, have four children: Clyde, Theo, Valerie, and Carol. Address: 1019 Broad St., Newark, NJ 07102

Mitchell, L. Pearl, humanitarian and civil rights leader, is known as "Miss NAACP" and "Miss AKA" for her long years of service to the NAACP and to her sorority, Alpha Kappa Alpha. She has received citations honoring her from the Ohio House of Representative and the Cleveland City Council. She was born in Wilberforce, Ohio, where her father, Samuel, was president of Wilberforce College, from which she received her B.A. degree. Later, she completed courses in supervisory public school music at the Oberlin Conservatory, and eventually studied sociology and recreational services at other institutions. She was honored in a poem "I Dream," dedicated to her by Langston Hughes. From 1915 until 1923, she worked as a teacher and youth camp director in Iowa, Michigan and Florida, teaching music, drama and tennis. She moved to Cleveland in 1924 and for 20 years served as a juvenile probation officer. After retiring from that position in the 1940s, she was chosen director of membership campaigns by the NAACP, leading mammoth drives in major cities in both the North and South. In 1965, Miss Mitchell was chosen as coordinator of an AKA drive which raised $440,000 in life memberships for the NAACP. Address: 13800 Terrace Rd., East Cleveland, OH 44106

M. Mitchell-Bateman, M.D.

Mitchell-Bateman, Mildred, M.D., psychiatrist, is director of the West Virginia Department of Mental Health. The first woman to head such a department in the U.S. and the first black in West Virginia history to direct an executive department, she has held her post since 1962. Born in 1922 in Cordele, Ga., she earned degrees at Johnson C. Smith University (B.S., 1941) and Women's Medical College of Pennsylvania (M.D., 1946). She interned in New York City and conducted private practice in Philadelphia. At Lakin State Hospital, W. Va., she served as physician, clinical director and superintendent. Dr. Mitchell-Bateman completed a three-year psychiatric residency and fellowship in the Menninger School of Psychiatry and was certified for practice in 1957. Under her directorship, West Virginia's mental health programs in local communities have increased from four to 54, Federal spending for mental health in her state rose from $268,000 in 1958 to over $6 million in 1968. Dr. Mitchell-Bateman is married and has two daughters. Address: West Virginia Department of Mental Health, Charleston, WV 25305

Rep. Parren J. Mitchell

Mitchell, Parren J., congressman, is a member of the U. S. House of Representatives. He was elected in 1970 from the 7th Congressional District in Baltimore, Md. Previously, he was professor of sociology and assistant director of the Urban Studies Institute at Morgan State College (1968–70); executive director of the Community Action Agency in Baltimore, Md. (1965–68); executive secretary of the Maryland Committee on Interracial Problems and Relations (1963–65), and supervisor of a program for Post Sentence Case Work for the Domestic Relations Division of the Supreme Bench of Baltimore (1956–63). He also has served as a sociology instructor at Morgan State College and as a probation officer. Born April 29, 1922 in Baltimore, Md., he is a graduate of the University of Maryland (M.A., sociology, 1952), and Morgan State College (A.B., sociology, 1950), and has taken courses at the doctoral level in sociology at the University of Connecticut. Awarded the Purple Heart in World War II, he was a leader of anti-war protests sponsored by the Moratorium Committee and John Hopkins University in 1970. Rep. Mitchell is a member of numerous professional and civic organizations, and is author of several books. He is single. Address: 1228 Longworth Bldg., Washington, DC 20515

Archie Moore

Moore, Archie, former heavyweight champion, is director of training and activities for the Any Boy Can clubs, which he founded. He was born Dec. 13, 1916 in Benoit, Miss., and was the world light-heavyweight boxing champion for ten years. For a number of years, he has been motivating youngsters to find a better way of life through "proper mental, moral, spiritual and physical training," using what he has learned through personal experiences as a guide. He is a member of the NAACP, the Urban League, the Optimists Club, and is a Seventh-Day Adventist. He enjoys table tennis, billiards and "day-dreaming about bettering racial relations." He and his wife, Joan, have six children: Anthony, D'Angelo, Hardy, Joanie, Rena and Billy. Address: 3517 E. St., San Diego, CA 92102

Daniel A. Moore

Evelyn K. Moore

George A. Moore

Moore, Daniel A., film company executive, is the founder, president and executive producer of Omega Films in Philadelphia, Pa., and has 12 years of film-making experience. Born Nov. 20, 1935 in Philadelphia, he developed his talent by working with major film crews for several years before striking out on his own. His clients include many major corporations. His work has been favorably reviewed in several publications and his films have been shown on network television programs. Some of his community service films have been *On Patrol For God* (aimed at juvenile gangs), *Sign Here* (dealing with consumer education), *The Fourth Floor* (on black nurse recruitment) and *Mr. President, We Are Ready*, (a film on Liberia's President Dr. William Tolbert Jr.) He is president of Christians United Reaching Everyone (a Philadelphia self-help agency which he founded), executive director of Community Motivation Center, and a lecturer on contemporary religion and on audio-visual communications. He also organizes, directs and distributes films for non-profit, self-help organizations. He is divorced and has one child, Daniel A. Jr. Address: P.O. Box 7566, Philadelphia, PA 19101

Moore, Evelyn K., agency executive, is director of the Black Child Development Institute in Washington, D.C. (there is a branch office in Atlanta, Ga.). She was born July 29, 1937 in Detroit, Mich. and grew up in rural Baldwin, Mich. She is a graduate of Eastern Michigan University (B.S., 1960) and the University of Michigan (M.A., 1960). She was chosen as "Outstanding Young Woman of the State of Michigan" in 1970. She has been director of BCDI for two years and finds satisfaction in coordinating activities of the first independent non-profit national black agency devoted to meeting the developmental needs of black children. She is a member of the board of directors of Children's Lobby and is a member of the National Association for Education of Young Children. Address: 1028 Connecticut Ave., N W, Washington, DC 20036

Moore, George Anthony, a television producer, is the first black producer and director for a U.S. television station. His responsibilities include much of the organization and smooth operation of a variety of telecasts, his chief responsibility being the Dorothy Fuldheim program, "Highlights of the News", which has been chosen as the outstanding Cleveland television news show in many newspaper surveys. Born Feb. 8, 1914 in Cleveland, Ohio, he graduated from Ohio State University (B.A.) and the University of Iowa (M.A.). Prior to becoming producer-director of Cleveland station WEWS, he worked five and a half years for the Scripps-Howard Cleveland Press and eleven years at Scripps-Howard's only television station starting from news director to his present position. He was also associate regional director for the Cleveland chapter of the National Conference of Christians and Jews. He was founder and director of the Catholic Theater of Cleveland, the Ohio State University Playmakers, (a black student drama group) and has appeared as actor in over a dozen live stage productions. He has travelled extensively throughout the United States, Europe, Africa and South America. He is a member of Karamu House, Project Equality, Project Peace, founder and president of the Catholic Commission on Community Action, and a member of the National Academy of Television Arts and Sciences. He is unmarried. Address: 1836 Euclid Ave., Cleveland, OH 44115

Hilliard T. Moore

Howard Moore Jr.

Parlett L. Moore

Moore, Hilliard T. Sr., city official and educator, is mayor of Lawnside, N. J. and is a social studies teacher in Camden, N.J. Born Aug. 18, 1925 in Kingston, N.C., he attended Fayetteville (N.C.) State University and earned a B.S. degree in education. He served as mayor of Lawnside for five consecutive two-year terms, and is serving a new four-year term. He has been elected for two three-year terms as a director of the Union Federal Savings and Loan Association, which has assets of $540 million. He and his wife, Gloria, have three children: Hilliard Jr., Stephen and Donna. Address: Hatch Middle School, Camden, NJ 08103

Moore, Howard Jr., attorney, is senior associate attorney with Moore, Alexander and Rindskopf, a law firm in Atlanta, Ga. The firm specializes in criminal law, civil rights, civil liberties and labor law. Since participating in the defense of Angela Davis during 1971-72, Mr. Moore has also established a law practice in Berkeley, Calif. Born February 28, 1932 in Atlanta, he is a graduate of Morehouse College (A.B., 1954) and Boston University School of Law (LL. B., 1960). He is national co-chairman of the National Conference of Black Lawyers and is a member of the National Lawyers Guild. He represented Georgia State Rep. Julian Bond during his successful 1966 efforts to be seated in the Georgia Legislature after having been barred because of anti-war statements. He also secured freedom for Preston Cobb Jr., a 15-year-old youth who had been accused of rape and sentenced to death in 1961. Mr. Moore secured removal of Georgia's insurrection statute and participated in the movement to abolish capital punishment in the state. He and his wife Jane, have three children: Grace, Constance and Kojo. Address: 1880 San Pedro, Berkeley, CA 94707

Moore, Parlett Longworth, educator and administrator, is president emeritus of Coppin State College in Baltimore, Md. He was president of the college from 1956 to 1970. During his administration, Coppin became fully accredited, the number of students increased from 293 to 2,656, a graduate school was added, and a number of new buildings were built. He now is national president of Phi Beta Sigma fraternity. He was born Sept. 17, 1907 at Wetipquin, Md. and is a graduate of Howard University (A.B., 1930), Columbia University Teachers College (M.A., 1935) and Temple University (Ed. D. 1952). He has done advance graduate work at the University of Pennsylvania, Columbia University, Catholic University, the University of Chicago, and Stanford University. He was a high school principal for 26 years (1930-56) before becoming president of Coppin. He is a member of numerous professional, civic, church and fraternal organizations. He and his wife, Thelma, have three children: Mrs. Thelma M. Smith, Partlett Jr. and Daniel. Address: 7410 Rockridge Rd., Baltimore, MD 21208

Richard V. Moore

Ronnie M. Moore

Winston E. Moore

Moore, Richard V., educator, is president of Bethune-Cookman College in Daytona Beach, Fla. Previously, he was Florida state supervisor of secondary schools for Negroes (1945-47) and a school principal (1932-45) before accepting his present position in 1947. Born Nov. 20, 1906 in Quincy, Fla., he is a graduate of Knoxville College (A.B., 1932) and Atlanta University (M.A., 1944). He has studied for a Ph.D. degree at New York University. He has honorary LL.D. degrees from Edward Waters College (1947), Knoxville College (1950), Morris Brown College (1969) and Syracuse University (1969); hon. LH.D. degree from Claflin College (1969); honorary Doctor of Pedagogy degree from Ohio Northern University (1971) and honorary Sc.D. from Fla. Institute of Technology (1972). He has received numerous other honors and awards and is a member of many professional, civic, business, church and fraternal groups. He is past president of the Council of Presidents of the Board of Education of the United Methodist Church and past president of the Florida Association of Colleges and Universities. He and his wife, Beauford, have nine children: Richard Jr., Rosalyn, Gene, Charles, Patricia, Reginald, Ethel, Barbara and David. Address: Bethune-Cookman College, Daytona Beach, FL 32015

Moore, Ronnie Malcolm, administrator, is executive director of the Scholarship, Education and Defense Fund for Racial Equality (SEDFRE) in New York City, a non-profit training and technical assistance arm of the civil rights and community development movement. Born Dec. 31, 1940 in New Orleans, La. he attended Antioch College, Washington/Baltimore campus. As of 1973, he was vice chairman of Alliance for a Safer New York and board member of the Workers Defense League Afram Association, Inc. He has written and published articles on community relations. Prior to his present position, he was a field secretary in charge of the Louisiana State Project on Community Organization & Voter Registration. He and his wife, Carol, have three children: Desimonae, Melissa and Ronnie. Address: SEDFRE, 315 7th Ave., New York, NY 10001

Moore, Winston E., penologist, is executive director of the Cook County (Ill.) Department of Corrections. Born Sept. 5, 1929 in New Orleans, La., he is a graduate of West Virginia State College (B.A., 1952) and the University of Louisville (M.A., 1954, psychology). He worked for two years as a psychologist for the Louisville Juvenile Court. Moving to Chicago, he worked nights at the post office while continuing his studies at the Illinois Institute of Technology. He was a psychologist at the Illinois Youth Commission's Reception and Diagnostic Center for juvenile delinquents (March–November, 1961) and its clinic director until 1966. He was staff psychologist with the Youth Opportunity Center of the Illinois State Employment Service (1966–68) and was County Jail superintendent (warden) from 1968 to 1970. There, he inherited what a newspaper called "a veritable jungle of sexual perversion, dope traffic, extortion and bestial violence." Today, because of his humane and progressive policies, Cook County Jail serves correction officials in the U.S. and abroad as an example of effective and enlightened jail management. He enlisted at sixteen in the U.S. Army and served three years (1946–49) in the Pacific. His wife, Mabel, teaches in the Chicago public schools. Address: 2600 S. California Ave., Chicago, IL 60608 **See article on Winston E. Moore in Volume II**

Rose Morgan

Judge Ernest N. Morial

John F. Morning Sr.

Morgan, Rose, businesswoman, is founder and president of Rhodelia Corp., and Rose Morgan House of Beauty in New York, N.Y. She is an internationally noted pioneer in modern beauty culture, primarily for black women. She was born in Shelby, Miss. and attended the Morris Beauty Academy in Chicago, Ill. Four months after moving to New York, she opened her own beauty salon with two operators; since then she has built a successful business, employing 200 operators. Her salons have served some two million women, including such celebrities as Lena Horne, Nina Simone, Marian Anderson and Diahann Carroll. During 1972, she began franchising a new business, Trim-Away Figure Contouring, Ltd. She has traveled extensively in the U. S. and abroad speaking and demonstrating her techniques at fashion shows and beauty clinics. Miss Morgan is a member of numerous professional and civic land organizations. She is a member of the board of directors of Freedom National Bank of New York, the Interracial Council for Business Opportunity, Kilimanjaro African Coffee Company, and Mt. Morris Park Hospital. She was formerly married to boxing champion Joe Louis. Address: 507 W. 145th St., New York, NY 10031

Morial, Ernest N., jurist, is a judge of the Orleans Parish Juvenile Court in New Orleans, La. He has won election to the 4th Circuit Court of Appeals for a term beginning in January 1974. He was born Oct. 9, 1929 in New Orleans and is a graduate of Xavier University (B.S., 1951) and Louisiana State University Law School (J.D., 1954). He is also a graduate of the National College of Juvenile Justice University of Nevada (J.D.). He was appointed in 1970 by the governor of Louisiana and was elected in 1972 without opposition. He was the first black to receive a degree from Louisiana State University Law School, the first black to serve in the Louisiana Legislature since Reconstruction (he was elected in 1967) and was the first black juvenile court judge in Louisiana. He is a past national president of Alpha Phi Alpha fraternity. He is a member of the Lawyers Committee for Civil Rights and the Louisiana Commission on Law Enforcement. He serves on the board of governors of Tulane University Medical Center and the board of directors of Loyola University. Judge Morial and his wife, Sybil, have five children: Julie, Marc, Jacques, Cheri, and Monique. Address: 421 Loyola Ave., New Orleans, LA 70112

Morning, John Frew Sr., administrator, is associate director of the National Insurance Association, which has headquarters in Chicago, Ill. He accepted the position in 1968 upon his retirement from Supreme Life Insurance Co. of America. He had been associated with Supreme Life for 44 years (1924–68) in various capacities—agent, district manager, agency director, vice president and director of public affairs, and member of the board of directors. At NIA, he is involved in a number of programs aimed at improving of the 46 black-owned member firms and developing new insurance markets for them. Born March 25, 1924 in Logan County, Ohio, he is a graduate of Wilberforce University (A.B., 1924). He lived in Cleveland, Ohio for a number of years and was the first black elected as a member of the Cleveland Board of Education. In 1949, he moved to Detroit, Mich. to manage three districts for Supreme Life. While there he was a director of the Home Federal Savings and Loan Bank, president of the Detroit Executive Insurance Council and president of the Wilberforce University Alumni Association. In 1956, he moved to Supreme Life's home office in Chicago as a vice president, agency manager and board member—position he held until his retirement. He is a member of numerous professional and civic groups. He and his wife, Juanita, have two daughters, Mrs. Roberta Martin and Mrs. Maurita Chisholm, and a son, John F. Morning Jr. Address: 2400 S. Michigan Ave., Chicago, IL 60616

R. D. Morrison

E. Frederic Morrow

John A. Morsell

Morrison, Richard David, educator, is president of Alabama A&M University in Normal, Ala. Elected in 1962, the name of the institution was changed from "College" to "University" and was completely reorganized. A number of undergraduate and graduate courses have been added, student enrollment has increased by 60 percent, numerous new buildings have been constructed, and the school has gained full accreditation (in 1963). It now shares in $16.83 million that Dr. Morrison helped secure for extension and research work at the 17 black land-grant colleges. (The school has an extensive agricultural extension program.) Born Jan. 18, 1910 in Utica, Miss., Dr. Morrison was urged by the late Dr. George W. Carver to enroll at Tuskegee Institute. He did, and earned a B. S. degree in agricultural education in 1931. He also studied at Cornell University (M.S., education and economics, 1941) and Michigan State University (Ph.D., ed., 1954). He has been associated with Alabama A&M since 1937. He is a former chairman of its Division of Agriculture, a member of the advisory committee of Farmers Home Administration and is a member of the advisory committee of Marshall Space Flight Center. He is affiliated with numerous professional and civic groups. He and his wife, Ethel, have no children. Address: Alabama A&M University, Normal, AL 35762

Morrow, E. Frederic, bank executive, is a vice president of the Bank of America, the world's largest bank, with $35 billion in assets. He is head of the Communications and Public Affairs Division in the New York, N.Y. office. Mr. Morrow was born April 20, 1909 in Hackensack, N.J. and has degrees from Bowdoin College (A.B., 1930; honorary LL.D., 1970) and Rutgers University School of Law (LL.B.; J.D.). In 1955 he became the first black man to serve as a White House aide when President Eisenhower appointed him administrative assistant. Previously he had been a field secretary for the NAACP, a public relations analyst for the Columbia Broadcasting System, and vice president of the African-American Institute. He joined the Bank of America in 1964. He is author of *Black Man in the White House*. He and his wife, Catherine, live in New York City. Address: Bank of America, 41 Broad St., New York, NY 10004

Morsell, John A., administrator, is assistant executive director of the NAACP. He shares with Executive Director Roy Wilkins the job of supervising the work of the nation's oldest civil rights organization. He was born April 14, 1912 in Pittsburgh, Pa. and has degrees from City College of New York (B.S.S., 1934) and Columbia University (M.A., social legislation, 1938; Ph.D., sociology, 1951). He is a member of Phi Beta Kappa. Dr. Morsell spent 10 years in sociological research prior to joining the NAACP in 1956 as assistant to the executive secretary. He was a member of a field team that investigated racial integration in the U.S. Army (1951). He is the author of more than 40 published articles, chiefly on aspects of civil rights. He is a Fellow of the American Sociological Association and is a member of the Eastern Sociological Society and the American Association for Public Opinion Research. In 1970, he was appointed to a six-year term as a member of the New York City Board of Higher Education, which governs the 21 colleges and other units of the City University system. He and his wife, Marjorie Ellen, have one child, Frederick Albert. Address: NAACP, 1790 Broadway, New York, NY 10019

Rev. Charles E. Morton

Rev. Otis Moss

Judge Constance B. Motley

Morton, The Reverend Charles E., clergyman and educator, is pastor of Metropolitan Baptist Church in Detroit, Mich. and adjunct professor of philosophy at Oakland University in Rochester, Mich. He served for eight years (after election in 1946) on the Michigan State Board of Education. Among many clerical and educational posts he has held are chairman, Division of Humanities and Philosophy, Dillard University, New Orleans, La., associate professor of philosophy, Albion College, Albion, Mich., and minister, Ebenezer Baptist Church, Poughkeepsie, N.Y. He is a member of the board of directors of First Independence National Bank of Detroit, Mich. Cancer Fund, Credit Counseling Center, and Detroit Industrial Mission. He is also vice chairman, Inner City Business Forum of Detroit; president, Metropolitan Housing Corporation; member, Governor's Commission on Higher Education, and treasurer, Urban Training Center for Christian Missions (Chicago, Ill.). He has authored several articles for religious journals. Born Jan. 31, 1926 in Bessemer, Ala., he has degrees from Morehouse College (B.A., 1946), Union Theological Seminary (B.D., 1949) and Columbia University (Ph.D., 1958). He and his wife, Jean, have two daughters, Joan and Carla. Address: 13110 Buena Vista, Detroit, MI 48238

Moss, The Reverend Otis, clergyman, is pastor of Mt. Zion Baptist Church in Lockland, Ohio, and is considered one of America's great preachers. Born Feb. 26, 1935 in LaGrange, Ga., he is a graduate of Morehouse College (A.B., 1956; B.D., 1959). He is founder and a member of the board of directors of the Mt. Zion Lockland Federal Credit Union, and a member of the board of directors of the University of Cincinnati. He is also a national board member of the SCLC and a trustee of the Martin Luther King Jr. Center for Social Change. He writes a weekly column for the Atlanta *Inquirer* and has written articles which have appeared in *Home Missions* magazine. His sermon, "Going From Disgrace to Dignity," was chosen for the book *Best Black Sermons,* published by Judson Press (1972). He has travelled throughout the United States as an evangelist and civil rights speaker, and has lectured on many college campuses. He has served as pastor of Mt. Olive Baptist Church in LaGrange, Providence Baptist Church in Atlanta, and as co-pastor with Dr. M. L. King Sr. of Ebenezer Baptist Church in Atlanta. He and his wife, Edwina, have three children: Kevin, Daphne and Otis III. Address: Mt. Zion Baptist Church, 325 Wayne Ave., Lockland, OH 45246

Motley, Constance Baker, jurist, is U.S. district judge for the Southern District of New York. She was appointed on Sept. 9, 1966 by President Lyndon B. Johnson. Born Sept. 14, 1921 in New Haven, Conn., she is a graduate of New York University (A.B., 1943) and Columbia University Law School (LL.B., 1946). Prior to her appointment, she was a member of the NAACP Legal Defense and Educational Fund, Inc. (1945–65). She served in the New York State Senate in 1964, having won a special election to fill a vacancy in her Manhattan district Feb. 4, 1964. She was reelected in Nov., 1964 and served until her special election in Feb., 1965 by the New York City Council to fill a vacancy in her Manhattan district February 4, 1964. She was reelected in November, 1964 and served until her special election in February, 1965 by the New York City Council to fill a vacancy in the office of the borough president of Manhattan. She was reelected in the city-wide direct elections of November, 1965 to a full four-year term with tri-party endorsement: Democratic, Republican and Liberal. She was the first woman and the first black person to hold that elective office. She was chief counsel for James Meredith in his long fight to enter the University of Mississippi. From October, 1961 to December, 1964, she argued 10 civil rights cases before the U.S. Supreme Court and won nine of them. She has received more than 70 awards from organizations and eight honorary degrees from universities. She and her husband, Joel Wilson Motley, have a son, Joel Jr. Address: U.S. Courthouse, New York, NY 10007 **See article on Constance Baker Motley in Volume II**

Judge H. Carl Moultrie

John W. Moutoussamy

Louis L. Mudd

Moultrie, H. Carl, jurist, is judge of the Superior Court of the District of Columbia. Born April 3, 1915 in Charleston, S. C., he is a graduate of Lincoln University (B.A., 1936), New York University (M.A., 1952), and Georgetown University Law School (J.D., 1956). He was national executive secretary of Omega Psi Phi fraternity (1949-72) and practiced law in Washington from 1957 to 1972 when he was appointed to the Superior Court by President Richard M. Nixon. Since 1941, Judge Moultrie has been a member of more than 75 committees, organizations, etc. He is a member of the D. C. Bar Association, Free Press Committee; member, board of directors, Opportunities Industrialization Centers; member, advisory council, Independence Federal Savings & Loan Association. He is a former president of the D. C. Branch NAACP and former vice-president of the Urban Coalition. He and his wife Sara, have one son, H. Carl Moultrie II, a physician. Address: D. C. Superior Court, 451 Indiana Ave., N. W. Washington, DC 20001

Moutoussamy, John W., architect, is a senior partner and 25 percent owner of Dubin, Dubin, Black and Moutoussamy, a major architectural firm in Chicago, Ill. He designed the Johnson Publishing Company building that was opened in 1971 in Chicago. Mr. Moutoussamy was born Jan. 5, 1922 in Chicago and has a B.S. degree in architecture from Illinois Institute of Technology (1948). He has worked as construction superintendent and architect with Chicago firms since 1948. He is a member of the American Institute of Architects. He is on the board of directors of the Chicago Urban League and is a trustee of Loyal University and a member of the Appeals Board of the Chicago Department of Environmental Control. He and his wife, Elizabeth, have three children: John, Claude and Jeanne Marie. Address: 228 N. LaSalle St., Chicago, IL 60601

Mudd, Louis L., marketing specialist, is assistant to the product planning manager at Brown & Williamson Tobacco Corp. in Louisville, Ky. The firm manufactures cigarettes and other smoking and chewing tobacco products. Mr. Mudd is second in command in a brand group responsible for development of new products. Previously, he was assistant brand manager on Kool cigarettes. Born July 29, 1943 in Louisville, he is a graduate of Tennessee State University (B.S., chemistry) and has attended a number of marketing seminars and workshops. He and his wife, Marcella, have three children: Latonya, Darron and Bryan. Address: 1600 W. Hill St., Louisville, KY 40201

Hon. Elijah Muhammad

The Rt. Rev. E. Murchison

John H. Murphy III

Muhammad, The Honorable Elijah, is spiritual leader (Messenger of Allah) of the Nation of Islam, which has thousands of adherents and is headquartered in Chicago, Ill. Born Elijah Poole in 1897 in Sandersville, Ga., he worked as a field boy and sawmill helper as a child. Later, In Macon, Ga., he was a laborer for the Southern Railroad and a foreman at the Cherokee Brick Co. He moved to Detroit, Mich., in 1923 and worked for a while at the Chevrolet plant. In 1930, he met Master W. D. Fard who began teaching him the principles on which he later built the Nation of Islam. The Temple Number Two he organized in Chicago in 1932 is the largest and most impressive of the Nation's mosques throughout the U.S. The Nation also constructs numerous businesses—restaurants, supermarkets, cleaning and laundry establishments, meat processing plants, farms and orchards, clothing stores, a national newspaper, etc. A widower, Mr. Muhammad is the father of six sons and two daughters: Emmanuel, Nathaniel, Elijah Jr., Herbert, Akbar, Wallace, Mrs. Ethel Sharrieff and Mrs. Lottie Muhammad. Address: 7450 S. Stony Island Ave., Chicago, IL 60649

Murchison, The Rt. Reverend Elisha, clergyman, is a bishop of the Christian Methodist Episcopal Church. He presides over 107 churches in Ohio, Kentucky, southern Indiana, West Virginia and western Pennsylvania. Born June 18, 1907 in Fort Worth, Tex., he is a graduate of Clark College (B.A.), Gammon Theological Seminary (B.D.), Boston University (M.A.) and the University of Chicago (D.D.). Beginning in 1920, he served pastorates in Georgia, Texas, Massachusetts and Illinois. In 1949, he was elected as editor of the church's weekly publication, *Christian Index*, and 12 years later was elected to the Episcopacy. As a bishop, he has organized CME churches in Ghana and Nigeria, which had two conferences with a membership of 43,600 in 1972. In 1948, he was a representative to the first assembly of the World Council of Churches. As an active supporter of ecumenical movements, he attended the First Assembly of the World Council of Churches in 1948 and is currently a member of the Executive Committee of the Consultation on Church Union. He is a former president of the National Fraternal (formerly National Negro) Council of Churches and is now vice-president-at-large of the National Council of Churches of America. He and his wife, Imogene, have two children, Marcia and Elleen. Address: Christian Methodist Episcopal Church, 6322 Elwynne Dr., Cincinnati, OH 45236

Murphy, John H. III, newspaper executive, is president of the Afro-American Co., newspaper publishers in Baltimore, Md. There are branch offices and local editions in Washington, D.C., Richmond, Va. and Newark, N.J. The paper was founded by Mr. Murphy's great-uncle, John Murphy Sr. Born March 2, 1916 in Baltimore, Mr. Murphy grew up in Philadelphia, Pa., where he had an *Afro-American* paper route when he was 10. He is a graduate of Temple University (B.S., business administration, 1937) and has attended American Press Institute Seminars at Columbia University. He joined Afro-American Newspapers in 1937 and has worked in almost every phase of the business. In more recent years, he worked under the direct supervision of Dr. Carl Murphy, son of the founder, and chairman of the board of directors. He became president in 1967. He is a member of the board of directors of Amalgamated Publishers, Inc., St. Augustine's College, Baltimore Art Museum and Council on Equal Business Opportunities. He is a member of the the U. S. Civil Rights Commission and the Maryland Advisory Committee of the U. S. Civil Rights Commssion. He and his wife, Alice, have two children, Mrs. Sharon V. Moore and Daniel. Address: 628 N. Eutaw St., Baltimore, MD 21201

Murray, Joan, communications specialist, is a television news correspondent on WCBS-TV in New York, N.Y., and is executive vice president of Zebra Associates, a black-owned New York advertising agency. Born November 6, 1941 in Ithaca, N.Y., she attended the New School for Social Research and Hunter College both in New York. She joined WCBS-TV in 1965. Miss Murray has received numerous awards, including "Media Woman of the Year," the John Russwurm Award and the Mary McLeod Bethune Achievement Award. With Raymond A. League, she formed Zebra Associates in 1969. The agency has a number of major clients, including Coca-Cola, Chrysler Corp. and AT&T, and currently bills more than $3 million a year. Miss Murray wrote *The News* (1968), an autobiography. She is single. Address: Zebra Associates, 18 E. 50th St., New York, NY 10022

Murray, Pauli, educator and attorney, is Stulberg Professor of Law and Politics at Brandeis University. She was born Nov. 20, 1910 in Baltimore, Md., and has degrees from Hunter College (A.B., 1933), Howard University (LL.B., 1944), the University of California (Berkeley) Law School (LL.M., 1945) and Yale University Law School (J.S.D., 1965). She has been admitted to practice in New York and California and before the U.S. Supreme Court. An early black activist, she was imprisoned in Virginia in 1940 for resisting segregation on an interstate bus. Dr. Murray was a pioneer advocate of women's rights and a founder of the National Organization of Women (NOW). She has taught at several schools, including the Ghana School of Law, and has served on national and international commissions. She has written several books, including *Dark Testament and Other poems* (1970), *Proud Shoes* (1956) and *States' Laws on Race and Color* (1951). She co-authored (with Leslie Rubin) *The Constitution and Government of Ghana* (1961), and has written numerous articles and monographs. Dr. Murray is single. Address: Brandeis University, Waltham, MA 02154

Myers, Samuel L., educator, is president of Bowie State College in Bowie, Md. Born April 18, 1919 in Baltimore, Md., he is a graduate of Morgan State College (A.B. social science, 1940), Boston University (M.A., economics, 1942), Harvard University (M.A., economics, 1948; Ph.D., economics, 1949) where he was a Rosenwald Fellow. He was a postdoctoral Ford Foundation Faculty Fellow at the University of Pennsylvania in 1960. In 1966, he attended the Foreign Service Institute, U.S. Department of State. Other honors include membership in Alpha Kappa Mu Honor Society and a Morgan State College honorary LL.D. (1968). From 1942–46, he served in the U.S. Army (Pacific Theatre) and was discharged as a captain. From 1950 to 1963, he was associate professor, professor and chairman of the division of social sciences, Morgan State College. From 1963–67, he was with the U.S. Department of State as advisor for regional integration and trade. In 1967, Dr. Myers was named president of Bowie State College. He and his wife, Marion, have three children: Mrs. Vvette Myers May, Tama and Samuel. Address: Bowie State College, Bowie, MD 20715

Joan Murray

Pauli Murray

Samuel L. Myers

N

Samuel M. Nabrit   M. Maceo Nance Jr.   Earl L. Neal

Nabrit, Samuel Milton, administrator, is executive director of the Southern Fellowship Fund of the Council of Southern Universities, with headquarters in Atlanta, Ga. He screens applicants for 300–600 annual fellowships averaging $5,500 each. Born Feb. 21, 1905 in Macon, Ga., he is a graduate of Morehouse College (B.S., 1925) and Brown University (M.S., 1928; Ph.D., 1932) and has eight honorary degrees, including a doctor of science from Brown (1962). Dr. Nabrit was a professor of biology at Morehouse College, chairman of the biology department and dean of the graduate school at Atlanta University, president of Texas Southern University (1955–66), and a member of the Atomic Energy Commission (1966–67). One of about four black foundation heads in the nation, Dr. Nabrit raised nearly $17 million in 1972 for various scholarship programs. He is a member of Phi Beta Kappa, the American Society of Zoologists and the board of trustees of Brown University, and was the third president of the National Institute of Science. He and his wife, Constance, live in Atlanta. Address: 795 Peachtree St., SW, Atlanta, GA 30314

Nance, M. Maceo Jr., administrator, is president of South Carolina State College. Born March 28, 1935 in Columbia, S.C., he enrolled at South Carolina State College (1942) but left to enter the U.S. Navy (1943) where he served until 1946. He is a graduate of South Carolina State College (B.S., 1949) and New York University (M.S., 1953), and has an honorary degree (LL.D., 1968) from Morris Brown College. He is a member of the executive committee of the National Association of State Universities and Land Grant Colleges, and is a member of the Urban League College Presidents Advisory Council and numerous other professional and civic groups. He is a former president of Sigma Pi Phi. He and his wife, Julie, have two sons, Irwin and Robert. Address: South Carolina State College, Orangeburg, SC 29115

Neal, Earl Langdon, city official, is special attorney for the Corporation Council of the City of Chicago (Ill.). He is also general counsel on the Service Federal Savings & Loan Corporation in the city. Born April 16, 1928 in Chicago, he is a graduate of the University of Illinois (B.A., political science, 1949) and the University of Michigan (J.D., 1952). He is an elected member of the board of trustees of the University of Illinois. He is also a member of the board of trustees of the Metropolitan (Chicago) YMCA and chairman of the association's Washington Park branch. He is a member of the United Cerebral Palsy Drive and the Merit Board of the state of Illinois. He and his wife, Isobel, have a son, Langdon. Address: 111 W. Washington St., Chicago, IL 60601

Edward O. Nelson

G. Leon Netterville

Richard H. Newhouse Jr.

Nelson, Edward O., technician, is engineering technician at the U.S. Environmental Protection Agency in St. Louis, Mo. He operates, maintains and field tests air monitoring instruments which detect air pollution. Born Feb. 2, 1925 in Johnsonville, Tenn., he attended St. Louis University and Rankin Technical Institute, and is taking courses in computer electronics at Washington University. He was the first black admitted to the International Brotherhood of Electrical Workers, and is a member of the American Radio Relay League. He and his wife, Pauline, have six children: Stanley, Michael, Michelle, Cozetta, Richard and Viola. Address: C.A.M.P. Station, 215 S. 12th St., St. Louis, MO 63102

Netterville, George Leon, educator and administrator, is president of the Southern University System, whose three campuses are in Baton Rouge, New Orleans and Shreveport, La. Born July 16, 1907 in Dutchtown, La., he is a graduate of Southern University (B.A.) and Columbia University (M.A.). He has honorary degrees from Wiley College (Litt.D.) and Centenary College (LL.D.). Prior to assuming his present position in 1969, he was business manager, vice president in charge of business affairs, and acting president of Southern University. Dr. Netterville is a member and officer of a number of organizations, including the International Affairs Committee and the National Association of State Universities and Land Grant Colleges. He is a member of the executive committee of the Louisiana Capital Area Health Planning Council, is treasurer of the National Association for Equal Opportunity in Higher Education, and is a member of the board of trustees of Gammon Theological Seminary. He and his wife, Rebecca, have a son, George Leon III. Address: Southern University, Baton Rouge, LA 70813

Newhouse, Richard H. Jr., legislator, is an Illinois state senator from the 24th District (Chicago). Born Jan. 24, 1924 in Louisville, Ky., he is a graduate of Boston University (B.S., 1949; M.S., 1951) and the University of Chicago (J.D., 1961). A Democrat, he is president of the Black Legislators Association, which he founded. He is director of the Black Legislative Clearing House in Chicago, a Fellow of the Adlai Stevenson Institute, and serves on the Intergovernmental Relations Commission and the Council on the Diagnosis and Evaluation of Criminal Defendants. He is a member of numerous civic groups. He has been named "Best Legislator" by both the Independent Voters of Illinois and the American Legion, "Outstanding Public Servant" by the Cook County Bar Association, and "Senator of the Year" by the Baptist Ministers Conference of Chicago. He is a practicing attorney. He and his wife, Kathi, have three children: Suzanne, Richard and Holly. Address: State Capitol, Springfield, IL 62706

Lionel H. Newsome

Huey P. Newton

Edwin J. Nichols

Newsome, Lionel H., educator and administrator, is president of Central State University in Wilberforce, Ohio. Born Nov. 11, 1919 in Wichita Falls, Tex., he is a graduate of Lincoln University (B.A., history, *cum laude*), the University of Michigan (M.A., sociology) and Washington University in St. Louis, Mo. (Ph.D., sociology and anthropology). He received an honorary degree from Davidson College in Davidson, N.C. He has taught at Lincoln University, Luther College, Morehouse College and Southern University. He was president of Barber-Scotia College (1964–66) and was president of Johnson C. Smith University (1969–72). He was appointed to the National Defense Executive Reserve by Secretary of Labor Willard Wirtz, and served as chairman of the Georgia Council on Human Relations and on the executive council of the Atlanta Negro Voters League. He is a former general president of Alpha Phi Alpha fraternity (1964–68), and is a member of numerous professional societies and civic groups. He and his wife, Maxine, have a daughter, Jacqueline. Address: Central State University, Wilberforce, OH 45384

Newton, Huey P., administrator, is leader, co-founder (with Bobby Seale) and chief theoretician of the Black Panther party. Born Feb. 17, 1942 in Monroe, La., his family soon moved to Oakland, Calif. where he has spent most of his life. He has an A.A. degree from Merritt College and has also studied at the San Francisco School of Law. He founded the Black Panther party "to provide the people of Oakland with a new method for resolving the problems they faced on the streets." The Party is now national in scope. Mr. Newton is presently a student at Merritt College. Address: 8501 East 14th St., Oakland, CA 94612

Nichols, Edwin J., administrator, is chief of the center for studies of child and family mental health of the National Institute of Mental Health in Rockville, Md. Born June 23, 1931 in Detroit, Mich., he is a veteran of the Korean War. He studied psychology at the University of the Assumption in Canada (1952–55) and completed his clinical and industrial internship at Eberhardt Karls Universität in Tübingen, Germany. He was appointed a Fellow by the Austrian Ministry of Education and graduated with honors (Ph.D., clinical psychology, 1961) from Leopoline-Franciscea Universität, Innsbruck, Austria. Dr. Nichols has taught at the Kansas Neurological Institute, Cleveland State University, Meharry Medical College and Fisk University. Since he acts as a liaison between the National Institute of Mental Health and various national organizations, he has had a wide range of academic, clinical, and administrative experiences, including membership on a number of community boards. He and his wife, Sandra, have two children, Lisa and Edwin. Address: 5600 Fishers Lane, Rockville, MD 20852

Herbert Nipson

Rep. Robert N. C. Nix

George E. Norford

Nipson, Herbert, journalist, is executive editor of *Ebony* magazine. Born July 26, 1916 in Asheville, N.C., he moved with his family to Clearfield, Pa. at age two. After graduating from Clearfield High School, he attended Pennsylvania State University (B.A., journalism, 1940) and the University of Iowa (M.F.A., creative writing, 1949). At Penn State, he won a letter in cross-country track, was on the staffs of the school newspaper and literary magazine and was named to Phi Eta Sigma, the freshman scholastic honorary fraternity, and to Sigma Delta Chi, the national journalistic honorary fraternity. In 1940-41, he was editor of *Brown American* magazine in Philadelphia. Drafted into the armed forces in 1941, he was discharged in 1945 with the rank of master sergeant. While a graduate student at Iowa, he won statewide Iowa Press Photographers Association awards and worked for a year as a correspondent for the *Cedar Rapids Gazette.* Named an associate editor of *Ebony* in 1949, he became co-managing editor in 1951, managing editor in 1964 and executive editor in 1967. He received the Capital Press Club's award as outstanding journalist in 1965 and was named a Distinguished Alumnus of Penn State in 1973. He is chairman of the board of directors of the South Side Community Art Center and a member of the Illinois Arts Council, The Joseph Jefferson Committee and the Board of Governors of Urban Gateways. Married to E. Velin Campbell of Philadelphia in 1942, he is the father of two children, Herbert and Maria. Address: 820 S. Michigan Ave., Chicago IL 60605

Nix, Robert N. C., congressman, has been a member of the U.S. House of Representatives since 1958. He represents the 2nd District of Pennsylvania (Philadelphia). He is a member of the House committees on Foreign Affairs, and Post Office and Civil Service. Born Aug. 9, 1905 in Orangeburg, S.C., he is a graduate of Lincoln University (A.B., 1921) and the University of Pennsylvania Law School (LL.B. 1924), and has been a practicing attorney since 1925. He is a member of numerous professional and civic organizations, including the Philadelphia Bar Association, the NAACP, the YMCA and Omega Psi Phi fraternity. He was elected as 44th Ward executive committeeman, 9th division, in 1923 and has been consistently reelected. He was a delegate to the Democratic National Convention in Chicago

Norford, George E., administrator, is vice president-general executive and a member of the board of directors of Westinghouse Broadcasting Co. in New York, N.Y. Born Jan. 18, 1918 in New York City, he worked on the staff of his high school newspaper as a sports reporter and later studied journalism and playwriting at Columbia University and attended the New School for Social Research. He was an associate editor of the first *Negro World Digest* published and, during World War II, was the only black correspondent on the staff of *Yank* magazine, the army weekly. He has written several short stories and plays about black life, six of which were produced in off-Broadway theaters. He began writing for television in 1951, was a press writer on "The Today Show" and later became the first black producer of network television programs at NBC (1957). He is a member of the Academy of Television Arts and Sciences and is a board member of seven civic organizations. He and his wife, Thomasina, live in New York. Address: 90 Park Ave., New York, NY 10016

O

Edwin E. Oliver

Frederick O'Neal

John O'Neal

Claude H. Organ Jr., M.D.

Oliver, Edwin E., pharmacist, is president of the National Pharmaceutical Association and is owner of Oliver's Pharmacy in Spartanburg, S.C. Born Feb. 15, 1926 in Montgomery, Ala., he served in the U.S. Navy, then attended Xavier University and graduated in 1950 from its College of Pharmacy. He is involved in numerous civic and political affairs of his community and serves as chairman of the Mayor's Committee on Human Relations, president of the board of directors of the Minority Businessmen's Development Corp. and president of the South Carolina Resources Development Corp. He is a member of Omega Psi Phi Fraternity, the American Pharmaceutical Assn., Palmetto Medical and Dental Association and the South Carolina Pharmaceutical Association. He and his wife, Deloris, have one child. Address: 375 So. Liberty St., Spartanburg, SC 29301

O'Neal, Frederick, administrator, is president of the Actors' Equity Association, international president of the Associated Actors and Artists of America and president of the Schomberg Collection of Black History, Literature and Art. Born Aug. 27, 1905 in Brooksville, Miss., he studied at the New Theatre School and the American Theatre Wing. He also has an honorary degree from Columbia College (D.F.A., 1966) and a certificate from Loeb Student Center of New York University (1967). Before assuming his present position in 1963, Mr. O'Neal organized the Aldridge Players in St. Louis (1927), founded the American Negro Theatre in New York (1940), served with the Armed Forces (1942–43) and established the British Negro Theatre in London (1948). He was a visiting professor at Southern Illinois University (1962) and at Clark College (1963). He has conducted theater seminars in various parts of the country and has written a number of feature articles for leading magazines. He and his wife, Charlotte, live in New York City. Address: 165 W. 46th St., New York, NY 10036

O'Neal, John, theatrical director, is producing director of the Free Southern Theater in New Orleans, La., which he co-founded with Gilbert Moses in 1963. A non-profit troupe, the FST tours small cities and dirt-farm towns in Alabama, Georgia, Mississippi and Louisiana, presenting excellent productions of such plays as *Waiting for Godot, In White America, George Dandin* and *Purlie Victorious* to integrated—largely black and poor—audiences. The stages are found in church auditoriums, school gyms or— lacking these—in cotton fields. Typical salary for talented directors and actors alike has been $35 per week. No admission is charged, the company relying on monies from contributions and benefits which have come largely from the North. A New York critic called FST's *Godot* "as good as any we have seen in this city (NYC)." Born Sept. 25, 1940 in Carbondale, Ill., Mr. O'Neal is a graduate of Southern Illinois University (B.A. philosophy, 1962). He has been field secretary of SNCC and has worked extensively in youth, child care and adult training programs in the New York, N.Y. area. Mr. O'Neal—who is also a playwright and poet—and his wife, Marilyn, live in New Orleans. Address: 1240 Dryades St., New Orleans, LA 70113

Organ, Claude H. Jr., M.D., educator, is professor and chairman of the department of surgery at Creighton University School of Medicine in Omaha, Neb. Author of numerous scientific papers, he recently travelled to Poland as a guest of that country's medical society to lecture to surgeons. He was also invited to Paris, France to read his paper entitled, "Surgical Procedures Upon the Drug Addict." Born Oct. 16, 1927 in Marshall, Tex., he graduated from Xavier University (B.S., 1948), the Creighton University School of Medicine (M.D., 1952) and Creighton University (M.S., surgery, 1957). Dr. Organ is responsible for the establishment of a Health Sciences Minority Recruiting Committee at Creighton and persuaded Creighton's health science schools to reserve a 10 percent quota of each entering freshman class for minorities. He is a member of the boards of Fontbonne College, Xavier University, and Boys Town. He is also a member of the President's Council at Creighton University and a member of the Medical Educational Committee of the American Medical Association. Dr. Organ and his wife, Betty, have seven children: Claude Jr., Brian, Paul, Gregory, David, Sandra and Rita. Address: Creighton University School of Medicine, Tenth and Martha, Omaha, NB 68108

George A. Owens

Jesse Owens

Leroy Ozanne

Owens, George A., administrator and educator, is president of Tougaloo (Miss.) College. Although Tougaloo is a predominantly black college, Dr. Owens in 1965 became the first black president of the more than a century-old institution. Born Feb. 9, 1919 in Hinds County, Miss., he attended Jackson (Miss.) State College (high school) and Tougaloo College (A.B., economics, 1941). In 1941, he enlisted as a private in the U.S. Army from which he was honorably discharged with the rank of captain in 1946. Before enrolling at Columbia University (M.B.A., accounting, 1950), he worked briefly (in 1946) as a clerk for the Security Life Insurance Co. in Jackson; as a bookkeeper for a hardware store in Jersey City, N.J. (1947–48), and as a junior executive for Saks in New York City. In 1949, he accepted the post of business manager and chief financial officer at Talladega (Ala.) College, a post he held until 1955 when he took a similar position with Tougaloo College. In September, 1964, he was made acting president and less than a year later president. He has been awarded four honorary doctorates (LL.D., Bethany College, 1967; LL.D., Houston-Tillotson College, 1967; LL.D., Brown University, 1967, and L.H.D., Wilberforce University, 1970). He is a board member of College Placement Services, Inc. in Bethlehem, Pa.; Communication Improvement, Inc., Channel 3-WLBT-TV, Jackson, Miss.; Higher Education Compact, New York City; the Institute of Politics in Mississippi, Jackson, Miss.; the National Council of Churches; the Southern Regional Council; the United Church Board for Homeland Ministries, United Church of Christ, and the United Negro College Fund. In addition, he is a member of the NAACP, the National Urban League, and Phi Delta Kappa fraternity. He and his wife, Ruth, have two children, Paul Douglas and Gail Patrice. Address: Tougaloo College, Tougaloo, MS 39174

Owens, Jesse, marketing executive, is a former Olympic and collegiate track star. He is president of Jesse Owens, Inc. and Jesse Owens & Associates in Chicago, Ill. The firms analyze consumer marketing problems and develop marketing plans for a number of clients. Born Sept. 12, 1913 in Danville, Ala., he was one of 11 children. The family moved to Cleveland, Ohio in 1924, and he found his rural Alabama education a real handicap, but by hard work he caught up with his class by age 14. Working afternoons and weekends at a shoe-shine stand to help out the family, he became a "one-man track team" in high school. At the National Interscholastic Championships in Chicago he won the 100-yd. dash in 9.4 seconds, equaling the world record, and won the 200-yd. dash and the broad jump. He worked his way through Ohio State University, where he received his B.S. degree and continued his track exploits. In just 75 minutes at the 1933 Big Ten Championships, the "Buckeye Bullet" set three world records and tied another. His broad jump record stood for 25 years, longest of any track and field record. At the 1936 Olympics in Berlin, Mr. Owens was the first athlete to win four gold medals in one Olympiad. He and his wife, Ruth, have three adult daughters: Gloria, Beverly and Marlene. Address: 333 N. Michigan Ave., Chicago, IL 60601

Ozanne, Leroy, contractor, is owner of Ozanne Construction Co., Inc., in Cleveland, Ohio. He was the first black person to become a member of the Cleveland chapter of the Associated General Contractors of America. Mr. Ozanne was born Oct. 30, 1926 in Beaumont, Tex. He studied pre-engineering at John Carroll University and architecture at Fenn College, Cleveland College and John Huntington Polytechnical. During this time, he was employed by the City of Cleveland as a building inspector. In 1956, he formed his own firm. He is a member of the Cleveland Growth Board and is vice president of the Society of General Contractors. He is active in civic affairs, and is a member of the Catholic Interracial Council. He and his wife, Betty, have four children: Dominick, Mark, Lisa and Jeff. Address: Ozanne Construction Co., E. 21st St. and Euclid Ave., Cleveland, OH 44115

P

Claude A. Parker Jr.

Gordon Parks Sr.

Henry G. Parks Jr.

Parker, Claude A. Jr., administrator, is quality-control manager at the Four Roses Distilling Co., in Dundalk, Md. He is responsible for all chemical, physical and taste and odor control on alcoholic beverages produced by the company, a subsidiary of Joseph E. Seagram & Sons, Inc. Previously, he was a chemist, materials supervisor and distillery production coordinator with the company. Born Oct. 24, 1938 in Branchville, Va., he is a graduate of Baltimore Community College (A.A., pre-engineering) and Morgan State College (B.S., science education). He and his wife, Constance, have a son, Claude. Address: P.O. Box 357, Baltimore, MD 21203

Parks, Gordon Sr., photo-journalist, author, composer and movie director, was director of the 1971 number one box-office hit film, *Shaft,* and its sequel a year later, *Shaft's Big Score.* Born Nov. 30, 1912 in Fort Scott, Kan., he is a graduate of Maryland Institute (A.F.D.). He was a cameraman for the U.S. Farm Security Administration under a Rosenwald Fellowship (1942–43) for the U.S. Office of War Information (1944), for Standard Oil Co. of New Jersey (1945-48) and for *Life* magazine (1948–72). He has been a color and black-and-white consultant on motion picture productions in the United States and Europe since 1954. His photography for *Life* ran the gamut from the raw realism of stories on a Harlem gang leader to graceful fashion portraits—an art that earned him the A.S.M.P. Magazine Photographer of the Year award in 1961. He has written several musical compositions, including *First Concerto for Piano and Orchestra*, performed in 1953, and three piano sonatas performed at Philadelphia in 1955. He has written the books, *Flash Photography, Camera Portraits, The Learning Tree* (1963) *A Choice of Weapons* (1966) and *Photos and Poems* (1968). In 1968, he brought *The Learning Tree* to the screen, writing the screenplay, directing it, casting and producing it and writing the music. Mr. Parks has four children: Gordon Jr., Toni (Mrs. Jean-Luc Brouillaud), David and Leslie. Address: Warner Brothers Seven Arts, Hollywood, CA 90028 **See article on Gordon Parks Sr. in Volume II**

Parks, Henry G. Jr., is president of H. G. Parks, Inc., a sausage company in Baltimore, Md. Born Sept. 20, 1916 in Atlanta, Ga., he is a graduate of Ohio State University (B.S. with honors), where he also pursued postgraduate studies in marketing. Before founding his company in 1951, he had experience in a variety of fields. After graduation, he went to work with Dr. Mary McLeod Bethune at the Resident War Production Training Center in Wilberforce, Ohio. He moved to New York and owned and operated several enterprises including a theatrical booking agency. In Baltimore, he engaged in a drug store operation, in real estate and in cement block production. Then, together with several other young men, he decided that there was a growing demand for a "Southern style, well-seasoned sausage." The fledgling company had every problem: financing, production, distribution, sales and raw materials. But special salesmanship and showmanship including a barker dressed as "Parky the Pig," parading the streets and passing out free sausage created a demand in the black community. Then, Mr. Parks signed up his first chain in Washington, D.C. and later won over every major chain on the East Coast. In 1971 the company's sales reached $10.4 million. Mr. Parks is vice president and board member of the Chamber of Commerce of Metropolitan Baltimore and of Tuesday Publications and a director of several corporations including First Pennsylvania and Magnavox. Divorced, he has two daughters, Grace (Mrs. L.D. Johnson) and Cheryl. Address: 501 W. Hamburg St., Baltimore, MD 21230 **See article on Henry G. Parks, Jr. in Volume II**

Rosa Parks

Judge James B. Parsons

Cecil A. Partee

Parks, Rosa, civil rights leader, is the woman who, in December, 1955, decided she wasn't going to give up her bus seat to a white passenger, and triggered a bus boycott in Montgomery, Ala. That boycott resulted in the outlawing of segregation on city buses in Montgomery and paved the way for the subsequent civil rights movement that followed throughout the South. She was born Feb. 14, 1913 in Tuskegee, Ala., but was raised in Montgomery. She attended Alabama State College. She worked as a clerk and an insurance saleswoman prior to taking a job as a tailor's assistant. Aside from her job, she was actively involved with the youth of her community and spent several years serving as youth advisor for the Montgomery NAACP. When she lost her job in 1955 as a result of her bus protest, she devoted all of her time to volunteer work to help carry on the boycott. In 1957, she moved her family to Detroit and became active with the SCLC and the Women's Public Affairs Committee, an interracial social action group. She is known as "The Mother of the Modern Civil Rights Movement," and SCLC sponsors an annual Rosa Parks Freedom Award. In July, 1971, she was honored by the Women's Missionary Society of the A.M.E. Church at the Quadrennial Convention held in Los Angeles and she was awarded an honorary degree from Shaw College in Detroit. She is presently a staff assistant to Rep. John Conyers. Address: 305 Federal Bldg., 231 W. Lafayette, Detroit, MI 48226

Parsons, James Benton, jurist, is U. S. District Judge for the Northern District of Illinois. He was appointed by President John F. Kennedy in 1961. He was born August 13, 1911 in Kansas City, Mo. and grew up in Decatur, Ill. He is a graduate of James Millikin University and Conservatory of Music (B.A., 1934), and the University of Chicago (M.A., political science, 1946; LL.D., 1949). He also studied political science during summers at the University of Wisconsin Graduate School (1935-40). He taught at Lincoln University (Mo.) and was acting head of the Music Department (1938-40). He was a supervisor for Greensboro, N.C. public schools (1940-42) and taught constitutional law at John Marshall Law School (1949-51). He was assistant corporation counsel of Chicago (1949-51); assistant U. S. district attorney (1951-60), and judge of Cook County (Ill.) Superior Court (1960-61) before becoming a federal judge in 1961. He is a member of numerous professional and civic groups. In 1967, the Parsons Elementary School in Decatur, Ill. was dedicated in his name. He is a widower and has a son, Hans-Dieter. Address: 219 S. Dearborn St., Chicago, IL 60604

Partee, Cecil A., legislator, is minority leader of the Illinois state senate. Prior to assuming the position on Jan. 10, 1973, he was president pro tem (majority leader) of the Senate. A Democrat, he represents the 26th District (Chicago). Born April 10, 1921 in Blytheville, Ark., he is a graduate of Tennessee State University (B.S., business administration, 1944) and Northwestern University (J.D., 1946). He was elected to the Illinois House of Representatives in 1956 and served five terms before being elected to the senate in 1966. Earlier, he served eight years as a Cook County (Chicago) assistant state's attorney. He is a member of Partee & Green, a law firm in Chicago. In 1967, he was named Outstanding Freshman Senator by his peers. In 1969, he was named Outstanding State Senator. He is a member of numerous civic organizations, including the Chicago City Club and the Jane Dent Home. He and his wife, Paris, have two daughters, Paris and Cecile. Address: State Capitol, Springfield, IL 62706

Patrick, William T. Jr., administrator, is director of community relations for the American Telephone & Telgraph Co. in New York, N.Y. Born March 28, 1920 in Washington, D.C., he has degrees from Howard University (A.B., 1942), University of Michigan (LL.B., 1946) and the University of Detroit (L.H.D., 1972). He is former director of environmental affairs for Michigan Bell Telephone Co. and has served as a visiting lecturer in political science at the University of Michigan (1965–67) and as consultant-lecturer at the University of Detroit (1960–71). He has received several awards, including the Howard University Outstanding Alumni Award (1964), the University of Michigan Regents Award (1965), the Beta Gamma Sigma Honorary Scholastic Society Award, Honorary Membership (1967) and the Wayne County Community College Outstanding Service Award (1971). He is a member of various professional societies and serves as a board member of several organizations, including the Center for Governmental Studies (in Washington, D.C.). He is board chairman of the Longwood Housing Association in Cleveland, Ohio. He and his wife, Betty, have a daughter, Michelle. Address: 195 Broadway, New York, NY 10007

Patterson, Frederick D., educator, is chairman of the board of the Robert R. Moton Memorial Institute, an educational service agency in New York City. Born Oct. 10, 1901 in Washington, D.C., Dr. Patterson attended Iowa State College (D.V.M., 1923; M.S., 1927) and Cornell University, (Ph.D., 1932). He holds honorary degrees from 12 colleges and universities including New York University, Morehouse College, Howard University, Tuskegee Institute and Atlanta University. An honored educator at Tuskegee Institute for some 30 years, Dr. Patterson has served as instructor, head of the veterinary division, director of the School of Agriculture and finally as president of the institute. Founder (in 1943) and honorary president of the United Negro College Fund, Dr. Patterson has contributed much to the survival and growth of the black college in America. He has contributed articles to several scientific and educational journals and is co-author of *What the Negro Wants*. Dr. Patterson and his wife, Catherine, have a son, Frederick Jr. Address: 527 Madison Ave., New York, NY 10022

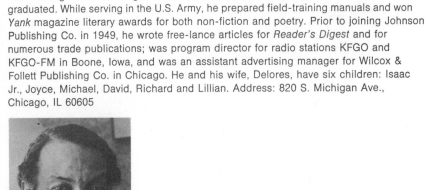

Payne, Isaac Newton, publishing executive, is advertising production manager and a vice president of Johnson Publishing Co., Inc. in Chicago, Ill. Born Jan. 29, 1920 in Fraser, Iowa, he studied social sciences and literature at Kansas State University and the University of Illinois, pre-law at John Marshall Law School, and script writing, newscasting and advertising at the Radio Institute of Chicago, from which he graduated. While serving in the U.S. Army, he prepared field-training manuals and won *Yank* magazine literary awards for both non-fiction and poetry. Prior to joining Johnson Publishing Co. in 1949, he wrote free-lance articles for *Reader's Digest* and for numerous trade publications; was program director for radio stations KFGO and KFGO-FM in Boone, Iowa, and was an assistant advertising manager for Wilcox & Follett Publishing Co. in Chicago. He and his wife, Delores, have six children: Isaac Jr., Joyce, Michael, David, Richard and Lillian. Address: 820 S. Michigan Ave., Chicago, IL 60605

William T. Patrick Jr.

Frederick D. Patterson

Isaac N. Payne

Benjamin F. Payton

Sallyanne Payton

John A. Peoples

Payton, Benjamin F., administrator, is officer in charge of higher education and minority affairs for the Ford Foundation's $100 million program of assistance to minorities in higher education. Born Dec. 27, 1932 in Orangeburg, S.C., he has degrees from South Carolina State College (B.A., 1955), Harvard University (B.D., 1958), Columbia University (M.A., 1960) and Yale University (Ph.D., 1963). Dr. Payton is the former president of Benedict College in South Carolina, where he rebuilt the school into an academic institution of national stature. He has served as executive director of the Commission on Religion and Race; the department of social justice of the National Council of Churches (1966-67); the Office of Church and Race (1966), and as an assistant professor at Howard University (1963-65). He was awarded the Harvard Billings Prize (1957) and was named South Carolinian of the Year (1972). He and his wife, Thelma, have a son, Mark Steven. Address: 320 E. 43rd St., New York, NY 10017

Payton, Sallyanne, White House aide, is staff assistant to the president of the United States. Born May 18, 1943 in Los Angeles, Calif., she has degrees from Stanford University (A.B., 1964; LL.D., 1968). Miss Payton is one of seven blacks working in various capacities on the White House staff. Her work involves policy analysis and recommendations for the president's use in domestic areas of concern, especially the District of Columbia affairs, such as housing and education policy. Miss Payton was formerly a social caseworker for the Los Angeles County Bureau of Public Assistance and an attorney for Covington & Burling in Washington, D.C. She is a member of several professional organizations and serves on the boards of organizations, including the Commission on the Organization of the Government of the District of Columbia, the Southeast Neighborhood House and the Health and Welfare Council of the National Capital Area Committee on Federal Legislation. She is a member of the California and District of Columbia bars. Address: The White House, Executive Office Building. The Domestic Council, 17th and Pennsylvania Ave. NW, Washington, DC 20500

Peoples, John A., educator and administrator, is president of Jackson State College in Mississippi. Born Aug. 26, 1926 in Starkville, Miss., he received degrees from Jackson State College (B.S., mathematics, 1950) and the University of Chicago (M.A., mathematics, education, 1951 and Ph.D., educational administration, 1962). In 1951, he became an instructor of mathematics in Gary, Ind., the first black to teach integrated classes in that city. Mr. Peoples became president of Jackson State in 1967, after having served for two years as professor of mathematics and as vice president of the school. He is a member of the American Association for Higher Education, the Institute for Educational Management and the Advisory Committee on Accreditation and Institutional Eligibility, United States Department of Health, Education and Welfare. He also holds membership in the Alpha Kappa Mu honor society as well as numerous civic organizations. Mr. Peoples and his wife, Mary, have two children, Kathleen and Mark. Address: P. O. Box 17179, Jackson State College, Jackson, MS 39217

Benjamin L. Perry Jr.   Brock Peters

Perry, Benjamin Luther Jr., educator and administrator, is president of Florida A&M University in Tallahassee, Fla. Under his administration, the school has erased the mediocre academic status it had held among Florida state schools. Born Feb. 27, 1918 in Eatonville, Fla., he is a graduate of Florida A&M College (B.S. agriculture education, 1940), Iowa State College (M.S., agriculture economics, 1942) and Cornell University (Ph.D., land economics, 1954). He has served at Florida A&M University in various capacities, including professor of economics, director of research and grants, and dean of men. He has authored numerous articles, including "Black Colleges—Past, Present, and Future," "Higher Education for Disadvantaged Students" and "FAMU at the Crossroads." He was honored by the president of the Republic of Nigeria for outstanding services to the University of Nigeria (1964) and has received, among other awards, the Phi Delta Kappa Man of the Year award (1970). His affiliations include president of the Southern Associations of Land-Grant Colleges and Universities; chairman of the board of directors of the Carnegie Program, University of Florida; member of Kappa Alpha Psi, and founder of Alpha Phi Omega. He and his wife, Helen, have one daughter, Kimberly. Address: Office of the President, Florida A&M University, Tallahassee, FL 32307

Peters, Brock, is a vocalist, musician, actor and producer. Born July 2, 1927 in New York City of a Senegalese father and a West Indian mother, he entered the Music and Arts High School as a violinist and vocalist, later studying at New York City College where he was a top athlete. At an audition for a revival of *Porgy and Bess*, Mr. Peters sang eight bars of "Old Man River," which convinced the producer that he should give him the role of Jim. He left college to tour the United States in a troupe that included the great Avon Long. There followed numerous featured roles on and off Broadway, in road and stock companies, nightclubs, television and a long run in Chicago as the juvenile lead in *Anna Lucasta*. Mr. Peters finished his college education at the University of Chicago. He has appeared in many films including *To Kill a Mockingbird*, *The L-Shaped Room*, *P.J.*, *The Daring Game*, *The Pawnbroker*, *The Incident* and *Black Girl*. He has won major film awards internationally and has been an "Emmy" nominee for the past seven years. Mr. Peters is a founding member of the Arthur Mitchell Dance Theatre of Harlem and is president of the Free Southern Theater. He is also the co-owner of two businesses with his wife, Dolores, who serves as his publicist. The Peters have one daughter, Lise. Address: MGM, 10202 W. Washington Blvd., Culver City, CA 90230

"Gene" Raymond Peters

Wilbert C. Petty

Basil O. Phillips

Peters, "Gene" Raymond, airline executive, is co-founder and president of New World Airways, Inc. and also executive director and founder of New World Aviation Academy, Inc. Born Aug. 24, 1933, in New Haven, Conn., his formal education consists of courses audited in business law and journalism at San Diego City College and economics courses at the University of Chicago. One of only five blacks who own an aviation transportation firm in the United States, he is first vice president of the Southern California Chapter of Negro Airmen International. The non-scheduled cargo airline operates throughout California. Editor and Publisher of *Profiles in Black American History*, he is co-founder and president of the National Afro-American Historical Society and organized California's first OEO War On Poverty agency. Author of *Prime Thoughts for Black Folks* (1969) and *Five Minutes to Freedom* (1963), he is currently writing a major motion picture script, *Eagles Don't Cry*. He and his wife, Mabel, have three children: Christopher, James and Patricia. Address: Suite 207, 953 8th Ave., San Diego, CA 92101

Petty, Wilbert C., foreign service officer, is the cultural attaché at the U.S. Embassy in Stockholm, Sweden, a diplomatic position he has held since 1960. Previous to this, he was a public affairs officer for the embassy. Born October 12, 1928 in Asheville, N.C., he attended Howard University (B.A., art, *cum laude*); Catholic University (M.F.A.); the University of Paris (Sorbonne); the Georgetown Institute of Foreign Languages; UCLA and the Foreign Service Institute. An accomplished sculptor in his own right, Mr. Petty owns a collection of more than 300 outstanding pieces of African sculpture, now on loan to Morgan State College in Baltimore, Md. He and his wife, Irene, have one daughter, Mariama. Address: American Embassy, Stockholm, Sweden

Phillips, Basil Oliphant, administrator, is photo editor at Johnson Publishing Co., Inc. in Chicago, Ill. He heads a staff which catalogues and maintains the picture library (about 500,000 photographs, drawings, color transparencies, etc.) of the world's largest black-owned publishing firm *(Ebony, Jet, Black World, Black Stars* and *Ebony Jr.*). He is also director of special markets and promotions for the JPC Book Division. Previously, he was sales manager. Before joining Johnson Publishing Co. in 1950, he was employed by Chicago's well-known Abraham Lincoln Bookstore. Born Feb. 19, 1930 in Kansas City, Mo., he attended Roosevelt University and the Institute of Design at Illinois Institute of Technology. He is single. Address: 820 S. Michigan Ave., Chicago, IL 60605

Rev. Channing E. Phillips

Judge Vel R. Phillips

Thomas M. Picou

Phillips, The Reverend Channing E., administrator, is president and director of the Housing Development Corp. in Washington, D.C. He directs the company in land acquisition, sales and property management in the Washington metropolitan area. Born March 23, 1928 in Brooklyn, N.Y., he has degrees from Virginia Union University (A.B., 1950), Colgate Rochester Divinity School (B.D., 1953), and honorary degrees from Mary Holmes College (D.D.), the Pacific School of Religion (D.D.) and Elmhurst College (L.H.D.). From 1945 to 1947, he served in the U.S. Air Force. Following graduate study at Drew University, he was lecturer at American University and Virginia Episcopal Seminary (1957–58). He was an instructor at the Howard University school of religion (1956–58) and minister of the Grace Congregational Church in New York (1958–59). A United Church of Christ clergyman, he is active in several civic and community organizations and was Democratic national committeeman for Washington, D.C. (1968–72). He was the first black nominated for U.S. president at the 1968 Democratic National Convention in Chicago. He and his wife, Jane, have five children: Channing, Shelah, Tracy, Jill and John. Address: Suites 800-821, 1010 Vermont Ave., NW Washington, DC 20005

Phillips, Vel R., jurist, is a Milwaukee County judge, Branch 13 of Children's Court. She is also a member of the law firm, Phillips & Phillips, in association with her husband, and a visiting lecturer for the Department of Afro-American Studies, University of Wisconsin. Previously, she was the first black elected to the Milwaukee Common Council (1956) where she was reelected to four terms, and was the first black person in the United States ever elected to serve on the National Committee of either of the major parties. She served for six years on the Democratic National Committee and in 1960 was named co-chairman of the National Democratic Convention's Committee on Rules and Order of Business. Born Feb. 18, 1924 in Milwaukee, Wis., she is a graduate of Howard University (B.S., 1946), University of Wisconsin Law School (LL.B., 1951) and a 1971 graduate of the Summer College for Juvenile Court Judges at the University of Nevada. The recipient of numerous awards including Woman of the Year by Milwaukee Marquette University Chapter of Theta Sigma Phi Sorority (1968) and the 1967 Milwaukee Star Award for service to Milwaukee youths, she was named one of the Doers of the Decade by Theta Sigma Phi sorority. She is a board member of the NAACP, Day Care and Child Development Council, John F. Kennedy School and is on the advisory board of the Department of Local Affairs as well as being a member of Delta Sigma Theta sorority, the American Association of University Women and the Women's International League for Peace and Freedom, among others. She and her husband, Dale, have two children, Dale and Michael. Address: 2218 N. Third St., Suite 209, Milwaukee WI 53212

Picou, Thomas Maurice, journalist, is managing editor of the *Chicago Daily Defender,* a black-owned newspaper in Chicago, Ill. He began his association with the *Defender* in 1961 as sports editor. His jobs on the newspaper have included assistant news editor, director of advertising and promotions, director of circulation, and assistant to the editor. Born Oct. 25, 1937 in Los Angeles, Cal., he attended Los Angeles City College (A.A., 1957), UCLA and Roosevelt University (B.A., 1959). He is president of the board of directors of Building Consultant, Inc. and a member of the board of directors of Leisure Development Corp., both in Chicago. He is chairman of the Chicago Blood Donor's Drive, and is a member of the board of directors of several civic groups. Divorced, he has a daughter, Tracey. Address: 2400 South Michigan Ave., Chicago, IL 60616

Ponchitta Pierce   Samuel R. Pierce Jr.

Pierce, Ponchitta, journalist, is a contributing editor of *McCall*'s magazine in New York, N.Y. Born August 5, 1942 in Chicago, Ill., she studied at Cambridge University in England and is a graduate of the University of Southern California (B.A., journalism, 1964). She was a CBS News special correspondent (1968–71), chief of the New York editorial bureau for Johnson Publishing Co. (1967–68) and an editor of *Ebony* (1964–68). Her awards include the Penney-Missouri Magazine Award for Excellence in women's interest journalism (1967), the New York Urban League John Russwurm Award for "sustained excellence in interpreting, analyzing and reporting the news" (1968) and the Headliner Award, presented (1970) by National Theta Sigma Phi for "outstanding work in the field of broadcasting." Miss Pierce attended the First Asian-American Women Journalists Conference in Honolulu in 1965, tri-sponsored by Theta Sigma Phi, the State Department and East-West Center. She is a member of Theta Sigma Phi, the American Federation of Television and Radio Artists, American Women in Television and the National Academy of Television Arts and Sciences. She is director of the African Student Aid Fund and director of the American Freedom From Hunger Foundation. She is single. Address: 230 Park Ave., Room 733, New York, NY 10017

Pierce, Samuel R. Jr., attorney, is the general counsel of the Treasury of the United States. Born Sept. 8, 1922 in Glen Cove, N.Y., he holds degrees from Cornell University (A.B., J.D.) and New York University (LL.M. and an honorary LL.D.). His appointment as principal advisor to the secretary of the treasury on policy matters, and head of the department's legal division, consisting of over 900 lawyers, marked the first time a black had ever been appointed to a subcabinet position in the treasury. Before being appointed by President Nixon in July, 1970, he was a judge of the Court of General Sessions in New York City, and a partner in the law firm of Battle, Fowler, Stokes, & Kheel. He serves on the board of directors of U. S. industries and on numerous boards of trustees, including Cornell University, Hampton Institute, the Institute for International Education, and the Executive Board of the Boy Scouts of America. Mr. Pierce and his wife, Barbara, a physician, have one daughter, Mrs. Victoria Pierce Ransmeier. Address: The General Counsel of the Treasury, U. S. Treasury Dept. Washington, DC 20220

Lois M. J. Pierre-Nöel

Arnold R. Pinkney

Peggy D. Pinn

Pierre-Noël, Lois Mailou Jones, artist and educator, is professor of design and watercolor painting at the College of Fine Arts of Howard University in Washington, D.C. Born Nov. 3, 1905 in Boston, Mass., she is a graduate of the Boston Museum School of Fine Arts (1927) and also has certificates from the Designers Art School (1928) and the Boston Normal Art School (1928). She attended Columbia, Harvard and Howard universities and received an A.B. degree, *magna cum laude*, from Howard. She also has certificates from the Academia Julian (1938) and the Academie 10 Grande Chaumière (1962) in Paris, France. Although Mrs. Pierre-Noël's paintings were exhibited and acclaimed by the world-famous Societé des Artistes Français in Paris as early as 1938, it was not until 1953 that one of her canvasses was hung in the Corcoran Gallery of Art in Washington, D.C.—and then only after it had been entered by one of her white friends. Her work is in 16 permanent collections in the U.S and several foreign countries. She has some 20 one-woman shows to her credit and has participated in more than 30 group exhibitions. In 1962, she was elected a fellow of London's prestigious Royal Society of Arts. After graduation from the school in Boston, she was turned down for a vacant teaching position there and told to "go South and help your people." In 1930, she began teaching at Howard and has been there ever since. Her husband, Vergniaud Pierre-Noël, is also a distinguished artist. Address: Box 893, Howard University, Washington, DC 20001 **See article on Lois Mailou Jones Pierre-Noël in Volume II**

Pinkney, Arnold R., business executive, is president of Arnold R. Pinkney Consulting Services and board chairman of Pinkney-Perry Insurance Agency in Cleveland, Ohio. He is involved in consulting on educational matters as related to urban areas and the selling of all lines of insurance. Born Jan. 6, 1931 in Youngstown, Ohio, he is a graduate of Albion (Mich.) College (B.A., education). He was appointed executive assistant to Cleveland Mayor Carl B. Stokes in 1970, and elected president of the Cleveland Board of Education two years in succession (1971-72). He is a life member of the NAACP, a member of the National Life Underwriters Association and was elected chairman of Central State University's board of trustees. He was an unsuccessful candidate for mayor of Cleveland in 1971. He and his wife, Betty, have one child, Traci. Address: 2131 Fairhill Rd., Cleveland, OH 44106

Pinn, Peggy D., film-maker, is director of the film training laboratory at the Howard University School of Communications in Washington, D.C. She instructs students in the art of film-making and has trained many blacks who are currently making feature films. Born Oct. 9, 1936 in Brooklyn, N.Y., she is a graduate of the City College of New York (B.S., education, 1953). She was head of the circulation department of *Our World* magazine (1954–55), a secretary at CBS television (1955–62), assistant director of a summer institute for teachers at City College of New York (1965), assistant to the producer of the ABC television documentary, "Africa" (1966–68), director of her own film school (1968–72) and assistant to the executive producer of "Black Journal Workshop" (1968–72). She is divorced. Address: 2600 4th St., NW, Washington, DC 20024

Lucius H. Pitts

Willa B. Player

Pitts, Lucius H., educator, is president of Paine College in Augusta, Ga. He is the first black man to serve as president of the 88-year-old school. Born in James, Ga., he has degrees from Paine College (B.A., 1941), Fisk University (M.A., 1945) and completed additional graduate work at Atlanta University, Peabody College and Western Reserve University. The recipient of numerous honorary degrees, Mr. Pitts started his career in education as the principal of Milan Public School, Georgia (1936–39). He was a teacher at Paine College (1933–48), principal of Holsey Cobb Institute (1948–55) and was the executive secretary of Georgia Teachers & Education Association (1955–61). He became the president of Miles College in Birmingham, Ala. in 1961 and president of Paine College in 1971. He developed Miles College as an accredited institution and raised $1,250,000 for its improvement. He has been a leader for social change in Birmingham, Ala. and the state of Georgia. During the early sixties, he worked with student protesters and acted as a race relations mediator. Mr. Pitts is a member of many educational, religious and civic organizations. He and his wife, Dafferneeze, have four children: Mrs. Eleanor Johnson, Lucius Jr., Etha Paulette and John Eugene. Address: 1235 Fifteenth St., Augusta, GA 30901

Player, Willa Beatrice, educator and government official, is director of College Support, a division of the U. S. Office of Higher Education in Washington, D. C. Born Aug. 9, 1909 in Jackson, Miss., she is a graduate of Ohio Wesleyan University (B.A.), Oberlin College (M.A.), Columbia University (Ed.D., 1964), the University of Grenoble in France (Certificat d'Études). She has honorary degrees from Lycoming College (LL.D.; 1962), Morehouse College (LL.D., 1963) and Albion College (LL.F., 1963). She is former president of Bennett College in Greensboro, N.C. In her present position, she serves as the chief administrator of grants for program support to colleges and universities. She has served as president of the National Association of Schools and Colleges of the Methodist Church, 1962; secretary, board of directors of Piedmont University Center; member board of trustees, Ohio Wesleyan University. She has received the Superior Service Award, Department of Health, Education and Welfare (1970) and the Distinguished Service Award from the same department in April 1972. She is single. Address: Office of Education, Department of Health, Education and Welfare, 7th & D Sts., SW, Washington, DC 20202

James O. Plinton Jr.

Alex C. Poinsett

Sidney Poitier

Plinton, James O. Jr., administrator, is vice president (special marketing affairs) of Eastern Airlines, Inc. in Miami, Fla. He accepted the position in 1971 after serving as an administrative and sales executive with Trans World Airlines (1951–71). Born July 22, 1914 in Westfield, N.J., he is a graduate of Lincoln University (B.S., 1935). He later completed aeronautics and pilot training programs at the University of Newark Division of Aeronautics to become a commercial pilot with a flight instructor's rating. He joined the famed all-black 99th Pursuit Squadron as a flight instructor. After World War II, he helped reorganize ANDESA, the national airline of Ecuador, then went to Haiti and established Quisqueya, Ltd., an inter-island air service, and operated Haiti's largest wholesale dry cleaning and laundry chain. He became the first black executive of a major U.S. airline when he joined TWA, and became the first black vice president of a major airline when he was elected at Eastern. He is a member of Negro Airmen International Association and is active in the YMCA, Boy Scouts of America and other professional and civic groups. He is a life member of the NAACP and Alpha Phi Alpha, and is secretary of the International Management Development Institute. He and his wife, Kathryn, have two children, Kathy Ann and James Jr. Address: Eastern Airlines, Miami International Airport, Miami, FL 33157

Poinsett, Alex C., journalist, is a senior staff editor of *Ebony* magazine, published by Johnson Publishing Co., Inc. in Chicago, Ill. Born Jan. 27, 1926 in Chicago, he is a graduate of the University of Illinois (B.S., journalism, 1952; M.A., philosophy, 1953). He completed all work except a thesis for a master's degree in library science at the University of Chicago. In his twenty years with Johnson Publishing Co., he has travelled more than one million miles, covering stories ranging from politics and education to housing and business in the black community. In 1965, he was invited to the Republic of Haiti and Kenya as a guest of the governments. He toured Moscow, Leningrad, Kiev and Sochi in the Soviet Union in 1969. He is the author of *Black Power: Gary Style*, a political biography of Gary's Mayor Richard Hatcher, and is the mayor's speechwriter. He is presently working on a book entitled *Black Politics in the Seventies*. He received the J. C. Penney–University of Missouri Journalism Award (1968) for his August, 1967 *Ebony* story, "Ghetto Schools: An Educational Wasteland." He is an associate of the Institute of the Black World. He and his wife, Norma, have two children, Pierette and Pierre. Address: 820 S. Michigan Ave., Chicago, IL 60605

Poitier, Sidney, actor, is the first black ever to win an Academy Award (for *Lilies of the Field*, 1964). Born Feb. 20, 1927 in Miami, Fla., he was educated by private tutors and in public high school in Nassau, New Providence, Bahamas. He had to leave school at 15 and seek work, first in Miami and then in New York City, where he was a drug store clerk, parking lot attendant, ditch digger, trucker and longshoreman. In World War II, he enlisted and served four years in the U.S. Army. After discharge, he became janitor at the American Negro Theater, slowly learned acting, worked on his diction and began to get small parts. Through a producer, James Light, he won a Broadway bit part. Roles in *Lysistrata*, *Freight*, and *Anna Lucasta* followed. His part of Miller in the film *The Blackboard Jungle* (1956) made him nationally known. Among his many films have been *Edge of the City* (1957), *Patch of Blue* (1966), *In the Heat of the Night* (1967), *Guess Who's Coming to Dinner* (1968) and *The Lost Man* (1969). Once able to choose his vehicles, he starred in *For the Love of Ivy* (1968) and *In a Warm December* (1973). With complete control of production now in his hands, he and Harry Belafonte produced and starred in *Buck and the Preacher*. He has helped establish First Artists Productions which includes Paul Newman, Barbra Streisand and Steve McQueen. Mr. Poitier was married April 29, 1950 to Juanita Hardy and has four children: Beverly, Pamela, Sherri and Messenger. Address: Columbia Pictures, 1438 Gower St., Los Angeles, CA 90004 **See article on Sidney Poitier in Volume II**

Pompey, Maurice, jurist, is a judge of the Circuit Court of Cook County (Ill.) Born May 14, 1923 in South Bend, Ind., he attended Howard University and Roosevelt College (now University) and is a graduate of DePaul University Law School in Chicago (J.D., 1951). During World War II, he commanded a B-25 bomber crew with the 477th Bombardment Group in the Pacific. He has been an assistant corporation counsel in Chicago, a trial judge in the city's municipal court and magistrate in the circuit court. He became a judge in 1972. He is a member of the Cook County, Illinois and American bar associations and the Original Forty Club. He and his wife, Josephine, have two children, Maurice Jr. and Tina Marie. Address: Cook County Circuit Court, Civic Center, Chicago, IL 60601

Porter, Albert S., jurist, is judge of the Cook County Circuit Court. His judicial duties include civil, housing and felony cases. Born Dec. 15, 1930 in Laurel, Miss., he is a graduate of the University of Illinois (B.S., chemistry, 1955) and John Marshall Law School (LL.B., J.D., 1962). He has also studied at Wilson Junior College, Roosevelt University, Illinois Institute of Technology, and has a criminal law certificate from Northwestern Law School. Before assuming his present position in 1970, he was deputy commissioner of the Chicago Department of Investigation (1966–70), trial attorney with the State Attorney's Office (1962–66), teacher (1957–62), service station proprietor (1958–59), chemist with Argonne National Laboratories (1955–57) and a U.S. Post Office clerk (1952–53). He is a member of the Chicago Bar Association, Illinois Bar Association, Cook County Bar Association and National Bar Association. He is a member of the National Honor Society and has received the American Legion Award for Scholarship. He and his wife, Mildred, have four children: Alvita, Darryl, Richard and Kimberly. Address: Chicago Civic Center, Chicago, IL 60602

Porter, Dorothy, library administrator, is librarian of the Moorland-Spingarn Collection of the Howard University Library in Washington, D.C. The collection, devoted to the history and culture of persons of African descent, contains more than 165,000 catalogued and indexed items—books, microforms and photographic materials. Born May 25, 1905 in Warrenton, Va., Mrs. Porter is a graduate of Howard University (A.B., (1928) and Columbia University (B.S., library science 1931; M.S., library science, 1932) and was awarded an honorary LL.D. degree from the University of Susquehanna (1971). She has a certificate in the Preservation and Administration of Archives from American University (1937), and has taken graduate courses at Howard University and American University. She has written numerous articles on black history for books and various publications. She is a member of Phi Beta Kappa and a number of professional and civic organizations. Among the awards and honors she has received was a Distinguished Service Award presented in 1971 by students of Howard's College of Liberal Arts. A widow, she has a daughter, Mrs. Constance Porter Uzelac. Address: P.O. Box 824, Howard University, Washington, DC 20001

Judge Maurice Pompey

Albert S. Porter

Dorothy Porter

E. Melvin Porter

Ersa H. Poston

Porter, E. Melvin, attorney and legislator, is a senator in the Oklahoma legislature in Oklahoma City, Okla. Born May 22, 1930 in Okmulgee, Okla., he has degrees from Tennessee State University (B.S., 1956), Vanderbilt University School of Law (LL.B., 1959), and an honorary degree (LL.D.) from Shorter College, Little Rock, Ark. Sen. Porter was elected to the Oklahoma State Senate as a Democrat in 1964 and became the first black to serve in the State Senate of Oklahoma. He is presently chairman of Social Welfare Committee, vice chairman of the Rules Committee and a member of the Judiciary Committee. He drafted the Anti-discrimination Act which is now law in Oklahoma, and a bill requiring a history of black Americans to be included in various textbooks throughout Oklahoma. He recently authored a bill requiring the state of Oklahoma to test for sickle cell anemia and the sickle cell trait, which carried with it an appropriation of more than $100,000. He is co-owner and publisher of *Black Voices* magazine, is a member of the Oklahoma County Bar Association, Oklahoma Bar Association, American Bar Association, American Judicature Society, life member of the NAACP (president of NAACP in Oklahoma City, 1961–64), 32° Mason and has received numerous civil rights awards and commendations. He and his wife, Leona, have six children: E. Melvin Jr., Damita, Soyna, Joel, Larry and Dion. Sen. Porter has two sons from a previous marriage. Address: 2116 N.E. 23rd St., Oklahoma, City, OK 73111

Poston, Ersa Hines, state official, is president of the New York State Civil Service Commission. She holds the highest appointive position ever given a black person in the state. She presides over a department of 900 people, with a $9.7 million annual budget. Born May 3, 1921 in Paducah, Ky., she is a graduate of Kentucky State College (B.A., 1942) and Atlanta University (M.S.W., 1946). She has an honorary LL.D. degree from Union College. Mrs. Poston was with the Hartford (Conn.) Tuberculosis and Health Association (1946–47). She was involved in YWCA and other community and city youth work in New York City until she became area director of the New York State Youth Commission (1957–62) and became its youth work program director (1962–64). She was confidential assistant to New York's Governor Nelson A. Rockefeller (1964–64) and was director of the New York State Office of Economic Opportunity (1965–67). She assumed her present position in 1967. She has received 33 awards and honors from organizations, colleges and universities. She declined a "high civil service post" offered by President-elect Richard M. Nixon in 1968 to continue her work for New York state. In 1957, she married Theodore "Ted" Poston, a well-known journalist with the *New York Post*. Address: Civil Service Building, State Campus, Albany, NY 12226 See article on Ersa H. Poston in Volume II.

Alvin Poussaint, M.D.

C. Clayton Powell

Carey M. Preston

Judith Price

Poussaint, Alvin, M.D., psychiatrist, is associate professor of psychiatry and associate dean of students at the Harvard University Medical School. Born May 15, 1934 in New York, N.Y., he is a graduate of Columbia University (B.A., 1956) Cornell University (M.D., 1960) and the University of California at Los Angeles (M.S., 1964). Before assuming his present position, he was an assistant professor of psychiatry at Tufts University Medical School (1966–69). He is author of the book *Why Blacks Kill Blacks* (1972) and has published numerous articles and was a founding fellow of The Black Academy of Arts and Letters. Address: Harvard Medical School, 25 Shattuck St., Boston, MA 02115

Powell, C. Clayton, optometrist, is founder and president of the National Optometric Association, an organization of black optometrists which has received a federal grant of $150,000 for recruitment of black college students for the optometric field. He also is in the private practice of optometry, is director of the Northwest Community Health Group and is director of optometry at the Southside Comprehensive Health Center—all in Atlanta, Ga. Born April 11, 1927 in Dothan, Ala., he is a graduate of Morehouse College (A.B.) and the Illinois College of Optometry (B.S. and O.D.). He has taken graduate courses at Atlanta University and through the Optometric Extension Foundation. He is founder and president of the Lincoln-Douglass Republican Club of Fulton County and the Lincoln-Douglass Republican Clubs of Georgia. He is an official of the State Republican Party of Georgia. He is a member of numerous professional civic and political groups. He and his wife, Romae, Georgia's first black woman judge (Fulton County Juvenile Court) have two children, C. Clayton Jr. and Rometta. Address: 565 Fair Street SW, Atlanta GA

Preston, Carey Maddox, administrator, is executive secretary of Alpha Kappa Alpha sorority, which has headquarters in Chicago, Ill. She heads a staff that provides liaison services between chapters of the international women's organization. She assumed her duties in 1949. Born April 28, 1915 in Columbia, Miss., she is a graduate of Tougaloo College (B.A., political science, 1937) and Atlanta University (M.S.W., 1939). She has been president of the Chicago Urban League since 1970 and vice president of the Chicago Board of Education since 1969. She is on the board of the Hyde Park Federal Savings & Loan Association in Chicago and the women's board of the University of Chicago. She is a widow. Address: 5211 S. Greenwood Ave., Chicago, IL 60615

Price, Judith, business executive, is a vice president and director of James B. Beam Import, Corp., a subsidiary of James B. Beam Distilling Co. in New York, N.Y. Born Feb. 10, 1937 in New York, N.Y., Mrs. Price attended City College of New York and the Bernard Baruch School of Business Administration. Before assuming her present position in 1972, she served the company as administrative director and assistant secretary. As an executive administrator, she has been employed within the alcoholic beverage industry for 15 years, starting as a secretary for a wine importer. She also spent many years in the field working with customs brokers and international shippers. She is a member of the Traffic Association of the Liquor Industry. She and her husband have two children, Toni and Marc. Address: 5800 Arlington Ave., Riverdale, NY 10471

Leontyne Price

Charley Pride

Thomas J. Pride

Rt. Rev. Q. E. Primo Jr.

Price, Leontyne, opera singer, is *prima donna assoluta* of the Metropolitan Opera Company in New York, N.Y. Born Feb. 10, 1927 in Laurel, Miss., she is a graduate of Central State College (B.A. 1949) and studied on a scholarship at the Juilliard School of Music in New York City (1949–52) and privately with Florence Page Kimball. She has honorary degrees from several schools, including Dartmouth College (L.H.D., 1962), Howard University (Mus.D., 1962) and Rust College (L.H.D., 1968). Cast as the heroine of George Gershwin's *Porgy and Bess* in 1952, she toured Europe with the company and was hailed in Vienna, Berlin, London and Paris. An eight-month Broadway run followed. After a concert tour in 1954, her *Tosca* performance with the NBC Opera Theater was a memorable television event. In 1957, she made her debut with the San Francisco Opera. In the first seven operas in which she was presented at the Metropolitan, critical response ranged from "Stradivarius of singers" to "pure velvet." She has been decorated with Italy's Order of Merit, has received 12 Grammy awards, and has been the recipient of numerous other honors. She married William Warfield in 1952 and was divorced in 1957. Address: 1133 Broadway, New York, NY 10010 **See article on Leontyne Price in Volume II**

Pride, Charley, entertainer, is the first black star of country music and was voted Entertainer of the Year in Country Music and Male Vocalist of the Year in 1971 by the once lily-white Country Music Association. Born March 18, 1939 in Sledge, Miss., he is a high school graduate. At first wanting to be a professional baseball player, he distinguished himself in the now-defunct Negro American Baseball League and made it to the major leagues with the Los Angeles Angels. Between seasons, he worked in Great Falls, Mont. as a copper smelter and as a nightclub singer in the evenings, singing the Grand Ole Opry songs he had always loved on radio. In 1963, the late Red Foley caught his act and said, "I don't care whether you're black, green or purple; you ought to go to Nashville." Rejected for the New York Mets by Casey, he stopped off in Nashville on his way home and charmed the country-western record producers. With his recording "Just Between You and Me," he launched into super-stardom. He has become the idol of country music concert fans. Mr. Pride's many hits includes such ballads as "Does My Ring Hurt Your Finger," "I Know One" and "Let Me Live." His country gospel hit, "Did You Think to Pray," won him the coveted Grammy award in 1971. He and his wife, Rozene, have three children: Kraig, Dion and Angela. Address: Jack D. Johnson Talent, Inc., Box 40484, Nashville, TN 37204 **See article on Charley Pride in Volume II.**

Pride, Thomas J., advertising executive, is the vice president of Ross Roy, Inc., an advertising agency which plans and implements marketing and advertising strategies for Chrysler corporate advertising in Detroit, Mich. He was born in Highland Park, Mich. on Jan. 18, 1940. Mr. Pride is associated with several professional and civic organizations including the National Association of Market Developers, Together Communications Bureau, Blacks Against Racism, the Adcraft Club of Detroit, and the Black Executive Exchange Program. He and his wife, Vernester, have three children: Leslie, Alesia and Tommy. Address: 2751 E. Jefferson, Detroit MI 48207

Primo, The Rt. Reverend Quintin E. Jr., clergyman, in 1971 became suffragan bishop of the Episcopal Diocese of Chicago. He was the fifth black ever elected as a bishop of the church. Born July 1, 1913 in Liberty County, Ga., he is a graduate of Lincoln University (B.A., sociology, 1934; S.T.B., 1937), Bishop Payne College (M.V.D., 1941) and Seabury-Western Seminary (M.V.D., 1972). He also has honorary degrees from General Theological Seminary of New York and Virginia Theological Seminary. Before assuming his present position, he was rector of St. Matthew's and St. Joseph's churches of Detroit, Mich., and was dean of the Woodward Convocation of the Michigan Episcopal Diocese. He has also served pastorates in Florida, North Carolina, New York and Delaware. He and his wife, Winifred, have three children: Cynthia, Quintin III and Susan. Address: Episcopal Diocese of Chicago, 65 E. Huron St., Chicago, IL 60611

Barbara G. Proctor

Rev. S. D. Proctor

Charles W. Pruitt

Proctor, Barbara Gardner, business executive, is president and creative director of Proctor and Gardner Advertising, Inc. in Chicago, III. Born Nov. 30, 1932 in Asheville, N.C., she is a graduate of Talladega College (B.A., English literature and secondary education, 1954; B.A., sociology and psychology, 1954). She is the founder and owner of her agency which has annual billings of $2 million. Previously, she was international director of VeeJay Records. She was an international jazz critic and served twelve years as feature writer, contributing editor, record reviewer and critic for *Downbeat* magazine. She is a member of the board of directors of the Better Business Bureau of Chicago, the Cosmopolitan Chamber of Commerce and the Chicago Economic Development Corp. She has received numerous awards, including the American TV Commercial Award (1968), the International Film Festival Award (1969) and the Cosmopolitan Chamber of Commerce Achievement Award (1972). Divorced, she has a son, Morgan. Address: 111 E. Wacker Dr., Chicago, IL 60611

Proctor, The Reverend Samuel DeWitt, clergyman and educator, is pastor of Abyssinian Baptist Church in New York, N.Y. and is Martin Luther King Distinguished Professor of Education at Rutgers University. With more than 12,000 members, Abyssinian is reportedly the world's largest Protestant congregation. Born July 13, 1921 in Norfolk, Va., Dr. Proctor is a graduate of Virginia Union University (B.A., 1942), Crozer Theological Seminary (B.D., 1945) and Boston University (Th.D., 1950). He has also done graduate study at the University of Pennsylvania (1944–45) and Yale University Divinity School (1945–46). He has honorary degrees from a number of colleges and universities. He was ordained as a Baptist clergyman in 1943, and was pastor of Pond Street Baptist Church in Providence, R. I. (1945–49). At Virginia Union University, he was professor or religion and ethics, and dean of the School of Religion (1949–50), vice president (1953–55) and president (1955–60). He was president of North Carolina A&T College (1960–64), associate director of the Peace Corps (1963–64), associate general secretary of the National Council of Churches (1964–65), director of the Northeast Region (later special assistant to the national director) of the Office of Economic Opportunity (1965–66), president of the Institute for Services to Education (1966–68) and dean of special projects at the University of Wisconsin (1968–69). He began teaching at Rutgers in 1969 and became pastor of Abyssinian Church (formerly pastored by the late U.S. Congressman Adam Clayton Powell Jr.) in 1971. He is a trustee of Meharry Medical College, the National Urban League, Ottawa University and St. Paul's College. He is a member of the National Education Association, Kappa Alpha Psi and numerous other professional and civic groups. He is author of *The Young Negro in America, 1960–80* (1966). He and his wife, Bessie, have four sons, Herbert, Timothy, Samuel and Steven. Address: 132 E. 138th St., New York, NY 10030

Pruitt, Charles W., legislator, is a senator in the Tennessee State House, representing the 58th District, and an employee of Western Electric Co. Born May 29, 1929 in Huntsville, Ala., he attended school in that city. He has introduced legislation aimed at improving the plight of the state's poor and working people, and is known particularly for his stands on welfare and credit reform. A mason, Mr. Pruitt has been active in the National Tenants Organization, the NAACP and the State Black Caucus. He and his wife, Mary, a school teacher, have two children: Renaldo and Marilyn. Address: G-19 War Memorial Bldg., Nashville, TN 37203

Roderick W. Pugh

Pugh, Roderick W., practicing psychologist, is professor of psychology at Loyola University in Chicago, Ill. Born June 1, 1919 in Richmond, Ky., and reared in Dayton, Ohio, he has degrees from Fisk University (B.A., 1940), Ohio State University (M.A., 1941) and the University of Chicago (Ph.D., 1949). Dr. Pugh teaches graduate courses in both individual and group psychotherapy at the Loyola University Guidance Center, has lectured extensively throughout the United States, and served as guest lecturer at Chung Chi College in Hong Kong, China. He is the author of numerous articles on psychological aspects of black adjustment and revolt and has published a book, *Psychology and the Black Experience.* He is a member of the American Psychological Association and the Association of Black Psychologists, and serves as secretary on the board of trustees at Fisk University. He is divorced. Address: 30 N. Michigan Ave., Suite 1515, Chicago. IL 60602

Royal W. Puryear

Puryear, Royal W., educator, is president of Florida Memorial College, Miami, Fla. When he took over leadership of the Baptist-related school in 1950, it was a two-year institution, Florida Normal and Industrial College, located in St. Augustine. He succeeded in building a four-year, Southern Association-accredited senior college, changing its name and moving it to Miami. A new campus was built from the ground up with completely new buildings, equipment and furnishings. The 300-mile move was made in 1968, and the college's enrollment was doubled. Born March 15, 1912 in Winston-Salem, N.C., Mr. Puryear has degrees from Howard University (A.B., 1933) and Indiana University (M.S., 1939). He also pursued studies in religion at Union Theological Seminary and Columbia University and studies in college administration at the University of Michigan. He has received five honorary degrees. He was a public school teacher in Winston-Salem for several years and has had 11 years' experience in YMCA work in many states. Just before heading Florida Memorial College, he was associate pastor of the St. John the Baptist Church in Dallas, Tex., and then president of Butler College in Tyler, Tex. An ordained Baptist minister, Mr. Puryear is active in community work and has been president of the Florida Institutions of Higher Learning. He and his wife, Pearl, live in Miami. Address: 15800 NW 42nd Ave., Miami, FL 33054

Benjamin A. Quarles

Quarles, Benjamin Arthur, educator, is professor of history at Morgan State College in Baltimore, Md. Born Jan. 23, 1904 in Boston, Mass., he is a graduate of Shaw University (B.A.) and the University of Wisconsin (M.A. and Ph.D.). A former Guggenheim Fellow, Dr. Quarles is perhaps the foremost authority today on the life of Frederick Douglass, the black nineteenth-century abolitionist leader. He has written and edited many books, articles and other pieces on black history. He currently is honorary consultant in American history of the Library of Congress. He is a member of the Committee on Civil Rights Documentation of the Ford Foundation, the editorial board of the *Journal of Negro History,* and is a founding member of the Black Academy of Arts and Letters. Address: Morgan State College, Baltimore, MD 21212

Leon D. Ralph

Ralph, Leon D., legislator, is a member of the California State Legislature. Representing the 55th District (Los Angeles), he was elected for the first time in 1966. Born Aug. 20, 1932 in Richmond, Va., he studied engineering at the University of Colorado, and is a graduate of Valley College in Los Angeles. He was administrative assistant (1964–66) to Jesse Unruh, former speaker of the California State Assembly. He is a member of the American Academy of Political Science and County Chairman of the Los Angeles Conference of Elected Black Officials. He and his wife, Pamela, live in Los Angeles. He has three children, from a previous marriage: Martha, Ruth and Leon. Address: State Capital, Sacramento, CA 90002

Dudley Randall

Randall, Dudley, librarian, poet and publisher, is a librarian at the University of Detroit (Mich.) His poems and short stories have appeared in *Midwest Journal*, *Milestone*, *Black World*, *Free Lance*, and *Negro History Bulletin*. He has edited several anthologies, including *Poems on the Life of Malcolm X*, and is currently working on a novel, "Paradise Valley." In 1965, he founded Broadside Press and published such noted poets as Gwendolyn Brooks, Don L. Lee and Sonia Sanchez. Mr. Randall attended public schools in Washington, D. C., East St. Louis, Ill., and Detroit. He was a librarian at Lincoln University (Missouri) from 1951-54, at Morgan State College from 1954-56 and at Wayne County Federated System from 1956-69. Since August 1969, he has been the resident librarian and poet-in-residence at the University of Detroit. Mr. Randall is a graduate of Wayne State University (B.A., English, 1949), the University of Michigan (M.A., library science, 1951), and has done post-graduate work in humanities at Wayne State University. Address: 12652 Livernois, Detroit, MI 48238

A. Philip Randolph

Randolph, Asa Philip, retired labor leader, organized the Brotherhood of Sleeping Car Porters in 1925 in New York, N.Y. and was president until his retirement in 1968. He became a vice president of the AFL-CIO in 1957 and now serves on its executive council. Born April 15, 1889 in Crescent City, Fla., he attended City College in New York City. Howard University awarded him an honorary LL.D. degree in 1941. Active in labor and civil rights since the 1920s, he was organizer and director of the first March On Washington (1941) which led President Franklin D. Roosevelt to start the Committee on Fair Employment Practice. He was also a leader (with Dr. Martin Luther King Jr.) of the 1963 March on Washington. For decades, he fought for racial integration of labor unions and advocated—in White House talks with presidents, in public meetings, etc.—the cause of equal opportunity. He was organizer of numerous movements, conferences and programs on behalf of black people, including the League for Non-Violent Civil Disobedience Against Military Segregation (which led to desegregation of the armed services), the National Negro Congress and the Non-Partisan League of the CIO. He is a member of the Masons, Elks and other fraternal and civic organizations, and has received numerous awards for his work. A widower, he lives in New York City. Address: The A. Philip Randolph Institute, 260 Park Avenue South, New York, NY 10010

Lloyal Randolph

Randolph, Lloyal, legislator, is a member of the Maryland House of Delegates, elected in 1968 from the 4th Dist. (Baltimore). He is a member of the House Judiciary Committee and is vice chairman of the Committee on Human Rights. Born April 6, 1904 in Keyser, W. Va., he has been in business (he is owner of York Lounge and Bar), civic affairs and politics in Baltimore for more than 30 years. He was the first black named as chief clerk of Baltimore's Board of Supervisors of Elections. He served five terms as Exalted Ruler of Monumental Elks Lodge No. 3 and Grand Trustee of Improved Benevolent and Protective Order of Elks of the World. He is chairman of the Business Committee of Upton Planning Commission, an urban redevelopment group. He and his wife, Cornelia, have two daughters, Bonnie and Lisa. Address: 1502-04 Pennsylvania Ave., Baltimore, MD 21217

M. Athalie Range   Rep. Charles B. Rangel   E. E. Rankin

Range, M. Athalie, former state official, resigned in 1973 as secretary of the Florida Department of Community Affairs. Her work involved the administration of the divisions of economic opportunity, technical assistance, migrant labor, emergency government, veterans affairs and the division of training and professional development. Born Nov. 7, 1918 in Key West, Fla., she is a licensed embalmer and funeral director. Mrs. Range was elected to the Miami City Commission in 1966, and served for a year as vice mayor of the commission. She is president of the Martin Luther King Boulevard Corporation, formed to rebuild (with a model cities grant) the site of the 1968 racial riot in Miami. Mrs. Range is a member of Dade County's Model Cities Governing Board, the Democratic Women's Club, Links of America, Inc. and of numerous other civic and professional organizations. Among her many awards are the Catholic Diocese of Miami Award for Meritorious Service, the Sojourner Truth Award of the Business and Professional Negro Women's Club and the National Association of Christians and Jews Award. A widow, she is the mother of Mrs. John L. Lee, Patrick, Oscar and Gary. Address: Howard Bldg., 2571 Executive Center Circle, East Tallahassee, FL 32301

Rangel, Charles B., congressman, is a U. S. representative from New York City. Born June 11, 1930 in New York City, he is a graduate of New York University School of Commerce (B.S., 1957) and St. John's University School of Law (1960). In 1961, he was appointed assistant U. S. attorney for the Southern District of New York, and served as associate counsel to the speaker of the New York State Assembly as well as being the general counsel to the National Advisory Commission on Selective Service. In 1966–70, he served two terms in the New York State Assembly, the 72nd Assembly District (Central Harlem), and in 1969 he was a candidate for president of the New York City Council in the Democratic primaries. Rep. Rangel is married to the former Alma Carter and they have two children, Steven and Alicia. Address: U. S. House of Representatives, Washington, DC 20515

Rankin, Edgar Everett, educator, is president of Mississippi Industrial College in Holly Springs, Miss., a liberal arts school supported by the Christian Methodist Episcopal Church. It is the only senior college in the state of Mississippi owned and operated by black people and serving underprivileged youths. Born April 25, 1914 in Holly Springs, he attended Mississippi Industrial College (B.S., chemistry, 1936; honorary L.H.D., 1960) and Springfield (Mass.) College (M.S., health and education, 1953). He was an instructor at Newton Vocational High School (1936-41) and was a science teacher and coach at Mississippi Industrial College (1941-57) before becoming president in 1957. He is a member of Omega Psi Phi, Phi Delta Kappa, the American Association of Independent College and University Presidents, and the American Association of Higher Education. He is a master Mason. He and his wife, Robbie Evelyn, have three children: Dr. Edward A. Rankin, Atty. Michael Rankin and Janet Evelyn. Address: Mississippi Industrial College, Holly Springs, MS 38635

Raspberry, William J., journalist, is urban affairs columnist for the *Washington Post* and a nationally syndicated political affairs writer. Born Oct. 12, 1935 in Okolona, Miss., he is a graduate of Indiana Central College (A.B., history, 1958). Prior to assuming his present position, he was a reporter and later editor for the *Indianapolis Recorder*. He joined the *Washington Post* in 1962 as a library assistant, later working as a teletype operator, a general assignment reporter, a copy editor and assistant city editor. He became urban affairs columnist in 1965. Mr. Raspberry's coverage of the 1965 Los Angeles riot earned him the Journalist of the Year award from the Capital Press Club. He also has been awarded a Citation of Merit in Journalism by Lincoln University in Jefferson City, Mo., and a Front Page Award by the Washington-Baltimore Newspaper Guild. He and his wife, Sondra, have two children, Patricia and Angela. Address: *The Washington Post*, 1150 15th St., Washington, DC 20016

Ray, The Reverend Sandy Frederick, clergyman, is vice president of the National Baptist Convention, USA, president of the Empire Missionary Baptist Convention in New York State and pastor of the 3500-member Cornerstone Baptist Church in Brooklyn, N.Y. Born Feb. 3, 1898 in Marlin, Tex., he earned degrees from Arkansas Baptist College (D.D., 1936) and Morehouse College (D.D., 1958) and holds an honorary LL.D. from Bishop College. Dr. Ray was appointed in 1967 by New York's governor to the New York State Council on Youth and in 1972 to the Governor's Task Force on Deserting Fathers. He is also a member of the State Commission Against Discrimination. Dr. Ray is chairman of the Brooklyn Advisory Council of the New York State Commission for Human Rights and a member of the boards of the Southern Christian Leadership Conference, the Martin Luther King Memorial Center for Social Change, Morehouse College, Andover-Newton Theological Seminary and the Carver Federal Savings and Loan Association in New York. He and his wife, Cynthia, live in New York, N.Y. He has a son, Sandy Jr., and a daughter, Dorothy. Address: 562–74 Madison St., New York, NY 11213

Reddick, Lawrence Dunbar, educator, is a professor of history at Temple University in Philadelphia, Pa. Born March 3, 1910 in Jacksonville, Fla., he is a graduate of Fisk University (B.A., 1932; M.A., 1933) and the University of Chicago (Ph.D., 1939). He has taught history at Kentucky State College, Dillard University, Atlanta University, Alabama State College and Coppin State College. Dr. Reddick served for nine years as curator of the Schomburg Collection of the New York Public Library and seven years as chief librarian at Atlanta University. He is the author of *Crusader Without Violence, A Biography of Martin Luther King, Jr., Our Colleges and the Industrialization of the South* and other works. He has also served as the editor of several scholarly journals. He and his wife, Marjorie, have two children, Brian and Frances. Address: Temple University, Department of History, Room B-33, Philadelphia, PA 19122

William J. Raspberry

Rev. Sandy F. Ray

Lawrence D. Reddick

259

Saunders Redding

Thomas J. Reed

Garth C. Reeves Sr.

Redding, Saunders, a well-known figure in American letters, is an Ernest I. White professor of American Studies and Humane Letters at Cornell University in Ithaca, N.Y. Mr. Redding is author of several books, including *To Make a Poet Black, No Day of Triumph* and *Cavalcade*, an anthology he co-edited with Arthur P. Davis in 1971. He has been a visiting professor at Brown University, Rosenfeld lecturer at Grinnell College, and AMSAC lecturer in Africa. He has twice been awarded the Guggenheim Fellowship. Mr. Redding was born in Wilmington, Del. and attended Brown University in Providence, R.I., where he received both undergraduate and graduate degrees (Ph.B, 1928; M.A., 1932, D.Litt., 1963). He and his wife, Esther, have two children, Conway and Lewis. Address: 239 Goldwin Smith, Cornell University, Ithaca, NY 14850

Reed, Thomas J., legislator, is a member of the Alabama Legislature. Elected in 1970, he was the first black to serve as a representative in the Alabama legislature since Reconstruction. Born Sept. 17, 1927 in Brookhaven, Miss., he attended Tuskegee Institute (B.S.; M.S.) where he majored in economics. Bills introduced in the legislature by Mr. Reed include one which created sixty scholarships for needy black students at Tuskegee Institute's School of Nursing and one preventing law enforcement officers from jailing youths under the age of eighteen. He also was instrumental in getting the legislature to hire the first black page. He has presided over public hearings on the maltreatment of Alabama prison inmates, and has pressured the state's Department of Public Safety to hire 350 blacks in various positions, including that of state trooper. He also filed charges against 17 federal agencies in the state, demanding that blacks be given 25 percent of all federal jobs in Alabama. He is chairman of the Black Elected and Appointed Officials of Alabama, and state president of the NAACP. He and his wife, Sereeta, have three children: Thomas Jr., Ava and Evelyn. Address: Drawer EE, Tuskegee Institute, AL 36088

Reeves, Garth C. Sr., publisher and banking executive, is editor and publisher of *The Miami Times*, a weekly newspaper founded in Miami, Fla. in 1923. He is also chairman of the board of the National Industrial Bank in Miami, and president of the National Newspaper Publishers Association. Born Feb. 12, 1919 in Nassau, Bahamas, he is a graduate of Florida A&M University (B.S., 1940) and Mergenthaler Institute in Brooklyn, N.Y. (1947). He has been a reporter, columnist and managing editor on *The Miami Times* since 1940 and helped organize the first integrated national bank in the South in 1964. He and his wife, Beatrice, have two children, Rachel and Garth Jr. Address: 6503 NW 15th Ave., Miami, FL 33126

Maude K. Reid

Charles M. Reynolds Jr.

Judge Hobson R. Reynolds

Reid, Maude K., administrator, is supervisor of Adult Home Education for the Dade County Public School system in Miami, Fla. She is responsible for planning and developing the adult home economics program. Born in Georgetown, S.C., she is a graduate of Florida A & M University (B.S., 1936) and Columbia University (M.A.). She has also studied at the University of Miami. Before assuming her present position in 1965, she was a teacher of home economics education, home demonstration agent, teacher trainer in home economics for the Florida State Department of Education, social columnist for the *Pittsburgh Courier*, summer workshop consultant at Bethune-Cookman College and Florida A & M College, and the first field secretary of Negro Programs of the Florida Tuberculosis and Health Education agency. She is a member of the American Vocational Association, National Education Association, American Home Economics Association, Florida Education Association, American Association of University Women and the League of Women Voters. She is president of the Council of United Fund Women, and past president of several other organizations, including the Greater Miami Urban League Board, National Council of Urban League Guilds, Links, Inc. and Greater Miami Urban League Guild. She is a member of the boards of directors of the YWCA, Senior Centers, and League of Women Voters. She is a member of the executive committee of the National Council of Jewish Women. She has received several awards, including the Links, Inc. ''Woman of the Year'' award and the Meritorious Achievement Alumnae award of Florida A & M University. Divorced, she has a son, Kennedy. Address: Dade County Public Schools, Office of Adult Vocational Education, 1450 N.E. 2nd Ave., Miami, FL 33132

Reynolds, Charles McKinley Jr., administrator, is president and chief executive officer of Citizens Trust Bank in Atlanta, Ga. He is responsible for the total operation of the firm, including supervision of a $10 million investment bond account and a $16 million loan portfolio. Born Jan. 11, 1937 in Albany, Ga., he is a graduate of Morehouse College (B.A., economics, 1961), and attended Wayne State University (mortuary science certificate, 1962) and Albany State College (middle grades certificate, 1964). He has done additional study in business administration at Wayne State and at Atlanta University. Before assuming his present position in 1971, he was a social studies teacher (1962–65), an assistant national bank examiner (1965–69) and a national bank examiner (1969–71). He was executive vice president and acting president of Citizens Trust Bank (1971). He is a member of Alpha Phi Alpha. Mr. Reynolds and his wife, Estella, have two children, Eric and Gregory. Address: 175 Houston St., NW, Atlanta, GA 30311

Reynolds, Hobson R., organization head, is Grand Exalted Ruler of the Improved Benevolent Protective Order of Elks of the World with headquarters in Philadelphia, Pa. Born Sept. 13, 1898 in Winston, N.C., he graduated from Waters-Normal Institute and Echols Business College in Philadelphia, Pa. Mr. Reynolds has honorary degrees from Bethune-Cookman College (LL.D.) and Allen University (LL.D.). He is chairman of the trustee board of Cheyney State College and a trustee of Bethune-Cookman College. He was elected in 1960 to head the organization's 500,000 members from 1,500 local units. Before his election, he served as Grand Adjunct General (1935–38) and Grand Director of Civil Liberties (1938–60) with the Elks. Additionally, Mr. Reynolds is a Prince Hall F. & A. Mason and has achieved the 33rd Degree, the highest in masonry. Mr. Reynolds, a funeral home director, was elected to the Pennsylvania General Assembly in 1934 and 1938. Appointed by President Dwight Eisenhower as assistant to the Commissioner of Federal Housing, Mr. Reynolds was selected by the *Afro-American* newspaper and placed on its honor roll for distinguished and outstanding service. He is listed in *Who's Who in American Politics* and was selected by *Ebony* magazine as one of the most influential black men in the country. He says that his most significant achievement was the passage of the Reynolds Equal Rights Bill in Pennsylvania during his first term as a legislator. He and his wife, Evelyn, live in Philadelphia. Address: 2044 Ridge Ave., Philadelphia, PA 19104

June A. Rhinehart

Vernon M. Rhinehart

Joseph Rhodes Jr.

Rhinehart, June Acie, publishing executive, is a vice president of Johnson Publishing Co., Inc. in Chicago, Ill., and is assistant to the publisher of *Ebony*, *Jet*, *Black Stars*, *Black World* and *Ebony Jr!* magazines. Her work involves administration of all departments—editorial, advertising, personnel, financial, etc.—of the largest black-owned publishing company in the world. She was promoted to her position in 1971 after 17 years as secretary and administrative assistant to the company's president and editor, John H. Johnson. Mrs. Rhinehart was born July 1, 1934 in McKeesport, Pa. She studied business law and political science at Wilson Jr. College in Chicago (A.B., 1962) and is a graduate of Roosevelt University in Chicago (B.A., 1968). She has also studied at Northwestern University. She is a member of Cook County Bar Auxiliary and Chicago Focus, and serves on the boards of directors of Planned Parenthood of Chicago, Leadership Resources Program, Lawrence Hall/Randall House and Women's Division of Chicago Economic Development Corp. Address: 820 S. Michigan Ave., Chicago, IL 60605

Rhinehart, Vernon Morel, attorney, is engaged in the practice of civil law in Chicago, Ill. Born Sept. 27, 1935 in Kansas City, Kan., he is a graduate of Boston University (B.A., history, 1958) and Howard University Law School (J.D., 1966). He employs his corporate experience with International Harvester Corporation (industrial relations) and the First National Bank of Chicago (corporate loan officer training) in his practice, which includes corporate law, business transactions, drafting and negotiations and real estate development, sales and purchase. He is a recipient of the American Jurisprudence Prize for Excellence in Federal Jurisdiction, and is a member of the American, Chicago, Illinois State, National and Cook County bar associations. He is also a member of the Judicature Society, Alpha Phi Alpha and Sigma Delta Tau legal fraternities, and the board of governors of the City Club of Chicago. His wife, the former June Acie, is an executive at Johnson Publishing Co. Address: 29 S. LaSalle St., Suite 429, Chicago, IL 60603

Rhodes, Joseph Jr., legislator, is a member of the Pennsylvania House of Representatives from the 24th District (Pittsburgh). He was elected to the office in November, 1972. Born Aug. 14, 1947 in Pittsburgh, Pa., he is a graduate of the California Institute of Technology (B.S., history, 1969) and was a junior fellow in intellectual history at Harvard University in 1970. At Caltech, he was president of the student body, a board director of the school's YMCA and earned the Extraordinary Service Award and the Heinrich Memorial Award. He also directed a tutoring program at the school. He was an instructor at the Massachusetts School of Education and California State College and has taught history at the University of Pittsburgh. He was a consultant to the secretary of the U.S. Department of Health, Education and Welfare (1968–71), the President's Commission on Volunteer Service (ACTION, 1969), the President's Commission on Campus Unrest (1970) and to four cabinet officers in two federal administrations. He has done staff research for the Ford Foundation and has attended NATO conferences in Europe and defense conferences at the Naval War College. He has visited South Africa under Ford Foundation auspices. He is single. Address: Pennsylvania House of Representatives, Harrisburg, PA 17120

Stanley C. Rich

George C. Richardson

Judge Scovel Richardson

Rich, Stanley C., police official, is second deputy commissioner of the Detroit, Mich. Police Department. He is chairman of the police trial board, equal employment officer, and small and minority business enterprises officer for the department. Born Feb. 25, 1920, Mr. Rich graduated from Morris Brown College (A.B.) and Wayne State University (M.A.). He has been a private accountant, a junior accountant for the Detroit Health Department (1947–50), senior accountant for the Mayor's Committee for Human Resources Development (1964–65), administrator for the Small Business Development Center (1965–67) and assistant director of program planning, research and evaluation for the Mayor's Committee for Human Resources Development (1967). He is a member of Kappa Alpha Psi fraternity, the United Community Services of Metropolitan Detroit, and the board of directors of St. Peter Claver Community Center. He and his wife, Coralie, have a son, Stanley Jr. Address: 1300 Beaubien, Detroit, MI 48226

Richardson, George C., legislator, is assistant minority leader of the New Jersey State Assembly. He was first elected in 1961. In 1971, he became chairman of the New Jersey Black Legislative Caucus. As a member of the assembly, he served on the New Jersey State Narcotics Division, the Committee on Institutions and Agencies, the Committee on Transportation and Public Utilities, the Sub-committee on Highways and the Committee on Taxation. Born Feb. 19, 1929 in Newark, N.J., he is a graduate of the United States Air Force Administrative School and has attended the Jersey City Technical Institute. He served in the Air Force during the Korean War. He is president of Periscope Associates, a Newark-based public relations agency. Divorced, he has a son, George Jr. Address: 455 Elizabeth Ave., Newark, NJ 07112

Richardson, Scovel, jurist, is a judge of the United States Customs Court in New York, N.Y. He presides over cases involving disputes between the federal government and importers over the classification and valuation of imported merchandise. Born Feb. 4, 1912 in Nashville, Tenn., he has degrees from the University of Illinois (A.B., 1930; M.A., 1934), and Howard University (LL.B., 1937). In 1938, he was admitted to the Illinois Bar and practiced law in Chicago. In 1939, he became a professor of law at Lincoln University in Missouri. He was named dean of the school of law in 1944 and was admitted to the Missouri bar the next year. In 1953, he was appointed to the U.S. Board of Parole in the Department of Justice by President Dwight D. Eisenhower. He was named chairman of that board in 1954. Judge Richardson became the first Howard University law graduate to be appointed a federal judge when he was named to the U.S. Customs Court in New York in 1957. He is the recipient of numerous awards, including the C. Francis Stradford Award from the National Bar Association (1967). He and his wife, Inez, have four daughters: Elaine (Mrs. Lawrence B. Harrisingh, Alice Inez, Mary (Mrs. Derek C. Brown) and Marjorie (Mrs. Michael A. Bogen). Address: U.S. Customs Court, Federal Plaza, New York, NY 10007

Wilson C. Riles

Clayton Riley

Edward E. Riley Jr.

Riles, Wilson C., state official, is superintendent of public instruction of the state of California. Born June 27, 1917 in Alexandria, La., he is a graduate of Arizona State College (B.A., 1940; M.A., 1947). He was elected to his position in 1970 with 3.25 million votes, the largest number ever cast for a black man in any single election in U.S. history. After three years in the Army Air Corps in World·War II, and after earning his master's degree in school administration at Arizona State, he entered the California school system as a teacher and compiled a distinguished record. In 1965, he was named associate superintendent of the California State Department of Education to head a $100 million-a-year Federal Compensatory Education Program for children of low-income families. He was second in command to state superintendent Max Rafferty. Highly critical of Mr. Rafferty's outlook and methods, Mr. Riles quietly talked up the idea of someone running against the incumbent. When no one qualified came forth, he took a leave of absence, telling Mr. Rafferty that he was going to seek his job in 1970. In a run-off, he swept into office with a 500,000 majority out of nearly six million votes cast. He launched a six-point plan for easing California's crucial education problems and has caused the hiring of numerous black personnel. He and his wife, Mary Louise, have four children: Michael, Narvia, Wilson Jr. and Phillip. Address: 721 Capitol Mall, Sacramento, CA 95814 **See article on Wilson Riles in Volume II.**

Riley, Clayton, writer and educator, is a free-lance journalist—mainly in the areas of television, radio and theater—whose articles have appeared in *Ebony,* the *New York Times, The Liberator,* the *Chicago Sun-Times* and other publications. He also teaches a course, "Arts and Humanities in the Urban Setting," at Fordham University Graduate School of Education, and a course, "Theater and Critical Writing," at Sarah Lawrence College. Mr. Riley was born May 23, 1935 in Brooklyn N.Y. Until 1965, he was involved with theater and film as a performer and technician. He was production assistant on the film, *Nothing But A Man.* He is a member of Drama Desk and the Harlem Writers Guild. He and his wife, Nancy, have two children, Hagar Lowine and Grayson. Address: 523 W. 112th St., New York, NY 10025

Riley, Edward E. Jr., educator and administrator, is academic dean at Dillard University in New Orleans. Born Aug. 27, 1926, in Greenville, S.C., he is a graduate of Syracuse University (B.A., zoology), Oberlin College (M.A., zoology) and Brown University (Ph.D., biology, 1955). Since 1958, he has been an advisory panelist and consultant to the National Science Foundation, and since 1968 he has been a consultant to the U.S. Office of Education (Title III and Title VI) on the Higher Education Act of 1965. He has been an advisor and/or consultant on numerous other education and scientific programs. From 1958 to 1961, he received more than $40,000 from the National Cancer Institute, U.S. Public Health Service and the Greater New Orleans Cancer Association for scientific investigations. He is a member of the American Association of Higher Education, the American Society of Zoologists, the American Institute of Biological Sciences, and several other professional organizations. His fraternities are Sigma Pi Phi and Omega Psi Phi. He has published scientific papers in national and international journals. He and his wife, Phyllis, have three children: Carole, Marcie and Edward III. Address: Dillard University, New Orleans, LA 70122

Millard D. Robbins Jr.   Elliott C. Roberts   William B. Robertson

Robbins, Millard D., Jr. mortgage banker, is president of Robbins Mortgage Company and Robbins Insurance Agency, Inc. in Chicago, Ill. Born Oct. 17, 1919 in Columbus, Ohio, he studied economics at Roosevelt University (B.A.). Prior to going into business for himself, he worked for the U. S. Treasury Department and Veterans' Administration. He is vice chairman of the Independence Bank of Chicago; a director of Peoples Gas Company; Home Investment Fund; Chicago Mortgage Bankers Association; a Chicago Board of Underwriters; Dearborn Real Estate Board, Inc., and of the Insurance School of Chicago. His wife, Alma, is vice president of the mortgage company and secretary of the insurance company. They have four children: Elizabeth Ann, Jean Marie, Millard Mark and John Hugo. Address: 8224 S. King Dr., Chicago, IL 60619

Roberts, Elliott C., administrator, is Commissioner of Hospitals for the City of Detroit, Mich. He is responsible for over-all decision-making regarding hospital operations and budgetary and personnel practices. Born Jan. 20, 1927, in Baltimore, Md., he is a graduate of Morgan State College (B.S., business administration, 1951) and George Washington University (master's degree in hospital administration, 1963). Before assuming his present position in July 1972, he was executive director of Harlem Hospital in New York, N.Y. He has been in the field of hospital administration since 1953. He is a member of the American College of Hospital Administrators, a member of the board of trustees of the American Hospital Association and a member of the National Association of Health Services, an organization of black hospital administrators. He and his wife, Shirley, have five children: Elliott Jr., Jay Timothy, Charles, Sondra and Erroll. Address: 326 St. Antoine, Detroit, MI 48226

Robertson, William Bernard, governmental aide, is special assistant to the governor of Virginia in the areas of consumer protection and minority economic development in Richmond, Va. His duties involve the upgrading and expanding of employment opportunities for blacks in state government and in private enterprises. He is also in charge of establishing camps for retarded children. Born Jan. 31, 1933 in Roanoke, Va., he is a graduate of Bluefield State College (B.S., elementary education, 1954; B.S., secondary education, 1956); Radford College (M.S., administration and supervision, 1965). He has an honorary doctor of arts degree from Virginia College (1972). Mr. Robertson taught school in Roanoke for 10 years and was an elementary supervisor for two and a half years. He has won many honors and awards, among them Outstanding Young Educator in Roanoke, 1965; Distinguished Service Award, Roanoke Area, Association for Retarded Children, 1970; Citizen of the Year, Omega Psi Phi fraternity, 1969; Man of the Year Award, 1972; Outstanding and Distinguished Service Award, Cardoza Jaycees, Washington, D.C., 1972 and National Conference of Christians and Jews, 1972. He is a member of the National Advisory Highway Safety Committee; and a member of the National Education Association; a member of the board of directors, State Mental Health and a member of the Virginia State Chamber of Commerce. Mr. Robertson and his wife, Johnnie Lucille, have two children, Bernice Victoria and William Allen. Address: State Capitol, Richmond, VA 23219

265

Prezell R. Robinson

S. Benton Robinson

Spottswood W. Robinson III

Robinson, Prezell R., educator, is president of Saint Augustine's College in Raleigh, N.C. Born Aug. 25, 1925 in Batesburg, S.C., he is a graduate of Saint Augustine's College (A.B., 1946), and Cornell University (M.A., educational psychology and sociology, 1956; Ed.D., sociology and administration, 1966). He was an instructor and administrator at Bettis Junior College and was registrar, teacher, dean and social science instructor at Voorhees Junior College from 1946 to 1956. He returned to Saint Augustine's in 1956 as dean of instruction and professor of sociology. In 1965, Dr. Robinson studied in India on a Fulbright Fellowship. In 1966, he was appointed to his present position. He is a member of the American Council on Education, a member of the National Association for Equal Opportunity in Education; a member of the North Carolina Association of Independent Colleges and Universities. He was named Tarheel of the Week in 1971 and was the first black member of the board of directors of Wachovia Bank and Trust Company. He and his wife, Lula, have a daughter, JesSanne. Address: Saint Augustine's College, Raleigh, NC 27611

Robinson, S. Benton, insurance executive, is senior vice president of Supreme Life Insurance Co. of America, headquartered in Chicago, Ill. Born June 5, 1928 in Parsons, Kan., he is a graduate of West Virginia State College (B.S., business administration, 1950) and the University of Chicago (M.B.A., 1970). He began his career at Supreme Life in 1950 as a management trainee. Within three months he was a district manager. Mr. Robinson was field auditor (1954–55), internal auditor (1955–62), controller (1962–69) and vice president (1963–68). He was appointed first vice president in 1968, and was elected to the board of directors in 1971, and was appointed to his present position in January, 1973. He is vice president of the board of directors of United Charities of Chicago and is a member of the board of directors of the Cosmopolitan Chamber of Commerce (Chicago). He is a member of Alpha Phi Alpha. Mr. Robinson and his wife, Dymple, have three children: Benton, Karen and Arthur. Address: Supreme Life Insurance Company of America, 3501 King Dr., Chicago, IL 60653

Robinson, Spottswood William III, jurist, has been a judge of the U.S. Court of Appeals in Washington, D.C. since 1966. Previously, he was a judge of the U.S. District Court in Washington, D.C. (1964–66); NAACP southeast regional counsel (1951–60) and Virginia legal representative for the NAACP Legal Defense and Educational Fund (1948–50); an attorney in Richmond, Va. (1943–60); dean of the Howard University Law School (1960–64) and a professor of law at Howard (1945–64), and a member of the Howard faculty (1939–49). Born July 26, 1916 in Richmond, he studied at Virginia Union University (1932–34 and 1935–36; hon. LL.D., 1955) and is a graduate of Howard University (LL.B., magna cum laude, 1939). He was vice president and general counsel of the Consolidated Bank & Trust Co. of Richmond (1963–64), and a member of the U.S. Civil Rights Commission on Civil Rights (1961–63). He has received numerous achievement awards and citations for civil rights work and civic activities. He is a member of various bar associations and is a vestryman of the Episcopal Church. He and his wife, Marian, have two children, Spottswood IV and Nina (Mrs. Oswald G. Govan). Address: U.S. Court House, Washington, DC 20001

William P. Robinson Sr.

Robinson, William P. Sr., legislator and educator, is a member of the General Assembly of Virginia and chairman of the department of political science at Norfolk State College in Norfolk, Va. Born March 15, 1911 in Norfolk, Va., Mr. Robinson studied political science at Howard University (B.A., 1932; M.A., 1935) and New York University (Ph.D., 1950). Elected on Nov. 4, 1969, Mr. Robinson was the first black to represent Norfolk in the general assembly since Reconstruction. He introduced into the legislature of Virginia the first open housing bill which was passed in 1972, making Virginia the first state in the South to adopt an open housing law. He is a member of the American Political Science Association, the Association for the Study of Afro-American Life and History and a member of the American Association of University Professors. His son, William P. Robinson Jr., is an attorney. Address: 2401 Corprew Ave., Norfolk, VA 23504

W. "Smokey" Robinson Jr.

Robinson, William Jr. ("Smokey"), record executive and songwriter, is vice president of the Motown Record Corp. in Los Angeles, Calif. Born Feb. 19, 1940 in Detroit, Mich., he has an honorary doctorate from Shaw College. At 13, he began singing with four classmates, all from the Detroit ghetto. They dubbed themselves Smokey Robinson and the Miracles. During a talent audition, they impressed the president of Motown, Berry Gordy Jr., who later signed them to a contract. In 1968, their first record and subsequent "Got A Job" marked a sharp upshoot for Mr. Robinson, the group and the Motown record empire. To date, Mr. Robinson has composed at least 250 songs. During his 15 years with the group, he recorded such hits as "Ooo Wee Baby," "Going to A Go-Go," "You've Really Got a Hold On Me," "The Tracks of My Tears" and "I'll Try Something New." He is the recipient of a BMI award and numerous gold records. He and his wife, Claudette have two children, Berry and Tamla. Address: Motown Record Corporation, 6464 Sunset Blvd., Hollywood, CA 90028

Calvin B. Rock

Rock, Calvin Bovell, clergyman, educator and administrator, is president of Oakwood College in Huntsvillle, Ala. The college is a Seventh Day Adventist institution with about 850 students (its enrollment increased by 54 per cent—from 551 to 854—during 1970-72). Born July 4, 1930 in New York, N.Y., Elder Rock (he is a Seventh Day Adventist clergyman) is a graduate of Oakwood College (B.A., religion, 1954) and the University of Detroit (M.A., sociology, 1966) and has studied for a doctorate at Michigan State University and St. John's University. He has an honorary LL.D. degree (1970) from Union Baptist Seminary in Birmingham, Ala. Prior to assuming his present position in 1971, he was pastor of the largest (2,4000 members) Seventh Day Adventist Church in the U.S., the Ephesus Church in New York City. He is author of the book *Our God Is Able*. He and his wife, Clara, have three daughters: Cheryl, Celia and Connie. Address: Oakwood College, Huntsville, AL 35806

John W. Rogers

Rogers, John W., city official, is a member of the board of trustees of the Metropolitan Sanitary District of Greater Chicago. He is also treasurer and general counsel of Sivart Mortgage Co. in Chicago. Born Sept. 3, 1918 in Knoxville, Tenn., he is a graduate of Chicago Teachers College (B.A., 1941) and the University of Chicago (J.D., 1948). He was admitted to the Illinois Bar in 1948 and has been admitted to practice before the United States Supreme Court. He was a pilot (second lieutenant) with the 99th Pursuit Squadron during World War II. He is a member of the boards of directors of the Chicago Council on Human Relations and the Ada S. McKinley Community Services. Divorced, he has a son, John Jr. Address: Sanitary District, City of Chicago, 100 E. Erie St., Chicago IL 60611

Timmie Rogers

Joseph W. Rollins Jr.

David P. Ross

Rogers, Timmie, entertainer, is a comedian, dancer, singer, composer and musician. Born in Detroit, Mich., he began his career as an entertainer more than 30 years ago on the streets of that city where he tap-danced for pennies. In 1948, he launched the first all-black show, "Sugar Hill Times," on the CBS television network. Mr. Rogers, who gained fame with his "Oh Yeah!" trademark some 20 years ago, has since made television appearances with Sammy Davis Jr., Melba Moore, Jackie Gleason, Ed Sullivan, Merv Griffin, Johnny Carson, and has delighted audiences in Las Vegas, Canada, London, Vietnam, New York and Miami. Sometimes referred to as the "dean of black comedians," Mr. Rogers has inspired such black entertainers as Nipsey Russell, Dick Gregory, Redd Foxx and Slappy White. In his performances, Mr. Rogers battles racism with humor. For years, he wrote song hits for Nat King Cole, Tommy Dorsey and Sarah Vaughan. Mr. Rogers and his wife, Barbara, have two daughters, Joy and Gaye. Address: William Morris Agency, 1350 Avenue of the Americas, New York, NY 10019

Rollins, Joseph W. Jr., manpower expert, is personnel representative for Arthur Little, Inc. in Cambridge, Mass. Born March 10, 1920 in Beggs, Okla., he attended Roosevelt University in Chicago (B.A.) and graduate school in personnel management and economics at Loyola University in the city. Prior to joining the firm, Mr. Rollins was manpower expert and director of a minority talent bank and talent search program for the U.S. Equal Employment Opportunity Commission in Washington, D.C. He worked with then Vice President Hubert H. Humphrey on the President's Council on Youth Opportunity and was an original member of a task force helping the U.S. Civil Service Commission organize and institute the "Executive Inventory Program." Mr. Rollins helped to establish the Chicago Small Business Development Corporation and has worked in advertising and magazine space sales, as founder and operator of a national cosmetic company and as an officer in a federally chartered savings and loan association. He also was assistant to the president of a black-owned and operated insurance company. He is single. Address: Acorn Park, Cambridge, MA 02199

Ross, David P., publisher, is founder and president of the Afro-Am Publishing Company in Chicago, Ill. Born Feb. 21, 1908 in St. Louis, Mo., he studied art at the Art Institute (1930–31), University of Kansas (1933–35) and LaSalle Extension University (1935-36). Mr. Ross publishes books and other educational materials aimed exclusively at the black studies school market. He supervises the company, selects material for publication and handles preliminary editing, promotion and sales. One of his aims has been to produce educational materials that instill pride and motivation in black youths. Mr. Ross is a member of the South Side Community Art Center, the Hyde Park-Kenwood Conference, the Association for the Study of Afro-American Life and History and a member of the African Association for Black Studies. He and his wife, VerLita, have two daughters, Jacquelyn Jane and Danelle Lita. Address: 1727 S. Indiana Ave., Chicago, IL 60616

Diana Ross

Richard Roundtree

Carl T. Rowan

Ross, Diana, entertainer, one of America's most popular singers and actresses, was born March 26, 1944 in Detroit Mich., where she graduated from Cass Technical High School in 1960. She sang with the Olivet Baptist Church choir and "for fun" with her girl friends. Rejected for a school musical, she defiantly formed her own singing group with Mary Wilson and Florence Ballard. They thumbed rides to "sock hops" and talent shows, earning about $15 a week. They auditioned for Motown Records' Berry Gordy Jr. who advised them to finish high school before pursuing a career. They did, and on their second audition Mr. Gordy signed them as the Primettes. After being renamed the Supremes, their record, "Where Did Our Love Go" hit the top of the charts with Miss Ross singing the lead. Other hits followed, including, "Baby Love," "Stop in the Name of Love" and "Come See About Me." Throughout the 1960s, the Supremes remained the top pop style-setters and the best-selling recording artists in musical history. Leaving the group in 1970, Miss Ross, as a single, became a great nightclub attraction and television star. In 1972, she starred as Billie Holiday in the film *Lady Sings the Blues* and was nominated for an Academy Award. She and her husband, Beverly Hills public relations man, Robert Silberstein, have two daughters, Rhonda Suzanne and Tracee Joy. She has received eight other awards, including *Cue* magazine's Entertainer of the Year (1973). Address: 6464 Sunset Blvd., Los Angeles, CA 90028 **See article on Diana Ross in Volume II**

Roundtree, Richard, actor, won overnight success as a film actor in the title role of the 1971 movie *Shaft*, followed by the sequel, *Shaft's Big Score*, in 1973. Born July 9, 1942 in New Rochelle, N.Y., he attended Southern Illinois University where he had a part in a campus theater production of the play, *A Raisin in the Sun*. He quit SIU after two years and returned home to a succession of odd jobs. After he was hired as a suit salesman at Barney's, a men's store in Manhattan, a friend urged him to try modeling. He made the rounds of modeling agencies and in 1967 was hired as a model for the Ebony Fashion Fair. During a Fashion Fair visit to Los Angeles, he met comedian Bill Cosby who advised him to return to New York and learn acting. Joining the Negro Ensemble Company, he appeared in *Kongi's Harvest*, *Man, Better Man* and *Mau Mau Room*. He got some movie bit parts and appeared in the Philadelphia stage production of *The Great White Hope*. He competed against 200 actors for the *Shaft* role. Having completed *Shaft's Big Score* and *Shaft in Africa,* Mr. Roundtree became involved in putting together a "Shaft" series for network television. He has made three TV movie features and has recorded several songs. Divorced, he is the father of Kelly and Nicole. Address: Metro-Goldwyn-Mayer, Inc., 10202 W. Washington Blvd., Culver City, CA 90230 **See article on Richard Roundtree in Volume II**

Rowan, Carl T., journalist, is a widely syndicated newspaper columnist. Born Aug. 11, 1925 in Ravenscroft, Tenn., he is a graduate of Oberlin College (A.B., 1947) and the University of Minnesota (M.A., journalism, 1948). He also studied at Tennessee State University (1942–43) and Washburn University (1943–44). He has 13 honorary degrees. He was an ensign in the U.S. Navy in World War II. He was a copy writer and later staff writer for the *Minneapolis Tribune* (1948–61); deputy assistant secretary of state for public affairs, U.S. State Department (1961–63); U.S. ambassador to Finland (1963–64), and director of the U.S. Information Agency (1964–65). He has been a syndicated columnist for the *Chicago Daily News* and Publishers-Hall Syndicate since 1965, and has received more than a dozen awards and honors for his professional work. He is author of *South of Freedom* (1953), *The Pitiful and the Proud* (1956), *Go South to Sorrow* (1957) and *Wait till Next Year* (1960). He and his wife, Vivien, have three children: Barbara, Carl and Geoffrey. Address: 1101 17th St., NW, Washington, DC 20036 **See article on Carl T. Rowan in Volume II**

Russell, Herman Jerome, builder and land developer, is president and owner of H. J. Russell and Companies in Atlanta, Ga. His numerous businesses employ some 450 persons. Born Dec. 23, 1930 in Atlanta, he took construction industry courses at Tuskegee Institute. He is president and owner of H. J. Russell Plastering Co., H. J. Russell Construction Co., Paradise Apartments Managing Co., Inc., Georgia-Southeastern Land Co., Inc., Metro-Finishers, Inc., and R. & K. Drywall Co. He is chairman of Enterprise Investments, Inc., chairman of the board of directors of the Atlanta Enquirer Newspaper, Inc., vice-chairman of the board of directors of Citizens Trust Co. Bank, member of the board of directors of Atlanta Mortgage Brokerage Co., Inc., and participating owner in The OMNI Group, holders of the franchises for the Atlanta professional basketball (Hawks), hockey (Flames) and soccer teams. OMNI also owns the Atlanta Coliseum Management Co. He is a member of the board of directors of a number of civic and professional organizations., and has received numerous awards, including the National Association of Market Developers Award (1968) and the Meritorious Business Achievement Award of the Atlanta Community Relations Committee (1969). He and his wife, Otelia, have three children: Donata, Michael and Jerome. Address: 504 Fair St., SW, Atlanta, GA 30313

Russell, James A. Jr., educator, is president of Saint Paul's College (Lawrenceville, Va.), a liberal arts school which also offers degrees in education and business administration. Dr. Russell, a third-generation president of the college, was born Dec. 25, 1917 in Lawrenceville and has degrees from Oberlin College (B.A., mathematics), Bradley University (B.S., electronics technology; M.S., technical education) and the University of Maryland (Ed.D., educational administration and industrial education). He attended the National Science Foundation Institute in engineering electronics at the University of Illinois. For 21 years he was a member of the faculty at Hampton Institute where he developed engineering and technology programs in which many black young men and women received training for positions in industry. He is a member of numerous professional and civic organizations. He received the Outstanding Educators of America Award in 1971. He and his wife, Nellie, have two children, Charlotte and James. Address: Saint Paul's College, Lawrenceville, VA 23868

Russell, Louis B., businessman and teacher, is owner of Louis B. Russell Fashions, a women's apparel shop, and an industrial arts teacher in the Indianapolis Public School System in Indianapolis, Ind. Born April 26, 1925 in Terre Haute, Ind., he studied industrial education at Indiana State University (B.A., M.A.). Mr. Russell received a heart transplant on August 24, 1968 in the Medical College of Virginia at Richmond, Virginia and is the longest living heart transplant patient in the world. He is a member of the Indiana State Heart Association, chairman of the Indiana Heart Fund Drive and is associated with the Indiana State Mental Health Program. He and his wife, Thelma, have four children: Charles, Connie Sue, David and Helen. Address: 5423 E. 38th St., Indianapolis, IN 46218

Herman J. Russell   James Alvin Russell Jr.   Louis B. Russell

Wendell P. Russell

Bayard Rustin

S. E. Rutland

Russell, Wendell Phillips, educator, is president of Virginia State College in Petersburg, Va. Born June 2, 1926 in Middlesex County, Va., he has received degrees from Virginia Union University (B.A., B.D., 1949), Case Western Reserve University (M.A., 1950) and the University of Virginia (Ed.D., 1970). Before accepting his present position in 1970, Dr. Russell was dean of students (1957–63) and dean of the college at Virginia Union University (1963–69). He is a member of the Special Advisory Committee on Public Opinion for the U.S. Department of State, the Army Advisory Committee, the executive committee of the Southern Regional Education Board and the National Laboratory for Higher Education. He and his wife, Eleanor, have three children: Vernon Lee, Shelley and Wendell Jr. Address: Virginia State College, Box T, Petersburg, VA 23803

Rustin, Bayard, administrator, is executive director of the A. Philip Randolph Institute in New York, N.Y. He is responsible for determining the institute's priorities, coordinating its fund-raising programs and legislative activities and coordinating its activities with those of other civil rights organizations. Mr. Rustin was born March 10, 1910 in West Chester, Pa., and attended Wilberforce University, Cheyney State College and City College of New York. He has honorary degrees from the New School for Social Research in New York, Montclair State College in New Jersey and Brown University in Rhode Island. In 1941, he was youth organizer for A. Philip Randolph's March on Washington. From 1943 to 1953, Mr. Rush served as race relations secretary of the Fellowship of Reconstruction. In 1947, he participated in the first Freedom Ride, The Journey of Reconciliation, designed to test enforcement of the 1946 Irene Morgan case decision outlawing discrimination in interstate travel. Arrested in North Carolina, he served 30 days on a chain gang. His report of this experience appeared in the *New York Post* and prompted an investigation which led to the abolition of the chain gang in North Carolina. In 1953, Mr. Rustin became executive secretary of the War Resister's League, a pacifist organization. In 1954, he helped Dr. Martin Luther King Jr. organize both the Montgomery bus boycott and the Southern Christian Leadership Conference. In 1957, he coordinated the 35,000-strong Prayer Pilgrimage to Washington for civil rights. In 1958 and 1959, he directed The Youth Marches for Integrated Schools. In 1963, he was deputy director of the March on Washington, which brought over 25,000 persons to the nation's capital and paved the way for passage of the 1964 Civil Rights Act. In 1964, Mr. Rustin directed the New York School Boycott. Mr. Rustin has been arrested 24 times in the struggle for civil rights. He is a bachelor. Address: 260 Park Ave., South, New York, NY 10010

Rutland, S. Edward, educator and administrator, is president of Paul Quinn College in Waco, Tex. Born March 17, 1916 in Forsyth, Ga., he is a graduate of Fort Valley State College (B.S., education, 1947) and Northwestern University (M.A., 1948). He has done graduate work at Northwestern, the University of Minnesota and the University of Colorado. He is a member of the National Council of Social Science, the American Academy of Political and Social Science, the American Educational Research Association, and other professional groups. He has been a consultant to the Georgia State Department of Education, a consultant and liaison official for the Tennessee Valley Authority and a consultant for the U.S. Department of Health, Education and Welfare. With a background of 33 years as a teacher and administrator, Mr. Rutland became president of Paul Quinn in 1970. He succeeded in securing accreditation for the college (his predecessors had been trying to achieve this for some 100 years). He and his wife, Lavesta, have three sons: S. Edward, Kenneth and Alfred. Address: Paul Quinn College, 1020 Elm St., Waco, TX 76704

S

Owusu Sadaukai

Raymond St. Jacques

Judge Edith S. Sampson

Sadaukai, Owusu (formerly Howard Fuller), educator, is the Mwalimu Mkuu (administrator) at Malcolm X Liberation University in Greensboro, N. C. He is responsible for overall administration of the school in accordance with policies determined by its political committee. He was born Jan. 14, 1941 in Shreveport, La. He says that he has "no specific education for this job beyond day-to-day work with black people" although he has a master's degree in social work. "Very little of that training prepared me for my present position," he says. His position is "very rare because there are very few independent Black educational institutions inside the U. S." He believes that future opportunities in his field "depend on how black people move over the next few years as it relates to developing independent institutions." He is a member of the Black Peoples Union Party (in N. C.); the National Black Assembly and the African Liberation Support Committee. He helped organize the African Liberation Day demonstration and visited in Mozambique with freedom fighters of the Mozambique Liberation Front. He and his wife, Rabia, have three children, Y'arAmashi, Kwesi and Kuumba. Address: P.O. Box 21045, Greensboro, NC 27420

St. Jacques, Raymond, actor, is a director and producer as well as a stage and screen actor. Born in Hartford, Conn., he graduated from Hillhouse High School in New Haven, Conn. and studied at the Actors Studio in New York City and at the American Shakespeare Festival Academy in New York and Connecticut. He also studied acting privately with Herbert Berghof in New York City. By 1973, he had appeared in 13 motion pictures and had founded a filmmaking company, the St. Jacques Foundation, Inc., which produced the film, *Book of Numbers*. He produced, directed and starred in the film. His first motion picture appearance was in *Black Like Me*. Other film appearances include *The Pawnbroker*, *The Comedians*, *Mr. Moses*, *The Green Berets*, *Up Tight*, *If He Hollers, Let Him Go*, *Cotton Comes to Harlem* and *Come Back Charleston Blue*. Mr. St. Jacques, who was the first black actor featured as a cowboy in a television series, "Rawhide," has appeared in numerous network television shows. He has two sons, Raymond and Sterling. Address: William Morris Agency, 151 El Camino Dr., Beverly Hills, CA 90212

Sampson, Edith Spurlock, jurist, is a judge of the Municipal Court of Chicago, Ill. Born Oct. 13, 1901 in Pittsburgh, Pa. she attended the New York School of Social Work, and the School of Social Service Administration, University of Chicago and is a graduate of John Marshall Law School of Chicago (LL.B.) and Loyola University of Chicago (LL.M.). She also has honorary degrees from John Marshall Law School (LL.D.) and MacMurray College (L.H.D.) She was admitted to the Illinois Bar in 1927. Before assuming her present position, she practiced law in Chicago and served as assistant corporation counsel of the city. In 1950 and in 1952, she received a presidential appointment as a member of the United States delegation to the United Nations. As a member of the World Town Hall of the Air, she visited more than 20 countries in 1949, participating in open debate on current political questions with leading citizens in each country visited. In 1951, she was a guest lecturer of the U.S. State Department in Germany and Austria and lectured extensively in Finland, Norway, Denmark, Sweden, Holland, France and England. In 1955, she was the recipient of an award given by the American Friends of the Middle East to travel and lecture in Turkey, Egypt, Iran, Iraq, Lebanon, Jordan, Israel and Syria. In the fall of 1958, she joined members of the International Seminar group on a "People to People Discussion Tour" to Venezuela, Columbia, Chile, Peru, Uruguay, Argentine and Brazil. She is a trustee of Roosevelt University, a member of the Chicago Bar Association, the National Association of Women Lawyers, the Chicago Council of Foreign Relations and the United Nations Association of Chicago. Judge Sampson is a widow. Address: 1502 Civic Center, Chicago, Ill. 60602

Charles L. Sanders

J. Stanley Sanders

Diana Sands

Sanders, Charles Lionel, executive, is management consultant of Mudsand, Inc., in Asbury Park, N.J., and is adjunct professor at Atlanta University and at Hunter College in New York City. Born Aug. 10, 1938 in Lakeland, Fla., he is a graduate of Howard University (B.A., 1959; M.S.W., 1961) and New York University (Ph.D., 1972). A former social worker, he became associate professor of management and assistant to the dean of the graduate division of Atlanta University in 1970. He has also served as administrative director of the community psychiatry division of St. Luke's Hospital in New York City. His articles have appeared in the *Journal of the National Medical Association, Black World,* and *Black Caucus.* He is co-editor of the *Directory of National Black Organizations*, published by Afram Associates in New York City. He was selected as one of the Outstanding Young Men of 1972. He is divorced. Address: 230 W. 139th St., New York, NY 10030

Sanders, J. Stanley, attorney, is a partner in Sanders, Tisdale, English & Tooks, the first black law firm in southern California. He was born Aug. 1, 1942 in Los Angeles, Calif. A Rhodes scholar, Mr. Sanders has degrees from Whittier College (B.A., political science, 1963), Oxford University (B.A., M.A., 1965) and Yale Law School (LL.B., 1968). In 1969, he became an associate in a Beverly Hills law firm until he formed his own partnership two years later. In 1969, he was named executive director of the Lawyers' Committee for Civil Rights Under Law in Los Angeles, a position he still holds. An active community worker, he was a co-founder of the Watts Summer Festival in 1966 and has served as director of the Black Arts Council. His law firm specializes in corporation law, and represents businesses from aircraft plants to quick service food franchises in Watts. Working through his law firm, he has contributed to the rebuilding of parts of Watts that were destroyed after the 1965 riots. He and his wife, Phyllis, enjoy skiing and tennis. Address: 5900 Wilshire Blvd., Suite 2700, Los Angeles, CA 90036

Sands, Diana, actress, is the recipient of several important awards for her dramatic performances on stage, television and film. They include New York's Outer Circle Critics Best Supporting Actress award (1959) for *A Raisin in the Sun*, the Obie Off-Broadway award (1964) for *The Living Premise* and the New York area Emmy award (1964) for *Beyond the Blues* on television. She has also been nominated twice for the Tony award for *Blues for Mr. Charlie* and *The Owl and the Pussycat* (1964). She was nominated for the Emmy award for the segment, "Who Do You Kill?" in the "East Side/West Side" TV series. She has received the award of the Black Academy of Arts and Letters for "a young artist's contribution to the black experience in the theater." Also among her stage triumphs are *Two for the Seesaw, Macbeth, Caesar and Cleopatra* and *Phaedra* (1967). Among her films are *A Raisin in the Sun* (1960) and *An Affair of the Skin* and *Mr. Pulver and the Captain* (1963). More recently she appeared in *The Landlord* and *Doctors' Wives* and *Georgia, Georgia.* Born Aug. 22, 1934 in New York City, she is a graduate from the Performing Arts High School in 1952 and studied at the New Dance Group and the International Dance Studio, all in New York City. She also received private teaching in acting, speech and singing in New York. She studied classical theater in England in 1966. Address: c/o the William Morris Agency, 1301 Avenue of the Americas, New York, NY 10019

Doris E. Saunders

Nelis J. Saunders

Granville M. Sawyer

Saunders, Doris Evans, publishing executive, is director of the Book Division of Johnson Publishing Co. Inc., in Chicago. She is responsible for developing, coordinating and supervising the book publishing aspect of the firm. Born Aug. 8, 1921 in Chicago, she attended Northwestern University (1938-40); Central YMCA College (1940-41) and received a certificate in library science (Chicago Public Library training class, 1942); graduated from Roosevelt University (B.A., philosophy, 1950). She did graduate work in Library Science at Rosary College and Chicago State University. She worked at the Chicago Public Library (1942-49) and in 1946 became the first black reference librarian (Principal Reference Librarian, Grade 4) in Chicago. She joined Johnson Publishing Co. in 1949 as librarian, a post she held until the establishment of the book division in 1961. In 1966, she established her own public relations firm (The Plus Factor) and became a columnist (*Chicago Daily Defender*, 1966-1970; *Chicago Courier*, 1970-73); was host of "The Doris Saunders Show" (1967) and "The Think Tank" (1970-72) and was writer/associate producer of "Our People" on WTTW-TV. She was director of community relations and institutional development at Chicago State University (1968-70) and was staff associate (1970-72) in the Office of the Chancellor of the University of Illinois (Chicago Circle Campus). She is the editor of *The Day They Marched* (1963) and *The Kennedy Years and the Negro* (1964). She is a board member of the Black Academy of Arts and Letters and is a member of the board of the Illinois Chapter, ACLU and the Chicago Leadership Resource Program. She belongs to the National Association of Media Women, the Chicago Publicity Club and Alpha Gamma Pi sorority. Divorced, she has two children, Mrs. Ann Camille Vivian and Vincent E. III. Address: 820 S. Michigan Ave., Chicago, IL 60605

Saunders, Nelis J., legislator, is a member of the Michigan Legislature, representing the 11th District (Detroit). Born Sept. 3, 1923 in Orlando, Fla., she graduated from Florida Memorial College (A.A., English and business administration, 1943). She also studied journalism at Wayne State University and law at the Detroit Institute of Technology. Elected in 1968, Rep. Saunders is chairman of the legislature's city corporations committee, vice chairman of the mental health committee, and is a member of the civil rights, labor, and youth care committees. As of 1972, she had authored or co-sponsored more than 300 House bills and more than 175 House resolutions. Previously, she was a church reporter with the *Michigan Chronicle* for 26 years. She was cited as an outstanding legislator by the Detroit Minister's and Laymen's Council of Metropolitan Spiritual Churches of Christ in 1969, the Wolverine State Baptist Convention in 1970, the Civil Liberties Department of the Michigan State Association of Elks in 1970, the National Supreme Council in 1971, and by the Women's Auxiliary of the National Baptist Convention, U.S.A., in 1971. She is divorced. Address: P.O. Box 119, State Capitol Bldg., Lansing, MI 48901

Sawyer, Granville Monroe, educator and administrator, is the president of Texas Southern University. Born May 7, 1919 in Mobile, Ala., he is a graduate of Tennessee A&I State College (A.B., 1947) and the University of Southern California (M.A., 1952; Ph.D., 1955). He was the dean of Huston-Tillotson College from 1947 to 1956 and was a professor of speech and drama there. Dr. Sawyer also is the former vice president of Tennessee A&I State University. He serves on the board of directors of the National Space Hall of Fame, is a vice chairman of the Council of Presidents of Texas Senior Colleges and Universities, a trustee of the Southern Association of Colleges and Schools, a board member of the Standard Savings Association and on the advisory committee of the Federal Facilities and Equipment Grants Program of the Texas College and University system. He has also published articles on black academies and student dissent on black college campuses. He and his wife, Maxine, have two children, Patrecia and Granville. Address: Office of the President, Texas Southern University, 3201 Wheeler, Houston, TX 77004

Gale Sayers

Anderson M. Schweich

George S. Schuyler

Sayers, Gale, former professional football player, is assistant athletic director at the University of Kansas at Lawrence. He is also co-chairman of the Legal Defense Fund of the NAACP Sports Commission, coordinator of the Chicago Reach-Out program and is a member of the President's National Advisory Council for Drug Abuse Prevention. He serves as a commissioner of the Chicago Park District. Born May 30, 1943 in Wichita, Kan., he attended the University of Kansas, where he won All-America honors in football. As a running back for the Chicago Bears of the National Football League, he was named Rookie of the Year in 1965, a season in which he scored 22 touchdowns, including six touchdowns in one game, an NFL single season record. In 1966 and 1969, he led the NFL in rushing. He is co-author of the book, *I am Third*, which was later adapted into the film, *Brian's Song*. He and his wife, Linda, have three children: Gale, Scott and Timothy. Address: University of Kansas, Lawrence, KS 66044

Schweich, Anderson M., insurance executive, is president of the Chicago Metropolitan Mutual Assurance Co. in Chicago, Ill. He joined the company in 1951 as data processing manager. He later was office manager, assistant secretary in charge of systems and procedures, vice president and controller and in 1969 was elected executive vice president. On March 1, 1971, he was elected president. Born June 12, 1923 in Chicago, he is a graduate of Loyola University (B.S., accounting, 1951), and has studied at Northwestern and Stanford universities. He is a member of the boards of directors of the Independence Bank of Chicago, the Chicago Alliance of Businessmen, the Joint Negro Appeal and Lawrence Hall/Randall House. He is active with the Insurance Accounting and Statistical Association, the Chicago Mortgage Bankers Association and the National Association of Accountants. He is also on the board of the Rehabilitation Institute of Chicago. He and his wife, Mary, live in Chicago. Address: 4455 S. King Dr., Chicago, IL 60653

Schuyler, George S., journalist is literary editor of The *Manchester Union Leader*, contributing editor of *Review of the News*, and contributing editor of *American Opinion*. Schuyler was born in Providence, R.I. on Feb. 25, 1895. *The Manchester Union Leader* is a daily newspaper with a circulation of 60,000; *Review of the News* is a weekly publication with a circulation of 45,000; and *American Opinion* is a monthly publication of 45,000. Mr. Schuyler has served as assistant editor of *The Messenger* 1923–28; also as a columnist and editor for *The Pittsburgh Courier* 1924–66. He has received several awards including a citation of merit from Lincoln University School of Journalism in 1952. He is the author of the novels *Black No More*, and *Slaves Today*, and an autobiography *Black and Conservative*. He is a widower and the father of Phillipa Schuyler, now deceased. Address: 230 Convent Ave., New York, NY 10031

Hugh J. Scott

Rev. Nathan A. Scott

Roland B. Scott, M.D.

Scott, Hugh Jerome, educator and administrator, is the superintendent of public schools in Washington, D.C. He coordinates a school system consisting of 131 elementary schools, 30 junior high schools, 11 senior high schools, 5 vocational high schools and 15 special schools. Born Nov. 14, 1933 in Detroit, Mich., he is a graduate of Wayne State University (B.S., education, 1956; M.Ed., education, 1960), and Michigan State University (Ed.D., education, 1966). He is the first black superintendent of schools for the District of Columbia. He estimates that out of about 22,000 superintendents in the country only 30 are black, while among the 22 major city superintendents, only two are black. He is the author of a number of published books and played a major role in the Academy award nomination film, *Children Without.* He and his wife Florence, have two children, Marvalisa and Hugh. Address: 5426 27th St., NW, Washington, DC 20004

Scott, The Reverend Nathan A., educator, is Shaller Mathews Professor of Theology and Literature at the University of Chicago. He was born April 24, 1925 in Cleveland, Ohio; raised in Detroit, Mich., and attended public schools in that city. He attended Michigan University (A.B., 1944); Union Theological Seminary (B.D., 1946); Columbia University (Ph.D., 1949); Ripon College (Litt.D., 1965); Wittenberg University (L.H.D., 1965); Philadelphia Divinity School (D.D. 1967); General Theological Seminary (S.T.D., 1968); Saint Mary's College and Notre Dame (Litt.D., 1969). He is the co-editor of *The Journal of Religion*; a priest of the Episcopal Church; canon theologian of the Cathedral of Saint James in Chicago; a former Kent Fellow of the Society for Religion in Higher Education; former adjunct professor of English at the University of Michigan (1969), and Walter and Mary Tuohy Visiting Professor of Religious Studies at John Carroll University (1970). He has written more than 20 books. He and his wife Charlotte have two children. Address: 5517 S. Kimbark Ave., Chicago, IL 60637

Scott, Roland B., M.D., physician, is chief pediatrician at Freedmen's Hospital, chairman of pediatrics and a professor in the Howard University College of Medicine and the director of the Center for Sickle Cell Anemia, all in Washington, D.C. He is certified both in pediatrics and in pediatrics allergy. Born April 18, 1909 in Houston, Tex., Dr. Scott received both his pre-medical and medical education at Howard University (B.S., chemistry, 1931; M.D., 1934). He interned at Kansas City General Hospital in Kansas City, Mo. and served his pediatric residency at Provident Hospital in Chicago, Ill. Dr. Scott has spent years researching sickle cell anemia and many of his 179 published papers have dealt with the disease. Dr. Scott considers his research in the areas of sickle cell anemia and in the growth and development of black children his most significant contributions. A widower, he has three children: Roland Jr., Mrs. Venice Carlenius and Mrs. Irene Gardner. Address: Freedmen's Hospital, Department of Pediatrics, Sixth and Bryant Sts., NW, Washington, DC 20001

Stanley S. Scott

Bobby Seale

Arthur Sears Jr.

Scott, Stanley S., journalist, is special assistant to President Richard M. Nixon and is the highest-ranking black in the White House. Born July 2, 1933 in Bolivar, Tenn., he is a graduate of Kansas University (B.A., 1953) and Lincoln University (M.A., 1959). Before assuming his present position, he was assistant to Herbert Klein, director of communications for the Executive Branch, the second black man to serve as a White House press aide. In 1960, he was editor and general manager for the *Memphis World* in Tennessee. His journalism career began at the *Atlanta Daily World* as a reporter in 1959. In 1964, he became the first black full-time general assignment reporter for United Press International. He received a Pulitzer nomination in 1965 for his eye-witness account of the assassination of Malcolm X. Mr. Scott became the first full-time black news announcer for all-news radio station, WINS, in New York City in 1967. He is recipient of the Russwurm Award for Excellence in Radio News Reporting and the New York Silurians Award. He and his wife, Bettye, have two children, Susan and Stanley II. He has a son, Kenneth, by a previous marriage. Address: The White House, 1600 Pennsylvania Ave., Washington, DC 20500

Seale, Bobby, political activist, is the chairman of the Black Panther Party for Self-Defense. He served as minister of information for the party after he helped organize it in October, 1966. Born Oct. 22, 1936 in Dallas Tex., he has served three years in the United States Air Force. Mr. Seale was also a student at Merritt College where he met Huey P. Newton, co-founder of the Black Panther Party. Mr. Seale was charged with conspiracy to foment a disruptive demonstration during the 1968 Democratic Convention and incurred a four-year contempt sentence in the subsequent trial. He was also among those Panthers charged with the murder of an alleged informer in New Haven, Conn. The charges were dismissed and the murder trial ended in a hung jury. Mr. Seale, who introduced a new political style in his "sure win" bid for mayor of Oakland, is a gifted orator and author of the book, *Seize the Time.* He and his wife, Artie have a son, Malik Nkrumah Stagolee. Address: 8501 East 14th Street, Oakland, Calif. 94621

Sears, Arthur Jr., communications specialist, is a consultant to corporate educational communications and corporate public relations of the General Electric Co. His duties as educational communicator include recruiting college and high school students for the industry. In 1970, he was awarded the Columbia University Mike Berger Award for a series of articles, "Kelly Street Blues," about slum life in the Bronx. The series appeared in the *Wall Street Journal.* Born July 1, 1928 in Pittsburgh, Pa., he is a graduate of the University of Pittsburgh (B.A., journalism, 1951). In 1954, he was a reporter for the *Norfolk Journal and Guide* in Virginia. Three years later, he went to the *Cleveland and Cincinnati Call & Post* where he worked his way up to district manager-editor. He became an associate editor for *Jet* magazine in 1959, rising to New York *Jet* editor. In 1966, he became a public relations director for the National Urban League, and two years later, became a reporter for the *Wall Street Journal.* He joined General Electric in 1972. He and his wife, Bettie Jean, have five children: Norma, Arthur III, Galana, Jory and Ryan. Address: 570 Lexington Ave., New York, NY 10022

John H. Sengstacke

Frank M. Seymour

Betty Shabazz

Sengstacke, John H., publishing executive, is president of Sengstacke Enterprises, Inc., Sengstacke Publications and the Pittsburgh Courier newspaper chain, and is publisher of the *Chicago Daily Defender* and other newspapers. Born Nov. 25, 1912 in Savannah, Ga., Mr. Sengstacke is a graduate of Hampton Institute (B.S., 1933) and was a postgraduate student at Ohio State University (1933). After graduation from Hampton, he became assistant to his uncle, Robert S. Abbott, and took courses at the Chicago School of Printing and at the Mergenthaler Linotype School. As the *Defender* grew, the Abbott company produced two affiliated papers, the *Louisville* (Ky.) *Defender* (1933) and the *Michigan* (Detroit) *Chronicle* (1936). Mr. Sengstacke became vice president and general manager of the company. He wrote editorials for all three papers and articles for the *Chicago Defender*. During World War II, he was chairman of the advisory committee on the Negro press to the U.S. Office of War Information, and chairman of Chicago's war rationing board. In 1944, he began one of his three terms as president of the Negro Newspaper Publishers Association, which he was instrumental in founding. He controls three major communications enterprises: the Abbott Company, Sengstacke Enterprises and Amalgamated Publishers, Inc. His holdings include the *Pittsburgh Courier* newspaper chain and the *Tri-State Defender* of Memphis, Tenn. He and his wife, Myrtle, have three sons: John, Robert and Lewis. Address: 2400 S. Michigan Ave., Chicago, IL 60616 **See article on John H. Sengstacke in Volume II**

Seymour, Frank M., public relations executive, is president of Seymour & Lundy Associates, Inc. in Detroit, Mich. He founded the firm in 1965 as Frank Seymour Associates. Among the agency's clients have been a dozen major corporations in the food, utilities, insurance and banking fields. Mr. Seymour was born Dec. 16, 1916 in Detroit. Self-styled as "the original high school dropout," he quit Detroit's Northwestern High School in 1936 after the 10th grade and obtained his diploma some 40 years later while earning more than $35,000 a year. In 1945 he was elected to the Ypsilanti (Mich.) City Council; he was the first black official elected in Washtenaw Co. He has been a newspaper owner, public relations manager of a brewing company and general manager of a black-owned radio station. He is an accredited member of the Public Relations Society of America, a member of Detroit Adcraft Club, member of Detroit Press Club, and member of the executive council of Detroit Area Boy Scouts. Mr. Seymour is a Christian Science practitioner. He and his wife, Edith, have two daughters, Ruth and Magda. Address: 20025 Greenfield Rd., Detroit, MI 48235

Shabazz, Betty, activist, is the widow of Malcolm X (El Hajj Malik El Shabazz), black leader assassinated in 1965. Mrs. Shabazz devotes most of her time to her children—carrying out her late husband's definite ideas on preparing them for life—and is involved in community affairs. Born May 28, 1936 in Detroit, Mich., she attended Tuskegee Institute, Brooklyn State Hospital School of Nursing (R.N.), Jersey City State College (Certified School Nurse and B.A., Public Health Education). She has certification in early childhood education and is completing her thesis, *Sickle Cell*, for her master's degree. She works as a volunteer in early child care education, is on the Sickle Cell Telethon Advisory Board and is involved in local P.T.A. work and in a high school for pregnant students. She is a director of the African-American Foundation, the Women's Service League and the Day Care Council (all of Westchester County), and is a trustee of the National Housewives League. She is a member of the board of education of the Union Free School (District 13) and is co-chairman of the advisory board of the *Amsterdam News* newspaper in New York City. She has six daughters: Attallah, Qubilah, Ilyasah, Gamilah, Malikah and Malaak. Address: 234 E. Fifth St., Mount Vernon, NY 10553

Shaw, The Reverend Alvia A., clergyman, is pastor of St. James A.M.E. Church in Cleveland, Ohio. Born May 7, 1915 in Duarte, Calif., he is a graduate of the University of Southern California (B.A.) and the Pacific School of Religion (M. Div.). He also has an honorary degree from Payne Theological Seminary (D.D.). Before assuming his present pastorate in 1968, he was pastor of St. Paul A.M.E. Church in Columbus, Ohio. He is a member of the Ohio A.M.E. Conference and the NAACP, and is a consultant with the National Council of Churches. He and his wife, Ruth, have two children, Alvia Jr. and Wendell. Address: St. James A.M.E. Church, 8401 Cedar Ave., Cleveland, OH 44103

Shaw, The Right Reverend Herbert Bell, minister, is presiding bishop of the First Episcopal District of the African Methodist Episcopal (A.M.E.) Zion Church. His conference includes New York, Cape Fear, the Bahama Islands, Jamaica (West Indies) and London-Birmingham (England). Bishop Shaw was born Feb. 9, 1908 in Wilmington, N.C., and received his college training at Fisk University, Nashville, Tenn., his graduate training in the School of Religion at Howard University, Washington, D. C., and was awarded the honorary Doctor of Divinity degree at Livingstone College, Salisbury, N.C. He was ordained an elder in the A.M.E. Zion Church in 1928 and was a pastor from 1929 until 1937. In 1952, he was elected bishop. He is a member of the General Commission on Army and Navy Chaplains and is chairman of the board of directors of the National Committee of Black Churchmen having previously served as president of that organization. He is the deputy grand master of the Masonic Lodge of North Carolina, in addition to being a member of numerous other organizations. Bishop Shaw was a delegate to the Eighth World Methodist Conference (England, 1950) and took an around-the-world trip to visit A.M.E. conferences in 23 countries. He and his wife, Mary Ardelle, have two children, John and Marla. Address: 520 Red Cross St., Wilmington, NC 28401

Sheffield, Horace L., labor union official, is administrative assistant to Nelson Jack Edwards, international vice president of the United Auto Workers in Detroit, Mich. With the union since 1944, he has been an organizer and a political action representative. He was a founder of the Trade Union Leadership Council in 1957 and now serves on a volunteer basis as TULC executive vice president. He is chairman of the board of trustees of Detroit General Hospital, a member of the executive committee of the Detroit Medical Center Corporation, member of the board of directors of Boulevard General Hospital, member of the Wayne University Clinics Building Committee, member of the program advisory committee of Detroit Public School, and president of the TULC Education Foundation of Michigan. He was awarded an honorary LL.D. degree by Wayne State University in 1972. A widower, he is the father of Horace L., LaVonne Marie, Kathryn Rose and Mrs. Corliss Williams. Address: 8000 E. Jefferson Ave., Detroit, MI 48214

Rev. Alvia A. Shaw

Rt. Rev. Herbert Bell Shaw

Horace L. Sheffield

Ulysses Shelton

Rt. Rev. O. L. Sherman

Kenneth N. Sherwood

Shelton, Ulysses, state legislator, is a Democratic member of the Pennsylvania House of Representatives (181st District, Philadelphia). He was first elected in 1960. Born July 1, 1917, he attended Mastbaum Vocational School. He served in the U.S. Air Force and later held various positions, including magistrate's clerk, department of records clerk and aide to U.S. Congressman Michael Bradley. He is a beer distributor and club owner. He is a member of the Yorktown Civic Association and the North Philadelphia Model City Program. He and his wife, Pearl, have two children, Charles and Frederick. Address: 1132 W. Jefferson St., Philadelphia, PA 19122

Sherman, The Right Reverend Oddie Lee, clergyman, is a retired bishop of the African Methodist Episcopal Church. He was elected the 78th bishop of his church by the delegation of the general conference in Miami, Fla. in 1956. Born in Jacksonville, Tex., he attended Jackson Theological Seminary in Little Rock, Ark. and Texas College in Tyler, Tex. He has honorary degrees from Wilberforce University (D.D.) Shorter College (D.D.) and Monrovia College in Monrovia, Liberia (D.D.). Bishop Sherman served as chancellor of Paul Quinn College in Waco, Tex., a school that was accredited by the Southern Association of Secondary Schools and Colleges in December, 1972. He is affiliated with the National Council of Churches, The World Methodist Conference and the American Bible Society. He and his wife, Edna Othenia, have two children, John Oliver Davis and Mrs. Mary Etta Gipson. Address: 2525 Chester St., Little Rock, AR 72206

Sherwood, Kenneth N., businessman, is president and chief executive officer of the Kenwood Corporation in New York, N.Y. Born Aug. 10, 1930 in New York City, he is a graduate of St. John's University (B.B.A., accounting, 1951). After honorable discharge (S/Sgt.) from the U.S. Army with which he served in Japan and Korea during the Korean War, he became credit manager and then accountant for a national retailing company, the Busch Corporation, from which he resigned in 1962 after 11 years. He was vice president in charge of the accounts division of the Reter Furniture Corp. in New York City (1962–65). In 1965, with a $20,000 personal investment and a $200,000 Small Business Administration loan, he bought the Reter company, located on Harlem's 125th St., and founded the Kenwood Corporation. The largest black-owned store of its type in the city, it employs 125 people and has sales of more than $6 million a year. The Kenwood conglomerate has eight divisions. Mr. Sherwood has held some 20 city, state and federal advisory appointments and has received 17 honors and awards from various organizations. He and his wife, Gloria, have two children, Michelle and Kendra. Address: 144 W. 125th St., New York, NY 10027 **See article on Kenneth N. Sherwood in Volume II**

Shirley, George, operatic singer and music teacher, is a lead tenor of New York's Metropolitan Opera. Born April 18, 1934 in Indianapolis, Ind., he received a bachelor's degree in education from Wayne State University in 1955. One of the first black singers hired by the Metropolitan Opera Company and the first black man to sing leading roles, Mr. Shirley has sung more than 30 roles with great distinction and has won recognition for his versatile performances in such operas as *Simon Boccanagra*, *La Boheme*, *Magic Flute*, *Oedipus Rex*, and *Madame Butterfly*. He has won acclaim at Covent Garden where he sang his first David in Wagner's *Die Meistersinger* amd with his first performance as Pelleas in *Pelleas and Melisande*. He had been hailed as a "thrilling recitalist" internationally. His records are available on the RCA and Columbia labels. Mr. Shirley and his wife, Gladys, have two children, Olwyn and Lyle. Address: c/o Shaw Concerts, 233 W. 49th St., Suite 800, New York City NY 10019

Short, Bobby ("Robert Waltrip"), entertainer, has kept alive the art of cafe singing. He specializes in songs of the 1920s and 1930s by such composers as Duke Ellington, Cole Porter, and George and Ira Gershwin. Born Sept. 15, 1924 in Danville, Ill., his career embraces appearances at New York City's Café Carlyle (where he has appeared almost nightly since 1968), on television and radio, on stage and in films. In 1970, he appeared at the White House. Mr. Short learned to pick out tunes on the piano at the age of four and began his musical career at 11 in Chicago, Ill. Besides working in supper clubs throughout the United States, he performed for a year in Paris and London. In May, 1968, he and singer Mabel Mercer teamed for a highly successful concert in New York City's Town Hall. A recording of the concert was a best-seller. He wrote an autobiography of his childhood, *Black and White Baby* (1971). He is single. Address: c/o Bessie Lee Hunt Associates, 234 W. 44th St., New York NY 10036

Shuttlesworth, The Reverend Fred L., clergyman, is the pastor of the Greater New Light Baptist Church in Cincinnati, Ohio. He is also the national secretary of the Southern Christian Leadership Conference. A minister for 24 years, he has been in his current position for seven years. Born March 18, 1922 in Montgomery, Ala., he received his education in Montgomery. He is a graduate of Selma University (A.B.); Alabama State College (B.S., secondary education, 1955) and Birmingham Baptist College (LL.D., 1969). He has an honorary degree from Cincinnati Baptist Bible College (D.D., 1971). Rev. Shuttlesworth was a former top aide to the late Dr. Martin Luther King Jr., and worked extensively with him. Today he still advances Dr. King's ideals. He considers his most significant achievement to be his formation and leadership of the Alabama Christian Movement for Human Rights from 1956 to 1962. The organization joined SCLC between 1962 and 1965 to bring about basic civil rights laws in this country. A widower, he has four children: Patricia, Ruby, Fred Jr. and Carolyn. Address: 710 N. Crescent, Cincinnati, OH 45229

George Shirley   Bobby Short   Rev. F. L. Shuttlesworth

Leonard Simmons   Carole Simpson   Naomi Sims

Simmons, Leonard, public official, is commissioner of civil service for the state of New Jersey. Born May 2, 1920 in Goldsboro, N.C., he graduated from Bowne Business School in New York City in 1941. Appointed in 1972 by New Jersey Gov. William T. Cahill, Mr. Simmons was the first black in the history of New Jersey to be named to the State Civil Service Commission. He has served as a city councilman, president of the council and police commissioner in the borough of Roselle. A former president, and a member of the Roselle Board of Education for 13 years, he helped adopt that city's present civil service system. He and his wife, Claudia, have seven children: Patricia, Leonard Jr., Gloria, Dennis, Jeffrey, Pamela, Zeno. Address: 1019 Chandler Ave., Roselle, NJ 07203

Simpson, Carole, journalist, is a news correspondent for WMAQ-TV, the NBC affiliate in Chicago, Ill. She joined the station in September 1970. Born Dec. 7, 1940 in Chicago, she is a graduate of the University of Michigan (B.A.) and the University of Iowa (M.A., journalism). She worked for the University of Iowa's radio station, WSIU and joined WCFL Radio in Chicago as a reporter and film and book reviewer, later working as a reporter for WBBM Radio in Chicago. She was editor of the information bureau at Tuskegee Institute where she was a journalism instructor, advisor to the college newspaper, and a stringer correspondent for the "Voice of America." She and her husband, Jim Marshall, an engineer at Argonne National Laboratory, have a daughter, Mallika. Address: WMAQ-TV, The Merchandise Mart, Chicago, IL 60654

Sims, Naomi, fashion model, is the recipient of 10 awards and honors for her work and for community service. Born March 30, 1949 in Oxford, Miss., she attended the Fashion School of Technology in New York City and studied psychology at New York University. She was the first black model to appear in a television commercial and on the cover of a major women's magazine, *Ladies Home Journal.* At age nine, she left Oxford for Pittsburgh, Pa., and graduated from Westinghouse High School in 1967 with a B-plus average. She went to New York with three scholarships: one to the Fashion School of Technology, one to New York University and a third for subsistence as she tried a modeling career. Photographer Gosta Peterson, husband of the fashion editor of the *New York Times*, photographed her on her first interview, thinking she was an experienced model. She appeared on the cover of the paper's fall fashion supplement. A few months later, she did a television commercial for American Telephone and Telegraph Co., launching a career that has spanned continents. She was the first black to be featured in a multi-color magazine spread in *Vogue,* and she often appears in *Harper's Bazaar.* She was on the cover of *Life.* In 1969 and 1970, she was voted Model of the Year by International Famous Mannequins. She is author of a beauty book, *The Beautiful Black Woman*, and a children's book, *The Gum Tree Monster.* She is a columnist for *Essence* magazine. Address: c/o Ford Modeling Agency, 344 E. 59th St., New York, NY 10022 **See article on Naomi Sims in Volume II**

William E. Sims

Sims, William E., educator and administrator, is president of Langston University in Oklahoma. Born March 28, 1921 in Chickasha, Okla., he is a graduate of Lincoln University in Missouri (A.B., music education and secondary education, 1949) and Colorado State College (M.A., music and educational psychology, 1952; D.Ed., music education and higher education, 1963). He has done additional study at Kansas University. From 1942 to 1946, he served in the United States Navy as a musician second class. After teaching in public schools in Tulsa, Okla. (1945–53), he joined the Langston faculty as a professor of music and band director in 1953. He became chairman of the department of music in (1963), dean of academic affairs in 1965, acting president in 1969 and president in 1970. He is a member of the Adult Education Association, Kappa Delta Pi, a professional education society, and Phi Delta Kappa, a men's professional education society. He has served as a member of the Oklahoma Humanities Task Force. His hobbies are athletics, music and reading. He and his wife, Muriel, have one daughter, Dana Rae. Address: Langston University, Langston, OK 73050

Mary L. Singleton

Singleton, Mary L., legislator, is a member of the Florida Legislature (Democrat, 16th District). Born Sept. 20, 1926, she attended Hampton Institute and is a graduate of Florida A & M University (B.S., 1949). She is the owner of Singleton's Bar-B-Que stores in Jacksonville. She was the first black since Reconstruction and the first woman to be elected to Jacksonville City Council. She is a former teacher of local and state government at Edward Waters College, and also served as hostess of a weekly radio program, "Progress Report." She is a member of Zeta Phi Beta and the Florida Restaurant Association. She has served on the Jacksonville Government Study Commission, as vice president of the City Council, and as director of the executive board of Northeast Florida Drug Control Program. She has received numerous awards for her legislative and civic work. She is the mother of two children, Mrs. Charles Scott and Isadore. Address: 1353 33rd St., Jacksonville, FL 32209

Moneta J. Sleet Jr.

Sleet, Moneta J. Jr., photographer, is a staff photographer for Johnson Publishing Co., publishers of *Ebony*, *Jet*, *Black Stars*, *Black World* and *Ebony Jr!* magazines. He works in the company's New York office and has traveled on assignment over most of the United States and to Africa, Europe, South America and the West Indies. Born Feb. 14, 1926 in Owensboro, Ky., he is a graduate of Kentucky State College (B.A., business administration, 1947) and New York University (M.A., journalism, 1950). He also attended the School of Modern Photography in New York and Columbia University. Before assuming his present position in November, 1955, Mr. Sleet was staff photographer for *Our World* magazine (1950–55), reporter for the *Amsterdam News* (1950) and an instructor in photography at Maryland State College (1948–49). He served in the U.S. Army during World War II and attained the rank of staff sergeant. In 1969 he received the Pulitzer Prize in Feature Photography for his photograph of Mrs. Martin L. King Jr. and her daughter, Bernice, at the funeral of her slain civil rights leader husband. He is a member of the Black Academy of Arts and Letters and has had his works exhibited in the Detroit Public Library, the City Art Museum of St. Louis and the Black History Museum, Hempstead, N.Y. He has also participated in exhibitions at the Studio Museum in Harlem and the Metropolitan Museum of Art. He and his wife, Juanita, have three children: Gregory, Michael and Lisa. Address: Johnson Publishing Co. Inc., 1270 Avenue of the Americas, New York, NY 10020

Fred J. Smith

Herman B. Smith Jr.

James Oscar Smith

Smith, Fred J., legislator, is an Illinois state senator from the 22nd District (Chicago). Born July 4, 1899 in Chattanooga, Tenn., he attended the Christian Institute, Roger Williams University and Fisk University. Before his election to the first of five senate terms, Mr. Smith, a Democrat, had served six terms in the Illinois House of Representatives. Sen. Smith is a deputy clerk of the Municipal Court of Chicago. He and his wife, Margaret, live in Chicago. He has two sons, Raymond and Frank. Address: State Capitol, Springfield, IL 61106

Smith, Herman B. Jr., administrator, is director of the Office for Advancement of Public Negro Colleges of the National Association of State Universities and Land-Grant Colleges in Atlanta, Ga. He plans, develops and executes a variety of programs and activities designed to assist the nation's black colleges and universities in increasing their visibility and, subsequently, their financial support from private voluntary sources. Born Feb. 12, 1927 in Mansfield, Ohio, he has degrees from Knoxville College (B.A., 1948) and the University of Wisconsin (M.S., 1955; Ph.D., 1960). He is a member of Alpha Phi Alpha, Phi Delta Kappa, and the National Society of Fund-Raisers. He and his wife, Annie, have two children, Gregory and Terry Lynn. Address: 805 Peachtree St., NE, Suite 577, Atlanta, GA 30311

Smith, James Oscar "Jimmy", musician, is a jazz organist who heads his own jazz group, the Jimmy Smith Trio. He was born Dec. 8, 1928 in Norristown, Pa., and studied string bass at the Hamilton School of Music. Later, he studied piano at the Ornstein School of Music. He began his musical career in 1952, playing piano, and later organ, with Don Gardner and His Sonotones. Two years later, he began performing as a single act during intermissions at the Harlem Club in Atlantic City, N.J. By 1954, he had formed his own jazz trio. When a category for organ was first included in the *Downbeat* Magazine Jazz Poll in 1964, Jimmy Smith won first place by a two-to-one margin. He has won recognition in the poll every year since then. He won the *Playboy* Jazz Poll when it first included a category for organ in 1969, and has been listed in that poll every year since. In 1964, he won the Grammy Award for his album *The Cat*. He made his vocal debut in 1966 on the album *Got My Mojo Working*, and in 1971 did an all-vocal album, *In a Plain Brown Wrapper*. He has two children, Jimmy Jr. and Jia. Address: 6355 Topanga Canyon Blvd., Suite 307, Woodland Hills, CA 91364

Rev. K. M. Smith Sr.

Rev. Kenneth B. Smith

Nate Smith

Smith, The Reverend Kelly Miller Sr., clergyman and college administrator, has been pastor of First Baptist Church in Nashville, Tenn. since 1951 and is assistant dean of the Vanderbilt University Divinity School. He accepted the position at Vanderbilt in 1969 after serving for a year as the first black faculty member of the divinity school. He teaches graduate courses in church ministry and the community, and administers a program on black church relations. Born Oct. 28, 1920 in Mound Bayou, Miss., he is a graduate of Morehouse College (A.B., religion and music, 1942) and Howard University School of Religion (B.D., 1945). He was Dr. Martin Luther King Jr.'s associate in Nashville during the civil rights struggle of the 1960s. He was elected in 1967 to the American Baptist Foreign Mission Societies (now called the Board of International Ministries). He is a member of the Society for the Study of Black Religion, the American Academy of Political and Social Science, and the National Committee of Black Churchmen. He was editor (1958–59) of the *Young Adult Quarterly*, published by the Sunday School Publishing Board, and was for a time pastor of Antioch Baptist Church in Cleveland, Ohio. He is a contributor to the books *The Pulpit Speaks on Race* (Abingdon Press, 1964) *and Best Black Sermons* (Judson Press, 1972) and was editor of *Racism, Racists and Theological Education* (Vanderbilt Divinity School, 1971). He and his wife, Alice, have four children: Joy, Adena, Kelly Jr. and Valerie. Address: 900 James Robertson Parkway, Nashville, TN 37203

Smith, The Reverend Kenneth B., clergyman, is chairman of the national executive council of the United Church of Christ and is pastor of the Church of the Good Shepherd (Congregational) in Chicago, Ill. Born Feb. 19, 1931 in Montclair, N.J., he is a graduate of Virginia Union University (B.A., history, 1953) and Bethany Theological Seminary (1960). He has also attended Drew University and has an honorary D.D. degree from Elmhurst College, of which he is a trustee. He is secretary of the board of the Chicago Urban League and board chairman of Opportunities Industrialization Centers in Chicago. He is on the board of directors of the Chicago Theological Seminary and the Community Renewal Society. He traveled to Africa in 1970 as a delegate to the World Conference of Churches and to Southeast Asia in 1972 for the United Church of Christ. He is a recipient of the DeVella-Mills Foundation Award. He and his wife, Gladys, live in Chicago. He has a son, Kenneth Jr. Address: 5712 S. Prairie Ave., Chicago, IL 60637

Smith, Nate, labor activist, is executive liaison officer (Manpower Division OEO Community Action Program) and project director of Operation Dig in Pittsburgh, Pa. The program was created in 1967 to help train blacks as craftsmen for jobs in the construction industry. Mr. Smith was named to head the project following a two-year movement he had started in 1965 to protest racial discrimination in the building trades labor unions. Mr. Smith was born Feb. 23, 1929 in Pittsburgh. Though he only has a sixth grade education, he has been a successful leader in efforts to develop training schools (Pittsburgh Plan and Operation Dig) for young blacks. About 70 men were being trained for jobs in the beginning of 1973. Smith "bluffed" his way into the U. S. Navy at age 12 and became a middleweight boxer at age 15. He fought 125 matches before he was 30 years old. Mr. Smith and his wife, Minnie, have three children: Reneé, Sabrina and Nate Jr. Address: 107 Sixth St., Pittsburgh, PA 15222

Otis M. Smith

Robert L. Smith, D.D.S.

Vernel Hap Smith

Smith, Otis M., attorney, is a member of the legal staff of General Motors Corporation in Detroit, Mich. Born Feb. 20, 1922 in Memphis, Tenn., he is a graduate of Catholic University of America (LL.B., 1950). He has also studied at Fisk University (1941–42) and Syracuse University (1946–47). Before assuming his present position in 1967, Mr. Smith was a partner of the Mallory and Smith legal firm (1951–57), an assistant prosecutor for Genesee County, Mich. (1954–55), public administrator (1955–57), a member of the Flint Election Board (1956–57), chairman of the Michigan Public Service Commission (1957–59), auditor general of Michigan (1959–61), the first black man to be appointed a justice of the Michigan State Supreme Court (1961–66) and a member of the University of Michigan Board of Regents (1967–71). He is a member of the executive committee of the Michigan United Fund, a board director of the Partners of Alliance, Children's Aid Society, Catholic Charities, and the Urban League of Michigan. He is also a member of the board of trustees of Oakland University. He has received the Distinguished Service award from the Flint Junior Chamber of Commerce, the National Alumni award for government from Catholic University of America and the Silver Beaver award from the Boy Scouts of America. He is a member of the American Bar Association, the State Bar Association of Michigan and the American Judicature Society. He and his wife, Mavis, have four children: Vincent, Raymond, Anthony and Steven. Address: General Motors Building, Detroit, MI 48202

Smith, Robert L., D.D.S., dentist, is president of the National Dental Association and a dental practitioner in West Palm Beach, Fla. He was born Nov. 5, 1918 in Waycross, Ga. Dr. Smith is a graduate of Morehouse College (B.S., 1942), Howard University (D.D.S., 1946), and holds an honorary (LL.D., 1970) from Bethune-Cookman College. He is a member of the Florida Medical, Dental and Pharmaceutical Association, the Southeastern District Florida Medical, Dental and Pharmaceutical Association, the National Dental Association, the American Dental Association, the Howard University General Alumni Association, the Bethune-Cookman Board of Trustees and Alpha Phi Alpha fraternity. A practicing dentist in West Palm Beach since 1949, Dr. Smith is active in various civic organizations. He and his wife, Bettye, have two children, Mrs. Barbara S. Mott and Robert L. Smith Jr. Address: 431 Rosemary Ave., West Palm Beach, FL 33401

Smith, Vernel Hap, city official, is recreation services manager for the city of Oakland, Calif. He has held the post since 1966. He administers a 1,000-employee department with a wide range of programs and facilities: community centers, pools, athletic fields, lake operation, mountain camps and in-city camps. His work involves planning, design, safety aspects, implementation of programs, development of viable delivery systems and personnel. He has applied social work practices to the department's work and has instigated selective hiring to achieve employment parity for minorities, especially blacks. Born Nov. 12, 1924 in Waycross, Ga., he has degrees from Ohio University (B.S., group work and recreation and Ohio State University (M.A., social administration). He did graduate work in social welfare at the University of California (Berkeley). His career includes broad experience in social welfare as administrator, lecturer, teacher and trainer in small towns and metropolitan areas, both in the United States and overseas. Divorced, Mr. Smith has two sons, Randy and Kevin. Address: 1520 Lakeside Dr., Oakland, CA 94612

Willi Smith

Kenneth Snipes

Frank M. Snowden Jr.

Smith, Willi, fashion designer, is the designer for Digits, Inc., a women's fashion house in New York, N.Y. Born Feb. 29, 1948 in Philadelphia, Pa., he attended the Parsons School of Design in New York City under a Philadelphia Board of Education scholarship. In high school, he did drawings and illustrations of clothes by other designers. After school and on Saturdays he worked at the Prudence and Strickland Boutique, the first black-owned business of its kind in Philadelphia. His first fashion design job in New York was at Arnold Scassi. He worked in several other Seventh Avenue houses, including Glenora Jr., where he received his first public recognition as a designer of pre-teen clothes. Two buyers, Frank Trigg and Irving Yanus, saw his designs and when they started Digits, Inc., they made him house designer. He now designs for women between age 16 and 35. Sales are soaring. Digits and Willi Smith have become nationally known, and Mr. Smith has gained a percentage of the firm. Actress Melba Moore and *Cosmopolitan* magazine editor Helen Gurley Brown are among the many women who wear his clothes. Address: 525 7th Ave., New York, NY 10018 **See article on Willi Smith in Volume II**

Snipes, Kenneth, administrator, is executive director of Karamu House, the nation's oldest resident community arts workshop, in Cleveland, Ohio. Born Oct. 13, 1938, he is a graduate of Philadelphia Museum College of Art (B.F.A, 1962). He also studied voice at the Philadelphia Settlement Music School (1958–63), attended a management training seminar at Case-Western Reserve University (1969) and attended the Harvard University Institute in Arts Administration (summer 1970). Before assuming his present position in May 1969, Mr. Snipes served as executive administrator (1968–69) and art director (1965–68) of Karamu House. He was art director of Wharton Center in Philadelphia, Pa., (1964–65) and an extension program art teacher with the Philadelphia Board of Education (1962–63). He is president of the Fairfax Foundation, Inc., a development corporation in Cleveland, and is a member of the Mayor of Cleveland's Council on Youth Opportunity and the Cleveland Junior League Program Committee. He has lectured at numerous colleges and other institutions. He is the former moderator-host of a program on WKBF-TV in Cleveland, and has had many of his paintings exhibited at museums in both Cleveland and Philadelphia. He and his wife, Jean, have three children: Kevin, Kyra and Julie. Address: 2355 E. 89th St., Cleveland, OH 44106

Snowden, Frank Martin Jr., educator, since 1945 has been chairman of the Department of Classics at Howard University in Washington, D.C. Previously he was an instructor in Latin, French and English at Virginia State College (1933–36) and an instructor in classics at Spelman College (1936–40). In 1940, he joined the faculty of Howard University. He was dean of the college of liberal arts (1956–68) and director of the evening school and adult education (1942–48). Born July 17, 1911 in York County, Va., he is a graduate of Harvard College (A.B., 1932; A.M., 1933; Ph.D., 1944). The author of *Blacks in Antiquity: Ethiopians in the Greco-Roman Experience* (1971), as well as numerous articles on various aspects of education, he is a member of the American Philological Association, the Classical Society of American Academy (Rome) and the Archaelogical Institute of America. The recipient of many awards, appointments and honorary positions, including the Medaglia d'oro from the Italian government, he is also secretary-editor of the American Conference of Academic Deans and vice president of the Washington Society of the Archaeological Institute of America. He and his wife, Elaine, have two children, Jane S. Lepscky and Frank III. Address: Howard University, Washington, DC 20001

Dora B. Somerville   H. H. Southall Sr.   Mark T. Southall

Somerville, Dora B., administrator, is correctional programs executive with the Illinois Department of Corrections. She is the first black woman ever to hold the position. Appointed in November, 1971, she serves as liaison between the department and colleges and universities across the state in the coordination of curricula involving criminal justice. Born Nov. 29, 1920 in Greensboro, Ala., she is a graduate of Ursuline College in Cleveland, Ohio (B.S., education, 1939), the Catholic University of America (M.A., child study, 1942) and Loyola University in Chicago, Ill. (M.A., social work, 1947). Prior to assuming her present position, she was a member of the Illinois Parole and Pardon Board. She is co-author (with Dr. Clyde Vedder) of the study, "The Delinquent Girl" (1970), and has written papers for a number of professional journals. She is a member of the American Correctional Association, the National Association of Social Workers and the National Council on Crime and Delinquency. In 1970, she was named as a technical consultant to the White House Conference on Children and Youth. She has been awarded citations of merit by Ursuline College and Loyola University. She is single. Address: Illinois Department of Corrections, 160 N. LaSalle St., Chicago, IL 60601

Southall, Herbert Howardton Sr., insurance executive, is the president of the Southern Aid Life Insurance Co., Inc., Richmond, Va. He was born March 7, 1907 in Richmond. He has been employed with Southern Aid Life Insurance Co. since 1926, where he started as a stenographer. He attended Tennesse State A & M University and Virginia State College. Mr. Southall is a member of the boards of directors of Richmond Community Hospital and the Greater Richmond Chamber of Commerce; he is listed in *Who's Who in Insurance* and *Who's Who in the South and Southwest*. He feels that the insurance field has opportunities for black people because of the untapped market for life insurance with the interest in the security of people. Mr. Southall sees his rise from a stenographer to president of his company as his greatest accomplishment. He and his wife, Louise have two children, Herbert H. Jr., and Louise Y. Forrest. Address: 2723 Fendall, Richmond, VA 23222

Southall, Mark T., state legislator, is a member of the New York State Assembly from the 74th district in New York City. Born June 1, 1911 in Norfolk, Va., Mr. Southall was elected an assemblyman in 1963 after many years of community service. He received his education at the Collegiate Institute in New York; POHS Institute of Insurance and Henry George School of Social Science in New York. He and his wife, Joanne, have one daughter, Joanne. Address: 274 W. 145th St., New York, NY 10031

Spaulding, Asa T. Sr., business executive, consultant and retired president of North Carolina Mutual Life Insurance Co. in Durham, is now president of Asa T. Spaulding Consulting and Advisory Services with headquarters in that city. Born July 22, 1902 in Columbus County, N.C., he has degrees from New York University (B.S., 1930), University of Michigan (M.A., 1932) and honorary degrees from Shaw University (LL.D., 1958), North Carolina College (LL.D., 1960), Morgan State College (D.B.A., 1961), University of North Carolina (LL.D.) and Duke University (LL.D.). Mr. Spaulding, who retired as president of the largest black-owned insurance company in the world in 1968, formed a consulting firm which provides advisory services to numerous corporations across the country. He had worked at North Carolina Mutual for 36 years. In 1964, he was named the first black director of W.T. Grant Co. Mr. Spaulding continues to serve on several federal and state government commissions and works with many professional, philanthropic and youth organizations. He is author of numerous papers on various aspects of life insurances as well as historical writings which have been placed in the *Congressional Record.* Mr. Spaulding and his wife, Elna, have four children: Asa Jr. Aaron, Kenneth and Mrs. Patricia S. Moore. Address: A. T. Spaulding Consulting and Advisory Services, 104 W. Parrish St., Durham, NC 27701

Speller, John Finton, M.D., is the secretary of health for the state of Pennsylvania. His appointment by the governor marks the first itme in American history that two black people (C. Delores Tucker, secretary of state) have served in any governor's cabinet at the same time. Dr. Speller was born April 13, 1910 in Philadelphia, Pa. He attended Lincoln University (A.B., 1932), and Howard University (M.D., 1940). He was a delegate to the White House Conference on Aging and was formerly with the Philadelphia department of health as a medical specialist. He is a member of the Pennsylvania Medical Society, the American Medical Association, the American College of Surgeons and a diplomate of the American Board of Urology. He and his wife, Dorothy, also a physician, are both licensed pilots, operate their own 50-ft. yacht and a 40-acre farm. They have three children: Sandra, Marsha and Jeffrey. Address: Harrisburg, PA 17101

Spellman, Karen Edmunds, educator, is director of the Southern Education Program, Inc. in Atlanta, Ga. It is the only black teacher recruitment service in the country operated by black people for predominantly black institutions. Born Sept. 9, 1943 in San Antonio, Tex., Mrs. Spellman is a graduate of Howard University (B.A., French, 1964), where she also did graduate work. Beginning in 1966, she served for two years as a research officer for the Student Non-violent Coordinating Committee (SNCC). She is currently a member of the Association for African Education and serves on the board of directors of the Atlanta Center for Black Art and the Martin Luther King Scholarship Committee of Woodrow Wilson Fellowships. Mrs. Spellman and her husband, poet A. B. Spellman, have a daughter, Toyin. Address: 859 Hunter St., Atlanta, GA 30310

Asa T. Spaulding Sr.

J. F. Speller, M.D.

Karen Edmunds Spellman

289

Rt. Rev. S. G. Spottswood   Thaddeus H. Spratlen

Spottswood, The Reverend Stephen Gill, clergyman, is chairman of the national board of directors of the NAACP and was a bishop of the African Episcopal Zion Church for 20 years until his retirement in 1972. Bishop Spottswood was born July 18, 1897 in Boston, Mass., and was educated at Albright College, Gordon Divinity School and Yale University. He holds an honorary degree from Livingstone College (D.D., 1939). Bishop Spottswood joined the NAACP in 1919 and was a member of the branch executive committees in every city where he was pastor. From 1947 to 1952, he served as president of the Washington D.C., chapter, and in 1955, he was named to the association's national board. He was elected national chairman in 1961. A past president of the Ohio Council of Churches, he is currently a member of his denomination's Commission on Housing and Community Development, the Chaplain's Commission and the Board of Transportation. Bishop Spottswood is married to the former Mrs. Mattie Brownita Johnson Elliott. He has five children by his late wife, Viola: Mrs. Virginia Simon, Rev. Stephen P., Mrs. Constance Miller, Mrs. Viola Cabaniss and Alleyne. Address: 1931 16th St., NW, Washington, DC 20009

Spratlen, Thaddeus H., educator, is adjunct associate professor of management at UCLA, associate professor of marketing at the University of Washington, director of the Black Economists Development Project in Los Angeles and is secretary-treasurer of the Caucus of Black Economists, Inc., headquartered in Washington, D.C. Born May 28, 1930 in Union City, Tenn., he is a graduate of Ohio State University (B.S., business administration, 1956; M.A., economics, 1957; Ph.D., marketing, 1962). In 1972, he was a panelist for the Second Annual Symposium on the State of the Black Economy and was chairman of the workshop on transportation and marketing at the Black Enterprise Conference sponsored by the Congressional Black Caucus. He has written many articles and papers for professional journals and magazines, and has served as a consultant to a number of organizations. He is a member of the American Economic Association and the American Marketing Association. He is married to the former Lois Price. Address: School of Business Administration, University of Washington, Seattle, WA 98105

Edward S. Spriggs

Jeanne Spurlock, M.D.

Alma G. Stallworth

Spriggs, Edward S., museum executive, is the executive director of The Studio Museum of Contemporary Black Art in Harlem in New York, N.Y. He has been administrator and creative head of the museum's programs, exhibitions, fund-raising and public relations since 1969. Born Dec. 6, 1934 in Cleveland, Ohio, he attended the San Francisco Art Institute (1953–55) and San Francisco State College (B.A., fine arts and art history, 1965). Mr. Spriggs was formerly a postal clerk in San Francisco 1958–65), freelance graphic artist, caseworker and a freelance sound technician and film editor (1965–69) in New York, N.Y. He is a consultant to the New York State Council on the Arts, editor of *Black Dialogue* magazine, a member of the American Association of Museums and the International Council of Museums. He is a published poet and writer of articles. Mr. Spriggs has exhibited his works in numerous art shows, founded Bay Artists and Craftsmen United and is a volunteer art director for the Negro Historical and Cultural Society in the San Francisco Bay area. He was also an instructor in silk screen design and processing and a member of the administrative staff of Harlem's Black Arts Repertory Theater/School, directed by Imamu Amiri Baraka Mr. Spriggs is divorced and the father of two daughters: Tracey Lynne and Lisa Kelly. Address: 2033 Fifth Ave., New York, NY 10035

Spurlock, Jeanne, M.D., physician, educator and administrator, is chairman of the Department of Psychiatry at Meharry Medical College. She was born in Sandusky, Ohio and is a graduate of the Howard University School of Medicine (M.D., 1947). She completed post-graduate study at the Chicago Institute for Psychoanalysis. Before assuming her present position in 1968, Dr. Spurlock taught at numerous medical schools across the country and was chief of the Child Psychiatry Clinic at Michael Reese Hospital in Chicago. She is a member of the National Medical Association, the American Academy of Child Psychiatry and the board of directors of the National Urban League. Dr. Spurlock is the first black to receive the coveted Edward Strecker award from the Institute of Pennsylvania Hospitals (Philadelphia) for her outstanding ability as a clinician, educator and community leader. She is listed in *Who's Who in Medicine.* Address: Dept. of Psychiatry, Meharry Medical College, 1005 18th Ave. N., Nashville, TN 37208

Stallworth, Alma G., legislator, is a member of the House of Representatives in Lansing, Mich. (4th District). Born Nov. 14, 1932 in Little Rock, Ark., she studied at Highland Park (Mich.) Junior College, Wayne State University and Merrill Palmer Institute in Detroit. Mrs. Stallworth, who represents 80,000 people in the northwestern section of Detroit, was elected to office in 1970. As a legislator, she has served as secretary of the majority Democratic caucus and sponsored numerous bills, including one seeking tax exemption of fees paid for child care by working mothers. Mrs. Stallworth is active in various community, church and women's rights groups. She and her husband, Thomas, have two children, Thomas and Keith. Address: State Capitol Bldg., Lansing, MI 48901

Frank L. Stanley Sr.

Robert C. Stepto, M.D.

Rev. Darneau V. Stewart

Stanley, Frank L. Sr., publishing executive, is editor-publisher of the *Louisville Defender*. The newspaper has won numerous national and state awards for excellence and public service. Born in Chicago, Ill., he is a graduate of Atlanta University (A.B., English) and took graduate courses at the University of Cincinnati. He has an honorary L.H.D. degree from Allen University. He won All-American honors in football and was a football and baseball coach at Jackson (Miss.) State College. His 1946 tour of American Military bases in Europe and his subsequent documentation of segregation in the U.S. armed forces paved the way for desegregation of the Army. He also authored the bill which desegregated higher educational institutions in Kentucky. He was a founder of the National Newspaper Publishers Association and has served five terms as its president. Mr. Stanley was president of Alpha Phi Alpha fraternity (1955–57). He was selected as a juror for the Pulitzer Prize awards in 1969 and 1972. He has received numerous honors and awards and is a member of a number of professional and civic groups. He and his wife, Vivian, live in Louisville. He has two sons, Frank Jr. and Kenneth. Address: 1720 Dixie Highway, Louisville, KY 40210

Stepto, Robert C., M.D., physician, educator and administrator, is professor and chairman of the Department of Obstetrics and Gynecology at the Chicago Medical School in Chicago, Ill. His job is the direction and organization of a teaching program for students, medical residents and attending staff in the field of obstetrics and gynecology, and providing health care and maintenance in his department. He was born Oct. 6, 1920 in Chicago, Ill. He received his undergraduate degree from Northwestern University (B.S. 1942), his medical degree from Howard University (M.D., 1944) and his doctorate from the University of Chicago (Ph.D 1948). He did three years of residency training in obstetrics and gynecology and spent two years in post residency training. He is the regional director of the largest obstetrical and gynecological unit in the United States. He was also influential in developing an in depth program for scholarships for minorities in medicine. He is a member of the American Medical Association, the American College of Surgeons, the Chicago Urban League and the NAACP. His leisure interests include art, opera and golf. He and his wife Ann have two children, Robert and Jan. Address: 15th & California, Chicago IL 60615

Stewart, The Reverend Darneau V., clergyman, is pastor of the People's Community Church in Detroit, Mich. Born Aug. 21, 1928 in Chicago, Ill., he is a graduate of Wilberforce University (B.S.) and Payne Theological Seminary (B.D.). Before assuming his present pastorate in 1967, he was assistant pastor (1959–67). Earlier, he was pastor of the Bethel A.M.E. Church in Des Moines, Iowa. He is a member of the board of trustees of the National Council of Community Churches, a member of the Neighborhood Health Planning Board, member of the Detroit Board of Education (regional and central boards) and a member of the Wayne County Intermediate School District. He is a past president of the Great Cities Research Council, past president of the National Council of Community Churches, and is a member of Kappa Alpha Psi. He is a life member of the NAACP. He and his wife, Christine, have a daughter, Sandra. Address: Peoples Community Church, 8601 Woodward Ave., Detroit, MI 48202

William Grant Still

Carl B. Stokes

Rep. Louis Stokes

Still, William Grant, composer and conductor of symphonic and orchestral music, is hailed by his peers as the "dean of black composers." Mr. Still, whose compositions now number over 150, became the first black man to conduct a major symphony orchestra in the country when he directed the Los Angeles Philharmonic in 1936. In 1935, he became the first black man to conduct an orchestra in the Deep South when he directed the New Orleans Philharmonic Symphony at Southern University. His numerous compositions for orchestra, band, chorus, piano, voice and stage reflect many aspects of black life. In 1933, his "Afro-American Symphony" became the first full length work by a black composer to be recorded by a major record company. Mr. Still was born May 11, 1895 in Woodville, Miss., and studied at Wilberforce University where he was originally preparing for a career in medicine, and Oberlin College Conservatory of Music in Ohio. He learned to orchestrate by playing many instruments, including the violin, cello and oboe. Mr. Still's career has spanned the century and he still continues to compose, lecture, conduct and travel throughout the country. He has won many awards, fellowships and grants, including a number of honorary doctoral degrees. Mr. Still and his wife, Verna, have two children, Duncan and Judith. Mr. Still also has four children by a previous marriage. Address: 1262 Victoria Ave., Los Angeles, CA 90010

Stokes, Carl Burton, communicator, is news anchorman for the NBC television network in New York City. In 1967, Mr. Stokes became the first black to be elected mayor of a major American city. He accepted his present job in 1972 after serving two, two-year terms as chief executive of Cleveland, Ohio. Mr. Stokes is the first black to anchor a weekly evening television news show in New York City. Born June 21, 1927 in Cleveland, Ohio, he has degrees from the University of Minnesota Law School (LL.B., 1954) and Marshall Law School, Cleveland, Ohio (LL.D., 1956). He holds honorary degrees from numerous other educational institutions. After graduating from Marshall Law School, he and his brother, Louis, formed a law partnership in Cleveland. In 1958, he was appointed assistant city prosecutor, a position he held until 1962. In 1962, he became the first black Democrat elected to the Ohio Legislature. He served in the state legislature until he was elected mayor in 1967. As mayor, Mr. Stokes helped open employment and political opportunities for minority groups and poor people. On the national level, he sought to find solutions to the problems of America's inner cities. Mr. Stokes and his wife, Shirley, have three children: Carl Jr., Cordi and Cordell. Address: NBC, 30 Rockefeller Plaza, New York, NY 10020

Stokes, Louis, legislator, is a member of the U.S. House of Representatives from the twenty-first Congressional District in Cleveland, Ohio. Congressman Stokes, a brother of former Cleveland Mayor Carl Stokes, is the first black to serve on the House Appropriations Committee. On Feb. 8, 1972, he was elected chairman of the congressional Black Caucus, consisting of the fifteen black members of the House of Representatives. Born Feb. 25, 1925 in Cleveland, he has degrees from Western Reserve University (B.A.) and Cleveland Marshall Law School (J.D.). In addition, he holds honorary degrees from Wilberforce University and Shaw University. Prior to being elected to his first term in office in November, 1968, Congressman Stokes was a practicing attorney in Cleveland. Active in civil rights and legal groups, he is currently on the executive board of the Cleveland branch of the NAACP and a member of the American Civil Liberties Union. He is on numerous other boards, including that of the Cleveland Bar Association and Cleveland State University. He and his wife, Jeanette, have four children: Shelley, Louis, Angela and Lorene. Address: 315 Cannon House Office Bldg., House of Representatives, Washington, DC 20515

Rembert E. Stokes

Herman Stone Jr.

Judge Juanita Kidd Stout

Stokes, Rembert Edwards, educator and administrator, is president of Wilberforce University in Wilberforce, Ohio. Founded in 1856, Wilberforce is the only privately-supported, predominantly black college in the North that is owned and operated by blacks. Born June 16, 1917 in Dayton, Ohio, he is a graduate of Wilberforce University (B.S., sacred theology) and Boston University (S.T.B. and Th.D.). He is the 1966 recipient of the Alumni Award for Distinguished public service from Boston University. He was an African Methodist Episcopal minister in Jamestown, R.I., Cambridge, Mass. and Canton, Ohio before going to Wilberforce where he first served as dean of the Payne Theological Seminary. He was named president of the university in 1956. Dr. Stokes is currently a member of the Ohio Mental Health Association and a trustee of the Cleveland Chapter of the National Conference of Christians and Jews. He is also a member of the National Council of Churches, the Association for Higher Education and the American Association for the Advancement of Science. He and his wife, Nancy, have three children: Linda, Deborah and Celeste, Address: Wilberforce University, Wilberforce, OH 45384

Stone, Herman Jr., educator and administrator, has been president of Lane College in Jackson, Tenn. since 1970 and has been a professor and administrator there for the past 26 years. Dr. Stone came to Lane in 1947 as a biology instructor, later became chairman of the division of natural science and then dean of instruction. He has received, among other awards, the Professor of the Year Award (1963), the Distinguished Service Award (1972) for 25 years of service to Lane College, and the Student Government Association Award (1972) for dedicated concern for students. Born Dec. 12, 1919 in Tupelo, Miss., he holds degrees from Lane College (B.S., 1946), Howard University (M.S., 1950) and the University of Colorado (Ph.D., 1962). He and his wife, the former Mary Frances Houston, have a son, Maurice Rene. Address: Office of the President, Lane College, Jackson, TN 38301

Stout, Juanita Kidd, jurist, is a judge in the Court of Common Pleas in Philadelphia, Pa. The first elected black woman judge in the U.S., Judge Stout has served in her current position since 1969. She was a judge of County Court of Philadelphia from 1959-68. She is one of twelve black women judges and of five hundred black judges in the country (as of 1972). As judge of a court of general jurisdiction, she tries homicides, major felonies and civil cases involving more than $10,000. Born March 7, 1919 in Wewoka, Okla., she has degrees from the University of Iowa (B.A. 1939) and Indiana University (J.D. 1948; LL.M., 1954). She has honorary LL.D. degrees from Ursinus College (1965), Indiana University (1966), Lebanon Valley College (1969) and Drexel University (1972) and Russell Sage College (Litt., D. 1966). A member of the American, Pennsylvania and Philadelphia Bar associations, Judge Stout has written numerous articles for legal publications. Before becoming a judge, she taught in public schools, practiced law and served as an assistant district attorney. She and her husband, Charles Otis Stout, a retired educator, live in Philadelphia. Address: Room 512, City Hall, Philadelphia, PA 19107

Earl E. Strayhorn   John H. Stroger Jr.   Ariel P. Strong

Strayhorn, Earl E., jurist, has been a judge of the Circuit Court of Cook County (Ill.) since 1970. Previously, he was a trustee of the Metropolitan Sanitary District of Greater Chicago and was associated with the law firm of Rogers, Strayhorn and Harth (1952–1966) and with R. Eugene Pincham and Charles B. Evins (1966–1970). He served as assistant state's attorney of Cook County (1948–1952) and was a member of the Civil Service Commission of the City of Chicago (1959–63). Born April 24, 1918 in Columbus, Miss., he is a graduate of the University of Illinois (A.B., 1941) and DePaul University College of Law (J.D., 1948) He was a U.S. Army artillery officer in Italy during World War II. He is a lieutenant colonel and commander of the 1st Battalion, 178th Infantry of the Illinois Army National Guard. He is a member of the American Judicature Society, the Cook County Bar Association, the Chicago Bar Association and the American Bar Association. He and his wife, Lygia, have two children, Donald and Earlene. Address: Civic Center, Chicago, IL 60616

Stroger, John H. Jr., public official, is a member of the Cook County (Ill.) Board of Commissioners. He is chairman of the board's Public Aid Committee, and is a member of the Finance and Rules Committees. Born May 19, 1929 in Helena, Ark., he is a graduate of Xavier University (B.A., business administration, 1952) and De Paul University (J.D., 1965). Between 1952 and 1953, he was a basketball coach, high school business instructor and a securities salesman. He was assistant auditor of the Municipal Court of Chicago (1953–55), personnel director at Cook County Jail (1955), deputy clerk of the Cook County Superior Court (1959), assistant to the auditor of Municipal Court (1959–61), an examiner (1963–67) for the Illinois Department of Financial Institutions and chief examiner (1967–68) of the Department's Sales Finance Agency Division. He has served as a member of the board of directors of the Gateway National Bank in Chicago. He is a member of the Illinois Academy of Criminology. He and his wife, Yonnie Rita, have three children: Yonnie Lynn, Hans and Todd. Address: Civic Center, Chicago, IL 60601

Strong, Ariel Perry, editor, is managing editor of *Black Stars* magazine, published by Johnson Publishing Co., Inc. in Chicago, Ill. Born in Social Circle, Ga., she studied English at Spelman College and specialized in printing at Tuskegee Institute (B.S.). She was a linotype operator and proofreader for the *Atlanta Daily World* and the *Chicago Defender* before joining the Johnson Publishing Co. in 1953 as a proofreader for *Tan* (now *Black Stars*), *Ebony* and *Jet* magazines. In 1963, she became the first woman to head *Tan* magazine as managing editor. In 1971, *Tan* was incorporated with *Black Stars* magazine. Mrs. Strong is divorced. Address: 820 S. Michigan Ave., Chicago, IL 60605

Rev. Leon H. Sullivan

William E. Summers III

Percy E. Sutton

Sullivan, The Reverend Leon H., clergyman and organization head, is pastor of Zion Baptist Church in Philadelphia, Pa. and is founder (1964) and board chairman of Opportunities Industrialization Centers of America, Inc. He is also a director of General Motors Corporation. Born Oct. 16, 1922 in Charleston, W. Va., he is a graduate of West Virginia State University (B.A., 1943) and Columbia University (M.A., religion, 1947). He took postgraduate courses at Union Theological Seminary (1943–45). He has more than a dozen honorary degrees, including D.D. degrees from Virginia Union University, Dartmouth College and Princeton University, and LL.D. degrees from Swarthmore College, Bowdoin College and Temple University. He was ordained as a Baptist minister in 1941. Becoming pastor of Mount Zion Church in 1950, he persuaded a number of church members to pledge $10 each per month to fund enterprises such as a housing complex, a shopping center, a garment factory and an aerospace factory. From this start, he developed the national movement of OICs which by 1973 was active in manpower training and minority economic development in 104 cities. The Reverend Sullivan is also a director of the Girard Bank and the Pennsylvania Savings Fund Society in Philadelphia. He has received numerous honors, including the Freedom Foundation award (1960), the American Exemplar Medal (1969) and the Russwurm Award (1963). He and his wife, Grace, have three children: Howard, Julie and Hope. Address: 3600 N. Broad St., Philadelphia, PA 19140 **See article on the Reverend Leon H. Sullivan in Volume II.**

Summers, William E. III, broadcast executive, is president of Summers Broadcasting, Inc. and general manager of Radio Station WLOU in Louisville, Ky. Mr. Summers is also pastor of St. Pauls A.M.E. Church in Louisville. He was born Oct. 17, 1918 and attended Kentucky State College, the College of Scriptures in Louisville, and the University of Rome. In 1951, he joined Radio Station WLOU as a sports announcer when it was owned by an Atlanta-based company. He held virtually every position at the station until 1972. In March of that year, Summers Broadcasting, Inc. purchased the station for $850,000. Summers Broadcasting, Inc. is owned by three men, including William Summers, and has an interracial board of directors. An active community member, Mr. Summers is chairman of the economic advancement committee of the Louisville branch of the NAACP. He is a board member of the National Foundation of March of Dimes and the National Association of Television and Radio Announcers. He and his wife, Georgia, have three children: William IV, Seretha and Sherryl. Address: 2549 S. Third St., Louisville, KY 40208.

Sutton, Percy E., city official, is president of the borough of Manhattan (New York, N.Y.). Born Nov. 24, 1920 in San Antonio, Tex., he is a graduate of Brooklyn Law School (LL.B.) and has an honorary degree from Morgan State College (LL.D., 1969). He also studied at Prairie View College, Tuskegee Institute, Hampton Institute and Columbia University. He enlisted in the U.S. Air Force in 1942, served as a World War II combat intelligence officer and was promoted to captain. He won combat stars for service in the Italian and Mediterranean theaters. During the Korean conflict, he was an intelligence officer and later a trial judge advocate. He has practiced law in New York City. He was elected to the New York State Assembly in 1964, and was chosen Manhattan Borough president by the City Council for an unexpired term in September, 1966. In November 1966, he was elected by an overwhelming majority of the popular vote and was reelected in 1969. He is a director of the New York branch NAACP, the American Museum of Natural History and the Museum of the City of New York. He is a national director of the Urban League, Martin Luther King Democrats and Operation PUSH. He and his wife, Leatrice, have two children, Pierre and Cheryl. Address: Municipal Bldg., New York, NY 10007 **See article on Percy E. Sutton in Volume II.**

Weathers York Sykes   Edward C. Sylvester Jr.

Sykes, Weathers York, insurance executive, is senior vice president of Supreme Life Insurance Co. of America in Chicago, Ill., and is in charge of the firm's administration service division. Born May 13, 1927 in Pond, Miss., he is a graduate of the University of Wisconsin (B.S., 1950). Prior to joining Supreme in 1962 as an assistant claims manager, he was a senior claims consultant (1958–61) for Prudence Mutual Casualty Co. in Chicago, director of field adjusters of the Exchange Casualty and Surety Co. in Chicago (1955–58) and a member of the Organic-Tritium Group of Argonne (Ill.) National Laboratory's Chemistry Division (1950–55). He is a member of Sigma Xi, an honorary scientific society, Kappa Alpha Psi, Phi Sigma Delta and Zeta Beta Tau fraternities, the International Claim Association, the Original Forty Club of Chicago, the Illinois Accident and Sickness Forum and the Chicago Home Office Life Underwriter Association. His civic activities include membership of the boards of Michael Reese Hospital and Medical Center in Chicago, the Michael Reese Research Foundation, the Community Renewal Society (vice president and member of the executive committee). He is a member of the Chicago Urban League and the NAACP; and is an associate of the Adlai E. Stevenson Institute of International Affairs and director of the Pullman Bank and Trust Co. in Chicago. He and his wife, Carol Elaine, have three children: Michael Gregory, Lori Denise and Stephen York. Address: Supreme Life Insurance Co. of America, 3501 S. King Dr., Chicago, IL 60653

Sylvester, Edward C. Jr., administrator, is president and trustee of the Cooperative Assistance Fund (CAF) in Washington, D.C. CAF is a tax-exempt institution through which foundations can make investments for enterprises which benefit minority and poverty groups. Born in Detroit, Mich. in 1923, he is a graduate of Wayne State University (B.S., civil engineering, 1949). After graduating, he became a civil and structural engineer for the city of Detroit. He served as president and manager of the Liberia American Enterprises, Inc. in Liberia, West Africa in 1959. From 1961 to 1968, he held several positions in the U.S. Department of Labor, including director of the Office of Federal Contract Compliance. He was chairman of the U.S. delegation to the United Nations International Labor Organization in Geneva, Switzerland in 1964. In 1960, he was on the national presidential campaign staff for Sen. Stuart Symington and was national campaign coordinator for the Democratic McGovern-Shriver ticket in 1972. He and his wife, Lucy, have three children. Address: 1325 Massachusetts Ave., NW, Suite 303, Washington, DC 20005

T

Gerald E. Talbot

Ervin Tarver

Comer L. Taylor Jr.

Talbot, Gerald Edgarton, legislator, is a member of the Maine House of Representatives. A newspaper compositor, he was born Oct. 28, 1931 in Bangor, Maine. He is the first black ever elected (1972) to the Maine Legislature in 152 years. In 1973, he introduced legislation to make the birthday of Dr. Martin Luther King Jr. a legal holiday in Maine. There are about 2,800 blacks among the state's population of 993,663. Mr. Talbot was a Bangor City Council candidate in 1971. He is a member of the U.S. Commission on Civil Rights, the Maine State Committee on Aging; Rescue, Inc.; the Democratic City Committee; the Greater Portland Federated Labor Council; the Maine Association for Black Progress, and the Maine Conference on Human Services. He has received a number of awards, including the 1970 Hall of Fame Certificate of the Laurel, Miss. NAACP; the 1969 NAACP Portland Branch award, and the 1967 Golden Pin Award of the Portland NAACP, which he organized in 1965. He and his wife, Anita, have four daughters: Renee, Rachel, Regina and Robin. Address: House of Representatives, Augusta, ME 04330

Tarver, Ervin, stockbroker, is a registered representative (in San Diego, Calif.) of Blyth Eastman Dillon & Co., Inc., stockbrokers, with headquarters in New York, N.Y. In 1957, he began work at the San Diego office as a janitor. He became a messenger, then a clerk. By 1966 he was head of the margin department. He took correspondence courses on stock markets and passed tests given by the New York Stock Exchange and the National Association of Security Dealers. In 1971, he became the first black registered representative—or "customer's man"—in San Diego. (Less than 1 percent of registered representatives in the U.S. are black.) Born Oct. 8, 1933 in Somerville, Tex., Mr. Tarver graduated from high school in Tucson, Ariz. He and his wife, Johnnie Mae, have three children: Mark, Teresa and Byron. Address: 2550 Fifth Ave., Suite 100, San Diego, CA 92103

Taylor, Comer L. Jr., administrator, is regional planner for the Tennessee Valley Authority in Knoxville, Tenn. He was born Oct. 12, 1949 in Fort Lauderdale, Fla. and has degrees from Alabama A&M College (B.S. and M.S.). His master's degree was completed in 1972 while he was working as a planner with the Top of Alabama Regional Council of Governments. In July, 1972, he assumed his present position at TVA and also enrolled in the graduate Planning Program and the University of Tennessee. At TVA, he is involved in a variety of regional and community planning assignments designed to relate TVA's Resource Development Program to the plans and program of states, counties and cities within the seven-state Tennessee Valley region. These activities include developing proposals for community improvement through local flood control and planning for industrial site location. He also works with TVA's Townlife Community Improvement Program, a program designed to help cities develop long-range growth plans. He and his wife, Crystal, have one child, Tracy. Address: Tennessee Valley Authority, Regional Planning Staff, Knoxville, TN 37902

Hobart Taylor Jr.

James C. Taylor

Lynnette D. Taylor

Taylor, Hobart Jr., attorney, is a partner in Dawson, Quinn, Riddell, Taylor & Davis, a law firm in Washington, D.C., and is a member of the board of directors of Aetna Variable Annuity Life Insurance Co., Great Atlantic & Pacific Tea Co., Standard Oil Co. (Ohio), Westinghouse Electric Corp., Urban National Corp. and Anchor Group of Mutual Funds. Born December 17, 1920 in Texarkana, Tex., he was educated at Prairie View (Tex.) A&M College (A.B., 1939), Howard University (A.M., 1941) and the University of Michigan (J.D., 1943) where he was editor of *The Michigan Law Review.* Admitted to the Michigan Bar in 1944, he has been research assistant to the Chief Justice of Michigan; assistant prosecuting attorney of Wayne (Detroit) County, Michigan; special counsel of the President's Commission on Equal Employment Opportunity (1961–62); special assistant to the Vice President of the United States (1962), executive vice-chairman of the President's Commission on Equal Employment Opportunity (1962-65), associate counsel to the President of the United States (1964-65), and a director of the Export-Import Bank of the U. S. (1965-68). He and his wife, Lynnette, have two sons, Albert and Hobart III. Address: 723 Washington Bldg., Washington, DC 20005

Taylor, James C., legislator, is an Illinois state representative from the 26th District (Chicago) and ward committeeman and superintendant of the city's 16th Ward. Born Feb. 8, 1930 in Crawfordsville, Ark., he is a member of the assembly's Banking, Savings and Loans Committee; Registration and Regulations Committee, and Personnel and Veterans Committee. He has introduced legislation to help purchasers of homes on contract get fair financial settlements when their property is condemned. He has also introduced a "Right of Eminent Domain" bill which makes it a felony to solicit by force, threat or harm any person under 17 years of age to enroll in any organization which promotes good citizenship among young people. He and his wife, Ella, have three children: Richard, Cassaundra and Cynthia. Address: Illinois General Assembly, Springfield, IL 62706

Taylor, Lynnette Dobbins, administrator, is executive director of Delta Sigma Theta, an international women's sorority. She is a former program analyst for the Office of Economic Opportunity (Washington, Virginia and Maryland areas) and a former principal of Roosevelt Elementary School (2,300 students; 90 teachers) in Detroit, Mich. She also served on curriculum committees for the Detroit Public School System and on the committee to select teachers and administrators. Earlier, she was New York editor of the *Chicago Defender* and the *Detroit Tribune.* She is a member of the boards of directors of the National Friends of Public Broadcasting Corporation and the National Center for Voluntary Action; director of college and youth activities for the American Red Cross; member of the Public Committee on Truth In Lending Legislation (an appointment from the Federal Reserve Board), and vice president of Women In Community Service (a combination of the National Council of Church Women, National Council of Negro Women, National Council of Jewish Women and National Council of Catholic Women). Born in Birmingham, Ala., she is a graduate of Alabama State Teachers College (B.S., 1939) and Wayne State University (M.S., 1948). She and her husband, Hobart Taylor Jr., an attorney, have two sons, Albert and Hobart III. Address: 1707 New Hampshire Ave., NW, Washington, DC 20008

Stuart A. Taylor   William Edward Taylor   Herbert Temple

Taylor, Stuart A., educator, is an associate professor at the Graduate School of Business, Harvard University, and a management consultant to various major corporations. Born July 2, 1936 in Providence, R.I., he received degrees from Oakwood College, Huntsville, Ala. (B.S., accounting and business, 1960); the Graduate School of Business, University of Rhode Island (M.S., industrial management, 1963), and the Graduate School of Business, Indiana University (Ph.D., industrial management and psychology, 1967). He was the first black to become a licensed public accountant in Rhode Island and to teach full-time at Harvard Business School. Selection in 1969 as one of the outstanding young men to participate in the White House Fellows Program enabled him to do research for the U.S. Department of Urban Development and to study aboard. A member of the Academy of Management and the board of advisors to the National Urban League, he is also the founder of Rhode Island's Committee for the Advancement of Negro Education. Dr. Taylor and his wife, Ella Marie, have four children: Sandre, Stuart, Sabrina and Scott. Address: School of Business, Harvard University, Boston, MA 02163

Taylor, William Edward, broadcast executive and entertainer, is general manager of radio station WLIB in New York City. He is responsible for overall operation of the black-owned station. Born July 24, 1921 in Greenville, N.C., he received a B.A. degree from Virginia State College, and holds honorary degrees from Fairfield University and Virginia State College. Mr. Taylor is also a pianist, composer and author. His group, the Billy Taylor Trio, is world renowned and he has written over 300 songs (among them, "I Wish I Knew How It Would Feel To Be Free"). Along with his songs, he has published twelve books on jazz and jazz piano playing. He has also performed as the leader of the 12-piece orchestra for "The David Frost Show." Mr. Taylor and his wife, Theodora, have two children, Duane and Kim. Address: 310 Lenox Ave., New York, NY 10463

Temple, Herbert, graphic artist, is art director of *Ebony, Ebony Jr!* and *Black World* magazines, published by Johnson Publishing Co., Inc. of Chicago, Ill. He is responsible for design of all covers and editorial pages in the three magazines and does illustrations for articles. He has conceived almost all covers for *Ebony*'s annual special issue in August. He also designs special advertising and promotional material and packaging for a Johnson subsidiary, Supreme Beauty Products Co., and has illustrated a number of books, including *The Ebony Cook Book, Negro Firsts In Sports* and *The Legend of Africana*. He was chairman of the art committee which selected and purchased $250,000 worth of painting, sculptures and other art objects by black artists around the world for permanent exhibition in the new Johnson Publishing Company Building. He has been a judge for numerous art shows throughout the U.S. Born July 6, 1919 in Gary, Ind., he attended the art school of The Art Institute of Chicago (1945–48). He and his wife, Athelstan, have a daughter, Janel. Address: 820 S. Michigan Ave., Chicago, IL 60605

Harold W. Thatcher, M. D.

Brig. Gen. Lucius Theus

Alvin I. Thomas

Thatcher, Harold W., M.D., physician, is a dermatologist in Chicago, Ill. Born July 7, 1908 in Kansas City, Kan., he is a graduate of the University of Minnesota (B.S., 1929; M.B., 1931; M.D., 1932). He was a longtime associate of the late Dr. Theodore K. Lawless, a world famous dermatologist. Dr. Thatcher interned at Provident Hospital in Chicago and spent a year on the staff of University Hospital and Bellevue Hospital in New York, N.Y. During World War II, he was chief of medical service for regional and station hospitals at Fort Huachucha, Ariz. and received the Legion of Merit for meritorious conduct from the U.S. Department of War. He is a member of the board of directors of the Service Federal Savings & Loan Association in Chicago and is on the board of trustees of Cook County (Chicago) Hospital Nursing School, the YWCA of Metropolitan Chicago and Dillard University in New Orleans, La. He is a member of the Chicago Metropolitan Dermatological Society and is a consultant to Provident Hospital's medical staff. He and his wife, Marjorie, have a son, Harold W. Jr. Address: 200 E. 75th St., Chicago, IL 60619

Theus, Brig. Gen. Lucius, military officer, is special assistant for social actions in the U.S. Air Force. Among his duties in this capacity is supervision of the Air Force Social Actions Program, which includes guidelines for equal opportunity and treatment; race relations education; drug and alcohol abuse control, and domestic actions. Gen. Theus was born Oct. 11, 1922 in Madison County, Tenn. He is a graduate of the University of Maryland (B.S., 1956) and George Washington University (M.B.A., 1957). On Jan. 27, 1972, he became the third black officer in Air Force history to be promoted to the rank of brigadier general. He believes that "opportunities were never greater in the Air Force for blacks and other minorities." Gen. Theus also holds the Legion of Merit medal awarded him at the same time that he received his general's star. He and his wife, Gladys Marie, live in Virginia. Address: HQ USAF/DPX, Washington, DC 20330

Thomas, Alvin .I., educator and administrator, is president of Prairie View A & M College in Prairie View, Tex. Born Sept. 7, 1925 in New Orleans, La., he attended the city's Xavier University in 1943, Kansas State College (B.S., 1948; M.S., 1949), Pennsylvania State College in 1951, Ohio State University (Ph.D., 1957) and the University of Michigan in 1963. Dr. Thomas was industrial arts instructor, woodwork instructor, director of industrial education (1952–63) and dean of the school of Industrial Education and Technology (1963–66) at Prairie View before he became its president in 1966. He has been a consultant for the public schools of Texas, Kansas, Ohio, California and Indiana, and for the Dow Chemical Co., Litton Industries, Westinghouse Management Services and the U.S. Office of Education. Dr. Thomas is a member of numerous professional, community and national organizations, including the National Education Association, the Texas Industrial Education Association and the Texas Rural Development Commission. He is a director of the Federal Reserve Bank of Dallas (Houston, Tex. branch). He and his wife, Iris, have two sons and twin daughters: Kenneth, Michael, Janet and Julie. Address: P.O. Box 2513, Prairie View, TX 77445

Charles C. Thomas

Franklin A. Thomas

Rt. Rev. James S. Thomas

Thomas, Charles Columbus, educator and administrator is director of African and Afro-American Studies at Richmond College of the City University of New York (N.Y.). He is also an actor, dancer, writer, musician and model. He holds the rank of assistant professor and serves on the College Personnel and Budget Committee, the President's Advisory Council, the Academic Committee and the Admissions and Standing Committee. His area of specialization is ethnomusicology, theater and dance. Previously, he was an adjunct assistant professor at New York Community College. Born in McAlester, Okla., he is a graduate of Langston University (B.A., music, 1962) and Brooklyn College (M.F.A., theater, 1972). He is author of The *Black Brother Goose: Rinds for Revolution.* (Wilhelmina Publications, 1971) and contributed to *We Speak As Liberators: Young Black Poets.* (Dodd, Mead, 1971) and *Probes—An Introduction to Poetry* (MacMillan Co., 1973). He is preparing two music anthologies and a work on African design. He has made numerous appearances as an actor and dancer. He is a member of the Screen Actor's Guild, the Music Educators National Conference, Big Brothers of America, Jazz Interactions, Afro-American Folkloric Troupe, Egbe Omo Nago Folkloric Ensemble and the Chuck Davis Dance Company. He is single. Address: 130 Stuyvesant Place, Staten Island, NY 10301

Thomas, Franklin A., administrator, is president and executive director of the Bedford-Stuyvesant Restoration Corporation in Brooklyn, N.Y. He is also the first black director of the First National City Bank in Brooklyn. Born May 27, 1934 in Brooklyn, N.Y., he graduated from Columbia College (B.A., 1956) and Columbia Law School (LL.B., 1963) and has honorary degrees from Fordham University (LL.D., 1972) and Yale University (LL.D., 1970). He served in the United States Air Force (1956–60) as a navigator with the Strategic Air Command (SAC). He has been an attorney for the Federal Housing and Home Finance Agency in New York (1963–64); assistant U.S. Attorney for the Southern District of New York (1964–65), and deputy police commissioner in charge of legal matters (1965–67). He became president of the Bedford-Stuyvesant Restoration Corp. in 1967. The corporation is presently planning for the construction of a $6 million commercial center in Bedford-Stuyvesant. Mr. Thomas sees a very great need for more blacks in positions similar to his. Address: 1368-90 Fulton St., Brooklyn, NY 11216

Thomas, The Right Reverend James S., clergyman, is resident bishop of the Iowa Area of the United Methodist Church. His responsibilities include the spiritual and temporal direction and supervision of 987 churches in Iowa and the administration of programs of social amelioration and the interpretation of issues. Bishop Thomas was born April 8, 1919 in Orangeburg, S.C. He graduated from Claflin College (A.B.) and attended Gammon Theological Seminary (B.D.), Drew University (M.A.) and Cornell University (Ph.D.). Bishop Thomas has been a pastor, seminary professor and a higher education director for the Board of Education of the United Methodist Church. He has numerous honorary degrees and was author of the article, "The Rationale Underlying Support of Negro Private Colleges by the Methodist Church," in *The Journal of Negro Education.* He is a member of Phi Kappa Phi, Kappa Delta Pi and Omega Psi Phi. He was the director of a program by which eleven of the black colleges of the Methodist Church were accredited when the Southern Association of Schools and Colleges desegregated. Bishop Thomas and his wife, Ruth, have four daughters: Claudia, Gloria, Margaret and Patricia. Address: 1019 Chestnut Street, Des Moines, IA 50309

Albert W. Thompson

Era Bell Thompson

John D. Thompson Jr.

Thompson, Albert W., legislator, is a Democratic member of the Georgia Legislature (District 86, Columbus). Born June 29, 1923 in Ft. Benning, Ga., he is a graduate of Savannah State College (B.S., 1942) and Howard University Law School (J.D., 1950). He has practiced law in Columbus since 1951. He is chairman of the Legal Redress Committee of the Muscogee County NAACP, a charter member of the Columbus Human Relations Council, and is a member of the boards of Goodwill Industries, the Chamber of Commerce, the Georgia Retardation Association and The Community Counseling Center in Columbus. He is secretary of the Muscogee Legislative Caucus and treasurer of the Georgia Association of Citizens Democratic Clubs. He has received numerous citations, including the Progressive Club's "Man of the Year" award. He and his wife, Dorothy, have three children: Eloise, Charles and Albert Jr. Address: 4154 Swann St., Columbus, GA 31903

Thompson, Era Bell, journalist, is international editor of *Ebony* magazine in Chicago, Ill. She specializes in on-the-spot coverage of foreign places and personalities. Prior to assuming her present duties in 1964, Miss Thompson was for thirteen years one of two co-managing editors of *Ebony.* She joined Johnson Publishing Co. in 1947 as managing editor of *Negro Digest* (now *Black World*) magazine. Born in Des Moines, Iowa, she is a graduate of Morningside College in Iowa (B.A., 1933) and studied at Medill School of Journalism at Northwestern University. In 1945, she received a Newberry Fellowship to write her autobiography, *American Daughter.* She also wrote *Africa, Land of my Fathers* (1954) and co-edited (with Herbert Nipson) *White on Black* (1963). Among her many awards and honors are a Bread Loaf writer's fellowship (1949), honorary doctorates from Morningside College (1965) and the University of North Dakota (1969), and the Patron Saints Award of the Society of Midland Authors (1968). In 1972, the town of Driscoll, N.D., honored her by declaring three "Era Bell Thompson Days." She is a member of the Urban League, NAACP, Chicago Press Club and the Chicago Council on Foreign Relations. She is a member of the board of directors of the Society of Midland Authors. Address: 820 S. Michigan Ave., Chicago, IL 60605

Thompson, John D. Jr., legislator, is a member of the Ohio House of Representatives (Democrat, Cleveland, District 15). Elected in 1970, he was reelected for a second term in 1972. Born Aug. 23, 1927 in Cleveland, Ohio, he attended Cleveland Engineering Institute and Fenn College, where he took night courses in real estate. He also took a Life Underwriters training course and is currently enrolled at Franklin University School of Law. Following three years of U.S. Army service, he worked as a sub foreman for United States Steel (1951–66); insurance consultant for the Metropolitan Life Insurance Co. (1966–69); air pollution control officer for the City of Cleveland (1969–70), and real estate broker (1960–63). A member of Democratic Party Executive Committee, the Lee Harvard Community Association and the Mount Pleasant Area Council, he is a 32nd degree Mason and Shriner, and a trustee of the Advent Lutheran Church in Cleveland. He and his wife, Doris, have two children, Joni and Janet. Address: 15611 Stockbridge Ave., Cleveland, OH 44128

Thompson, Leon, legislator, is minority leader of the Arizona House of Representatives, serving his sixth term of office. He became minority leader in 1972. A Democrat, he represents the 23rd District (Phoenix). Born Oct. 26, 1917 in Albuquerque, N.M., he attended the University of Arizona (1938–40). He is a retired policeman in Phoenix. He is a member of the Fraternal Order of Police, the Salvation Army Auxiliary Council, St. Mary's Home and School Association, and the Elks Club. He and his wife, Jane, have six children: Yvonne, Sharon, Leon Jr., Stephen, Nolan and Frederick. Address: Arizona House of Representatives, Phoenix, AZ 85007

Thorpe, Marion Dennis, educator and administrator, is chancellor of Elizabeth City State University in Elizabeth City, N.C. Born Sept. 25, 1932 in Durham, N.C., he has B.A. and M.A. degrees in psychology from North Carolina College (now North Carolina Central University) and a Ph.D. degree in counseling psychology and administration from Michigan State University. Under President Lyndon B. Johnson, he was appointed assistant director of the Neighborhood Youth Corps of the U.S. Department of Labor. While in this capacity, he was responsible for effecting and implementing the funding of over $350 million for Neighborhood Youth Corps projects in the United States, Guam, Puerto Rico and the Virgin Islands. He is the author of numerous scholarly papers and reports, including "One State's Program for Traditionally Negro Colleges" and "The Role and Significance of the Black Colleges in the Desegregation Process." He is a member of numerous professional societies and civic groups. He and his wife, Lula, have two children, Pamela Monique and Marion Dennis. Address: Elizabeth City State University, Elizabeth City, NC 27909

Thurman, The Reverend Howard, clergyman, author and lecturer, is dean emeritus of Marsh Chapel at Boston University and founder-minister emeritus at the Church for The Fellowship of All Peoples in San Francisco. Born Nov. 11, 1900 in Daytona Beach, Fla., he attended Morehouse College (B.A.), Colgate-Rochester Theological Seminary (B.D.) and Haverford College. He holds honorary doctorate degrees from 12 universities, including Morehouse College (D.D.), Howard University (D.D.), Wesleyan University (D.D.), Tuskegee Institute (L.H.D.) Oberlin College (D.D.), and Boston University (D.D.). During his career of exemplary religious leadership, Dr. Thurman has served as professor of religion and theology at Morehouse and Spelman College, Howard University and Boston University and is the founder of the Church for the Fellowship of All Peoples, the first church completely integrated in leadership and membership in the United States. He has written 19 books, including *The Greatest of These, Deep is the Hunger, Luminous Darkness,* and *The Search for Common Ground.* The much honored minister, named one of the World's Ten Greatest Preachers by *Ebony* magazine, has also published numerous articles and recorded several long-playing records. Dr. Thurman and his wife, Sue, have two daughters, Olive and Anne. Address: 2020 Stockton St., San Francisco, CA 94133

Leon Thompson   Marion D. Thorpe   Rev. Howard Thurman

Edward E. Tillmon   Johnnie L. Tillmon   James Tilmon

Tillmon, Edward E., banker, is president of the Bank of Finance in Los Angeles, Calif.
He joined the bank in 1968 and became its president in 1972. Born Jan. 5, 1923 in
Kansas City, Kan., he is a graduate of the University of Kansas (B.S., 1947), did
graduate study at the University of Nebraska (1947-48) and was certified by the
Graduate School of Banking. University of Wisconsin in Madison. A past president
of the National Bankers Association, he is a member of the board of directors of the
Los Angeles Area Chamber of Commerce, Group Five California Minority Capital
Corporation. He is also a member of the American Bankers Association, California
Bankers Association, Independent Bankers Association and Kappa Alpha Psi fraternity.
He and his wife, Barbara, have three children: Mrs. Conie Payne, Edward and Bobbi.
Address: 2651 S. Western, Los Angeles, CA 90018

Tillmon, Johnnie Lee, welfare worker, is the executive director of the National Welfare
Rights Organization. Her work involves the supervision of the national office,
administrative duties and promoting community support. Born April 10, 1926
in Scott, Ark., she took courses in social work at the University of California. She was
national chairman of NWRO (1967–71) and assistant executive director (1971–72).
She has been active in political and community affairs since 1963 when she organized
the first welfare rights group. She formed the Mothers Anonymous group, which surveys
areas such as Watts in Los Angeles to educate welfare recipients about their
rights, contacts county welfare departments to try to obtain necessary help for
needy people. In 1968, Mrs. Tillmon attended the International Conference on Social
Welfare, observing similar programs in England, Finland and the Netherlands. She is
on the board of directors of the Women's Action Alliance and the National Association
for Community Development. Mrs. Tillmon has six children: Marsha, Ronald,
Auluvance, Josalyn, Tanya and Caffie. Address: 1424 16th St., NW, Washington. DC
20036

Tilmon, James, business executive, is president of Tilmon Productions, Inc., an
audio-visual production firm; host of the NBC television show "Tilmon Tempo"
(produced by Tilmon Productions) in Chicago, Ill., and a first officer with American
Airlines, flying as a co-pilot. Born July 31, 1934 in Guthrie, Okla., Mr. Tilmon majored
in music education at Lincoln University (Mo.) and joined the ROTC. After graduation
in 1957, he received a reserve commission in the U.S. Army and entered the Corps of
Engineers. He served eight years in the U.S. Army, during which he attended flight
school, and was discharged in 1965. In his leisure, he plays clarinet in two symphony
orchestras in Illinois. His wife, Louise, teaches mathematics at Highland Park (Ill.) High
School. They have three children: James, John and Thera. Address: 1434 Old Skokie
Rd., Highland Park, IL 60035

T. N. Todd   Shirley A. Tolentino

Todd, Thomas Nathaniel, attorney, is executive vice president of Operation PUSH, which is headquartered in Chicago, Ill. He is also assistant professor of law and assistant director of the Center for Urban Affairs at Northwestern University. Born Sept. 24, 1938 in Demopolis, Ala., he is a graduate of Southern University (B.A., political science, 1959; LL.B., 1963). In 1969, he developed research leading to the citing of the Chicago Board of Education for faculty segregation and established the first civil rights division of a local U.S. Attorney's office in the country. He was also coordinator of the African-American Colloquy in Nigeria, a participant in the International Law Student Conference in Mexico, and a guest of the president of Liberia in 1972. He has been the subject of numerous articles in leading periodicals, and has received several awards, including the 1971 Certificate of Achievement of the Kappa Alpha Psi fraternity at Northwestern University, the 1971 Activist Award of Operation Breadbasket, the 1971 Certificate of Achievement of the Afro-American Patrolmen League of Chicago, and the Outstanding Alumni Award of Southern University in 1972. He belongs to a number of organizations, and is a board member of the Legal Opportunity Scholarship Program, the Lawyers Action Committee, the American Civil Liberties Union Ghetto Project, the Black Legislative Clearing-House and the Afro-American Patrolmen League. He and his wife, Janis, reside in Chicago. Address: 930 E. 50th St., Chicago, IL 60653

Tolentino, Shirley Ann, state official, is a deputy attorney general in the State of New Jersey Division of Law and Public Safety in Trenton, N.J. She is counsel to the Board of Review of the Department of Labor and Industry. Born Feb. 2, 1944 in Jersey City, N.J., she is an honor graduate of the College of St. Elizabeth in Convent, N.J. (B.A., 1965) and Seton Hall University (J.D., 1971), and is presently working toward an LL.M. degree at New York University. She was admitted to the New Jersey Bar in 1972 after teaching high school Latin and English (1965–67) and serving as assistant project director of an Upward Bound program that permitted underprivileged high school students to take courses for the College of St. Elizabeth (1967–71). She attended law school at night. She is a member of the American Bar Association, New Jersey Bar Association and Delta Sigma Theta (Graduate Division). She and her husband, Ernesto, a physician, have a daughter, Aña-Ramona. Address: State House Annex, Trenton, NJ 08624.

Judge Edward B. Toles

Anne W. Toliver

A. P. Torrence

Toles, Edward B., referee in bankruptcy, was appointed in 1968 by the judges of the U. S. District Court in Chicago, Ill., and is one of the two blacks among the 216 federal referees in the United States. Born Sept. 17, 1909 in Columbus, Ga., he attended the University of Illinois (A.B., 1932), University of Illinois Law School and Loyola Law School (J.D., 1936). His private practice of law (1936-68) was interrupted when he served (1943-45) as a war correspondent in Europe for the *Chicago Daily Defender.* He was president of the Cook County (Ill.) Bar Assn. (1961-62) and was active in obtaining nominations of more black attorneys for Cook County judgeships and for appointment to the federal bench. He has written a number of articles about discrimination against black men seeking such posts. Mr. Toles is a member of several professional organizations and has received a number of honors and awards. He is a former president of the Chicago Bar Association. He and his wife, Evelyn, have one son, Edward Jr. Address: Dirksen Federal Bldg., 219 S. Dearborn St., Chicago, IL 60604

Toliver, Anne W., administrator, is executive director of the National Association of Real Estate Brokers, Inc. in Washington, D.C. She directs and supervises administrative programs of the NAREB and plans and coordinates its national conventions, conferences and special meetings. Born in Atlanta, Ga., she is a graduate of Howard University (B.A. and M.S.W.). She has taken graduate courses at the University of Heidelberg (Germany) and has attended seminars and workshops at the Real Estate Management Broker's Institute. She is a former real estate broker who owned her own firm, Reliance Realty Co., in Washington. She is a member of numerous professional and civic organization, including the American Association of University Women, the Institute of Executive Associations and Alpha Kappa Alpha sorority. Mrs. Toliver is a charter member of the Association of Notary Publics. She and her husband, James, have a daughter, Patricia Anne. Address: 1025 Vermont Ave., NW, Suite 1111, Washington, DC 20005

Torrence, Andrew Pumphrey, educator, is president of Tennessee State University in Nashville, Tenn. He was elected in 1968. He was born Nov. 20, 1920 in Little Rock, Ark. and has degrees from Tennessee State University (B.S., 1948) and the University of Wisconsin (M.S., 1951; Ph.D., 1954). From 1954 to 1968, he was at Tuskegee Institute as associate professor and head of the Department of Agricultural Education (1954-62), professor and dean of academic affairs (1962-67) and vice-president for academic affairs (1967-68). He is the author of numerous articles and is co-author of three books: *Leadership for Action in Rural Communities* (1960), *Teacher Education in Agriculture* (1967) and *New Careers and Curriculum Change* (1968). He is a member of numerous professional organizations. He is on the Advisory Committee of the U.S. Army Command and General Staff College. He was a U.S. Army warrant officer (1942-46). He and his wife Marian, have two chilidren, Kenneth and Andrea. Address: Tennessee State University, Nashville, TN 37203

Ronald Townsel

William H. Townsend, O.D.

Dempsey J. Travis

Townsel, Ronald, correctional executive, is superintendent of adult parole for the State of Illinois. He is responsible for the operation of the state's entire adult parole program. Some 135 persons are on his staff. He was appointed in 1970 and is the first black to hold the office. In 12 years he rose through the ranks from parole agent to casework supervisor. He has developed special programs to deal with ex-offenders who are violence-prone, or who have alcohol or narcotics problems or language barriers. He is a former schoolteacher and social worker with Chicago youth gangs. Born Nov. 25, 1934 in Chicago, Ill., Mr. Townsel has a B.S. degree in education from George Williams College. He has also taken postgraduate courses in social group work there. He is on the executive board of Interstate Compact Administrators and is a member of five other professional organizations. He and his wife, Ruby, have two sons, Raynard and Randall. Address: 160 N. La Salle St., Chicago, Il 60601

Townsend, William H., O.D., legislator, is a member of the Arkansas House of Representatives. He is also a practicing optometrist in Little Rock. Born July 30, 1914 near West Point, Miss., he is a graduate of Tuskegee Institute in Alabama (B.S., agriculture, 1941) and Northern Illinois College of Optometry in Chicago, Ill. (O.D., 1950). He also attended pre-medical courses at Howard University in Washington, D.C. In 1950, he passed the state Optometric Board to become the first black licensed optometrist in Arkansas. He is president of the Arkansas Council on Human Relations, second vice president of the Arkansas Optometric Association, treasurer of Professional Services, Inc., a local business enterprise, and chairman of the personnel committee of the Little Rock Urban League. He is a member of the local, state and national optometric associations and the Arkansas state board of directors (of optometrists). He is financial secretary of Pi Lambda chapter of Alpha Phi Alpha fraternity and a trustee of Mt. Zion Baptist Church in Little Rock. He and his wife, Billye, have three daughters: Yolanda, Terezenha and LaJuan. Address: Arkansas House of Representatives, Little Rock, AR 72201

Travis, Dempsey J., businessman, is president of Sivart Mortgage Corp., Travis Realty Co., Freeway Mortgage and Investment Co. and Dempsey J. Travis Securities and Investment Co.—all in Chicago, Ill. Born Feb. 25, 1920 in Chicago, he is a graduate of Roosevelt University (B.A.). Prior to building his companies, he was leader of a musical combo, and a stockyards worker. Drafted into the U.S. Army in 1942, he completed Quartermaster School for non-commissioned officers and became, successively, clerk of the Aberdeen (Md.) Proving Ground post exchange, assistant manager, manager and then supervisor of all post exchanges in the Aberdeen area. After graduation from Roosevelt, he studied at Chicago's Kent College of Law but quit and went into business for himself selling real estate. In 1961, his Sivart company became the first black-owned concern to qualify as an FHA-VA-approved company. Active in civic affairs, he is past president of the Chicago Branch NAACP, a director of the Cosmopolitan Chamber of Commerce, a trustee of Northwestern Memorial Hospital, a member of the Mayor's Commission for the Preservation of Chicago's Historic Buildings, and a member of the Board of Governors of the Chicago Assembly. He is married to the former Moselynne Hardwick. Address: 840 E. 87th St., Chicago, IL 60619 **See article on Dempsey J. Travis in Volume II**

William J. Trent   C. Delores Tucker

Trent, William J., business executive, is assistant personnel director at Time, Inc. in New York, N.Y. His responsibilities include recruiting students from black colleges for employment, financing minorities students, working with inner-city school groups, and personnel affairs within the company. He is also former executive director of the United Negro College Fund. He was born March 8, 1910 in Asheville, N.C. and received degrees from Livingstone College in Salisbury, N.C. (B.A., 1930) and the University of Pa. (M.B.A., 1932). He later did graduate work at the University of Pa. and the University of Chicago. He was race relations officer for the Federal Works Agency for five years, then joined UNCF (1944-64). In 1965, Mr. Trent served on the Nineteenth Selections Boards of the U.S. Dept. of State and in 1967 served on a Foreign Service Inspection Team in Japan. He is president of St. Luke's Hospital and treasurer of the Urban League in New York City. He is also a member of Metropolitan Applied Research Center and of College Placement Services, Inc. He and his wife, Viola, have three daughters, Toni, Judy and Kay. Address: Time, Inc., New York, NY 10020

Tucker, C. Delores, state official, is secretary of the Commonwealth of Pennsylvania (secretary of state). Born Oct. 4, 1927 in Philadelphia, Pa., she attended Temple University and the University of Pennsylvania. She is the first black and the second woman ever named to a cabinet-level post in Pennsylvania history, and she holds the third-highest ranking governmental office in the state, following the governor and lieutenant governor. By law, she is a member of the boards of Pardons, Property and Finance, and Revenue. She is also a member of the State Athletic Commission, keeper of the Great Seal of the State, custodian of the laws and resolutions passed by the general assembly, and custodian of the governor's proclamations. She records all sentences and other official acts in connection with the penal system. She registers and keeps records on the more than 500,000 corporations in Pennsylvania, and licenses and regulates 19 occupations and professions. She has brought many able black technicians into her administration. She is married to William L. Tucker. Address: Department of State, Room 303, North Office Bldg., Harrisburg, PA 17120 **See article on C. Delores Tucker in Volume II**

Lemuel Tucker

Robert L. Tucker

Alvin A. Turner

Tucker, Lemuel, broadcast journalist, is a television news correspondent for ABC News in New York City. His responsibilities include gathering, collating, writing, filming and broadcasting of news by use of film. The news is filmed under his direction and edited under his supervision. He also appears on television live to report the news. From 1965 to 1970, Mr. Tucker was with NBC News as a television and radio news correspondent. His wide-ranging assignments included the 1968 Republican and Democratic presidential nominating conventions and the Nigerian Civil War. He has also won an Emmy Award for his stories on "Hunger in America." Born May 26, 1938 in Saginaw, Mich., he is a graduate of Central Michigan University (B.A.) and has done work on his master's degree at the University of Michigan and at Central Michigan University. He is a member of the American Civil Liberties Union, the Reporters Committee for Freedom of the Press, the New York Civil Liberties Union and the American Federation of Television and Radio Artists. He is a bachelor. Address: 175 W. 13th St., New York, NY 10011

Tucker, Robert L., attorney and educator, is a partner in McCarty, Watson & Tucker, a law firm in Chicago, Ill.; a member of the faculty of Northwestern University School of Law, and general counsel for Operation PUSH (People United to Save Humanity). Born Feb. 14, 1929 in Chattanooga, Tenn., he is a graduate of Tennessee State University (B.S., 1951) and Northwestern University School of Law (J.D., 1956). He was a member of the noted Chicago law firm, McCoy, Ming & Leighton, for a number of years, and was assistant regional administrator for equal opportunity in the Chicago-Midwest Regional Office of the U.S. Department of Housing and Urban Development (he was head of the Office of Equal Opportunity from 1968 to 1971 when he resigned to become general counsel of SCLC's Operation Breadbasket in Chicago. When the Reverend Jesse Jackson formed Operation PUSH in December, 1971, Mr. Tucker joined the organization as general counsel. He is a member of the boards of directors of the Illinois Division of the American Civil Liberties Union, the National Association of Community Legal Counselors, and other organizations. He and his wife, Shirley, have one child, Teri. Address: 11 South LaSalle St., Suite 1732, Chicago, IL 60603

Turner, Alvin A., jurist, has been a judge of the Circuit Court of Cook County (Ill.) since July, 1970 when the new Illinois constitution abolished the position of magistrate, a post he had held since January, 1964. Born Feb. 2, 1910 in Calvert, Tex., he attended Paul Quinn Junior College and is a graduate of Bishop College (B.A., 1935) and Robert H. Terrell Law School in Washington, D.C. (LL.B., 1942). He served as a referee in Traffic Court (1962–64) and as a member of the Cook County Board of Tax Appeals (1962). He was an attorney in the Chicago law firm of Ellis & Westbrooks (1947–62). He is a member of the Cook County and Illinois Bar associations and the Varsity Club of Chicago. He was field director in Australia, the Philippines and Japan for the American Red Cross during World War II. He is divorced. Address. Civic Center, Chicago, IL 60601

Turner, Morrie, cartoonist, writes and draws two cartoons for King Features Syndicate in New York City. Born Dec. 11, 1923 in Oakland, Calif., he started his career as a free-lance cartoonist, doing comic strips for black newspapers. In 1964, he created the comic strip "Wee Pals," the world's first integrated comic strip. "Wee Pals," influenced by Charles Schultz's "Peanuts," soon became nationally syndicated, appearing in all of the large daily and Sunday comic pages. Mr. Turner now does the writing and drawing for the national animated television series, "Kid Power," which is based on the "Wee Pals" comic strip. He also hosts a local San Francisco television show, based on his comic strip, called "We Pals On The Go." Mr. Turner teaches cartoon classes once a week at Laney College in Oakland. Although his profession is a very rare one for blacks, Mr. Turner sees limitless possibilities for young blacks in the cartoon field. He and his wife, the former Letha Harvey, have one son, Morris. Address: 375 Jayne Ave., Oakland, CA 94610

Twyman, Luska J., city official, is the mayor of Glasgow, Ky. Born May 19, 1914 in Hiseville, Ky., he holds degrees from Kentucky State University (A.B.), Indiana University (M.S.), and Simmons University (LL.D.). He served 22 years as principal, teacher and coach at the Ralph Bunche School in Glasgow. Then, in 1969, he became the first black in the state of Kentucky's history to ever be elected mayor of one of its cities. He rates his work in race relations and human understanding among his top achievements. He advises, for young people, that "preparation" is the "key to success." He is married to the former Gladys Woodson. Address: 1208 S. Lewis St., Glasgow, KY 42141

Tyson, Cicely, actress, received rave reviews for her role in the film, *Sounder*, released in 1972. Born in New York, N.Y., she attended New York University and studied acting at the Actors' Playhouse. Following her high school graduation, she worked as a secretary for the American Red Cross for a time but quit to try modeling. After a brief, lucrative stint as a cover girl, she enrolled at New York University but soon quit to study acting. She won a role in the short-lived play *The Spectrum* and later made her Broadway debut in *The Dark of the Moon.* In 1962, she appeared in *The Blacks* and received the coveted Vernon Rice Award. She won that award again for *Moon on a Rainbow Shawl.* She was in *Tiger, Tiger, Burning Bright* and had a regular feature role in the TV series "East Side/West Side." Among her other TV appearances were on a special, "Americans: Portrait in Verse, "Naked City," "Camera Three," "The Nurses," "Slattery's People," "I Spy," "Frontiers of Faith," and "To Tell the Truth." Following her first major movie role in *Twelve Angry Men*, she starred with Sammy Davis Jr. in *A Man Called Adam.* She had six other film roles before *Sounder.* Address: c/o William Morris Agency, 1515 El Camino Dr., Beverly Hills, CA 90212 **See article on Cicely Tyson in Volume II**

Morrie Turner

Luska J. Twyman

Cicely Tyson

Leslie Uggams

Uggams, Leslie, entertainer, made her show business debut at age six, acting with Ethel Waters on the "Beulah" television show. Born in the Washington Heights section of New York, N. Y., she performed on stage until she was 11, then retired temporarily in order to concentrate on her schooling. In her senior year at the Professional Children's School in New York City, she was elected president of the student body. A long-time star of the "Sing Along With Mitch" show on television, Miss Uggams has guest-starred on numerous variety and dramatic programs on television and has appeared in nightclub and Broadway shows. For a while, she had her own television variety show, "The Leslie Uggams Show," and was featured in the TV special, "Hallelujah Leslie." She has won the Tony Award (1967), the Theatre Critics Award (1966-67) and Fame Award (best female singer on TV). She appeared in the movies *Two Weeks in Another Town* (1962), *Skyjacked* (1972) and *Black Girl* (1973), and sang the theme for the soundtrack of the film *Inherit the Wind*. She and her husband, producer Grahame Pratt, have a daughter, Danielle. Address: M-G-M, Inc., 10202 W. Washington Blvd., Culver City, CA 90230

Earl Vann

Vann, Earl, legislator, is a Democratic member of the Pennsylvania House of Representatives (186th District, Philadelphia). Born Oct. 18, 1913, he attended the University of Pennsylvania. He served in the U.S. Coast Guard during World War II, 1942–45. He was first elected to the legislature at a special election in 1964 and has been reelected in consecutive elections. He is a member of Phi Beta Sigma, the American Legion and the Pennsylvania Athletic Commission, and is secretary of the 36th Ward Democratic Executive Committee. He is married to the former Ada Gladden. Address: 1329 South 22nd Street, Philadelphia, PA 19121

Melvin Van Peebles

Van Peebles, Melvin, writer, actor, composer, film director, performed all these functions as well as those of producer and distributor in making a success of the film *Sweet Sweetback's Baadasssss Song*. The 1971 movie grossed about $12 million, broke the white film pattern and spawned the subsequent rash of black movies. Born Aug. 21, 1932 in South Chicago, Ill., he is a graduate of Ohio Wesleyan University (B.A., 1953). After graduation in 1953, he joined the U.S. Air Force and served three years. After discharge, he worked as a grip man on the San Francisco cable cars and wrote a book about cable cars, *The Big Heart*. He later moved to Holland and toured with the Dutch National Theater. Moving to Paris, he danced and sang black spirituals in the streets for a few *centimes*, keeping himself alive for 10 years while writing five novels, four of them in self-taught French: *A Bear for the FBI*; *The True American*; *The Party in Harlem* (which became the play *Don't Play Us Cheap*) and *La Permission*, (which became the movie *The Story of a Three-day Pass*). In 1970, he directed *Watermelon Man* for Columbia Pictures. Determined to do his next film without studio backing, he put up $70,000 and sweet-talked additional funds from others. With an amateur cast, a non-union crew and rented equipment, he filmed *Sweet Sweetback*. Turning to Broadway, he produced the musical, *Ain't Supposed to Die a Natural Death* in 1971 and *Don't Play Us Cheap* in 1972. Divorced, he has two children, Mario and Megan. Address: 132 rue d'Assas, Paris 6, France **See article on Melvin Van Peebles in Volume II**

Jackie Vaughn III

Vaughn, Jackie III, legislator, is a Michigan state representative and also a part-time teacher at the University of Detroit. Born Nov. 17, 1930 in Birmingham, Ala., he has a B.A. degree from Hillsdale College and an M.A. degree from Oberlin College. He studied at Oxford University in England as a Fulbright Scholar and Fellow (1960) and became one of the few Americans to receive a State Department extension of the award, thereby making it possible to graduate from Oxford University (Oxon B.Litt., social science). He was the first black to be elected president of the Young Democrats of Michigan. He is also the author of the historic 18-Year-Old Voting Rights Bill in Michigan. He is a bachelor. Address: 2625 W. Grand Blvd., Detroit, MI 48208

Abraham S. Venable

Nathaniel Vereen Sr.

Shirley Verrett

Venable, Abraham S., corporate executive, is director of urban affairs of General Motors Corp., Detroit, Mich. He coordinates and directs activities of the corporation relating to minorities and its role in resolving social problems. Previously, he was director of the U.S. Commerce Department's office of minority enterprise. Born April 10, 1930, in Washington, D.C. he earned his degrees in economics and business administration at Howard University (B.A., M.A.) and studied urban affairs under a fellowship at Princeton University. In late 1972, he completed a book, *Building Black Business—an analysis and a plan*, and assigned rights, title and proceeds to the Graduate School of Business at Howard University at a $1,000-a-plate benefit dinner. The $33,000 dinner proceeds and those from the book established a student revolving loan fund at his alma mater. He and his wife, Anna, have three children: Stephen, Douglas and Karen. Address: 3044 W. Grand Blvd., Detroit, MI 48202

Vereen, Nathaniel Sr., city official, is mayor of the town of Eatonville, Fla. Born March 3, 1924 in Forest City, Fla., he is a graduate of Savannah State College (B.S., 1949) and Bradley University (M.A., 1952). He is chairman of the Orange County Council of Local Government; a member of the Florida Construction Industry Licensing Board, Region III; Florida League of Cities; Greater Orlando Chamber of Commerce, and the Criminal Justice Council of Florida. Entering politics as a councilman in 1958, Mr. Vereen became a part-time mayor in 1963 and assumed full-time responsibilities Nov. 1, 1972. He has served five terms as mayor of Eatonville and has supervised the construction of a complete sewer system for the town. Mayor Vereen and his wife, Rosetta, have five children: Nathaniel, Gloria Ann, Valerie, Mark and Roslyn. Address: P.O. Box 2163 Eatonville, FL 37251

Verrett, Shirley, concert artist, is one of America's most distinguished opera singers. Born in 1933 in New Orleans, La., she graduated from Ventura College in California (A.A., 1951) and Juilliard School of Music (Voice, 1961). She made her recital debut at Town Hall in New York City (1958) and has appeared as a soloist with the New York Philharmonic Orchestra (1961–62), the Washington Opera Society (1962), the Chicago Symphony (1963), the Minneapolis Symphony Orchestra (1963), at the New York Philharmonic Hall (1963), at the Lausanne (Switzerland) Festival (1964) and as Carmen at the Bolshoi Theatre in Moscow (1963). She made her television debut on the "Ed Sullivan Show" in 1963, and her recording debut in 1964, producing such albums as *How Great Thou Art, Precious Lord* (1964, Kapp Records), *Carnegie Hall Recital* (1965, RCA Records), *Seven Popular Spanish Songs* (1965) and *Singing in the Storm* (1966). She has won many awards, grants and honors, including the Marian Anderson award (1955), the National Federation of Music Clubs award (1961), the Martha Baird Rockefeller Aid to Music Fund Fellowship (1959–61) and a Ford Foundation Fellowship (1962–63). She and her husband, Louis LoMonaco, live in London. Address: c/o Basil Horsfield, Artists International Management, 5 Regents Park Road, London, NW 1 England

W

Rev. C. T. Vivian   Rev. Charleszetta Waddles   Melvin R. Wade

Vivian, The Reverend Cordy Tindell, minister, is presently university minister at Shaw University in Raleigh, N.C. Born July 30, 1924 in Boonville, Mo., he received a bachelor of education degree from Western Illinois University, and a bachelor of theology degree from the American Baptist Theological Seminary. During the past 25 years, he has been active in each stage of the evolving movement for black freedom the Reverend Vivian was chairman of the board of the Institute of the Black World, Atlanta, Ga. He served as vice president of the Peoria, Ill. NAACP, was an organizer of the Nashville Christian Leadership Council, and rode on the first freedom bus to enter Jackson, Miss. He has authored a book entitled *Black Power and the American Myth*, an Ebony Book Club selection. Rev. Vivian has conceived and implemented such major programs as the National Black Training Center, presently training black clergymen, urban activists, and community organizers. Rev. Vivian's wife, Octavia, has written *Coretta*, a biography of Mrs. Coretta Scott King, which has been translated into two foreign languages. The Vivians have six children: Joanna, Cordy, Denise, Mark, Kira, Albert, and Charisse. Address: Shaw University 11 W. South, Raleigh, NC 27602

Waddles, Mother Charleszetta, clergywoman, is director of Mother Waddles' Perpetual Mission, which she founded in 1956 in Detroit, Mich. She conducts worship services and supervises the mission's emergency service program which deals with "the total needs of the poor." On a 24-hour, seven-days-a-week basis, the mission provides food, shelter, transportation, clothing, medical and dental care, financial aid and other help to 50 to 100 individuals and families each day. It conducts classes in practical skills from sewing and knitting, household and business budgeting, typing, and remedial education to salesmanship, basic electronics, aircraft maintenance, photography and basic political science. The mission's staff is largely volunteer. It is not funded by government or foundation sources; it operates on funds from individual and group contributions. Mother Waddles, born Oct. 7, 1912 in St. Louis, Mo., has received more than 50 honors and awards. Widowed once and divorced once, she married Dayton Waddles in 1956. She is the mother of 10 children: Bea, Leroy, Letheda, Annette, Lorraine, Andrea, Jackie, Charles, Dennis and Theresa. Address: 3700 Gratoit, Detroit, MI 48207

Wade, Melvin R., business executive, is owner and chairman of the board of Eastern Rubber Reclaiming Co., Inc., which reprocesses scrap rubber and which has capabilities of producing 100,000 lbs. of rubber per day, in Chester, Pa. The firm is the only black-owned plant of its type in the world and is one of only seven such enterprises in the U. S. His clients include General Motors Corp. and Mohawk Carpets. Born May 16, 1936 in Chester, he worked as a sheet metal fabricator at Boeing Aircraft after graduation from Chester High School and later as a technician at General Electric. Using his house as collateral he purchased the Eastern Rubber Reclaiming Co. in 1971. He has studied business administration at Temple University, technology at Drexel University and real estate at Delaware County Board of Realtors School. He is single. Address: 1 Flower St., Chester, PA 19013

John A. Wagner

E. C. Walden, M.D.

A. Maceo Walker

Wagner, John A., educator, is professor of biology and coordinator of the undergraduate programs at Morehouse College in Atlanta, Ga. He counsels and advises biology majors and directs the independent research of students. As consultant, Dr. Wagner travels to universities throughout the country explaining the various educational programs at the Argonne National Laboratory, Argonne, Ill.; Oak Ridge Associated Universities, Oak Ridge, Tenn.; and Savannah River Laboratory, Aiken, S.C. During the summer, he serves as director of the Summer Honors Research Program at Argonne National Laboratory. Born Jan. 7, 1923 in Sipsey, Ala., he is a graduate of Southern University, (B.S., 1948); Duquesne University (M.S., 1951); Michigan State University (Ph.D., 1962). Dr. Wagner was a junior biologist with the U.S. Public Health Service in Toyko, Japan (1948–50); assistant professor of biology Benedict College (1951–53); associate professor, South Carolina State College (1953–56); head, Department of Biology, Bay City (Mich.) Junior College (1956–63); visiting professor, Wayne State University (1961); chairman and professor of Department of Biology, Southern University, 1963–64. He is a member of Omega Psi Phi fraternity, Beta Kappa Chi, the American Society of Cell Biology, the American Society of Zoologists and the National Institute of Science. He and his wife, Adelle, have a son, Eric. Address: 223 Chestnut St., S. W., Atlanta, GA 30311

Walden, Emerson Coleman, M.D., physician, in private practice in Baltimore, Md., is a past president of the National Medical Association. Born Oct. 7, 1923 in Cambridge, Md., he is a graduate of Howard University (M.D., 1947). He served as chief of the surgical service of the United States Air Force Hospital at Mitchell Air Force Base, Long Island, N.Y. (1951–53), and was chief of surgery at Provident Hospital in Baltimore (1964–68). He is an attending surgeon at Lutheran, Johns Hopkins, Provident and South Baltimore General hospitals and is a part-time school physician in the Baltimore City Health Department. He is director of health services at Providence Comprehensive Neighborhood Health Center in Baltimore. He is president of the Maryland Medical Association, vice president of the Monumental City Medical Society, and a member of the Baltimore City Medical Society. Dr. Walden is chairman of the board of trustees of NMA, and was one of the NMA physicians who toured the People's Republic of China in 1972. He is a member of numerous boards, commissions and organizations. He and his wife, Celonia, have three children: Emerson C. Jr., Thomas E. (both students at the University of Maryland School of Medicine) and Celonia. Address: 4200 Edmondson Ave., Baltimore, MD 21229

Walker, A. Maceo, administrator, is president of Universal Life Company and president of Tri-State Bank, both of which are located in Memphis, Tenn. He was born June 7, 1909 in Indianola, Miss., but moved to Tennessee when he was eleven years old. His father was a physician, but gave up the practice of medicine and devoted himself to the life insurance business. He is a graduate of Fisk University (A.B., business administration, 1930) and New York University (M.B.A., 1932). He has studied actuarial mathematics at the University of Michigan School of Mathematics. Mr. Walker was elected president of Universal Life in 1952. Since he has been president, incomes and assets of the company have quadrupled and their operations have spread from coast to coast. Mr. Walker was ambassador to Mali, Africa in 1964. He is vice chairman of the Tennessee Commission on Civil Rights and a board member of Fisk University, Jarvis College, and the Memphis State University Foundation. Mr. Walker and his wife, Harriette Ish, have three children: Patricia, A. Maceo Jr., and Harriette Lucile. Address: 480 Linden St., Memphis, TN 38101

Rt. Rev. John T. Walker

Rev. Lucius Walker Jr.

William M. Walker, M.D.

Walker, The Rt. Reverend John Thomas, clergyman, in 1971 became suffragan bishop of the Episcopal Diocese of Washington, D.C. His election made him the first black bishop of the diocese and the third black ever elected as a bishop of the church. Born July 27, 1925 in Barnesville, Ga., he is a graduate of Wayne State University (B.A., history, 1951) and Virginia Theological Seminary (B.D., 1954). He was rector of St. Mary's Church in Detroit, Mich. (1955–57) and was a member of the faculty at St. Paul's School in Concord, N.H. (1957–66). He became canon of the Washington Cathedral in 1966 and served until he was elected a bishop. In Washington, he has been active in education and community service, particularly as chairman of the Negro Student Fund, which supports black students in independent schools in the Washington area. He has served as secretary of the Standing Committee of the Diocese and is host of "Overview," a weekly program on Washington's WRC-TV. He is chairman of the boards of trustees of Absalom Jones Theological Institute in Atlanta, Ga., St. Paul's School in New Hampshire, the National Cathedral School for Girls in Washington, D.C. and the Association of Independent Schools. He is a member of a number of church and civic organizations, including the Union of Black Episcopalians. He and his wife, Rosa Marie, have three children: Thomas, Ana Maria and Charles. Address: Episcopal Church House, Mt. St. Alban, Washington, DC 20016

Walker, The Reverend Lucius Jr., clergyman, is executive director of the Interreligious Foundation for Community Organization in New York, N.Y. IFCO gives financial support to the effort of renewing and developing black communities, with headquarters in New York, N.Y. Born Aug. 3, 1930 in Roselle, N.J., he is a graduate of Shaw University (A.B.), Andover Newton Theological Seminary (B.D.) and the University of Wisconsin (M.A., 1963). He has an honorary L.H.D. degree from Malcolm X College in Chicago, Ill. He is a member of the boards of trustees of Shaw University, and Andover Newton Theological School, and is a member of the Black Foundation Executives. He and his wife, Mary, have five children: Lucius, Donna, Gail, Richard and Edythe. Address: 475 Riverside Dr., Room 560, New York, NY 10027

Walker, William McAlpine, M.D., surgeon, is in the private practice of medicine in Chicago, Ill., and is chief of the Breast Service Clinic at Northwestern Memorial Hospital in Chicago and a member of the surgery faculty at Northwestern University. He is a noted cancer surgeon and specialist on diseases of the breast. He developed the thermal rake procedure for treatment of cancer, and the upper-outer quadrectomy procedure for treatment of pre-cancerous lesions of the breast. Among his other developments in the field is a technique for contrast media study for lesions resulting in bleeding from breast nipples. He is in demand as a lecturer at leading universities and medical schools. He has lectured at the University of Austria on pancreatic diseases and breast diseases and at Keio University in Japan on pre-cancerous and cancerous breast diseases. Born in Selma, Ala., he is a graduate of Morehouse College (B.S., chemistry and biology, 1941) and the University of Illinois (M.D., 1945). He served his internship at Los Angeles General Hospital and took post-graduate courses in surgery at the University of Southern California (1946–48). He was a resident in surgery under the famed Dr. Karl A. Meyer at Cook County Hospital in Chicago (1949–53). He has been a member of the staffs of Columbus, Wesley Memorial, Passavant and Provident hospitals in Chicago. He is a member of various medical associations, including the American Medical Association and the National Medical Association, ans is a diplomate of the American Board of Surgery and a Fellow of the American College of Surgeons and the International College of Surgeons. He is medical director and chief of the Underwriting Department of Supreme Life Insurance Company of America, and is a member of numerous civic and professional groups. He is a member of Alpha Phi Alpha, the Forty Club of Chicago and the Snakes Club of Chicago. He and his wife, Elizabeth, have two children, William M. and Eunice Elizabeth. Address: 55 E. Washington St., Chicago, IL 60602

William O. Walker

Rev. Wyatt Tee Walker

Rev. Frederick P. P. Wall

Walker, William O., publisher, is president of P-W Publishing Co. and publisher-editor of the *Call & Post* in Cleveland, Ohio. He took over the newspaper, which had no assets or equipment, in 1932 and developed it into a highly profitable business. Born Sept. 19, 1896 in Selma, Ala., he attended Wilberforce University (B.S., business, 1916) and Oberlin Business College (1918). Before taking over the *Call & Post*, he had worked as secretary to the director of the Urban League in Pittsburgh, Pa., as city editor of the *Pittsburgh Courier*, and as the first black manager of a branch of the Fair Department Store in Baltimore, Md. He then returned to the newspaper field and became an owner (later sole owner) of the *Call & Post*. He is a former president of the National Newspaper Publishers Association, and was director of the Ohio Department of Industrial Relations (1963-71). He is a member of numerous professional and civic organizations, and has been active in Cleveland and Ohio politics for many years. He and his wife, Naomi, enjoy gardening. Address: 1949 E. 105th St., Cleveland, OH 44101

Walker, The Reverend Wyatt Tee, clergyman and administrator, is minister of the Canaan Baptist Church of Christ in New York, N.Y. He is also special assistant to the governor of New York on Urban Affairs and has been involved in the construction of the Harlem State Office Building and Pilot Cultural Center. Born Aug. 16, 1929 in Brockton, Mass., he attended Virginia Union University (B.S., chemistry and physics, 1950, B.D., 1953). The Reverend Walker served as chief of staff to Martin Luther King Jr. and planned and executed the Birmingham campaign in the spring of 1963. Appointed minister of Canaan Baptist Church in 1967, he established the "tithers' fellowship" which has added considerably to the church's physical and financial growth. Under his direction, the church subsidizes the operation of an Anti-Narcotics Center which provides quarters and rehabilitation to ex-addicts. The Reverend Walker is a member of numerous civic and national organizations and is in constant demand as a preacher, human relations specialist and lecturer. He has conducted sensitivity seminars for big corporations such as IBM, AT&T, New York Bell Telephone Co., and Consolidated Edison, which introduced realities of the racial polarization in America. The Reverend Walker and his wife, Theresa Ann, have four children: Ann Patricia, Wyatt Jr., Robert and Earl. Address: 132 W. 116th St., New York, NY 10026

Wall, The Reverend Frederick Pinkney Pickering, publishing executive, has been editor and publisher of the *Chicago (Ill.) Courier*, a black weekly newspaper, since 1968. Previously, he was general manager of the Chicago edition of the *Pittsburgh Courier*. Born June 22, 1915 in Long Branch, N.J., he attended Bethune-Cookman College, Northwestern University and John Marshall Law School in Chicago. From 1942 to 1955, he was secretary to U.S. Congressman William L. Dawson (D., Ill.). He was vice president of the Democratic State Central Committee of Illinois from 1946 to 1950. He was employed in supervisory capacities at the *Chicago Defender* newspaper and at S. B. Fuller Products, a cosmetics company. He became an ordained minister in 1971 and is assistant pastor of Progressive Baptist Church in Chicago. He is a member of the board of the John Howard Association and Operation PUSH, and is a member of the Joint Negro Appeal, the Chicago Media Reps, the Cosmopolitan Chamber of Commerce and the Chicago State University Foundation. He and his wife, Etta, have two children, Irene and Frederick. Address: 4647 King Dr., Chicago, IL 60653

Kelvin A. Wall   William J. L. Wallace   Arthur M. Walters

Wall, Kelvin A., businessman and educator, is president of Kabon Consulting, Inc. in New York, N.Y., and is president of Thursday Development Corporation in Atlanta, Ga. Kabon specializes in marketing consulting while Thursday is a fast foods company with $1.3 million in annual sales. Before founding Thursday in 1971, he was a senior consultant with Arthur D. Little Co. of Boston, Mass. (1970–71); vice president, market development department, Coca-Cola USA (1966–71); director of advertising, N.Y. *Amsterdam News* (1958–62) and merchandising manager, *Ebony*, 1962–66. Born June 14, 1933 in New York City, he is a graduate of St. John's University (B.B.A.) and studied at New York University. He is a member of several professional and civic organizations, including the American Management Association, the American Marketing Association, the National Association of Market Developers and the Institute of Management Sciences. He is author of a number of studies, articles, etc. in the sales and marketing fields. Address: 110 E. 37th St., New York, NY 10016 or 800 Peachtree St., Suite 664, Atlanta, GA 30308

Wallace, William J. L., educator, is president of West Virginia State College in Institute, W. Va. He was named acting president of the college in November, 1952 and president in June, 1953. Dr. Wallace was born Jan. 13, 1908 in Salisbury, N.C. He is a graduate of the University of Pittsburgh (B.S.), Columbia University (M.A.) and Cornell University (Ph.D.). He has honorary degrees from Livingstone College (LL.D.), Concord College (L.H.D.) and Alderson-Broaddus College (D.Sc.). He received the Outstanding Civilian Service Medal of the Department of the Army in May, 1972. He is a member of the West Virginia Advisory Committee; a member of the U. S. Commission on Civil Rights; a member of the Advisory Committee, Farmers Home Administration, and a member of the Kanawha Home For Children. Dr. Wallace and his wife, Eleanor, have a daughter, Mrs. Eleanor Wallace Hill. Address: West Virginia State College, Institute, WV 25112

Walters, Arthur M., social service administrator, is executive director of the Louisville, Ky. Urban League, responsible for the administration and program operation of the agency. He is the league's former director of economic development and employment. Born Nov. 6, 1918 in Magnolia, Ky., he has a degree from Colorado College (B.A.), took graduate training at the University of Louisville and attended the Army Engineer School at Fort Belvoir, Va. He served for 20 years in the U.S. Army, retired as a lieutenant colonel with decorations for heroism and bravery, received the AFL-CIO community service award and is a member of numerous civic and professional organizations. He helped to develop the league's on-the-job training project, anti-dropout and jobs and opportunities programs. He and his wife, Noralee, have three children: Reginald, Artye and Michele. Address: 209 W. Market St., Louisville, KY 40202

Mary D. Walters

Ronald Walters

George L. Washington

Harold Washington

Walters, Mary Dawson, librarian, is head of the acquisition department and associate professor of library administration at Ohio State University in Columbus, Ohio. As administrator, she supervises a budget that exceeds one million dollars and maintains and adapts the library's extensive collection of all media used to support the university's curriculum. Mrs. Walters was born Oct. 6, 1923 in Mitchell County, Ga. She studied home economics at Savannah State College (B.S., 1949) and library science at Atlanta University (M.S., 1957). She has also studied at Ohio State University and Ohio Historical Society. Before accepting her present position in 1961, she was librarian at Albany State College where she taught courses which were necessary for the certification of teacher-librarian in the state of Georgia. Mrs. Walters is the first black associate professor of library administration as well as the first black professional librarian to head a department in the Ohio State University libraries. She received the Who's Who in Library Service Award in 1965 and the Two Thousand Women of Achievement Award in 1972. Mrs. Walters is married to Vincent Walters. She has two children by a previous marriage, Marjorie McCoy Smith, a physician, and Robert H. McCoy. Address: Ohio State University Library, 1858 Neil Ave., Columbus, OH 43210

Walters, Ronald, educator, is chairman of the department of political science at Howard University. He was born July 20, 1938 in Wichita, Kan. Dr. Walters is a graduate of Fisk University (B.A., history, 1963) and American University (M.A., 1966; Ph.D., 1971 degrees in African studies). Formerly chairman of the department of African and Afro-American studies at Brandeis University (1969–71), he also taught at Georgetown and Syracuse universities. Dr. Walters speaks and writes frequently on education and U.S. foreign and domestic policie , and has published articles in *Current History, The Negro Educational Review, Africa Today* and *Black World*. He is a member of the American Political Science Association, the African Heritage Studies Association, and the National Conference of Black Political Scientists. He and his wife, Patricia Ann, live in Silver Springs, Md. Address: Howard University, Washington DC 20001

Washington, George L., is president and executive director of the College Service Bureau, Inc. in Washington, D.C. The bureau was organized in 1969 to serve as a "Washington office" for the Cooperative College Development Program of UNCF college and the Phelps-Stokes Fund. Born Jan. 17, 1903 in Norfolk, Va., Mr. Washington is a graduate of the Massachusetts Institute of Technology (B.S. and M.S.). He has been dean of engineering and technical instruction at North Carolina Agricultural & Technical State University, dean of the technical education and training division at Tuskegee Institute, assistant to the president of Tuskegee Institute and Howard University, and business manager and chairman of the University Computer Committee at Howard. During World War II, he pioneered the training of blacks as military pilots, was a consultant to the U.S. Air Force in the establishment of Tuskegee Army Air Field and served as general manager of the AAF Primary Flying Training School in Tuskegee. He is married to the former Ruby Evans. Address: 1026 17th St., NW, Suite 809, Washington, DC 20036

Washington, Harold, legislator, is an Illinois state representative from the 26th District (Chicago), serving his fifth term. Born April 15, 1922 in Chicago, Ill., he is a graduate of Roosevelt University (B.A., political science and economics, 1949) in the city and Northwestern University (J.D., 1952) in Evanston, Ill. He is a practicing attorney in the firm of Washington and Washington, founded by his father. A first sergeant in the Air Force Engineers, he spent two years in the South Pacific during World War II. He was an assistant corporation counsel for the city of Chicago for four years and from 1961 to 1964 served as an arbitrator with the Illinois Industrial Commission. He is a member of the Cook County, the Illinois and the National Bar Association. He is single. Address: Illinois General Assembly, Springfield, IL 62706

Walter Washington

Washington, Walter, educator and administrator, is president of Alcorn A & M College in Lorman, Miss. Born July 13, 1923 in Hazlehurst, Miss., he is a graduate of Tougaloo College (B.A.), Indiana University (M.A.) and the University of Southern Mississippi (D.Ed.). He also has an education specialist degree from George Peabody College (1958). He was awarded an honorary LL.D. degree by Tougaloo College in 1970. Dr. Washington was successful in getting the state legislature to appropriate $12 million in 1971 for the general improvement of Alcorn, the oldest land-grant school in the nation; it was founded in 1871. He is a member of the Mississippi Advisory Commission on Vocational Education, the state board of directors of the Boy Scouts of America and Phi Delta Kappa, and is a vice chairman of the secondary commission of the Southern Association of Colleges and Schools. He is general president of Alpha Phi Alpha fraternity, and is a member of the Mississippi Teachers Association and the National Alumni Council of the United Negro College Fund. He is married to the former Carolyn Carter. Address: Alcorn A&M College, Lorman, MS 39096

Walter E. Washington

Washington, Walter E., city official, is mayor of Washington, D.C. Born April 15, 1915 in Dawson, Ga., he is a graduate of Howard University (A.B., 1938; LL.B., 1948). After graduating from college, he became a junior aide with the National Capital Housing Authority and took night law courses at Howard. He was admitted to the District of Columbia Bar in 1948 and was admitted to practice before the U.S. Supreme Court in 1949. He was appointed executive director of the National Capital Housing Authority by President John F. Kennedy in 1961, and was appointed chairman of the New York City Housing Authority by Mayor John V. Lindsay in 1966. He was appointed mayor of Washington, D. C. by President Lyndon B. Johnson in 1967. Among his many advisory posts and organizational affiliations, he is a member of the advisory board of the U.S. Conference of Mayors, vice chairman of the National League of Cities, and a trustee of the John F. Kennedy Center for the Performing Arts. He has received numerous honors and awards from organizations and universities. He and his wife, Bennetta, have a daughter, Mrs. Bennetta Jules-Rossette). Address: 14th and E Sts., NW, Washington DC 20004 **See article on Walter E. Washington in Volume II**

Levi Watkins

Watkins, Levi, educator, is president of Alabama State University in Montgomery, Ala. He was born in Montgomery, Ky. Dr. Watkins is a graduate of Tennessee A&I College (B.S.) and Northwestern University (M.A.). He has an honorary degree from Arkansas Baptist College (LL.D.). Prior to accepting his present position, Dr. Watkins was an administrative assistant to the president of Alabama State College. In 1969, the college was elevated to university status and the name was changed to Alabama State University. He was founder and president of Owen College at Memphis, Tenn. (1953–59). Dr. Watkins is a vice president of the Council of University Presidents (Alabama Commission on Higher Education); a member of the Alabama Advisory Committee of Alabama Higher Education Facilities Commission; a member of the Alabama Education Association and a member of the Advisory Board on Health and Environmental Quality. He has many other professional and civic affiliations. He and his wife, Lillian, have six children, among them a Ph.D., a cardiac surgeon, an attorney, a teacher, an airline revenue controller and a medical student. Address: Alabama State University, Montgomery, AL 36101

Barbara M. Watson

André Watts

Rodney S. Wead

Watson, Barbara M., federal official, is administrator of the Bureau of Security and Consular Affairs of the U.S. State Department in Washington, D.C. Born Nov. 5, 1918 in New York, N.Y., she is a graduate of Barnard College (A.B., 1943) and New York Law School (LL.B., 1962). She was an interviewer for the United Seamen's Service in New York City (1943–46), operated a successful modeling school (1946–56), was an attorney with the New York City Board of Statutory Review (1962–63), an assistant attorney in the law department of the Office of the Corporation Counsel of the City of New York (1963–64), and executive director of the New York City Commission to the United Nations (1964–66). She began her State Department career in 1966 as a special assistant to the U.S. deputy undersecretary of state for administration. She became deputy administrator of the Bureau of Security and Consular Affairs in 1966, acting administrator in 1967, and was appointed administrator in 1968. She is a member of the board of directors of the United Mutual Life Insurance Co., is an ex officio member of the women's advisory board of the Office of Economic Opportunity, and is active in a number of other professional and women's organizations. Address: U.S. Department of State, Washington, DC 20520 **See article on Barbara M. Watson in Volume II**

Watts, André, concert pianist, has been called "an artist who transcends all known limits of virtuosity." Born June 20, 1946 in Nuremberg, Germany, he studied at Peabody Institute in Baltimore, Md. and at the Philadelphia (Pa.) Music Academy. In 1962, at age 16, he performed on conductor Leonard Bernstein's "Young People's Concerts" television show. Three weeks later, Mr. Bernstein asked him to substitute as guest artist with the New York Philharmonic for Canadian pianist Glenn Gould, who was ill. Young André's flawless rendition of Liszt's *Concerto No. 1 in E-Flat Major* drew the season's wildest ovation and made the front page of *The New York Times.* Mr. Watts performs as soloist with major U.S. and European orchestras and appears on concert tours around the world. He is single. Address: c/o Judd Concert Artists, 127 W. 69th St., New York, NY 10023 **See article on André Watts in Volume II**

Wead, Rodney Sam, administrator, is executive director of the United Methodist Community Center (Wesley House) in Omaha, Neb. He is also director of Urban Business Development Center, a project (supported by a 1972 Office of Minority Business Enterprise grant) for development and funding of various community businesses. He is also chairman of the board and president of Reconciliation, Inc., which operates Omaha radio station KOWH AM-FM, the only black community-owned and operated radio station in the United States. With $1,000 from the Nebraska Methodist Conference, he raised $500,000 for purchase of the radio station. He has also established a community credit union, a legal defense fund, a scholarship program for minority students, an Afro-American library, a black television program, a $170,000 urban-rural crisis fund for education and economic development for blacks, Chicanos and Indians of the state (which has produced $1.5 million in business assets), a black newspaper and a black community bank. Mr. Wead was named Omaha's Man of the Year for 1971 by the *Omaha Sun* newspapers. Born June 28, 1935 in Omaha, he is a graduate of Dana College (B.S., education, 1957). He and his wife, Angeline, have four children: Denise, Eugene, Lineve and Melissa. Address: 2001 N. 35th St., Omaha, NB 68111

George L.-P. Weaver

Robert C. Weaver

Albert S. Webb

Weaver, George Leon-Paul, a labor consultant, is the special assistant to the director-general of the International Labor Organization, Geneva, Switzerland (United Nations Agency). He is based in Washington, D.C. He also fulfills special assignments for the director-general and he has been with the organization since September, 1969. Born May 18, 1912 in Pittsburgh, Pa., he received his education at Roosevelt University (1940–42), Howard University Law School (1942–43) and Howard University (1962). He was a member of the CIO War Relief Commission (1941–42), assistant to the secretary-treasurer of CIO (1942–55), executive secretary of AFL-CIO (1955–58), special assistant to the Secretary of Labor (1961), assistant secretary of Labor International Affairs (1961-69), and finally appointed to his current position on Sept. 1, 1969. He is a board member of the United Negro College Fund. He and his wife, Mary, live in Washington, D.C. Address: 3819 26th St., NE, Washington, DC 20018

Weaver, Robert C., economist and educator, has been a professor of urban affairs at Hunter College in New York City since January, 1969. He is the former secretary of the U.S. Department of Housing and Urban Development and was the first black man ever to hold a cabinet position in the United States government. He was born Dec. 29, 1907 in Washington, D. C. and was educated at Harvard College (B.S., 1929) and Harvard University (M.A., 1931; Ph.D., 1934). Mr. Weaver entered government in 1933 and continued to serve in Washington for 10 years working in housing and labor recruitment and training. During that time, he held many advisory and administrative positions through World War II. In 1944–45, he was executive secretary to the Mayor's Committee on Race Relations in Chicago. He has since held various positions in the education field on the East coast. He is the author of four books, and holds thirty honorary degrees from institutions throughout the nation. He and his wife, Ella, live in New York City. Address: 215 E. 68th St., New York, NY 10021

Webb, Albert S., business official, is executive vice president and secretary of American Federal Savings & Loan Association of Greensboro, N.C. Born May 5, 1930 in Greensboro, Ala., he is a graduate of Hampton Institute (B.S.) and the Graduate School of Savings and Loan at Indiana University. When Mr. Webb joined American Federal in 1959 (when it opened), the firm's assets were $350,000. In 1973 its assets were more than $47 million. Previously, he was supervisor of the Statistics, Issue and Underwriting Department at Dunbar Life Insurance Co. in Cleveland, Ohio. He is the only black on the seven-member North Carolina Commission of Correction. He is also a member of the Trends and Economic Policy Committee of the U. S. Savings and Loan League, a member of the American Savings and Loan Institute, the Greensboro Citizens Association and a number of other civic groups. He is single. Address: 701 E. Market St., Greensboro, NC 27401

James O. Webb

Kenneth L. Webster

Robert Wedgeworth Jr.

Webb, James O., business executive, is a vice president of Blue Cross/Blue Shield in Chicago, Ill. As administrator of product and project management, he is responsible for the development and implementation of all new health insurance products and other related administrative procedures and control of corporate product portfolio. He is also chairman of the Home Investments Fund, which provides financial assistance to black families buying homes in "open housing" areas. He was born Nov. 25, 1931 in Cleveland, Ohio. Mr. Webb studied business administration at Morehouse College (B.A., 1953) and actuarial science at the University of Michigan (M.A., 1957). He has served in an actuarial capacity in New York with Mutual of New York and in Chicago with Supreme Life Insurance Company of America, where he held the position of vice president and actuary. Mr. Webb was appointed to the Glencoe (Ill.) School Board in 1970. He was appointed by Governor Richard Ogilvie to the Illinois Commission on Urban Area Government in 1970. He is a member of the American Academy of Actuaries, the Chicago Actuary Club and the Association for Corporate Growth. A former member of the Glencoe Human Relations Committee, he and his wife, Frankie L., have two daughters, Pamela and Lisa. Address: Blue Cross/Blue Shield, Hospital Service Corporation, 233 N. Michigan Ave., Chicago, IL 60601

Webster, Kenneth L., legislator and administrator, is a member of the Maryland House of Delegates, and is one of the first of three black legislators to be elected from his district as a House member for the Fifth Legislative District of Baltimore, Md. He is also community relations assistant for the Model Cities Housing Development. Mr. Webster was born April 29, 1935 in Baltimore, Md. After the completion of his enlistment as a member of the Strategic Air Command team, he attended Morgan State College (Baltimore, 1958-61) majoring in political science and history. He has lectured at Loyola College and Community College of Baltimore. His organizational affiliations include memberships in the Black United Front, the Baltimore Advisory Council of Vocational Education, and the New Democratic Coalition of Maryland. He and his wife, Phoebe, have no children. Address: 100 St. Paul St., Baltimore, MD 21202

Wedgeworth, Robert Jr., administrator, is executive director of the American Library Association in Chicago, Ill. Born July 31, 1937 in Ennis, Tex., he is a graduate of Wabash College (B.A., English literature) and the University of Illinois (M.S., library science). He is a doctoral candidate and was assistant professor at Rutgers University Graduate School of Library Service. He has studied Spanish literature at Washington University. Before assuming his present position, he was editor of *Library Resources and Technical Services*, an official ALA journal. He was a cataloger at the Kansas City Public Library (1961–62); assistant librarian (1962–63) and acting head librarian (1963–64) at Park College in Parkville, Mo.; head librarian of Meramec Community College in Kirkwood, Mo. (1964–66); assistant chief order librarian of the Brown University Library (1966–69), and staff member of Library 21 at the Seattle World's Fair (1962). He is a member of the American Society of Information Science. He has written scholarly articles for the *Library Journal* and the *Wilson Library Bulletin*. He and his wife, Chung Kyun, live in Chicago. Address: American Library Association, 50 E. Huron St., Chicago, IL 60611

Leonard 12X Weir

Weir, Leonard 12X, patrolman, is a policeman in New York, N.Y., and is president of the National Society of Afro-American Policemen. He founded the society in 1964 and has helped organize black policemen in other cities. Born Feb. 28, 1931 in New York City, he is a member of the Nation of Islam and is owner of Lenny's Books 'n' Things, a store which sells books and natural foods. A policeman since 1959, he has been a uniformed patrolman in Harlem and Brooklyn, an undercover officer for the Narcotics Bureau, an undercover investigator in the district attorney's office, and community relations consultant to the assistant chief of police and the Department of Justice. He is now assigned to the Internal Affairs Division; he investigates complaints of police corruption. He has appeared on numerous radio and television shows to discuss his work on behalf of black policemen. He and his wife, Teresa 14X, have seven children: Leonard, Roland, Ronald, Rosemarie, John, Larry and Don. Address: 240 Centre St., New York, NY 10014.

Verda F. Welcome

Welcome, Verda F., legislator, is state senator of the Fourth Legislative District in Baltimore, Md. Mrs. Welcome was born in Lake Lure, N.C. and graduated from Morgan State College (B.S., 1936) and New York University (M.A., 1943). Honorary degrees have been conferred on her from Howard University (J.D., 1968), and the University of Maryland (Doctor of Social Sciences, 1970). She was elected state senator (1963) becoming the first woman and the first black to be so honored. Mrs. Welcome's list of legislative accomplishments is long and includes the introduction and implementation of a bill requiring equal pay for equal work; the sponsoring of the "Miscegenation Bill" repealing the banning of interracial marriage (1967), and the sponsoring of the bill to prohibit racial discrimination in the sale of new housing (1968). She and her husband, Dr. Henry C., a surgeon, have a daughter, Mary Mercer. Address: 3423 Holmes Ave., Baltimore, MD 21217

Frances Cress Welsing, M.D.

Welsing, Frances Cress, M.D., child psychiatrist, is an assistant professor of pediatrics at Freedmen's Hospital and Howard University School of Medicine in Washington, D.C. Born March 18, 1935 in Chicago, Ill., she is a graduate of Antioch College and Howard University School of Medicine (M.D.) Dr. Welsing is a third generation physician in her family; both her grandfather, Dr. Henry Clay Cress, and her father, Dr. Henry N. Cress, were physicians. She is author of *The Cress Theory of Color-Confrontation and Racism.* Dr. Welsing is a member of the National Medical Association, the American Medical Association and the American Psychiatric Association. She is divorced. Address: Freedmen's Hospital, Department of Pediatrics, Washington, DC 20001

Charles H. Wesley

Wesley, Charles H., educator, is executive director emeritus of the Association for the Study of African-American Life and History, headquartered in Washington, D.C. He retired in 1972. He has also served as president of Wilberforce University (1942–47) and Central State College (1942–65). Born Dec. 2, 1891 in Louisville, Ky., he earned degrees from Fisk University (B.A., 1911), Yale University (M.A., 1913) and Harvard University (Ph.D., 1925). Author of twenty books and editor of the ten-volume *International Library on Negro Life and History,* Dr. Wesley holds honorary degrees from nine colleges and universities. He is a presiding elder of the AME Church, a member of the American Historical Association, the National Council of Social Studies, the National Education Association, the American Association of School Administrators, the American Association of University Professors and other learned societies. He was president of Alpha Phi Alpha fraternity (1931–40). He is a widower and has a daughter, Mrs. Charlotte Hollomon. Address: 1824 Taylor St., NW, Washington, DC 20011

Logan H. Westbrooks

Kim Weston

Clifton R. Wharton Jr.

Westbrooks, Logan H., business executive, is director of special markets for Columbia Records Co. Born Aug. 28, 1937 in Memphis, Tenn., he attended LeMoyne College in Memphis for two years and graduated from Lincoln University in Missouri (B.A.). As director of special markets at Columbia, he provided special marketing direction in all aspects of black products—including advertising, selling and promotion—for all black productions on Columbia, Epic and Custom labels. Mr. Westbrooks entered the record industry in 1965 as a tape specialist with RCA Distributing Corp. in Des Plaines, Ill. He joined Capitol Records Distributing Corp. in 1967 and became administrative assistant to the vice president for R&B marketing for that company. He served as director of national promotion for Mercury Records in Chicago before assuming his present position. He and his wife, Geraldine, have a daughter, Babette. Address: 51 W. 52nd St., New York, NY 10023

Weston, Kim, entertainer, is a singer and actress. Born Dec. 20, 1939 in Detroit, Mich., she began singing in the choir of her church (where her father was the minister) and later with a gospel group, the Wright Specials. In 1961, she went to Motown Records and recorded a string of near-hits, including "Love Me All the Way," "Just Loving You," and "It Takes Two." The latter was a duet with singer Marvin Gaye. She then went to New York to study acting at the Herbert Berghof studio. The training led to a starring role in the road-show company of *Hallelujah, Baby!* And to other roles on Broadway. In 1967, she left Motown, was associated briefly with MGM Records, then signed with Stax Records. She has gained national popularity for her recording of "Lift Ev'ry Voice And Sing," known as the "black National Anthem." She is a life member of the National Council of Negro Women, and is a member of SCLC and Operation PUSH. Address: Stax Records, 98 N. Avalon Ave., Memphis, TN 38104

Wharton, Clifton Reginald Jr., educator and administrator, in 1970 became the first black president in the 114-year history of Michigan State University in East Lansing, Mich. The university's 1972–73 budget was about $200 million, and it had 41,500 students and 8,500 faculty members and other employees. Born Sept. 13, 1926 in Boston, Mass., Dr. Wharton is a graduate of Harvard University (B.A., history, 1947), Johns Hopkins University (M.A., international studies, 1948) and the University of Chicago (M.A., economics, 1956; Ph.D., economics, 1958). He is a specialist in the economic and human problems of agricultural development, and has worked for both private and U.S. government agencies in Latin America and Asia. He is a member of several boards of directors, including those of Ford Motor Co., Burroughs Corp. and Equitable Life Assurance Society. He and his wife, Dolores, have two sons, Clifton III and Bruce. Address: President's Office, Michigan State University, East Lansing, MI 48823 **See article on Clifton R. Wharton Jr. in Volume II**

Wheeler, John H., banker, is president of the black-owned Merchants and Farmers Bank in Durham, N. C. Born Jan. 1, 1908 in Kittrell, N. C., Mr. Wheeler holds degrees from Morehouse College (A.B., 1929) and North Carolina Central University (LL.B., 1947). He has received honorary degrees from colleges and universities including Duke University, Shaw University and Tuskegee Institute. One of the most influential black men in the South, he has long been firmly committed to combatting racial discrimination in his state while also acting as trusted liaison between the black and white communities. Mr. Wheeler has been involved in a broad range of activities. Most recently, as president of the Low Income Housing Development Corporation of North Carolina, he was instrumental in the development of 1,500 units of low income housing in the state. Mr. Wheeler is a member of several boards of directors including those of Morehouse College, Atlanta University (chairman), Southern Regional Council, Lincoln Hospital, the Durham Committee on Negro Affairs and the National Corporation for Housing Partnerships. Mr. Wheeler and his wife, Selena, have two children, Mrs. Julia W. Taylor and Warren. Address: P. O. Box 1932, Durham, NC 27702

Wheeler, Lloyd G., executive, is senior vice president and secretary of Supreme Life Insurance Company of America, headquartered in Chicago, Ill. and is a member of its board of directors and its executive committee. He has been with the company since 1923. Born Aug. 26, 1907 in St. Joseph, Mo., he is a graduate of the University of Illinois (B.S., insurance, 1932) and has studied at John Marshall Law School in Chicago and at Northwestern University. He is a former board member of the Chicago chapter of the American Red Cross and the Juvenile Institute of Chicago, and is a former executive vice president of the National Insurance Association. In 1972, he was named Man of the Year by his Supreme Life colleagues. He and his wife, Margaret, live in Chicago. Address: 3501 S. Dr. Martin Luther King Jr. Dr., Chicago, IL 60616

White, Charles Wilbert, artist, is represented in some of America's most prestigious museum and private collections. Born April 2, 1918 in Chicago, Ill., he studied at The Art Institute of Chicago as an Institute Scholar (1937), the Art Students League in New York, N.Y. (1942), the Taller de Grafica and Esmeralda School of Painting and Sculpture in Mexico City, Mexico (1947). He has honorary Doctor of Art and L.H.D. degrees from Columbia College in Chicago (1969). He was an instructor at the South Side Community Art Center in Chicago (1939–40), artist-in-residence at Howard University (1945), instructor at the Workship School of Art in New York City (1950–53) and at the Otis Art Institute in Los Angeles, Cal. (1965). He has exhibited in numerous group shows in the U.S. and abroad, and has had a number of one-man shows. He is a member of the executive board of the Black Academy of Arts and Letters and the National Center for Afro-American Artists. He has won numerous awards and has contributed to a number of art books and publications. He and his wife, Frances, have two children, Jessica and Ian. Address: Heritage Gallery, 718 N. La Cienega Blvd., Los Angeles, CA 90069

John H. Wheeler

Lloyd G. Wheeler

Charles W. White

Judge William S. White

Matthew J. Whitehead II

Judge Willie Whiting

White, William Sylvester, jurist, is presiding judge of the nation's oldest juvenile court system, the Cook County Juvenile Court in Chicago, Ill. He was appointed as presiding judge in 1968 after four years on the bench—two as a Circuit Court judge (he was elected in 1964) and two years in the court's Law-Jury division. Some 25,000 young persons—delinquents, children in need of supervision, dependent children, neglected children, etc.—each year are brought to the attention of the judges and other court officials supervised by Judge White. Born July 27, 1914 in Chicago, he is a graduate of the University of Chicago (A.B. 1935; J.D., 1937). He practiced law for two years before being appointed an assistant U.S. attorney in 1939—a position he held for 16 years except 1943–46 when he was in the U.S. Navy. (He was one of the first 12 blacks to be commissioned as navy officers; he was a lieutenant junior grade.) He was assistant state's attorney (1955–56), attorney for the Chicago department of investigation (1957–61), and director of the Illinois Department of Registration and Education (1961–64). He once served as chairman of the Illinois Board of vocational Education and Rehabilitation. He is a member of various bar associations and civic groups, and has received a number of awards during his professional career. He and his wife, George Vivian, have twin daughters, Marilyn and Carolyn. Address: 2240 W. Roosevelt Rd., Chicago, IL 60608

Whitehead, Matthew J. II, attorney, is midwestern regional counsel at International Business Machines Corp. in Chicago, Ill. He provides legal counsel to IBM's Data Processing Division management for the midwestern third of the U.S. Since joining the corporation in 1966, Mr. Whitehead has been plant counsel at IBM's Brooklyn plant and senior attorney of its Service Bureau Corp. He accepted his present position in 1970. Born Feb. 11, 1940 in Wilson, N.C., he has degrees from Tufts University (B.A., 1962) and Howard University (LL.B., 1965). He is a member of the American, National and New York Bar associations, Illinois State Chamber of Commerce, NAACP, Urban League and Kappa Alpha Psi fraternity. He and his wife, Adrienne, have a son, Matthew J. III. Address: One IBM Plaza, Chicago, IL 60611

Whiting, Willie, jurist, is associate judge of the Circuit Court of Cook County, Ill. Born in Chicago, she attended Fisk University, Roosevelt University and John Marshall Law School (LL.B., 1950). Prior to assuming her present post in 1970, she was a magistrate of the Circuit Court. Admitted to the Illinois Bar in 1951, she was a law clerk and attorney in the George J. Harkness law firm (1950–55). She was a caseworker and resources consultant for the Cook County Department of Public Welfare, (1955–56); executive secretary of the Chicago branch of the NAACP (1957–59), assistant corporation counsel of the City of Chicago (1959–61), an assistant Cook County state's attorney (1961–65) and an assistant U.S. attorney assigned to criminal litigation (1965–66). Judge Whiting is a member of the Cook County, National and Women's bar associations, the advisory board of the Midwest Community Council, the American Veterans Committee and the 2nd Ward (Chicago) Regular Democratic Organization. She is a member of the board of the Chicago branch of the NAACP, a past president of the Professional Women's Club and a resident agent of Zeta Phi Beta sorority. She is single. Address: Cook County Circuit Court, Civic Center, Chicago, IL 60601

Joseph C. Wiggins, M.D.

Lawrence D. Wilder

Henry T. Wilfong

Rt. Rev. W. R. Wilkes

Wiggins, Joseph C., M.D., physician, is chief of the Department of General Medicine at Forest City Hospital in Cleveland, Ohio and is in the private practice of medicine. Born Sept. 19, 1909 in Petersburg, Va., he is a graduate of Fisk University (B.A., 1932) and Meharry Medical College (M.D., 1940). He has taken postgraduate courses at Case Western Reverve University and Ohio State University. He was a three-time All-American football halfback at Fisk (he was called "Jumping Joe" Wiggins) and played professional baseball (under the name "Jody Chevalier") with the Baltimore Black Sox and the New York Black Yankees (1929–32). He is a charter member and former director of the Cleveland Academy of General Medicine, and is a member of a number of medical and civic organizations. He is assistant secretary, member of the board of directors and member of the executive committee of Supreme Life Insurance Co. of America. He is a co-founder of the Quincy Savings & Loan Co. of Cleveland and serves as vice president (former president) and member of its board of directors. He is a trustee and member of the executive committee of Fisk University, a member of the Cleveland Growth Association, the Cleveland Citizens League, the Cleveland Council on World Affairs and Omega Psi Phi. He formerly published the *Cleveland Courier* newspaper. He and his wife, Constance, have a daughter, Jolynn. Address: 5707 Woodland Ave., Cleveland, OH 44104

Wilder, Lawrence Douglas, legislator, is the only black state senator in Virginia. Born Jan 17, 1931 in Richmond, Va., he attended Virginia Union University (B.S., chemistry, 1951) and the Howard University School of Law (J.D., 1959). In addition to duties in the state legislature, he maintains a private law practice, specializing in criminal and personal injury law. He was a floor leader for the Virginia open housing bill, sickle cell anemia bill, drug paraphernalia bill and has served as chairman of the Virginia Legislative Council Sub-Committee. He and his wife, Eunice, have three children: Lynn, Lawrence Jr. and Loren. Address: 3020 P St., Richmond, VA 23222

Wilfong, Henry T., accounting executive, is managing partner of Wilfong, Morris & Co. in Los Angeles, Calif. Born Feb. 22, 1933 in Ingals, Ark., he has degrees from UCLA (B.S., M.S.). The firm audits most of the major community action anti-poverty agencies throughout California, the Oakland school district (with funding in excess of $80 million per year) and the city of Berkeley. Before joining the company, Mr. Wilfong was a corporation tax auditor for the state of California. He is president and organizer of the National Association of Minority CPA (Certified Public Accountants) firms and holds memberships in the California Society and American Institute of CPA's. He and his wife, Aline, have two children, Bernetta and Brian. Address: 3700 Wilshire Blvd., Suite 520, Los Angeles, CA 90010

Wilkes, The Right Reverend William R., clergyman, has been bishop of the 13th Episcopal District (Kentucky and Tennessee) of the AME Church since 1972. Previously, he was bishop of the Third District, which included Wilberforce University where he supervised large amounts of new construction on the campus. He has also presided over the 16th, 12th and 6th districts. Born April 10, 1902 in Eatonton, Ga., he is a graduate of Morris Brown College (A.B.) and attended Garrett Theological Seminary and Northwestern University. He has an honorary D.D. degree from Morris Brown and honorary D.D. and LL.D. degrees from several other schools. He and his wife, Nettie Julia, have two sons, William and Alfred. Address: 1002 Kirkwood Ave., Nashville, TN 37204

Roy Wilkins

Frederick D. Wilkinson Jr.

Rev. A. Cecil Williams

Wilkins, Roy, organization administrator, is the executive director of the NAACP. He was born Aug. 30, 1901 in St. Louis, Mo. He is a graduate of the University of Minnesota (A.B., 1923) and holds honorary doctorates from more than 18 schools, including Atlanta, Howard, Boston and Notre Dame universities, and Tuskegee Institute. Active in civil rights most of his life, Mr. Wilkins was a delegate to the first national NAACP convention in Kansas City, Mo. in 1923. He was then the managing editor of the *Kansas City Call*, a weekly newspaper. In 1931, he joined the national staff of the NAACP as assistant secretary and, while filling that position, was also (1934–49) editor of the *Crisis*, the official organ of the NAACP. Early in his career with the NAACP, he spent four weeks hitchhiking in Mississippi and Louisiana as a laborer so that he could investigate the treatment of blacks on army-supervised flood control projects. His reports on this situation led to reforms instituted by President Hoover. He is the author of numerous articles which have appeared in leading newspapers and magazines. He also has a syndicated column which appears in daily newspapers across the country and a bi-weekly column with the *New York Amsterdam News*. He is the recipient of the Spingarn Medal (1964), Freedom House Award (1967), Theodore Roosevelt Distinguished Service Medal (1968), the Medal of Freedom (1969) and numerous other awards and citations. He is married to the former Aminda Badeau. Address: NAACP, 1790 Broadway, New York, NY 10019

Wilkinson, Frederick D. Jr., business executive, is vice president of R. H. Macy, Inc., a department store chain in New York, N.Y., and is manager of the Macy's store in Jamaica, N.Y. Born Jan. 25, 1921 in Washington, D.C., he is a graduate of Howard University (A.B., 1942) and Harvard University (M.B.A., 1948). While in the U.S. Army (1942–46), he was a trial judge advocate and received a certificate in business law and accounting from the Army University Center of Oahu, Hawaii. He began his career with Macy's in 1948 and held a number of successively more responsible positions before being elected a vice president in 1968. He is a director and member of the executive committee of the Freedom National Bank in Harlem and a trustee of the National Urban League, and is a director or member of numerous other civic groups. He and his wife, Jeane, have two daughters, Sharon and Dayna, and a son, Frederick III. Address: 89–22 165th St., Jamaica, NY 11432 **See article of Frederick D. Wilkinson Jr. in Volume II**

Williams, The Reverend A. Cecil, clergyman, is pastor of the Glide Memorial United Methodist Church in San Francisco, Cal. Born Sept. 22, 1929 in San Angelo, Tex., he received his A.B. degree in sociology from Huston-Tillotson College (1952). He was one of the first five black students to be admitted on a full-time basis to Perkins School of Theology at Southern Methodist University (B.D., 1955). He taught and served as chaplain at Huston-Tillotson College. He pastored St. James Methodist Church in Kansas City, Mo., for three years. During that time, he was also co-chairman for the Congress of Racial Equality. In 1964, he joined the staff of the Glide Foundation's Glide Urban Center in San Francisco to serve as director of community involvement. His wife, Evelyn, a pianist, helps in many of his endeavors. They have two children, Kim and A. Cecil Jr. The Reverend Williams calls his services "celebrations" and gives his official title as "Minister of Involvement and Celebration." Address: Glide Memorial United Methodist Church, 330 Ellis St., San Francisco, CA 94102

Albert W. Williams   Judge David W. Williams   Eddie N. Williams

Williams, Albert W., executive, is chairman of the board of directors of North Carolina Mutual Life Insurance Co. Born July 25, 1902 in Augusta, Ga., he attended the Wharton School of Commerce of the University of Pennsylvania and the University of Illinois. He has an honorary LL.D. degree from Allen University (1958). He has been president and board chairman of Unity Mutual Life Insurance Company, founded in 1928, and Unity Funeral Parlors, Inc. in Chicago, which he still serves as president. He was one of the founders of the Illinois Federal Savings & Loan Association in Chicago, which he serves as president and chairman of the executive committee. He is a member of the executive committee of the Chicago Urban League. He has served four consecutive terms on the Chicago Civil Service Board. He and his wife, Ruth, have two daughters, Mrs. Lillian Ward and Mrs. Barbara Halfacre and a son, Norman. Address: North Carolina Mutual Life Insurance Co., Mutual Plaza, Durham, NC 27701

Williams, David W., jurist, is judge for the Central District of California. Born March 20, 1910 in Atlanta Ga. Judge Williams attended Los Angeles Junior College, UCLA (A.B., 1934) and the University of Southern California Law School (LL.B., 1937). He was elevated to the federal bench in 1969 after 13 years as a judge of the Los Angeles Municipal Court and Los Angeles Superior Court. Judge Williams is a member of the American Bar Association, the American Law Institute, the Los Angeles Bar Association, the American Judicature Society and the Board of Councilors—University of Southern California Law School. He has a number of citations, including the 1958 Russwurm Award presented by the National Association of (Negro) Newspapers for outstanding civic work and the 1969 Citizen of the Year award of the Guardians of the Jewish Home for the Aged, Los Angeles. He and his wife, Ouida, have two sons, David Jr. and Vaughn. Address: U.S. District Court, Los Angeles, CA 90012

Williams, Eddie N., executive, is president of the Joint Center for Political Studies in Washington, D. C. The center is a non-profit, tax exempt organization co-sponsored by Howard University and the Metropolitan Applied Research Center. It is affiliated with the National Black Caucus of Local Elected Officials. Funded by a grant from the Ford Foundation, it provides research, education technical assistance and information for minority elected officials on a non-partisan basis. Before accepting his present position in 1972, Mr. Williams was vice-president for public affairs at the University of Chicago (Ill.). He was also director of the University of Chicago Center for Policy Study. Born August 18, 1932 in Memphis, Tenn., he has a B.S. degree in journalism from the University of Illinois (1954) and has done graduate work in political science at Howard University and Atlanta University. He is a member of the board of directors (and chairman of the Fellowship Committee of the National Drug Abuse Council, and is vice-chairman of the board of trustees of the National Children's Television Workshop. He and his wife, Sallie, have two children, Traci and Larry. Address: 1426 H St., NW, Suite 926, Washington, DC 20005

Williams, Franklin H., administrator, is president of the Phelps-Stokes Fund in New York, N.Y. Born Oct. 22, 1917 in Flushing, N.Y., he is a graduate of Lincoln (Pa.) University (A.B., 1941) and Fordham Law School (J.D., 1945). He was NAACP assistant special counsel (1945–50), NAACP West Coast director (1950–59), assistant attorney general of California (1959–61), African regional director of the Peace Corps (1961–63), U.S. representative to the UN Economic and Social Council (1963–65), U.S. ambassador to Ghana (1965–68) and director of the Urban Center at Columbia University (1968–69). He is a director of the Consolidated Edison Co. in New York, Fordham University, Lincoln University, Carver Federal Savings and Loan Association (in New York), the African Descendants Association Foundation, Praeger-Kavanagh & Waterbury, Inc. (in New York) and several other firms and organizations. He is chairman of the N.Y. State Advisory Committee to the U.S. Commission on Civil Rights, and is president of the African Student Aid Fund. He is active in numerous other groups. He and his wife, Shirley, have two children, Franklin Jr. and Paul. Address: 22 E. 54th St., New York, NY 10022

Williams, Gertrude Johnson, publishing executive, is vice president of Johnson Publishing Co. in Chicago, Ill. The mother of the firm's founder and president, John H. Johnson, she is active in numerous civic and religious groups. She is a member and one of the founders of Emmanuel Baptist Church in Chicago where she serves as general treasurer. Mrs. Williams is also a member of the church's board of trustees, the deaconess board and finance committee. She holds life membership in the Federated Women's Club and the NAACP and is a member of the League of Women Voters. She is a vice president of the Grace Lee Stevens Local Federated Club and has been president for more than three decades of the Pep-It-Up Club. Born Aug. 4, 1891 in Lake Village, Ark., she and her son came to Chicago in 1933 to attend the Century of Progress Exposition. She had planned to stay only two weeks but, believing her son's opportunities would be greater in the northern city, she decided to stay. Mrs. Williams, a widow, lives in Chicago. Address: 820 S. Michigan Ave., Chicago, IL 60605

Williams, Hardy, legislator, is a member of the Pennsylvania legislature (Democrat, Philadelphia). Born April 4, 1931 in Philadelphia, he is a graduate of Pennsylvania State University and the University of Pennsylvania (LL.B.). He was elected in 1970. He is a practicing attorney in Philadelphia and is active in the city's black community. He is a member of Community Legal Services, the Lawyers Committee for Civil Rights, the Philadelphia Council for Community Advancement, and Omega Psi Phi fraternity. He and his wife, Carole, have three children, Lisa, Anthony and Kelly. Address: 5939 Cobbscreek Parkway, Philadelphia, PA 19143

Franklin Hall Williams

Gertrude Johnson Williams

Hardy Williams

Joseph W. Williams Sr.

Kenneth R. Williams

Oscar Spencer Williams

Williams, Joseph W. Sr., business executive, is industrial relations consultant for Loews Hotels and Theatres, Inc. in New York, N.Y. He is responsible for implementation of equal employment policy and represents the company at the highest level of negotiations with federal and city-state agencies. Born July 25, 1921 in Wilmington, N.C., he is a graduate of North Carolina A&I College (B.S., 1940), did graduate work at Boston University (1941-43) and was a student at Bloomberg Criminal Law School. Mr. Williams was an officer with the Boston Police Department (1944-57), a case investigator for the Edward Brooke law firm (1961–63), a community relations specialist and research consultant for Florence Heller Graduate School of Social Studies at Brandeis University (1963-64), and a probation officer with Dorchester Municipal Court in Boston, Mass. (1966-67). He was owner and operator of ALSTA Travel Agency in Boston (1957-60). He is a member of numerous civic and professional organizations and is a past commander of AMVETS Post 128 of Boston. He was appointed as a life companion of the Tuborg League of Denmark by the Lord Mayor of Copenhagen in 1963. He is the author of *Mobility of Minorities Undergoing Urban Renewal,* published by Brandeis University. A widower, he has a son, Joseph Jr. Address: 666 Fifth Ave., New York, NY 10019

Williams, Kenneth Raynor, educator and administrator, is chancellor of Winston-Salem State University in Winston-Salem, N.C. He is the chief executive of the university. He was born Aug. 16, 1912 in Norfolk, Va. He is a graduate of Morehouse College (A.B., 1933) and Boston University (M.A., 1936; S.T.B., 1952; Ph.D., 1961). He received an honorary LL.D. from Wake Forest University in 1962. Prior to becoming chancellor, he taught at Winston-Salem University for 25 years. He is listed in *Who's Who in America*, *Who's Who in The South and Southwest* and *Who's Who In American Colleges and University Administration*. He was chaplain in the United States Army, and honorably discharged with the rank of major. Dr. Williams received from the Danforth Foundation a short-term leave grant and took a two-month tour of sixteen foreign countries and forty cities. He was also awarded the Freedom Foundation Award in 1952. He is a board member of the Association of American Colleges for Teacher Education, Piedmont University Center, Inc., the Urban Academic Affairs Consortium, the Winston-Salem Chamber of Commerce and the Winston-Salem Chapter Rotary Club. He and his wife, Edythe, have three children: Kenneth III, Ronald and Norman. Address: Winston-Salem State University, Winston-Salem, NC 27102

Williams, Oscar Spencer, bank executive, is president of Guaranty Bank & Trust Co. in Chicago, Ill. The bank (March, 1973 assets: $5.2 million) was purchased in 1972 by the Honorable Elijah Muhammad's Nation of Islam. Born Dec. 24, 1937 in Chicago, Ill., he attended evening classes for 11 years at Roosevelt University (B.S., business administration, 1971). Prior to being selected for his present position, he was special assistant to the midwest regional director of the Small Business Administration. He worked to develop minority business opportunities in the six-state region. Mr. Williams was a tax manager at Continental Illinois Bank, a trust administrator at State National Bank of Evanston, Ill., and a commercial loan officer at Chicago's Exchange National Bank. Listed in *Outstanding Young Men* for 1969–70, he has served on the Finance Commission of the Chicago Girl Scouts and as vice chairman of the Illinois Advisory Council to the SBA. Mr. Williams and his wife, Nadine, have two children, Cheryl and Reginald. Address: 6760 S. Stony Island, Chicago, IL 60649

Paul R. Williams

Wallace C. Williams

Walter H. Williams

Williams, Paul R., architect, is president of Paul R. Williams & Associates, an architectural firm that plans homes and commercial buildings. Mr. Williams has designed some 400 houses in California, among them residences for Tyrone Power, Frank Sinatra, Bill Robinson, Betty Grable, Lon Chaney, Julie London and Cary Grant. He has designed several large estates in South America and the Virgin Islands. Born Feb. 18, 1896 in Los Angeles, Calif., Mr. Williams attended the University of Southern California and Beaux Arts Institute of Design and has honorary degrees from Howard, Lincoln and Atlanta universities and Tuskegee Institute. He was appointed to the National Monument Commission by President Calvin Coolidge and the National Housing Advisory Commission by President Dwight Eisenhower. Mr. Williams was associate architect for the planning of the Federal Customs Building in Los Angeles and the Los Angeles Airport. He has planned some 3,000 homes in the United States and South America. He has been a fellow of the American Institute of Architects since 1957. Mr. Williams married to the former Della M. Givens in 1922 and has two daughters, Marilyn (Mrs. Elbert T. Hudson) and Norma (Mrs. Frank Harvey). Address: 3440 Wilshire Blvd., Los Angeles, CA 90010

Williams, Wallace C., economic development executive, is director of the Office of Minority Business Enterprise of the Michigan Department of Commerce in Detroit Mich. His office helps members of minority groups to open, maintain and expand businesses. Mr. Williams holds community meetings on minority economic development and arranges university workshops and training programs for minority entrepreneurs, and works with industry and labor to secure on-the-job training for minority workers. Born Sept. 23, 1921 in Kannapolis, N.C., he studied accounting and law at Pace College (1947–48), economics and English at Columbia University (1948–50), Wayne State University (1969–70), and studied for a degree in urban affairs at the University of Detroit. Before assuming his present position in 1969, he was an employment security executive and a prison fiscal officer. He and his wife, Carrie, live in Detroit. He has two children, Wallace Jr. and Joyce. Address: 1200 Sixth St., Detroit, MI 48226

Williams, Walter H., insurance executive, is president of The Security Life Insurance Company of the South in Jackson, Miss. Born Feb. 19, 1906 in Gurdon, Ark., he has degrees from Clark College (B.S.) and the University of Wisconsin (M.S.) and did graduate study at Columbia University, Northwestern University and Georgia Technical University. In 1930 he moved to Jackson as a biology teacher and coach at Tougaloo College. While attending Clark College, he worked part-time for a black-owned insurance company in Atlanta. Finding no such company in Mississippi, he decided to start his own. With ten other prominent black men, he formed a corporation and in 1938 Security Life received its charter from the State Insurance Commission. The company has grown from assets of $27,000 to assets of well over $1 million. Mr. Williams is president of the Advisory Committee on Public Education, and a member of numerous organizations, including the Jackson Chamber of Commerce, the National Business League, the Jackson Educational Task Force, the Industrial Development Task Force and the Mississippi Industry and Special Service. He and his wife, Nellie, have three children: Walter, Byron and Ruth Marie. Address: 1328 Lynch St., Jackson, MS 39205

Charles V. Willie

Charles Z. Wilson

Clerow (Flip) Wilson

Willie, Charles V., educator, is vice president for student affairs at Syracuse University in New York. He directs and supervises the work of the Office of Student Affairs which serves some 15,000 students. He is also a professor of sociology. He was chairman of the sociology department (1967-71). Born Oct. 8, 1927 in Dallas, Tex., he has degrees from Morehouse College (B.A., sociology, 1948), Atlanta University (M.A., sociology, 1949) and Syracuse University (Ph.D., sociology, 1957), and was a research training fellow of the National Opinion Research Center at the University of Chicago (1956). He is a Fellow of the American Sociological Association, and is a member of many professional and community organizations, including the American Public Health Association and the Social Science Research Council. He is vice president of the House of Deputies of the Episcopal Church. He has an honorary L.H.D. degree from Berkeley Divinity School of Yale University (1972). He is a member of Phi Beta Kappa, Alpha Kappa Delta and Theta Beta Chi. He is the author of *Church Action in the World* (1969), and *The Family Life of Black People* (1970), and is co-author of *Black Students at White Colleges* (1972). He is a co-editor of *Racism and Mental Health* (1972) and has a book in progress, *Affluent, Marginal and Poor Black Families*. He has contributed chapters to 10 other books and has written numerous monographs and articles for professional journals and religious and public affairs magazines. He and his wife, Mary Sue, have three children: Sarah, Martin and James. Address: 306 Steele Hall, Syracuse University, Syracuse, NY 13201

Wilson, Charles Z., educator, is the vice chancellor of academic programs at UCLA. Born April 21, 1929 in Greenville, Miss., he has degrees from the University of Illinois (B.S., economics and business, 1952, and Ph.D., economics and statistics, 1956) and has taken postgraduate studies. Before appointment to his present position in 1970, he was a research assistant, economic analyst, lecturer and professor. He is a member of the President's Advisory Council on Minority Business Enterprise and chairman of the Education Committee; a consultant to the Economic Ph.D. Program Development at Howard in Washington, D.C.; on the executive committee of the Interracial Council for Business Opportunity and a member of numerous other professional, governmental and civic organizations. Mr. Wilson teaches and does research in economic theory, managerial economics, statistical decision and organizational theory, business policy, corporate finance and educational planning. In these areas, he is the author of articles, papers and reviews that have been published in leading business and educational journals. He and his wife, Doris Jean, have four children: Charles, Joyce, Joanne and Gary. Address: 405 Hilgard Ave., Los Angeles, CA 90024.

Wilson, Flip (Clerow), entertainer, is a world-famous comedian and the star of his own weekly television segment, "The Flip Wilson Show." Born in 1933 in Jersey City, N.J., he began his career as a night club comic at the Manor Plaza Hotel in San Francisco (1954). Before assuming his present stature in 1970, he appeared on numerous television shows, including the "Johnny Carson," "Ed Sullivan," "Mike Douglas," "Merv Griffin" and "Today" shows. He has recorded several comedy albums, including *Cowboys and Colored People* (1967), *Flippin'* (1968), and *Flip Wilson, You Devil You* (1968). He has received numerous honors, including the 1971 "Grammy" award for Best Comedy Record. He is divorced and has four children. Address: c/o National Broadcasting Company, 3000 West Alameda, Burbank, CA 90205 *See article on Flip Wilson in Volume II*

John Wilson

Judge Kenneth E. Wilson

Rev. Mannie L. Wilson

Mary Wilson

Wilson, John, artist, is associate professor in the fine arts department of Boston University. Born April 14, 1922 in Boston, Mass., he is a graduate of Tufts University (B.S., 1947). He has studied at Fernand Leger's School in Paris France, 1949; Institute Politecnico, Mexico City, 1952; Esmeralda School of Art, Mexico City, 1952, and Escuela de las Artes del Libro, Mexico City, 1954–55. Mr. Wilson taught anatomy at Pratt Institute and art in the New York Public Schools before accepting his present position at Boston University in 1964. He has received numerous awards for his work in national exhibitions, among them seven first and two second prizes awarded by Atlanta University's national annual exhibit of John Hope Awards. His work is owned by Smith College Museum of Art; Boston Public Library; Museum of Modern Art; Atlanta University; Carnegie Institute, Bezalel Museum, Israel; Howard University, and the Department of Fine Arts of the French government. He is listed in *Who's Who in American Art*. He and his wife, Julia, have three children: Rebecca, Roy and Erica. Address: 44 Harris St., Brookline, MA 02146

Wilson, Kenneth Emerson, jurist, is a judge of the Circuit Court of Cook County (Chicago), Ill. Born Sept. 24, 1919 in Tacoma, Wash., he is a graduate of Hampton Institute (B.S., social studies, 1942) and the University of Chicago Law School (J.D., 1948). He was a Cook County Commissioner (1964–68), an assistant attorney general of Illinois and assistant states attorney for Cook County (1951–55); and a member of the Illinois House of Representatives (1955–64). During World War II he served four years in the U.S. Army Corps of Engineers in England, France and Germany. He is a member of the American Bar Association and the judicial council of the National Bar Association, Alpha Phi Alpha, and trustee board of the Church of the Good Shepherd. He and his wife, Orestes, have a daughter, Kay Michelle. Address: Circuit Court of Cook County, Civic Center, Chicago, IL 60602

Wilson, The Reverend Mannie L., clergyman, is pastor of the Convent Avenue Baptist Church in New York City. Born in O'Brien, Fla., The Reverend Wilson attended Roger Williams University and American Baptist Theological Seminary in Nashville. He has an honorary degree from Benedict College (D. D.). An outstanding minister, the Reverend Wilson preached a sermon at the White House at the request of President Richard M. Nixon on February 1, 1970. He has many affiliations, including chairman of the board of council of Churches of the City of New York and member of the executive committee of the Southern Christian Leadership Conference. He is president of the board of trustees of Knickerbocker Hospital in New York City and a member of the board of trustees of Union Theological Seminary in New York. The Reverend Wilson is a recipient of many honors including the Silver Beaver Award of the Boy Scouts of America and Man of the Year for the Harlem Branch YMCA. He and his wife, Bettie, have two children: Mrs. Ruth C. Witherspoon and Mrs. Alicia C. Petersen. Address: 420 W. 145th St., New York, NY 10031

Wilson, Mary, entertainer, is the only original member still appearing with the popular Supremes singing group. Born March 8, 1944 in Greenfield, Miss., she was educated in the public schools of Detroit. She sang in her church choir and in her high school glee club before beginning her professional career. In 1959, she became a member of the Supremes, along with Florence Ballard and Diana Ross. The group skyrocketed to international fame through their recordings on the Motown record label and through personal appearances in theatres, concert halls, night clubs and television. She has a son, Willie. Address: Motown Record Corp., 6464 Sunset Blvd., Hollywood, CA 90028

Wade Wilson

LeRoy Winbush

Stevie Wonder

Wilson, Wade, educator and administrator, is president of Cheyney State College in Cheyney, Pa. He is responsible for planning, directing and coordinating all the activities of the college. He also administers a broad program for the education and training of teachers and liberal arts students as well as business administration and the allied health fields. Dr. Wilson was born July 29, 1914 in Birmingham, Ala. He has degrees from Cheyney State College (B.A., 1936), Pennsylvania State University (M.A., 1937), New York University (Ph.D., 1954). Dr. Wilson has written numerous articles dealing with industrial arts education and engineering and with professional education in general. He is co-author of a training manual, *Workshop for the Maintenance Engineering Student*, for the U.S. Air Corps Technical School at Chanute Field, Ill. He is a member of the National Education Association and Educational Facilities Corporation. He is also past president of the Pennsylvania State Education Association, and the Cheyney Education Association. He has travelled abroad since 1966 representing the National Education Association in seven countries in Africa, Asia and Europe. Dr. Wilson and his wife, Naomi, have a son, Glenn. Address: Cheyney State College, Cheyney, PA 19319

Winbush, LeRoy, graphic designer, is the owner of the firm, Winbush Design, and is a design consultant specializing in visual communications, exhibits and displays. Born Dec. 7, 1915 in Memphis, Tenn., he is a high school graduate. His design agency serves clients in the financial field including the American National Bank and Trust Company of Chicago, United of America Bank and the Chicago Title and Trust Company. Mr. Winbush formerly was art director of Goldblatt Brothers department stores (1938–45), art director for Johnson Publications (1945–55), president of Winbush Associates, Inc. and assistant professor of visual communications at the Art Institute of Chicago. He has received awards from the Chicago Society of Communicating Arts, the Society of Typographic Arts, *International Display World* magazine and the Chicago Committee of One Hundred. He is a member of the *Chicago Defender* Round Table of Commerce, The National Society of Communicating Arts, The Chicago Artists Guild, exhibit chairman of the International Design Conference and president of Twenty Fathom Skin and Skuba Divers Club. Mr. Winbush is married to the former Frances A. Robinson. Address: 540 N. Lake Shore Drive, Chicago, IL 60611

Wonder, Stevie, entertainer, is a singer, musician and composer with Motown Records, Inc. in Hollywood, Calif. Born May 13, 1950 in Saginaw, Mich., he is a graduate of the Michigan School for the Blind (1968). A professional entertainer since the age of twelve, he was the first Motown artist to perform overseas (England, France, Japan, Okinawa), the first to appear in motion pictures (*Bikini Beach* and *Muscle Beach Party*), and the first to perform on network television, including the *Ed Sullivan, Mike Douglas* and *Tom Jones* shows; *American Bandstand,* and *Where The Action Is.* He has recorded more than twelve gold records, including "I Call It Pretty Music," "Fingertrips," and "Uptight." He has also recorded such hits as "High Heel Sneakers," "Nothing's Too Good For My Baby," "Blowing In The Wind," "Alfie," "A Place In The Sun," "Traveling Man," "My Cherie Amour," "For Once In My Life," "Heaven Help Us All," and "Superstition." He has received numerous honors, including the Show Business Inspiration and the Distinguished Service awards. Address: Motown Records, Inc., 6464 Sunset Blvd., Suite 700, Hollywood, CA 90028 **See article on Stevie Wonder in Volume II.**

Thomas A. Wood

Hale A. Woodruff

Howard B. Woods

Rev. S. H. Woodson Jr.

Wood, Thomas Alexander, business executive, is founder, president and a director of TAW International Leasing Corporation, which is headquartered in New York, N. Y. The firm leases construction equipment, trucks, farm machinery to privately-owned firms and governments in a number of African countries. Born Jan. 26, 1926 in New York City, Mr. Wood is a graduate of Columbia University (A.B., 1949) and the University of Michigan (B.S., electrical engineering, 1951) and has done postgraduate work at Massachusetts Institute of Technology (1958), and Wayne State University (1953–54). He is a computer systems expert who was president and a director and founder of Decision Systems, Inc. in Teaneck, N. J. before founding TAW in 1968. He is a member of the boards of directors of Chase Manhattan Bank (North America), Fecor Industries and Greer Children's Community, and is a trustee of the National Urban League. He is a member of various professional and civic groups. He and his wife, Barbara, have three children: Kaye, Eric and Victoria. Address: 866 United National Placa, New York, NY 10017 **See article on Thomas A. Wood Volume II**

Woodruff, Hale A., artist and educator, is a professor emeritus of New York University in New York City. He has also been a famous artist for many years. While he was actively engaged at New York University, he taught undergraduates and graduates in the philosophies, practices, techniques of art and the teaching of art. He was born Aug. 26, 1900 in Cairo, Ill. He studied at the John Herron Art Institute in Indianapolis, Ind., the Fogg Art Museum, Harvard University, and the Academie Scandinave and the Academie Moderne in Paris, France. He has exhibited in numerous places including the New York World's Fair, the Art Center of New York, the Chicago Art Institute and Howard University. His important works are *The Amistad Mutiny* and the *Founding of Talladega*, both at Talladega College, and the *History of California*, *The Art of The Negro* and the *Red Landscape* at Johnson Publishing Co. He is the author of seven publications on art and art education. He is a member of the New Jersey Society of Artists, the Society of Mural Painters, and the Committee on Art Education of the Museum of Modern Art in New York City. Mr. Woodruff was awarded an honorary degree at Atlanta University (L.H.D., 1972) where he once served as art director. He and his wife, Theresa, have a son, Roy. Address: 22-26 E. 8th St., New York, NY 10003

Woods, Howard B., publisher, is the founder-editor-publisher of the *St. Louis Sentinel* in St. Louis, Mo. He was born in Perry, Okla., where he attended high school. Since entering the newspaper field some thirty years ago, he has worked in a wide variety of jobs—reporter, radio news commentator, advertising salesman, nightlife columnist and editor on various newspapers, including the *Chicago Daily Defender*, the *Michigan Chronicle*, the *New Pittsburgh Courier* and the *St. Louis Argus*. In addition to his newspaper work, he has participated in many government, civic and welfare activities. He was a member of President John F. Kennedy's Committee on Equal Employment Opportunity from its inception in 1961 until its abolition in 1965. He also served as chairman of the board of commissioners of the St. Louis Housing Authority. Mr. Woods and his wife, Jane Elizabeth, have four daughters: Mrs. Joanne Austin, Judy, Patricia and Gail. Address: 5 S. Rock Hill Rd., St. Louis, MO 63119

Woodson, The Reverend S. Howard Jr., state legislator and clergyman, is a member of the General Assembly of the state of New Jersey and pastor of the Shiloh Baptist Church in Trenton, N.J. The Rev. Woodson was born May 8, 1916 in Philadelphia, Pa. He studied at Philadelphia State College and Morehouse College. He began his political career in 1955, running as a Republican. In 1957, he switched parties, ran for the city commission and lost. In 1962, he was nominated a candidate for the city council by an interracial organization. In 1964, he was elected to the New Jersey General Assembly, the only black serving in the Lower House. He was nominated in 1967 by the governor for the position of minority leader in the Lower House, where he served two consecutive terms. The recipient of numerous awards, the Rev. Woodson, a widower, has two children, Mrs. Jean Woodson Mitchell and Howard III. Address: 340 Calhoun St., Trenton, NJ 08618

Benjamin H. Wright

Charles S. Wright

Edward W. Wright

Jane C. Wright, M.D.

Wright, Benjamin H., business executive, is manager of ethnic development and urban affairs at Clairol, Inc. in New York, N.Y. He develops and oversees affirmative action programs involving hiring and upgrading of minorities and women. He was born in Shreveport, La. and later moved to Cincinnati, Ohio. He received a B.B.A. degree from the University of Cincinnati in 1950 and an M.A. degree in economics in 1951. He has done further graduate work in economics at the State University of New York and at New York University. He was awarded an LL.D. (honorary) in 1970. He has served with the U.S. Department of State, lecturing on economics at the College of Liberia in Africa. Upon returning to the states, he became sales promotion and merchandising manager of Johnson Publishing Co. Address: Clairol, Inc., 342 Park Ave., New York NY 10010

Wright, Charles S., business executive, is president of Charles S. Wright, Inc., in New York, N. Y. The firm, founded by Mr. Wright in 1968, specializes in development of community-sponsored, non-profit housing projects in the New York Metropolitan Regional Area. Born Sept. 18, 1935 in New York, N. Y. he attended Howard University (architecture major), City College of the City University of N.Y. (B.S., industrial management and engineering) and New York University (M.P.A., city and regional planning). Prior to forming his own organization, he was director of housing and planning at the Bedford-Stuyvesant Restoration Corp. in Brooklyn, N. Y. (1967-69). Earlier, he was associate director for neighborhood planning at the United Planning Organization in Washington D.C. (1965-67) and was a lecturer at Howard University School of Architecture and Engineering. He is a member of Phi Beta Sigma, the International Federation for Housing and planning, and other professional organizations. He is single. Address: 110 E. 42nd St., New York, NY 10017

Wright, Edward W., publicist, is president of the Edward Windsor Wright Corp., a public relations, advertising and marketing organization in Los Angeles, Cal. The company has handled careers of such notables as Bobby Womack, Bill Cosby, the Temptations, Billy Paul and Ramsey Lewis. Mr. Wright was born Oct. 14, 1940 in Cincinnati, Ohio. At thirteen, while still in junior high school, he worked as a disc jockey at WCIN radio station in Cincinnati. In 1964, he was elected president of the National Association of Radio Announcers, a black disc jockey organization. Mr. Wright, who is single, attended the College Conservatory of Music, Radio & TV Arts in Cincinnati. Address: 6430 W. Sunset Boulevard, Suite 502, Hollywood, CA 90028

Wright, Jane C., M.D., administrator, is associate dean and professor of surgery at New York Medical College, the highest post in medical administration ever attained by a black woman physican. Born Nov. 30, 1919 in New York City, she is a graduate of Smith College (B.A., pre-medicine, 1942) and New York Medical College (M.D., 1945). Before assuming her present position in 1967, she was a New York City public school physician and a visiting physician at Harlem Hospital, a clinician at the Harlem Hospital Cancer Research Foundation, director of the Harlem Hospital Cancer Research Foundation, assistant professor at the New York University Medical Center and adjunct associate professor of research surgery at the New York University Medical School. She was also associate dean and professor of surgery at the New York Medical College. She is a consultant at St. Luke's Hospital and St. Vincent's Hospital. She is a member of the American Association for Cancer Research, the American Medical Association and the National Advisory Cancer Council. She is a member of the board of directors of the American Cancer Society and is vice president of the African Research Foundation. She is on the editorial board of the *Journal of the National Medical Association*. She and her husband, David, an attorney, have two daughters, Jane and Alison. Address: New York Medical College, 106th St. and 5th Ave., New York, NY 10025

Nathan Wright Jr.

Stanley V. Wright

Stephen J. Wright

Wright, Nathan Jr., educator and author, is professor of urban affairs at State University of New York in Albany. Previously, Dr. Wright was a columnist for the Newark *Star-Ledger*, executive director of the department of urban work for the Episcopal Diocese of Newark, N.J., chairman for the 1967 and 1968 National and International Conferences on Black Power in Newark and Philadelphia, and a founding member of the National Committee of Black Churchmen. Born Aug. 5, 1923 in Shreveport, La., Dr. Wright graduated from the University of Cincinnati (B.A., 1947), the Episcopal Theological School in Cambridge, Mass. (B.D., 1950), Harvard University (S.T.M., 1951), Massachusetts State College (Ed.M., 1961), and Harvard University (Ed.D., 1964), and received an honorary LL.D. from Upsala College (1969). An award-winning author, his ten books include *Black Power and Urban Unrest*, *Ready to Riot*, and *What Black Educators Are Saying*. He has also contributed more than 300 articles to numerous books, magazines and journals. He is a member of the National Association of Urban and Ethnic Directors and the National Association of Professional Group Workers, and participated in the "Journey of Reconciliation" in the freedom ride of 1947 under the auspices of the Congress of Racial Equality. Dr. Wright and his wife, Carolyn, are parents of five children. Address: 24 Rector St., Newark NJ 07102

Wright, Stanley V., educator, is professor of physical education and head track coach at California State University in Sacramento. Born Aug. 11, 1921 in Englewood, N.J., he is a graduate and has degrees from Springfield College (B.S., 1949), Columbia University (M.A., 1950) and took graduate study at the University of Texas (1954–56) and at Indiana University (1968). As an asst. track coach at the Mexico City Olympic Games, he was responsible for the athletes who won six gold medals, setting five world records and tying one in six events. He has been appointed for the second time to the U.S. Olympic Track & Field Committee and to the U.S. Olympic bd. of dir. for the next quadrennial. Mr. Wright has received many honors and awards and is a member of numerous professional organizations. His articles such as "Techniques Related to Sprint Racing" have appeared in leading athletic journals, and he has participated in over 200 high school and college clinics. Mr. Wright and his wife, Hazel, have four children: Stanley, Toni, Sandra and Tyran. Address: 6000 Jay St., Sacramento, CA 95819

Wright, Stephen Junius, education specialist, is vice president of the College Entrance Examination Board. Born Sept. 8, 1910 in Dillon, S.C., Dr. Wright, attended Hampton Institute (B.S., 1934), Howard University (M.A., 1939) and New York University (Ph.D., 1943). The respected educator has received honorary degrees from Colby College, the University of Notre Dame, College of St. Thomas, Morgan State College, New York University, Michigan State University, University of Rhode Island, Morehouse College and Manhattan College. He began his teaching career in 1934 in the public schools of Maryland, and was president of Bluefield State College (1953–57), president of Fisk University (1957–66) and president of the United Negro College Fund (1966–69). He is a member, trustee or director of numerous professional and civic organizations and has published many scholarly articles. Dr. Wright is married to the former Rosalind Person. Address: College Entrance Examination Board, 888 Seventh Ave., New York, NY 10019

Y

Joseph P. Yeldell

Yeldell, Joseph Phillip, social service administrator, is director of the District of Columbia Department of Human Resources. Born Sept. 9, 1932 in Washington, D.C., he has degrees from D.C. Teachers College (B.S.) and the University of Pittsburgh (M.A.). Appointed to his position in 1971, he directs the dispensing of a wide range of social services, including public welfare, health care, mental health, narcotics treatment and vocational rehabilitation. Before his appointment, Mr. Yeldell was a mathematical statistician in the U.S. Bureau of Labor Statistics, an IBM marketing representative, an educational planner, and a director of programs for the under-privileged. In 1967, he was appointed by President Lyndon B. Johnson to serve on the District's City Council. He was reappointed in 1971 by President Richard M. Nixon. Mr. Yeldell is a member of the President's Councils at Howard University and at Federal City College, the Computer Science Advisory Committee, and the District of Columbia Health and Welfare Council. He and his wife, Gladys, have two daughters, Gayle and Joi. Address: District Building, Room 420, 14th and E Sts., NW, Washington, DC 20004

Andrew J. Young

Young, Andrew J., congressman, was elected in 1972 as a Democratic member of the U.S. House of Representatives from Georgia. Born March 12, 1932 in New Orleans, La., he attended Dillard University (1947–48) and is a graduate of Howard University (B.S., 1951) and Hartford Theological Seminary (B.D., 1955). He is an ordained minister in the United Church of Christ; he was pastor of various churches from 1952 to 1957. He was associate director of the Department of Youth Work of the National Council of Churches (1957–61), administrator of the Citizen Education Program of SCLC (1961–64), executive director of SCLC (1964–68) and executive vice president of SCLC (1968-70). He has won numerous awards for his civil rights work. He is chairman of the board of the Delta Ministry of Mississippi and is a board member of a number of organizations. He and his wife, Jean, have three daughters: Andrea, Lisa and Paula. Address: House of Representatives, Washington, DC 20515 **See article on Andrew J. Young in Volume II**

A. S. "Doc" Young

Young, A. S. ("Doc"), journalist, is executive editor of the *Los Angeles Sentinel* and is director of public information at Pepperdine College in Los Angeles, Calif. Born Oct. 29, 1924 in Virginia, he is a graduate of Hampton Institute (B.S., business administration) and studied journalism at California State University and Pepperdine College. He is the author of seven books, has written a number of radio commercials and has made numerous radio-television appearances. He was sports editor, feature writer and producer of special editions for the *Chicago Daily Defender*, and was sports editor, assistant editor, and managing editor of *Jet* magazine. His articles have been published in more than 100 newspapers and magazines. He is a member of the Baseball Writers Association of America, Sigma Delta Chi, the Publicists Guild of Hollywood, and other professional and civic groups. He and his wife, Hazel, have two children, Norman and Brenda. Address: The Sentinel, 112 E. 43rd St., CA 90011

Claude "Buddy" Young

Young, Claude ("Buddy"), sports executive, is player relations representative for the National Football League. He is a former collegiate and professional football star. Born Jan. 5, 1926 in Chicago, Ill., he attended the University of Illinois (1944–47), where he was the world 40-yard dash champion and the Illini star in the 1947 Rose Bowl football game. He was a scout and assistant personnel director for the Baltimore Colts (1956–65). From 1954–65, he was sports editor, announcer and assistant to the general manager of radio station WEBB in Baltimore, Md. He and his wife, Geraldine, have four children: Claude Jr., Paula, Jeffrey and Zollie. Address: 410 Park Ave., New York, NY 10022

Harding B. Young

Lawrence T. Young

Rev. Rufus K. Young Sr.

Young, Harding Bernett, college professor, is a professor of management at Georgia State University in Atlanta. He is also founder and director of the Southeastern Institute of Entrepreneurship and Management in Atlanta. Born Jan. 16, 1922 in Rosston, Ark., he received his B.S. in mathematics from Arkansas AM&N College (1944), his B.C.S. in management from Boston University (1948) and his D.C.S. in control and management from the Harvard University Graduate School of Business Administration (1955). He was dean and professor of business administration at Atlanta University (1961–69). He is a member of the Georgia District Advisory Council of the Small Business Administration, the President's Commission for Minority Business Enterprise, and numerous other professional and civic groups. In September, 1972, he was elected to the Board of Citizens and Southern National Bank, Atlanta, Ga. He is a member of the American Economic Association. He and his wife, Sadye, have four children: Sybil, Angela, Gregory, and Harding. Address: 2391 Sewell Rd., Atlanta, GA 30319

Young, Lawrence T., administrator, is executive secretary of Alpha Phi Alpha fraternity, Inc., an organization with 382 college chapters and 228 alumni chapters throughout the United States and in Europe, Africa, Vietnam and the Virgin Islands. Born Nov. 3, 1905 in West Medford, Mass., he is a graduate of Ohio University (A.B., commerce) and John Marshall Law School (J.D.). He also has a Certificate of Proficiency from the National Shorthand Reporters Association of America. Prior to assuming his present position, he was for 25 years official court reporter for the coroner of Cook County, Ill., and the Cook County State's Attorney's Office. He was the first black court reporter assigned to the coroner's office in 1930, and rose to the rank of chief court reporter. He is a member of the NAACP, Chicago Urban League, and the Old Tymers Club. He and his wife, Rebecca, have two children, Lawrence Jr. and Mrs. Grace Y. Bruce. Address: National Headquarters, Alpha Phi Alpha, 4432 King Dr., Chicago, IL 60653

Young, The Reverend Rufus King Sr., clergyman, has been pastor of Bethel A.M.E. Church in Little Rock, Ark. since 1953. Born May 13, 1911 in Durmott, Ark., he is a graduate of Shorter College (B.A.) and Payne Theological Seminary (B.D.). He has honorary doctor of divinity degrees from Shorter College and Wilberforce University. He was pastor of Visitor's Chapel A.M.E. Church in Hot Springs, Ark. 1950–53), president of Daniel Payne College in Birmingham, Ala. (1948–50), pastor of Pearl Street A.M.E. Church in Jackson, Miss. (1946–48), pastor of Bethel A.M.E. Church in Baton Rouge, La. (1944–46) and dean of the Edward W. Lampton School of Religion in Jackson, Miss. (1940–44). He is president of Glenview Improvement League in Little Rock, treasurer of the Arkansas Annual A.M.E. Conference, a board member of the Arkansas Service Organization, and a member of the Little Rock Civic League. He and his wife, Essie, have five children: Mrs. Essie Norman, Rufus Jr., James, Mrs. Ellen Fizer and Allena. Address: 815 W. 16th St., Little Rock, AR 72202